DISCARDED

D1570863

The Collective and the Individual in Russia

Studies on the History of Society and Culture

Victoria E. Bonnell and Lynn Hunt, Editors

The Collective
and the Individual
in Russia
A Study of Practices

OLEG KHARKHORDIN

University of California Press
BERKELEY   LOS ANGELES   LONDON

University of California Press
Berkeley and Los Angeles, California

University of California Press, Ltd.
London, England

© 1999 by the Regents of the University of California

Three publishing houses have courteously granted me permission to use
pieces of my previous articles that appeared in other edited collections
and journals: "Reveal and Dissimulate: A Genealogy of Private Life in
Soviet Russia," in *Public and Private in Thought and Practice: Perspec-
tives on a Grand Dichotomy*, ed. Jeff Weintraub and Krishan Kumar
(Chicago, 1997) © by The University of Chicago, all rights reserved;
"The Soviet Individual: Genealogy of a Dissimulating Animal," in *Global
Modernities*, ed. Mike Featherstone, Scott Lash, and Roland Robertson
(Sage Publications, 1995) © Sage Publications Ltd., all rights reserved;
and "Civil Society and Orthodox Christianity," *Europe-Asia Studies* 50,
no. 6 (1998): 949–968 (University of Glasgow; Carfax Publishing Ltd.,
P.O. Box 25, Abingdon, Oxfordshire OX14 3UE, United Kingdom).

Library of Congress Cataloging-in-Publication Data

Kharkhordin, Oleg, 1964–
   The collective and the individual in Russia : a study of practices
 / Oleg Kharkhordin.
     p.   cm. — (Studies on the history of society and culture ; 32)
    Includes bibliographical references and index.
    ISBN 0-520-21604 (alk. paper)
    1. Social psychology—Soviet Union. 2. National characteristics,
 Russian. 3. Social control—Soviet Union. 4. Political culture—
 Soviet Union. 5. Foucault, Michel—Contributions in social
 sciences. I. Title. II. Series.
 HN523.K48   1999
 306'.0947—dc21   98-31931

Manufactured in the United States of America

9 8 7 6 5 4 3 2 1

The paper used in this publication meets the minimum requirements of
American National Standard for Information Sciences—Permanence of
Paper for Printed Library Materials, ANSI Z39.48-1984.

Contents

viii / *Contents*

Illustrations

Acknowledgments

First of all, I would like to thank my four *directeurs de conscience:* Hanna Pitkin, the only person who ever taught me to write; Ken Jowitt, without whose lectures I would not have even thought of writing on Russia and whose zeal kept me going; Paul Rabinow, who provided constant methodological inspiration and who knew what the art of existence meant; and Reggie Zelnik, who unobtrusively but sternly held my theoretical fantasy within empirical bounds. Victoria Bonnell's graduate research seminar at the University of California, Berkeley, was the place where for the first time I tried out my ideas on Foucault and Russia, and I owe her and other seminar participants my greatest thanks for their willingness to experiment.

I also thank those who were part of the background for writing this book: Vadim Volkov, in constant interaction with whom my thinking evolved, and the four kindred spirits—Valerie Sperling, Jeff Sluyter, David Woodruff and David Montgomery—who, by their joint corrective effort and especially by inserting the right articles in the right places, embodied themselves in this text and thus became part of the book.

Research and writing were supported by an SSRC-MacArthur Fellowship in Peace and Security in a Changing World, and by a particularly timely grant from the Berkeley Program in Soviet and Post-Soviet Studies. The Harvard Academy for International and Area Studies provided a very encouraging environment for discussing and making an unending stream of revisions that this manuscript had to undergo in the last couple of years. I thank all those who contributed their substantial remarks and reviews to this exercise in constant change: Luc Boltanski, Robert Crummey, Hubert Dreyfus, Boris Firsov, Sheila Fitzpatrick, Martin Jay, Edward Keenan, Stephen Kotkin, Colleen Lye, Tim MacDaniel, Laurie Manchester, Irina Paperno, Michael Rogin, Monique de Saint-Martin, Adam Seligman, Bill

Todd, Michael Urban, Veljko Vujacic, and Jeff Weintraub. My multiple shortcomings and their numerous misgivings clearly emerged into the open after our interaction; if I kept the former and sustained the latter, they are not to blame.

Finally, I thank all of my colleagues at the Faculty of Political Sciences and Sociology at the European University at St. Petersburg and the class of 1996–97 for making me believe that speech acts really matter.

1 Introduction

Individualism and the Study of Practices

This book started with a puzzle. Interviews with new Russian entrepreneurs conducted in 1992–93 revealed a substantial number of people who espoused individualist ideals, a surprising finding for the country that was presumed to have been overtly collectivist for centuries.[1] Could the "individualism" in question be exactly the same as Western individualism? It was hard to believe that the people who had shared collectivist ideals for so long could radically change their preferences in a couple of years following the collapse of the Soviet Union. Of course, Milton Friedman and Friedrich von Hayek seemed the most popular authors for the Russian public of the early 1990s, with their statements on the unconditional value of individual economic freedom endlessly repeated, but this radical change in discourse did not correspond to any obvious corollary change in the everyday life of the majority of the Russian population.

Observers were divided on the interpretation of this sudden emergence of individualism in discourse. Many took this discursive shift as indicating a deep change in values that must have occurred sometime during the perestroika years, when the old Communist doctrines were progressively challenged and a demand for "freedom" became the mood of the day. Even more suspected that the new predominance of individualism in discourse was just a part of the fashionable jargon of the day, disguising the essential collec-

---

1. According to the enterpreneurs, they shared an ethic of "self-reliance." It is closer to the German *Selbstständigkeit* with its Lutheran connotations than to Emerson's concept. See Oleg Kharkhordin, "The Corporate Ethic, the Ethic of *Samostoiatelnost'*, and the Spirit of Capitalism: Reflections on Market-Building in Post-Soviet Russia," *International Sociology* 9, no. 4.

tivism of the Russian people, which would reassert itself with time. Elections in 1993 and 1995 seemed to support the latter point of view. Stories of a "Communist legacy" pervaded many newspapers, which recast it as an almost insurmountable obstacle to any radical political and social reform in Russia. Then Boris Yeltsin's victory in the 1996 presidential elections restored the ambivalence: perhaps, this legacy from the Soviet days does not hold an iron grip, after all.

The question of whether Russia is collectivist or individualist is still troubling. Should we take the growing number of people who express preferences for personal dignity, individual autonomy, and inviolability of the private sphere to indicate a decisive social change ushering in an era of individualism, or should we regard these statements with suspicion and look for continuation of the age-old mechanisms of a collectivist lifestyle? Formulated in these terms, the question is hard to answer. Even the growth of the middle class will not dispel the ambiguity of current conditions. Given the fact that many new successful entrepreneurs were part of the Communist *nomenklatura,* it is hard to believe that they have suddenly wholeheartedly adopted liberal ideals.

The problem may lie with the concepts rather than with the country. Perhaps "collectivism" and "individualism" are not very useful concepts for examining social and political changes in the Union of Soviet Socialist Republics or in Russia today. These grand terms, which often designated nothing more than ideological commitments, may not advance scientific analysis. Claiming that some instance of human behavior is "collectivist" or "individualist" is too gross a classification to add much to our knowledge. Offering an interpretation of the Russian historical experience in terms of more subtle distinctions is one of the aims of the present investigation.

So far, researchers of the two formerly dominant schools in interpreting Soviet history—the totalitarians and the revisionists—seemed to agree, even if they contradicted one another on most other points, that a curious individualization of the populace happened under Joseph Stalin. Thus, Raymond Bauer, echoing Hannah Arendt's thesis that totalitarianism was based on atomization of the masses, stated in his classic 1952 study that the Soviet concept of man was characterized by "responsibility, rationalism, individualism, all seeming contradictions in a totalitarian society."[2] Similarly, works of revisionist historiography that appeared some decades later noted

2. Raymond A. Bauer, *The New Man in Soviet Psychology* (Cambridge, Mass.: Harvard University Press, 1952), 177.

the extreme individualization of the workforce that was brought about by Stalinist industrialization and the Stakhanovite movement.[3] Perhaps Donald Filtzer has recently summed up the shared beliefs of all, when he wrote: "economic and political life in the Soviet Union became characterized by extreme individualism, for it was only as individuals . . . that people could function."[4] Few, however, would claim that this individualism had a lot in common with its Western counterpart.

The present investigation addresses this curious status of individualism in Russian culture, but from a specific angle, examining the practices of individualization rather than discourse about individualism. Let me first clarify the meaning of the terms and describe their relationship. Oversimplifying a bit, we may say that practices of individualization are captured by the term "individualism," but they constitute only one of the four main components of meaning usually ascribed to this term. In the most comprehensive study to date, Steven Lukes, working in Arthur Lovejoy's tradition of the history of ideas, has distinguished four core component ideas "variously expressed and combined" in the term "individualism."[5] The first one is respect for persons, "the supreme and intrinsic value, or dignity, of the individual human being." The second is independence or autonomy, "according to which an individual's thought and action is his own, and not determined by agencies or causes outside his control." The third aspect of individualism is the notion of privacy, "an area within which an individual is or should be left alone by others and able to do or think whatever he chooses." The fourth is the notion of self-development, which now "specifies an ideal of the lives of individuals—an ideal whose content varies with different ideas of the self on a continuum of pure egoism to strong communitarianism."[6] The four core ideas, Lukes argues, are logically and conceptually interrelated and are all strongly linked to the ideas of liberty and equality. "The idea of human dignity . . . lies at the heart of the idea of equality, while autonomy, privacy and self-development represent the three faces of liberty and freedom."[7]

3. See, e.g., Hiroaki Kuromiya, *Stalin's Industrial Revolution* (Cambridge: Cambridge University Press, 1988); and Lewis H. Siegelbaum, *Stakhanovism and the Politics of Productivity in the USSR, 1935–1941* (Cambridge: Cambridge University Press, 1988).

4. Donald Filtzer, *Soviet Workers and De-Stalinization* (Cambridge: Cambridge University Press, 1992), 125.

5. Steven Lukes, *Individualism* (London: Blackwell, 1973), 42.

6. Ibid., 45, 52, 59, 71.

7. Ibid., 125.

Self-development, the fourth component in Lukes's conceptualization, is the closest to the topic of our study. However, we will study it not as an idea but, following Michel Foucault, as a set of practices of self-perfection and self-fashioning. Juxtaposing Lukes's to Foucault's conceptualization is rather challenging. Foucault himself distinguishes among at least three components of the meaning of the word "individualism." First, writes Foucault, there is an individualistic attitude, which assigns absolute value to human individuals in their uniqueness and opposition to a primary group to which they belong. Second, there is a positive valuation of private life, defined as family relations and the domestic activity attached to them. Third, there is a certain intensification of one's relationship with oneself, that is, of the ways in which a human being is called upon to make him/herself an object and a field of action (so that one can know, correct, and purify oneself, for example).[8]

Though Foucault calls these components "attitudes," they almost replicate the last three "core ideas," directly linked to freedom in Lukes's conceptualization. The first attitude is close to the value of autonomy, the second to that of privacy, and the third spells out the program of self-development. These three elements, argues Foucault, combine in certain cultures or for certain groups within a given culture but not universally. For example, following the historians Peter Brown and Paul Veyne, Foucault finds that among the Stoic philosophers and later among early Christians, the relation to the self intensified and developed without an immediate parallel rise of the value of individual autonomy or the valorization of private life, which only appear to us to be necessary corollaries of this intensification of the relation to the self.[9] Foucault's conceptualization shifts emphasis from the substance called "individualism" to the process of "individualization": that is, from the study of the core ideas of individualism, or of the internalized values and attitudes, to the study of practices of self-development and self-fashioning, the "core practices" that make possible the adoption of individualist ideas and attitudes.

If we apply Foucault's conceptualization of individualism to the Russian case, it seems to explain the puzzle that initiated this work. Indeed, by making continuous efforts to emphasize the practice of self-perfection, the Bolsheviks intensified the relation to the self among Party members, and then among the rest of the Soviet citizens. This self was made an object to care

8. Michel Foucault, *The History of Sexuality*, vol. 3, *The Care of the Self*, trans. Robert Hurley (New York: Pantheon, 1986), 42.
    9. Ibid., 43.

about, to reflect upon, to perfect. Peasants who became workers who became Communists started for the first time in their lives to think and write about themselves, to care about the possession and development of an individual self. But this intensification of relation with the self proceeded without the concomitant assertion of the values of individual autonomy and private life, since such statements were hardly possible in official discourse. According to a Foucaultian conceptualization, the post-1985 development would then seem to be only the recognition in discourse of this profound individualization, in the sense of self-concern, that took place under the auspices of the Soviet regime. That is, official discourse that had so far banned the values of the individual autonomy and privacy was simply radically reversed and its opposite was adopted.

This application of a Foucaultian framework to the Russian experience immediately encounters two serious problems. Soviet individualization hardly happened in a way described by Foucault for the case of Western Europe. First, Christian confession—a primary means of the individualization in the West, according to Foucault—did not play the same central role in Russia. Foucault argues in the first volume of *The History of Sexuality* that once confession spilled over the walls of the monasteries, where it had been primarily practiced in the Middle Ages, and was adopted by the wider population for confessing secrets of the fictional entity called "sex," the Western individual was produced. We are witnesses to the current predominance of the method:

> one confesses one's sins, one confesses one's thoughts and desires, . . . one sets about telling with the greatest precision what is most difficult to tell; one confesses in public and in private, to one's parents, to one's teachers, to one's doctor, to those one loves; one confesses to oneself, in pleasure and in pain, things that it would be impossible to tell anyone else. . . . Western man has become a confessing animal.[10]

Recent historical studies seem to support Foucault's stress on the centrality of confession to the formation of the Western individual. For example, Colin Morris, one of the medieval historians who have challenged Jakob Burckhardt's classical thesis that the development of humanism and individualism in Europe started in Renaissance Italy, has posited the origins of individualization in the eleventh and twelfth centuries, with confession as one of the most important means of this process. A novel con-

---

10. Michel Foucault, *The History of Sexuality*, vol. 1, *An Introduction*, trans. Robert Hurley (New York: Pantheon, 1980), 59.

cern with self-discovery and the increased sensitivity of the boundary between the self and the other developed on the basis of restored Augustinian confession.[11] In another influential study, the historian Thomas Tentler came to the conclusion that Christian confession was used in the Middle Ages simultaneously as a means of social discipline and as a means of individual self-fashioning.[12] On the one hand, official dogmatic theology developed "a novel stress on intention in assessment of conduct."[13] In 1215 the Lateran Council institutionalized annual auricular confession for all Christians. Abelard's emphasis on "inner contrition" as essential to exculpation, which greatly fostered self-analysis, became part of Catholic dogma after the Council of Trent in 1551.[14] On the other hand, autobiographies of such monks as Otloh of St. Emmeram, Guibert of Nogent, or Abelard himself all presented instances of "genuine self-expression" in the twelfth century, following the Augustinian model of confession to God.[15]

A Russian reader is surprised by these descriptions of the centrality of confession. The history of the Orthodox Church does not know any decisive date similar to 1215; Eastern Christianity did not have any equivalent to the Lateran Council. Gratian, the famous eleventh-century Western canonist who first collected eighty-nine opinions of the church fathers on matters of confession, thought that the Eastern Church did not practice private confession at all! Given the fact that confession was of course universally practiced in the Eastern Church, Russian historians later explained Gratian's curious statement in the following way:

> Western schoolmen could speak about the absence of private confession among the Greeks, because they were little acquainted with the practice of the Eastern Church, or perhaps because in the West private confession was treated in practice as a necessary condition for the absolution of sins and admittance to the Eucharist for all, while in the East private confession was not demanded with such resoluteness either theoretically or practically, not to mention its legal institutionalization.[16]

11. Colin Morris, *The Discovery of the Individual, 1050–1200* (New York: Harper and Row, 1973).

12. Thomas N. Tentler, *Sin and Confession on the Eve of the Reformation* (Princeton: Princeton University Press, 1977).

13. Morris, *Discovery of the Individual,* 73.

14. In a related argument Tentler stresses Peter Lombard's emphatic defense of confession to a priest as instrumental to its use throughout the West by the end of the 13th century (Tentler, *Sin and Confession,* 21).

15. Morris, *Discovery of the Individual,* 85.

16. N. Suvorov, *Ob"em distsiplinarnogo suda i iurisdiktsii tserkvi v period vselenskikh soborov* [Scope of disciplinary court and church jurisdiction in the time of the universal councils] (Iaroslavl', 1884), 119–120.

Private confession, rarely stressed as an essential part of Orthodox Christianity, was downgraded even further in modern times under Peter the Great, who obliged priests to violate the secrecy of private confession in matters of state treason. Annual confession to a priest was also used as a means of locating religious dissenters and enforcing Orthodoxy, which contributed to its image as a disciplinary means rather than as a private channel of self-expression. Secular confession that came to flourish in the eighteenth and nineteenth centuries did not fare much better than its church counterpart after 1917. Lay confessional techniques, so popular among the propertied classes before the revolution, seem to have been swept away together with these classes. In Soviet days, with a notable exception of the judicial confession, extorted to vindicate the truth "discovered" during the preliminary investigation, we do not find many instances when secular confession played a role comparable to its Western equivalent. Furthermore, the meager number of psychoanalysts in Russia until the late 1980s may owe less to the political suppression of psychoanalysis in the 1930s than to the lack of habit among Russians to discover one's own essence by means of confessing desires, if not to their wholehearted aversion to wordy outpourings.

Foucault's framework, thus, would seem questionable in its application to Russia, if we search for confession, the essential Western technique of individualization. But non-Western cultures may employ other practices to transform and work on the self. Thus, this study could apply Foucault's methodology to Russia, without expecting to duplicate his findings on the mechanisms of individualization in the West. Using his method of genealogy, we could examine the cultural practices that served as the background for the general individualization of the population in Soviet Russia and analyze the resulting cross-cultural comparisons.

Even with this objective in mind, we face another serious difficulty with applying a Foucaultian framework to interpret Russian individualization. The methods of the formation of the Soviet individual draw on the specific Soviet way of arranging a human group, that is, the basic social unit of Soviet society that was conveniently transliterated into English as the *kollektiv*. In the early days of the Soviet regime, the *kollektiv* eclipsed the individual as the singular focus of attention and unit of action, while the practices of group-formation intertwined with practices of self-development. By contrast, Foucault's studies of individualization mostly neglect the issues of group formation and interaction between the individual and the group.

This neglected dimension of the study of the group may be essential for the study of individualization. As some historians would argue, even in the

West the formation of the individual went hand in hand with the formation of the group. Caroline Walker Bynum has disputed Morris's opinion (still indebted to Burckhardt in this respect) that in the twelfth century the affirmation of the individual happened against and at the expense of the community. In her words, "the twelfth-century person did not 'find himself' by casting off inhibiting patterns, but by adopting appropriate ones."[17] Examining him- or herself, the medieval person discovered an *imago Dei*, a universal divine pattern of Christian life. However, at that time several religious orders and groups, "lives" or "vocations" in medieval parlance, competed to be the correct model of Christian life. For example, the Cistercians and the Carthusians argued which order correctly embodied Christian virtue. Conceiving oneself apart from or in opposition to a group was largely impossible. Even when Abelard wrote his famous autobiography, he presented it as a description of a vocation called "philosopher" rather than of the unique individual named Pierre. Bynum concludes: "In the twelfth century, turning inward to explore motivation went hand in hand with belonging to a group that not only defined its own life by means of a model but also was itself—as a group and as a pattern—a means of salvation and evangelism."[18] Similarly, Natalie Zemon Davis points out in her analysis of individualization in sixteenth-century France that "the exploration of the self . . . was made in conscious relation to the groups to which people belonged. . . . Embeddedness did not preclude self-discovery, but rather prompted it."[19]

Thus, perhaps, we need to supplement the Foucaultian attention to the practices of individual self-fashioning with attention to the practices of group formation. In the Russian case in particular we must construct parallel genealogies of the collective and of the individual, if only to do justice to a system that always claimed the collective, and not the individual, as the primary unit of society. With this objective in mind I now turn to Foucault's methods. Readers who are not interested in Foucault may skip the examination of the "how" of this study and proceed straight to the end of this chapter discussing the general layout of the book.

17. Caroline Walker Bynum, *Jesus as Mother* (Berkeley: University of California Press, 1982), 90.
18. Ibid., 105.
19. Natalie Zemon Davis, "Boundaries and the Sense of Self in Sixteenth-Century France," in *Reconstructing Individualism*, ed. Thomas C. Heller, Morton Sosna, and David E. Wellbery (Stanford: Stanford University Press, 1986), 53, 63.

METHOD

Hubert Dreyfus and Paul Rabinow have produced the most powerful and exhaustive account of Foucault's methodology to date. They consider it to be the most radical step beyond both theoretical explanation, as exemplified in positivist or structuralist theories that provide objective analysis of things "as they are," on the one hand, and the interpretive understanding of shared subjective meanings, as exemplified in hermeneutic or phenomenological approaches, on the other. Foucault's method, they say, is best seen as "an interpretive analytics": "analytics," because it follows in the footsteps of Kantian and Heideggerian studies of the conditions of possibility of the "real," rather than the "real" itself; and "interpretive," because it shares in the meanings of the culture studied, rather than positing an external explanation. Still the resulting interpretation is not an expression of these shared meanings but is "a pragmatically guided reading of the coherence of the practices" of this culture.[20]

Now, some clarifications are in order, lest the previous paragraph sound mystical. What Dreyfus and Rabinow, following Kant, call conditions of possibility of the "real," can also be more simply seen as "background," a concept that originally came from Gestalt psychology and is now used in some versions of phenomenology and in John Searle's theory of speech acts. The idea of the background is very widespread in the twentieth-century philosophy and the sociology of knowledge, in various efforts to articulate the unarticulated preconditions for speech and intentional communication of meaning. Possible examples include Wittgenstein's "language games" and "forms of life," Polanyi's "tacit knowledge," Ryle's knowing how as opposed to knowing that, and Goffman's "frames" of everyday reference.[21] Searle's is just one of the more recent attempts that address the same set of issues.[22]

20. Hubert L. Dreyfus and Paul Rabinow, *Michel Foucault: Beyond Structuralism and Hermeneutics*, 2d ed. (Chicago: University of Chicago Press, 1983), 122, 124 (hereafter HDPR).

21. Ludwig Wittgenstein, *Philosophical Investigations*, trans. G. E. M. Anscombe (Oxford: Blackwell, 1953); Michael Polanyi, *Personal Knowledge* (Chicago: University of Chicago Press, 1958); Gilbert Ryle, "Knowing How and Knowing That," *Proceedings of the Aristotelian Society* 46 (1945–46): 1–16; Erving Goffman, *Frame Analysis* (New York: Harper and Row, 1974).

22. E.g., John Searle, "The Background," in *Intentionality* (Cambridge: Cambridge University Press, 1983); and an extensive discussion in John Searle, *The Construction of Social Reality* (New York: Free Press, 1995).

Building on the basic finding of Gestalt psychology that visual perception of a figure is possible only against a background, when the "figure-background" composite is perceived as a whole, Searle argues that a similar "background" functions in verbal communication to make understanding possible. A background for any pictorial representation delineates the figure but itself temporarily stays unnoticed as such, unless the Gestalt is switched and the background becomes the foreground figure, while the former foreground recedes into the background, as in certain puzzle pictures and paintings by M. C. Escher. Similarly, a background for the communication of meaning in an utterance consists of a set of "assumptions" about ways of dealing with words and their referents, taken for granted in a given culture. There is a difference between pictorial and discursive backgrounds, however, in that no one is ever able to put the discursive background into the foreground completely, that is, to spell this set out fully.[23] We may recognize this discursive background only when it shifts, when those assumptions we take for granted are suddenly revealed to be inadequate.

In order to illustrate his concept, Searle supplies a series of extravagant stories involving the claim "a cat is on the mat," shifting the background from one that most Americans find familiar to one that appears outlandish, so that the meaning of the same claim changes radically, depending on this shifting background.[24] The resulting confusion when the background expectation based on the previous story is challenged by a new one, manifests the shift in the discursive background. Instead of repeating these stories, I offer a more mundane example: the puzzlement a Russian tourist experiences in the bathroom of a Boeing aircraft on reading a sign asking the passenger to wipe the washbasin after its use, as a courtesy to the next passenger. The background for dealing with washbasins is different in Russia and the West. Russians wash under running water and do not touch the basin, which therefore normally does not have a plug; the English fill the basin, while some Anglo-Americans fill it only while shaving, which makes understanding the point of the sign difficult for a Russian. Without background knowledge of dealing with washbasins in a different culture, the Russian may engage in long speculations on excessive courtesy requirements, or, perhaps, strange hygienic standards in the United States.

23. Participants in most verbal interaction are unaware of the background. In pictorial representation, by contrast, an artist is usually aware of background features while creating the work, but viewers often perceive only the composite "figure-background" unless Gestalts are switched.

24. John Searle, "Literal Meaning," in *Expression and Meaning* (Cambridge: Cambridge University Press, 1979).

Searle's colleague and opponent, Dreyfus, proposed that the background is better understood as a set of practices that members of a given culture normally share, practices that embody their typical skills for coping with objects and people.[25] Background practices, as he calls them, are not explicitly taught, nor do they have explicit rules. The practitioners may not even be aware that there is a pattern to what they are doing (when, for example, they maintain normal conversational distance, a normal way of walking, facial expressions, and the like), or sometimes even that they are doing anything. Children, imitating adults, simply pick up these patterns. Cultures differ not only in these aspects of physical comportment, which are easily revealed when members of different cultures meet—as in the washbasin example[26]—but also in other, more subtle background ways of dealing with objects and people.[27]

In the language of interpretive analytics, background practices supply the "conditions of possibility" for the correct understanding of an uttered sentence. According to Dreyfus and Rabinow, Foucault studies these practices so as to reveal their coherence, and to call attention to the shared background that endows words in a given culture with sense.[28] Foucault uses the term "background" frequently, but not necessarily in Dreyfus's sense of the term. He employs it mostly in the idiomatic phrase "against the background," often used interchangeably with synonymous idioms. Thus,

25. Hubert L. Dreyfus, *Being-in-the-World* (Cambridge, Mass.: MIT Press, 1991), 4.

26. Recurrent situations at international conferences reveal differences in background expectations as pairs of interlocutors "dance" around the hall, constantly readjusting their normal conversational distance: an interlocutor from Latin America tends to approach closer than a North American normally allows; the second backs off as the first advances to restore a "normal" distance, and so on. For this and other cross-cultural encounters see Edward T. Hall, *The Silent Language* (Garden City, N.Y.: Doubleday, 1959), 209 and passim.

27. Increased interaction between cultures highlights differences in conceptual language and ways of doing complex things. For early attempts at intercultural analysis, see R. A. Brower, *On Translation* (Cambridge, Mass.: Harvard University Press, 1959). On the Sapir-Whorf hypothesis of the incommensurability of languages see David D. Laitin, *Politics, Language, and Thought* (Chicago: University of Chicago Press, 1977).

28. In this interpretation I read "the background practices" approach into Dreyfus and Rabinow's argument because they often refer to it even when they do not state it explicitly. One such reference is "No doubt [Foucault] would agree with writers from Wittgenstein to Kuhn to Searle that the specific understanding of the specific speech acts involves a taken for granted shared background of practices, since no one can ever fully say what he means so as to exclude in advance every possible misunderstanding" (HDPR, 49; and see xxi, 47, 77, 94).

he writes that reflection on the origin of a phenomenon always starts "against the *background* of the already begun";[29] and he asserts the necessity to write the history of punishment against the *background* of a history of bodies.[30] *The Care of the Self* claims to demonstrate that "it was against the *background* of this cultivation of the self, of its themes and practices, that reflection on the ethics of pleasure developed in the first centuries of our era."[31] Only once does Foucault use the concept of the background as such, outside idiomatic usage. The last sentence of *Discipline and Punish* states that the book is "a historical *background* for different studies of normalization."[32] In other words, Foucault here claims to have described the configuration of disciplinary practices, against the background of which future, better documented, and more specific histories can be written.

It would be also untrue to say that Foucault gives precedence to the term "background" over other metaphors for the relationship between practices and the content of discourse. In his earlier writings, which were still very heavily influenced by Heidegger's use of spatial metaphors, he employs such terms as "surrounding," "periphery," "operational domain," and "field" to identify the conditions of possibility for discourse. Thus, in *The Archaeology of Knowledge* he writes that analysis of language "is surrounded on all sides by an enunciative field," and that "elements of language always emerge in the operational domain of an enunciative function."[33] These spatial metaphors give Gilles Deleuze grounds to interpret Foucault's analytics in highly metaphoric Nietzschean language as a surface-oriented study of the "base" or "curtain" on which statements of a given discourse appear, and behind which no essential meaning is hidden, but which constitutes the condition of possibility for statements to appear.[34]

Whether or not Foucault is using the concept of background practices,

29. Michel Foucault, *The Order of Things*, trans. Alan Sheridan (New York: Pantheon, 1971), 330. Rather than the original French texts and terms, I cite their English-language translations that were instrumental in Dreyfus's construction of the "background practices" interpretation of Foucault's work.

30. Michel Foucault, *Discipline and Punish*, trans. Alan Sheridan (New York: Pantheon, 1978), 25.

31. Foucault, *Care of the Self*, 66; emphasis added.

32. Foucault, *Discipline and Punish*, 308.

33. Michel Foucault, *The Archaeology of Knowledge*, trans. A. M. Sheridan Smith (New York: Pantheon, 1972), 112. In Dreyfus's terms, they emerge against the background of practices of the production of serious utterances.

34. "Each age says everything it can according to the condition laid down for its statements. . . . Behind the curtain there is nothing to see, but it was all the more important each time to describe the curtain, or the base. . . . Statements become readable or sayable only in relation to the conditions which make them so and

he is surely studying very specific practices, and here the interpretation of Dreyfus and Rabinow is supported by Foucault's texts. He explicitly states that the target of his analysis is "the practices . . . understood here as a place where what is said and what is done, rules imposed and reasons given, the planned and the taken for granted melt and interconnect."[35] His definition of practices is very reminiscent of Wittgenstein's concept of a language game, as a combination of deeds and words. Like many other commentators on Foucault, Thomas Flynn notes the resemblance and writes: "Similar to Wittgenstein's 'game,' a practice is a preconceptual, anonymous, socially sanctioned body of rules that govern one's manner of perceiving, judging, imagining and acting. . . . Neither a disposition, nor an individual occurrence, a practice forms an *intelligible background* for actions" by its double function of setting standards for normal behavior and of making possible distinctions between truth and falsehood.[36]

The standard methodological procedure for this study of background, which Dreyfus and Rabinow call interpretive analytics, starts with a diagnosis of some urgent problem in the analyst's culture. Having identified this problem, the analyst proceeds to study the conditions that made the appearance of this problem possible, by paying attention to those background practices that provided grounds for its formation and its discursive articulation. Having explored the internal coherence of these background practices by means of the method that Dreyfus and Rabinow, following Foucault, call "archaeology," the analyst then studies how this current configuration of practices has come about, by means of "genealogy," another method frequently mentioned in Foucault's writings. Let us look in greater detail at these two constituent components of Foucault's method.

Archaeology

Facing the difficult task of accounting for the changing meanings of Foucault's terms "archaeology" and "genealogy," Dreyfus and Rabinow pro-

which constitute the simple inscription on [this] 'enunciative base'" (Gilles Deleuze, *Foucault,* trans. Sean Hand [Minneapolis: University of Minnesota Press, 1988], 54).

35. Michel Foucault, "Questions of Method," in *The Foucault Effect,* ed. Graham Burchell et al. (Chicago: University of Chicago Press, 1991), 75.

36. Thomas Flynn, "Foucault's Mapping of History," in *The Cambridge Companion to Foucault,* ed. Gary Gutting (Cambridge: Cambridge University Press, 1994), 30; emphasis added. See also another formulation of explicit affinity between Wittgenstein and Foucault: "that which presents itself as subjective arises out of the common (public) transformable practices" (John Rajchman, "Foucault: the Ethic and the Work," in *Michel Foucault Philosopher,* trans. Timothy J. Armstrong [New York: Routledge, 1992], 218).

pose the following formulation: "from his earliest days Foucault has used variants of a strict analysis of discourse (archaeology) and paid a more general attention to that which conditions, limits and institutionalizes discursive formations (genealogy). . . . However, the weighting and conception of these approaches has changed during the development of his work."[37] Let us clarify this succinct formulation.

For Foucault, archaeology deals primarily with written discourse but treats it as a set of background practices for dealing with words. *The Archaeology of Knowledge,* which was allegedly intended to serve as a methodological commentary to the three books written during the "archaeological" period of Foucault's development, insists on this treatment of texts several times: rather than analyze what the texts say, treating them as "documents," Foucault chooses to analyze texts as "monuments," as certain embodiments of practices for producing knowledge. The set of these discursive practices, which constitutes the background of a given discourse, defines its four principal features: what can be taken as an object of this discourse, who can take the position of a speaking subject, what kind of concepts may be accepted, and what kind of theories may be constructed within a given discourse. However, in order to see the background of present-day discourse (in which the author shares), we must take "an archeological step back," a kind of estrangement technique that renders our most obvious ways of doing things with words problematic by comparing them with something outlandish, either the discursive practices of a foreign culture or those of an earlier epoch in our own culture. Foucault usually follows the second strategy, which is why he calls his work "archaeology."

Thus, in *The Order of Things* Foucault studied, among other discourses, "natural history," a precursor of modern biology. Legitimate ways of producing scientific statements in natural history were different from ways of producing them in the biological sciences nowadays. In the foreground of natural history, different statements from opposing theories—for example, from Linnaeus's "fixist" or Buffon's "evolutionist" theories—could contradict each other, but they both conformed to the same practice at the background level. Both theories were predicated on a certain manner of description, which took as its object the whole structure of visible organs (in contrast, say, to the earlier practice of looking for manifest resemblances between some part of the plant and some human organ—a walnut and a brain) and then classified results in tabular form, with a regular table con-

37. HDPR, 104.

taining a definite number of cells (in contrast, say, to the later construction of trees of evolution), that were supposed to exhaust all possible creation.[38]

Foucault claims that this finite number of ways of doing things with its statements characterized the enterprise of natural history. These discursive practices made up the very specific background for what could be said within natural history.[39] He points out that bigger groupings of discourses also had common backgrounds. Three discourses of the classical period in French culture—natural history, analysis of wealth, and general grammar—shared practices of attribution, articulation, designation, and derivation.[40] This common set of practices for producing legitimate serious statements, which had remained unnamed until Foucault, formed an enunciative background for all the pursuits and research of grammarians, logicians, and linguists at the time: "Against this *background* of enunciative coexistence, there stand out, at an autonomous and describable level, the grammatical relations between sentences, the logical relations between propositions, the metalinguistic relation to an object language and one that defines the rules, the rhetorical relations between groups (or elements) of sentences."[41]

In order to clarify what archaeology does, Dreyfus and Rabinow compare it to Searle's theory of speech acts. Though both study how people do things with words, they differ in one important respect. While Searle deals with any ordinary utterance, Foucault deals primarily with statements from scientific and quasi-scientific discourses, with philosophical and political treatises. Dreyfus and Rabinow call these objects of Foucault's attention "serious speech acts" and claim that they are modeled on the statements of normal science in Kuhn's conception of a paradigm. A paradigm comprises a number of cases of exemplary solving of problems in a given science and thus unobtrusively prescribes acceptable ways of doing things

38. Foucault, *Archaeology of Knowledge*, 152.
39. The word "could" in this sentence may be taken as too strong an assertion but I choose to retain Foucault's usage because he shares with Heidegger a conception of *Waltens*, a "governing" quality of the Clearing of Being [*Lichtung*] that sets the conditions of possibility for phenomena to appear as they do. Common sense, in this theorization, has forgotten about this quality and ascribes the act of "prohibition" or "suppression" only to human beings; while Foucault and Heidegger hold it to be the quality of the discursive practices. On *Waltens*, see Hubert L. Dreyfus, "Foucault and Heidegger on the Ordering of Things," in *Michel Foucault Philosopher*, trans. Timothy J. Armstrong (New York: Routledge, 1992).
40. Ibid., 60.
41. Ibid., 99; emphasis added.

in this discipline. "Serious speech acts" are similarly produced by a very specific and finite number of acceptable ways of doing things with words. What makes them serious, however, is not the rigidity of their production per se, but their authentication as legitimate means of producing truth in a given culture. Serious speech acts are different from ordinary utterances in that they are supported by a whole network of institutionalized power relations that grant them a superior status of truth claims. In the example of Dreyfus and Rabinow, when I say "It's going to rain," this is an ordinary speech act; when a University of Michigan scientist, or spokesman of the National Weather Service, utters the same statement, it is a "serious" speech act.[42]

Archaeology, therefore, is a method for revealing the background practices governing the production of serious speech acts. It starts with an estrangement technique, a certain step back from the practices to be analyzed, at least if those practices are contemporary. This step is already made for the archaeologist, if these practices belong to the distant past. Next, this method becomes one of "pure description,"[43] almost of a positivist kind: an archaeologist simply enumerates and registers a finite number of ways of doing things with words discerned in the studied texts, those practices that were employed by the speaking subjects in their construction of serious statements in a given discourse. Having enumerated them, an archaeologist posits no unifying sense among the practices, nor any reason that brought these practices together. For example, Foucault simply registers that medieval thinking employed four practices of finding resemblances in order to produce serious sentences in medicine—*convenientia*, emulation, analogy, and "sympathy"—but finds no underlying logic beneath this grouping.[44] Perhaps some of these practices could have been mixed with some of the four practices that made up the background of natural history of the seventeenth century and could have been combined in a strange discursive formation of their own—derivation and designation coupling, say, with emu-

---

42. The authors' focus on one meaning of the term "serious" when they construct their definition of the "serious speech act" makes their definition difficult to handle. If the president makes a joke during a presentation to Congress, or a weather scientist makes a mistake, is this "serious" or "unserious"? The decision depends on whether a sentence produces "truth": the frivolity of a joke excludes it from "serious speech acts," but even a mistake of an authorized pronouncer of truth on the weather does not make the speech act "unserious."

43. Ibid., 27.

44. Foucault, *Order of Things*, 18–23.

lation and analogy. But archaeology does not inquire why these very background practices, and not others, were linked.[45]

Genealogy

Later, however, the question of "why these practices together?" becomes central for the interpretive analytics of Foucault. Many commentators agree that his "genealogical" period (roughly, the 1970s) was ushered in by the events of May 1968 in France, along with his subsequent interest in issues of power. In a sense, political engagement forced Foucault to consider the question of why certain speech acts—and not others—are deemed to be serious in a given culture, which in turn became connected to the question of why only certain practices form the background for the production of serious speech acts. Foucault's method of answering these questions is genealogy: it traces the development of practices and their interconnection in time.

According to Dreyfus and Rabinow, a genealogist practices the archaeological method but subordinates it to genealogical tasks. Archaeology still defines the background practices of the seriously sayable in a given culture, but then genealogy steps in to trace the external, nondiscursive conditions that shaped the given configuration of discursive practices. A broader social background is considered, including the analysis of the reception of discourse by nonprofessional users, and the analysis of institutional and social practices that conditioned the choice of discursive practices which in their turn serve as the background for the production of serious speech acts.

> The genealogist sees that cultural practices are more basic than discursive formations (or any theory) and that the seriousness of these discourses can only be understood as part of the society's ongoing history. The archaeological step back that Foucault takes in order to see the strangeness of our society's practices no longer considers these practices meaningless.[46]

Furthermore, genealogy is a way of analyzing such ensembles of nondiscursive practices as institutions (such as the prison or the clinic), or of such complex patterns of behavior as sexuality. Genealogy studies the "conditions of possibility" that allowed practices to form these ensembles and

---

45. In Foucault's archaeological project, as in Thomas Kuhn's scientific paradigm, he tries to describe the finite number of practices used to provide the model solution of a problem.

46. HDPR, 125.

thus allowed, for example, modern prison or modern sexuality to emerge as phenomena of this world. In *Discipline and Punish* Foucault discerns some practices that underlie what he calls "disciplinary power." By means of archaeology he discovers that these practices were the practice of normalizing judgment and the practice of hierarchical observation. By means of genealogy, he traces how each of these practices developed in time and points to the multiple origins of each of these practices in different spheres and to the diverse nexuses of their interconnection (a merger, say, of hierarchical observation with normalizing judgment that yielded such a universal and seemingly obvious technique as the examination).

Similarly, "the task of the genealogist of the modern subject is to isolate the constituent components and to analyze the interplay of these components."[47] If modern individuals are produced by searching for the truth of who they are individually in repeated confessions of matters of sex, an archaeologist has to isolate at least three constituent elements of this intertwining of practices and discourses. These are, first, confessional practices; second, the object of confession called "sexuality"; third, those nondiscursive practices that constituted conditions of possibility for the formation of discourse on this object, which united such diverse and heretofore unrelated elements as certain desires, comportments, pleasures, and bodily excretions.[48] A genealogist then examines how it became possible to merge such unrelated elements in order to constitute the novel object of discourse; and then he or she examines the merger of the practices of confession with the nondiscursive practices underlying the production, study, and analysis of the novel discursive object called sexuality.[49]

Foucault calls this method of looking for origins of the current configuration of practices "genealogy" because of its clearly Nietzschean overtones. Dreyfus and Rabinow hold that in his single brief essay that specifically

47. Ibid., 175. "Subject" here stands for "the individual," since Foucault is interested in how human beings become subjects of action. He relies on the Continental European philosophical tradition that frequently equates the two.

48. Before political and social institutions concerned with population growth and with procreation made these diverse elements the object of their analysis in the 18th century, confession did not and could not focus on "sex"; "what we had before that was no doubt the flesh" (Michel Foucault, "The Confession of the Flesh," in *Power/Knowledge*, ed. Colin Gordon [New York: Pantheon, 1980], 211).

49. As Wahl says, "from the practices of discourse to the practices of action, and always in terms of changing rules which cause them to act upon one another," Foucault's thought is "a pragmatics of diversity" (François Wahl, "Inside or Outside Philosophy?" in *Michel Foucault Philosopher*, trans. Timothy J. Armstrong [New York: Routledge, 1992], 79).

dealt with methodological ramifications of genealogy, Foucault demonstrated the interconnections between Nietzschean genealogy and his own version of it.[50] First, both reveal the multiple origins of the current configuration of practices, the many points and historical contingency of their interconnection, demonstrating thus that the current configuration is far from being the only one possible. Second, both try to uncover the "lowly origins" of the current configuration, indicating that it came about through violence and bloodshed, that base interests and motives lay at the foundation of this configuration. As a result they destabilize it and, perhaps, move people to rework their practices.

Method in Question

Dreyfus and Rabinow's description of Foucault's method has been under attack during the last decade. First, some of its elements remain ambiguous. For example, what are the relations between discursive and nondiscursive practices in serving as the background for discourse? Do nondiscursive practices condition discursive practices (as penal discipline conditions "objective positive description" of a prisoner)—which in turn condition what can be meaningfully said in a given discourse—or do nondiscursive and discursive practices simultaneously condition what may be said? Why do no nondiscursive practices figure in the background for discourse on life, labor, and language in the eighteenth century, as is seen in *The Order of Things*, and as it is once again stated in the introduction to *The Use of Pleasure?*[51] If on the one hand, archaeology deals primarily with discourse, while genealogy deals primarily with what conditions it, and on the other hand, "all archaeology reconstructs systems of practices," does this mean that archaeology deals with discursive practices, while genealogy deals with nondiscursive practices?[52] If this is true, then how is the archaeology of nondiscursive practices possible at all? Dreyfus and Rabinow would seem to owe us answers to these questions.

Second, other commentaries have produced differing sequences in Foucault's methodological development. Flynn discerns three consecutively employed methods: archaeology, genealogy and problematization. He writes that Foucault initially practiced archaeology as a study of the configuration

50. Michel Foucault, "Nietzsche, Genealogy, History," in *Language, Counter-Memory, Practice*, ed. Daniel Bouchard (Ithaca: Cornell University Press, 1977).
51. Michel Foucault, *The History of Sexuality*, vol. 2, *The Use of Pleasure*, trans. Robert Hurley (New York: Pantheon, 1985), 11.
52. HDPR, 104, 256.

of practices; then, with growing attention to power and its influence on the body, he shifted to genealogy; and the end of Foucault's career is marked by the use of "problematization" as a methodological tool appropriate to the study of the practices of the self.[53] Davidson makes a similar argument but calls the three respective "forms of analysis" archaeology, genealogy, and ethics.[54]

Third, many would question whether Foucault had a coherent vision of his method at all. Paul Veyne, Foucault's colleague at the Collège de France, says that "he preferred to preach by example, to exemplify his method in history books rather than setting it out."[55] Indeed, Foucault rarely commented on his methods, unless pressed to do so by his interlocutors. His only essay dealing with genealogy, mostly of a Nietzschean kind, was written in 1970, well before Foucault did any of his famous studies of the "genealogical" period. *Archaeology of Knowledge* stands out, of course, as a methodological tour de force, but a close study of other books from his "archaeological period," *Madness and Civilization, The Birth of the Clinic,* and *The Order of Things,* reveals that he used very different methodological procedures in each book, united perhaps only in their common origin in the normative basis of the "history of concepts" that Foucault learned from Georges Canguillhem.[56] All of these procedures are hardly connected to the method spelled out in *The Archaeology of Knowledge,* which seems more of a beautiful exercise in applying structuralist language to describe a Heidegger-inspired view of the Clearing of Being, or of what Dreyfus calls the background for discursive statements. Last, but not least, Foucault sometimes directly contradicted the opinion of Dreyfus and Rabinow that he employed two consecutive methods, archaeology and genealogy, in the course of his career. Thus, he once called constructing a genealogy of the subject as "the aim" of his project, while the method of arriving at this genealogy was designated as archaeology.[57]

Given all these reservations, we might wonder whether Foucault had a

53. Flynn, "Foucault's Mapping of History," 28.
54. Arnold I. Davidson, "Archaeology, Genealogy, Ethics," in *Foucault: A Critical Reader,* ed. David Couzens Hoy (Cambridge: Blackwell, 1986), 221.
55. Paul Veyne, "Foucault and the Going Beyond (or the Fulfillment) of Nihilism," in *Michel Foucault Philospher,* trans. Timothy J. Armstrong (New York: Routledge, 1992), 342.
56. Roberto Machado, "Archaeology and Epistemology," in *Michel Foucault Philosopher,* trans. Timothy J. Armstrong (New York: Routledge, 1992), 17.
57. Michel Foucault, "About the Beginning of the Hermeneutic of the Self," *Political Theory* 21, no. 2 (May 1993): 223.

clear methodology. Thus, Gary Gutting in his recent overview chooses to challenge the most powerful interpretation of Foucault's method:

> Dreyfus and Rabinow offer a general interpretation in that they read the whole of Foucault's work as directed toward the development of a single, historico-philosophical method that has a privileged role in contemporary analysis. . . . I am uneasy with this and other general interpretations of Foucault because they deny the two things that, to my mind, are most distinctive and most valuable in his voice: its specificity and marginality.[58]

Notwithstanding the disputable claims of the value of specificity and marginality, it seems plausible to defend Dreyfus and Rabinow's methodological exposition in two other respects. On the one hand, the overview of Foucault's own statements from the late period of his work suggests that after 1979 a certain methodological collusion has developed between him and his primary interpreters. Of course, Gutting is correct that the "whole work" of Foucault was not directed toward elaborating "the single historico-philosophical method." At the same time Foucault's statements from the late period indicate that he came closer to a uniform rationalization of his method, supplied by Dreyfus and Rabinow, and thus unwittingly helped them maintain their stance. Foucault's own methodological remarks, unambiguously supporting the interpretation of Dreyfus and Rabinow, may prove that their representation of his method is correct—at least for those readers who still believe that the author's own statements still count, even in the current age of "the death of the author."

On the other hand, for those readers who cannot take Foucault's own words at face value and who tend to think that the "rules of Foucaultian method" are impossible to find (and its "application" to the study of a specific culture impossible to undertake), I suggest the following argument. Instead of following the rigid "rules," we may point out and follow Foucault's typical "strategy" of dealing with source material, which we will call "nominalist critique." In this version of defense of Dreyfus and Rabinow, we recognize their description of the typical moves in this strategy as useful for further practitioners.

Before we consider the relevance of Foucault's "methods" or "strategies" to the study of Russian individualism, let us look at the rare methodological remarks that Foucault made in the last years of his life. Respond-

58. Gary Gutting, introduction to *The Cambridge Companion to Foucault,* ed. Gary Gutting (Cambridge: Cambridge University Press, 1994), 3.

ing in 1977 to the questions of a group of French historians discussing his *Discipline and Punish*, Foucault admitted his predilection for asking "how" rather than "what." "It's a method," he conceded, "which seems to me to yield, I wouldn't say the maximum of possible illumination, but at least a fairly fruitful kind of intelligibility." This method, in Foucault's opinion, involved two steps: the first is a "breach of self-evidence" that aims to shake assumptions about what seems obvious. A close study of historical sources reveals that it is far from obvious, for example, that locking up criminals is the "natural" or the universal way to treat them, or that the only means for the study of disease is a singling out and analyzing the individual body. The second step is "rediscovering of connections . . . , plays of forces, strategies and so on, which at a given moment establish what subsequently counts as being self-evident, universal and necessary." [59] The first step, estrangement from what is most familiar, corresponds to archaeology, in the terminology of Dreyfus and Rabinow, while the second, tracing the interrelations of practices that provided the conditions for the appearance of the familiar, is genealogy. [60]

In his 1980 remarks on methodology during his Howison lectures at Berkeley, Foucault made a similar suggestion. He stated that he predominantly studied sources from the human sciences, concentrating "on regressive history that seeks to discover the discursive, institutional and social practices from which these sciences arose." [61] Though on this occasion Foucault called this exercise "archaeological history," he was describing both what Dreyfus and Rabinow call archaeological dimensions (a study of practices that form the background for discourse) and what they call genealogical (a regressive study of their origins). It seems very likely that a detailed description of Foucault's method, already contained in the first edition of *Beyond Structuralism and Hermeneutics* (1979), and the conversations that Dreyfus and Rabinow had with Foucault while writing their book, influenced his own methodological reflections. However, this two-step procedure appears in his own methodological remarks only later.

In the introduction to *The Use of Pleasure* (1983), Foucault gave the latest, and perhaps the most detailed, version of relations between archaeology and genealogy. He said that he aimed

---

59. Foucault, "Questions of Method," 76.

60. This perfect coincidence of Foucault's words with Dreyfus and Rabinow's description of his method is not surprising: the authors must have been aware of this exchange at the time of writing HDPR. In its 2d ed. they quote from *L'impossible prison*, where this exchange appeared in French in 1980.

61. Foucault, "About the Beginning," 223.

at analyzing not behaviors or ideas, nor societies and their ideologies, but the problematizations through which being offers itself to be, necessarily, thought—and the practices on the basis of which these problematizations are formed. The archaeological dimension of the analysis made it possible to examine the forms themselves, the genealogical dimension enabled me to analyze their formation out of the practices and the modifications undergone by the latter. There was the problematization of madness and illness arising out of social and medical practices, and defining a certain pattern of "normalization"; a problematization of life, language and labor in discursive practices that conformed to certain "epistemic rules"; and a problematization of crime and criminal behavior emerging from certain punitive practices conforming to a "disciplinary" model.[62]

The method, as described by Dreyfus and Rabinow—archaeology individualizes and analyzes the configurations of discursive or nondiscursive practices that constitute the background for discursive formulations, while genealogy studies the permutations of these practices—finds new support in this lengthy passage. It adds the term "form of problematization," which refers to a configuration of practices (as the author clarified in an interview):

> Problematization doesn't mean a representation of the pre-existing object, nor the creation by discourse of an object that does not exist. It is the totality of discursive and nondiscursive practices that introduces something into the play of true and false and constitutes it as an object for thought (whether in the form of moral reflection, scientific knowledge, political analysis, etc.).[63]

Thus, the *Use of Pleasure* starts with an analysis of thematic similarities of contents of the Christian and classical Greek prescriptions on sexual austerity. Then Foucault shows that the forms of problematization—the practices that underlay these formulations—were radically different: if Christianity imposed a universal moral code to be followed by everybody, in Greece practicing sexual austerity was the choice of the exceptional few who so fashioned their lives out of concern for "the aesthetics of existence." Foucault as archeologist uncovers different practical backgrounds that support the same discursive formulations in Greek and Christian dis-

---

62. Foucault, *Use of Pleasure*, 10–11.
63. Michel Foucault, "The Concern for Truth," in *Politics, Philosophy, Culture. Interviews and Other Writings, 1977–1984*, ed. Lawrence D. Kritzman (New York: Routledge, 1988), 257.

course; Foucault as genealogist will then trace how the Greek practical background shifted to become the radically different Christian background: he will study the permutations of background practices or, as he chooses to call them now, "forms of problematization."[64]

Foucault's late opinions on his methods include an article on Foucault written in 1983 for the encyclopedia of French philosophers. A search for the real author hidden behind its pseudonym "Maurice Florence" has yielded no results so far; given the article's style and paraphrasing of what Foucault said in his last interviews, we might suspect that it was Foucault himself or, at least, a person who was intimately familiar with Foucault's manner of writing. This brief entry in the encyclopedia contains an overview of "methodological choices." The specificity of Foucault's method, claims "Florence,"

> resides in appealing to practices as the domain of analysis, of approaching one's study from the angle of "what was done." He first studies the practices—ways of doing things— . . . through which one can grasp the lineaments of what was constituted as real for those who were attempting to conceptualize and govern it, and of the way in which those same people constituted themselves as subjects capable of knowing, analyzing, and ultimately modifying the real. These "practices," understood simultaneously as modes of action and of thinking, are what provide the key to understanding a correlative constitution of the subject and object.[65]

The last sentence in this elegant synthesis of Foucault's oeuvre suggests yet another observation on the methodological collusion between Foucault and his interpreters. In their interactions with Foucault in Berkeley in the late 1970s, Dreyfus and Rabinow proposed to him that, generally speaking, he primarily studied two types of practices.[66] On the one hand, there are "objectifying practices," like the small techniques used in natural sciences or penal discipline, which serve as the background for making objective

64. Even in Foucault's new vocabulary of problematizations, the archaeological practice of estrangement is easily recognizable: "Thought . . . is what allows one to step back from this way of acting or reacting, to present it to oneself as an object of thought and question it as to its meaning, its conditions, its goals" ("Polemics, Politics, and Problemizations," in *The Foucault Reader*, ed. Paul Rabinow [New York: Pantheon, 1984], 389).

65. Maurice Florence, "Foucault, Michel, 1926–," in *The Cambridge Companion to Foucault*, ed. Gary Gutting (Cambridge: Cambridge University Press, 1994), 318.

66. Paul Rabinow, personal communication. On subjectifying and objectifying practices, see HDPR, 160–167, 178–183.

statements about the world and people, and thus contribute to the formation of the objective world. On the other hand, he also studied "subjectifying practices," such as techniques of hermeneutics or different techniques of self-perfection, which serve as the background for the production of interpretations of oneself and help form human subjectivity. Foucault seems to have accepted this general overview and repeated it, to an extent, in his article specifically written for the afterword to Dreyfus and Rabinow's book.[67]

The physical being of a Frenchman named Foucault seems to support in plain speech the claims of Dreyfus and Rabinow on the availability of a certain method, or at least, certain "methodological dimensions" in his own work. For those of us who still hold on to the modern understanding of authorship, what else, if not the direct and unambiguous confession of the author himself concerning his methods, may support his interpreters' claim that he had consciously applied this very methodology in his work?

Therefore, if we accept the "methodological interpretation" of Dreyfus and Rabinow, we should do a Foucaultian study of Russian culture by seeking its characteristic subjectifying and objectifying practices. In so doing, we should rely on archeological description of the set of background practices of Russian culture and then on genealogical investigation of subjectifying and objectifying practices that constitute this set.

NOMINALIST CRITIQUE AS A PRACTICAL SKILL

Even within this general interpretation, Gutting's anti-methodological argument may find our support for a different reason, namely for being true to Foucault himself. And if we follow the methodological premise of archeology—even in the general version of Dreyfus and Rabinow—we should not look for a single feature underlying all of Foucault's diverse studies. His is not an oeuvre that has a single object, and the titles of his books demonstrate this clearly. Apart from the reference to the same physical being, we cannot posit the same subject behind his statements. Foucault changed himself with each new book, to such an extent that the books seemed to be written by different authors. "Do not ask me who I am and do not ask me to remain the same," he replied in a famous statement to

---

67. "I have studied the objectivizing of the subject in what I shall call 'dividing practices'. . . . Finally, I have sought to study . . . the way a human being turns him- or herself into a subject" (Michel Foucault, "Why Study Power: The Question of the Subject," afterword to *Michel Foucault,* by Hubert L. Dreyfus and Paul Rabinow, 2d ed. [Chicago: University of Chicago Press, 1983], 208).

those who would try to establish the continuity between the radically different authors of *Madness and Civilization* and *The Order of Things;*[68] this
plea applies to his later work as well. There is hardly any unifying conceptual apparatus or "theoretical strategy" also. For example, the "theory" of
the first volume of the *History of Sexuality*—a study of confessions on
matters of sex—is obliterated in favor of a new one in the second volume
—a study of the hermeneutics of desire—that appears eight years later,
hence such a formidable time gap between the two volumes.

If we cannot find unity on all of these levels, then should we search for
it on the level of methodology? This search seems to run counter to what
Foucault said and did. Rather than looking for a single method in Foucault,
an archaeologist could uncover a set of diverse discursive practices that serve
as the background for this body of writing, practices that have a certain coherence and intelligibility. A genealogist could discover how these practices
came to coexist. However, since neither an archaeology of discourse united
under the heading "Foucault," nor a genealogy of Foucault's practice are
the aims of this book, I leave them to others and get back to the problem of
how to practice Foucault's type of study in relation to the Russian source
material, even if there is no single universal "Foucaultian method."[69]

Gutting considers Foucault not as a methodologist but as "an intellectual artisan," who over the years constructed a number of diverse artifacts,
"the intellectual equivalents of the material objects created by a skilled gold-
smith or a cabinetmaker."[70] We may use them accordingly, but we may also
put them to different further uses, not even imagined by their creator. Second, Gutting's formulation gives us grounds to reconceptualize Foucault's
methodology as a "skill" that he perfects over time, as every artisan does.
Or, we may say, Foucault consistently performs a certain practice—of doing archaeology, genealogy, problematization, however he and other people
may choose to call it—that comes into being through his texts.

Two passages from Foucault may illustrate this hypothesis. He is open
about his nomadic habit of applying his skills to different concerns in diverse milieus: "I like to open a space of research, try it out, and if it does

---

68. Foucault, *Archaeology of Knowledge*, 17.
69. Flynn makes a first attempt at this archaeological "pure description" of Foucault's earlier practices: shocking the reader with a phenomenological image of an
alien reality; stating a bold thesis that challenges received opinion; restructuring
the evidence at hand on the basis of this claim (see Flynn, "Foucault's Mapping of
History," 32).
70. Gutting, introduction, 6.

not work, try again somewhere else."[71] As a consequence Foucault is often not clear about the relations among his various categories, but he may disregard this lack of clarity (perhaps, only temporarily, since he was usually forced to supply it eventually by his interviewers), if his products attract attention:

> On many points—I am thinking especially of the relations between dialectics, genealogy and strategy—I am still working and don't yet know whether I will get anywhere. What I say ought to be taken as "propositions," "game openings" where those who are interested are invited to join in; they are not meant as dogmatic assertions that have to be taken or left *en bloc*.[72]

As a traveling tinkerer, an intellectual artisan, Foucault approaches different sets of problems, applies his skills, seeing whether they work, and abandons the half-finished artifact if it bores him. Thus, in response to a question from his puzzled assistant about the radical change of subject from the first to the second volumes of *The History of Sexuality*, Foucault answers:

> When a piece of work is not also an attempt to change what one thinks and even what one is, it is not very amusing. I did begin to write two books in accordance with my original plan, but I very soon got bored. It was unwise of me to embark on such a project and run counter to my *usual practice* . . . out of laziness.[73]

"Usual practice" here means changing what one thinks and changing oneself while writing a new book, and this practice seems to be the only kernel of continuity uniting the ever-changing "selves" that implicitly stand behind the author's various works. The point now is to grasp the kernel.

There are different ways of approaching this task. For example, a scientific study of "practical sense," developed by such sociologists as Pierre Bourdieu, would recommend revealing the *habitus* of Foucault the artisan, that is, the representation of his typical coping techniques in a diagram of his skill.[74] Perhaps it would be my objective if I wanted to put into words what Foucault did. But my aim is different: to employ his skill in a different cultural setting, to analyze the birth of Russian individualism using his research techniques.

---

71. Foucault, "Questions of Method," 74.
72. Ibid.
73. Foucault, "The Concern for Truth," 255; emphasis added.
74. Pierre Bourdieu, *The Theory of Practice* (Stanford: Stanford University Press, 1990).

Bourdieu's theory of practical sense is helpful for this enterprise also, but in another respect. His criticism of the structuralist attempts to explain practical sense in terms of fixed "rules," rather than open-ended "strategies," suggests an approach to earlier studies of Foucault's methodology. Rules, according to Bourdieu, are produced by an inquiry that asks the respondents to objectify what they do or observes them; while "strategies are the product, not of obedience to a rule, but of a feel for the game," which leads the players to choose the best move possible, given the assets available to them and the "skill with which they are capable of playing." Rules are rationalizations of action, arrived at post factum. If however, they are then stated explicitly, and adopted by the players themselves, the rules supply guidance for further action. In a slightly misleading metaphor, "the explicit rule of the game . . . defines the value of playing cards." [75]

The methodological interpretation of Dreyfus and Rabinow laid down the "rules of a Foucaultian game," by assigning values to different ways of doing research. Thus, there are archaeology, genealogy, techniques of estrangement such as "stepping back," and techniques of revealing the background—all within a certain hierarchy: for example, archaeology is subservient to genealogy, estrangement is part of the archaeological procedure, and so on. This description is very useful because it defines the field of possible actions in a "Foucaultian game" and the means available to players in this game. Provided with a description of the rules, we may now start imitating Foucault's skills, practicing them, trying out the most successful "strategic" move, using the learned skill and available assets.

Now, if the assets and their ranking are more or less clear, following the exposition of Dreyfus and Rabinow, we need a "feel" for the basic Foucaultian skill as a lived practice. Following many interpretations of Foucault's work, I propose to call it "a nominalist critique." It may come in different guises, employ different moves, but the end product will be the same: the criticism of things taken to be self-evident and universal. Let me now give a preliminary description of this skill, before attempting to practice it in the following study.

The methodological nominalism of Foucault is an obvious feature of his writing. Many prominent commentators, except perhaps Dreyfus and Rabinow, repeatedly point it out. For example, David Hoy speaks about "pragmatic nominalism"; Gilles Deleuze about "repudiation of the universals";

75. Pierre Bourdieu, "From Rules to Strategies," in *In Other Words* (Stanford: Stanford University Press, 1990), 64.

Thomas Flynn about "historical nominalism."[76] Foucault himself uses the term explicitly a few times. Explaining his method in the mid-seventies, Foucault defines it as "the nominalist critique itself arrived at by way of historical analysis."[77] *The History of Sexuality* contains the most famous nominalist claim: "One needs to be nominalistic, no doubt: power is not an institution, and not a structure; neither is it a certain strength we are endowed with; it is the name that one attributes to a complex strategical situation in a particular society."[78]

"Nominalism," of course, is a philosophical position in the famous medieval scholastic debate about universals, claiming that general concepts are mere names without any corresponding reality. This claim opposed the claim of the philosophical school of "Realism," that what abstract concepts stand for has real, objective, and absolute existence. A nominalist would say that universals exist only as *universalia in re*, that is, they do not have separate existence from singular things. In the passage from Foucault quoted above, power is exactly this: the name that unites a myriad of interacting forces in a given society—between a traffic police officer and a driver, between a doctor and a patient, between a teacher and a pupil, between a father and a son, and so on. Nominalism requires, however, taking even these "typical" relations of forces apart down to the most singular interactions, for example an interaction between a driver "X" and an officer "Y" in a city "Z" at a time "T." "Power" therefore becomes a name that is attributed to all of these singular interactions in a given moment of time.[79]

76. David Couzens Hoy, "Power, Repression, Progress: Foucault, Lukes, and the Frankfurt School," in *Foucault: A Critical Reader*, ed. David Couzens Hoy (Cambridge: Blackwell, 1986), 135, 139; Gilles Deleuze, "What is a *dispositif*?" in *Michel Foucault Philosopher*, trans. Timothy J. Armstrong (New York: Routledge, 1992), 162; Flynn, "Foucault's Mapping of History," 39.
77. Foucault, "Questions of Method," 86.
78. Foucault, *An Introduction*, 93.
79. This paragraph oversimplifies the Nietzschean perspective that Foucault takes, in which the human individual is also a product of power, not the indivisible smallest foundation of interactions. Rather, Nietzschean "forces" clash to mold and remold this unstable set of practices called a particular human individual. Foucault's nominalist analysis of the situation of a traffic police officer stopping a motorist would describe their interaction in terms of forces (forces that individuals exert on others; forces that form them as these very individuals; ones that reinforce and disturb their formation as individuals in the outcome of this present confrontation, etc.), not in terms of individual subjects.
But what interaction of forces is nominalist analysis to take as the most singular and concrete, as indubitably real? A fist hitting a cheek? Or is it a quasi-automatic handing over of a driver's license at an officer's demand instead of even considering

In a similar manner,

> Sexuality must not be thought as a kind of a natural given which power tries to hold in check, or an obscure domain which knowledge tries gradually to uncover. *It is the name* that can be given to a historical construct: not a furtive reality that is difficult to grasp, but a great surface network in which a stimulation of bodies, the intensification of pleasures, the incitement to discourse, the formation of special knowledges, the strengthening of controls and resistances, are linked to one another.[80]

A comparison with Walter Benjamin, another great nominalist of the twentieth century, may better illuminate certain qualities of Foucault's practice. Benjamin's nominalism, which laid the foundation for the negative dialectics of the Frankfurt School, treats universals as arising out of the configurations of elements, out of "constellations," to use the famous term of both Benjamin and Theodor Adorno.[81] Universals then are denied an existence separate from their constituent elements, similar to the way a mosaic exists only as a configuration of particular elements. Concern for the particular was a driving passion for the theorists of the Frankfurt School, who aimed at eschewing "the terrorism of the universal" that subjugated a particular will to the will of majority. By contrast, mosaic constellations, which could not oppress the constituent elements in such a manner, were therefore preferable since each element kept its full particularity in this aesthetic universal.

Benjamin's method subdivides the existing phenomena into constituent elements and then regroups these elements, not into conventional classes

---

hitting him in response to this usual claim of power? Foucault's position, which uncovers an interaction of forces, is only relatively more nominalist than the conventional description that posits an interaction of individuals. In a sense, Foucault goes just "one level" deeper in his nominalist descriptions, but that move allows him to get rid of the notion of the human individual as an indubitably real atom of action. On his concept of power as a constellation of "forces acting on forces" see his "Why Study Power?"; and on Nietzsche's concept of forces, which influenced Foucault, see Gilles Deleuze, "Active and Reactive," in *The New Nietzsche*, ed. David B. Allison (Cambridge, Mass.: MIT Press, 1985).

80. Ibid., 105–106; emphasis added.

81. I follow the superb description of constellations in Susan Buck-Morss, *The Origins of Negative Dialectics* (New York: Free Press, 1977), esp. ch. 6. See also Richard Wolin, *Walter Benjamin, an Aesthetic of Redemption* (New York: Columbia University Press, 1982); and Martin Jay, *Adorno* (Cambridge, Mass.: Harvard University Press, 1984).

of elements sharing an abstract characteristic, but into new constellations of an aesthetic, nonoppressive kind. The closest cultural model for this practice of constructing constellations, which both Benjamin and Adorno employed in their work, was a new original piano interpretation of a classical musical piece or a jazz improvisation: elements remain the same, but a reconfiguration of them brings out a different universal. This reconfiguration, however, is not a simple reshuffling of the elements, as in rotating of the kaleidoscope. The image of the mosaic or of a jazz improvisation is somehow misleading, since in Benjamin's conception constellations do not depend so much on visible or audible unities, as they do on the power of naming. A researcher reconfigures the elements of the phenomena and then names the resulting constellation, since only naming finally brings the new constellation into existence and gives it meaning.[82]

Whether or not Foucault shared the aspirations that founded this search for constellations among the Frankfurt theorists, his practice is to a certain extent similar to Benjamin's. For example, *Archaeology of Knowledge* starts with the repudiation of the great existing universals—"tradition," "influence," "evolution," "the spirit of the time"—that usually serve as a common ground for a given discourse: "All these syntheses that are accepted without question, must remain in suspense."[83] Foucault wishes to find new, different unities underlying the discourse, by analyzing discourses as practices. As a result he finds universals that subsume the diversity of discourse without reference to a single abstract characteristic common to all elements.[84] These are not hard to find, since they are given in the names of existing discourses. Foucault reveals discourses to be constellations of practices. He first individualizes a set of discursive practices that serve as a background for a particular discourse and then shows that the title of this particular discourse is just a name of the constellation of

82. Of course, the new name has a meaning only if I give it one. Benjamin's view of naming reflects his background in Jewish mysticism and refers to giving proper names for things rather than to inventing strange new words with shared meanings. On "divine naming" in pre-Adamic language, much like "giving proper names," see Walter Benjamin, "On Language as Such and on the Language of Man," in *Reflections*, trans. Edmund Jephcott (New York: Harcourt Brace Jovanovich, 1978).

83. Foucault, *Archaeology of Knowledge*, 25.

84. The commonsense notion of the universal as a shared feature of a set of objects still reigns in conventional science. Foucault attacks this commonsensical notion in the French context, as Wittgenstein did in the Anglo-American context with his "family resemblances" and Benjamin did in the German one.

these practices. The name "doctor" in the nineteenth century referred to a constellation of practices of "qualitative descriptions, interpretation, and cross-checking of signs, reasoning by analogy, deduction, statistical calculations, experimental verification, and so on."[85] Constellations of other practices found other discourses.

Some European commentaries in their very language suggest this affinity between Benjamin and Foucault. Thus, Rainer Rochlitz writes that Foucault's standard procedure was "stepping back and reconstituting the genealogy of present constellations," while François Wahl claims that Foucault describes a "history of problems and a redistribution of practices which order them."[86] However, there are two important differences between Benjamin and Foucault. The first consists simply in the orientation of analysis: if Benjamin tries to reveal novel constellations by means of reconfiguration and naming, Foucault reveals the already existing universals as constellations, hiding behind the conventional image of a concept that captures a set of abstract general features common to each element of a given class.[87] In other words, he is reinterpreting those entities that seem unproblematic simple generalizations by showing the multiplicity of their constituent elements. In his later, "genealogical" works, not only titles of discourses but such universals as "power" and "sexuality" are each in turn subject to nominalistic analysis and are revealed as constellations of disparate practices. The second difference between Foucault and Benjamin consists in their answers to the question of what brought these disparate practices together. Foucault suspects the "lowly origins" of every such merger, in contrast to the ethical impulse of Benjamin, who always considered constellations to be of benign nature. Once more quoting "Florence" on Foucault, "the first methodological rule . . . is . . . to circumvent anthropological universals to

85. Ibid., 50. Foucault's "nominalism of degree" uses terms that are universals themselves (a radically nominalist position is hardly tenable) but subvert the existing self-evident generalizations by being just a bit more nominalist than convention allows.

86. Rainer Rochlitz, "The Aesthetics of Existence: Post-Conventional Morality and the Theory of Power in Michel Foucault," and Wahl, "Inside or Outside Philosophy?" both in *Michel Foucault Philosopher*, trans. Timothy J. Armstrong (New York: Routledge, 1992), 248 and 78.

87. What makes a discourse of general grammar a unity is not an abstract feature common to all its statements but a finite number of practices for producing these statements. And to produce each statement some practices are activated, others are not. Seen as a whole, general grammar is a constellation of these practices—a universal that exists only through the co-presence of its particular constitutent elements.

the greatest extent possible, so as to interrogate them in their historical constitution."[88] We should treat "madness," "delinquency," "sexuality" as sets of practices whose content varies with time, but we should also ask what conditions, in a given time, make it possible to recognize a subject as "mentally ill" or what makes it possible for people to search for the truth of their individuality in a strange construct called "sexuality."

Foucault's nominalist critique is applied to different objects, destroying the illusion of their "essential nature" or "necessity." It is part of both genealogy and archaeology. When applied to a certain historical problem, it may also be said to uncover a "problematization," a set of practices that made possible the appearance of this problem in the form it did. Attacking grand anthropological universals, it reveals a background diversity of practices that made possible the appearance and use of these very universals. Following Foucault, we will study the set of practices that provided the conditions for the appearance and meaningful use in contemporary Russian life of the universal called *individualizm*.

DOMAIN

Having reviewed the methods, I am now able to restate my objectives in finer detail and map out the domain of this study of individualization in Soviet Russia. Because attempts to relate the Foucaultian methods of archeology and genealogy to the Russian case constantly bring up the topic of the functioning of the primary group to which an individual belongs, I explore collective group-formation as well as individual self-fashioning. I practice nominalist critique in the relation of two of the most obvious and mundane phenomena of Russian culture—the individual (*lichnost'*) and the collective (*kollektiv*)—and identify the background practices that constituted the conditions of possibility for Russian thinking about them, as well as of constructing and transforming them in Russia. In the end, I reflect on the constellation of practices that enabled the term *individualizm* to make sense for the majority of the Russian population, when applied to describe their life by the time of the collapse of the Soviet Union.

The primary sources of data for this study are the minor, pragmatic discourses of the Soviet period: manuals and instructions on how to conduct a purge or a self-criticism session in a Party cell, how to create a *kollektiv* out of a chaotic human group, how to work on oneself to become a true

88. Florence, "Foucault, Michel, 1926–," 317.

Communist, and so on. Following Dreyfus and Rabinow's distinction between "subjectifying" and "objectifying" practices, I examine a set of practices that made it possible for people to be known objectively and to know
themselves as individuals in Soviet Russia and compare this local background with the one Foucault found in the West.

Outlining a general context, chapter 2 articulates a certain congruence
between some Orthodox Christian practices and those ushered in by the
Russian Revolution of 1917. It shows how this general quasi-religious background set the conditions for changes in the language and practices of the
epoch. Taking up the *kollektiv*, chapter 3 describes how it became an object
of knowledge and action and analyzes the discourse on the *kollektiv* and the
pragmatic techniques for *kollektiv*-building proposed by the educationalist
Anton Makarenko. Turning to the *kollektiv* as a subject of knowledge and
action, chapter 4 puts discourses on self-criticism and purges, the activities
of a *kollektiv* purifying itself, against the background of practical methods
of searching out "Party illnesses."

Taking up the individual, chapter 5 observes the emergence of the individual as the object of knowledge and action in Party discourse on the "individual approach" to Party members and against the general background
of practices of conducting a purge in the 1930s. Chapter 6 deals with the individual as the subject of knowledge and action, analyzing the discourse of
Soviet educational literature (including books of guidance for youth) on
practices of self-fashioning, or "working on oneself," as it was then called.
Chapters 7 and 8 integrate the results into a general description of the practices of formation of the individual and of the collective in mature Soviet
society. A conclusion reviews the general results of studying Russian background practices, and the problems of practicing this Foucaultian style of
inquiry.

2   Reveal, Admonish, Excommunicate
Ecclesiastical Courts and the Central Control Commission

PARTY JUSTICE

B., a member [of the Russian Communist Party] since 1917, of peasant origin, barely literate and politically uneducated, a former People's judge. Expelled from the Party for discrediting it and the Soviet state by drinking while performing his functions (appeared at the court hearings drunk); for threatening the People's assessors with arrest when they did not agree with his opinion; for forcing female subordinates into sexual intercourse with him.

In the Terentiev district the chairman of the Committee of Poor Peasants, comrade M., dressed in female attire, drank among women in order to hide his systematic alcoholism but became drunk to such a degree that peasants found him asleep on the street and took the makeup off.

P., a member since 1912, of worker origin, primary education, a director of an industrial plant, politically developed and active, a worthy manager. Accused of systematic alcoholism and staging drinking bouts with his female subordinates. . . . District Control Commission has expelled him from the Party as corrupt. The Moscow Control Commission and the Central Control Commission, having taken into consideration his positive and negative features, as well as that his drinking and intercourse with women had a character of license rather than of total corruption, have expelled P. for a term of one year, together with relieving him of the job of director of an enterprise, and sent him to work on the shop floor, for "refreshing."[1]

---

1. Emelian Iaroslavsky et al., eds., *O bor'be s naslediem proshlogo (p'anstvo i religioznye predrassudki sredi chlenov partii)* [Fighting the residues of the past (alcoholism and religious prejudices among Party members)] (Moscow: TsKK, 1925), 20, 11, 19.

These are just three typical cases that involved Russian Communist Party members tried in 1924–25 by the Party's Control Commissions on charges of alcoholism and sexual misdemeanor. The charges brought against them were not uncommon. Brutal conduct and methods of operating by assault and attack, fostered by the tumultuous conditions of the Civil War, seem to have hardened into established patterns of behavior for the victors.[2] Although these examples, taken from the anti-alcoholism campaign, were far from the most important cases tried by the Control Commissions—crimes related to property were considered the most corrupting—they represent some typical concerns of the day with which the winning Party had to deal, lest its image of virtue be smeared by such examples.

First, they present us with the curious logic by which the Party classified misdeeds and allocated appropriate punishment. The nomenclature of misdeeds changed with time but remains surprising to a modern reader, since categories frequently seem to lack a common logical denominator. Thus, in the most detailed formulation of the seven "Party illnesses" adopted by the plenum of the Central Control Commission in October 1924, and in order of their decreasing gravity, the categories were careerism and squabbling within the Party (*sklochnichestvo*); marrying or entering into close personal contact with petty bourgeoisie (*oNEPivanie*); expanding one's holdings of land or other primary economic assets (*khozobrastanie*); excesses in personal habits (*izlishestva*); alcoholism; sexual license; participating in religious rites.[3]

Second, these cases demonstrate the puzzling insistence on curing rather

2. Instead of securing law and order, militiamen in one provincial city "chased peaceful citizens brandishing their drawn sabers" (for which 12 of the 30 were disciplined); when in another city the militia were called to arrest a Communist who, while drunk, broke into a private apartment and fell asleep in the bath, they recognized the head of the military section of the local Party committee and "guarded his sleep" until he woke in the morning; another Communist, not content with activities at a party he attended, "arrested all the girls," put them in a barn, used the butt of his gun to hit a Komsomol member who tried to defend them, shot at the executive of the local Soviet, and so on (see ibid., 21, 16, 11). In the mid-1920s the "extravagant" stories in this brochure read alone make the general scene look unsightly: Communists fight during meetings and bite off fingers, vomit while delivering speeches, collectively rape cleaning women, spend public resources on gypsy bands and restaurants, and so on.

3. Emelian Iaroslavsky, "O partetike: Predlozheniia prezidiuma TsKK II Plenumu TsKK 3 oktiabria 1924 g." [On Party ethics: proposals of the CCC presidium to the 2d CCC plenum, October 3, 1924], in *Partiinaia etika: Dokumenty i materialy diskussii dvadtsatykh godov* [Party ethics: documents and materials of Party discussions of the 1920s], ed. A. A. Guseinov et al. (Moscow: Politizdat, 1989), 57; terms *oNEPivanie* and *khozobrastanie* were invented to cover these very specific

than punishing. What we see is the wish not only to eradicate misdeeds, which besmirch the image of the Party, but even more to correct Party members guilty of misdeeds. In considering each malefactor, the commissions took account of specific mitigating circumstances and authorized "gentler" disciplinary measures when possible, as in the reassignment "to work on the shop floor" mentioned above. Curing the illness, rather than punishing the transgressor, was the general aim. This curious therapeutic impulse and the strange nomenclature of Party crimes require explanation.

Let us recount the history first. The Central Control Commission (CCC), initially created in November 1920 to offset dangerous status differentiation within the Party, was not specifically intended to fight crimes. The creation of the CCC was one among many efforts attempting to democratize Party life, including more frequent meetings and rotation of Party officials, their criticism by the Party rank and file, and so on. As the resolution of the Ninth Party Conference, founding the CCC, stated in September 1920, "war conditions forced us to establish 'shock' (and therefore in fact privileged) offices and groups of officials. After the war this takes the form of the problem of 'top' and 'bottom' [layers] within the Party, which is unacceptable."[4] The CCC was created to deal with this problem of certain Party members being "more equal" than others. The founding resolution appealed to the Party cells to file complaints with the CCC about any abuse of Party office that seemed to violate the professed egalitarianism of the Party. Swamped by the resulting denunciations, the newly created CCC and its subsidiary provincial Control Commissions swiftly acquired the unintended status of permanent Party courts.

The CCC was an independent Party body, equal in status only to the Central Committee. In practical terms, it functioned as the Party's judicial branch, separate from the executive power vested in the Central Committee. Members of the CCC could not serve on Party committees at any level or on its administrative bodies. They were recruited from the "most honorable," "trusted," and "conscientious" workers whose reputation stood unblemished from prerevolutionary days.[5] Of the 150 people initially com-

---

"illnesses," and ordinary terms ("squabbling" and "excesses in personal habits") were given new meanings (see chapter 4).

4. "Ob ocherednykh zadachakh partiinogo stroitel'stva" [Current tasks of party building], resolution of the IX Party Conference, in *Voprosy partiinogo stroitel'stva: Materialy i dokumenty* [Problems of party building: materials and documents], ed. A. Mel'kumov (Moscow: Gosizdat, 1927), 167.

5. Solts, a lifetime member of the CCC who often served as its chairman, had the nickname "the Conscience of the Party" (*Sovest' partii*). See the idealized lit-

prising the CCC, 70 full-time functionaries staffed its permanent offices, 50 members of the CCC were ordinary workers in plants and factories appointed so that the CCC retained "contact with the masses," and 30 chaired its regional Control Commissions. Members of the CCC had unlimited access to the offices and plenums of the Central Committee and could speak there but not vote. However, at any joint plenum of the Central Committee and the CCC, they had full voting rights.[6] Local Control Commissions tried the misdeeds brought to the Party's attention in a given region. A typical "Party collegium," that is, a section of the local Control Commission, charged with dealing with the illnesses of the Party, consisted of the three staff members of the local Control Commission and two invited People's assessors.[7] Special "Party investigators" who prepared cases for the consideration of the collegium were employed in some regions. The verdict of the local Control Commission could be appealed to the Party collegium of the CCC in Moscow, which usually diminished the penalty.

erary portrait that reflects this image in Anatolii Rybakov's novel *The Children of Arbat,* and in his biography (note 12 below).

6. "Polozhenie o TsKK RKP(b)" [The CCC statute], in *Spravochnik dlia KK RKP(b) i organov RKI* [Reference book for the Control Commissions and bodies of the Worker-Peasants' Inspectorate] (Moscow, 1924), 8 (hereafter *RBCC*, with year of its amended ed.).

In 1923, following Lenin's last instructions, the CCC was merged with the Worker-Peasants' Inspectorate, a commissariat of the state control. The WPI's fledgling status was to be boosted by this union with the most powerful body of the Party, according to Lenin's thought. The WPI conducted raids on Soviet and industrial offices, fought "bureaucratism," sought to effect the "rationalization of socialist production," and thus served as "the school of government" for the workers who were frequently recruited ad hoc for a given raid. Part of the presidium of the CCC served on the board of the WPI; the posts of chair of the local CCC and head of the local WPI were combined. But the lower WPI staff was not supposed to interfere with the functioning of the Party collegium, the main section of the local Control Commission, dealing with "Party illnesses" as such. I thus concentrate only on the functioning of the CCC branch of the CCC-WPI. For further accounts of the CCC see Paul M. Cocks, "Politics of Party Control: The Historical and Institutional Role of Party Control Organs in the CPSU" (Ph.D diss., Harvard University, 1969). Standard works in Russian are I. M. Moskalenko, *TsKK v bor'be za edinstvo i chistotu partiinykh riadov* [CCC in the struggle for the unity and purity of Party ranks] (Moscow: Politizdat, 1973); and S. N. Ikonnikov, *Sozdanie i deiatel'nost' ob"edinennykh organov TsKK-RKI v 1923–1934 gg.* [Creation and activities of the CCC-WPI in 1923–34] (Moscow: Nauka, 1971).

7. "Instruktsiia o rabote partkollegii mestnykh KK" [Instruction on the work of Party collegiums of the local CCs (May 11, 1926)], in *RBCC 1932,* sec. 3, par. 4; "Polozhenie o Partkollegii TsKK VKP(b)" [CCC Party collegium statute (January 18, 1926)], in *RBCC 1927,* sec. 3.

The fact that the CCC soon became an effective Party court is not surprising; special bodies called "Party courts" existed even before 1920 on an ad hoc basis. Although the 1918 Party Statute authorized only the creation of certain special disciplinary commissions and prohibited maintaining "permanent Party courts," the Central Committee circular (August 18, 1920) established the temporary guidelines for the ad hoc courts: "Every Communist bears double responsibility because for his actions that violate the laws of the republic he is subject to both civil and Party courts."[8] Those who committed serious criminal offenses were subject to automatic expulsion from the Party and were to be handed over to the People's courts. "However, Communists who and Party organizations that violate only Party discipline or commit an act contrary to the general opinion within the Party, are subject to the Party court only."[9] The ad hoc Party courts were to be guided in their deliberation by paragraph ten of the 1918 Statute of the Party, and by two circulars of the Central Committee.[10] Given the fact that the Central Committee later issued a special appeal against spontaneous creation of "Party investigative commissions"—which allegedly violated the 1918 statute—transforming ad hoc Party courts into permanent judicial bodies was rather widespread also.[11]

8. "O dvoinoi otvetstvennosti kommunistov za prostupki" [On the double responsibility of Communists for their misdeeds], in *RBCC* 1931, par. 18 (dropped in later eds.), 122–123.

9. Ibid.

10. See the 1918 Party statute and the October 21, 1919 circular ("O merakh nakazaniia za narusheniia partdistsipliny" [On means of punishment for violations of Party discipline], in *Spravochnik partiinogo rabotnika* [Reference book of Party officials], 1st ed. (Moscow, 1921), 16 and 88. I cite the second circular above in note 8.

11. See the Central Committee circular in *RBCC*, 2d ed., 1922, par. 24, 82.

The Party courts, antedating the creation of the CCC, seem to have come into being rather spontaneously during the years of the Civil War. The offenses considered are similar to those later tried by the Control Commissions. Thus, in St. Petersburg 354 Communists were expelled from the Party in the first half of 1920 on the basis of these Party courts' decisions. The main bulk of the expelled included those who did not attend party meetings or pay their dues (29 percent of the expelled), those who did not pick up new party cards at the exchange of documents (24.5 percent), and those convicted of stealing (12 percent). Party offenses strictly speaking included breaking Party discipline (7.2 percent), deserting the ranks of the Red Army (7.2 percent), private speculations on the black market (1.8 percent), demonstrated avarice (2.3 percent), and alcoholism and card playing (3.9 percent) (M. Pol'tov, "Partiinyi sud" [Party court], *Sbornik materialov Peterburgskogo komiteta RKP, vypusk 1: ianvar'–iiul'* [A collection of the documents of the Petersburg Party committee] 1 (January–July) (Petersburg, 1920), 27.

Granted its proclaimed task of adjudication in internal Party conflicts, and the pressing social need of curtailing violations of the Party statute, the CCC easily took over the functions of the preexisting Party courts. The kind of delicts that the CCC sought to address differed over time. Aaron Solts, one of the first chairmen of the CCC, delivering the first summary report of this body to the Party Congress (March 1921), said that the CCC already dealt primarily with three kinds of Party "defects." [12] These were separating oneself from the broad Party masses, abuse of Soviet offices for private gain, and fomenting intra-Party quarrels and factionalism. [13] Interestingly, all the defects mentioned were assigned to the Party and not to a specific individual and were accordingly called "Party illnesses." Because these defects threatened to subvert the supposedly tight unity of the Party, they were subject to correction.

The period of the New Economic Policy (NEP) brought radical changes. The loosening of political controls over the market visibly restored a capitalist spirit in the country. As a consequence, the report of the CCC to the Eleventh Party Congress in 1922 stated that now the most important issue was the problem of corruption by petty-bourgeois elements, which had infiltrated the Party. [14] Issues of everyday conduct of individual Party members in diverse mundane situations moved to the forefront, giving rise to prolonged debates in 1923–25 over the question of "Party ethics." A list of seven "Party illnesses" (mentioned above) was compiled to give some standard directions to the work of the local Control Commissions. As a re-

---

12. Aaron Solts (1872–1945). Born into a merchant's family, graduated from the law department of St. Petersburg University; revolutionary activist since 1898. Distributed Lenin's illegal newspaper *Iskra* in 1901, arrested and exiled. Participated in 1905 revolution; arrested and exiled. In 1917, member of the Moscow Party Committee; in 1918, a "Left Communist" (demanded the export of revolution into Germany). In 1921–34, member of the CCC, and a member of its ruling presidium after 1923. Member of the International Control Commission of the Comintern. Delegate to the IX (1920)–XVII (1934) Party Congresses. During the last years of his life worked in the USSR Procuracy. For further details see P. I. Roshchevsky, *Skvoz' Grozy* [Through the storms] (Sverdlovsk, 1967); and *Geroi Oktiabria* [Heroes of the October Revolution] (Moscow, 1967). One of Solts's important speeches is translated in William G. Rosenberg, *Bolshevik Visions* (Ann Arbor, Mich.: Ardis, 1984), 42–54.

13. Aaron Solts, "Doklad Kontrol'noi Komissii na X s"ezde RKP(b)" [CCC report to the 10th Party Congress], in *Partiiniaia etika,* ed. A. A. Guseinov et al. (Moscow: Politizdat, 1989), 132.

14. Aaron Solts, "Iz otcheta Tsentral'noi Kontrol'noi Komissii na XI s"ezde RKP(b)" [CCC report to the 11th Party Congress], in *Partiinaia etika,* ed. A. A. Guseinov et al. (Moscow: Politizdat, 1989), 142.

sult, similar classifications, compiled by local Control Commissions to account for the specificity of their local tasks, proliferated.[15]

During 1925–27 attention turned from Party ethics to left oppositionism. For those who wanted to see the party as a living body, nothing could be more ghastly than such a grand schism within it. After open factional struggle erupted at the Fourteenth Party Congress in 1925, the main focus of activity by the local Control Commissions in 1925–27 was rounding up and disciplining the "unstaunch" and "vacillating elements."[16] The left opposition was eliminated by 1927, and the right opposition became the new scapegoat in the late 1920s. Economic crimes by Party members also steadily gained the attention of the Control Commissions, displacing the question of ethics.[17] In 1931 the Control Commissions were reoriented by Stalin to become tools in the struggle for collectivization and industrialization.[18] Punishing transgressions connected with this vast revolution in

15. Thus the Moscow Control Commission had eight categories of misdeeds against Party ethics. Out of 7,010 cases brought to the Party collegiums of Moscow between October 1926 and September 1927, "only" 3,299 concerned the violation of ethics. These included squabbling (372 cases), alcoholism (1,938 cases, by far the largest category), participation in religious rites (72), "sexual license with a refusal to support the child" (95 cases), un-Communist treatment of subordinates (94), nationality conflicts (19), ties to "alien elements" (94), and others (612) (Guseinov et al., eds., *Partiinaia etika*, 444–445).

16. For example, in the first half of 1927 the number of processed cases in all the categories of Party illnesses decreased or stayed the same relative to 1926, while the only substantial increase (from 4.4 to 6.6 percent of those prosecuted) was in oppositional activities ("Iz otcheta TsKK-RKI SSSR XV s"ezdu VKP[b]" [CCC-WPI report to the 15th Party Congress], in *Partiinaia etika*, ed. A. A. Guseinov et al. [Moscow: Politizdat, 1989], 452).

17. In 1926–27, authorizing "unproductive expenditures" and plain embezzlement of official funds accounted for 27–28 percent of cases tried by the Control Commissions (ibid.). The joint resolution of the Central Committee and the CCC of October 1923, dealing with the general matter of "excesses" in spending, was not reprinted in the subsequent editions of *RBCC* after 1931; perhaps it sounded too vague and general. Instead, a section dealing with "Party illnesses" was mostly devoted to detailing economic crimes. Among those enumerated in 1933 were the CCC instructions on the inadmissibility of spending public funds for banquets and presents; on thrifty spending of funds for business trips abroad; on prohibiting solicitation of financial "help" from industrial enterprises for Party organizations; on prohibiting use of public funds to furnish the apartments of Party officials; on prohibiting allocation of funds for unspecified "travel needs"; on prohibiting appointment of cliques of cronies from an old job after move to a new one, and so on (see *RBCC* 1933, pars. 29–34, 181–183).

18. See *RBCC* 1932, sec. 3 ("The Work of Party Collegiums"), par. 3 (resolution of the CCC plenum, June 1931, following Stalin's "New Tasks" speech).

the economic life of the country constituted the bulk of their activities in 1931–33. As commentators have noted, this fervent anti-crime campaign was wide-ranging: 30 percent of the leaders of the local Control Commissions themselves were subsequently dismissed and punished for "over-zealous deviations" in 1933.[19] Apart from these changing functions, which depended on the changing priorities of Party policy, the Control Commissions were always assigned the task of carrying out the general Party purges (in 1921, 1929, and 1933) and of conducting intermittent partial screening campaigns in 1924 and 1925. They were responsible for initiating the majority of Party prosecutions until 1934, when the CCC was disbanded.[20]

Three rather puzzling features of the CCC should be now stressed. First, given the number of cases tried, and of people continuously screened at its sessions, it is surprising that the CCC consistently rejected being compared to a court and resolutely refused to call itself one.[21] Solts, in his first CCC report to the Party Congress, almost immediately after the creation of the CCC, stated that "we do not conduct trials, and we do not have defendants; we have comradely conversations on the subject of the accusation presented."[22] The resolution of the Thirteenth Party Congress on the Control Commissions (1924) again stated that the Party collegiums, a section of the Control Commission specifically engaged in curing Party illnesses,

19. Kuromiya, *Stalin's Industrial Revolution*, 296.

20. In 1934 the CCC-WPI was disbanded for reasons that are unclear, being supplanted by two new bodies, the Committee of Soviet Control and the Committee of Party Control. These new committees were supposed to take care of these two branches of control more effectively, with the help of extensive permanent staffs, rather than recruiting rank-and-file members on an ad hoc campaign basis to help the few permanent CC-WPI officials. The last general purge of 1933–35 was finished by the special "purge commissions," whose members not infrequently were former Control Commission officials. Soviet commentators, particularly in the Khrushchev era, suspected a hideous Stalinist plot of eliminating the CCC—a body of "genuine Party democracy." Indeed, the CCC successors—the CPC and the CSC—played a very small independent role after 1936, since they effectively became part of the state apparatus, until Khrushchev salvaged them from oblivion (see chapter 7 for a discussion of the KPGK, the committee of Party-state control).

21. For example, in 1924 the Control Commissions "considered" 46,600 Communists, that is, 5.1 percent of the whole membership (Guseinov et al., eds., *Partiinaia etika*, 427). Between the XIV and XV Congresses (18 months in 1926–27) they "made answerable" 93,300 Communists or 7.6 percent of membership, with 2.6 percent expelled as a result (449). The general purge of 1933 ended with 17 percent of the total membership expelled and with another 6.6 percent demoted to the then existing special rank of "sympathizers" (*XVII s"ezd VKP[b]: Stenograficheskii otchet* [17th Party Congress: stenographic report] [Moscow, 1934], 287) (hereafter *XVII Steno/34*, page).

22. Solts, "Doklad Kontrol'noi Komissii," 134.

"should not be transformed into judicial bodies dealing with violations of the Party statute and Party ethics."[23] Instead, the Party collegiums were supposed to study the illnesses and work out concrete measures for their elimination. These measures were to be of an "educational," and not of a punitive character.[24] Better still, stated the 1924 resolution, "casual small misdeeds of a Party member that do not harm the Party organization and do not indicate the corruption of this Party member" should not be brought to the attention of the Control Commission at all but should be handled "in the comradely environment."[25]

The CCC considered its quasi-judiciary functions an anomaly. How could it be normal for a comrade, asked Solts during the discussion of the "Party ethics" campaign, to bring another comrade before a Party prosecution, instead of guiding the faltering comrade into righteous conduct by comradely advice and admonition? He insisted: "If your brother or your wife, your close friend makes a mistake, I'm sure you don't summon him immediately to the C[ontrol] C[ommission], but you try to resolve the problem among yourselves, because it would be strange if a son brought his father to the CC or to judicial prosecution."[26]

These quotes also indicate the second puzzling feature of the CCC: its curious aversion to expulsion. Expulsion was always to be the last measure, for use when all other educative measures fail. Thus, the 1920 circular on the Party courts distinguished between "expulsion" proper (a forced excommunication), "stepping down" (a voluntary departure from the Party), and "removal from the ranks" (resulting from nonpayment of dues). "Expulsion from the Party is the highest measure of punishment, because it leads to the civil and political death of the expelled, according to the circu-

23. "Rezoliutsia XIII s"ezda o rabote KK" [13th Party Congress resolution on the work of Control Commissions], in *RBCC 1924*, 4.

24. Compare this description of the aim of the Party collegium with the statement of one of the CCC's general aims: "Broad systematic study of morbid phenomena in the Party, in the sphere of ideology and in the organizational practices and everyday life of Party members as well, and the working out of joint measures together with the Central Committee aimed at eliminating the conditions that bring these morbid phenomena about, with the employment of predominantly educative measures" ("Polozhenie o TsKK," par. 6, *RBCC 1924*, 8). Of course, the primary official aim of the CCC as a single body was to recruit the best representatives of the working class into the Party and maintain its unity. Study of illnesses and their cure was made a special central objective of the Party collegium, a subdivision of the CCC.

25. Ibid.

26. Aaron Solts, "O partinoi etike" (1924) [On Party ethics], in *Partiinaia etika*, ed. A. A. Guseinov et al. (Moscow: Politizdat, 1989), 278.

lar of December 21, 1919, and is applied by the Party courts only for the gravest misdeeds"—or when other measures of influence fail.[27] The following devices were proposed in the preceding Central Committee circular of October 21, 1919, on disciplinary measures: censure at the Party committee meeting; censure at the general membership assembly, censure with subsequent publication in the local press, temporary relief from duty in Soviet and Party work. Only when these failed was expulsion authorized.[28]

Admonition, rather than expulsion, was stressed as the most appropriate means for the work of the CCC throughout its existence. Thus, Emelian Iaroslavsky, another co-chairman of the CCC, reasoned during the Party ethics campaign:[29]

> We do not differ over what to do with those who have incorrigibly succumbed to the negative influences of NEP. But if this is a valuable comrade and we see that we may save him by adopting different measures . . . , then we should do it. We should constantly watch such vacillating comrades, and when we see the slightest signs of danger threatening this comrade, we should warn him, help him get out of this situation, only [of course] if this comrade is one who may still be helped.[30]

27. *RBCC* 1931, 123 (for full title see note 8). I was unable to find this circular in printed sources. The circular from October 21, 1919 (note 10) states almost the same, however. It seems that in 1919–21 expulsion very often automatically resulted in a dismissal from work (since Party members were exclusively occupied in Soviet and Party offices); later, when Communists could be employed by nongovernmental or non-Party bodies, this practice was repealed and even prohibited. See note 41.

28. *Spravochnik partiinogo rabotnika* 1921, 88 (for full title see note 10).

29. Emelian Iaroslavsky (Gubel'man), 1878–1945, member of the Party since 1898. After participating in the revolution of 1905, imprisoned, then exiled to Siberia; in 1917, member of the Moscow Party Committee, one of the leaders of insurrection in Moscow in October 1917; elected to the Central Committee in 1921, then member and co-chair of the CCC in 1923–34, member of the Committee of Party Control in 1934–39. One of the most prominent Party ideologists, editor of the journal *The Marxist Historian,* and author of the *History of the CPSU;* chairman of the League of the Militant Godless in the 1920s, published five (!) volumes of anticlerical works and wrote the hugely popular Soviet catechism of atheism, *The Bible for Believers and Non-Believers.* His article in *Pravda* (June 23, 1941) supplied the Soviet title for the Second World War, "the Great Patriotic War of the Soviet People." For more information see P. S. Fateev, *E. M. Iaroslavsky* (Moscow, 1980); and B. G. Grigoriev, *Boets i letopisets revolutsii* [The warrior and chronicler of the revolution] (Moscow, 1960).

30. Emelian Iaroslavsky, "O partetike: Doklad na II Plenume TsKK RKP(b)" [On Party ethics: report to the 2d CCC plenum (October 5, 1924)], in *Partiinaia etika,* ed. A. A. Guseinov et al. (Moscow: Politizdat, 1989), 175.

Valerian Kuibyshev, who delivered the report of the CCC to the Fourteenth Party Congress in 1925, rejected the criticism of the CCC being "too soft" on transgressors (since the CCC annulled half of the expulsion verdicts of the lower Control Commissions in the period between the congresses), by telling a critic to try it himself: expelling a live human being who stands in front of you robs him of the dearest thing he has, "the political life." This was why, reasoned Kuibyshev, the CCC was becoming more and more like a "comradely organization" that aimed not to punish but to educate and correct.[31]

The Bulletin of the CCC, discussing the cases of "lack of staunchness" (*nevyderzhannost'*, a euphemism most frequently used in the Party press to designate oppositional activities) in 1927, reported that "the majority of those not staunch were shown the lack of staunchness in their behavior by comradely reproof" only, and most of the expulsion verdicts in these cases were overruled by the CCC.[32] Sergo Ordzhonikidze, presenting the CCC report to the Fifteenth Party Congress in 1927, implied that even in treating the oppositionists, the CCC wished to be an admonishing rather than a punishing agency, and thus lifted 90 percent of penalties and expulsions imposed on the oppositionists by the local Control Commissions.[33] This tactic, however, turned out to be counterproductive, he reasoned, since the oppositionists took it as a sign of weakness and resumed their factional activities. After this disregard for the CCC's care Ordzhonikidze recom-

31. *XIV s"ezd VKP(b): Stenograficheskii otchet* [14th Party Congress (December 1925): stenographic report], 3d ed. (Moscow: Gosizdat, 1926), 537 (hereafter *XIV Steno/26*, page).

32. Other activities grouped under this generic term *nevyderzhannost'*, which covered 4,523 cases considered by the 27 Control Commissions in the first six months of 1926, included not paying dues, not attending Party meetings regularly, discontinuing Party membership because of a wish to stop paying dues, and attempted suicide (O. Zortseva, "O partdistsipline i partnevyderzhannosti" [On Party discipline and the lack of Party staunchness], *Biulleten' TsKK VKP(b)* [CCC bulletin] 2–3 [1927]: 17).

The radical diversity of these activities makes obvious the arbitrary character of their grouping, and the highly fictitious character of the overarching generic term. What power relations would have made the term seem natural or as obvious for us as, say, "sex"? For example, if people had been shot or promoted to power on the basis of being "staunch" or "unstaunch" in the course of at least one generation's lifetime, then, we may suspect—in full accordance with Berger and Luckmann's description of habituation—later generations could have taken it as part of the stable institutionalized reality into which they were socialized in their childhood, and thus, as a most obvious description of the essence of human nature.

33. *XV s"ezd VKP(b): Stenograficheskii otchet* [15th Party Congress (December 1927): stenographic report] (Moscow: Politizdat, 1961), 1:430–466.

mended harsher measures. But if the main punitive energy was henceforth centered on fighting the oppositionists, the role of admonition and educative work in settling all other Party disputes and correcting minor transgressions increased.

Though the April 1931 conference of the Control Commission secretaries and the following plenum of the CCC in July 1931 primarily aimed at heightening vigilance against the factional activities of the right and left oppositions, they nevertheless both stressed the need to deal with smaller offenses in the cells, "in a comradely environment," invoking the resolution of the Thirteenth Party Congress.[34] When the gravity of a crime required harsher penalties, yet the CCC did not want to expel the member, a new institutional solution—temporary demotion—was proposed. During the general Party purges of 1929 and 1933 the Control Commissions could temporarily demote the member to the status of a candidate, or to the newly invented status of a "sympathizer." Having undergone appropriate rehabilitating exercises, like studying Party literature or demonstrating zeal in the practice of socialist construction, members could then be restored to their previous full status.

In a similar vein, in September 1929 the Komsomol (Young Communist league) restructured the Conflict Commissions—set up in 1926 to deal primarily (as the name itself suggests) with appeals of expulsions and penalties[35]—on the model of the Party Control Commissions in order to conform to the mood of the day and fight alien elements infiltrating the ranks of Young Communists, who brought into the Komsomol "a self-seeking attitude to production, nationalism, religiosity, petty-bourgeois individualism, . . . slackening of discipline, and noncomradely relations toward young women."[36] Yet these refashioned Conflict Commissions were still required to practice measures of an educative and preventive nature, and to authorize expulsion only when all other measures failed. The description

34. "O zadachakh i metodakh raboty partkollegii" [On the tasks and methods of the work of Party collegiums (April 21, 1931)], and "O zadachakh partkollegii KK" [On the tasks of Party collegiums of the Control Commissions (July 6–10, 1931)], both in *RBCC* 1932, sec. 3, pars. 2–3. For the original resolution of the 13th Party Congress see note 23.

35. "O konfliktnykh kommissiiakh TsK VLKSM" [On the Conflict Commissions of the Central Committee of Komsomol], the CCC resolution adopted on May 31, 1926, in *RBCC* 1927, 19.

36. "O zadachakh konfliktnykh kommissii VLKSM" [On the tasks of the Conflict Commissions of Komsomol], joint resolution of the Central Committee and the CCC, September 9, 1929, in *RBCC* 1932, 129.

of the tasks of the Komsomol Conflict Commission said that its main objective was to "train proletarian, revolutionary internationalists, Bolsheviks of the growing generation," rather than to punish or expel.[37]

Even during the Great Terror (1935–38), doctrinal logic required such people as Nikolai Ezhov to claim that one needed now "to practice more broadly such measures of training and strengthening of discipline among Party members as patient comradely explanation of the mistake committed by a Party member, warning him, issuing a reprimand."[38] Stalin himself had to allude to the necessity of admonitory measures even in his most ferocious speech, ushering in the height of terror. "Soulless treatment of people" was what he called the immediate expulsion from the Party of someone who showed up late for work once. Such a person should be warned first, the wise Leader reminded his audience.[39] When the terror abated, Andrei Zhdanov named at the Eighteenth Party Congress in 1939 the practice of "mass expulsions" as the main disadvantage of the method of the general purge. The Party should practice expulsion only as a last resort, sounded the familiar motif; while "the flexible scale of Party influences," neglected during the last three years, should be reinstated. The recommended list of disciplinary penalties included, in order of mounting pressure, "putting into the open" (*postavit' na vid*), declaration of censure (*poritsanie*), notice of a misdeed, reprimand, strict reprimand, strict reprimand with warning.[40]

The third puzzling feature of the CCC was its insistence that with expulsion, its jurisdiction ceased. The CCC did not punish: once it expelled a Communist, it had nothing further to do with his or her fate. Of course, CCC officials knew that expelled Communists almost always risked being dismissed from their jobs and might end up in an NKVD prison. But the official discourse tried to insist that this should by no means be automatic.

---

37. Ibid., 127, 125.

38. *III Plenum KPK pri TsK VKP(b)* [3d Committee of Party Control plenum] (Rostov-on-Don, 1936), 18. Nikolai Ezhov was the head of the dreaded NKVD (Narodnyi Komissariat Vnutrennikh Del [People's Commissariat of Internal Affairs]) in 1937–38; at the time of this statement (the summer of 1936) he was still the head of the Committee of Party Control, a successor body to the CCC.

39. I. V. Stalin, "Zakliuchitel'noe slovo na Plenume TsK VKP(b) 5 marta 1937 g." [Concluding remarks at the Central Committee plenum, March 5, 1937], in *I. V. Stalin, Sochineniia* [Works], ed. Robert H. McNeal (Stanford: Hoover Institute, 1967), 1 (XIV):246–247 (hereafter *Sochineniia*, volume: page).

40. *XVIII s"ezd VKP(b): Stenograficheskii otchet* [18th Party Congress (March 1939): stenographic report] (Moscow, 1939), 524 (hereafter *XVIII Steno/39*, page).

The 1919 Central Committee circulars on the double responsibility of the Communist that linked "civil and political death" were effectively repealed by the establishment of the Party collegiums, the whole raison d'être of which was the segregation of Party and civil offenses. In August 1926 the CCC even issued a special circular prohibiting the automatic layoffs of those expelled, unless they held Party jobs.[41] The CCC also held that Soviet state punitive bodies should not automatically follow its sanctions. Even during mass terror, in 1936, Ezhov stubbornly insisted (in a formulation that now seems either cynical or foolish) that the widespread practice of quasi-automatic turning over of expelled Party members to administrative prosecution should be stopped.[42] Expulsion from the Party did not necessarily indicate that someone worked poorly, said Ezhov; he might have been expelled simply for hiding from the Party some dubious biographical facts that were revealed during the purge. His deception of the Party by no means implied that he was failing to meet his job obligations.

Set against the background of perhaps the twentieth century's most brutal and bloody political regime, these three features of CCC discourse—the commissions' aim of curing, rather than punishing; admonition as their primary means of action; bloodless expulsion as their ultimate resource—demand an explanation. One suggestion comes to mind immediately: humane words, particularly coming from such people as Ezhov or Stalin, lose all their sense and become a cynical ruse, a ritual incantation that covers up slaughter. A popular myth, that of the "old Communists," is another alternative. The idealistic old Communists who actually abided by these humane words during the relatively peaceful 1920s were superseded and assassinated after 1934 by bloodthirsty villains, who however took over their gentle discourse.

The fact is that, contrary to the myth, CCC discourse did not conform to reality even before 1934. The CCC effectively played the role of a Party court and administered all verifications and purges while it existed, turning Communists over to NKVD prosecution and thus putting them under "the sword of the revolution," whether the CCC liked it or not. Therefore the rationale for the CCC discourse did not reside in its correspondence to real life. We find startling parallels between the discourse of the CCC and the discourse of the Russian Orthodox Church when it spoke about ecclesias-

41. "O nedopustimosti mekhanicheskogo sniatiia s raboty v nepartiinykh uchrezhdeniiakh lits, iskliuchaemykh KK" [On the inadmissibility of mechanical layoffs of the expelled in non-Party institutions], in *RBCC 1927*, 99.
42. Ezhov, quoted in *III Plenum KPK pri TsK VKP(b)*, 60.

tical courts: neither corresponded to reality, but both reasserted the same need to cure rather than punish, to admonish rather than expel, and both abhorred physical execution. Here, perhaps, lies the secret of the apparent "humanity" of CCC discourse.

ECCLESIASTICAL COURTS

In the first chapters of *The Brothers Karamazov* is an episode that may seem a little strange to modern readers. Ivan Karamazov speaks for the first time in the novel in a discussion of the future of ecclesiastical courts. He has just published a journal article outlining a grand plan to reform Russian society and humanity as a whole. In opposition to an opponent's plan for totally withdrawing church courts from secular affairs, Ivan's article proclaimed that church courts should regulate all aspects of social life. Thus the Russian Church would be able to fulfill its mission in this world: to expand so as to supplant the state and substitute its own benign authority for the bloody laws of the secular government.

Says Karamazov,

> When the pagan Roman Empire desired to become Christian, . . . it included the Church but remained a pagan State in very many of its departments. . . . The Christian Church entering into the State could, of course, . . . pursue no other aims than those which have been ordained and revealed by God Himself, and among them that of drawing the whole world, and therefore the ancient pagan State itself, into the Church. In that way . . . every earthly State should be, in the end, completely transformed into the Church and should become nothing else but a Church, rejecting every purpose incongruous with the aims of the Church. . . . If everything became the Church, the Church would exclude all the criminal and disobedient, and would not cut off their heads.[43]

Ivan also distinguishes his radical project from Catholicism, where he says the Church took over the state functions of repression of crime and sustaining political life. In his project, the Church would not punish, it would not become the state: rather, it would recast all social relations in accord with the New Testament. The elder Zossima, who participates in the conversation, supports Ivan:

> If anything does preserve society, even in our time, and does regenerate and transform the criminal, it is only the law of Christ speaking in his

---

43. Fyodor Dostoyevsky, *The Brothers Karamazov*, trans. Constance Garnett (New York: Modern Library, 1960), 61, 63.

conscience. [I]f the jurisdiction of the Church were introduced in practice in its full force, that is, if the whole of the society were changed into the Church, not only the judgment of the Church would have influence on the reformation of the criminal such as it never has now, but possibly also the crimes themselves would be incredibly diminished. And there can be no doubt that the Church would look upon the criminal and the crime of the future in many cases quite differently and would succeed in restoring the excluded, in restraining those who plan evil, and in regenerating the fallen.[44]

Father Paissy, present at the conversation, sums up the shared prophecy: "the Church is not to be transformed into the State. That is Rome and its dream. That is the third temptation of the devil. On the contrary, the State is transformed into the Church, will ascend and become a Church over the whole world—which is . . . the glorious destiny ordained for the Orthodox Church. This star will arise in the east!"[45]

It is curious to note that in this seemingly abstract discussion Fyodor Dostoyevsky not only introduces important theological issues on the difference between the aspirations of Eastern and Western Christianity but also sets out a vital topic of the day. At that time, in the mid-1870s, the question of ecclesiastical courts was in the forefront of attempts at government-initiated church reform in Russia. Reformers hoped to bring elements of modern secular rationality into the conduct of chaotic and ailing ecclesiastical justice. They aimed to separate the judicial from the administrative powers of bishops and to create independent diocesan courts, with lawyers and the participation of laity. They also aimed to install a uniform, codified system of canon law, to be applied systematically and solely to the clerical estate. Those few secular affairs—like some cases of marriage and divorce, or involuntary manslaughter—that remained in church courts after Peter the Great had removed almost all other issues from the Church's jurisdiction—were to be turned over to the secular courts.[46] Apparently, the reformists' viewpoint was represented in the position of Ivan's opponent in the novel. Dostoyevsky clearly endowed Ivan with a highly idealistic religious position, with which to oppose the mundane utilitarianism of secular Russian church reformers.

In reality the proposed rationalizing reform collapsed. A couple of

44. Ibid., 65.
45. Ibid., 66.
46. Gregory L. Freeze, *The Parish Clergy in Nineteenth-Century Russia* (Princeton: Princeton University Press, 1983), 329–345, 401–404.

influential clerical pamphlets appeared, discussing the proposed reforms in relation to apostolic teachings, and demonstrating that the reforms were clearly incompatible with the New Testament.[47] The bishops, who stood to lose the most in the implementation of the reforms since their judicial power was to be shared with both "white priests" and laity, firmly resisted the reforms.[48] They stalled the reforms, and—following the change of the secular supervisor of the Holy Synod in 1880—dismissed the liberal reformers and canceled their plans. As a result the unreformed ecclesiastic courts fell into oblivion: by the beginning of the twentieth century their activity was hardly noticeable, and church courts led a dormant existence on the outskirts of social life.

Whether or not the principles of canon law played an important role in late nineteenth-century Russia, it is surprising to find them apparently embodied in the functioning of the CCC fifty years later. At least, the parallels are striking. First, the church courts did not aim to punish, unlike the secular courts. Dostoyevsky stated it nicely in the words of the Elder Zossima quoted above: the Church must not judge, as the secular courts do, and must not assign punishment; it warns, remonstrates, and redeems a fallen Christian. This seems to be the predominant opinion at the time of the novel. Secular liberal reformers, in their insistence on abolishing the church court jurisdiction over such matters as divorce, appealed to this opinion, claiming that the Church may influence sinners in their souls, while the secular courts take care of the remaining legal issues. In its essence, claimed liberal historians of canon law, church penance (*epitimiia* in Russian) was only "prohibition" and not "punishment," according to the Greek meaning of the word.[49] Therefore, the liberals argued, the Church as such does not and should not ever have courtlike institutions that judge and punish the laity. Those clerics, who—like Elagin in his pamphlets against the proposed liberal reform—attempted to justify the existence of church

---

47. N. Elagin, *Predpolagaemaia reforma tserkovnogo suda* [Proposed reform of the church court] (St. Petersburg, 1873), vols. 1–2.

48. The clerical estate in Russia consisted of the "white clergy" (parish priests who were allowed to marry) and "black clergy" (celibate monks who held the chief posts in the church hierarchy, including bishoprics).

49. Originally *epitimion* meant denial of Holy Communion—the only penalty noted in the writings of such church fathers as St. Basil the Great—but later included fasting, prostrations, and other penitential deeds and came to designate the practice of penance itself (see N. Suvorov, *O tserkovnykh nakazaniiakh: Opyt issledovaniia po tserkovnomu pravu* [On church penalties: an investigative essay on ecclesiastical law] [St. Petersburg, 1876], 75).

courts in the Russian Orthodox Church, could hardly appeal to anything but the declarations and practice of the nineteenth-century Holy Synod in Russia,[50] a justification that many found inadequate, since it disregarded the more profound experience of the early Christians.

The second feature of the CCC finds its parallel in the principles of the Orthodox church court also: admonishing rather than expelling is its aim. Therefore one should apply all the possible measures of admonition and exhortation before resorting to the ultimate threat of excommunication. An Orthodox bishop, allocating penalties to a sinning brother, could choose among several admonitory measures of different degrees of severity. Thus, in the end of the nineteenth century a bishop's usual *instrumentarium* of twelve penalties included a remark, a simple or resolute reprimand, imposition of penitential prostrations, monetary fines, constant surveillance, demotions (of various degrees) to a lower job, temporary "monastery pacification" (detention); penance with temporary denial of the right to participate in liturgy, penance with temporary expulsion from the clerical estate, permanent expulsion from the clerical estate, excommunication.[51]

The standard primer on Orthodox canon law gave the following list of penalties imposed on the clergy by the decision of the church court: denial of communion from the hands of the bishop; denial of rights and immunities pertaining to a member of the clerical estate; demotion to a lower status; demotion to the lowest status; removal from clerical profession, but retention in the clerical estate; full defrocking, and excommunication.[52] Historians find the same admonitory measures practiced in reality. Thus, in 1753 Tikhon, the metropolitan of Moscow, authorized the following system of admonitory penalties in a convent. An abbot was supposed first to call the brethren and condemn the sinning monk by pointing to the precepts of Holy Writ. If the sinner did not agree with the abbot's verdict, the abbot could assign penitential prostrations in front of the brethren. If the sinner did not obey and repent, the abbot—on the advice of the brethren— could put the sinner in chains and send him to perform "rigorous works." Flagellation as an admonitory measure was recommended only if the unanimous demand of the brethren supported it, never on the abbot's decision alone. If none of the above measures worked, and the sinner persisted in his

50. Elagin, *Predpolagaemaia reforma*, 1:6.

51. Ibid., 2:241.

52. N. Suvorov, *Uchebnik tserkovnogo prava* [Introduction to ecclesiastical law], 5th ed. (Moscow, 1913), 289. The order of penalties is changed in the direction of increasing severity.

defiance, the abbot had to send the sinner to the Consistory (a diocesan church administration, established in 1744) for excommunication.[53]

Third, the Church, like the CCC, could not execute sinners. As many apologists of the Russian Orthodox Church claimed, its jurisdiction did not exceed the words of Jesus:

> if thy brother shall trespass against thee, go and tell him his fault between thee and him alone: if he shall hear thee, thou hast gained thy brother. But if he will not hear thee, then take with thee one or two more, that in the mouth of two or three witnesses every word may be established. And if he shall neglect to hear them, tell it unto the church: but if he neglect to hear the church, let him be unto thee as an heathen man and a publican. (Matthew 18:15–18)

Concerning heretics, this was amended to include the precept that "a man-heretic should be denied after two admonitions" (Titus 3:10–11). "This almost exhausted the jurisdiction of the Church, as such, over apostates from the true faith," wrote one of the apologists, who tried to prove that execution was alien to the nature of the Russian Orthodox Church, and that this Church had never had institutions comparable to the Inquisition.[54]

The logic of the New Testament underlying the functioning of ecclesiastical courts required three consecutive steps: first, denounce the deeds of the sinner and point them out to him or her (*oblichit'*); second, admonish him or her to return to righteousness (*uveshchat'*); and only if all these measures fail is the third step then authorized: excommunication (*otluchit'*). Of course, in accordance with the "harmonious" relations between Church and state characteristic of Eastern Christianity, princes frequently applied political laws from the Justinian code to heretics, following their own sense of their saintly duty, and in order to prevent the corruption of the state as a result of confusion of minds. But church spokesmen insisted that this was not required by the Church.[55] Its authority was purely moral. The Church did not impose punishments in the sense of the civil law, and excommunication from the Church was by no means automatically followed by a withdrawal of civil or political rights.

53. Ardalion Popov, *Sud i nakazaniia za prestupleniia protiv very i nravstvennosti po russkomu pravu* [Court procedure and punishment for crimes against faith and morals in Russian law] (Kazan, 1904), 234. Flagellation is taken here as an admonition rather than punishment. In a later, "more humane" age, the Church will exclude it from the list of penalties (see Elagin, *Predpolagaemaia reforma*, 2:241).

54. N. I. Barsov, *Sushchestvovala li v Rossii inkvizitsiia?* [Did the Inquisition exist in Russia?] (St. Petersburg, 1892), 7.

55. Ibid.

Three kinds of excommunication procedures were practiced in Russian church history. Before the seventeenth century the excommunicated was simply prohibited from partaking in sacraments and in any means of communion with the Church. The establishment of the Moscow Patriarchate radicalized the practice by introducing an "all-house" excommunication: an anathematized individual could not enter any Church or house in a given settlement apart from his own. The Spiritual Reglament (1722) of Peter the Great sought to install a two-step excommunication procedure, copying the Catholic practice of imposing lesser excommunication as a preliminary censure and following the Catholic idea that persistence in sin rather than the sin itself led to excommunication. The lesser excommunication was, according to the Reglament, to be itself preceded by a triple private warning of the cleric to a sinner, and a public warning in the Church. If these warnings and the subsequent lesser excommunication did not work, a letter requesting excommunication of the sinner was to be sent to the Spiritual Collegium, which, if it agreed, finally anathematized the sinner.[56]

All these examples from Russian church history indicate a startling similarity, if not a congruence, of the authorized practices of the Communist Control Commissions and the Orthodox church courts. The triple logic of the church court—reveal, admonish, excommunicate—underlay the functioning of the secular Party bodies too. However, before the revolution this logic, captured in the exchange between Ivan, Zossima, and Paissy in Dostoyevsky's novel, also founded the widespread aspirations of those who dreamed on reforming Russian society in accord with just and benign principles, inherent—but not fully realized, in their opinion—in the life of the Orthodox Church.[57] Apart from belles lettres these aspirations were expressed also in Russian religious philosophy. Such prominent thinkers as Semyon Frank considered the project of transforming Russian society (*mir*)

---

56. Suvorov, *O tserkovnykh nakazaniiakh*, 149. As always, practice differed. Western-oriented innovations did not take root, and 18th-century clerics still practiced "all-house" excommunication. In the next century the Russian Church did not excommunicate at all (the famous case of Leo Tolstoy in 1901 was the only prerevolutionary exception; see 160–167).

57. Some would consider this project as representing radical monasticism and opposed to other available strains of Christian orientation toward the world. For example, pastoral care and attention to the needs of the day rather than reform of the world according to the ancient ideal was another powerful orientation among the Russian clergy. See Laurie Manchester, "The Secularization of the Search for Salvation," *Slavic Review* 57, no. 1 (spring 1998). She draws a somehow different picture, distinguishing between "proto-intelligent" and "otherworldly" archetypes.

according to the norms of the Church an ultimate goal of human development and based this project in the original yearning of the Christian Church.[58]

Ironically, the Bolsheviks, supposedly the most secular of revolutionaries, seem to have carried out what I, for lack of better designations, may call "the Karamazov project": their organizations embodied and intensified the practices of the defunct ecclesiastical courts. The CCC came to constitute one of the main features of the Soviet system in its early years: admonishing standards of saintly conscience in human behavior, it regulated a large portion of Party life and thus made it inaccessible to the non-Party state courts. But as the following exposition will suggest, this reformation of secular life according to saintly standards happened not only in the CCC, which perhaps was only its starkest manifestation. Other milieus in Soviet society—indeed, almost all factories, offices, and schools—were to be remade as if in accordance with these practices of life in the ideal church congregation.[59]

SOZNATELNOST' AND CONSCIENCE

The conception of Bolshevism as a religion is hardly novel in Russian studies. Nikolai Berdiaev, an émigré Russian philosopher, gave a classic rendition of the thesis. According to him, the Bolsheviks channeled the religious energy of the Russian people to suit Bolshevik aims and in so doing became the malignant outcome of the benign millennial development of the Russian Orthodox Church. The Bolsheviks' facade of atheism should not deceive the astute observer, he said, for it covers up the essentially re-

58. See S. L. Frank, *Dukhovnye osnovy obshchestva: Vvedenie v sotsial'nuiu filosofiiu* [Spiritual foundations of society: introduction to social philosophy] (Moscow: Respublika, 1992), 97; but he warned against attempts to carry out the project of transforming the world into a church by this-worldly means.

59. I make no essentialist argument: the Party was *not* in essence a Church, even if the analogies are striking. Moshe Lewin, of course, noticed these analogies and reinterpreted the Bolshevik experience in accordance with Ernst Troeltsch's famous thesis: the revolutionary sect aimed at becoming a church (see his *Making of the Soviet System* [New York: Pantheon, 1985], 305–307). Neither do I call the Soviet regime a theocracy, though parallels prompt interesting ideas, for example Stephen Kotkin's analysis of theocratic aspects of the Stalinist civilization (*Magnetic Mountain* [Berkeley: University of California Press, 1995], ch. 7). Finally, widespread assertions on Marxism as essentially yet another form of religion usually stress doctrinal similarities; I eschew the analysis of doctrine and am more interested in the transformation of practices that occurred after the Russian Revolution and went unaccounted for in official Soviet ideology.

ligious mechanisms that explain the advent and dynamics of communism in Russia.[60]

Berdiaev pointed out the background of Soviet culture, but he did not concentrate on the specific change in religious practices that the Bolsheviks inaugurated. This change, however, lies at the heart of Bolshevik successes. It is similar to what another renowned Russian thinker, Pavel Miliukov, called the transition "from ritualized piety toward the religion of the soul."[61] In his study of religious sectarianism in Russia during the eighteenth and nineteenth centuries, Miliukov outlined what he saw as a central feature of "spiritual progress" at the time: the change from mass rituals of worship, the essence of traditional Orthodoxy, toward a deep individual faith, which was characteristic of the sectarians. But whether a parallel conversion occurred within individual Bolsheviks—whether a fervent individual belief replaced the stale sacramental piety of Orthodoxy—is not clear. We may only point to the indubitable preoccupation with matters of individual faith, characteristic of the Bolshevik discourse, which eventually led to the atrocious institutionalized practice of testing faith called "the general purge."

This preoccupation with individual faith centered on the same category as in the Western religious reforms—the notion of individual conscience. In Christian tradition the notion of conscience is usually traced back to the writings of Saint Paul, who is credited with having envisaged an internal court of conscience, and with discerning its three elements—divine judgment, moral self-evaluation, and troubled forays into the deep recesses of one's heart.[62] The Middle Ages, however, saw conscience as a capacity that people practiced in life to a greater or lesser extent, or as a shared knowledge embedded in practical forms of life. The decision of the Lateran Council in 1215 to institutionalize annual confession aimed at establishing an internal "tribunal of conscience," as opposed to mere outward conformity to the demands of Christian ethics.

Nevertheless, the true internalization of conscience in the West occurred only with the Reformation, which made conscience an individual rather

60. Nikolai Berdiaev, *Istoki i smysl russkogo kommunizma* [Origins and meaning of Russian communism] (Paris: YMCA-Press, 1955).

61. Pavel Miliukov, *Ocherki po istorii russkoi kul'tury: Tserkov' i shkola* [Sketches on the history of Russian culture] (Moscow, 1897), 93 (translated as *Outlines of Russian Culture* [Philadelphia: University of Pennsylvania Press, 1942]).

62. My exposition follows the argument of Michel Despland's article on "conscience" in *The Encyclopedia of Religion*, ed. Mircea Eliade (New York: Macmillan, 1987), 4:45–52.

than a common capacity, and a fact of psychic life. Later, modernity separated "conscience" and "consciousness": consciousness became the site of the cognitive capacities and judgments of fact, while conscience became a purely moral faculty, robbed of any pretensions of giving objective information on the external world. The nineteenth century sharpened Saint Paul's depiction of conscience as "an obsessive inner court," and conscience in its most radical conceptualizations could become "a purely retrospective solitary self-condemnation."[63]

The Russian revolutionaries did not speak of "conscience" as such; rather, they brought heightened attention to the Russian concept of *soznatelnost'*. Its analysis shows that *soznatelnost'* is closer to the Protestant understanding of Conscience—as an individual, and yet undifferentiated, capacity of moral and factual judgment, exercised in accordance with the Holy Word—than to both modern consciousness as a source of factual judgments and modern conscience as a source of moral judgments. The term *soznatelnost'* is usually translated into English as "consciousness," though this is not necessarily the best translation. On the one hand, the word "consciousness" that figures in many English-language books on the Russian Revolution is the rather unsuccessful result of an attempt to translate *soznatelnost'* literally, holding onto one of its meanings common to both the Russian and the English language—"the quality of those who are conscious." But the English word "consciousness" has its closest Russian equivalent in the word *soznanie*, designating the cognitive processes of the mind. On the other hand, the translation of *soznatelnost'* as "consciousness" ignores all the direct connotations of Holy Conscience. For example, the most authoritative dictionary of modern Russian defines the adjective *soznatelnyi* as "convinced of the rightness of one's deeds," and gives the following clarificatory example from Furmanov's essay *The Conscious Hero*: "The heroism of Communists stems from their deep conviction of the righteousness of their cause."[64] The last edition of the Soviet dictionary of ethical terms tells us that *soznatelnost'* is the highest form of development of *sovest'*, a capacity to act in accord with revolutionary doctrine.[65]

Sovest' means "conscience" in English, and both words are translations of the Greek word *syneidesis;* the Latin equivalent of this Greek term be-

---

63. Ibid., 48.

64. Article on *soznatelnyi*, in *Slovar' sovremennogo russkogo literaturnogo iazyka* [Dictionary of contemporary Russian literary language] (Moscow: Institut russkogo iazyka, 1955–68), vol. 14 (hereafter *Slovar'*, with specific article).

65. I. S. Kon, ed., *Slovar' po etike* [Dictionary of ethics] 3d ed. (Moscow: Politizdat, 1975), 289.

ing *conscientia*.[66] Both have the connotation of co-knowing, partaking in the higher, holy truth. Therefore, the ethical sense of *soznatelnost'* (its habitual use in revolutionary rhetoric) is tightly connected to the notion of conscience, and it seems better to translate it in this way. Even if the discourse of the Russian Revolution rarely mentioned *sovest'* but was suffused by *soznatelnost'*, it was the saintly conscience that mattered when the word was used.[67] I capitalize it to translate *soznatelnost'* in order to stress the religious roots of this Russian concept, and in order to distance it from "consciousness" as used in modern science.

Bolshevik discourse came to be infused with the term *soznatelnost'* through what is now commonly translated as the "consciousness/spontaneity" dialectic, the main contrast in Lenin's manifesto, *What Is To Be Done?* (1902). The dichotomy appeared in the discourse of revolutionary intelligentsia from the 1860s on. Historians trace it to Nikolai Chernyshevsky's revolutionary novel of 1863, which bore the same title. According to a standard interpretation, Chernyshevsky was the first to outline the image of the New Man who would "consciously" reshape the world in accord with his vision of a better future.[68]

> Whenever and wherever 'consciousness' was discussed . . . it had almost invariably stood for the affirmation of the *intelligent*'s distinctive identity . . . : it had stood for an effort on his part to interpret, organize, and, thus, in a sense, control his experience by the delineation in the process of reality of a logic and a purpose different from the predominant patterns in the existing world. 'Spontaneity' had stood for a refusal or a failure on his part to so mediate his responses to the world and to his own impulses, it had stood for a desire to give free rein to his own feelings and to the 'elemental' forces in the external world.[69]

"Consciousness" was offered to the intellectual as a radical way of remaking himself and the world, as a self-affirmation against a world full of "elemental" passions and strong instincts. Irina Paperno has noted that

66. Max Vasmer, *Etimologicheskii slovar' russkogo iazyka* (Moscow: Progress, 1986), 3:705.

67. Perhaps revolutionaries preferred *soznatelnost'* to *sovest'* because of the overtly Christian and moralizing overtones of the latter word; secular Bolshevik discourse could not tolerate such a word as its central concept. And their choice sounded "scientific," suggesting an origin in the scientific laws of historical materialism, not blind faith.

68. Leopold Haimson, *The Russian Marxists and the Origins of Bolshevism* (Cambridge, Mass.: Harvard University Press, 1955), 11.

69. Ibid., 210–211.

Chernyshevsky's model for revolutionary behavior was characteristic of the postreform Russia of the 1860s.[70] Another leader of the Russian radicals in the 1860s, Dmitrii Pisarev, may have captured the process of transformation into a "conscious" person in his central essay, "The Realists." He contrasted Russian Realists (read: New Men) with those people who immediately translate every feeling and outside impulse into a reaction, without reflection. Realists, according to Pisarev, mediate and guide all of their actions by principles.[71] A similar "rigidification" of behavior has been noted by many scholars as the core of the transition to "saintly conscience" among various revolutionary religious sectarians, for example, the Puritans.[72]

Both versions of *What Is To Be Done?*, then, may be interpreted as dealing with the process of spiritual progress from the state of the unenlightened chaotic soul to Higher Conscience, that is, as a process of conversion. If Chernyshevsky deals with conversion occurring in the soul of an individual revolutionary, Lenin describes the political strategy for producing conversions among the workers, by bringing them to the state of Conscience. Later this narrative of the ascent to Higher Conscience became what Katerina Clark calls the "masterplot of Socialist Realism,"[73] repeated in almost every novel of this genre: a disciple, under the guidance of a wise teacher, overcomes enormous difficulties, learns to control his or her chaotic passions by doctrinal insight, and thus rises to Conscience (*soznatelnost'*).[74]

Later *soznatelnost'* became a mass phenomenon, rather than a quality of the few New Men. This "popularization of Conscience" followed the 1917 Revolution, after which every Party member was expected to reflect on this internal quality. For example, the resolution of the Ninth Party Conference, establishing the CCC, ascribed it to each Communist and specified it as the only legitimate ground for differentiation among Party members: "Distinguishing among Party members only on the basis of the

70. Irina Paperno, *Chernyshevsky and the Age of Realism* (Stanford: Stanford University Press, 1988), 28.

71. Dmitrii Pisarev, "Realisty," in *Sobranie sochinenii* [Collected works] (Moscow, 1956), 3:8.

72. See Robert N. Bellah, *Beyond Belief* (Berkeley: University of California Press, 1970), 44. For general analysis of sectarian revolutionaries see Michael Walzer, *The Revolution of the Saints* (New York: Atheneum, 1968).

73. Katerina Clark, *The Soviet Novel* (Chicago: University of Chicago Press, 1981).

74. Clark notes that literary techniques employed in these novels were virtually identical to the techniques of 19th-century Russian hagiography (ibid.). What she does not say is that the plot itself was a narrative of conversion, the endlessly reiterated narrative of Protestant literature.

degree of their *soznatelnost'*, dedication, endurance, political maturity, and readiness to sacrifice themselves, the Party fights any other attempts to distinguish among the members of the Party on the basis of any other principle: top and bottom, intelligentsia and workers, nationality, and so forth."[75] This formulation of the principle of revolutionary Conscience, together with its synonyms in this passage, is very close to the usage among the intelligentsia described by Leopold Haimson. As the Party ethics campaign reasserted, a worker endowed with *soznatelnost'* could never simply "float down the stream," yielding to instinct.[76] Instinctual drives had to be checked by the doctrinally informed moral agency that affirmed or forbade them.

The Party preoccupation with individual *soznatelnost'* became embodied in the work of the Control Commissions. But it became particularly central to Party concerns after the general purge aimed to test *soznatelnost'* in each Communist, or—in the words of Ian Rudzutak, a chairman of the Central Control Commission who reported on the peculiarity of the 1933 purge at the Seventeenth Party Congress—the main emphasis was now focused on "how Communists revealed themselves in their deeds as really active Bolsheviks . . . , to what extent each member of the Party 'Conscientiously' [*soznatel'no*] takes part in the building of socialism."[77]

Now, how could one test the possession of Conscience by a given Communist? We might provisionally single out some criteria for assuring a Bolshevik's possession of Conscience from the obituaries published in the early postrevolutionary era. These obituaries of Bolsheviks and Conscientious workers, hailing them as examples of *soznatelnost'*, said that they lived like saints. Scholars studying these sources have found that what became the normative Soviet moral requirement—sacrifice without reward in pursuit of the common good—had in prerevolutionary narratives been an exceptional feat, characteristic only of religious and military heroes and usually demonstrated by the loss of life.[78]

75. See resolution of the IX Party Conference, in A. Mel'kumov, ed., *Voprosy partiinogo stroitel'stva*, 168 (its title was "Ob ocherednykh zadachakh partiinogo stroitel'stva").

76. See Iaroslavsky, "O partetike: Predlozheniia," 167.

77. *XVII Steno/34*, 285.

78. Jeffrey Brooks, "Revolutionary Lives" in *New Directions in Soviet History*, ed. Stephen White (Cambridge: Cambridge University Press, 1992), 31; he identifies two early models for Bolsheviks: professional revolutionaries' ascetic heroic struggle against the Old Regime and "conscientious" workers' martyrlike performance. On self-fashioning through the imitation of Christ, see chapter 6.

The demonstration of *soznatelnost'* before death, however, was a different and more difficult task. The Bolsheviks, preoccupied with the problem of the individual saintly Conscience, practiced methods for establishing possession or loss of Conscience on a mass scale, very similar to those practiced by the Orthodox Church for ages. These background practices of their culture conditioned the outcome of Bolshevik reformation of the soul. Rather than focus on the confessional practices that underlay analysis of the individual soul in Western Christianity, the Bolsheviks intensified penitential practices that were essential for knowing the individual Conscience in Eastern Christianity.

Instead of endowing each individual with an internal *forum conscientiae,* a "tribunal of conscience," Russian Communists subjected each individual to the external *forum judiciale,* a Party tribunal that deliberated on matters of Conscience.[79] An overview of the penitential background of Orthodox Christianity will help us understand the cultural resources that the Bolsheviks found at hand when they intensified their tests of Conscience.

PUBLIC PENANCE AND PRIVATE CONFESSION

In his sketch of the origins of techniques of self-knowledge in Christianity, Foucault distinguished between *exomologesis* and *exaugoresis,* terms signifying two distinct ways of arriving at self-knowledge. The first signified the early Christian ritual of public penance (described by such authors as Tertullian); the second applied to auricular confession, practiced by some early monks following the precepts of one of the founders of Western monasticism, John Cassian.[80] Foucault suggested that in the West private confession eclipsed public penance as the practical way of coming to know the self. After the Lateran Council introduced compulsory annual auricular confession in 1215, and the Council of Trent attempted to intensify the technique of private confession further in 1551, confession became central for Western culture. In *The History of Sexuality* Foucault argued that once confession spilled over the walls of the monasteries, where it primarily was practiced in the Middle Ages, and the wider population adopted it to confess the secrets of the fictional entity called "sex," the Western individual was produced. We are witnesses to the current predominance of the method:

79. Distinction between private confession as *forum conscientiae* and church court as *forum judiciale* follows Suvorov, introduction to *O tserkovnykh nakazaniiakh.*

80. Foucault, "About the Beginning," 223.

one confesses one's sins, one confesses one's thoughts and desires, . . . one sets about telling with the greatest precision what is most difficult to tell; one confesses in public and in private, to one's parents, to one's teachers, to one's doctor, to those one loves; one confesses to oneself, in pleasure and in pain, things that it would be impossible to tell anyone else. . . . Western man has become a confessing animal.[81]

Of course, many view this description of developments in the West as unacceptable simplification and blame Foucault for uncritically taking specific French Catholic techniques to be representative of all Christianity. Indeed, Protestant churches were ambiguous over the issue of confession, in contrast to the Catholic Church. Though some radicals like William Tyndale, the first translator of the Bible into vernacular English, rejected private confession outright since "shrift in the ear is verily a work of Satan,"[82] many followed Martin Luther who deemed confession useful, even if it had not been mentioned in the Bible. Zwingli radicalized his point, clearly stating that confession may be used for consultation, but never for absolution from sin. Calvin, following the New Testament (James 5 : 16), recommended mutual confession but also added that it should be preferably directed to a minister.[83] Notwithstanding this initial ambiguity, private confession, whether to a minister or to a diary, or in meditation while preparing for the Holy Supper, seems to have become firmly rooted among many Protestants with time.[84] For example, the Church of England since the mid-sixteenth cen-

81. Foucault, *An Introduction,* 59. This grand historical generalization seems to be supported by a classic study that Foucault never cites: Henry Charles Lea, *A History of Auricular Confession and Indulgences in the Latin Church,* 3 vols. (Philadelphia: Lea Brothers, 1896).

82. Stephen Greenblatt, *Renaissance Self-Fashioning* (Chicago: University of Chicago Press, 1980), 85.

83. Geoffrey Rowell, "The Anglican Tradition," in *Confession and Absolution,* ed. Martin Dudley and Geoffrey Rowell (London: SPCK, 1990), 92–93. Calvin's predilection for public confession points to another ambiguity, whether confessions allowed by the Reformers were to be of the private or public kind. In the early Massachusetts Bay colony the community of the elect required "tests of relation"—a rite of public confession of one's conversionary experience—from all new members (Adam Seligman, *Innerworldly Individualism* [New Brunswick, N.J.: Transaction, 1994], 88). The use of private confession to arrive at inner knowledge of the self in Protestantism may perhaps follow distinct Lutheran, Calvinist, and Anabaptist models: see Ernst Troeltsch, *The Social Teaching of the Christian Churches,* vol. 2 (Louisville, Ky.: Westminster/John Knox Press, 1992).

84. On Puritan meditational manuals see Seligman, *Innerworldly Individualism,* 169. On confession in a Puritan diary see William E. Paden, "Theaters of Humility and Suspicion," in *Technologies of the Self,* ed. Luther H. Martin, Huck Gutman, Patrick H. Hutton (Amherst: University of Massachusetts Press, 1988).

tury required compulsory general confession and absolution but allowed additional private confession for those wishing to undergo it. And by the end of the nineteenth century, after the Oxford Movement had led to the reintroduction of Catholic confession to the fullest degree, it not only tolerated but approved private confession. Also, although initially connected to their religious origins, confessional techniques soon disengaged themselves to become a widespread technology of the self in secular life.

These widespread confessional techniques usually equate with Christian technologies of the self as such. Yet the curious practice of *exomologesis*, described by Foucault as a way of knowing oneself that was abandoned in the West, encountered a different fate in Orthodox East. There it gave rise to the prevalence of public penance as the means of assuring possession of a Christian self. The ritual of *exomologesis*, or "full confession," from the verb *exomologeuo*, originally meant "to agree, to promise"; its later relevant meanings were "to confess guilt," "to own up completely."[85] *Exomologesis* is used by the early church fathers in two senses: first, as the whole feat of prolonged penance, and, second, as an act of verbal confession that constituted part of this penitential discipline.[86] Nikolai Suvorov, one of the renowned Russian church historians, described its use by Irinaeus and Tertullian, "to designate the open, public confession, and . . . also all the totality of penitential works, in which the sinner's feeling of grief . . . and fiery wish to reunite with the Church were expressed."[87]

In early Christianity penance was allowed only once and was a rather lengthy procedure that lasted several years. The origin of penance as a sacramental ritual is usually dated back to the Decian persecutions (250–251 A.D.) and the problem of the relapsed. Those Christians who lapsed back into paganism under pressure from Roman emperors, but wished to rejoin the

85. The Greek term appears in the *Oxford English Dictionary*, since many church fathers used it without translating into Latin or English.

86. See the dated but still useful commentary on the frequency of usage and the meanings of the term in *Tertullian: Apologetic and Practical Treatises*, trans. C. Dodgson (Oxford: John Henry Parker, 1842), note L on 376–379. Among contemporary theologians, Erickson stresses verbal confession as integral to the whole ritual of public penance: "penance itself involves not just a change in attitude, but calls for the fruits of repentance, manifested in diverse outward ways. Among these —along with prostrations, sackcloth and ashes—is confession (*eksomologesis*). It is chiefly a penitential exercise, and not part of a judiciary procedure," as it will happen later (John H. Erickson, "Penitential Discipline in the Orthodox Canonical Tradition," in *Challenge of Our Past* [Crestwood, N.Y.: St. Vladimir's Seminary Press, 1991], 27).

87. Suvorov, *Ob"em distsiplinarnogo suda*, 39–40.

Church, were to be somehow absolved of their apostasy. Saint Cyprian gave the following justification for the severity and length of *exomologesis*, which became the means of rejoining the community of faithful Christians after a lengthy period of penance. Since those Christians who did not yield to the pressure from Roman emperors became martyrs, the ritual for the restoration of the relapsed had to be equally severe.[88] The martyrs were imitating Christ, so those repenting their inability to become a martyr had to be connected to the model of *imitatio Christi* also.

Later, *exomologesis* was imposed on anyone who voluntarily confessed his or her sins and wished to efface them through the ritual of public penance. The ritual involved bodily humiliation and maceration of flesh. Tertullian wrote that *exomologesis*

> is a discipline for man's prostration and humiliation, enjoining a demeanor calculated to move mercy. With regard also to the very dress and food, it commands [the penitent] to lie in sackcloth and ashes, to cover his body with mourning, to lay his spirit low in sorrows, to exchange the severe treatment for the sins which he has committed; moreover, to know no food and drink but such as is plain,—not for the stomach's sake, to wit, but the soul's; for the most part, however, to feed prayers on fastings, to groan, to weep and make outcries unto the Lord your God; to bow before the feet of the presbyters, and kneel to God's dear ones; to enjoin on all the brethren to be ambassadors to bear his deprecatory supplication [before God].[89]

Saint Jerome, in another renowned excerpt, described *exomologesis* as practiced by a Roman noblewoman Fabiola, who

> put on sackcloth to make public confession of her error. . . . It was then that in the presence of all Rome . . . she stood in the ranks of penitents and exposed before the bishop, presbyters and people—all of whom wept when they saw her weep—her disheveled hair, pale features, soiled hands and unwashed neck. What sins would such a penance fail to purge away? . . . She laid bare her wound to the gaze of all, and Rome beheld with tears the disfiguring scars which marred her beauty.[90]

88. St. Cyprian, epistles 25 and 29, in *The Ante-Nicene Fathers*, ed. Alexander Roberts and James Donaldson (Grand Rapids, Mich.: Eerdmans, 1951), 5:304, 307. See also his treatise "On the Lapsed" (in ibid., 437–447).

89. Tertullian, "On Repentance," ch. 9, in ibid., 3:664.

90. St. Jerome, letter 77, in *A Select Library of Nicene and Post-Nicene Fathers*, ed. Philip Schaff and Henry Wace (Grand Rapids, Mich.: Eerdmans, 1954), 6:159–160. Slightly inaccurate but vivid English translations of these excerpts from Tertullian and Jerome that Foucault apparently supplied himself are in Foucault, "About the Beginning," 214.

These are the two most renowned accounts of *exomologesis*.[91] Yet they do not provide answers to many questions concerning the details of the procedure. Other scattered remarks hardly help restore the clarity. For example, later interpretations differed on whether the initial practice of *exomologesis* necessarily involved public or private confession. Written sources are inconclusive in this respect. Catholics wished to prove that confession existed as part of the penitential ritual from the very start; Protestants doubted it.[92] Orthodox sources frequently quoted Origen, who had mentioned private confession but had not considered it compulsory, or Cyprian, who had deemed it a laudable exercise but only in addition to *exomologesis* itself.[93] The current scholarly source sums up the confusion: "To the dismay of an older generation of polemicists, whether Roman Catholic or Protestant, texts of this period show little interest in confession as such, whether 'public' or 'private.' For the most part, our texts suppose that the sin is manifest, known to all."[94]

Exomologesis seems to have declined in both East and West following a specific episode in 391 A.D. in Constantinople. Different scholars competed to interpret the rather cryptic lines of the two early church historians, Socrates and Sozomen, who described this episode known as the "scandal of the presbyter-confessor."[95] But all agreed on the end result: after patri-

---

91. The mid 19th-century Russian text that gave a detailed description of *exomologesis* seems to generalize from these two sources also. See "O publichnom pokaianii" [On public penance], *Pravoslavnyi Sobesednik* [Orthodox conversant] 5, no. 1 (January–April 1868): 289.

92. Cf. articles on Roman Catholic and Anglican penance in *Encyclopaedia of Religion and Ethics*, ed. James Hastings (New York: Scribner's Sons, 1908–26), 9:710–715, and 715–721; and a treatise that compares *exomologesis* in Tertullian and Cyprian and finds little evidence that "actual confession, or particularisation of sin, found place; [but] it is clear that some acknowledgement of the sin must have preceded the assignment of penance" (Oscar D. Watkins, *A History of Penance, Being the Study of the Authorities* [London: Longmans, Green, 1920], 1:193).

93. Suvorov, *Ob"em distsiplinarnogo suda*, 39–40.

94. Erickson, "Penitential Discipline," 26.

95. A noble lady, undergoing lengthy public penance under the supervision of the presbyter-confessor, publicly confessed another sin of lechery with a deacon (of the same temple or penitentiary). Nectarius, in order to stifle the resulting public turmoil, abolished the post of presbyter-confessor altogether. The episode appears in every Russian source on early Christian rituals and many Western ones, since Calvin took the episode as testimony to the spread of public confession among the early Christians—using it to advocate public confession as the primary means of Protestant penance (see A. I. Almazov, *Tainaia ispoved' v pravoslavnoi vostochnoi tserkvi: Opyt vneshnei istorii* [Private confession in the eastern Orthodox Church: an essay of external history] [Odessa, 1894], 1:60). Interpretations include curious

arch Nectarius abolished this special post in the church hierarchy, voluntary public penance waned. Parallel to that, the ecclesiastical courts began to codify and impose public penance in the fourth century by ecclesiastical courts.

The early church courts were simply community disciplinary gatherings, which censured sinners.[96] A famous passage by Tertullian describes their functioning: "In the same place also exhortations are made, rebukes and sacred censures are administered. For with a great gravity the work of judging is carried on among us . . . ; and you have the most notable example for judgment to come when any one has sinned so grievously as to require his severance from us in prayer, in the congregation and in all sacred intercourse. The tried men of our elders preside over us, obtaining that honour not by purchase but by established character."[97] Codification of canon law went hand in hand with the institutionalization of these courts.

The codification of the public penance ritual was carried out by the 12th canon rule of Saint Gregory the Neo-Caesarean, who had introduced four main gradations or ranks (*stationes penitentiales*) of penitents. The first rank comprised "the weepers," those who stood outside the church, since they were not allowed to enter, and lamented their fate, asking the entering parishioners to pray for them and shedding tears in order to be eventually permitted into the church. The second rank, "the auditors," stood in the church near its entrance, listening to the liturgy, but were required to leave first before the rite of communion. The third, "the genuflectors," kneeled behind the last row of the faithful, but in front of the auditors, and were required to leave the church after the auditors. The last gradation, "the bystanders," were penitents who had progressed through all the pre-

---

psychological guesses (she confessed because she believed the deacon was still immune from punishment; the presbyter's lenience toward the deacon outraged many people) and factual guesses (the deacon and the presbyter were the same person).

To my taste, Suvorov's explanation (in *Ob"em distsiplinarnogo suda*, ch. 1) is by far the best: the post of presbyter-confessor required supervision of penitents in a specific priest penitentiary; coming there regularly, the lady was spotted and corrupted by the vicious deacon. Hence the elimination of the post of presbyter after the public outcry kept other penitents from harm. A plausible modern reading—the lady's corruption occurred in a special place for secret confession of sins *before* the appointment of public penance—implies that private confession was already widespread and may reflect contemporary attitudes on ancient practice (see John Halliburton, "'A Godly Discipline': Penance in Early Church," in *Confession and Absolution*, ed. Martin Dudley and Geoffrey Rowell [London: SPCK, 1990], 45).

96. Suvorov, *Ob"em distsiplinarnogo suda*, 6.

97. Tertullian, "Apology," ch. 39, in *Ante-Nicene Fathers*, 3:46.

vious ranks and were allowed now to stand among the faithful, but not to partake of the sacraments.[98]

When these four gradations of public penitents were accepted into the body of canon law in the Eastern Orthodox Church, the punishments differed only in terms of the amount of the time to be spent in each rank. For example, the 87th canon rule of the Council in Trullo convicted women for illegal second marriages and ordered them to spend one year in the rank of weeper, two years in the rank of auditor, and three years among the genuflectors.[99] During the seventh year they were allowed to stand among the faithful, and upon its completion they were allowed to receive communion, "if they repented with tears."[100] The practice of imposing penance by decisions of ecclesiastical courts in the Eastern Church flourished until the fall of Byzantium in 1453.[101] For example, in the fourteenth century the Holy Synod imposed public penance on Epirean rebels and on suspected magi, with the same consecutive progression through the ranks of the weepers, auditors, genuflectors, and bystanders.[102]

In Western Europe, whether or not public confession was practiced as part of *exomologesis* before the fifth century, it was forbidden by the edict of Pope Leo the Great in 461. The founder of Western monasticism, John Cassian, was the first to introduce the practice of private confession instead. It was picked up in Irish and English monasteries in the sixth and seventh centuries and then gradually spread throughout Europe to eclipse public penance rituals.[103] Public penance was practiced in the West until the four-

98. Suvorov, *Ob"em distsiplinarnogo suda*, ch. 2. St. Gregory was also called Thaumaturgus, or the Wonderworker. See Erickson, "Penitential Discipline," 26, where he claims that the Neo-Caesarean ranks in their rigid form were initially applied only in Pontus, Cappadocia, and parts of Asia. See also a picturesque description of these ranks in "O publichnom pokaianii," 294. For Western variants of this procedure see Friedrich Frank, *Die Bussdisciplin den Kirche von den Apostolzeiten bis zum XVII Jahrhunderts* (Mainz: Kirchheim, 1867), 578–598; and Henry Barclay Swete, *Forgiveness of Sins: A Study in the Apostles' Creed* (London: Macmillan, 1916), 107.

99. The Council in Trullo (also called Quinisext, falling between the 5th and 6th ecumenical councils) gathered in Constantinople in 692 A.D. to codify the main sources of Eastern canon law—"85 apostolic rules" and "rules of the ecumenical councils"—and conducted its sessions in a hall with arches (*en trullo*, in Greek), hence the name. The Western church did not recognize its legitimacy.

100. Suvorov, *Ob"em distsiplinarnogo suda*, 127.

101. For data on the 13th century see Erickson, "Penitential Discipline," 30 and 37–38 n. 12.

102. Suvorov, *O tserkovnykh nakazaniiakh*, 76–77.

103. The general opinion of 19th-century Western European church historians was that this eclipse of public penance happened because of the widespread abhor-

teenth century but lost most of its raison d'être after the decisions of the Lateran Council in 1215 to install a requirement of compulsory annual confession; the practice of indulgences easily superseded it. Private confession became the primary sacrament that relieved and purified the individual conscience.

In the Eastern Church private confession did not progress to an extent comparable to its spread in the West. The institution of private confession existed, but its development is hard to describe. The first Eastern penitential is named after John the Faster but has "nothing to do with the sixth-century patriarch of that name."[104] The exact dating of the first available manuscript is disputed: Erickson puts it in the early or mid-ninth century, while some modern scholars date it as late as 1100.[105] The still extant 130 medieval Russian handwritten penitentials, studied by Almazov, appeared after that date and copied the penitential of "John the Faster" in 5 main versions.[106] It also seems that Eastern penitentials were modeled on or copied from penitentials coming from northern Europe in the seventh to ninth centuries rather than reflected actual Eastern practice. Furthermore, the Eastern "nomocanons" from that period—compilations of secular laws of the empire together with canon laws, used to define what penance should be imposed on sinning monks—were not employed to impose penance on laity, save for those ardent believers who came voluntarily to confess their sins to the monks.[107]

We have already mentioned that many Western canonists were unaware

---

rence of this humiliating procedure. By contrast, Russian church historians proudly quoted one of the few exceptions to this general opinion, contained in Löhning's analysis of *Kirchenrecht*, which stated that the baseness of mores of the Germanic tribes made it impossible to practice voluntary public penance. But after the collapse of the Roman empire, the Church had to conduct trials for spiritual crimes, and public penance came to be allocated according to penitential books, which were used as an ad hoc surrogate criminal code. Public penance was imposed by courts for open transgressions of Christian morality in the Frankish kingdom in the 9th century, while land disputes and other secular matters were settled by the law of ordeal. Wasserschleben, another 19th-century German canonist quoted by Russian sources, also stated that the Western Church had relied on colonization of internal conscience during the private confession, rather than on demanding public penance that no one would have observed, as the only way to enforce some standards of purity in the lax conditions of the early Middle Ages (Suvorov, *O tserkovnykh nakazaniiakh*, 132–138).

104. Erickson, "Penitential Discipline," 30.
105. Ibid.
106. Almazov, *Tainaia ispoved'*, 1:286.
107. Suvorov, *Ob"em distsiplinarnogo suda*, 119.

of the Eastern practice of private confession. Suvorov explains this curious fact:

> Western schoolmen could speak about the absence of private confession among the Greeks, because they were little acquainted with the practice of the Eastern Church, or perhaps because in the West private confession was treated in practice as a necessary condition for the absolution of sins and admittance to the Eucharist for all, while in the East private confession was not demanded with such resoluteness either theoretically or practically, not to mention its legal institutionalization . . . [108]

In his opinion, the first decisive introduction of private confession into the Eastern Church may be registered in the writings of the Byzantine canonist Theodore Balsamon in the twelfth century, who reinterpreted the rules of the Council in Trullo concerning public penance as also demanding private confession. The practice of private confession, which—we may suspect—was well underway, was finally legitimized in the written canon law.[109] Summing up, we may say that private confession existed but was accorded hardly any doctrinal or practical attention.

Public penance, however, was very much emphasized, and it did not decline in the East as it did in the West. For example, Eve Levin argues that—as part of regulation of the sexual mores in the typical medieval Russian settlement—confession was private, but penance remained public in order to ensure compliance with the dominant order.[110] Demonstration of penitential zeal supported the status quo. Also, the coexistence of secular and ecclesiastical punishment in the code of Prince Iaroslav (eleventh century), where monetary compensation and deeds of penance were of equal status, was abolished by the fifteenth century. No Russian equivalent of indulgences ever developed. Historians note the predominance of public penance in the fifteenth and sixteenth centuries as a means of punishment for the violation of church canons and communal mores.[111] The centrality of public penance persisted well into the Petrine reform period.

Three famous examples from Russian church history are usually quoted to illustrate the point. Maxim the Greek, a foreign monk who had arrived to correct defects in Russian church books, was—after being accused of conspiring with the Turks against Orthodoxy—condemned to "public pen-

---

108. Ibid., 119–120.
109. Ibid., 160.
110. Eve Levin, *Sex and Society in the World of Orthodox Slavs, 900–1700* (Ithaca: Cornell University Press, 1989), 300.
111. Popov, *Sud i nakazaniia*, 58.

ance" in 1526 under the supervision of his enemies, the Josephites of the Volokolamsk monastery. "Having suffered cold, and hunger, and smoke," so the chronicle goes, he was brought before the ecclesiastical court for the second time five years later. His new sins (miscorrecting the texts intentionally) were revealed during the second trial, but the official pretext for initiating the second trial was the testimony of the Josephite monks that he did not repent hard enough and, thus, did not reveal the possession of a reborn Christian soul.[112]

In another famous case, Deacon Viskovaty, a "secretary of the state" during the rule of Ivan the Terrible, shouted in the central cathedral of the Kremlin, denouncing the newly painted icons that, in his opinion, were made according to a blasphemous pattern. Having been warned by the Church hierarchs of the unacceptability of his behavior, which disturbed public order, he submitted a special thesis on iconography to the Church Council, asking the Council, presided over by Ivan the Terrible, to adjudicate. The Council ruled Viskovaty to be wrong, denounced him as a sinner, and ordered on January 14, 1554 that he undergo a three-year-long public penance at the entrance of the Kremlin church he had "defamed." His penance was appointed in accord with the 64th canon rule of the Council in Trullo (concerning commentary by a layman on matters of faith) and corrected according to the 102d rule (sincere contrition after the sin). Viskovaty was supposed to spend one year as a weeper, one year as an auditor, and one year as a bystander.[113] Ivan the Terrible himself had to undergo public penance for three years, imposed on him by a council of twenty-three hierarchs of the Russian Church in 1575 for his fourth marriage. The czar could partake of communion only upon finishing the necessary penitential deeds.[114]

Public penance became less visible after the practice of sending sinners to monasteries under the monks' surveillance became popular. "Monastery pacification" (*smirenie*), or "subordination"—in full accordance with its etymology, meaning subjection to order—was effectively becoming a form of imprisonment in the seventeenth century, with monasteries being

---

112. E. E. Golubinsky, *Istoriia russkoi tserkvi* [History of the Russian Church] (Moscow, 1900), vol. 2, pt. 2, 718–725, 842.

113. Ieronim Gralia, *Ivan Mikhailovich Viskovaty: kar'era gosudarstvennogo deiatelia v Rossii XVI v.* [Viskovaty: the career of a state official in 16th-century Russia] (Moscow, 1994), 125, 144. Signs of Viskovaty's actual penance are absent. The fact that in 1556 he kissed the cross while signing the treaty with the Lithuanians indicates that he was already absolved from his sin.

114. Elagin, *Predpolagaemaia reforma*, 1:29.

given clear directions from the ecclesiastical courts on what term and sort of penance the person, sent by the court to the monastery, should undergo. This practice lasted well until the Great Schism over matters of liturgy and sacraments (1667), which influenced treatment of those sent to the monasteries for "pacification." Repression of schismatics seemed to give the monks so much power that arbitrariness and torture became the rule of the day. But torture fit the mood of the epoch. Freeze, describing the functioning of the Russian church courts in the eighteenth century, notes that "the consistory used torture and physical abuse liberally, seeking not so much truth as full confession. To avoid subsequent appeals and claims of innocence, the consistory insisted upon a signed confession, and used whatever coercion seemed necessary to overcome the 'stubbornness' of clergy who denied their guilt."[115]

The Church reforms under Peter the Great and later Russian emperors did not challenge the primacy of public penance. But they managed to radically affect the status of private confession within the established Russian Church. For example, a special 1722 edict abolished the privileged secrecy of confession in matters of state treason: this edict required confessors to denounce traitorous parishioners to the state.[116] The ruling may have not been widely applied but, along with a later requirement of a compulsory annual confession to a priest—partly envisioned as a means of spotting multiple sectarians and schismatics—it contributed to a development of popular perception of confession as a means of official discipline. Of course, alternative modes of Christian confession proliferated (e.g., confession of laity to monk-"elders"), but these developments did not help confession in the official Church very much. It was regularly practiced, but probably more and more people who relied on confessional resources for self-analysis did so outside the Church. After the eighteenth century the role of secular voluntary confession radically increased, owing perhaps to the import of Enlightenment models of self-analysis.[117]

115. Gregory L. Freeze, *The Russian Levites* (Cambridge, Mass.: Harvard University Press, 1979), 67.

116. P. V. Verkhovskoi, *Uchrezhdenie dukhovnoi kollegii i dukhovnyi reglament; k voprosu ob otnoshenii tserkvi i gosudarstva v Rossii* [Establishment of the spiritual college and the Spiritual Reglament: on church-state relations in Russia] (1916; reprint, Farnborough: Gregg, 1972).

117. I refer to confessional and introspective modes of self-analysis, discussed in more detail in chapter 6. On its nonvoluntary counterpart, extracted by secular courts as the ultimate proof of truth obtained during the preliminary investigation see N. B. Golikova, *Politicheskie protsessy pri Petre I* [Political trials during the reign of Peter the Great] (Moscow, 1957).

By contrast to the adventures of confession, public penance was reasserted as the dominant ecclesiastical practice in the Spiritual Reglament in 1722. Peter the Great also allowed public penance to be appointed by secular courts, in such cases, for example, as an inadvertent homicide in the army. In fact, by demanding public confession as part of this penalty, Peter's reforms aimed at radicalizing public penance. Feofan Prokopovich, who wrote the Spiritual Reglament, was under German influence and included Pietistic practices of public confession in this document. In the most difficult cases, according to the Reglament, sinners were to confess their sins in public, answer the questions of the bishop in public, undertake the allocated deeds of penance with diligence and zeal in public; only then could they once more take part in the sacrament of the Eucharist.[118] Yet, suggested the Russian Church historians, because of its clearly German origins, public confession never took root.[119]

The historians also registered that the actual use of public penance was diminishing in the eighteenth and nineteenth centuries. In 1734 the Holy Synod adopted a decision centralizing the imposition of penance (each local decision had to be approved by a higher body), which resulted in long delays and, probably for that reason, in the gradual decline of the practice. The ordinances of 1799 and 1801 allowed substitution of "public" penance in the circle of one's family for "monastery subordination" and public penance in the local church.[120] Nineteenth-century practice is perhaps best captured by an 1852 synodal letter to local priests. Three measures were realistically advised in matters of appointing public penance: the penitent may come to church during Sundays and holidays and perform twenty-five or more penitential prostrations; he may engage in fasting and prayers at home under the surveillance of the visiting priest; and he may perform some works of charity depending on the wealth of the penitent.[121]

By 1903, when Ardalion Popov was finishing his magisterial history of punishment in the Russian Orthodox Church, public penance remained an existing punishment that could be imposed by both secular and ecclesiastical courts, but the instances of its actual use were negligible. However, the discursive insistence on the need to demonstrate faith by penitential deeds remained unchallenged. For example, in 1842 the journal *Khristianskoe chtenie* (Christian reading) reprinted the old epistles to the Luther-

118. Popov, *Sud i nakazaniia*, 206.
119. Suvorov, *Uchebnik tserkovnogo prava*, 289.
120. Suvorov, *O tserkovnykh nakazaniiakh*, 220.
121. Popov, *Sud i nakazaniia*, 443.

ans (1574) of Jeremiah II, patriarch of Constantinople, on differences in dogma and ritual, including the matters of penance, where the doctrine was stressed once again. The Russian Church required penitential deeds to attest to the real change undergone by the soul of the sinner, "to see and know whether the penitent has rejected the sin completely."[122]

Emelian Iaroslavsky, reporting on the preliminary results of the second general Party purge in 1929, gave the following lengthy rationalization for the subordinate character of confession in the purge proceedings:

> Of course, it is hard to call a Communist who deceives his wife a New Man in all respects. One cannot take him as a model. We can demand sincerity from him toward his wife, but expelling him just for this insincerity would be incorrect. Perhaps [even] every member of the Control Commission, if he had to recollect all of his life, would remember an instance when he was insincere toward an intimate friend.
>   But he will not go to Comrade Shkiriatov [a chairman of the CCC at that time] and say: 'I confess, Comrade Shkiriatov, I have committed this sin.' (Laughter in the audience). . . . We the Communists should banish from our relations everything that smells of petty bourgeois relations in the worst sense of the word, of sanctimony, of priesthood. . . . We have many more criteria, other measures for determining whether a Communist is ready to fight for socialism, so that we need not make this [confession] the main thing.[123]

In other words, readiness to confess infinitesimal sins to the Party should not be taken as the main sign of Conscience; rather, Conscience is to be determined by other means. As we shall see, the primary sign indicating possession of Higher Conscience will be not words but demonstrated deeds, in the totality of the official and private life of the Communist. Fifteen centuries after Christianity curtailed *exomologesis*, it reappears. In this restaging, however, not only those volunteering or cast out by the community will undergo it, but all will have to pass this demanding test. Another novelty is that since every deed in the construction of the Holy Common-

---

122. "Otvet liuteranam sv. Ieremii" [St. Jeremiah's response to the Lutherans], *Khristianskoe chtenie* [Christian reading (St. Petersburg)] 2 (1842): 244. These letters are translated in George Mastrantonis, *Augsburg and Constantinople* (Brookline, Mass.: Holy Cross Orthodox Press, 1982).
123. Emelian Iaroslavsky, *Rabota TsKK VKP(b): Doklad, zakliuchitelnoe slovo i rezoliutsii po dokladu XVII Moskovskoi gubpartkonferentsii* [Work of the CCC: report, concluding remarks, and resolutions on the 17th Moscow regional Party conference report] (Moscow-Leningrad, 1929), 122.

wealth on earth is to demonstrate Conscience, no specific penitential deeds will be needed. Castigation and maceration will be unnecessary; devotion and dedication will be manifest in every act of life.

The Lateran Council of the Western Church, which institutionalized annual confession in 1215, finally found its logical counterpart in the East, with regular public penance being institutionalized in Russia after the 1930s. This penance-based exercise became the primary means to reveal Higher Conscience of a Communist. Let us now investigate the plans for reconstructing this community of penitents, for building the holy congregation on the foundation of joint penance. The next two chapters will explore the logic of the construction and functioning of the *kollektiv*.

3 A "Technology of No Mercy"

The Collective as an Object
of Knowledge and Action

In 1984, collectives in the Soviet Union numbered about two and a half million.[1] Having come to designate the basic unit of Soviet society, the most familiar and mundane reality of Soviet life, the word *kollektiv* most often applied to a stable group of colleagues in a given factory, farm, or office. The most authoritative dictionary of Russian literary language defined it as "a group of people united by a common goal, by common activity" and added, "people united by constant joint labor and membership in the same organization, institution, enterprise, and so forth."[2] The abstractness of this explanation indicated that the word was so widespread as to become uninteresting for theoretical analysis. In common parlance, it constituted one term in the habitual pair of opposites, "the collective versus the individual"—a universal feature of life in any human society.

The task of this chapter is to estrange the notion of the *kollektiv:* to demonstrate that the *kollektiv* was a very culturally specific phenomenon, existing almost exclusively in Soviet society; that the term *kollektiv* had a long conceptual history with the currently predominant meaning being only one among many contingent others; and that the *kollektiv* started to seem a universal feature of human existence only after a prolonged sequence of fierce struggles to create it in every Soviet factory, school, or office. The chapter begins with the use of the word in discourse and then examines the practices of *kollektiv*-formation and of the scientific study of the *kollektiv*, which together form a pragmatic background for discourse

1. Vladimir Shlapentokh, *Public and Private Life of the Soviet People* (Oxford: Oxford University Press, 1989), 131.
2. Article on *kollektiv*, in *Slovar'*.

and explain why Anton Makarenko referred to the *kollektiv* as a "technology of no mercy."[3]

THE COLLECTIVE AND THE *KOLLEKTIV*

Terms translating the English word "collective" entered the Russian language rather late. An adjective *kollektivnyi* first appeared in translations of European books in the mid-nineteenth century, as in "collective ownership" or "collective enterprise."[4] The noun *kollektiv* was registered as part of stable usage only by dictionaries published after 1934, which is rather curious, given the fact that the related terms "collectivism" and "collectivist" had already appeared in Russian dictionaries before the revolution.

The noun *kollektiv* is usually said to have originated in and remained part of the professional jargon of social psychologists who tried to describe the new phenomena brought about by the years of the first Russian revolution (1905–07) and the First World War. For them, *kollektiv* was a signifier that captured the newly observed set of actions carried out by a group or spontaneous gathering, be it a crowd, a public, or an army. Before the 1917 Revolution this scientific usage did not penetrate wider social strata. By contrast, the noun *kollektivizm* appeared in translations of French socialists' writings and therefore circulated widely in the discourse of the workers' movement. It had already entered a popular dictionary, published in 1895, which took *kollektivizm* to be a synonym of socialism.[5] Soviet dictionaries similarly defined *kollektivizm* as the principle of the comradely cooperation of laborers, according to which the private interests of an individual were "consciously" subordinated to social ones.[6] This influence seems to have defined another initial meaning of the word *kollektiv*—a human group linked to the proletarian revolutionary cause. These were the word's two main meanings in the postrevolutionary years—coming from the discourse of social psychology, on the one hand, and from the discourse of revolutionary struggle, on the other. Hereafter I use the English word "collective" to translate those Russian usages that aimed at a connotation

3. Anton Makarenko, "Problemy shkol'nogo sovetskogo vospitaniia" [Problems of Soviet school training], in *Sochineniia* (Moscow: Academy of Pedagogical Sciences of RSFSR, 1951), 5:136 (hereafter Makarenko, volume: page).

4. The *Slovar'* article on *kollektivnyi* states that this word was first registered in the 3d ed. of Dal''s dictionary in the late 19th century.

5. *Entsiklopedicheskii Slovar'* (St. Petersburg and Leipzig: Brockhaus and Efron, 1895), article on *kollektivizm*.

6. Article on *kollektivizm*, in *Slovar'*.

of universality, like those in the early social psychologists' theories who considered the collective to be a universal human phenomenon, an object of study for general social science. I use the transliterated monstrosity *kollektiv* in translating those usages that primarily implied a connection to the doctrine of communism and thus connoted a human group organized in a very specific manner.

Let us trace both primary meanings. Many commentaries on the development of the term *kollektiv* state that it first appeared in Kopelman's *What Should Collective Psychology Be Like?* (1908). The definition of a collective in this book sounded almost tautological: "any single group united by a process of establishing psychic unity."[7] Later attempts to define a collective in Russian according to objective scientific methods were more pointed. The academician V. M. Bekhterev who strove to extend his work on the etiology of individual human reflexes into the field of what he dubbed "collective reflexes" (instances of spontaneous cohesive group behavior in public) defined a collective as "an assembled person."[8] His followers have provided extensive glosses to this short definition. As an example of these, we may cite one of the most famous formulations: "a collective is a group of interacting individuals who jointly react to these or those stimuli."[9]

In Bekhterev's tradition, a collective would be a small group, never the nation or the whole people. Bekhterev was very suspicious of terms like "group mind" and *l'esprit de la nation* after MacDougall's and Le Bon's speculations on the matter. He decided to stay within the strictly scientific borders of the objectivist method of the study of group reactions. The recurrent example of a collective in Bekhterev's book is of a crowd carried away by the oratory of a revolutionary demagogue. People get excited by assembling in revolutionary rallies or demonstrations, in armies, or simply in crowds that spontaneously coagulate around a street orator. The crowd, however, as a rule deserves to be called a "disorganized collective," because

7. A. Kopelman, *Chem dolzhna byt' kollektivnaia psikhologiia?*, 37, quoted in V. I. Aleksandrov et al., "K voprosu o poniatii *kollektiv*" [On the concept of the collective], *Uchenye zapiski MOPI* [Learned notes of Moscow Regional Pedagogical Institute] 302 (1971): 189–198.

8. V. M. Bekhterev, *Kollektivnaia refleksologiia* [Collective reflexology] (Moscow: Kolos, 1921), 422.

9. Zaluzhny's 1930 definition, quoted in G. V. Panasenko and Iu. N. Belokopytov, "Formirovanie poniatiia kollektiva v filosofii i drugikh obshchestvennykh naukakh" [Formation of the concept of the collective in philosophy and other social sciences] (Moscow University, 1985), Institute of Scientific Information on Social Sciences ms 20323, Russian Academy of Sciences.

it assembles randomly and haphazardly. The first level of organization occurs in a public meeting that gathers with a passive aim—to listen to somebody, to receive information, and the like. The higher level of collective life comes about in workers' co-ops and *artel's*, where people get together with an active aim and consciously interact to achieve a common goal.[10]

This tradition of defining a collective as a group jointly reacting to external stimuli was virtually eliminated after the June 1936 resolution of the Central Committee on the perversions of pedology. Scholars are still not sure what led to the adoption of this resolution in the days when greater matters were at stake in Party life: the height of the Great Terror was just about to arrive. "Pedologists" was the name given to those scientists in the 1920s and 1930s who studied a specific object called "childhood" and proposed methods for improving the upbringing of the future builders of communism. Many of them came from Bekhterev's school of reflexology, and they used his basic concepts and definitions when they tried to deal with the problem of the *kollektiv* in Soviet high schools. Makarenko's attack on the pedologists, published only posthumously but thereafter relentlessly quoted by all official sources, ridiculed the pedological definitions of the *kollektiv* and strove to eliminate these definitions from both scientific and vernacular usage. Before discussing the alternative definition proposed by Makarenko and canonized by official sources after his death in 1939, let us describe the everyday usage of the 1920s, which was largely unconcerned with the problems of social psychology.

As already mentioned, the term "collectivism" appeared in the Russian language earlier than the noun "collective," and the term *kollektiv* was thus largely shaped by the preexistent term. In his insightful essay on the origins of proletarian culture, Robert C. Williams discerns three predominant meanings of the word "collectivism" among the revolutionary Bolsheviks before 1917. First, it signified a religious and philosophical notion of life after death: through joining the collective, individuals could gain a kind of immortality. Even after physical death, their personal contribution to the common cause would remain. Second, "collectivism" was the name for a certain political strategy that aimed at fusing the workers into a unified fighting corps by means of a revolutionary myth. Third, the word signified the future culture of the victorious proletariat after the revolution.

The second meaning is very important for our concerns. According to Williams, the syndicalist experience of the Bolsheviks during the abortive

10. For a detailed exposition of *artel'* see the section below, "To Form a *Kollektiv*."

revolution of 1905 had made them receptive to the idea of the proletariat as a collective body. Sorelian themes of unity based on a revolutionary myth —popular among those who were actively involved in organizing strikes and armed resistance to the czarist regime—also fed into this notion. Many Bolsheviks wished "to organize their experience and energy around an ideology that would help them lose their sense of self and acquire the sense of the collective."[11] They endowed collectivism with an almost religious meaning. In fact, Maksim Gorky and Anatolii Lunacharsky became the two renowned leaders of this Bolshevik strain of thought called "God-building." Trying to reconstruct Marxism as a new religion in order to fuse the proletariat into a this-worldly equivalent of the supreme being, they spelled out their program in a series of essays on *kollektivizm* as a truly revolutionary philosophy. In 1907 they published a collection entitled "Essays on the Philosophy of Collectivism," issuing their manifesto together with "empiriomonist" Alexander Bogdanov—a Marxist philosopher who spearheaded a theoretical revolution of appealing to "collectively organized experience" as the ultimate ground of all knowledge and action.

Another classic by Lunacharsky, his two-volume *Religion and Socialism* (1908–10), may be the best example of the Bolshevik attempt to create a new religion of collectivism and give it to existing worker's groups. Published after the defeat of the first Russian revolution, the book sought to capitalize on its lessons and develop the ethical dimension of Marxism that had been thus far left in abeyance.[12] Lunacharsky decided to reinvigorate the doctrinally weak ethical component in order to strengthen the revolutionary movement. He argued that Marxism could focus powerful human emotions if revolutionaries used it as a religious doctrine. The needs that underlay the great religions of the past and constituted the "psychological axis of the nation's life"—questions of happiness, justice, power, immortality—have not disappeared, he said: they demand some satisfaction in the doctrine of the workers' movement.

11. Robert C. Williams, "Collective Immortality: The Syndicalist Origins of Proletarian Culture, 1905–1910," *Slavic Review* 39, no. 3 (September 1980): 393. Williams's sentence should not imply, however, that the Bolsheviks were using the word *kollektiv* widely at that time.

12. Anatolii Lunacharsky, *Religiia i sotsializm*, 2 vols (St. Petersburg: Shipovnik, 1908–10). After 1905 the Russian intelligentsia engaged in painful self-examination of what went wrong. Curiously, this work's introduction is a polemic against Berdiaev, who had been his friend and colleague: Berdiaev's answer to the ethical barrenness of Marxism was individual conversion to Orthodox faith whereas Lunacharsky sought to erect a new Marxist faith.

Now, the existing proletarian philosophy, reasoned Lunacharsky, could easily satisfy some of these needs. For example, the philosophical works of his friend Bogdanov stated that human beings could now acquire a sense of personal immortality if they fused themselves with revolutionary practice: "In the face of the relativity of the physical individual there is only one absolute—collective practice."[13] Marx, according to Lunacharsky, had pointed at this conclusion in his "Critique of the Hegelian Philosophy of Right": human emancipation as the abolition of alienation transforms individual human beings into a species endowed with all the human capacities. In the current situation, however, wrote Lunacharsky, it is the species who wages the war for emancipation, and individuals—if they are to become emancipated and acquire full human potential—have to submit to it for the time being: "the center is the species, the collective, and the individual [*lichnost'*] revolves around it."[14] This submission to the collective resolves "the damned issues of being" because it empowers and assures immortality, thus fulfilling the basic functions of any religion: "This human religious need—to find happiness in knowing oneself to be part of a greater whole, this yearning to elevate and expand your life by means of a very particular experience when the borders of personality collapse, and vital energy spills over the border of the body into the great force of the cordially intimate and incessantly loved elemental force—this need that played such a prominent role in religious emotional life is natural, fruitful, and is destined to develop."[15]

Lenin, who suddenly found himself in the minority in his own Bolshevik party because he opposed these "God-seeking tendencies," eventually managed to gain discursive supremacy and designate God-building as a deviation. But the collectivists still exerted extensive practical influence. Bogdanov, the author of the concept of "proletarian culture," Gorky, the epitome of a proletarian writer, and Lunacharsky, the People's Commissar of Enlightenment for the first ten years of the revolution, left their indelible marks on the development of Soviet culture. At the least, they firmly tied the term "collectivism" to the notion of the higher cause of communism, a tie that was also very important for the first widespread instances of the use of the term *kollektiv*.

The modern Russian reader is puzzled by reading sources from the early

13. Ibid., 2:376.
14. Ibid., 338.
15. Ibid., 363.

postrevolutionary era because their use of the notion of *kollektiv* is very different from its modern sense. Consider the following examples: "Concerning all everyday life questions, workers address the *kollektiv;* sometimes they address the *kollektiv* even on topics that have nothing to do with it."[16] Or "It is enough to mention that complaints . . . against the improper actions of the administration were directed to the *kollektiv,* and the *kollektiv* more than once successfully cleared up the confusion. This, of course, increased its authority. [But] the positive results of the work were achieved only after a whole series of meetings, open conferences, and lectures, by which the *kollektiv* managed to attract the attention of workers who are not members of the Party."[17]

The dominant contemporary meaning of the word *kollektiv* (any group of colleagues tied by constant labor ties into a stable professional group) is often useless in interpreting the quoted examples, because it lacks one of the central features that was taken as essential by the speakers in the 1920s. At that time, only groups intimately related to the Communist cause could earn the high name of *kollektiv.* These usually were only the Party cell (as in the two newspaper statements above) or some highly specific types of production units.

In most cases, immediately after 1917 the word *kollektiv* signified a Party cell.[18] Documents from the early postrevolutionary period of Party history include resolutions that describe the relations between "higher" and "lower organizational *kollektivy,*" and statements that use the expressions "factory cell" and "Party *kollektiv*" as synonyms. For example: "Each lower *kollektiv* submits to a higher organizational *kollektiv* every two months a list of 5–10 percent of the members of the lower organizational *kollektiv,* mentioning those assignments that the given *kollektiv* considers appropriate for the people on the list."[19] A special brochure published in 1922, *The Role of a* Kollektiv *of the Russian Communist Party in NEP,* concentrated on describing the changes in the Party cell's functions under the

16. "Spaika s bespartiinymi," *Petrogradskaia Pravda,* November 1, 1922, 3 (I am grateful to the St. Petersburg historian Sergei Iarov, who directed me to these sources from the early 1920s).

17. "Spiachka proshla," *Petrogradskaia Pravda,* November 25, 1922, 3.

18. This sense is unfamiliar, hence puzzling, to most contemporary Russian speakers.

19. "Resolutsiia IX s"ezda po org. voprosu" [9th Party Congress resolution on organization matters], in *Voprosy partiinogo stroitel'stva,* ed. A. Mel'kumov (Moscow: Gosizdat, 1927), 164. See also 258.

conditions of the New Economic Policy, when it had to abandon economic tasks altogether and concentrate solely on political work.[20]

Kollektiv and "cell" (*iacheika*) were used interchangeably for some time, with *kollektiv* being more appropriate for ideological reasons since it closely reflected the aims of the revolution, and "cell" appearing more technical. Competition between the two ended with "cell" winning by the mid-1920s. The term originated in the conditions of clandestine Party work after the defeat of the first revolution of 1905. "Cells . . . are small, very flexible groups," wrote Lenin, and this name in his opinion very appropriately reflected the flexible character of their combat tasks.[21] In 1907–12 outlawed Party cells adopted the goal of creating a "network" of legal workers' organizations around them in order to tie the few remaining clandestine Party organizations together, which boosted the image of the Party as a network. The 1919 Party Statute first introduced the term cell into official Party documents, and the Fifth Congress of the Comintern (1922) made the term compulsory for all member parties. According to its resolution, the Communist Party cell differed from the territorially based "primary Party organization" of the Second International, in that it was organized in every industrial enterprise in order to facilitate the seizure of political power.[22]

A specific "cell problem" became central to Party concerns after the huge influx of new members into the Party following Lenin's death. In November 1924 there was an all-union conference of the cell/*kollektiv* secretaries presided over by Stalin. The conference tried to deal with the appearance of many new cells and the transformation of their internal structure owing to the large number of new, inexperienced Communists within them. Probably because of the sudden increase in the amount of published discourse on matters relating to cells, and the confusion arising from using this term parallel to *kollektiv*, the Central Committee adopted a resolution on June 29, 1925 to standardize the usage. From then on, two official terms were to be used, "the factory cell," and the "workshop cell" as a subunit within it.[23] However, it was not easy to stamp out the formerly prevalent usage of

20. *Rol' kollektiva RKP pri novoi ekonomicheskoi politike* [The role of the collective of the Russian Communist Party during the New Economic Policy] (Petrograd, 1922).

21. See multiple references in V. I. Lenin, *Polnoe sobranie sochinenii* [Complete works], 5th ed. (Moscow: Gospolitizdat, 1967–70), 7:15, 10:193, and 20:35.

22. V. I. Ratner, *Pervichnye organizatsii partii* [Primary Party organizations] (Moscow, 1953).

23. "O rabote tsekhovyh iacheek" [On the work of the workshop cells], in *Voprosy partiinogo stroitel'stva*, ed. A. Mel'kumov (Moscow: Gosizdat, 1927), 270.

kollektiv. Even in 1928 a brochure on self-criticism within the Party still used the term to refer to the Party organization of an enterprise: "When the plenum of a *kollektiv* adopts a resolution, the plant manager goes to a higher Party body and does everything to overturn this decision."[24]

The early 1930s witnessed great social changes—industrialization and collectivization—which among other things rendered the previous usage of the word *kollektiv* more or less obsolete. I will not concern myself with the collectivization drive in agriculture since the new usage that originated there is almost transparent: "collective farms"—*kolkhozy,* or agricultural *kollektivy*—became ubiquitous, and have been much studied.[25] The similar changes in industry deserve more attention since they were part of the same collectivization-of-life drive, at least in discourse. These changes drew comparatively less scholarly scrutiny, except for a few articles that noted the appearance of industrial "production collectives" (*proizvodstvennye kollektivy*). The phenomenal proliferation of "production collectives" followed the industrialization-related appeals issued by the Sixteenth Party Conference in 1930 "to develop socialist competition" and "to adopt Communist forms of labor." As a brochure, Kollektivy *and Communes in the Struggle for Communist Forms of Labor,* claimed, after labor was transformed by shock workers from a burden into a matter of "honor, glory, and heroism," the emergence of production *kollektivy* became the next logical step in the "reconstruction [*perestroika*] of labor relations in production."[26]

24. G. Alikhanov, *Samokritika i vnutripartiinaia demokratiia* [Self-criticism and intraparty democracy] (Leningrad, 1928), 121–122. The term "cell" itself was also ordered out of Party discourse by the decision of the XVII Party Congress in 1934. The official term became "primary party organization."

25. See R. W. Davies, *The Industrialization of Soviet Russia,* vol. 2, *The Soviet Collective Farm, 1929–30* (London: Macmillan, 1980), esp. ch. 4. See also Moshe Lewin, *Russian Peasants and Soviet Power* (London: Allen and Unwin, 1968), 109–112, for a discussion of three basic forms of collective work units in agriculture. Among recent works, Sheila Fitzpatrick's account of collectivization seems unsurpassed (*Stalin's Peasants* [New York: Oxford University Press, 1994]).

In fact, the collectivization of Soviet agriculture was reflected in English and French as well. The *OED* article on "collective" registers its earliest usage as a noun in the meaning of "Soviet agricultural farm" in 1925. In French, the *Petit Larousse* cited the noun *collectif* as a financial term at least until 1958, but Soviet commentators proudly pointed to articles on the USSR in *L'Humanité,* citing a widespread usage in the Soviet sense of the word (S. G. Il'enko and M. K. Maksimova, "K istorii obshchestvenno-politicheskoi leksiki Sovetskogo perioda" [Toward the history of the social and political lexicon of the Soviet period], *Uchenye Zapiski LGPI* 165 [1958]: 292).

26. P. Dubner and M. Kozyrev, *Kollektivy i kommuny v bor'be za kommuni-*

What were these "production collectives"? Lewis Siegelbaum, who described the phenomenon in one of his articles, mentioned that the new *kollektivy* were not all that different from the production communes already existing in Soviet industry. In fact, those few original experimental communes that waged their uneasy life in the 1920s were superseded by a wave of communes and collectives that flooded Soviet industry in 1929 in the wake of the industrialization drive.[27] These newer entities were very similar. Communes, of course, following the doctrinal definition, had to be closer to the Communist future in their level of socialization of life, but both shared the ideological justification, which distinguished them from the rest of workers' brigades: production communes and *kollektivy* had a high "level of Communist Conscience among participants," expressed in production successes stemming from Communist collectivism. In practice, mentioned the author, one can distinguish the *kollektiv* (or a new production commune) from other organizational types of production units at the point where a workers' brigade adopts the slogan Five-Year Plan in Four Years![28] Distinguishing between a production *kollektiv* and a production commune in practice was even more difficult. Siegelbaum, following the Russian brochure by Kalistratov, proposed the following distinction: while a *kollektiv* distributed collectively earned income among its members according to skill grades, a commune divided it equally.[29]

The movement for the all-out collectivization of life reached its apex in the creation of "co-habitation collectives" (*bytovye kollektivy*) whose members were to share everyday facilities and housing. By March 1930, for example, according to one of the optimistic estimates, there were 110 co-habitation workers' and students' *kollektivy* in Leningrad, involving some 50,000 people. Here, as in industrial production, a *kollektiv* was considered to be an intermediary form on the way to a completely Communist form of life, that is, a commune. "*Kollektiv* in its essence . . . is a form of the partial collectivization of everyday life. . . . The goal of the *kollektiv* as a tran-

---

sticheskie formy truda [*Kollektivy* and communes in the struggle for Communist forms of labor] (Moscow-Leningrad, 1930), 9.

27. Also see Robert G. Wesson, *Soviet Communes* (New Brunswick, N.J.: Rutgers University Press, 1963).

28. Iu. Kalistratov, *Za udarnyi proizvodstvennyi kollektiv* [For the shock production collective] (Moscow, 1930), 13. Note that Conscience is revealed in expressed deeds.

29. Lewis H. Siegelbaum, "Production Collectives and Communes," *Slavic Review* 45, no. 1 (1986).

sitional form is rather narrow,"[30] stated the same brochure. The activities to be collectivized included shared cooking and procurements of food, common laundry, and child-care facilities.

The subsequent fate of *kollektivy* in production and in housing was similar. The June 1931 "New Tasks" speech by Stalin stressed the need to heighten the individualization of responsibility, and unbridled collectivism became suspect. Co-habitation *kollektivy* and communes were chided for their excesses, while production *kollektivy* were quietly reclassified as "self-accounting brigades," in order to stress their most important feature: the meticulous calculation of individual input into the collective outcome. Whether this reclassification entailed any changes in labor practices is not clear, according to Siegelbaum.[31] Apparently the collectivist principle was successfully challenged only after 1935, with the unleashing of the highly individualistic Stakhanovite movement.

The connection between *kollektiv* and Communist Conscience that existed in everyday usage became weakened in the mid-1930s.[32] We may suggest two reasons for this. First, with socialism officially proclaimed to have been built in the USSR by 1934, every group of state employees working in the same factory or office could claim to be part of the higher civilization (and Communist Conscience) and thus, establish its right to be called a *kollektiv*. Second, with the proclaimed destruction of alien classes, the Soviet Union itself and large-scale units of Soviet citizens acquired the quality of a homogenous, unified body imbued with Communist Conscience, so that even such bigger entities could then be called *kollektivy*.

In this respect it is interesting to note the examples given in the 1934 Ushakov dictionary that first registered the usage of the noun *kollektiv*. The dictionary article gave two separate meanings for the word: (1) "a

30. Iurii Larin, *Stroitel'stvo sotsializma i kollektivizatsiia byta* [Socialist construction and the collectivization of everyday life] (Leningrad, 1930), 24–25. In the 1920s the agents renting apartments from the state were also frequently designated as "*kollektivy* of tenants," which may imply that cohabitation was seen as a higher form of life. See Katerina Gerasimova, "Zhil'e kak sotsial'nyi institut: Leningrad, 1918–1941" [Habitat as a social institute: Leningrad, 1918–1941] (master's thesis, Faculty of Political Sciences and Sociology, European University at St. Petersburg, 1997).

31. Siegelbaum, "Production Collectives," 82.

32. Here as elsewhere I use a capital letter to translate *soznatelnost'* as "Conscience" and mark the revolutionary connotation separating the term from a standard meaning of "conscience" as moral agency or internal judgment (see chapter 2, which discusses the concept's religious origins).

group of people, united by common work, common activities" as in the following example—"the whole collective unanimously protested"; and (2) "a unit within some whole, a cell" as in "tightly fused [spaiannyi] collective," "Party collective," or "collective of the unemployed."[33] Still, the political dimension is prevalent in all these examples that, from the 1990s viewpoint, only describe organizational structures. Indeed: people united by common work do not primarily work but are engaged in unanimous protest; while the organizational subunits mentioned are all tied to class struggle and class analysis.

Only a few idealists could call the whole USSR "a multimillion person collective" in 1933, as Solts did in his essay on the coming Party purge.[34] He may have been justified in doing this only because he was writing as one of the chief architects of the decisive purge operation, that was intended to transform the impure body of the country into a pure and monolithic union of builders of communism. The mass purges also allowed Zhdanov to call the whole Party a kollektiv in his final report at the Eighteenth Party Congress in 1939: "Each Party member has begun to feel that he is a fully valued unit, who is tied to the general collective of the Party, and who is responsible for the whole."[35] By the 1950s both of these claims had become clichés. The country, the Party, a factory, a workshop, a shift—all came to be called kollektivy. In the end ordinary usage would call any contact group of people within the Soviet Union a kollektiv.[36]

However, being a kollektiv still retained, if only in the background, the residual necessary political and ideological qualities that were earlier ascribed only to certain groups. Thus in 1940, while describing people working in a rail company as a kollektiv, a pamphlet would say: "The kollektiv of the North Donetsk Railroad, fulfilling in the Bolshevik manner the directives of Stalin's People's Commissar L. M. Kaganovich, demonstrates the best examples of a truly socialist attitude toward labor."[37] In 1951, people working at a Sverdlovsk factory would be called a kollektiv because "in the

33. D. N. Ushakov, ed., Tolkovyi slovar' russkogo iazyka (Moscow: Sovetskaia entsiklopediia, 1934–40), 1:1403–1404.
34. Aaron Solts, Dlia chego partii nuzhna samokritika? [Why does the Party need self-criticism?] (Moscow: Partizdat, 1933), 11.
35. Zhdanov's speech in XVIII Steno/39, 527.
36. A kollektiv was (at least potentially) a contact group or single body, acting as a whole. Thus, a group of textile workers employed by an industrial ministry was a kollektiv and a group of blue-eyed blondes was not.
37. Kollektiv Severo-Donetskoi v bor'be s zimnei stikhiei [North Donetsk Railroad collective in the struggle with winter] (Moscow, 1940).

factory, in the *kollektiv*, each of us becomes a man in the best sense of the word—a Soviet man."[38] Note that "a socialist attitude to labor" was precisely what distinguished the original production *kollektivy* from other workers' groups in 1929. A tie with the higher cause was still in place in the 1940s and 1950s, even if obscured by the fact that every enterprise and every workshop could now boast of this connection.

The political connotation slipped into the background as the word *kollektiv* served more and more as a general term. To invoke the distinction drawn earlier, since everywhere in late Soviet society we find only *kollektivy*, they became collectives, a general sociological term for a group, as opposed to an individual. By 1975, "scientific" classification by a group of Soviet scholars yielded sixteen distinct types of Soviet collectives: a family (organized as a collective of equal members held accountable by society for the upbringing of children in the spirit of communism); children's collectives in different institutions of education—in daycare, in kindergarten, in secondary school, in vocational school; students' collectives; a set of production-based collectives—in industrial enterprises, in farms, in commerce, groups of seasonal workers, colleagues in scientific research institutes, and artists' collectives; military collectives (and pilots' collectives as a special case); collectives of sports enthusiasts (and collectives of chess players as a specific case); finally—and most curiously—a collective of Soviet tourists, traveling together on a trip abroad. Each type of collective merited a special chapter since it allegedly had features distinguishing it from other types.[39]

This proliferation of collectives was reflected in the most widespread meaning of the word in everyday life, captured in Ozhegov's 1972 dictionary: "a group of people united by common work, by common interests."[40] Collectives were everywhere. A Russian entered a collective as a small child, passed from one to another in the course of life, but was never (normally) outside a collective. The network of collectives constituted the entire terrain of social life, so ubiquitous that people stopped noticing them as a phenomenon. And perhaps this quality of immediate givenness to perception, this feature of the collective as a taken-for-granted generic form of Soviet life, hid an epochal shift that went largely unnoticed. Indeed, before

38. V. Ponomarev, *Nas vyrastil Stalin* [We were brought up by Stalin] (Sverdlovsk, 1951), 79.
39. See K. K. Platonov, ed., *Kollektiv i lichnost'* [The collective and the individual] (Moscow: Nauka, 1975).
40. S. I. Ozhegov, *Slovar' russkogo iazyka*, 9th ed. (Moscow, 1972), 260.

the collective became this generic form, every existing human group in the Soviet Union had in fact to turn itself into a *kollektiv*, that is, had to construct or reconstruct itself according to a very specific set of organizational principles.

An analysis of the 1970s scientific writings on the *kollektiv* shows that Soviet social science constantly stressed this thesis. Perhaps the assertion of the cultural specificity of the *kollektiv* merited this insistent emphasis because the general Soviet public did not share it. Most people would presume that everyone everywhere lived and worked in collectives, even in the country most famous for its individualism, the United States. Even if Americans did not call their small human groups "collectives," a Soviet would typically imagine the mechanisms working within such a small human group as like ones at home. Soviet social science aimed to dispel this unscientific prejudice.

One commentary on the conceptual development of the term "collective" criticized the 1972 dictionary definition quoted above as missing the most important feature of the Soviet *kollektiv*, namely that *kollektivy* do not have goals of their own that are superior to the goals defined by the whole society.[41] Stressing the socially useful goal of a human group was the most widespread element of definitions of *kollektiv* in social psychology. Artur Petrovsky, the author of the most famous synthetic psychological theory of the *kollektiv*, defined it as "a group where interpersonal relationships are mediated by the socially valued and personally significant content of group activity."[42] In other words, in order to become a *kollektiv*, a group had to serve general interests as defined by the wider society. This was seen as a generic feature of the *kollektiv*, because the tightly cohesive in-group that pursued its own group interest unrelated or contrary to wider societal concerns merited only the name of "corporation."[43]

The most widely read introduction to social psychology said in 1980: "The *kollektiv* is not simply a new object of study for social psychology, but a new phenomenon in social life itself."[44] This statement closely paral-

41. K. K. Platonov, "Obshchie problemy teorii grupp i kollektivov" [General problems of the theory of groups and *kollektivy*], in *Kollektiv i lichnost'*, ed. K. K. Platonov (Moscow: Nauka, 1975), 14.

42. A. V. Petrovsky, *Lichnost', deiatel'nost', kollektiv* [The individual, the act, the collective] (Moscow: Politizdat,1982), 47.

43. See Leonid Umansky, "Poetapnoe razvitie gruppy kak kollektiva" [Stages of development of a group as the collective], in *Kollektiv i lichnost'*, ed. K. K. Platonov (Moscow: Nauka, 1975), 80.

44. G. M. Andreeva, *Sotsial'naia psikhologiia* (Moscow: Moscow University, 1980), 300.

leled the claim of official philosophers that the *kollektiv* was a "historically novel type of human unity."[45] The following dialectical edifice was erected to house this claim: historically, the "primordial collectivism" of traditional tribes was negated by the "group principle" of capitalist society. However, true *kollektivy* could not exist there, as a rule, because of the profound separation between people wrought by private property. Finally this stage, too, was negated by the third stage of human history, marked by the advent of a socialist *kollektiv* where the essential "collectiveness" of human existence acquired a "systemic quality."[46] Scholastic debates would rage over such issues as whether a proletarian Party in a capitalist society could be properly considered a *kollektiv* or what was the relation between the essence called "collectiveness" and the principle of collectivism, and so on.[47]

What interests us here is the insistence on the difference between the basic Soviet social unit and a typical Western small group. Of course, it may be explained by an obvious doctrinal need for distancing the Soviet phenomena from comparable Western ones. Even if chimneys produce the same smoke in Sverdlovsk and Detroit, according to the great theorist of industrialism and systemic convergence, Raymond Aron, Soviet ideologists had to prove that smoke in one case was qualitatively different from that in the other, since they were produced in two radically different socioeconomic systems. But apart from this apologetic interest, many scientists, committed to the experimental method, genuinely perceived and perhaps to a certain extent captured something profoundly different in the way small human groups were organized in the respective societies.

Before examining some works on social psychology in order to characterize this profoundly felt difference, and the kind of epochal change that Soviet society underwent when it transformed every small human group into a *kollektiv*, let us return in greater detail to the original definition of *kollektiv*, which lies at the roots of the postwar Soviet social psychology.

45. V. P. Ratnikov, *Kollektiv kak sotsial'naia obshchnost'* [The collective as a social unity] (Moscow, 1978).

46. Panasenko and Belokopytov, "Formirovanie poniatiia kollektiva," pt. 4.

47. Ibid. In its dogmatic exegesis of classic Marxist-Leninist texts, Soviet political economy defined *kollektiv* as " an internal system of relations of comradely cooperation and socialist mutual help of co-workers, who are united by socialist property and the common goal of production" (ibid.)—somewhere between the philosophical and socio-psychological definitions. But disciplines that had to deal with empirical reality were less dogmatic: sociology studied the empirical problems of existing collectives rather than the ideal *kollektiv;* pedagogy dutifully repeated the orthodox statement of Makarenko and proceeded to invent new ways to study its object and perfect its tools.

KOLLEKTIV AS A FORM OF LIFE: MAKARENKO'S DEFINITION

All the principal postwar Soviet sociopsychological works incorporated Makarenko's definition of *kollektiv*, "a contact group built on the socialist principle of association," and repeated his line of argument to a certain extent.[48] We may attribute this remarkable fact to some moments in the origins of Soviet culture. Sheila Fitzpatrick, in an article on the main orthodoxies in Soviet life, enumerated the principal figures whose work in the 1920s and 1930s set up the terms of debate in each respective cultural field for decades to come. In literature, it was Gorky; in life sciences, Pavlov and Lysenko; and in education it was Makarenko.[49] After his untimely death in 1939 he was canonized almost immediately: the few published articles, a volume of scribbled notes, and transcribed public lectures of this diligent educationalist from Ukraine became the *corpus classicus* of educational thought in the Soviet Union.[50] Given the fact that Makarenko was a practitioner of education first and foremost, his works also constituted the core of thinking on the definition of *kollektiv* in the empirical social sciences.

The most concise, even if slightly tautological, statement on *kollektiv* comes from his 1938 public lectures, where he summed up his previ-

48. See O. I. Zotova, "Razvitie teorii kollektiva v sovetskoi nauke" [Development of the theory of the collective in Soviet science], in *Kollektiv i lichnost'*, ed. K. K. Platonov (Moscow: Nauka, 1975), 34.

49. Fitzpatrick notes that an editorial in *Pravda* (August 27, 1940) endorsed the cult of Makarenko, and that he gained full status of a canonic figure by 1950 (*The Cultural Front* [Ithaca: Cornell University Press, 1992], 252–253).

50. Born in Ukraine in 1888, Makarenko worked as a provincial teacher in a professional school before the revolution. In 1920 he started a children's labor colony for war orphans and street waifs near Kharkov. In 1927 he was hired by the Ukranian NKVD to run its model Dzerzhinsky labor colony, where teenagers produced cameras and automatic drills. National popularity came to Makarenko in the 1930s as a result of his novels that described his educational experience, and the film *A Road To Life*—made after *The Pedagogical Poem*—made him an international success in 1933; John Dewey provided an introduction for its American version. His main works were translated into English in the 1930s and 1950s. Western scholarly interest in Makarenko, which soared high in the days of scrupulous analysis of Soviet education in the late 1950s and early 1960s, has virtually disappeared. The only exception is the Makarenko laboratory in Marburg University in Germany, which has continued to study him over the last thirty years and even collected its own archive of Makarenko-related documents (see Gotz Hillig, ed., *Hundert Jahre Anton Makarenko: Neue Studien zur Biographie* [Bremen: Temmen, 1988]).

Five volumes in the standard Russian 7-vol. 1950–52 ed. of Makarenko's writings are literary works. Such Stalinist masterpieces as the novel *Honor* (1936) or the didactic *Book for Parents* (1938, translated as *The Collective Family*) await their deconstruction.

ous thoughts in the following form: "What is a *kollektiv?* It is not just an assembly, not simply a group of interacting individuals, as pedologists thought. A *kollektiv* is a goal-oriented complex of persons, who are organized, who possess the organs of the *kollektiv.*" A biological term, "organs" implies that the *kollektiv* is a sort of a body, which, the author adds, is tied not by relationships of love or friendship or neighborhood but, in Makarenko's famous phrase, by "relations of responsible dependency."[51] An earlier, more interesting and detailed elaboration on the definition of *kollektiv* occurs in the unfinished book entitled *Problems of Methodology of Work of a Children's Labor Colony,* drafted in 1932. Makarenko's text there, published after the author's death in its original draftlike form, was later quoted by Soviet social psychologists for decades because it stated the many points required for a more precise formulation.

Makarenko starts with a description of the field of scientific debates on *kollektiv* in 1932: "Some say: 'A collective does not exist. Only individuals are real.' Others say: 'An individual does not exist as an independent entity in social reality. Only society exists.' A third group [of scientists] are glad that there is all this nonsense, and write volumes about it. All are called 'learned people.'" We, says Makarenko, will not engage in such idle talk; because we know from our practical life that both entities—a collective and an individual—exist and we have to deal with them in our educational work. Whereas pointing at an individual in practical life is very simple, pointing at a collective is not, if we follow the definition that prevails in psychological science. And Makarenko cites the famous formulation of the pedologist Zaluzhny ("a collective is a group of interacting individuals who jointly react to these or those stimuli"), implying that real collectives, like his labor colony, do not fit this definition. On the other hand, a group of drunks, fighting in the street, who hear a militiaman's whistle and jointly react by running away, easily fall under this definition. Is this a collective? Makarenko asks mockingly. A reader from the late twentieth century might say "Yes, if we accept the perspective of pedologists." Makarenko, by contrast, simply cannot accept this definition, because what he sees as "collective" is not some abstract human group jointly reacting to external stimuli, but a group organized in a very specific manner, as a *kollektiv.*

For him, the objectivist method that pedologists espouse, following in the footsteps of scientists like Bekhterev, denigrates a human being to the level of an animal and misses what is essentially human in life: "Interaction and joint reaction—this is something not even human, not social—it

51. Makarenko 5:207.

smacks of biology at a distance of ten miles. This is a herd of monkeys or a colony of polyps, if you like, but not a collective of people, not human activity."[52] Pedologists' favorite examples of collectives include a group of playing children, a political rally, a random street crowd, and a gang of war orphans. Even the League of Nations or states might be called collectives at certain moments. A pedologist would then scientifically classify these objectively registered phenomena as "temporary" as opposed to "constant" collectives, or as "self-organizing" versus "imposed" collectives. This play of artificial classifications is far from what Makarenko considers to be real life.

Makarenko resorts to ordinary usage to define what a real collective is, posing the following argument that an immense number of his commentators would routinely repeat: "Only a social association that is built according to the socialist principle may be called a collective. At least our Russian language registers this exactly and definitely. We say: 'The collective of KhTZ [Kharkov tractor factory] should provide the country with a hundred tractors.' But we will never use an expression like 'a collective of the Ford plant.' We say: 'The collective of the GPU' [the name of the secret police at that time], but we will never say 'the collective of the French Ministry of Foreign Affairs'. . . . Thus our language is faultless in defining what a collective is. We may only add that our language tends to apply the word 'collective' only to unities arising in direct contact, distinguishing a collective from the more broad concept of union."[53]

A collective in Makarenko's definition is what we have earlier marked as the *kollektiv*, that is, an entity related to the higher cause of communism. The obvious opposition of a collective to the phenomena of life in capitalist countries shows that it can occur only in socialist society. Abbreviations, a sign of the revolutionary era in the Russian language, also stress this point, as do the examples chosen: KhTZ, the symbol of socialist changes in the Ukraine, where Makarenko worked (a giant factory built during Soviet industrialization, producing tractors for collectivized agriculture) and the secret police (a symbol of revolutionary unity for him, because, as he puts it elsewhere, they constantly feel a comradely presence and jointly work for a higher cause).[54]

52. Anton Makarenko, "Opyt metodiki raboty detskoi trudovoi kolonii," in Makarenko 5:470.
53. Makarenko 5:475.
54. Makarenko 3:380, quoted in James Bowen, *Soviet Education* (Madison: University of Wisconsin Press, 1962), 129.

Nevertheless, there is something startling about his definition, namely the way in which Makarenko chooses to prove his point. He relies on ordinary language usage to back up his definition of what is a collective, hardly the procedure we would expect in a society that uses dogmatic exegesis from the classical texts of Marxism to support its claims. And Makarenko too employs some doctrinally correct narrative, and in fact, the description of ordinary usage comes at the end of just such a narrative. According to Makarenko, the collective is the last in a historically evolving series of forms of human sociability. History witnessed a progression from patriarchal family to feudal serfdom, and then to capitalist enterprise. Now comes the new form of sociability, based on the "socialist principle," which in turn "is based on the principled position of the global unity of laboring humanity, . . . expressed not in declarations but in real forms of human sociability and activity."[55]

Makarenko's exposition between this passage and the concluding definition of a collective reads like a rapidly written first draft, never revised.[56] It mixes up "social" and "socialist" many times, using them interchangeably; it is often circular as in the quotation above ("principle . . . based on principled position"); and it is sometimes incoherent. Let me attempt the thankless task of making sense of this difficult passage in order to draw at least some conclusions about the general thrust of Makarenko's argument.

Makarenko gives an example in order to clarify his point. In the spirit of the relevant concurrent debates, he counterposes the Soviet *artel'*[57] to one directed and hired by a private contractor. The first, apparently, exemplifies the Soviet collective, organized according to the social (or socialist) principle, the second is a residue of the capitalist past. Both of these forms of sociability are voluntary, but members of the latter form accept the lawful right of the contractor to appropriate surplus value. The former, by contrast, "allows each member *to see the whole in a different perspective.*"[58]

This perspective includes three basic elements. First, the Soviet collective is not a contingent form of association, but a law of the socialist society, which asserts "the sovereignty of the social whole, of the collective over the individual." Second, this sovereignty of the collective rests on its being the primary legal subject of relations governing the allocation, dis-

55. Makarenko 5:474.
56. Makarenko 5:474–475.
57. A small workers' collective; see the section on forming a *kollektiv*.
58. Makarenko 5:474; emphasis added.

tribution, and use of resources. Third, different collectives do not compete or clash with one another because all of them cooperate in the building of socialism. And then comes a set of concluding phrases: "Social association is an actually existing *form of life* of humanity. . . . Only a social association that is built according to the socialist principle can be called a collective."[59] A reader is able to infer from this sequence that a collective is a specific form of life.

It is interesting to juxtapose this excerpt to a comparable one, published in the 1931 primer for the pedologists.[60] Elkonin, also writing during the all-out collectivization-of-life drive, compares Boy Scouts and Young Pioneers in order to arrive at the definition of *kollektiv*. In appearance their activities look the same, claims the author. But in essence, Boy Scouts are individualists who cooperate only in order to get individual merit badges. In Young Pioneers' collectives, by contrast, "collectivist aspirations, that is, yearnings to achieve a Communist classless society, combine with the collective forms of organization."[61] Thus, concludes Elkonin, a *kollektiv* exists only where we find the following features: "the principle of socially useful labor; an expressed class collectivist attitude; a goal common to all participants; organization, that is, knowledge by every member of his role and position (in the whole); the responsibility of each for collective work and of a *kollektiv* for the work of each of its members, together with the personal responsibility of each member for his own work;[62] mutual help in work; and a socialist attitude to labor."[63]

59. Makarenko 5:475; emphasis added.

60. D. B. Elkonin, "Detskie kollektivy" [Children's collectives], in *Uchebnik pedologii dlia pedologicheskikh tekhnikumov*, chast' 2: *Pedologiia shkol'nogo vozrasta* [Handbook of pedology for the students of pedological schools, pt. 2: Pedology of the school age], ed. M. N. Shardakov (Leningrad, 1931). A sign of the times appeared on the book's cover: its author was a *kollektiv*—a "brigade of pedologists" of the Leningrad Pedagogical Institute. A. I. Dontsov (*Psikhologiia kollektiva: Metodologicheskie problemy issledovaniia* [Psychology of the collective: methodological problems of research] [Moscow: Moscow University, 1984], 101) cites Elkonin's chapter as an example of an original definition of the *kollektiv*, subverting the orthodoxy that granted this honor to Makarenko.

61. Ibid.

62. This last point on individual responsibility was added, apparently, at the last moment for obvious political reasons: after Stalin's June 1931 speech, personal responsibility for the use of industrial equipment, not "depersonalizing" collective use of it, became the slogan of the day. Before that a point on mutual responsibility would do.

63. Elkonin, "Detskie kollektivy," 76–77.

Makarenko's definition is far less comprehensive than Elkonin's, though they are similar in many respects. The stress on common goals, on expressed collectivist attitudes, and on organization, which many commentators ascribed to Makarenko in later years, supporting it by assembling disparate quotations from his numerous works, is not yet there, though it is definitely present in Elkonin's definition. Perhaps Makarenko himself profited by reading the systematic Elkonin and later unwittingly incorporated bits and pieces of Elkonin's exposition into his own work. However, the central strategy of argumentation (comparing phenomena of capitalist and socialist societies in order to arrive at a definition) and the thrust of the conclusions (stressing the relation of *kollektiv* to the Communist future) are the same.

But what at first seem to be minor details in Makarenko's argument—the ordinary usage to justify his claims, the rhetoric—taken as a whole, provide very specific connotations. "To see phenomena in a different perspective"—does this not sound too Nietzschean? "A form of life"—does this not sound too Wittgensteinian? Perhaps. It would be improper to cast a humble rural schoolteacher as the greatest Soviet philosopher, based on the minor details of his scattered remarks here and there. Nevertheless, some points are noteworthy.

First, it seems plausible to argue that the term "forms of life" may come from Eduard Spranger's book *Lebensformen* (1928).[64] Makarenko may have known the book. At the minimum, being well versed in contemporary psychological literature, he must have been aware of this Austrian scholar's efforts, following Dilthey, to employ the method of *Verstehen* as opposed to the method of objective description in the human sciences. Makarenko also constantly stresses his difference with pedologists whose objectivist methods, in his opinion, obliterate everything human in the study of collectives. He insists that the starting point of the study must be a real human form of life, or forms of sociability characteristic of a real society, rather than some abstract, supposedly objective definition that subsumes everything.

There is a second curious point also. According to *Lebensphilosophie*, of which Dilthey and Spranger were notable representatives, we live primarily in language, and thus "forms of life" are given to us in everyday usage. Makarenko also relies on ordinary usage to support his definition of the collective as a form of life, whether or not he is following Dilthey and

---

64. I am grateful to the St. Petersburg historian Daniil Aleksandrov, who first suggested this link to me.

Spranger.[65] His form of life, however, allows people "to see the whole in a different perspective." That is, transferring to this new form of life, engaging themselves in this specific form of sociability, people inhabit a world that is different from the one founded in another form of life, if we understand "the world" as phenomenologists do—not as a spatial void filled with things, which develops over time, but as a unity of prospects for meaningful actions in their available interpretations.[66] We may even say, then, that coming to live in a *kollektiv* means completely changing individual experience and existence: it involves entering a new world, where many things show up and make sense differently than they did before.

Of course, evaluating this assertion from the standpoint of skeptical scientists positioned in the end of the twentieth century, we are bound to say that it involves reading too much into Makarenko's example. In terms of everyday functioning, the capitalist *artel'* seems little different from the socialist *artel'*, except for the latter's explicit collective effort to talk in accord with the dominant ideological discourse, and open and overt proclamations concerning its adherence to this discourse. This point accords with Kalistratov's 1930 comment on the practical difference between socialist production *kollektivy* and other production units, noted earlier: *kollektivy* adopted the slogan Five-Year Plan in Four Years! Allegedly, there is no change in practice, other than the addition of a practice of collectively expressing approval for collectivism.

Is this enough to found a new world? Intuitively, it does not seem so.[67] Perhaps there were some other changes involved, but in order to discern those, we must investigate the practices of the new collectivist "form of life"; we should examine what it took to create a *kollektiv* out of an *artel'*

---

65. Allan Janik and Stephen Toulmin claim that Wittgenstein picked up the term from Spranger also (see their *Wittgenstein's Vienna* [New York: Simon and Schuster, 1973], 230). Nicholas F. Gier carefully examines connections between Wittgenstein's concept of a form of life and the use of the same term in such authors as Spranger and Simmel in his *Wittgenstein and Phenomenology* (Albany, N.Y.: State University of New York Press, 1981), 55–60. According to his argument, Wittgenstein may have also followed *Lebensphilosophie* when he was rethinking his earlier philosophy in the 1930s and came to prioritize ordinary usage over formalized language.

66. See Dreyfus, *Being-in-the-World*, ch. 5.

67. If this is so, then members of a *kollektiv* should be assumed to be blatant collective dissimulators, not believing the slogans they emit for consumption by a broader public. Another version of this transformation would entail collective conversion to a new faith. Both are unlikely.

or another preexisting group, and what change in world perception this may have entailed.

SOCIAL PSYCHOLOGY: DISCOVERY OF DIFFERENCE

Soviet social psychologists in the 1970s and 1980s, while duly invoking the prescribed definitions coming from Makarenko, had some freedom when they formulated and enumerated distinct features of the *kollektiv*. Platonov gave perhaps the most orthodox version of it, assigning the *kollektiv* three main features: a common externally set goal, common activity to achieve this goal, and the availability of the ruling organs of the *kollektiv*.[68] A more interesting popular primer was written by Galina Andreeva, who was famous for her commitment to empirical studies and for her critical attitudes to ideological nonsense, which she was nevertheless sometimes obliged to repeat. It mentioned three features of the *kollektiv* similar to Platonov's (common goal approved by wider society, cohesion as a system of relations actively built by participants, and a functional differentiation of organs) but added a fourth: the *kollektiv* as a specific type of interaction that fosters the development of individual personality.[69]

Books on *kollektivy* published before 1979 lamented the absence of an integral psychological theory of the *kollektiv*. That year finally saw the appearance of a collection of essays under the editorship of Artur Petrovsky that introduced the "stratometric conception of the *kollektiv*." This conception was now hailed as a solid achievement in the development of the science of *kollektivy*, because it was said to have opened up new prospects for theorizing the *kollektiv* and studying it empirically. According to Petrovsky and his numerous colleagues, each *kollektiv* had an onionlike structure of three levels, each subject to empirical measurement; hence the name of the conception. The core of the *kollektiv* was common activity in material production pursuing a target set by society. The second level was activity mediated by shared values and formed into two distinct layers: one, of activity stemming from "value-orientational unity" (VOU), that is, from common attitudes toward shared abstract values, and another, less basic one, that included interpersonal communication on matters of production. The

68. Platonov, "Obshchie problemy," 13.
69. Andreeva, *Sotsial'naia psikhologiia*, 291. Inherent in this definition was a socially critical position: those units that stifle individuality cannot be called a *kollektiv*. See chapter 8 on development of individuality in informal *kollektivy* in the 1960s and 1970s.

third, outermost and most superficial, level involved interpersonal communication among members of a *kollektiv* that had nothing to do with the official aim of the *kollektiv's* business activities.[70] The ordering of the strata
was predicated on familiar Marxist assumptions: the closer to the core, the
closer to the basis of material production that defines the socioeconomic
formation, the further away from the core, the more superstructural.

The main impetus to the development of the stratometric conception came from the empirical measurements of the coefficient of VOU and
from the discovery of what was called the phenomenon of "collectivist self-
definition." This phenomenon was considered to be extremely representative of the attitudes prevalent in Soviet life. The original experimental
setting involved students of the pedagogical institute who were given ex-
tracurricular socially relevant collective assignments (an assignment was
given to each of their thirty study groups that held approximately four hundred people altogether). After several months, a pedagogue invited students
into his office one by one and insisted that the project already long underway must be stopped, citing objective necessity and a strong group opinion.
According to the research results, more than 60 percent of the respondents
still expressed their desire to continue working individually on the discontinued project, even if there were no immediate rewards involved in it.

The Petrovsky team interpreted the results of this experiment as indicating the thorough acceptance of group aims by most individuals in the
group. Even when the group discontinues activities, its members identify
with the collective goal to such an extent that they still individually feel a
psychological need to fulfill the adopted initial objective.[71] This type of individual behavior that voluntarily pursues group aims in the absence of
coercive threat or external reward was triumphantly proclaimed to undermine the opposition between conformist and nonconformist behavior that
underlay conventional social psychology in the West. In dominant scholarly opinion, here was a stark vindication of the widespread phenomenon
of individuals freely defining themselves through the adoption of collectivist values.

70. A. V. Petrovsky, ed., *Psikhologicheskaia teoriia kollektiva* [Psychological
theory of the collective] (Moscow: Pedagogika, 1979).
71. An obvious criticism of the experimental setting is that a boss demanded disconnection while the group might have informally discussed the boss's decision and
chosen to resist it. Another criticism suggests that the results would have been different if an individual had to make the decision in the silent presence of the group,
who, as the boss said, favored disconnection.

The main determinants in group dynamics, concluded Soviet psychologists, were the adoption of a common goal for a group and the subsequent individual identification with that goal. Dontsov, a student of Andreeva and Petrovsky, developed a whole comparative theory of the *kollektiv* that specifically aimed at distinguishing it in this respect from the empirical referent of Western social psychology—any small human group. Interpreting Makarenko's rift with pedologists as arising specifically over the pedologists' neglect of a shared group goal, Dontsov also concluded that Western researchers similarly missed this principal point in the study of small groups.

Analyzing standard works by George Homans, Leon Festinger, and Morton Deutsch, Dontsov singled out one notion of a group, common to them all.[72] Their shared assumption is that a group is a voluntarily unit in which people would stay because the utility of being part of the group exceeds that of being alone, or because cooperation brings satisfaction not otherwise achievable. This notion underlies all usual experiments that aim at calculating the interpersonal emotional attraction within the group, proximity of value orientations between individual members, and the like. These experiments seemed rather superficial to Soviet scholars. A most frequently invoked criticism stated that it seemed futile to study groups by assembling Yale students in artificial laboratory conditions, while ignoring real human groups active in capitalist production.[73] Furthermore, many rejected Western methodological individualism as a very primitive tool for analysis of human interaction. For example, Andreeva wrote that one should not seek the reasons for group maintenance and cohesion in individual psyches. The main feature of *kollektiv*, she asserted rather elliptically, is that the reasons for its creation and existence lie outside the wills of the participants.[74] Dontsov's argument may be seen as a clarification of these lines of his teacher: Western methodological individualism, he said, prevented recognition of the real basis of group cohesion—a socially approved common goal.

72. Dontsov, *Psikhologiia kollektiva*, 24–25. Another favorite point of reference throughout his book is a collected work of early American social psychology—Dorwin Cartwright and Alvin Zander, eds., *Group Dynamics*, 3d ed. (New York: Harper and Row, 1968).

73. See P. N. Shikhirev, *Sovremennaia sotsial'naia psikhologiia SShA* [Contemporary social psychology in the USA] (Moscow, 1979), 137, repeated in Dontsov, *Psikhologiia kollektiva*, 32.

74. Andreeva, *Sotsial'naia psikhologiia*, 248.

Of course, questions of whether a group engenders a systemic reality that is not explicable in terms of its constituent individuals, and of ways to evaluate this systemic quality, are subjects of long scholarly discussion. But in this particular case Soviet methodological diatribes also reflected an acute awareness of the general inadequacy of the Western psychologists' concepts and methods to the study of Soviet life, whose basic reality was not a freely assembled group of interacting equals but a unit of socialist production, assembled to pursue a socially defined goal. In other words, not a free congregation, but a labor camp.[75] Hence the difference in research methodologies.

This difference in methodologies may tell us a lot about the internal features of typical small groups in the respective cultures. Setting up experiments to calculate the coefficient of a group's density, Budassi started using the method of asking everybody within a group about everybody else's moral qualities and professional capacities. The resulting coefficient was calculated according to the extent of coincidence of opinions on a given member of a group.[76] Later studies concentrated on measuring VOU calculated as the coincidence of group members' opinion on abstract or actual personal qualities needed to attain a preset group goal.[77] For example, Dontsov's experiments initially dealt with the activity of pedagogical *kollektivy*, where he measured the coincidence of opinions among members of the single pedagogical *kollektiv* on the features of the ideal pupil; then the coincidence of opinion on specific real pupils in the school. Opinions on the ideal were found to diverge, while opinions on real people tended to converge. This finding proved, in Dontsov's opinion, that the goal of group activity—educating real pupils, not conversing about remote ideals—ensured the group's cohesion. Later he studied VOU within newly organized industrial workers' brigades. The goal of group activity was found to influence the interpersonal perception in these groups. The longer the group existed and the more closely workers had to cooperate in it, the more

75. In terms of relevant religious practices: not the Puritan congregation, but the Orthodox monastery. For difference in religious backgrounds, see this chapter's section on St. Joseph.

76. S. A. Budassi, "Modelirovanie lichnosti v gruppe (na veroiatnostnykh strukturakh)" [Modeling an individual within a group (in probability structures)] (abstract, Candidate of Science diss., Moscow State Pedagogical Institute, 1972). See also S. A. Budassi, "Sposob issledovaniia kolichestvennykh kharakteristik lichnosti v gruppe" [Means of studying the quantitative characteristics of an individual in a group], *Voprosy psikhologii* [Problems of psychology (Moscow)] 3 (1971).

77. Dontsov, *Psikhologiia kollektiva*, 123–124.

the professional qualities of a person were stressed as central in the description of a colleague, and the more frequently negative features were mentioned.[78]

Summing up these experiments on measuring group cohesion, we are struck not by the findings, but by the techniques. Festinger's classical experiments on group cohesion relied on measuring the number of people considered personal friends within a small group, on the emotional appeal of some members of the group to others, and on questions of the type "How do you like your group?"[79] Soviet respondents, by contrast, had to evaluate every single member of the group according to moral and professional standards. Cohesion—discursively proclaimed to be predicated on a common group goal—could in practice be calculated only on the basis of asking everybody to inform on everybody else, one by one.

Apparently, eliciting such information was rather easy, given the number and extent of experiments based on this practice. Perhaps this practice even seemed natural, since every respondent was already accustomed to constantly watching and evaluating colleagues. Accordingly, the contention of the remaining sections of this chapter will be that group cohesion within a *kollektiv* could be thought of and maintained only against this background of mutual surveillance.

TO FORM A *KOLLEKTIV*

According to a widely accepted thesis in Soviet social psychology, a randomly assembled group of people has to pass through certain stages of development in order to become a *kollektiv*. In the formulation of Umansky, they entail passing from "conglomerate" to "cooperative group" and then on to *kollektiv*. When a human conglomerate develops a stable structure and ruling organs, it forms a cooperative group. At this stage the group's task is to develop aims that do not contradict the broader aims of society;

78. Ibid., 124–125, 134–137.
79. Festinger asked group members (from a court community in MIT's Westgate housing project) to nominate three people they see most often socially. Then the criterion of group cohesion was calculated as a proportion of the number of friends who lived in a given court to a total number of friends living in the whole project. See Leon Festinger, Stanley Schachter, and Kurt Back, *Social Pressures in Informal Groups* (New York: Harper and Brothers, 1950), 37, 91. Other questions concerned appeal of the project tenants' organization, and emotional attraction between tenants. Dontsov quotes this classic study in *Psikhologiia kollektiva*, 41.

otherwise it turns into a "corporation," which favors group goals over so-cial ones.[80]

This scheme of group development follows the famous process of cre-ating a children's labor colony that Makarenko described in his numerous novels, based on his actual efforts to form such colonies.[81] Makarenko's writings yield two ways of examining this process: reconstruction of his actual historical experience from the novels, and his own explicit method-ological advice. Let us begin with the former, particularly with the most fa-mous *Pedagogic Poem* (1930) describing the experience of the Gorky chil-dren's labor colony in 1920–27. Luckily for us, Makarenko's experience was concisely summed up by James Bowen, one of the English-speaking commentators on his educational methods.

According to Bowen, setting up a *kollektiv* required four phases. In the first phase Makarenko had to consolidate the randomly assembled group into some kind of an aggregate by getting colonists engaged in collective action in response to some external threat (e.g., hunger). Then he arranged situations that presented additional outside challenges (scarcity of fire-wood, the hostility of neighboring peasants), so that the collective response to them became habitual and some "gang collective" appeared. At this stage "a mystique of the collective" emerged as colonists felt empowered by their joint effort. Simultaneously Makarenko had to combat alternative group-ings within the primary collective. At the third stage a socially approved goal was introduced to transform the gang collective ("corporation" in Umansky's terms) into a Soviet *kollektiv*. The fourth and final stage was achieved when colonists introduced a full system of self-governance, while Makarenko had to restrain the punitive power of the *kollektiv*.[82]

Makarenko himself described the stages of *kollektiv*-building in *Prob-lems of Soviet School Education*, saying that the first task is to formulate some simple external demands, backing them up by a threat of physical force if necessary. A pedagogue at this stage should not concern himself with explaining why he formulates these requirements; the important point is just to impose them. He should just say No to certain behavior, in Makarenko's words. The second phase entails the creation of an *aktiv*—a core group whose members earnestly support these demands. Makarenko

80. Umansky, "Poetapnoe razvitie gruppy," 80.
81. Children's labor colonies were set up to care for the *besprizorniki* (literally, "the unsurveilled"), war orphans and street waifs who numbered millions after the end of the Civil War.
82. Bowen, *Soviet Education*, chs. 6–7.

advised paying no attention to the personal deficiencies of these pupils and fully supporting their wish to carry out the pedagogue's demands. At stage three the *kollektiv* finally appears, insofar as group responsibility for individual transgression is introduced, and the *aktiv* starts to enforce the professed standards of behavior on the whole group, shaming and punishing their transgression. "Relations of responsible dependence" (in Makarenko's terms) thus take hold. Stage four involves curtailing of the punitive power of the *kollektiv*, as it could become ruthless: "the *kollektiv* gains speed and often demands too much from a particular person," Makarenko says. Self-policing also characterizes this stage, since everybody now realizes the unacceptability of certain behavior. Each starts controlling himself and "is interested in his own behavior more than in anything else."[83]

What is interesting in this methodology is the complete reversal of the pedologists' method prevalent before Makarenko. Pedologists strove to create an individual conscientious believer by arranging a suitable environment for each child, their objective being individual conversion to Communist faith. Only when an internalized conscious discipline was in place could each person join ranks with others in a free collective. Makarenko insisted that this method was utopian, if not counterproductive. He had to work with the damaged personalities of war orphans and street delinquents, who could almost never transform themselves individually into mature Communists. In the words of Bowen, there was not much to reform in the children with whom Makarenko worked;[84] they had yet to be formed, because—having been abandoned at a very early age to live on the street during the tumultuous years of revolution and civil war—they lacked basic social skills and habits. By using group coercion, Makarenko sought to inculcate basic habits in these children and get them to solve their problems through collective action. Strong in-group mechanisms would then produce conscientious believers far more successfully than all the pedological talk about arranging a suitable social environment.

83. Makarenko 5:147. In 1939 Soviet power in the newly occupied Polish territories relied on the *aktiv* to staff the offices of the Soviet administration, drawing on people willing to support the new regime for personal material or spiritual reasons —and, often, to profit from the spoils available in the new positions of power— which gave Jan Gross grounds to talk about "the privatization of the state" as the main feature of the Soviet regime. Yet, he noted, the *aktiv*'s members also became slaves to the collective machinery itself, because other citizens equally acquired the right to direct prosecution against their former masters (Jan T. Gross, "Social Control Under Totalitarianism," in *Toward a General Theory of Social Control*, ed. D. Black [New York: Academic Press, 1984], 2:59–78).

84. Bowen, *Soviet Education*, 52.

According to Makarenko, pedologists sought "to inculcate discipline by sermons," and half of their successes were questionable for this very reason. Once a child was out of the reach of imposed discipline, the power of the sermon would cease and old habits would reappear. Makarenko insisted, by contrast, that discipline should be taken not as a set of individually adopted and maintained techniques, but as a complex moral phenomenon produced by the entire system of relations within a tight primary group. Of course, pedologists and Makarenko strove for the same end result—"conscious discipline." But their objects of primary pedagogical influence were radically different. Pedologists would single out an individual who is to understand and conscientiously follow a discursively formulated disciplinary rule. Makarenko would insist that the primary object of education be not an individual, but a collective: "Discipline should be demanded from a *kollektiv*. . . . A task of discipline should be set up for the *kollektiv* directly, clearly, and resolutely."[85]

Apparently, at some stage—when justification was already necessary, as obedience had to rely on rational consent to some extent—the pedagogue had to articulate the task of discipline as a moral task for a *kollektiv* and supplement it with the following doctrinal justification. First, discipline is most effective in the achievement of common goals. Second, discipline liberates every individual within a *kollektiv* from the fear of abuse by the strongest because its requirements defend them equally. Third, because of the first and second points, the interests of the *kollektiv* should always be superior to individual interests. "The technology of no mercy" should be applied to enforce this rule in practice. Last, but not least, discipline is beautiful. Here two elements testify to it: clean children who march in orderly fashion through the city streets are more beautiful than a gang of sick, dirty street scum in libertine postures. Also, there is a specific beauty in meeting a worthy challenge, fulfilling the difficult task neatly and in time through the discipline that organizes the *kollektiv*.

Makarenko's recipes for *kollektiv*-building appeared in multiple milieus of Soviet life. Yet the forces that were charged with implementing these recipes in any given case were very diverse, their objectives contradictory, their individual intentions not entirely clear. Furthermore, it is not obvious whether these forces faithfully implemented Makarenko's policies in action or his writings simply supplied a vocabulary that was highly appropriate for description of the changes already long underway. Still, the end

---

85. Makarenko 5:134.

result of this complicated development was registered by the Platonov classification in stark clarity: the army, the prison, the school, the factory workshop and the Soviet office were all recast to become *kollektivy*. Though examples abound, I concentrate on changes in the school system as the most characteristic example of this epochal transformation. These changes defined the standards of what was to be taken as normal routine life, since they were inculcated in every Soviet citizen in the process of secondary socialization in compulsory schooling.

Tatiana Konnikova, the director of secondary school no. 210 in Leningrad, wrote a model book on the application of Makarenko's methods in postwar schools. The book was all the more notable because its setting was so extraordinary: 750 evacuated children from 526 different high schools had returned in 1945 to a city ravaged by a fierce siege, during which all standards of moral behavior had been seriously challenged.[86] Konnikova, who later defended a Ph.D. thesis based on her postwar experience, decided that the only way to get these war-affected kids back into normal life was by setting up a *kollektiv*. The school pedagogical council approved her plan, and it followed Makarenko's methodology in almost every detail.[87]

First, the teachers clearly articulated requirements to the incoming pupils in each class. Then a potential *aktiv* was formed in each class, which had the task of enforcing these demands together with the teacher. The third stage witnessed the introduction of disciplinary competition between classes and the subsequent transformation of the *aktiv's* opinion into the unanimous opinion of the entire class. Stage four was dedicated to individualizing the disciplinary influence of newly formed *kollektivy* and to the development of self-policing habits.

There was one innovation, however. The primary activity that brought each class *kollektiv* together in the Leningrad case was the conscious disciplining of its members, and disciplining members of the entire school *kollektiv*. If Makarenko had some other demands in mind (his initial demand in the famous scene at the beginning of *The Pedagogic Poem* is that the first six colonists who were former thieves and bandits should finally

---

86. Harrison Salisbury described the complete overturning of what counted as humane morals inside the city during the 900-day German siege, which resulted in 600,000 civilians dead of hunger and wounds (see his *900 Days: The Siege of Leningrad* [New York: Harper and Row, 1969]).

87. T. E. Konnikova, *Organizatsiia kollektiva uchashchikhsia v shkole* [Organizing the collective of pupils in school] (Moscow: Russian Academy of Pedagogical Sciences, 1957).

start working in the household simply to feed themselves), Leningrad pedagogues had only disciplinary demands to rely on. The main means of ensuring group cohesion became the activity of consciously demanding disciplined behavior from others; the practice of being on duty (of setting up
gardes du jour, as the Russian language would have it, following the French
idiom) fused classes and the whole school into a *kollektiv*.

Substantively different pedagogical demands in the initial stage of
kollektiv-building yielded to a single set of procedural demands: children
should observe standards of externally disciplined bodily behavior. "Guards
on duty," pupils from a class that held disciplinary duty for a given week
and competed with other classes for excellence in carrying out duty, would
patrol the school corridors, enforcing the following simple standards: def-
erential greeting at the sight of teachers; no arguments with teachers and
immediate fulfillment of their demands; orderly procession in and out of the
classroom and in the corridors of the school (usually, this boiled down to
"no running during class breaks"). In full accordance with Berger and Luckmann's description of the social construction of reality through habituation, this routine that seemed an imposed novelty to the beginning classes
became a normal institutional reality for those who commenced their
studies in successive years.

The Leningrad innovations were popularized by the press and prescribed
for others to follow. A few books enumerated other rituals contributing to
the creation of the *kollektiv*, invented in the years immediately following
the war, but by 1985 these rituals seemed immutable eternal mechanisms
of the everyday functioning of each secondary school in the Soviet Union.
Allegedly, in 1949 the first holiday of the "Last Bell" took place: all the
school's other *kollektivy* threw a surprise party for pupils of the graduating tenth grade on their last day of classes.[88] Similarly, the Last Bell celebration was introduced in school no. 152 in Moscow in 1951, and was popularized by the local press.[89] Annual August conferences of the practicing
kollektiv-builders in the Academy of Pedagogical Sciences in Moscow were
established, and their experiences were discussed on the pages of *Uchitel-
skaia gazeta* (Teacher's gazette). In the early 1950s, this helped to dissem-
inate the compulsory forms of postwar Soviet school life: a regular wall
newspaper, a regular school-wide assembly as the main moral agency, a
holiday in the school's honor, and the adoption of an individualized motto

88. Ibid., 326.
89. A. T. Kurakin, H. J Liimets, and L. I. Novikova, *Kollektiv i lichnost' shkol-
nika* [The collective and the personality of the pupil] (Tallin, 1981), issue 1:60.

by each *kollektiv*. Mottoes varied; to give but a few examples: "There is no union more sacred than friendship" (Gogol');[90] "To strive and seek, to find and never surrender" (Kaverin); "If to be—then to be the best" (Chkalov), and so on.

The important element also stressed by the pedagogues in the 1950s was a fight against "false *kollektivy*," subgroups that might challenge the supremacy of the *kollektiv* from within, or the devolution of the *kollektiv* into an in-group that did not aspire to support broader social values and pursued only narrow group interests. True *kollektivy* had to fight the false ones, in order to maintain their internal stability, and in order to bring the straying group-corporations back into line with societal interests.

One "false *kollektiv*" mentioned by Makarenko himself is the gang. He worked to break those residual ties from the thieves' networks that his colonists brought with them into their new lives. Assaulting the code of honor of thieves and expelling the recalcitrant colonists who continued to form stable subgroups based on this code of honor became the only means by which to vanquish this dangerous threat to Makarenko's concerns. But it was not only Makarenko who encountered this problem in the 1930s; real-life production *kollektivy* had to fight their equivalent, an enemy called the *artel'*. This opposition was at the forefront of debates on industrial policy at that time, which may explain why Makarenko chose to counterpose the Soviet *artel'* to the private *artel'* in his explanation of what a *kollektiv* is. Based on common geographical origin, or united on the basis of complementary skills, *artel'*s, or small voluntary groups of workers who collectively undertook to fulfill a certain task, were objects of suspicion to the Soviet authorities.

An *artel'* usually numbered twelve to fifteen people, with a paternalistic elder as its head. The official position on them was ambiguous throughout the 1920s. On the one hand, these were workers' collectives of some kind; on the other, they were not created in order to achieve societal goals and thus were frequently accused by the authorities of satisfying the private interests of the *artel'* elder or corporate interests at the expense of the social ones.[91] Tolerated until the late 1920s, *artel'*s were squeezed out by the industrialization drive. These small voluntary groups were no longer

90. This surprising motto referred to friendly relations of comrades united in a *kollektiv*. Interpersonal friendship, of course, was the most subversive force countervailing the pressure of the *kollektiv*. See chapter 7 on the role of friendship in mature Soviet society.
91. Hiroaki Kuromiya, "Worker's Artels," in *Russia in the Era of NEP*, ed. Sheila Fitzpatrick et al. (Bloomington: Indiana University Press, 1991).

acceptable because they were not set up under the guidance of Soviet power, whereas the same group mechanisms oriented toward achieving the goals of socialist construction were close to the dearest aspirations of the government. Kuromiya suggests that after the anti-*artel'* campaign began, *artel's* simply transformed themselves into an acceptable form of "shock brigades" by relabeling themselves, condemning the figure of the paternalistic elder in discourse while keeping some form of centralized leadership in practice, and openly adopting the socially approved image of contributing to socialist industrialization. Only the mechanization of labor in the mid-1930s finished off *artel'* traditions in reality.

In 1937, at the height of the purges, Stalin used the already derogatory term *artel'* to lash out against migrating teams of employees that followed powerful patrons transferred to other jobs.[92] Of course, his main concern was the practice of patronage, but the choice of usage is interesting also. Actually, this practice was widespread and was an outgrowth of the lack of qualified personnel. Managers transferred from one plant to another, distant, one would recruit their closest aides and assistants in order to ensure effective administration at the new site.[93] By labeling this practice *artel'*-building, Stalin inadvertently equated it with the instigation of false *kollektivy*, that, in Stalin's words, "send nauseating reports on their successes" to the center instead of effecting changes in reality with the help of their true *kollektivy*. Zhdanov similarly attacked the false *kollektiv* during the purge of the Komsomol leaders in 1938. He charged them with having abandoned the principled task of taking care of Komsomol members' *kollektivy* and having engaged in false drunken camaraderie instead. In 1950 Zhdanov levied the same charges against the editorial boards of the journals *Zvezda* and *Leningrad*.[94]

Searching for and fighting against patronage networks or networks of friends that could subvert the true collectivity of the *kollektiv* became the

92. Stalin, "Zakliuchitel'noe slovo na Plenume TsK VKP(b)," 1 (XIV):231.

93. See Kotkin, *Magnetic Mountain*, 76, on the arrival of a whole army of middle-level managers together with Gugel', the new director of Magnitogorsk Metal Works, in 1929. For the CCC-WPI instruction on fighting this widespread practice, see par. 34 in *RBCC* 1933, 184.

94. A. A. Zhdanov, "Rech' na Iubileinom Plenume TsK VLKSM" [Speech at the jubilee plenum of the Komsomol CC], *Komsomolskaia Pravda*, November 4, 1938; and A. A. Zhdanov, *Doklad o zhurnalakh* Zvezda i Leningrad (Moscow: Ogiz, 1946); see a bilingual edition of the second speech, *The Central Committee Resolution and Zhdanov's Speech on the Journals* Zvezda *and* Leningrad, trans. F. Ashbee and I. Tidmarsh (Royal Oak: Strathcona, 1978).

norm. For example, methodical instructions on setting up a class *kollektiv* in a primary school, issued by the Academy of Pedagogic Sciences in 1957, included the following. First, one had to outline "the clear attractive tasks" of future common activity to the class, unambiguously describe the rules of discipline, and enforce them personally. Second, a system of collective responsibility was to be introduced, by staging monthly review of the educational successes and failures of the class, measured in terms of competition with other classes, while pointing out the personal contribution of each pupil to the general result. Third, the teacher had to struggle with the "false camaraderie" of cheating on exams—in other words, networks of pupils sharing the right answers.[95] This set of instructions is reminiscent of Zhdanov's efforts to weed out the false *kollektivy* in the Komsomol and literary journals.

Let us finish this section on practices of *kollektiv*-building with another example that sums up the exposition and reveals all the mechanisms at work rather starkly. It concerns the curiously marginal type of Soviet *kollektiv*, the last one in Platonov's classification: the group of Soviet tourists on a trip abroad. Now, this group had to accomplish all the stages of forming itself as a *kollektiv* very quickly in a limited amount of time and maintain itself under conditions most unnatural for a *kollektiv:* namely, "surrounded by enemies." Its procedure of *kollektiv*-building follows the familiar steps. First, a common goal is presented to the group—"to honorably represent our country abroad." Then, the *aktiv* is formed, and the head of the group is named. Before the tourist group goes abroad, preliminary training is required; in the guise of introduction to the lifestyles and history of the visited country, experts give advice on the possible "provocations" that await a tourist group there. In the same preliminary sessions the workings of group opinion are tested in staging discussions of some hypothetical "difficult cases," implying the most widespread failure of the group—a defection of one of the tourists. Standards of appropriate and inappropriate behavior are discussed, and the signs of suspicious individual actions are clearly delineated.

The main element to ensure the success of the group trip abroad, says the chapter, is the personality of the leader. She or he should be "tactful"

95. M. D. Kostina, "Organizatsiia i vospitanie uchashchikhsia pervykh i vtorykh klassov" [Organizing and training of 1st- and 2d-year pupils], *Izvestiia Akademii Pedagogicheskikh Nauk* [Academy of Pedagogical Sciences reports] 94 (1957): 47–57.

but resolute in the application of power if the need arises. Apparently, a *kollektiv* was very likely to dissolve without this supervision and the threat of the broader society, personified in the group's leader. When the leader could not be physically present with all the members of the group simultaneously to represent this threat, the only means to ensure the success of the tourist *kollektiv* in fulfilling the honorable task of representing Soviet society abroad was to rely on the enforcement skills of the tourists themselves. The worst-kept secret that all Soviet tourists knew in practice, and probably the first organizational rule in the instructions to any group leader, was this: no Soviet individual may walk alone in a Western city. Soviet tourists, even on a leisurely evening stroll on the boulevard du Montparnasse, must always walk in threesomes!

MUTUAL SURVEILLANCE

This episode reveals what may have been the ultimate background of Soviet power. At times when all the other institutional arrangements fail, when no leader can enforce his or her will, the most basic technique is used in order to confound power: the group is entrusted with the task of controlling itself. Mutual surveillance is the reliable bedrock of Soviet power, the foundation on which pyramids and hierarchies are erected. But this surveillance of everybody by everybody else is not a clever institutional trick adopted as a last resort, when nothing else is working; on the contrary, this is the ever-present rock bottom that one reaches upon dismantling mountains of power. If this bedrock dissolves, Soviet power disappears: hierarchies crumble and pyramids collapse. Mutual surveillance sets the cornerstones of Soviet power: without it, the Soviet Union could never have existed.[96]

Mutual surveillance is hardly a novel invention. Practiced for centuries of rural life, it was part and parcel of the Russian peasant land commune. It was practiced with even more ferocious intensity in some Russian monasteries that espoused the ideal of cenobitism. But the Soviet Union employed mutual surveillance to create a new universally widespread phenomenon—a *kollektiv*, a unit imbued with a higher cause. Peasant communes relied on extensive surveillance but did not care about the saintli-

96. Stephen Kotkin was one of the first scholars to draw specific attention to the cooperation of Soviet people in their mutual surveillance, and to the interlocking web of state and popular surveillance (*Magnetic Mountain*, 196). I would like to stress the primary role of horizontal surveillance in this web.

ness of themselves or of their particular members. Some monasteries did use surveillance to enforce standards of saintly living but did not venture to penetrate the wider society. Only certain tiny enclaves in Russia used mutual surveillance to enforce saintly zeal before 1917; after the 1930s this mutual enforcement became the rule in every Soviet institution and thus constituted the bedrock of Soviet power.

Here is an example from a 1957 pamphlet of the Academy of Pedagogic Sciences on the arrangement of ordinary classroom life in an average secondary school—this very important classroom life that prepared each small Soviet citizen for what awaited him or her in wider society as a grownup. One of the innumerable commentators on how to replicate Makarenko's successes in every secondary school advises creating several different networks of surveillance. Apart from the usual *gardes du jour* who watchfully control general discipline, a "sanitary corps" should be also created to control the cleanliness and enforce standards of socialist hygiene (clean nails, hands washed, hair combed). To these, a pupils' commission checking on the condition of books that were distributed to the pupils at the beginning of school year should be added: how do pupils learn to maintain and preserve common property? Still a fourth special pupils' commission checks on the availability of pens, paper, and ink at each desk in the classroom and redistributes those resources if it finds some desk wanting.[97] Thus the school becomes a disciplinary paradise based on mutual surveillance: there are so many duties that each pupil always plays the roles both of the watcher and of the watched. Studies are forgotten; meaningful life is spent in a frenzy of checking up on one another, and in conflicts arising out of it.

In the 1950s the *kollektivy* may overlook installing mutual surveillance as a primary technique ensuring their existence, rather they are already concerned with perfecting its multiple applications and making its web more ubiquitous. By contrast, the *kollektivy* of the previous epoch did not consider mutual surveillance such an obvious feature and proudly cited it as an organizational innovation, distinguishing them from the non-Communist groups. For example, one brochure on production *kollektivy* insisted that they practiced a radical new type of discipline, which rejected hierarchical control and was predicated on workers' mutual enforcement. A section of this brochure, tellingly titled "One for all and all for one" says:

> Socialist self-discipline is based on socialist self-control and in turn facilitates it. The mutual control of participants in [production] *kollektivy*

97. Kostina, "Organizatsiia i vospitanie uchashchikhsia," 59.

and communes stems from proletarian collectivism in work, that is, from a yearning to collectivize all the available strength and personal capacities of the individual participants, in the interest of raising the common labor output.[98]

Statutes of production *kollektivy* published in 1930–31 recommended electing a governing body called the council that would subsequently enforce workers' discipline, addressing "cases of an unconscientious attitude toward labor," fighting absenteeism, and so on. Basically, all these statutes enacted the policy that Makarenko would recommend some years later: elect a ruling body, install joint responsibility, demand discipline of your comrades. Thereby, as another brochure put it, "in a *kollektiv* a new man is formed."[99]

A description of practices of mutual surveillance in the everyday life of Makarenko's ideal labor colony may reveal some important points about the structure and functions of mutual surveillance within a *kollektiv*. In the early 1930s this colony housed about five hundred children aged seven to fifteen within thirty-five to forty-five "detachments" (*otriady*). The name came from the jargon of the Civil War days and served to recast mundane tasks—such as sowing a field, or building a fence—as heroic missions. "Detachment no. 12 has stormed through its task in three days!" would be the usual report at the evening assembly of all the colonists. Each detachment elected a commander who was responsible for the activities of her or his unit and represented this detachment in the council of commanders, the supreme legislative and executive body of the colony. It is curious to note that Makarenko did *not* have veto power, and he had to accept the council's binding decisions if his appeals to the contrary were overruled.

All members of a detachment shared a bedroom and ate at the same table. They could be separated during the day, however, as colonists were frequently regrouped with members of other detachments to become parts of ad hoc "assembled detachments" that fulfilled some special task. During these work tasks discipline was enforced by an ad hoc commander, nominated for this particular task, but after hours, in their free time, the original detachment was responsible for the behavior, hygiene, and scholarly success of its members. Group responsibility was ensured by both punishments and rewards that were mainly meted out to the detachment as a

98. Kalistratov, *Za udarnyi proizvodstvennyi kollektiv,* 17.
99. Dubner and Kozyrev, *Kollektivy i kommuny,* 14.

whole. Thus, the detachment was a primary unit, a *kollektiv*.[100] Mutual surveillance and censure in these primary units functioned to the fullest. First and foremost, it penetrated every aspect of daily life. It became particularly fierce, however, when it concerned political or moral matters.

Discussing matters of discipline elsewhere, Makarenko claimed that in order to ensure the primacy of the *kollektiv* over the individual one should apply a "technology of no mercy."[101] He gives an example of a particularly "shocking" situation. A commander of some detachment on duty stole a radio from one of the colony inhabitants. After the loss was reported, the commander, addressing the regular evening assembly of all the colonists, "tactfully" admonished whoever had stolen the radio to return it. A colony-wide search was conducted, with personal belongings searched, but nothing was found. However, some days later he himself was identified as the thief and accused of stealing the radio. Young Pioneers searched all the possible hiding places in the colony, found the radio, and then waited in ambush until the thief came to check his new possession.

A meeting of the detachment members decided to expel the guilty commander from the colony. Makarenko tried to have the verdict repealed but failed to persuade the detachment. An extremely stern Young Pioneer, nicknamed Robespierre for his demonstrated zeal, formulated the opinion of the *kollektiv*: "Kick him out! Throw him down the stairs!" Robespierre supplied the following justification: the *kollektiv* had entrusted the accused colonist with the highest honor, but he had cynically cheated. If the colonists let the commander remain part of the *kollektiv*, it would collapse.

Expulsion, however, was not the primary means of individual punishment for Makarenko. He practiced other effective but nonexclusionary means. The highest threat was being called to account for one's actions in front of all the colonists assembled. In fact, this was not "in front," strictly speaking, but "under the chandelier": the accused was positioned right in the middle of the big circular hall, in the spotlight, with colonists standing in a circle around him. The rule was strict: commanders reporting about their detachment's activities of at the evening assembly would report standing in rank with the detachment in some part of the circular perimeter; if specific commanders had to account for their own misdeeds, they had to literally come out into the open and stand in the center of the circle. It is as if horizontal surveillance and admonition are intensified to the limit; the pro-

100. See Makarenko 5:167–171 stressing this point.
101. Makarenko 5:136.

cedure is a double inversion of the hierarchical scheme of Panopticon, presented by Foucault as the disciplinary paradigm of Western civilization.[102]

First, instead of all the prisoners being surveilled by one guard, as in the famous prison design of Jeremy Bentham, a single person is surveilled by all. Second, if the surveilled cannot see the surveillant in the Panopticon because of the physical obstruction to their gaze, here each one may see in every direction. This is perfect visibility, but of a strange kind: standing alone at the center and unable to look in all directions at once to see the surveillant, an individual at the center is a victim who can never see the "assembled personality." Each single person standing at the perimeter is clearly visible and thus may represent a potential friend from the old days. United together in a circle around the victim, single persons disappear; they become part of a physically invisible yet terrifying *kollektiv*, a "goal-oriented complex of persons that possesses the organs of the *kollektiv*,"[103] including eyes and strangling arms. There's nowhere to look for help, there's nowhere to run. The power of the corrective gaze increases a hundredfold.[104]

Mutual surveillance creates a curious "public opinion." This opinion is not an instance of Habermasian critical publicity formed as a result of rational discussion, but a corrective action, close to Locke's Law of Opinion.[105] According to the characteristic Russian usage from the epoch, it is formed "around" an individual, rather than on an issue. Thus, a book published at

102. Foucault discusses a similar circular arrangement in an orphanage (*Discipline and Punish*, 177), implying that the orphanage council (a micro-tribunal) assigns offenses and metes out corresponding punishments to individuals. Makarenko's technique differed in two respects: first, putting someone under the chandelier was not a courtlike proceeding but the colony's ultimate means of discipline; disagreement with the group's judgment caused the individual's expulsion. Second, handling offenses committed by detachments rather than individuals, the council of Makarenko's colony accused and punished a group as a whole (and if the detachment persistently failed to discipline a defiant individual, the individual was put under the chandelier at the colony assembly). On "advancing the individual" through group pressure see a section on Makarenko in chapter 4.

103. Makarenko 5 : 207.

104. Foucault briefly mentions "lateral" relations, on which surveillance may rest together with top-bottom and bottom-up relations (*Discipline and Punish*, 176) and discusses cultural models for modern discipline, claiming that a plague model had replaced the leprosy model: isolation of an infected individual rather than expulsion of an infected group. In contrast, I suggest a link between the cultural model for Soviet discipline and the collective sacrifice of a scapegoat. But the objective is to transform the victim *without* killing it.

105. Jürgen Habermas, *The Structural Transformation of the Public Sphere* (Cambridge, Mass.: MIT Press, 1989).

the time of high Stalinism to sum up the "experience of raising workers in the spirit of Communist Conscience" at Sverdlovsk enterprises referred, in an offhand manner, to "public opinion" as a means of enforcing labor discipline. In the example given, the *kollektiv* lamented that it had not "created a public opinion around the absentee" in a timely fashion. Therefore, an assembly of the *kollektiv* had to discuss the worker in question in a special meeting, and he subsequently changed for the better.[106]

Undoubtedly, this expression "public opinion around a person" used to describe the core means of the disciplinary enforcement, even if highly reminiscent of Makarenko's practice of positioning the accused "under the chandelier," is connected to him in a very convoluted manner.[107] But his commentators in the 1950s stressed this very practice of making individuals account for their misdeeds while surrounded by the *kollektiv* as one of the primary means of strengthening corrective public opinion. "The communard who condemns Chubakov [a transgressor discussed in this text] is hardly likely to adopt his point of view," wrote one of them.[108] The metaphor of adopting someone's point of view, as well as the metaphor of having an opinion wrapped around oneself, are very revealing. Few people in their sound senses would like to step into the focal point where all eyes, burning with comradely zeal, meet to condemn what they see. Few would like to adopt the position from which the transgressor Chubakov had to view the world: he meets a condemning gaze no matter where he looks. Perhaps the form of life called the *kollektiv* brings this phenomenological world into being.

It is rather curious that Makarenko himself did not pay frequent attention to the techniques of mutual surveillance. Apparently, for him the tal-

106. M. T. Iovchuk, ed., *Sotsialisticheskoe promyshlennoe predpriiatie—shkola vospitaniia kommunisticheskoi soznatelnosti* [Socialist industrial enterprise— training school for of the Communist conscience] (Sverdlovsk, 1953), 83.

107. In assessing "public opinion," Iaroslavsky used another revealing metaphor: "We need to create this public opinion, we should put the Communist under the bell jar [*stekliannyi kolpak*], in order to make him feel that the Party condemns him" (*VI Plenum TsKK sozyva XIII s"ezda, 11–13 dekabria 1925* [Sixth CCC plenum, December 11–13, 1925] [Moscow, 1926], 52). Curiously, this metaphor became part of common Soviet parlance in 1973, with the appearance of the cult film *Seventeen Moments of Spring,* in which the Gestapo head puts a suspected Soviet intelligence agent "under the bell jar." Film critics suggest that this movie's cult status stemmed from its critical view of Soviet reality disguised as the last days of the Third Reich.

108. M. D. Vinogradova, "Voprosy oranizatsii obshchego obrazovaniia v shkole kommuny im. FED" [Problems of educational organization in the Dzerzhinsky commune school], *Izvestiia Akademii Pedagogicheskikh Nauk RSFRSR* 102 (1959): 271.

ent of controlling one's neighbor is a quasi-natural given that children bring with them when they arrive at the colony. The point is, as we already said, to direct this capacity to the right objects, and to proportion its application. Makarenko is aware of certain virtuosi of surveillance in his colony, young children whom he calls "communication specialists," who know everything that's going on.[109] But he relies on their help and summons their information only when he has to make a disciplinary move or correct some *kollektiv* on the verge of devolving into false camaraderie. Transgressions that do not affect the purity of life in the colony may be left unattended for the time being.

Surveillance is stressed by Makarenko as a decisive means only when his colony has to deal with cases of distinct marginality entering its well-ordered life. Before the elements of this marginal life get well integrated into the comprehensive machinery of unobtrusive mutual control, they should be put under meticulous surveillance. Novices are incessantly followed by the commanders of the detachments to which they have been assigned, while in more serious cases, "scum"—those thieves who do not abandon their criminal habits upon arrival at the colony—are to be subjected to everyday surveillance by everybody and immediately reported on in case of even a minimal transgression. But apart from these marginal cases, mutual surveillance ought not be stressed as a specific tool; it is merely spread throughout the body social, always out there, handy.

To sum up, Makarenko's specific achievement was his demonstration of the potential for using this surveillance to enforce the standards of saintly living. Makarenko backed up higher Conscience with mutual surveillance and thus revealed a new form of life. I must stress this point. Makarenko did not create a novel form of life, since it already existed, he simply showed a way to universalize it. And in the concluding words to his 1938 public lectures on *kollektiv*-building, Makarenko said: "I think that what my colleagues and I were doing was also being done by many people in the USSR. I was different from them only to the extent to which I felt the need to demand these rules of everybody."[110] Conscientious behavior was demonstrated by certain willing individuals or was enforced in certain locales, but it was not demanded of everybody and everywhere. Enforcing such a demand was a daunting task. Any force poised to achieve this would fail in its project of imposing the standards of higher Conscience on a recalcitrant

109. Makarenko 5:182.
110. Makarenko 5:221.

population, if it had to rely on costly external physical coercion. But an extensive internal resource of mutual surveillance existed, to impose and enforce them.

MONASTIC IDEAL IN THE MIDST
OF THE SECULAR CIVILIZATION

Comparing Makarenko's achievement with the monastery statute of Saint Joseph Volotsky (1503) is very illuminating.[111] Joseph's statute is usually considered to be one of those documents that determined the development of the Russian Church in the direction of heightening means of external discipline rather than intensifying attention to means of internal control of the soul. It is said that after the followers of Joseph had defeated the followers of Saint Nil Sorsky—the main proponent of practices of internal analysis and training of the soul—in the famous debate in the beginning of the sixteenth century, and the Josephites had merged with the nascent Russian empire, legitimating its claim to theocracy, Joseph's statute became a model for many monasteries. Commentaries take Joseph as the main actor in what may be called the Russian counter-reformation of the sixteenth century;[112] they describe his statute as a detailed plan of setting up an institution that aimed at rekindling monastic life by radicalizing the standards of purity in order to fight the corrupting influences of the reform-oriented sectarians.[113] The main subject of this curious document is monastic discipline, enforced by constant surveillance.

Joseph explicitly calls a cloister a "single body,"[114] the integrity of which

111. St. Joseph Volotsky is also sometimes called St. Joseph of Volokolamsk, by the name of the monastery where he lived. The roots of the two names are related in Russian (see Tomas Spidlik, *Joseph de Volokolamsk, un chapitre de la spiritualité russe* [Rome: Institutum orientalium studiorum, 1956]).
112. See B. A. Rybakov, "Vointstvuiushchie tserkovniki XVI veka" [Militant clerics of the 16th century], *Antireligioznik* [The anti-religious] 3 (1934): 26, for parallels between Volotsky and Loyola.
113. Ia. S. Lur'e, "Kratkaia redaktsiia Ustava Iosifa Volotskogo—pamiatnik ideologii rannego iosiflianstva" [Short version of Joseph Volotsky's statute—a monument of the ideology of early Josephites], *Trudy otdeleniia drevne-russkoi literatury* [Works of the section on ancient Russian literature (Leningrad)] 12 (1956): 138.
114. [St.] Joseph Volotsky, "Dukhovnaia Gramota prepodobnogo Iosifa" [Spiritual Statute of St. Joseph], *Velikie Chetii Minei*, September 1–13, [St. Petersburg, 1868]), col. 576. The statute was not reprinted during Soviet days; see, however, the detailed discussion of its shorter and longer versions in Ia. S. Lur'e, "Iosif Volotsky kak publitsist i obshchestvennyi deiatel' " [St. Joseph as a moralist and public figure],

is supported by a network of mutual surveillance, described by him with some lyricism:

> Saint Ephraim says: it is appropriate to us, brethren [to act as follows] —the strong should raise the infirm, the industrious should console the exhausted, the vigilant should rouse those falling asleep, the orderly should punish the disorderly, the reverend will teach the outrageous, the abstinent should remonstrate the nonhesitant [to sin], the healthy should compassionate the sick—and holding ourselves in such manner, teaching good to one another, we will unanimously defeat our enemy, and glorify our God.[115]

Different metaphors are brought together to justify the same horizontal influence, peer pressure being presented as brotherly help. The end result is unanimous action, when all the souls act as one, when all the minds think as one, and the perfect body of Christ is realized in a given cloister: "the obligation of the pastured is the agreed and warmest harmony of minds."[116]

The statute authorizes a series of institutional practices that reminds us of Makarenko's colonies. First, the ultimate disciplinary threat is that of expulsion; the penultimate is condemnation and shaming in front of the brethren. Joseph repeats the quote from Matthew 18:15–18 ("If thy brother sins against thee, go and tell it to him alone," and so on), which the ecclesiastical courts used as their primary guidance in setting the familiar sequence of court actions: reveal, admonish, excommunicate.[117] Then he applies it to monastery life: "If someone does not listen to prohibition and condemnation [oblicheniia] coming from the abbot or cathedral brothers, then one should condemn [oblichati] him in front of all the brethren and if he remains insubordinate, banish him from the cloister."[118]

If there were a chandelier in the cloister, we might imagine that Joseph would willingly authorize putting the sinner under it. And if Bentham's Panopticon is based on the model of treating the physical disease of plague in a medieval European town, Joseph's cloister is organized on the model of treating a spiritual plague. Hence the difference: instead of compartmentalizing each body and individually treating it—in such a way that this body does not contaminate another one—a joint effort of all the souls, sur-

---

in *Poslaniia Iosifa Volotskogo* [Epistles of Joseph Volotsky] (Moscow-Leningrad, 1959), esp. 56–64.

115. St. Joseph, "Dukhovnaia Gramota," col. 575.

116. Ibid., col. 566.

117. This precept from the New Testament is invoked two times (ibid., cols. 576 and 579); for its role in ecclesiastical court procedure see chapter 2.

118. Ibid., col. 579.

rounding a sick soul, is preferred. Spiritual contamination fails when therapeutic pressure comes from all sides simultaneously; the cure combines the efforts of many and encircles the sinning soul with righteous ones, for there is no escape from this circle. When one cannot physically recreate the circle, one may effect it in an imaginary space, if each will treat the sinner in the same curative way. In the words of Saint John Chrysostom, whom Joseph quotes: "If you see someone undergoing penance, turn away from him more than an abbot; let the sinner fear you more than he fears the abbot. If he fears only the teacher he may sin again soon; if he fears many fathers and many lips, he will shrivel in many ways." [119] Coming from each healthy soul, the condemnation guarantees the cure of the sick one.

The second curious parallel between Makarenko and Joseph is that both stress the need to create the core group of the righteous, the *aktiv*, in order to enforce saintly standards. In Joseph's model, these righteous brothers are called the "cathedral" (*sobornye*), or "bigger" (*bol'shie* or *preimushchie*) brothers. These bigger brothers are allowed to condemn a sinner immediately, on the spot; other inhabitants of the monastery have to report a sinner to these bigger brothers or to the abbot himself. The bigger brothers also take care of the novices, by paying specific disciplinary attention to the novices' behavior. Joseph says that each monastery should have from ten to twenty of these bigger brothers, enforcing mores within the monastery.

Answering an imaginary interlocutor who is puzzled by this innovation (no such brothers were specifically appointed heretofore in Russian cloisters), Joseph gives the following justification for the appearance of this privileged group. Before, he says, monasteries were small and poor. Monks spent all their time struggling with nature, and this burdensome struggle equally shared by a small body of monks made it impossible to segregate between bigger and smaller brothers. Now, with the amelioration of living conditions and the increase in the number of brothers, admonitions and prohibitions coming from the bigger brothers to the others serve as a "light yoke," in order to train the novices to the profound hardships that await them in their future monastic life. [120] A less elevated reason is the inability of the abbot to police each himself as a result of the growth of the number of brothers. Since not all monks are equally assiduous in piety, the function of the correction of the infirm should be shared with the pious. [121]

Similar to Makarenko's *aktiv*, bigger brothers constitute the disciplinary

119. Ibid., col. 574.
120. Ibid., col. 585.
121. Ibid., col. 571.

core of the cloister. A part of Joseph's statute called "the precepts" details the tasks and origins of this disciplinary guard. Makarenko advises starting the formation of the *kollektiv* with the formation of the *aktiv*. The first precept of Joseph also advises immediate election of "those who are first in virtue and reason, willing and able to help the abbot in supporting the piety and well-being of the cloister."[122] Then Joseph enumerates the activities of the bigger brothers. For example, during the liturgy, they should stand in different parts of the cathedral (perhaps this is why they are sometimes called "cathedral brothers") and watch everybody else. During the service, two bigger brothers stand at the entrance of the cathedral and check the entrants and those who intend to leave, letting them out only if they have pressing physical needs. Two others are standing in the front left and right corners of the cathedral, facing the crowd, so that no one escapes their frontal gaze. There are two more bigger brothers standing in the church vestibule, and two more near the altar who enforce order and silence during the liturgy.

Outside the liturgy, the bigger brothers enforce order in the refectory, stop impious conversations, and check those who steal food. They make hourly walks around the territory of the monastery, searching for the idle and assigning them work. They check the material possessions of the monks in their cells and allow no more than two shirts, pants, cloaks, and so on. They fight thievery. They accompany peasants, and especially women and boys entering the monastery in order to prevent license. They look for monks who are drunk and discover the hidden potion. They police the courtyard at night so that nobody escapes from the cloister without the abbot's permission, and so on.

A routine not much different from other monasteries, we might say. Of course, this statement would be true. But few societies in modern European history—other than the Soviet Union—aimed at transforming schools in accord with the model of a cloister. And the model underwent some changes in its new milieu. Makarenko made a great contribution when he democratized the Josephite statute: anyone became a bigger brother while serving as a *garde du jour* and then became a smaller brother while off duty.[123]

The third similarity between Makarenko's colony and the Josephite mon-

---

122. Ibid., col. 588.

123. In Volokolamsk monastery, a bigger brother was supposed to be elected for life but could be deposed if he sinned; his brothers elected a successor. When an abbot died, bigger brothers also were to elect a new one, since an abbot was prohibited from appointing a heir (ibid., cols. 580–585).

astery lies in the socialization procedure for the novices. According to Joseph's statute, if the older monks may condemn sins, and the bigger brothers can both condemn the sin and enforce the standard of saintly living, the novices hardly have any rights in disciplining others. Their role is to be an object of discipline. In Joseph's words:

> If they see someone committing impiety . . . , they cannot prohibit or condemn, but should tell this in solitude to their elders, and if one of the novices does not have an elder, he should tell it to the abbot, or to one of the bigger brothers who conduct the monastery's governance, and should not tell anyone else.[124]

If some doubt whether denouncing a brother to an abbot is right, they should "learn the truth that this is not libel or condemnation but perfect love," because, as Saint Basil the Great said, those who refuse to denounce sinning brothers are equal to "fratricides."[125] The novices should concentrate on self-perfection only. Rather than looking for the misdeeds of others, they should train their own virtue to gain the right to police. "The young and the novices do not condemn and prohibit but only attend to themselves and accept advice from everywhere."[126]

The bigger brothers also train the younger brothers to submit their wills to God. Joseph recommends exercises from Paul the Simple and Basil the Great, meaningless feats with the sole aim of mortifying the will in obedience to divine will, as expressed by a bigger brother. Novices fill countless buckets of river water, only to pour it back; they tear their robes and mend them; they unweave the carpet on which they sleep and then weave it back; they stand for nine hours under the sun in incessant prayer.[127] Here Joseph's advice reveals the secrets of this power system in its stark reality. A new recruit is supposed to pass all these exercises in order to make his body unquestionably docile and let his soul overflow with the pleasure of obedience by the sheer fact of conforming to God's Will. Some time later this monk, no more a novice, willingly imposes the same meaningless but demanding exercises on later recruits; the relay system of enforcing obedience and docility continues without a break.[128]

124. Ibid., col. 578.
125. Ibid., cols. 575 and 614.
126. Ibid., col. 578. On attention to and work on the self after external condemnation see chapter 6.
127. Ibid., col. 534.
128. Surprisingly, the Soviet army used a similar system of *dedovshchina* (eldership); see its exposition in chapter 7. And, to enforce unquestioning obedience,

Eschewing moral judgment, I must stress the difference of this power system from the system of hierarchical surveillance in the West. The rhetoric of Joseph is very suggestive in this respect for it lets us glimpse the principle of horizontal discipline. There is no single Big Brother, but there are many bigger brothers. There is no single apex, where punitive and decision-making power culminate, but a network of surveilling peers, to whose arbitrariness in the enforcement of virtue the individual submits. These bigger brothers are not far away, there at the top; rather they constitute the most proximate environment, exerting immediate and physical pressure on a physical body. Instead of the tyranny of the sovereign, the tyranny of the *aktiv;* instead of a despotism of a person or of a principle, a despotism of a myriad of small sanctimonious bosses. In the most democratic version of this power system, since you are a boss yourself, at least for a day or an hour, this is your own tyranny of yourself, mediated by the *kollektiv.* You suppress, to be suppressed in turn. The corrective gaze returns, multiplied a hundredfold. Discipline is inescapable not because of hierarchy that enforces it, but because of what we may call "hierequacy," saintly virtue enforced by equals.

Joseph's rhetoric of bigger brothers allows us to recognize the sources of Makarenko's success in the USSR. But why does it still seem strange then that Soviet schools were so similar to factories, farms, and army units—and that all of them resembled labor colonies that resembled monasteries?

Makarenko punished colonists who made something good for the colony on their own initiative. A deed is good only if the *kollektiv* sanctions it; any other justifications are secondary.

4 Purge and Self-Criticism
The Collective as a Subject
of Knowledge and Action

In the summer of 1926 a student of the Leningrad Mining Academy named Davidson committed suicide. There was enough evidence to suppose that her partner in "civil marriage," Konstantin Korenkov, also a student at the same academy, was the reason for her suicide. Over the preceding year he had continuously humiliated her, calling her names like "rabble" and "Jewish creep," talking with his friends in her presence about his sexual relations with other women, and locking her up in their dorm room when she was a nuisance (such as when she was bleeding after one of three consecutive abortions). The day she committed suicide, Korenkov told Davidson he was leaving for the Crimea to spend a summer vacation alone: why did he need her there when he had other women to meet? He left a loaded revolver in the top drawer of the desk and went down into the dorm's backyard to play soccer.

Said a witness:

> I have known Korenkov and Davidson since 1925. . . . I am not aware of the details of their family life, but I heard from others that they did not do very well together. On the day Davidson died, before the shot sounded, we were playing ball, and Korenkov was among the players. When we finished, we parted, and in half an hour I was told that Davidson had shot herself. Initially I did not believe it, and as they live upstairs and I live downstairs, I did not even go to check it out.[1]

Korenkov could not be put on trial for murder. However, the local Komsomol cell, of which he was a member, excluded him from both the Kom-

---

1. Sofia Smidovich, "O Korenkovshchine" (1926) [On Korenkovism], in *Partiinaia etika*, ed. A. A. Guseinov et al. (Moscow: Politizdat, 1989), 382.

somol and the Party on the grounds of "moral responsibility for the suicide of a comrade." The district Party Control Commission overruled this
decision as too harsh a punishment and substituted a "severe reprimand
and warning." Shortly thereafter, in June 1926, Korenkov and his younger
brother staged a holdup of the cashier's office of the Mining Academy. They
stabbed the cashier to death and heavily wounded his wife. The brothers
needed money for a vacation in the Crimea.

These two related episodes did not surprise many readers of newspapers
at the time: 1926 was a year filled with press reports of such crimes as dis-
memberment and group rape. However, Sofia Smidovich, a former chair-
woman of the Zhenotdel, the section of the Party's Central Committee that
was specifically set up to deal with problems of women's liberation, and now
one of the co-chairs of the Central Control Commission, chose this story as
representative of the most serious illness corrupting the body social in 1926.

Of course, she was appalled by the way Korenkov had treated his wife;
of course, she linked his gangster behavior to this treatment. But the peculiar thing about her article was that these aspects were not her central concern: Smidovich wanted to expose a specific type of social illness she called
"Korenkovism." The most dangerous feature of Korenkovism, she wrote,
was that "young people who encounter him [Korenkov] every day and
watch his relations with poor Davidson, who perceive his unbelievable rude-
ness, cynicism, and humiliation of her, do not react to this fact at all and os-
tracize him only after the commission twice rules him guilty of Davidson's
death."

Smidovich found the essence of Korenkovism in the nonchalant reaction
of the dormitory inhabitants to their neighbors' private lives, the sphere
where dark and ominous forces lurk:

> The private life of my comrade is not of my concern. The students' col-
> lective watches how Korenkov locks up his sick, literally bleeding wife
> —well, this is his private life. He addresses her only with curse words
> and humiliating remarks—nobody interferes. What's more: in Ko-
> renkov's room a shot resounds, and a student whose room is one floor
> beneath does not even think it necessary to check out what's going on.
> He considers it a private affair of Korenkov and Davidson.[2]

What is interesting here is that Smidovich is more Bolshevik than fem-
inist in describing the case. She chooses to focus not so much on the case's
manifest misogyny as on the parlous condition of the *kollektiv* that does

2. Smidovich, "O Korenkovshchine," 383.

not interfere in private lives. What is most serious is that the *kollektiv* is tainted: it watches everything, as all the drama takes place in its sight, but it does not react. Consequently, what Smidovich is trying to cure is not the way men treat women, but the way *kollektivy* cohere and act. What she primarily seeks is the installation of mutual enforcement and collective action.

This narrative represented the typical concerns of the day: *kollektivy* existed on paper, but they did not act in real life. What would make them real was collective action by their members in punishing a transgressor or enforcing standards of comradely behavior. And what would make a group a *kollektiv*—imbuing it with Communist Conscience—was mutual surveillance to support this Conscience.[3]

Smidovich was not making any extraordinary statements when she insisted that action should come from the dorm's collective as a whole. In the early postrevolutionary Party discourse, the *kollektiv* was presented as the primary subject of action and knowledge. The Party cell was presumed to act as a whole, as, for example, it was stated in the 1921 pamphlet on the role of the *kollektiv* in NEP: it should politically direct the trade union local, it should control the possible malfeasance of the factory administration and report it to the local Control Commission; but, "aware of what's going on, the *kollektiv* must strictly remember that interference into the business of administrating itself is unacceptable." Finally, the *kollektiv* was supposed to influence non-Party workers and draw them into the Party.[4]

The balance of doctrinal attention also shifted decisively in favor of the collective. Indeed, in 1920, according to the "Regulation on the Unified Party Card" the personal contribution of every Communist to the cell's activity had to be recorded monthly. Examples given suggest records like "he attended two Party meetings and three *subbotniks*," as the level of information sought by the Party. By contrast, every district committee was at the same time required to compile its own "Personal Card" (*lichnaia kartochka*) and submit it to the provincial committee on a quarterly basis. The person in this case was the district committee, not the single individual. The proposed standard report form covered six pages and included several dozen questions (how many cells it comprised, what they carried out, collected, demonstrated, advocated, and so on).[5] The Statute of the Party Cell

---

3. On my translation of *soznatelnost'* as "Conscience"—and its revolutionary connotations—see chapter 2, which discusses this Russian concept's religious origins.
4. *Rol' kollektiva RKP,* 3–5.
5. See addenda to *Sbornik materialov Peterburgskogo komiteta RKP,* 50–51.

adopted in May 1927 marked the height of this prevalence of the collective as an actor. A cell was to be set up in a job-site whenever there were at least three Communists available, in order to elect its ruling body, the bureau, and to engage in revolutionary work. Several paragraphs on the activity of the Party cell describe it as a unitary subject of action and knowledge: the cell decides, the cell undertakes, the cell directs, the cell controls.[6]

Talking about the *kollektiv* acting and knowing seems a bit of a stretch in our own context, which takes solitary individuals as the principal objects of perception. However, it may have been justified in some theoretical traditions, for example, those connected with the name of Emile Durkheim, where the existence of *conscience collective* was taken for granted. This tradition influenced many Soviet social scientists who boldly talked about the *kollektiv* acting and reacting as if these statements were supported by solid empirical evidence. Liudmila Bueva, a social psychologist who was the most interesting late Soviet proponent of this viewpoint, stated the following: collective or group subject is not a mystical entity, it is a "reflection of the integrative qualities of the process of common labor."[7] When a Soviet group engages in common labor, researchers objectively record that the *kollektiv* that emerges adopts a socially defined work goal that differs from the aims of its individual members (that is, it superposes the goal of socialist construction on that of satisfying the basic subsistence needs of the workers). Also, its members' reactions to outside stimuli change, and differences among them occasionally level out. All these phenomena were visible in scientific experiments and justified talking about the *kollektiv* as an actor and knower.[8]

A set of the experiments that studied the emergence of a specific quality (emotional cohesion) characteristic of the existence of collective subjects relied on the following curious piece of machinery. It was constructed specifically for experimentation and was dubbed a "Sensory-Motor Integra-

---

6. "Polozhenie o rabote iacheiki VKP(b)" [Statute of the Party cell], in *Voprosy partiinogo stroitel'stva*, ed. A. Mel'kumov (Moscow: Gosizdat, 1927), 203.

7. Quoted in Dontsov, *Psikhologiia kollektiva*, 153.

8. In recent debates in analytical philosophy Searle claims that to assume the existence of "we intentionality" in cases such as "We are pushing the car out of the ditch"—and to ground it in ordinary usage—is more parsimonious than to puzzle out the coordination of individual consciousness in this mundane but very complicated activity (see John Searle, "Collective Intentions and Action," in *Intentions in Communication*, ed. Philip R. Cohen, Jerry Morgan, and Martha E. Pollack [Cambridge, Mass.: MIT Press, 1990]).

tor." [9] The SMI was a round table with an S-shaped curve cut in the middle of it. Inside this curvilinear cut of about 5 inches wide was a small vertical peg that moved in all directions when several people rotated six special handles set in the sides of the table. A complicated mechanism of relays made the peg move but not in a way directly accessible to any of the actors. What they did know was that in order to move it, everyone had to apply some force to their handles, and the cooperation of all was necessary for a successful completion of the experimental task assigned to the group: to drive the peg from one end of the S-curve to the other, without touching the sides.

The social psychologist Leonid Umansky invented this device in order to study the spontaneous emergence of a leader in a group working on a collective task: he compared randomly assembled groups and old *kollektivy* in their efforts to complete the task of driving the peg. However his device was "perfected" by others who introduced some elements reminiscent of the famous Milgram and Zimbardo experiments. Vadim Petrovsky (a son of the author of the stratometric theory of the *kollektiv*) introduced elements of punishment into the SMI: an unpleasant sound and a small electric discharge were emitted when the peg touched the side. Both means of punishment could be directed at all or at specific people, by rearranging electrodes and headphones.

The modified SMI was used in experiments on emotional cohesion. It was hypothesized that a systemic effect would be induced in tight cohesive groups: the pursuit of the group goal subdued individual egoistic interests to such an extent that even a possibility of individual gain would not upset the group unity. Conversely, in a loosely associated group individual aims of single members would always prevail over the group one. In order to test this hypothesis, the following arrangement was made: in phase one, all the members of the group were equally punished for mistakes; in phase two, only a specially designated member would get all the punishment, while the speed of the group's achievement would be rewarded. The results were close to the expectations: tight groups of colleagues (labor *kollektivy*) did not change their behavior in phases one and two, while loose groups (new *kollektivy* or groups assembled specifically for the experiments) or antisocial groups (a controlling experiment was conducted with the inmates of a corrective institution) increased their speed in phase two, disregarding

9. Leonid Umansky, A. S. Chernyshev, and B. V. Tarasov, "Senso-motornyi integrator," *Voprosy psikhologii* 1 (1969): 128–130.

the pain of a single member.[10] These experiments served to demonstrate that individual self-interested behavior changed after emotional unity was formed in a tight *kollektiv,* an indubitable sign of the existence of a different systemic reality that may be called a "collective subject." The pain of one of the members of the body of this collective subject prevented its other members from engaging in self-interested behavior.

The Soviet social psychologists' descriptions of the *kollektiv* as an actual subject of action do not seem very far-fetched. In real life (and experiments) Soviet people were reacting together differently than they would on their own, a fact that lies at the foundation of social psychology, East and West. Interpreting their findings as evidence of a powerful entity overshadowing its members' individual identity, the psychologists also drew on the fact that many situations in everyday life required sentences with the word "we" as the subject of action. Ordinary usage stressed the fact that individual actions were part of a group activity. In all of these senses Soviet citizens could claim that the *kollektiv* existed as a subject of action and knowledge.

The main test of the *kollektiv* as a subject of action arrived when it received the task of not only knowing itself or acting to transform the outside world, but of acting on itself, that is, of purging and cleansing itself. After many failed attempts to install mutual surveillance within Party cells, worker's units and groups of colleagues in Soviet offices, the years of the Great Terror set up surveillance everywhere and completely justified speaking of the *kollektiv* as a subject. The blood of the victims that the *kollektiv* sacrificed while acting on itself witnessed its success.

SMIDOVICH'S DILEMMA

In characterizing Korenkovism as a typical social illness of the *kollektiv,* Smidovich provided a second example of it. A certain Morgunov used his official position (as an employment instructor in a trade union) to obtain sexual favors. He granted employment assignments to young women only after they agreed to have sex with him. One of the victims refused him when she was brought into a basement in Moscow, and so he raped her. Hav-

10. V. A. Petrovsky, "Emotsional'naia identifikatsiia v gruppe i sposob ee vyiavleniia" [Emotional identification in a group and methods of its registration], in *K voprosu o diagnostike lichnosti v gruppe* [On diagnosing an individual within a group], ed. A. V. Petrovsky (Moscow, 1973). For detailed description of these experiments, also see A. V. Petrovsky and M. Turevsky, "Deistvennia gruppovaia emotsional'naia identifikatsiia" [Effective emotional identification in a group], in *Psikhologicheskaia teoriia kollektiva,* ed. A. V. Petrovsky (Moscow: Nauka, 1979).

ing been summoned to the preliminary investigation bodies, Morgunov denied the rape but did not care to deny that

> having met her in the district office of the trade union as a teenager for whom he, according to his professional obligations, was supposed to find employment, he engaged in sexual intercourse with her and did not attach "much significance to this fact as one that could produce excessive talk and suspicion; he considered it his personal affair."[11]

The worker Morgunov did not see an issue here. He had presumably had sexual relations with women before, in workers' dorms in the full sight of his comrades, and it had not produced talk or suspicion. He had behaved according to traditional patriarchal mores that prescribe subjugating a resisting female to an aggressive male, and these mores did not give rise to excessive talk. He did the same in this case and now honestly could not understand how a workers' state could punish him for such a trifle. However, had there been a conscientious comrade to admonish and instruct Morgunov before he slipped from sexual license into criminal rape, said Smidovich, corruption would never have occurred.

The Korenkov and Morgunov cases, as two instances of the illness of the *kollektiv*, called for applying mutual surveillance techniques to enforce issues of Conscience. But they did so in a different manner. In the Korenkov case the collective knew what standards of Conscience were but failed to enforce them. By contrast, in the Morgunov case workers could have enforced these, if they had honestly known what these standards were. These two cases thus constitute two respective parts of what may be called "Smidovich's dilemma": either the notion of Conscience is present, but people lack the surveillance to bring it about or the resolve to enforce it; or surveillance is abundant, but nobody cares to know what is characteristic of Conscientious behavior. Both cases, however, testify to the lack of one of the components of the combination needed to build a *kollektiv*, mutual surveillance enforcing standards of higher Conscience.

Smidovich's article is indeed representative of the concerns of the time. Attempts to fuse mutual surveillance and concern with higher Conscience, a feat that Makarenko achieved in a single colony and Smidovich hoped to see repeated everywhere, were not very successful. The reason for this outcome lay in a difference between the life situation of peasants and of workers of peasant origin, and that of urban people on the eve of the revolution —the former upper classes, professionals, intellectuals, students, qualified

---

11. Smidovich, "O Korenkovshchine," 385.

workers, and even simple clerks. Coming from the village, new workers considered mutual surveillance a natural phenomenon but did not care very much about higher Conscience. The educated strata, by contrast, may have cared about Communist faith and "Conscious discipline" but lacked the developed skills and habits of surveillance to enforce them. Furthermore, these strata often hated attempts at the installation of surveillance. Thus, in order to blend the two elements needed for the resolution of Smidovich's dilemma (mutual surveillance and concern with higher Conscience), two strategies were essential: workers must be taught to care about Communist faith, while techniques of mutual surveillance had to be disseminated and rooted among the educated strata.

The 1920s witnessed both. The working masses were continuously encouraged to apply their surveillance techniques when higher Conscience or high administrative posts were at stake. For example, they were called upon to check on new Communists entering the Party. A list of candidates to the Communist Party would be posted outside the office of a given Party cell, and members of this Party *kollektiv* would solicit possible denunciations from the masses against those aspiring to join. Only after a thorough discussion of any denunciations—or, if none arrived after a fixed period of time—could an aspirant become a full Party member in 1921.[12]

It is likely that urging workers to enforce matters of Conscience did not prove to be very successful. Denouncing future Party members was not as natural and easy as denouncing comrades in a workshop or office. Trotsky, who was the first to comment on the wave of "cant" in 1923, was startled by the frankness of workers' correspondents who used real names and stopped at nothing in their wish to vilify their fellow comrades in the workers' press.[13] The description of sexual mores is not the best way to use the workers' press, suggested Trotsky; perhaps, other types of activities should be in the spotlight of the critics. Mutual surveillance was there, but for many workers it was still unclear what deeds should be censured by the community.

In contrast, many intellectuals and professional revolutionaries knew how higher Conscience was supposed to be manifested and what constituted its corruption but were reluctant to apply the techniques of mutual surveillance to enforce it. Top Party leaders themselves were not of the

12. *Rol' kollektiva RKP pri NEPe*, 10.
13. Leon Trotsky, "Voprosy byta," *Pravda*, August 17, 1923 (translated in *The Problems of Everyday Life* [New York: Monad Press, 1973], 65).

same opinion on mutual surveillance, as the following exchange on the matter of denunciation (*donos*) demonstrates. Discussing the CCC report to the Fourteenth Party Congress (1925), Bakaev, the leader of the Leningrad Party organization that was the center of leftist opposition, charged the Central Committee and the CCC with introducing *donos*—an unacceptable mode of informing on comrades, strongly tied in Bolshevik collective memory to the methods of the czarist secret police—into Party life: "A friend cannot tell a friend a thought that is dear to his soul—what is this?"[14] He was referring to the fact of two Party members writing letters to the Central Committee denouncing the Leningrad Party leaders in their oppositional activities. These letters were later used by the CCC in its accusations of Leningraders. Bakaev also charged the CCC with partiality in adjudicating the dispute between two parts of the Central Committee, that is, siding with the majority. Nikolaeva, also from Leningrad, supported this claim, saying that CCC was becoming a Cheka (secret police) within the Party. This, in her opinion, led to a horrible condition: "If two people have spoken intimately on matters of life or politics, one will surely write to the CCC."[15]

Shkiriatov, one of the CCC co-chairmen, answering Bakaev, claimed that the Party should distinguish reporting on the matters of comrades' everyday life, which he held unacceptable, and reporting on factional activity. The latter was a duty. He was supported, by Gusev, another member of the CCC, who was even more straightforward:

> You are making a false note, old man Bakaev (*Bakaich*), you are, believe me. Lenin taught us . . . that every member should be an agent of the Cheka, that is, should watch and report (*donosit'*). I do not propose to introduce the Cheka in Party life. We [already] have the CCC, we have the Central Committee, but everybody should write denunciations (*donosy*).[16]

Solts was the only one who tried to appease everybody by saying that the CCC did not solicit denunciations as such; the denunciatory letters in question were intercepted by the militia. He did insist that because de-

14. Bakaev's speech, in *XIV Steno/26*, 566.
15. Ibid., 600.
16. Ibid. Readers familiar with the history of perestroika immediately recognize this tonality of stern but comradely frankness in the eye-to-eye interaction. It almost parodies, or anticipates, Ligachev's famous remark at the Central Committee plenum that expelled Yeltsin from the Politburo in 1988: "Boris, you are wrong."

nunciation was bad for the Party, then the members of the opposition were obliged to openly state their positions on their own initiative, and to sternly suffer the consequences that this move entailed. Kuibyshev, in his concluding remarks on the CCC report to the congress, stated what seemed to become the Party line for the next several years, at least until the era of Great Terror: reporting the content of a private conversation in a letter to the CCC is of course an unacceptable denunciation (*donos*), but if somebody sees in this content "a threat to the unity of the Party," reporting it becomes the duty of a Party member.[17]

This discussion shows that even the top functionaries of the Party were uneasy about the all-out introduction of mutual surveillance and denunciations into Party life. Communists with a higher educational background seemed to reject it even more vigorously. The Moscow Control Commission screening the Party cells in Soviet offices and institutions of higher education in April 1924 reported that "an overwhelming majority of Party members have shut down inside themselves, do not know one another, and seem not to wish to know." Intellectuals, until pressed to do so, failed to police one another. This, reported the commission, facilitates the blossoming of "intelligentsia individualism," detrimental to the Party, which produces an environment that "corrupts the collectivist . . . spirit of the cell members."[18]

Still, until the 1930s, appeals to introduce comradely admonition in Party and Soviet organizations seem to have been largely wishful thinking. Smidovich's articles only signified the beginning of a new persistent effort to bring it about. To spread mutual surveillance throughout the body social, and make Soviet power depend on it, mutual surveillance had to be at work in every Soviet factory, farm, and office, converting these sites into *kollektivy*. Each group of colleagues had to experiment with the practices of expulsion and mutual control, through criticizing and purging itself.

This merger of criticism and purging was very important. The Party discourse on self-criticism and purges was similar in its insistence on the collective character of the practices in question. Yet the practices themselves were very different, contrary to many accounts that tend to erase the distinction between them. Our analysis of this pragmatic difference will allow us to see the structure of the merger of practices of self-criticism and purging in a sharper light, and to evaluate the consequences of this merger.

17. Ibid., 615.
18. "Otchet Moskovskoi KK 15.04.24," in *Partiinaia etika*, ed. A. A. Guseinov et al. (Moscow: Politizdat, 1989), 424–425.

CLEANSING AND COHESION: DISCOURSE OF THE PURGE

According to the latter-day rationalizations, "self-purging" had constituted one of the features of the Russian Social Democratic Party since its inception, but the term itself, strictly speaking, was first officially used during the first general purge that occurred in 1921.[19] In Western literature the whole period of 1933–39 is usually subsumed under the title of the Great Purges, following the early studies of Brzezinski and Conquest, but Party discourse had a narrower definition. Getty was first to pay attention to this linguistic fact and noted that by "purge" (*chistka*) the Party designated a practice of "periodic membership screenings" that were aimed at "weeding out the undesirables who flooded the Party ranks."[20] Having this in mind, we will study the original sources for Brzezinski's description of the "permanent purge," in order to get a clearer understanding of what the term meant in Party discourse.[21]

The first general purge of all Party cells was conducted in 1921 in order to cleanse the Party ranks of those who managed to infiltrate them during the tumultuous years of the Civil War and resulted in 24.1 percent of the membership expelled. This figure included the cases of workers who left in a mass voluntary exodus, unwilling to pay Party dues and engage in time-consuming Party work. Partial purges were conducted in 1924–25 (a screening of the Party cells in Soviet offices and in higher education in order to weed out the Trotskyites; 25 percent of general membership screened, 6 percent expelled) and in 1926 (a verification of the rural cells to strengthen Party ranks before the collectivization campaigns). A second general purge was conducted in 1929, in order to cleanse the Party of "alien elements" during the socialist offensive in industry; 7.6 percent were expelled.

The third and last general purge was announced in April 1933, in order to regularize Party ranks after the Party had expanded almost twofold dur-

19. Emelian Iaroslavsky (*Za bolshevistskuiu proverku i chistku partii* [Bolshevik verification and purging of Party ranks] [Moscow, 1933]) faithfully quotes Lenin's essay "Party Organization and Party Literature" (1912) that uses the verb *ochishchat'* (to cleanse) in a statement asserting that the Party should periodically conduct self-cleansing (Lenin, *Polnoe sobranie sochinenii*, 12:103).

20. J. Arch Getty, *Origins of the Great Purges* (Cambridge: Cambridge University Press, 1985), 49.

21. Zbigniew Brzezinski, *The Permanent Purge* (Cambridge, Mass.: Harvard University Press, 1956), chs. 3 and 4. The next two paragraphs draw on an article on *chistka* in *Bol'shaia Sovetskaia Entsiklopediia* and on Iaroslavsky's brochure, *Za bolshevistskuiu proverku i chistku partii*, which Brzezinski used as the main sources of general information.

ing the mass entries of the chaotic years of the "broad socialist offensive" of 1929–33. The purge had managed to cleanse twenty-five regional Party organizations (18.3 percent of general membership expelled) by 1935, when it was announced that it had been successfully completed in the majority of Party organizations, with seventeen remaining regional Party organizations completing it during the verification and exchange of Party documents campaigns in 1935–36. Events that marked the height of terror—the Party reelection, self-criticism campaigns and "mass operations" of 1937—were *not* called "purges"; the purges were officially over with the end of the exchange of Party documents campaign of 1936. The Eighteenth Party Congress (1939) admitted that the method of mass purges had some severe handicaps—like unfounded mass expulsions—and ruled that the Party would now cleanse itself of the violators of the Statute and Program of the Party in the usual manner, through the activity of the Committee of Party Control, created in 1934 (together with the Committee of Soviet Control) to replace the CCC.

Brzezinski provided an account of the Party usage, more or less similar to the one presented in the last two paragraphs, but he curiously ignored the fact that, contrary to *The Great Soviet Encyclopedia*, Iaroslavsky pointed to the "reregistration" of Party documents in 1919 as the first instance of the Party purge, though carried out without a special resolution of the Central Committee. During this reregistration one-third of the Party members spontaneously abandoned the Party—which Iaroslavsky later dubbed an effective means of expulsion—when in mid-1919 the Party order sought to mobilize all the available Party members into the military to send them to the fronts of the Civil War. Iaroslavsky was supported by Nadezhda Krupskaia in calling this abrupt reduction of the members on the roll a real purge.[22] The people who stayed had few benefits to enjoy, and a lot to lose, in the dire conditions of the besieged Soviet state of 1919.

This curious "purge" of 1919 points to the general mechanism of the change in linguistic meaning. Conventional Soviet sources on the origins of the political term *chistka* claim that it was formed by endowing the mundane term (as in *chistka odezhdy*, a cleaning of clothes) with a new political meaning.[23] However, this Bolshevik reinterpretation was not partic-

22. See Nadezhda Krupskaia, "Kakim dolzhen byt' kommunist" [What a Communist ought to be (June 1933)], in *Izbrannye proizvedeniia* [Selected works] (Moscow: Politizdat, 1988), 331.

23. Il'enko and Maksimova, "K istorii obshchestvenno-politicheskoi leksiki," 271. This claim is supported by other evidence; Lenin's agenda of the first Soviet government in November 1917 included the purge of ministries (*chistka minis-*

ularly novel. The term "purging" had applied to recruiting the members of the Orthodox clergy to serve in the fighting army at least since Catherine the Great, who had enlisted the excess clerical estate in her wars against the Turks. This practice continued well into the nineteenth century (the last recruitment occurred in 1831) and even engendered the title of Gregory Freeze's recent book on the clergy in czarist Russia, *The Russian Levites.* Ancient Levites, of course, was the name given to a group of armed clerics, mentioned in the Old Testament; the ordinance of Paul I (1796) employed this reference to justify the czar's continuation of his mother's policy of re-cruiting the clergy into the military.[24] Freeze, discussing the vicissitudes of the recruitment of the clergy, does not notice the terms used by his Russian counterparts whom he quotes as sources, such as the historians Znamensky and Miliukov. They, relying on the imperial documents, employed *ochishchenie, chistka,* and *ochistka,* the terms also used in the Bolshevik discourse.[25]

Of course, it would be far-fetched to claim that such pious Bolsheviks as Krupskaia and especially Iaroslavsky, well versed in church history, trans-ferred its term into the Party setting because of the similarity in the situ-ations of the clergy and the Party members' recruitment to serve in the military to defend the true faith.[26] Rather, Bolsheviks may have reconcep-tualized the mundane word *chistka* to become the central term of their dis-course, much as church historians had done. The aim of the purge in the political sense of the word is taken to be the cleansing of the body—the Church's or the Party's—of malignant elements, so that in the end a tightly

---

terstv) but put the term in quotes. See Dmitrii Volkogonov, *Lenin* (Moscow, 1995), 1:306.

24. Paul was a better recruiter: in 1796 12,000 soldiers were taken; Catherine managed to extract "only" 9,000 in 1769 and 5,000 in 1787 (Freeze, *Russian Levites,* 38–40).

25. I. Znamensky, *Prikhodskoe dukhovenstvo v Rossii so vremeni reformy Petra* [Parish clergy in Russia since Peter's reforms] (Kazan, 1873), 341–344, uses *ochishchenie* and quotes "purging clergy of the indecent people" and "of the excessive people" as the two primary reasons for the recruitment of 1831; all jobless (that is, without a parish to service) members of the clerical estate aged 15 to 40 were to be sent to the army (in 1831 these potentially subject to cleansing amounted to 7,351 out of approximately 150,000 people in the clerical estate, according to synodal sta-tistics). Miliukov's usage is closest to the Bolsheviks: the subheading of one chapter uses the word *chistka* in the phrase "purging the clergy" (Miliukov, *Ocherki po isto-rii russkoi kul'tury,* 1994 revised edition, vol. 2, pt. 1, 162 and 412).

26. Iaroslavsky, apart from being the CCC chairman, was also the head of the League of the Militant Godless; his anticlerical writings (*Protiv religii i tserkvi,* 5 vols, 1932–35) vastly exceed anything else he wrote.

united corps, ready to preach or fight, is produced. Stress on the unity of the corporate body is a recurrent theme in early Bolshevik sources.

Thus, in 1921, the resolution on the first general purge of the Party stated that the penetration of the Party body by bourgeois elements made it necessary to conduct the purge so that "the Party would be cast as a monolith."[27] The CCC specifically was to fight for that monolithic unity with due energy, punishing various oppositionists and conducting purges. The Statute of the CCC, adopted by the Thirteenth Party Congress in 1924, as a matter of fact stated that one of its primary functions was "verifying the ranks of the Party: purging [*chistka*] the Party of ideologically alien, harmful, and corrupting elements."[28] The aim of the purge was cohesion, as one of the CCC co-chairmen, Solts, said in his commentary on the 1929 purge: "We should not only get rid of those who infiltrated the Party, but should become more tight and cohesive, should create a comradely fusion" (*spaika*).[29]

This "fusion" was a catchword for the desired ideal condition of the Party cell. *Spaika* was taken to be the sign of systemic unity and cohesion that distinguished the Communist Party from all the other parties, and, perhaps, all other human groups.[30] Before 1917 several terms served interchangeably for designating this quality. For example, Lunacharsky talked in 1910 about *sliianie* ("merging," literally—"confluence") as a "specific experience where the borders of personality crumble" and one feels like part of the greater whole.[31] By 1921 *spaika* was predominant, however. The cells of the Russian Communist Party were preoccupied with inducing it in themselves, since their members could not regularly meet, if they worked in different shops of the same factory. "Fusion," thus, was to be instituted by specific techniques: the cell leaders had to go and chat with the rank-and-file members, help them if need be, exchange letters with members if some of them were sent far away on Party assignment, and organize joint leisure and recreation activities.[32]

---

27. Literally, *vylita iz odnogo kuska*, "as one piece" (*K proverke, peresmotru i ochistke partii* [Toward the checking, screening, and purging of the Party] [Irbit, 1921], 7).
28. "Polozhenie o TsKK RKP(b)," 8, par. 8.
29. Aaron Solts, "K chistke" (1925) [Toward the purge], in *Kak provodit' chistku partii* [How to conduct the Party purge], ed. Emelian Iaroslavsky (Moscow, 1929), 29.
30. In the 1930s the *kollektiv* became the primary subject of this "fusion"; it comes from the verb *spaiat'*, which means "to fuse, to produce an alloy."
31. Lunacharsky, *Religiia i sotsializm*, 2:363.
32. *Rol' kollektiva RKP*, 8–9.

Reports of the Control Commissions who carried out the checks of the cells in 1924 centered primarily on the notion of *spaika*, the absence of which in the cells of Soviet institutions was duly lamented.[33] And yet cells in industrial factories were said, following the ideological education of the mass of new entrants in 1924, to be "transformed into tightly nailed and ideologically fused [*spaiannye*] *kollektivy.*"[34] Solts theorized "fusion" in 1924 in the following way. *Spaika* was the condition of "intimately friendly relations" that existed among the professional revolutionaries during the Party's underground struggle in 1903–17. This condition was ironically jeopardized by its victory, since the new Party members, joining after the Revolution, behaved differently.[35] However, the everyday struggle of the CCC and the purges could restore the lost intimate unity of the Party.[36]

The unity of the Party was at stake in many Party struggles. The most famous ones, the resolution of the Tenth Party Congress (1921) on the unity of the Party and the debate between Bukharin and Zinoviev at the Fourteenth Congress (1925), revolved around the same topic: the possibility of having a faction within the Party. The opponents frequently talked past each other: for example, Zinoviev would discuss the theoretical unacceptability of some Party programmatic statements, while Bukharin would not dispute the revealed doctrinal flaws but rather pointed to what the opposition was doing in practice, which seemed even more unacceptable. The oppositionists' activities seemed atrocious to Bukharin because they undermined the unity of the Party. The "authenticity of the Party line" countered "arguments of unity" and pragmatic reasoning, with the latter easily winning. Delegates to the congresses did not wish to listen to the doctrinal debates, when it was obviously clear that the opposition was corrupting Party unity from the inside. The Fifteenth Party Congress, which destroyed the leftist opposition completely, had speakers who decried the "criminal schismatic activity" and "attack of schismatics [*raskol'niki*] on

33. "There is no fusion: . . . a very harmful intelligentsia individualism is blossoming," concluded one of the Control Commissions ("Otchet Moskovskoi KK 15 aprelia 1924 g." [Report of the Moscow Control Commission, April 15, 1924], in *Partiinaia etika*, ed. A. A. Guseinov et al. [Moscow: Politizdat, 1989], 425).

34. Mel'kumov, ed., *Voprosy partiinogo stroitel'stva*, 252.

35. Compare the victory's effect to the change in the Church's purity (deplored by Christian theologians) when it emerged from underground and became part of the Roman empire.

36. Solts, "O partiinoi etike," 264–267; and Solts, *Dlia chego partii nuzhna samokritika?*

the Party." This usage was strongly reminiscent of the religious schism of 1667 in Russian church history.[37]

However, said one of the speakers at the Fifteenth Congress, the schismatic activity was defeated and the "historical moment" was achieved when the Party voted unanimously to approve the report of the Central Committee to the congress, with none abstaining.[38] It should have been put on film, lamented the speaker; such a rare occasion! The irony of history is that it really was a historical moment; unanimity was a rule for the next sixty years. After the oppositionists gained minimal support in provincial Party votes in 1926–27, with only small percentages of the Party body voting for them, their fate was sealed. The winning majority named the losers "single individuals" and dubbed their victory the triumph of *kollektivy* over "the Party aristocracy," as the few leaders who opted for an oppositional stance and dared to engage in an open factional struggle, were now called. "The place of singular individuals [in directing Party life] was taken over by *kollektivy*, most of all by the Central Committee and the CCC," said a speaker.[39] His words implied that the Party body was reconstituted as a unified whole, after an abominable threat of schism.[40]

When threats to Party cohesion appeared, so did the possibility of "corruption." The purge sources offer relevant examples of this dominant metaphor.[41] In 1928 the CCC plenum talked about "ulcers" and issued a

37. Speeches of Fabritsius and Afanas'ev in *Piatnadtsatyi s"ezd VKP(b), dekabr' 1927: Stenografricheskii otchet* (Moscow: Politizdat, 1961), 1:487. On the generally negative attitude of Party masses toward factional activities, see Sheila Fitzpatrick, "The Civil War as a Formative Experience," in *Bolshevik Culture*, ed. Abbott Gleason et al. (Bloomington: Indiana University Press, 1985), 63.

38. Ianson in *Piatnadtsatyi s"ezd VKP(b)*, 530.

39. Ibid.

40. In its preoccupation with unity, the Party may remind us of the Russian Orthodox Church theologians' concern for Church unity. They held that the Church —unlike the Protestants' "invisible community"—constituted a visible "body of Christ" with Jesus Christ as its actual head, not the pope (a fallen man). This "indivisible god-human organism" was unitary, holy, catholic (that is, assembled), and apostolic; any attempts to subvert the unity of the body of Christ were to be fought (see Evgenii Akvilonov, *Tserkov': Nauchnyia opredeleniia tserkvi i apostol'skoe uchenie o nei kak o tele khristovom* [The church: its scientific definitions and apostolic teaching on the body of Christ] [St. Petersburg, 1894]).

41. Medical and bodily metaphors in Party discourse merit a study, since the notion of the body politic never developed in Russia (for its Western origins see Ernst H. Kantorowicz, *The King's Two Bodies: A Study in Mediaeval Political Theology* [Princeton: Princeton University Press, 1957]). Noting recurrent reports on dismembered bodies that filled the criminal columns of Soviet newspapers in the 1920s, Eric Naiman finds in them an indirect reflection of the Party mood, displac-

call to "uproot the degenerate elements in our organizations."[42] Iaroslavsky in his 1933 brochure on the general purge interpreted Lenin's speech
from 1918 in the following way: "A cadaver of the bourgeois society . . . is
decaying in our environment, this cadaver rots and infects us." Another article by Lenin said that revolutionary workers were becoming infected with
diseases of petit-bourgeois corruption.[43] Iaroslavsky used the metaphor to
point to the need for the purge that would cleanse these rotting elements
from the Party. The Party was the subject of corruption, but it could become the subject of unity through the purge.

Solts also stated that the Party was the subject of diseases as early as
1921, in his report to the Tenth Party Congress. A rather flawed logic of his
argumentation to ensure cohesion within the Party does not concern us
here, but the doctrinal concern is expressed by Solts straightforwardly: "all
the trouble consists not in the crimes of individual comrades, but in those
instances of illness that are unavoidable for us as a ruling Party."[44] A broad
list of the Party's illnesses was compiled for the plenum of the CCC in October 1924, an exhaustive compendium to give directions to the local Control Commissions. The preface to the resolution, which was adopted after
long discussions, summed up the familiar thesis: the unity of thought and
action in the Party was the primary goal, and unity was to be ensured by
fighting the seven "Party illnesses." The CCC ideologists had to use some
neologisms to designate these seven deadly threats to the collective body.

The threats were careerism and squabbling within the Party (*sklochnichestvo*), which spoiled the relations among Party members; marrying or
getting into close personal contact with petty bourgeoisie (*oNEPivanie*),
which led to a change of heart; expanding one's land plots and other primary economic factor possessions (*khozobrastanie*), which put personal
interest over Party ones; excessive luxury in dress or spending habits
(*izlishestva*), which separated Communist officials from the rank and file;
alcoholism as an instance of false brotherhood contradicting conscientious

---

ing and playing out the threat to the unity of its collective body (Eric Naiman, *Sex
in Public* [Princeton: Princeton University Press, 1997]).

42. Speech of Lebed', *III Plenum TsKK sozyva XV s"ezda 25–29 avg. 1928* [3d
CCC plenum, August 25–28, 1928] (Moscow, 1928), 5 (hereafter *III Plenum/28*,
page).

43. Lenin, "O golode" [On hunger], in *Polnoe sobranie sochinenii*, 36:357–
364, quoted in Iaroslavsky, *Za bolshevistskuiu proverku i chistku partii*, sec. 3.

44. Aaron Solts, "Otchet TsKK na X s"ezde RKP(b)" [CCC report to the 10th
Party Congress], in *Partiiniaia etika*, ed. A. A. Guseinov et al. (Moscow: Politizdat,
1989), 140.

Party unity; sexual license as an instance of "exploitative" relations between man and woman; participating in religious rites as an unacceptable membership in an alternative sacred body.[45]

Altogether, the CCC was preoccupied with ties of and between Party members that threatened to corrupt the Party's body as a tight group with exclusive membership and unanimous opinion. Nothing signified preoccupation with the coherent collective body so well as the proposed treatment of homosexuality or masturbation. In cases of this "perversity," demonstrated by one of its members, the cell had to decide whether it would send the Communist for treatment or whether—given the comrade's indispensability for the urgent tasks of the day—it should tolerate the transgressor and accept collective responsibility for him or her.[46]

PRACTICING PURGES

The recommended practice of purging remained fairly constant over the 1920s and 1930s. A purge commission, consisting of some trusted comrades—usually sent by the higher Party body—would inform the cell of the aims of the purge and listen to the bureau's report on the general condition of the cell.[47] It would issue a call for denunciations, either oral or written, depending on the circumstances. Then at a special purge meeting individual members would be called to present themselves in front of the purge commission, with or without other people present, depending on the circumstances. Having adopted a decision on individual members and the condition of the cell as a whole, the commission would publicize its decisions.[48]

There were some remarkable variations in this procedure. For example,

45. Iaroslavsky, "O partetike: Predlozheniia," 157.
46. Ibid., 164.
47. Purge commissions were themselves subject to the purge before they purged others, by a higher level Purge Commission, with the pyramid culminating in the CCC. Members of the Central Committee and the CCC were not purged (see resolution of the Central Committee and the CCC authorizing the 1933 purge in *O chistke partii* [On the Party purge] [Saratov, 1935], 11).
48. This section relies on data from the following purge instructions: four instructions in *K proverke, peresmotru;* "Instruktsiia o proverke neproletarskogo sostava RKP," in *RBCC 1924;* and "Instruktsiia o proverke derevenskikh part'-iacheek," in *RBCC 1927;* "Instruktsiia po organizatsii i provedeniiu general'noi chistki i proverke riadov VKP(b)," in *Kak provodit' chistku partii,* ed. Emelian Iaroslavsky (Moscow, 1929); "Instruktsiia oblastnym, raionnym i nizovym komissiiam po chistke partii," in *O chistke partii* (Moscow: Partizdat, 1933).

during the 1921 purge industrial cells were supposed to be purged as a single body. They were gathered by the purge commission and asked whether there were causes for expelling somebody from the cell; responses were registered in the meeting's protocol and discussed immediately. Autobiographies were not required. Non-Party members were asked to inform on the cell's misdeeds also, but these denunciations were turned over for the cell's discussion, and, if needed, the allegations stated in these denunciations were tested by a vote of the members of the cell.[49] (The cell was also asked to inform on Communists working in the government or administrative offices that supervised it; this information was sent to the purge commissions working in these offices.) In the village cells the purge commission inquired in 1921 among peasants and Communists alike about "suspicious elements" in the purged cell before or at the beginning of the purge meeting. If found by this preliminary investigation, they were to be cast away from the meeting itself; their purge may have been conducted in absentio.[50] In army units, the soliciting of written denunciations was compulsory, and the soldiers were asked by the commission members about their commanders: the higher the commander, the more thorough the investigation. The 1921 purge instructions for the Soviet offices were notable for the fact that Communists working in these offices were the only ones required to supply an autobiography and three recommendations before the purge.

The 1929 general purge was special in that after the open purge meeting (where written and oral denunciations were presented and discussed following the presentation of the biography of each Communist), the commission discussed each Communist behind closed doors before arriving at a verdict. Also, before the arrival of the purge commission at a purged cell, the district committee supervising it had to issue a special written "characteristic" of the cell as a whole, stating "the quality of their [the cells'] work as a whole . . . and data on deviations from the Party line, violations of Party discipline, and the misdeeds of single members."[51] Obviously, the cell was still a primary actor. The 1933 purge instructions for the first time overtly required open purge meetings with the presence of non-Party members.

---

49. If a vote of the majority of the cell members held the denunciation to be a lie, the case was closed; purge commissions were required to listen only to a "substantial minority" within the cell (*K proverke, peresmotru,* 10)

50. See "Instruktsiia po krest'anskim iacheikam," in ibid., 11–12.

51. Iaroslavsky, ed., *Kak provodit' chistku partii,* 148.

They also stated that members themselves were to read their "autobiographies" (not "biographies presented" as in the 1929 instructions, which left a chance of interpretation), together with "information on [their] work in the past and in the present."[52]

The main point was that decisions of the purge commission could not be overturned by the cell, during any of the conducted purges. They could be appealed during a certain time to the higher purge commission or the CCC, but the final decision was left to the organization that represented the Party conscience, the CCC, not to the collective of Party members itself. It was the abandonment of this principle in 1935–37, and the entrusting of the *kollektiv* with the right to decide on the demonstrated Conscience of its own member, that contributed to the murderous outcome. The purge was blended with self-criticism and the cell, dutifully criticizing itself, found itself in a position where it had to start cutting off the bad members itself. But what was self-criticism exactly and how was it different from the purge?

DISCOURSE ON SELF-CRITICISM

For a contemporary Russian speaker, it seems part of common sense that the term "self-criticism" (*samokritika*) primarily reflects the activity of the individual self. However, in the Soviet days, it was hard to specify whether the word related to an individual person or a group criticizing itself. Of course, "self-criticism" was defined in the dictionary as "criticism of mistakes and flaws of one's action or one's behavior, " but the ambiguity of the "one" in question is easily illustrated by the dictionary quote from Leningrad Party chief Kirov, who said that Lenin "was not afraid to uncover the most serious of our illnesses, he perfectly mastered the weapon of Bolshevik self-criticism."[53] Lenin's writings more often represent self-criticism as an action of the whole Party rather than an action of an individual, as for example in the following quote from 1904: "Russian social democrats are already well tested in battle, and they do not notice these barbs, they continue—despite these barbs—the work of self-criticism and of merciless

52. "Instruktsiia" (1933), par. 14. The 1933 model is usually taken to be representative of how purges were conducted, since surprisingly many of the purge accounts in historical literature rely on the vivid description of the 1933 purge in the memoirs of Viktor Kravchenko, *I Chose Freedom* (New York: Scribner's, 1946), 132–47.
53. Article on *samokritika*, in *Slovar'*.

unmasking of their own deficiencies."[54] For Lenin, the last sentence was an opportunity to emphasize what subsequently became a dogmatic point: the Bolsheviks are different from the parties of the Second International in that they are not afraid to expose their own misdeeds and subject them to fierce criticism.

The term *samokritika* was registered by a Soviet academic dictionary in 1940, but it did not appear as such in *The Great Soviet Encyclopedia* at all. Instead, it figured there as part of the stable idiom "criticism and self-criticism," which was said to be a characteristic feature of Communist parties and the law of development of Soviet society. Only books printed at the twilight of the Soviet epoch attempted to separate "criticism" from "self-criticism," while the monstrous double "criticism and self-criticism" pervaded earlier literature as a strange malformation, possibly owing its existence to the needs of public incantation.[55] Thus, a pamphlet from 1989 said that "by criticism we understand the exposing of flaws and their perpetrators; condemnation, revelation [*oblichenie*], and uncovering those conditions that stand in the way of normal life in order to eliminate the former and train the latter. . . . By self-criticism we understand criticism directed by a man at himself, one's own activity and behavior."[56] No examples of individual self-criticism were provided, however, and a few pages later the pamphlet quoted Mikhail Gorbachev's speech at the Nineteenth Party Conference in 1988, which confused the proposed distinction immediately: "It should be said in a self-critical manner: during the last three years we could

54. Lenin quoted in *Bol'shaia Sovetskaia Entsiklopediia*, article on *kritika i samokritka*.
55. The Communist parties of Western Europe incorporated it in this double form (see an article on *critica e l'autocritica* in Italian: A. A. Kasatkin, "Novye slova ruskogo proiskhozhdeniia v italianskom iazyke" [New words of Russian origin in the Italian language], *Uchenye zapiski LGU* [Learned works of Leningrad University] 161 [1952]: 173–186). I have not discovered what made Party discourse blend "criticism" and "self-criticism"—perhaps the subtle difference depended on who did the criticism of the Party cell (coming from a Central Committee emissary, it was undoubtedly "comradely criticism" and from members of the cell themselves, "self-criticism"). Also, the image of joining top and bottom in a mutual critical attack on middle-level party functionaries may underlie it. But its repetitive rhythm tells more than any sense imputed by interpretation of its content. On the prominence of rhythm in political discourse see Eric Havelock, *Preface to Plato* (Cambridge, Mass.: Harvard University Press, 1962).
56. V. M. Ramazanov, *Vnoshu predlozhenie: O kritike i samokritike v rabote partiinykh organizatsii* [Making a motion: on criticism and self-criticism in the work of Party organizations] (Rostov-on-Don, 1989), 14.

have done significantly more on the main routes of perestroika." [57] Of course, in this statement Gorbachev could not be said to criticize his personal flaws, the subject of self-criticism being most clearly a "we."

This confusion needs some careful preliminary mapping before we move further on. Self-criticism as an activity of the individual directed at him- or herself should be segregated from self-criticism as an activity of the collective body. Let's concentrate on the individual's criticism of his or her own personal features first. Examples of this meaning can be found in Russian usage throughout the twentieth century, but they seem to be of secondary importance. Explaining this curious fact, Soviet sources claimed that the term *samokritika* had entered Russian language as a direct translation of the German term *Selbst-Kritik* in the mid-nineteenth century. It was taken to signify the inner process of an intellectual and did not gain much usage outside intelligentsia circles. [58] However, *samokritika* was used in a similar sense in the 1920s and 1930s, though it implied self-criticism of the individual performed in public, rather than in the depths of inner consciousness. Three versions of this individual self-criticism were possible.

As Inkeles noted in the first of the two definitions of self-criticism he gave in his famous article on the topic, it was "criticism of one's own mistakes and the deficiencies in one's conduct and work . . . —essentially a sham performance exacted from Soviet citizens in various organizational group contexts . . . as a way of setting an example for others and of exacting public penance from sinners against the Party line." [59] Indeed, this ritual was part of public penance procedures that required one to accept external comradely criticism of one's mistakes with gratitude and to repeat this criticism as now issued by oneself in the end of the shaming session. The procedure may have had some variation: several former oppositionists received a rare individual opportunity to recant their mistakes at the Seventeenth Party Congress, repeating the allegations against them, after they had been subjected to most fierce criticism at the previous congresses. [60]

---

57. *Materialy XIX Partkonferentsii*, quoted in Ramazanov, *Vnoshu predlozhenie*, 30.

58. V. V. Akulenko, "Iz istorii russkoi obshchestvenno-politicheskoi terminologii nachala XX veka" [Notes on the history of Russian social and political terms of the beginning of the 20th century], *Uchenye Zapiski Kharkovskogo Gosudarstvennogo Universiteta* [Learned works of Kharkov University] 109 (1960): 73.

59. Alex Inkeles, *Social Change in Soviet Russia* (Cambridge, Mass.: Harvard University Press, 1968), 291–292; this section first appeared as an article coauthored with Kent Geiger in *American Sociological Review* in 1952–53.

60. Also see Kotkin, *Magnetic Mountain*, 301, on "public acts of repentance, or 'self-criticism'" during the general purges.

Second, a comrade might engage in individual self-criticism of a spontaneous rather than of an elicited kind. This self-criticism could potentially incriminate the speaker individually, though this happened rarely, since it was usually voluntarily emitted by an individual in the quality of the nominal head of the *kollektiv*. Thus, the dreaded People's Commissar of Internal Affairs Nikolai Ezhov promised in a preliminary remark during the February–March 1937 Central Committee plenum to "to engage in self-criticism tomorrow," which could imply talking about himself individually.[61] However, when he gave a big speech on the instances of wrecking in his commissariat, he simply started with an "I have not worked enough" statement. The speech later dealt with the conditions of the Commissariat of Internal Affairs rather than with Ezhov's personal activities or state of mind.[62] This public confession of one's flaws was far from the intellectuals' inner self-analysis, as well as from the public analysis of the self. It was closer to a description of the work of the corporate body, to which the speaker belonged as its leader, who perfunctorily claimed that the flaws in the body's performance could also—among other factors—result from his or her "having not worked hard enough."

Third, self-criticism could mean spontaneous criticism by an individual Party member of his or her own faults, a kind of rare confessional outpouring before the group criticism. As a rule, this type of individual confession was not practiced at Party or *kollektiv* meetings in the Soviet Union. Of course, people were often required to give self-accounts in public in front of Party assemblies or purge gatherings, but nobody expected that they should incriminate themselves. The misleading view that attributes confessions of individual faults to Russian Communists may come from the uncritical extension of the patterns demonstrated during the Cultural Revolution in China[63]—or in self-criticism sessions of certain European Communist parties and in the Comintern that were in accord with Western expectations (of self-emanating confession).[64] Naturally, every rule has an exception and such confessions were demonstrated by a few Old Bolsheviks during the Great Trials of the 1930s, a practice later popularized by the

61. Ezhov's remark on March 1, 1937 in the stenographic record of this plenum, *Voprosy istorii* [Problems of history], February 1994, 19.
62. Ezhov's speech on March 2, 1937, in ibid., October 1994.
63. On Chinese patterns see Ezra Vogel, *Canton Under the Communist Rule* (Cambridge, Mass.: Harvard University Press, 1969): during self-criticism in 1952 all Chinese intellectuals criticized themselves personally.
64. Berthold Unfried, "Die Konstituierung des stalinistischen Kaders in *Kritik und Selbst-Kritik*," *Traverse* 3 (1995): 71-88.

great confessional novel by Arthur Koestler, which may have only added to the confusion.[65]

This usual equation of Soviet self-criticism with Rousseau-like self-emanating confession of individual faults or deficiencies not only overlooks the two predominant modes of individual self-criticism in Soviet Russia described above but also obscures another important fact. In Party discourse, the term "self-criticism" very rarely applied to a single person criticizing his or her own flaws. It normally meant collective criticism by Party members of the weaknesses of the Party. For example, the majority of statements from the 1920s and 1930s faithfully followed Lenin's original insistence that through a certain person speaking up, the whole Party criticized itself.[66] After 1917 not only the Party but also "the revolutionary working class" gained a discursive right to be called the subject of self-criticism. "Self-criticism," said a popular commentary, "means that the working class that upholds the proletarian dictatorship . . . criticizes and corrects its own mistakes and failures by itself."[67] An authoritative collection of essays on Soviet democracy gave the following definition: "By self-criticism we mean an open statement by the working masses of their opinions on the weaknesses in Soviet . . . administrative apparatus and life."[68]

Both quotes come from the days of the huge self-criticism campaign that followed the special appeal on self-criticism that the Party issued on June 3, 1928. This appeal stated that the Party alone could not solve the main problems of socialist reconstruction, without the masses overseeing the mal-

65. Arthur Koestler, *Darkness at Noon*, trans. Daphne Hardy (New York: Macmillan, 1941).

66. I focus here on face-to-face interaction rather than on letters sent to higher bodies. Public letter-writing was Inkeles's primary context in quoting from the 1940 Ushakov dictionary, which defined *samokritika* as "public criticism of the work defects of one's own enterprise or organization and the activity and conduct of individual workmen" (Inkeles, *Social Change in Soviet Russia*, 292). "Public" here meant "coming from society" (*obshchestvennaia*), rather than "open."

Secret denunciations might fall into the category of self-criticism, as a secret letter called *signal* also implies (see Sheila Fitzpatrick, "Signals from Below: Soviet Letters of Denunciation from the 1930s," in *Accusatory Practices*, ed. Sheila Fitzpatrick and Robert Gellately [Chicago: University of Chicago Press, 1997], 87). Still, I distinguish between self-criticism and secret letter-writing. For uneasiness on secret denunciations and their distancing from acceptable open criticism, see the Central Committee discussion of *donos* in the section "Smidovich's Dilemma."

67. S. Ingulov, *Samokritika v deistvii* [Self-criticism in action] (Moscow-Leningrad: Gosizdat, 1930), 97.

68. G. Viktorsky, "Samokritika v sisteme sovetskoi demokratii" [Self-criticism in the system of Soviet democracy], in *Sovetskaia demokratiia*, ed. Iu. M. Steklov (Moscow: Sovetskoe Stroitel'stvo, 1929), 266.

functioning industrial and government administration. The motto of self-criticism, the appeal said, should be the following: "Criticism coming from the bottom to the top and from the top to the bottom, without exempting anybody." "Self-verification and self-criticism" coming from the top to the bottom, clarified the appeal further, were already in place. The task of the day now was "to raise a mighty wave of self-criticism coming from the bottom up." The Party was to initiate this wave by starting self-criticism within itself: without the furtherance of internal Party democracy, the self-criticism campaign would be a sham, said the appeal.[69]

Stalin marked the specificity of the situation in 1928 in his speech in May, shortly before the appeal was published. Commenting on the necessity to unleash a campaign of self-criticism, Stalin singled out the following reasons. The Russian Communist Party was the only party in the USSR and thus had to criticize itself in order to eliminate its flaws. Leftist oppositionists, who had monopolized the practice of criticism in 1925–27, were defeated, and the Party now needed "not the hostile counterrevolutionary criticism but the honest, open, Bolshevist one," coming from its own ranks in a nonfactional way.[70]

The second urgent reason for self-criticism was the renewed attempt to mend the split between the leaders and the rank and file that had haunted the Party since the end of the Civil War. The Bolsheviks, said Stalin, needed "to organize as part of criticism and self-criticism of our flaws a broad public opinion of the Party, a broad public opinion of the working class, that will serve as a vigilant moral oversight, a voice to which even the most authoritative leaders should listen, if they wish to maintain the trust of the Party, the trust of the working class."[71] This statement was in line with previous resolutions, notably with the resolution of the Ninth Party Conference (1920) that decided to create the CCC to fight this dangerous split between the leaders and the masses. In fact, "criticism" was proposed already in 1920 as a means to fight the emergence of unassailable leaders, and a discussion leaflet containing criticism was to be published.[72]

69. "Obrashchenie TsK VKP(b) o samokritike," in *VKP(b) v rezolutsiiakh*, 6th ed. (Moscow, 1941), 2:808.

70. I. V. Stalin, "Doklad na aktive MO o rabote aprel'skogo ob"edinennogo plenuma TsK i TsKK 13 aprelia 1928 g." [Report on the April unified plenum of the CC and the CCC at the meeting of Moscow Party organization's *aktiv*], in *Lenin i Stalin o partstroitel'stve* [Lenin and Stalin on party building] (Moscow, 1941), 2:490.

71. Ibid., 491–492.

72. Resolution of this conference is in Mel'kumov, ed., *Voprosy partiinogo stroitel'stva*, 170. The following Party Congress (10th, in 1921) insisted that this

The third function of self-criticism was to preempt the possible "unexpected events" that might stall socialist construction, like the wrecking cases presented in the sabotage of state grain procurements or in the Shakhty affair.[73] Such events seem now to have been the most salient reason for a renewed thrust of mass criticism in 1928. The doctrinal justification, however, took a lot of textual space, and—even if Stalin did not intend that—could be taken by some local activists as a true command for an attack on the leaders. Together these three reasons (the one-Party system needs internal criticism, the mass/leaders split should be eliminated, preempting wreckers' malfeasance) laid the foundation for the standard Stalinist interpretation of self-criticism. This triplicate justification was frequently invoked in 1937.

The canonized Stalinist version of discourse on self-criticism appeared only in 1948, however, after the Higher Party School published a cathechistic brochure by Leonov, later translated into many languages in order to give a standard rendition of the issue.[74] Leonov condensed the plethora of quotes from Zhdanov, Stalin, and other leaders in a rigid dogmatic structure. Titles of the consecutive chapters in this brochure defined self-criticism as the new law of historical development (because the Bolshevik Party is not afraid to reveal its flaws—a novel phenomenon); as a new method of overcoming contradictions in Soviet society (by planned discussions and working out common solutions rather than through class struggle); as an instrument for the development of socialist culture (since science and art profit from criticism of their oeuvre); as the driving force of Soviet society (for even when it is not 100 percent correct, it produces novel perspectives).

Nikita Khrushchev repeated some of these formulations in his characterization of self-criticism as the new universal obligation of a Party member in his speech on the proposed changes in the Statute of the Party at the Nineteenth Party Congress, which still occurred in Stalin's lifetime (1952). The Twentieth Congress that denounced Stalin could not challenge the

---

leaflet be published rather more regularly in order to eschew the possibility of the formation of a hidden opposition. See the 1921 resolution "O edinstve partii," par. 4, in *KPSS v rezolutsiiakh i resheniiakh s"ezdov, konferentsii i plenumov TsK* [Resolutions and decisions of CPSU's congresses, conferences, and central committee plenums], 9th ed. (Moscow: Politizdat, 1983), 2:6.

73. The "Shakhty affair" (1928) was the first widely publicized trial of "bourgeois" engineers who were allegedly wrecking the socialist mining industry.

74. M. A. Leonov, *Kritika i samokritika—dialekticheskaia zakonomernost' razvitiia sovetskogo obshchestva* [Criticism and self-criticism—the dialectical law of the development of Soviet society] (Moscow: Pravda, 1948).

dogmatic foundations of Party discourse. And the Khrushchevian version of the Party brochure on self-criticism, published by Slepov in 1956, faithfully repeated Leonov's formulations, substituting the word "Party" for the word "Stalin," while still quoting the tropes from Stalin's 1928 speeches without mentioning his name ("we need self-criticism as we need air or water") and giving the Shakhty trial and the "Dizzy with Success" episode as the best examples of successful self-criticism in the Party.[75] In this form, with slight changes, it was preserved until the perestroika days.[76]

ATTACK THE LEADERS: PRACTICING SELF-CRITICISM

The practice of self-criticism, according to the late-Soviet era sources, involved three stages. A Party meeting on a certain subject of criticism would elicit many criticisms stated either in writing or in public oral reports. Then the Party secretary would compile a list of these critical remarks, report them to the higher Party body, and simultaneously assign members who would be responsible for the elimination of the registered flaws. During the next Party meetings, progress in correcting mistakes discovered by the previous sessions of self-criticism would be discussed.[77] This representation is truthful but does not address the most interesting question: who was criticizing whom, when the *kollektiv* criticized itself?

The Party continuously solicited self-criticism, which in practice meant urging rank-and-file members to criticize the top leaders, in order to make the body of the Party homogenous. For example, when the self-criticism campaign was begun in industry, workers were called upon to criticize managers in order to raise labor productivity. Among the students of the Soviet Union, representatives of both the "revisionist" and "totalitarian" schools, which are at war in other matters, seem to agree on this. "Urging people to criticize local conditions and their leaders" was always on the Party's agenda, according to Robert Thurston.[78] Brzezinski asserts the same: the Party called for constant critical evaluations of local conditions and local

75. L. Slepov, *Kritika i samokritika v rabote partiinykh organizatsii* [Criticism and self-criticism in the work of party organizations] (Moscow, 1956).

76. See S. P. Mezentsev, *Kritika uchit, pomogaet, vospityvaet* [Criticism teaches, helps, trains] (Moscow, 1976); and A. A. Khomiakov, *Kritika i samokritika v deiatel'nosti partiinykh organizatsii* [Criticism and self-criticism in the activity of Party organizations] (Moscow, 1984).

77. Ramazanov, *Vnoshu predlozhenie*, 71.

78. Robert Thurston, "Reassessing the History of Soviet Workers," in *New Directions in Soviet History*, ed. Stephen White (Cambridge: Cambridge University Press, 1992), 163.

leaders but never strove to develop the atmosphere of genuine criticism that would have put the Party doctrine itself under scrutiny.[79]

The intensity of this urge to criticize may be illustrated by eighteen neologisms related to the practice of criticism that lexicologists registered in the 1950s. These words pertained either to certain aspects of practice or to its objects. Curiously enough, only two of the eighteen are not defunct now—*sabotazh* and *podkhalimazh* (toadying)—others would now require a separate article explaining their precise meaning for a contemporary Russian speaker. Thus, *alliluishchina* (hallelujah-singing) was the designation for the behavior of those bosses who, tired of the futile protracted struggle of challenging unjust workers' accusations, later accepted any critical remark that came from them as true in order to quickly repent of the "misdeeds" and thus cut short the ordeal of criticism.[80]

Thurston, in his recent reassessment of the opportunities to criticize available to the Soviet populace, noted a discrepancy in the testimonies of the Russian émigrés, gathered by the Harvard Project in the 1940s and 1950s. Most of the émigrés talked about the "terrible fear of arrest" while simultaneously pointing out many cases of successful criticism practiced at the local level.[81] He concluded that this was the classical case of a discrepancy between a generic description, based on a value judgment, and descriptions of multiple concrete situations, when the necessity to abide by the stated value was absent. According to him, opportunities to criticize were widespread and were skillfully used by Soviet citizens in the 1930s.

Developing this critical capacity of the populace was no mean feat, however.[82] Mutual surveillance was practiced by the workers, as we have already stressed, but directing it at bosses was a different matter. The difficulties encountered in cultivating rank-and-file criticism may be fathomed

79. Brzezinski, *Permanent Purge*, 38.

80. The other neologisms, pronounceable with an effort in both Russian and English, are *deliachestvo, gruppovshchina, kulturnichestvo, obezlichka, kampaneishchina, samotek, prisposoblenchestvo, perestrakhovka, uravnilovka, partizanshchina, antiobshchestvennik, pererozhdenets, prisposoblenets, zagibshchik, stiliaga* (Il'enko and Maksimova, "K istorii obshchestvenno-politicheskoi leksiki," 272).

81. Thurston, "Reassessing the History." The article foreshadows the argument of his recent book, Robert W. Thurston, *Life and Terror in Stalin's Russia, 1934–1941* (New Haven: Yale University Press, 1996).

82. Kant's notion of *Kritik* as the ego's universal feature obscures the fact that developing critical capacity requires substantial effort and that not all life situations warrant its exercise. Rather, some human acts are possible only in the absence of criticism; see Luc Boltanski, *L'amour et la justice comme compétences: trois essais de sociologie de l'action* (Paris: Editions Metailie, 1990).

from some didactic stories presented in the brochures published in 1928–30 that aimed at developing and shaping the critical capacity of the masses. Here is one of them. A worker at the Klara Zetkin tobacco factory in Moscow raised her voice against the coming rationalization of production proposed by the management. Fadeeva believed rationalization would put the women at a serious disadvantage. The director of the factory disputed her opinion, called Fadeeva "a counterrevolutionary and an enemy of the working class," and demanded that her words be registered in the protocol of the meeting. As a result, Fadeeva "became possessed by the idea" that her words were "registered," fell ill, and died. Her funeral procession turned out to be a rally against the director and the factory Party cell.[83] Worker-correspondents, writing critical columns at the factory newspapers, were also said to have frequently committed suicide after vilification coming from the indignant managers. This, stated the brochure, was inadmissible: if rural correspondents were killed by kulaks in open battle so that one knew where the enemy was, here worker correspondents were being exterminated in a covert manner.[84] Coming from similar assumptions, Stalin stated in his May 1928 speech on the unleashing of self-criticism that even if a worker's allegation against a manager is only 5 or 10 percent true, it still should be aired. Because workers are afraid of ridicule by their fellow workers, or of punishment by the managers, the Party should support them in their wish to put everything out into the open, every single small claim, reasoned Stalin.[85]

The campaign of self-criticism that followed the 1928 appeal was primarily directed against bosses. The appeal specifically stressed the need of the Party cells to work with the simple folk against the bosses, for the *aktiv* to go down to the masses. With the heightening of attention to self-criticism, other forms of existing worker's control were to be intensified and new ones proposed. R. W. Davies enumerated six forms employed during the Stalinist industrialization of 1928–32.[86] These were promoting workers into administration; self-criticism; temporary Control Commissions created for specific ad hoc tasks; "light cavalry" (Komsomol Control Commissions); industrial conferences (workers discussing issues of raising labor productivity, similar to "quality circles" in postwar Japanese in-

83. S. Ingulov, *Samokritika i praktika ee provedeniia* [Self-criticism and the practice of its implementation] (Moscow: Gosizdat, 1928), 9.
84. Ibid., 49.
85. Stalin, in *Lenin i Stalin o partstroitel'stve*, 2:492.
86. R. W. Davies, quoted in Kuromiya, *Stalin's Industrial Revolution*, 114.

dustry); and shock work, which demonstrated the limits of the possible and thus "criticized" slow managers. Stalin's speech specifically stressed the revival of ad hoc Control Commissions and of the production conferences. Of course, there were curious instances, when workers did not lash out against managers but concentrated on themselves as a group, which may be properly called "self-criticism" according to common sense: "Workers also criticized themselves: one finds a mean relationship among workers when they deceive each other during rubber smelting. They work carelessly, manufacture the product unconscientiously. Being asked by the shop steward about who had smelted [this portion of rubber], nobody admits responsibility."[87] These instances of workers chiding themselves seem to be rare.

Yet the masses' critical impulse, once it was unleashed, proceeded in a rather skewed manner that had to be adjusted after only twenty-three days. This was the period that elapsed between the publication of the Central Committee appeal on self-criticism and Stalin's hurried article on the perversions of the slogan of self-criticism, which appeared in *Pravda* on June 26, 1928. Apparently, things were not going very smoothly. He mentioned "a tendency to redirect the campaign from a businesslike criticism of the flaws of socialist construction to fanfare screams against excesses in personal life," and of "criticism for the sake of criticism" that provided no positive contribution to production matters.[88] Then he turned to the main perversion, which was manager-bashing. Of course, one should allow statements that are true to an extent of 5 to 10 percent, said Stalin, repeating his older stance, but this did not mean that workers were free to hound down managers whom it usually took years to replace. A dialectical double was set into motion: on the one hand, one should encourage the workers to generate self-criticism even if the facts they quote are 95 percent libelous; on the other hand, one should not encourage manager-bashing.[89]

We may gain some insight on how self-criticism worked from the analysis of the records of the CCC plenum, dedicated to the problems of carrying out the self-criticism campaign, which gathered in August 1928. Some managers present at the plenum complained that 80 percent of self-criticism

87. Alikhanov, *Samokritika*, 115.
88. Stalin gave the Irkutsk newspaper *Power of Labor* as an example; there, he said, articles with titles like "Bandits of a Kingsize Bed" were published (I. V. Stalin, "Protiv oposhleniia lozunga samokritiki" [Against perverting the slogan of self-criticism], in *Lenin i Stalin o partstroitel'stve* [Moscow, 1941], 2:513).
89. How a party organizer was to combine them was unclear; Stalin put Party workers in a double-bind: they were to blame for any problems arising in the self-criticism campaign.

was directed against them. Others wished to harness the publication of critical (*oblichitelnye*) materials by requesting their obligatory prepublication approval by a workers' conference.[90] Iaroslavsky, representing the impartial CCC, defended the right of workers to criticize managers, because otherwise it would seem that the Party approved only of criticism that suited its taste.[91] Solts—the great inventor Solts!—proposed a peculiar psychological technique that would suit everybody, workers and managers. A worker was advised to imagine, before saying something critical of a manager, that the body he was kicking was not somebody else's but his own, since in the Party view he was assaulting a corporate body of which he was a part. Solts admitted that many workers rejoiced at watching their managers fall under the critical blows. This was unacceptable, because "certain people are Party property," reasoned Solts, and the Party could not allow this property to be wasted in mindless criticism. "One needs to criticize in such a way so that it feels that one criticized oneself," said Solts, then the force of a blow would be diminished.[92] History does not provide us with a clear answer as to whether anybody followed Solts's advice in real life.

In November 1929 the Central Committee adopted a resolution on the excesses of self-criticism. Manager-bashing was transferred from an arena of chaotic popular practices into a sound institutional setting. The Worker-Peasant Inspectorate (WPI) took it over.[93] Ingulov, one of the authors of the 1928 brochures that advertised goals and methods of the then beginning self-criticism campaign, wrote a sequel brochure in 1930, that may be exemplary in its change of emphasis. The Party decided to "guide" self-criticism, stated the brochure. But, said Ingulov, its methods did not agree with the claims of Tomsky and other leaders of the rightist opposition who had tried to defend managers against workers' criticism in 1928–29; the rightists struggled against the slogan of self-criticism as such, while the Party decided to "guide" it now through the WPI in order to stop petit-bourgeois perversions, of which, apparently, unconstrained manager-bashing was the main one.[94]

90. *III Plenum/28*, 27, 41 for speeches of Nazarov and Lezhava.
91. Ibid., 76.
92. Ibid., 69–71.
93. The WPI and CCC were fused after Lenin's death in 1924; the WPI dealt with "secular" matters like production control, and the CCC handled party illnesses. Under Ordzhonikidze in 1929–30, the WPI became one of the primary bodies that screened the industrial administrative staff and, with the secret police, "the most reliable apparatus of Stalin's revolution" (Kuromiya, *Stalin's Industrial Revolution*, 48).
94. Ingulov, *Samokritkia v deistvii*.

Self-criticism, once unleashed, seemed to be so powerful that Soviet authorities had first to harness it, and later to entrust to it to a safe bureaucratic organization. By the end of the chaotic first Five-Year Plan, discipline mattered more than criticism. In 1931, recruiting workers for all types of extraproduction activities like control raids was banned altogether.[95] The ban did not last long, though: the masses' critical capacity was solicited once again just a few years later.

THE MERGER OF SELF-CRITICISM AND PURGING

Sometime in the mid-1930s a deadly configuration fused the practices of self-criticism and purging and assigned them both to a subject that until then had not used them to their fullest extent—the *kollektiv*. According to doctrinal writings, the *kollektiv* did a lot and knew a lot; now it was entrusted with the activity of knowing itself in order to cleanse itself. The results of this collective self-scrutiny were to be implemented into action in the rearrangement of the *kollektiv by itself*.

Heretofore self-criticism was primarily practiced by the Party (for instance, correspondents writing to Party newspapers, or Communists speaking up at Party meetings), or by "the revolutionary working class" (workers of a given enterprise criticizing management for irregularities in production and supplies, etc.), but it was not principally entrusted to a professional or Party *kollektiv*. The rank and file would speak up against the bosses, when they dared to do it, or denounce the misdeeds of their fellow comrades; nevertheless the punitive and administrative decisions on the revealed flaws were undertaken by those who were in authority to do so. During the years of the Great Terror this procedure changed: each *kollektiv* had to decide which of its members were to blame for any failures in production and act accordingly. The whole collective body had to participate in the process of deliberation and then seal its results by vote. The reality of who was at fault for given organization failures was to be established and approved by the organization itself.

Before the mid-1930s, however, the Party explicitly prohibited the general vote. It cited some Cossack settlements in southern Russia as examples of inappropriate conduct in the 1925 verification of the rural Party cells, because there a village gathering would be called to vote on the demonstrated Conscience of each Party member. Another prohibited violation involved preliminary "mutual verification at the secret general assembly,

95. Kuromiya, *Stalin's Industrial Revolution*, 279.

when . . . Party members gave characterizations of each other, and the issue of retaining a given member in the Party was put to a general vote," with the purge commission conducting personal verification only afterwards.[96] The most important difference from the 1920s procedure, however, was not the general vote as such, but the link between the practices of self-criticism and purging: it joined denunciation and expulsion without the necessary intermediary, advised by canon law in cases of conscience, the practice of admonition.[97] Criticizing may or may not be damaging to the object of criticism, but when it is rigidly linked to expulsion from the Party following the collective verdict, it surely becomes atrocious. There is no way to correct one's mistakes or follow admonition into right behavior if expulsion comes immediately after criticism. Let us take a closer look at the dangerous merger of self-criticism and purging.

Its first step was the link between the practices at the level of the Party itself. Statements from 1933 tied both practices to the *kollektiv*—often meaning not a small human group but the whole body of the Party. The Party used self-criticism to point out those elements of taint that it had to purge in order to become a real body, a *kollektiv*. The purge is the best form of self-criticism, summed up Solts in the title of the first section of his 1933 brochure, *Why Does the Party Need Self-Criticism?* The same concerns led the Central Committee to state in the resolution authorizing the last general purge of on April 29, 1933, that "the purge is the expression of the Bolshevist self-criticism of our Party."[98] This merger of self-criticism and purge led later interpreters to think that they had always been indistinguishable, which was not the case throughout the 1920s.

Solts's clarificatory pamphlet on the tasks of the general purge of 1933 is rich with powerful rhetoric that may sound today like a revolutionary zealot's unnecessary embellishment. Yet it is very suggestive. According to Solts, one should never forget that "we are a collective master in our own socialist country," which requires that "all members of the multimillion person *kollektiv* watch the ongoing socialist construction with an eye of a master and eliminate its deficiencies, that is, engage in self-criticism."[99] Self-criticism during the purge helps achieve many brilliant results, says Solts. These amount to, first, purging the Party of all the enemies and

96. *Otchet TsKK RKP(b) XIV s"ezdu partii* [CCC report to the 14th Party Congress] (Moscow, 1925), 53.
97. See chapter 2 for a discussion of the logic of reveal-admonish-excommunicate, central to the functioning of the CCC and Orthodox ecclesiastical courts.
98. The 1933 resolution on purges, in *O chistke partii* (Saratov, 1935), 9.
99. Solts, *Dlia chego partii nuzhna samokritika?*, 10–11.

cheats who hold Party cards, of those who infiltrated the Party ranks or who "have wasted their revolutionaryness"; second, putting leaders under "the unmediated surveillance of the masses they are serving," the struggle with bureaucratic excesses. Self-criticism coupled with purge aimed to attain the same goals as those proposed by the 1928 self-criticism campaign, or the 1920 resolution on the problems of leaders and masses in the Party, now, however, more efficiently.

The second deadly step assigned a combination of self-criticism, with purging, to every *kollektiv* within the Party, from the tiniest cell to district, city, regional, and republican committees. For example, P. N. Pospelov, an academician and one of the official biographers of Lenin, linked self-criticism and the 1937 reelection campaign in his pamphlet *Bolshevist Self-Criticism — the Foundation of Party Action*.[100] The brochure, published in the middle of 1937, unambiguously summed up many of the topics discussed in a series of consecutive February and March editorials in *Pravda* (the brochure's title itself replicating the title of one of the February editorials) that linked self-criticism to purging. It urged the rank and file in every Party organization to thoroughly check the candidates' reports on their activities in the mid-election period, before the inclusion of their names in the new election ballot. Here was an example of self-criticism yet again, but different from the one practiced in 1928. Instead of just criticizing the leadership, the rank and file were urged to deprive the leaders of their dearly earned posts at the top of the hierarchy by not reelecting them, if these leaders were not worthy of these posts. Self-criticism was to be linked with denigration of leaders, or even outright expulsion, practiced by the *kollektiv* itself.

The linkage of self-criticism and purge is a repetitive topic for these editorials from 1937. Thus, self-criticism and vigilance—a central term of the purge proceedings—were said to be "blood sisters" because "real vigilance is possible only in those locales that practice extensive real self-criticism, not exempting anybody from it."[101] An editorial called "Truthfulness and Honesty" implied that these were the qualities of a comrade who will stop at nothing to report another to the Party.[102] Another editorial demanded that the reelection campaign be carried out "Under the

---

100. P. N. Pospelov, *Bol'shevistskaia samokritika — osnova partiinogo deistviia* [Bolshevist self-criticism—the foundation of party action] (Moscow: Partizdat, 1937).
101. *Pravda*, February 7, 1937.
102. *Pravda*, February 27, 1937.

Slogan of Self-Criticism and Unity with the Masses."[103] Yet another insisted that "self-criticism is a permanently functioning weapon of Bolshevism . . . without the new wave of self-criticism, secret ballot elections would not yield the needed results—only with the help of self-criticism will the masses nominate people who are really tested in action . . . and devoted to the Party cause." By implication, the writer meant that the Party would demote or expel the unworthy: purge and self-criticism were to go hand in hand.[104]

Pospelov's brochure and the *Pravda* editorials that it repeated only put into focus what was already underway during several preceding years. In a persuasive recent argument on the origins of the purges, Stephen Kotkin links them to attempts at the Party revival in the 1930s: "The mobilization of the party for the sake of mobilizing the country convulsed both party and country and threatened to overwhelm the success of the grand crusade itself."[105] This revival had many forms and expressed itself in different guises. For example, the verification of Party documents campaign of 1933–35 sought, among other things, to have the Party *aktiv* take a "more active role" in verification by discussing the decisions of the Party apparatchiks usually taken heretofore behind closed doors.[106] Of course, it is likely that little or no increase in actual participation happened in the majority of Party organizations, given subsequent Zhdanov's attacks on flawed and "bureaucratized" verification and the July 1935 Central Committee order to restage the verification campaign in certain areas, this time at open Party meetings.[107]

103. *Pravda,* March 6, 1937.

104. *Pravda* March 7, 1937. Many of these editorials were reprinted in another interesting brochure (*O perestroike partiino-politicheskoi raboty: K itogam Plenuma TsK Vkp(b) 26 fevralia 1937 g.* [On restructuring the Party's political work: results of the CC plenum, February 26, 1937] [Moscow: Partizdat, 1937]). Surprisingly, perestroika was the title of the 1937 self-criticism campaign; like the 1986–89 campaign, it called for *demokratizatsiia,* and both campaigns relied on unleashing the activity of Party masses. But with no link to purging, self-criticism in the 1980s led to a different result: Soviet power collapsed when untrammeled discussion of the leaders showed the system's blatant inequality.

105. Kotkin, *Magnetic Mountain,* 286.

106. Ibid., 304. During the verification campaign in Smolensk the Party masses were encouraged to speak up when the records in someone's documents contradicted their own experiences or information; at Party meetings 712 oral denunciations were made on 4,100 members under verification, and 445 were expelled (Merle Fainsod, *Smolensk Under Soviet Rule* [Cambridge, Mass.: Harvard University Press, 1958], 229–230).

107. Getty, *Origins of the Great Purges,* 105. In Magnitogorsk the leaders restaged verification and—one suspects—flushed out potential rank-and-file trouble-

The great show trials of 1936–37 supplied further impulses for intensive self-criticism and self-examination by Party organizations. First, a secret Central Committee letter, following the August 1936 trial of Zinoviev and Kamenev, brought about "boisterous primary Party organization meetings" that sought to find and weed out Trotskyites and other brands of oppositionists hidden among their ranks.[108] Then the January 1937 trial of Piatakov, Shliapnikov, Krestinsky, and other Party leaders who supervised industrial development—the second of the three great trials—set up the new model for self-criticism and began an indiscriminate hunt for enemies within Party ranks. The accused in the second trial were the best sons of the Party who had not taken part in any recent opposition, yet they allegedly had conspired against socialism and its leaders.

Of course, Stalin's main point in his speech at the February–March 1937 plenum was simple: the enemy could be anyone. But the reasoning is important also, since it reveals the shifting emphasis in how to define this enemy. The main enemy now, stated Stalin, was a double-dealer with clean Party documents—formal controls would not reveal him or her. This enemy replaced the previous enemies who were easily located by their social origin or by their former participation in factions and opposition groups. The new type of enemy was "one of us" who defected and became a spy working to destroy the Socialist Motherland.[109] Therefore a new screening

---

makers: of the 234 Communists expelled (8.6 percent of the total there), 28 people were immediately picked up for criminal prosecution (Kotkin, *Magnetic Mountain*, 308). But a factory in Smolensk, where ritualized verification had happened before, reordered public verification meetings in the presence of emissaries from the city Party committee and "raised self-criticism to a new height," with workers lashing out against top managers and their cronies, who controlled the factory Party cell (Getty, *Origins of the Great Purges*, 73). See examples in Kotkin of what seems to have become the rule in Party revival campaigns as in the presence of (and often after outright incitement from) higher level emissaries, the rank and file toppled their local leadership: Magnitogorsk Party boss Spirov's removal in the presence of Ordhonikidze, or first secretary of Cheliabinsk obkom Ryndin's removal after a visit by Kaganovich (*Magnetic Mountain*, 301 and 573–574 n. 225).

108. Kotkin, *Magnetic Mountain*, 312. Some prominent Communists were expelled at these meetings without prior authorization by the district Party committees. "Everyone knew that these low-level bodies did not normally take action on such major questions without written or verbal instructions from above. Thus the 'unauthorized' expulsions were a sign that Moscow's frequent calls to the 'party mass' to become 'active' were being heeded. . . . But short of complete reinterpretation of the political situation by Moscow, the process could not be stopped" (314).

109. Stalin, "O nedostatkakh partiinoi raboty i merakh likvidatsii trotzkistskikh i inykh dvurushnikov" [On weaknesses in Party work and measures for the liquidation of Trotskyites and other double-dealers], in *Sochineniia* 1 (XIV): 202–203.

technique was needed: only close scrutiny of the actual deeds of each Party member might reveal his or her true face. In his concluding remarks at the plenum, which advocated the first multicandidate Party election campaign with secret ballot (and the only one until 1989), Stalin reiterated the point: leaders should be evaluated by their deeds, not by the documents they might supply. Therefore "Party masses check their leaders by listening to their reports at meetings of the *aktiv*, at conferences and congresses, by criticizing the weaknesses, by electing or not electing them to the governing bodies."[110] The *kollektiv* was now to review and decide on the fate of each potential leader, by producing a verdict on the Conscience of a given Communist by means of a vote or a resolution— a public seal of approval or disapproval.

Consequently, the reelection campaign of March and April 1937 turned into a forum of public discussion of leaders during cell meetings. In Magnitogorsk, it led to "a dramatic turnover of lower-level officeholders": 83 of 118 Magnitogorsk Party secretaries and shop organizers were new, including 35 elected to such posts for the first time.[111] Some reelection meetings lasted for several days, if not weeks, in a row. A Party meeting at Elektrozavod in Moscow lasted eleven days. The work of the Party committee of this industrial enterprise was deemed unsatisfactory. During the three days of discussions of the committee's work only 62 people (out of 150 who signed up) managed to present their opinions on the committee's activities. The next seven days were spent in the individual discussion of candidates to be included in the ballot.[112] In extreme cases, a reelection conference could last for a month, as happened with the Rybinsk city committee; one of the top Party leaders, Malenkov, had to be sent from Moscow in order to stop the sessions.[113]

The character of discussions and the consequences they entailed were frequently very menacing. The four-day plenary meeting of the Magnitogorsk city committee to discuss the results of the February–March 1937 Central Committee plenum started with a criticism of the city committee leader, elicited by the powerful emissary of the Cheliabinsk regional committee (*obkom*), and resulted in a flurry of accusations and counteraccusations levied between representatives of different levels of Party and state

110. Stalin, "Zakliuchitel'noe slovo na Plenume TsK VKP(b)," 1 (XIV): 233.
111. Kotkin, *Magnetic Mountain*, 327 and 571 n. 215.
112. *Pravda*, April 13, 1937, quoted in Pospelov, *Bol'shevistskaia samokritika*, 15.
113. Gabor Rittersporn, *Stalinist Simplifications and Soviet Complications* (Philadelphia: Harwood, 1991), 130.

hierarchy, sometimes even implicating the Cheliabinsk committee itself. Of the 115 people signed up to speak, 48 were given the floor. Only 17 speeches were published or paraphrased in the city newspaper, however.[114] Nobody was expelled immediately, but within a few months of the March city committee meeting "most of the fourteen *gorkom* [city committee] speakers cited in the newspaper were expelled from the party and arrested; at least seven were executed. As for the three *obkom* representatives at the meeting, two were expelled and arrested," the third one—the second secretary of the Cheliabinsk *obkom*, an emissary who opened the deadly plenary discussion with calls for self-criticism—apparently committed suicide.[115]

Indeed, many leaders subject to denunciatory discussion during the re-election campaign disappeared in the whirlpool of sacrificial sessions that followed, together with their "collaborators" who were suggested at self-criticism meetings of the summer and the fall of 1937. Collaborators, who were said to be "recruited" by the revealed enemies to form spying networks, usually included all those who worked in close contact with the deposed leader, not to mention relatives and personal friends—but the connections could be forged completely artificially.[116] The background for this tragedy was an insistent pressure coming from Moscow that each *kollektiv* purge itself of impure Communists, who were revealed to be culpable for the setbacks of the *kollektiv*, which in the most widely used pragmatic interpretation of the day meant those who could have been contaminated by their ties with already revealed enemies. "The self-immolation of the Party," to borrow an astute term of Stephen Kotkin, followed an entrustment of each Party cell with a task to demonstrate the burning desire to examine, criticize, and purge itself.

Still, it would be far-fetched to argue, as some historians did, that the spring of 1937 saw an attempt at revolt by the Party rank and file, which was stopped only in the summer with great difficulty.[117] Surely many re-election and self-criticism meetings were still conducted according to an established pattern, when bosses easily scapegoated many rank-and-file

114. See the vivid account of this plenary meeting in Kotkin, *Magnetic Mountain*, 321–326, and 571 n. 210.
115. Ibid., 328.
116. Correspondingly, the most often repeated questions in the NKVD investigations in 1937 were "Who recruited you?" and "Whom did you recruit?" (W. Beck and F. Godin, *Russian Purge and the Extraction of Confession* [London, 1951], 45).
117. See Rittersporn, *Stalinist Simplifications*, 130–133.

members.[118] Also, a complicated dynamic of struggles between central and local Party apparatuses, and between different parts of state and Party apparatuses, played out in each concrete case and defined the outcome of self-criticism meetings. Even more important, the NKVD had its own specific agenda in 1937, and "mass operations"—the term for massive executions of undesirables, frequently requested in huge numbers supplied by the very top of the Party hierarchy—formed the grim backdrop to the talk of democratization and "renewal."[119] But, in the final account, "the party revival had served as the vehicle for the search of the nonexistent enemy" that, with the involvement of the NKVD, devoured millions of Communists.[120] The bickering and infighting within the Party eased the NKVD job of finding millions of spies and wreckers during the long hot summer of 1937. It may also have contributed to the atmosphere of omnipresent conspiracy and deep suspicion, which fed into Stalin's paranoia and supplied obvious justification with the help of which the NKVD officers explained their actions to themselves.

Historical interpretations of why purges happened seem to suffer the fate of being eternally incomplete. Given their referential data set, they tend to explain a partial complex of historical facts while ignoring others that provide a competing interpretation on the basis of an alternative data set. Kotkin was the first to propose concentrating on the "how" of the purges rather than on the "why": "Instead of seeking the origins of the terror, a problem that must await the detailed study of the NKVD and party secretariat archives, we can ask what made the terror possible, what forms it took, and what its effects were." He considered the adversarial character of Soviet industrialization, a sense of how the international context appeared in the minds of contemporary actors and observers, the institutional dynamics of the Party and the NKVD and their interaction, and the already

---

118. Milieus where bosses managed to stifle the rank and file's critical voices— village Party cells, which often consisted only of bosses who were unwilling to sacrifice one another, noted Rittersporn; or the army, argued Reese, whose hierarchy thwarted self-criticism—held terror in check and allowed Mekhlis, the army commander in chief, to boast in his speech at the 1939 Party Congress that mass purges did less ruin to the military than to the greater society (Roger Reese, "The Red Army and the Great Purges," in *Stalinist Terror*, ed. J. Arch Getty and Roberta T. Manning [Cambridge: Cambridge University Press, 1993], 208).

119. Kotkin, *Magnetic Mountain*, 328 and 334.

120. Ibid., 332.

discussed attempt at Party revival. The point was to discover a certain rationality underlying terror—"no matter how apparently bizarre or disgusting"—that made it sensible for many Soviet people to participate in the process that "often led to their own undoing."[121]

Kotkin's analysis uncovers the multiple facets of meaning of human action in terror-ridden environments, including acts to sustain or contribute to terror against others or oneself. To his so far unequaled account of how things happened in the foreground—that is, how they made sense for so many participants—I add only an emphasis on the changed pragmatic background, the different "how" that usually went unnoticed in everyday life, but against which the universe of subjective meanings made sense. This "how" made the contact group the subject of purging defined as self-criticism, linked the practice of revealing misdeeds to the practice of cleansing and expulsion, and simultaneously assigned both to each *kollektiv*. This background change structured the possibilities for disclosing the prospects for action that now made sense in the foreground.

A simple thought experiment may indicate the direction of this background change. The elimination of any of the three elements involved in a deadly constellation of purge, self-criticism, and the *kollektiv* would render terror difficult to accomplish, if not impossible. Withdrawing one of the elements of this constellation and evaluating the consequences proves the point. Without designating the *kollektiv* as the unit of self-criticism and purge, the Party could still criticize itself in a rather tender manner; that is, with one cell blaming another for the Party's general underachievement.[122] Without the function of self-purging, the *kollektiv* could criticize itself and still escape bloodshed: it would have the chance to not expel the guilty, and therefore fewer stigmatized scapegoats would be easily available for execution (a group often ended up in general criticism of itself without naming particular persons). Without self-criticism, the *kollektiv* could respond in a less chaotic manner to Moscow appeals to the Party masses to engage in assaults on the leadership, and the purge would go on as it did until 1933: the leaders would have flushed out the culpable rank and file

121. Ibid., 286.
122. The bulk of criticism in Inkeles's analysis of 127 published letters (where both subject and object were indicated) came from 70 organizations who blamed distant partner organizations for not meeting planned objectives and thus disrupting the complainants' functioning; only 12 dealt with their own organization, and 29 denounced another closely related organization (Inkeles, *Social Change in Soviet Russia*, 316).

on the planned orders of the secret police. Thus, the withdrawal of any one of these elements would have diminished the number of victims and eliminated the unpredictable and uncontrollable character of terror, which was at least partially conditioned by assigning a tight contact group the compulsory act of choosing a series of scapegoats among themselves by publicly discussing the misdeeds of its members.

The Sensory-Motor Integrator (mentioned at the beginning of this chapter) reveals the cultural paradigm for the background change, effected by the merger of self-criticism and purge assigned to the *kollektiv*. The younger Petrovsky, who "perfected" the original SMI by introducing elements of a punitive apparatus into it, stopped short of modeling the most basic mechanism of the Soviet society. If he had ever assigned the experimental group the task to discuss and decide who was to blame each time a peg touched the side of the S-curve, with the inescapable necessity of punishing somebody unless all were to suffer a far greater punishment together, he would have discovered one of the most important secrets of the Great Terror.

Such was the constellation of practices that inaugurated mass surveillance as the background of Soviet power. Later generations of Soviet people modified the deadly grip of purge cum self-criticism, by reintroducing the practice of admonition to mediate between denunciation and expulsion; but they did not eliminate the ultimate sanctioning of the whole edifice by terror, which was to be potentially invoked when admonition did not work well enough. The whole edifice seemed so benign and used so little violence because once a huge amount of violence had gone into its construction, very little of it was adequate to support its smooth functioning.

5 Revealing the Self
The Individual as an Object
of Knowledge and Action

Having traced the formation and development of the *kollektiv*, we turn to the formation and transformation of the individual. In looking at what Foucault called "individualization" we take a slightly more discriminating approach, distinguishing between two facets of the individualizing experience: the first one of "individuation," when human beings are separated from the primary group in which they were embedded and thus become units, to which personal responsibility for actions may be assigned and which may be studied as particular objects; and the second facet of "individualization proper," when these units become the subjects of independent action, including the acts of self-perfection and self-transformation. The present chapter deals with individuation, the next with individualization proper.

STALINIST INDIVIDUATION

Party discourse in the 1930s registered a steady increase in attention to the "individual approach" (*individual'nyi podkhod*) toward Party members. The origin of this tendency is usually dated to the "New Tasks" speech by Stalin in June 1931, in which he lashed out against "depersonalization" (*obezlichka*) in the use of equipment and called for clearly defined personal responsibility in order to ensure the most efficient use of the scarce machinery. Scholars noted an insistent "urgency of human problems" in his speeches of 1931–35, culminating in the famous "cadres decide everything" statement in 1935. This speech provided a canonical version of the injunction to be attentive to the common people, and to stop treating them in a "soulless and bureaucratic manner."[1]

1. Bauer, *New Man*, 46. Stalin's statement is in *Sochineniia* 1(XIV): 62.

The subsequent years of the Great Terror (1935–38) witnessed a real offensive in the Party press to urge this "individual approach" toward Party
members. Reproducing the discourse of these Party documents, J. Arch
Getty was the first to register a "direct line of succession" of six important
Party resolutions—in three years!—on implementing the "individual approach."[2] In June 1935 the Central Committee criticized the leadership of
the western administrative region for mishandling the verification of Party
documents campaign and for neglecting the "individual approach." Then
came criticism of the Saratov leaders for the same violations. In March 1936
the plenum of the Party Control Committee vigorously attacked those
who "subverted" the Party resolution on the careful handling of appeals by
previously expelled Party members, followed by the special June 1936 Central Committee letter on appeals. The famous resolution of the February–
March 1937 plenum of the Central Committee that unleashed the height
of terror in the Party accompanied speeches by both Zhdanov and Stalin,
once again calling for a most meticulous "individual approach" as opposed
to a "formal-bureaucratic" one. Finally, the resolution of the January 1938
plenum of the Central Committee on violations during the mass purges
blamed them on continuous local deviations from the line of successive
central Party resolutions on the "individual approach."[3]

All these resolutions took the local Party cadres to task for conducting
the business of the purge behind closed doors, and for the resulting mass
expulsions from the Party. The resolutions implied that local leadership
used some formal rationale to justify mass expulsions, the usual pretext
being charges of not showing up at a Party meeting or not knowing some
paragraph of a Party statute. Speeches and directives coming out of Moscow, on the contrary, continually insisted on the need to concentrate on the
personality of each screened or expelled Communist, while the local leaders seem to have consistently ignored these exhortations and resorted to
the tested practice of expulsion based on "formal-bureaucratic" criteria.

To get a fuller picture of the extent of the "individualization drive" of
1935–38 we must add a series of other measures to the succession invoked
by the January 1938 resolution. For example, an instruction on the exchange of Party documents in 1936 ordered secretaries of Party district

2. Getty's interpretation differs from the present one. See his *Origins of the
Great Purges*, 187.
3. "Ob oshibkakh partorganizatsii pri iskliuchenii kommunistov iz partii" [On
mistakes of Party organizations in expelling Communists from the Party], in *KPSS
v rezoliutsiiakh*, 9th ed. (Moscow: Politizdat, 1985), 7:8–10.

committees personally to hand over each new Party card after a member individually filled out the three new registration forms in the secretary's presence.[4] Before 1936 unidentified clerks handled the issuing and exchange of Party cards. There were widespread opportunities to obtain a Party card illegally, and many "dead souls" on the Party rolls, while many secretaries were not aware of the actual size of their organizations. And in 1936 cadres began to stress strictly individual Party recruitment.[5] Heretofore the procedure had been rather collectivist. In the early 1920s a list of those joining the Party hung on the wall, open to public scrutiny. If no denunciations arrived by a certain time, the Party cell would vote on the whole list at the next meeting and hand it over to the district committee for approval.[6] Apparently this practice persisted through the 1920s until the Central Committee finally decided to end it abruptly.

Another instance of growing individuation was supplied by the Party reelection campaign of spring 1937, when, dutifully following the decisions of the February–March plenum, Party cells and committees engaged in a strictly individual discussion of each candidate to be elected, "with no limits on the right to denounce the candidates."[7] This "preelection campaign" was to be followed by the only secret ballot in Party history, in which everyone could cross out the names of any individuals they considered unworthy of Party leadership. Finally, to further the political education of Party members, the Central Committee resolution of November 1938 demanded that "individual study" replace the political study circles of the *Short Course of the History of the VKP(b)* (Stalin's long-awaited catechism of communism).[8]

4. "Itogi proverki partdokumentov" [Results of the verification of Party cards], resolution of the CC plenum, December 21–25, 1935, in *Lenin i Stalin o partstroitel'stve* (Moscow, 1941), 2:874.

5. "O vozobnovlenii priema novykh chlenov v VKP(b)" [On restarting the admission of new members into the Party], in *Lenin i Stalin o partstroitelstve*, 877.

6. "Instruktsiia o novom prieme" [Instruction on the new admissions], in RKP(b), in *K proverke, peresmotru i ochistke partii* (Irbit, 1921).

7. A. A. Zhdanov, "Podgotovka k vyboram v verkhovnyi sovet SSSR po novoi izbiratel'noi sisteme i sootvetstvuiushchaia perestroika partiino-politicheskoi raboty" [Preparations for the elections of the USSR Supreme Soviet according to the new electoral system and the corresponding restructuring of the Party's political work], in *O perestroike partiino-politicheskoi raboty*, 29. Note the deliberate use of the term *perestroika* in Russian.

8. "O postanovke partiinoi propagandy v sviazi s vypuskom Kratkogo kursa istorii VKP(b)" [On staging party propaganda in connection with the publication of the Short course of the history of the Communist Party], in *VKP(b) v rezoliutsiiakh* [Communist Party in resolutions], 6th ed. (Moscow, 1940), 2:684.

This "individuation drive" in Party discourse stood in marked contrast to the relative indifference of the Party toward the individual in the 1920s. To put it more precisely, some doctrinal attention to the individual existed from the Party's inception, but the balance of attention in the 1920s was decisively on the collective, that is, the Party cell. In the early 1930s, however, the balance was restored and then shifted toward the individual. Already in 1929, a special "protocol of personal verification" of every Communist had to be compiled for the first time as a result of the purge. By the next purge, in 1933, doctrinal attention to the individual eclipsed attention to the condition of the collective. Thus, according to the 1933 instructions, the purge committee was first to publish its decisions on individual Communists, and only then on the Party cell as a whole.[9] This was hardly the case before, when the *kollektiv* was taken as a primary object undergoing the purge.[10]

Some interpreters have suggested reasons for this shift of the authorities' attention to the individual. For example, Bauer cited Vyshinsky's theory of individual crime, based on the "remnants from the past" that reside in every person's soul, to suggest that the authorities needed to blame delinquent individuals for the dysfunctions of the system, once the enemy classes had been destroyed during the industrialization and collectivization drives.[11] Rittersporn has recently argued similarly that the successful criminalization of existing popular practices (including Party practices) enabled the regime to escape their discursive articulation as instances of mass resistance or as an inescapable characteristic of the system itself, casting them instead as individual transgressions.[12]

Although these interpretations are quite persuasive, they fail to illuminate another background change, corollary to the obvious shift in doctrinal attention from the collective to the individual: a change in the doctrinally required practices for checking on the individual that also occurred somewhere between 1929 and 1933. Thus, Rudzutak, a chairman of the Central Control Commission, reporting on the 1933 purge at the Seventeenth Party Congress, clearly stated that the peculiarity distinguishing the last purge from the previous ones was that for the first time the main emphasis was put on "how Communists revealed themselves in their deeds as really active Bolsheviks (*na dele proiavliali sebia*) .. , to what extent each member

9. See "Instruktsiia" (1933), par. 15.

10. For doctrinal justifications for collectives being objects and subjects of purging practices, see chapter 4.

11. Bauer, *New Man*, 38–40.

12. Rittersporn, *Stalinist Simplifications*, 295.

of the Party conscientiously takes part in socialist construction."[13] His words implied that "revelation by deeds" was becoming the new method of verification of the Communist's true identity.

A comparison of the paragraphs of purge instructions from 1929 and 1933 that deal with individual verification procedures may illuminate this point. The protocol of personal verification that purge commissions compiled according to the instructions of 1929 concentrated on the past—individuals' "social origin," service in the Red or White armies, main occupation before 1917, membership in other parties—and only then proceeded to current Party assignment and to any violations of Party ethics, membership in the opposition, or ties with "alien elements."[14] Second, the 1929 instructions provided for some differential treatment of worker and peasant Communists and those currently in office and contained an insistent demand to be careful with those at the bottom of the Party hierarchy. Workers and peasants, conscientiously working in their posts, even if they failed to fulfill their Party tasks, could not be considered "passive" and expelled on these grounds.[15]

In comparison, the instructions from 1933 dropped the class differentiation altogether. Now everybody was to be checked for demonstrated zeal (*aktivnost'*) and could be expelled for "passivity." Even more interesting was the fact that the protocol of personal verification with its genealogy of an individual life was also dropped. What remained was a protocol of expulsion that concentrated on the misdeeds of the last two to three years, with required documentary proof attached. Some novel types of cardinal sins (e.g., participation in factional activities) were added to the list of misdeeds as well.[16] Commenting on the purge of 1933, Solts wrote: "A Communist is checked as to the way in which he fulfills the tasks that the Party has set for him, the plans that the Party has put forward. . . . A member of the Party should prove in action [*na dele*] that he is a conscientious builder of this country."[17]

In brief, between 1929 and 1933 "revelation by deeds" replaced a formal "genealogy of social origin" as the general method of arriving at the knowledge of an individual. Let us describe these methods of identification in finer detail. Tracking down a genealogy of current position was the preva-

13. *XVII Steno/34*, 285.
14. See "Instruktsiia" (1929), par. 30, 153.
15. Ibid., pars. 16–18, 149–150.
16. See "Instruktsiia" (1933), par. 17.
17. Solts, *Dlia chego partii nuzhna samokritika?*, 3–4.

lent method of identifying the individual in the 1920s, according to Sheila Fitzpatrick. The category of "social origin" (*sotsial'noe proiskhozhdenie*) was part of the definition of "social position" (*sotsial'noe polozhenie*), which allegedly reflected the class position of the individual, and was supposed to define voting rights and political status. The relation between origin and current position was precarious, however. In case of stigmatized identities, origin was the only thing that mattered: "a priest's son was always 'from the clergy,' regardless of occupation; a noble was always a noble." By contrast, workers of peasant origin were usually considered to be "workers" by their social position.[18]

In difficult cases certain ad hoc procedures for defining social position emerged and solidified. For example, as a rule of thumb, seven years of pre-revolutionary factory experience or volunteer service in the Red Army sufficed to make an individual a "worker" by social position.[19] Consideration of biography was institutionalized when according to the March 1928 Central Control Commission's resolution, a given Party cell was given the right to decide on the social position of its members after a consideration of their current employment and predominant labor activity before joining the Party; this decision of the cell had to be approved by a higher body.[20] Classifying individuals according to the formal criteria of their birth, previous jobs, and memberships seems to have been eagerly supported by the masses. Lynn Viola, describing a spontaneous purge of village soviets during the collectivization drives, notes that "political and social genealogy appears to have become a national pastime in the countryside" in the late 1920s.[21]

And yet within only four or five years, the Party leadership changed its mind completely and demanded in the 1933 purge instructions that now Communists should be evaluated according to their revolutionary deeds, demonstrated in recent years, rather than according to their social origin.

18. Sheila Fitzpatrick, "Ascribing Class: The Construction of Social Identity in Soviet Russia," *Journal of Modern History* 65, no. 4 (1993): 756.

19. Sheila Fitzpatrick, "The Problems of Class Identity in NEP Society" in *Russia in the Era of NEP,* ed. Sheila Fitzpatrick et al. (Bloomington: Indiana University Press, 1991), 16.

20. *RBCC* 1931, 152–153. This did not last for long, however; since 1932 "social status" was registered in internal Soviet passports, and was thus decided by the issuing body (Fitzpatrick, "Ascribing Class," 763).

21. Lynn Viola, "The Second Coming: Class Enemies in the Soviet Countryside, 1927–35," in *Stalinist Terror,* ed. J. Arch Getty and Roberta T. Manning (Cambridge: Cambridge University Press, 1993), 72.

This new technique of a public review of conscientious deeds performed by an individual is rather easy to describe, since Stalin himself urged it in his speech at the February–March plenum of 1937. The main enemy now, stated Stalin, was a double-dealer with clean party documents, and formal controls would not reveal him. This enemy replaced the previous enemies whose social origin or former participation in factions and opposition groups easily gave them away. The new enemy was "one of us" who'd defected and now plotted to destroy the Socialist Motherland. Of course, Stalin was more concerned about "unmasking the enemies" than about the new screening technique, but he asserted it inadvertently as he repeated the demand of the 1933 purge instructions: only close scrutiny of Party members' recent deeds might reveal their true face.[22]

To posit a radical change in the methods of arriving at knowledge of specific individuals on a contrast between the purge instructions from 1929 and 1933 runs the risk of oversimplifying historical complexity. We must qualify this assertion in two important ways. The first concerns the techniques of verifying Communist identity. Neither 1929 nor 1933 marked a decisive break in these techniques; both were at most landmarks in an ongoing transition, which spread to affect first the top, and then the bottom of the Party. Thus, the identification of Communists by their "conscientious" work existed already in the 1920s, but it had a rather marginal status and applied only in very special cases. For example, the purge instructions of 1921, the first ever to be published, surprise the modern reader by the differential treatment accorded to different social groups (workers, peasants, soldiers, officers, and Communist officials). The contrast between the treatment required for workers "from the shop floor" and for Communists in the office is most stark. Workers were not supposed to be subjected to any specific individual review unless a personal denunciation against them was made at the purge meeting. In the latter case accused workers were required to counter the allegations immediately, restore their reputation, and thus alleviate the burden of deliberation for the purge commission. No written documents were required for individual workers to pass the purge.[23]

Communists working in Soviet offices, by contrast, had to supply their biographies, verified by two other cell members, as well as three recommendations from other Communists with at least a three-year term of

22. See Stalin, "O nedostatkah partiinoi raboty," 1:211, 232–233.
23. "Instruktsiia po proverke i chistke lichnogo sostava RKP na predpriiatiiakh" [Instruction on screening and purging of Party members at industrial enterprises], in *K proverke, peresmotru i ochistke partii* (Irbit, 1921), 10–12.

membership in the Party, who could evaluate by what deeds and how a given Communist "has revealed himself in public and personal life." The purge commission was simultaneously ordered to check into the official's everyday life at home. For Communists whose office directly supervised workers, an inquiry into the workers' opinion of the official was also compulsory. The introduction to the 1921 purge instructions gave the rationale for such thorough verification procedures for Communist officials: the point was to purge all individuals in this sphere who might be suspect in the slightest degree, since they were particularly susceptible to corruption.[24] So, it would seem, the 1930s simply made applicable to everyone what had hitherto existed only as a means of assurance in difficult cases, in which certainty of possession of the revolutionary self was essential.

The second way we must qualify the assertion of radical change in the methods of arriving at the knowledge of a given individual concerns the contrasting methods themselves, the genealogy of social origin and the revelation by deeds. Both represent Weberian ideal types that rarely appear in historical phenomena as clearly as they do in the 1929 and 1933 purge instructions.[25] Outside the Party, change in the methods of screening an individual was not as fast (and demand for change was not as steadfast) as within the Party. Stephen Kotkin, for example, describes "reporting on one's work history" as a primary individualization technique among the workers of Magnitogorsk that pervaded all official documentation.[26] This technique of identification through personal work history is very interesting, since it concerned Communists and broader categories of the population as well. In fact, the examples of work histories Kotkin cites show the accounts' transitory methods of individualization: they combined elements of both social origin and deeds.

Thus the personnel cards of the deputies of the Magnitogorsk city So-

24. "Instruktsiia po peresmotru, proverke i chistke partii chlenov RKP, rabotaiushchikh v sovetskikh uchrezhdeniiakh" [Instruction on screening, checking, and purging of Party members working in Soviet institutions (1921)] and "K instruktsii" [On the instruction], in ibid., 14 and 2.

25. Many sources seem to superpose "analysis of deeds" on "the genealogy of origins"; Iaroslavsky identified it as the correct method of checking in 1933, noting that mass Party recruitments of 1929–33 ignored 3 Leninist ways to check every new entrant: the check on the individual's past, possession of the minimum of political knowledge, and "how he revealed himself as a Communist [*chem proiavil sebia kak kommunist*] . . . how he took part in the business of socialist construction." The latter was presented as a specific recent emphasis (Iaroslavsky, *Za bolshevistskuiu proverku i chistku partii*, 33).

26. Kotkin, *Magnetic Mountain*, 215–225.

viet in the 1930s are most representative of the formal genealogical approach: they state name, sex, nationality, membership in the Party, "social ancestry," shock worker (yes or no), service in the Red Army, place of work, and home address.[27] We can already see that shock work, typically a feature of a work effort demonstrated in the recent years, has already crept into this predominantly genealogical account. In comparison to these personnel cards, individual *kharakteristiki* of the Stakhanovites, issued in 1938, put more stress on deeds: along with such genealogical features as the time of commencement of comrades' working career or membership in the Party, they state such features as the average percentage of the fulfillment of production norms, and demonstrated public activism. Finally, the list of workers who were allotted "shock food rations" in Magnitogorsk in 1933–34 was predominantly compiled through the revelation by deeds technique. Apart from the usual records of membership and current profession, this list states the following information concerning each worker: instances of absenteeism, participation in production conferences (that aim at heightening the productivity of labor), study or course attendance, proposals on rationalization of socialist production, percentages of norm fulfillment, and the kinds of socialist competition entered.[28] It seems that the revelation by deeds technique was gradually spreading and squeezing out the residues of the genealogical approach, not only in identifying Party members, but also among the general populace. First the Communists, then the Stakhanovites, then just ordinary workers: the technique trickled from top to bottom.

The 1937 Party reelection campaign and the self-criticism sessions that followed it probably supplied a particularly strong impulse to the spread of the revelation by deeds technique. During this campaign, the Stalinist dictum "by deeds alone"—*solis actis*, we might say, parodying Luther's *sola fide*—that had been shared only by Stalin and a few zealous Communists at the top of the Party hierarchy until the mid-1930s, was now heralded as a universal doctrinal requirement and implemented in order to reveal enemies by their deeds.[29] It led to long discussions of the activities of many a

27. Ibid., 502 n. 105.
28. Ibid., 502 and 216.
29. Stalin often states that deeds alone truly reveal the essence of an individual; see his 1931 letter to the journal *Proletarskaia Revolutsiia* defending the authenticity of Lenin's Bolshevism, which other authors there had questioned: no matter what documents might demonstrate Lenin's vacillation at some points, argued Stalin, Lenin proved *by his deeds* that he was a true Bolshevik. And they were the ultimate proof, ruled Stalin (see his "O nekotorykh voprosakh istorii bol'shevizma" [Concerning some questions of the history of Bolshevism], in *Sochineniia* 13:84–103).

leader during the reelection meetings that were supposed to review each candidate individually. In the ensuing battle of denunciation between bosses and the rank and file, the losing side had to leave the battlefield exposed as "enemies of the people," with flocks of alleged collaborators of the denounced enemies soon to follow suit in the self-criticism sessions that raged through the summer and fall of 1937.

Of course, the outcome of each battle depended on the organizational assets of the local Party leaders and secret police chiefs, the firmness of their entrenchment, and the availability of connections to the top Kremlin leadership, their ability to stifle "the voice of the masses" that Moscow so insistently elicited in print, the presence or absence of emissaries from the center at a given reelection or self-criticism meeting, the dynamics of discursive exchange at this meeting, and so on. And of course, the scapegoats targeted by these meetings, and their numerous "collaborators" uncovered a bit later, do not comprise all the victims of mass terror. As other evidence suggests, the NKVD arrested millions on trumped-up charges under pressure from the top Party leadership.[30] But the fantasies of secret police agencies that invented connections between alleged conspirators do not explain all the notably chaotic acceleration of mass terror. Its wild course owed something to the mechanism of revelation by deeds, which allowed the search for enemies during the 1937 self-criticism campaign to use denunciation itself as a "deed," that is, a speech act that demonstrated either a true Bolshevik self or a traitorous self. Comrades could be denounced by others for not having denounced enough or for having denounced too much, for recklessly overlooking an enemy working next to them, or for leveling irresponsible libelous charges against honest Communists. In other words, the search for deeds to unmask the enemy helped to turn the Party during the spring and summer of 1937 into a vast slaughterhouse, with animals fighting under external pressure to decide who would be sacrificed in the next round of butchery, the basis for decision being deeds during the previous round.[31]

30. Kotkin, *Magnetic Mountain*, 334 and 579 n. 259.
31. Of course, some may argue, the Great Terror was not about deeds but revelation of the true essence of a man—"I suddenly knew he was a spy"—which no logic or impersonal evidence could overrule. If the deeds mattered, then people could defend themselves, according to this line of reasoning. Its weak point is to posit some impersonal technical criteria to define the "deed." But when public assemblies or secret police bodies define "deeds" according to whim, people cannot defend themselves against their evidence. According to George Kennan, the Bolshevik experience had discovered very disturbing truths about the human exis-

The mechanism of revelation by deeds that contributed to the frantic pace of mass terror was not challenged even when the terror abated. On the contrary, the mechanism came to constitute a part of the pragmatic *instrumentarium* of mature Soviet society. After 1939 it was imposed on the whole populace rather than on the Communists alone, and institutionalized in such familiar and widespread rites as discussions of each individual's *kharakteristika* by the collective; or, in a slightly modified form, in an evaluation of an individual's contribution to a joint effort at regular meetings of workers' brigades; or in compulsory review of each individual pupil at the public gathering during the annual Lenin Pass ceremony in each Soviet high school, and the like.[32] These procedures became routinized and almost meaningless by the end of the Soviet epoch, no doubt. However, they contributed to the Soviet citizens' background understanding of how people naturally came to know who they were as individuals: those wishing to get this knowledge of themselves had to subject their deeds to evaluation by the relevant community.

Let us sum up the exposition thus far. In the 1930s, revelation by deeds became the supreme authorized method of Soviet individuation. By the 1933 purge, revelation by deeds had been doctrinally fixed as the way to arrive at the knowledge of the individual self, and attempts to implement it in practice were carried out in the successive campaigns of 1933–38. Every Bolshevik was to pass this individualizing ordeal, officially either in the purge of 1933–35 or in the verifications and exchanges of Party documents of 1935–36, informally in the frenzy of meetings to foster mutual vigilance, develop self-criticism, or reelect leaders in 1935–38. But it would be simplistic to claim that this individuation of the Party members proceeded after a sudden installation of revelation by deeds. Rather, it had existed only as a means of reassurance in difficult cases—where certainty of the

---

tence; in Stalinist Russia, he wrote, there are "no objective criteria of right or wrong. There are not even objective criteria of reality or unreality. . . . We mean that right and wrong, reality and unreality, are determined in Russia not by any God, not by any innate nature of things, but simply by men themselves. . . . The reader should not smile. This is a serious fact. It is the gateway of comprehension of much that is mysterious in Russia" (Kennan, *Memoirs* [Boston: Little, Brown, 1967], 529). With this insight in mind—and chapter 4's experiments with the Sensory-Motor Integrator—readers can imagine a group of people tied into the SMI who must determine who's to be punished this time by discussing what each one did during the SMI's previous round . . .

32. See more in chapters 7 and 8 on instances of routinized revelation by deeds in the 1960s–1980s.

subject's Conscience was essential—and now became applicable to everyone. The doctrinal acceptance of the practice of revelation by deeds was obvious from the start; what stalled its widespread application was the lack of any need to individuate the masses.

Kotkin has recently argued that the ideological revival of the Party in the mid-1930s was one of the chief preconditions for the unleashing of mass terror.[33] I would like to suggest that this revival of ideological purity also implied an evaluation of each Communist's effort in socialist construction. Aiming at evaluating the purity of each, Communists subjected themselves to an intensive individualizing procedure—a public discussion of each individual's deeds—that later became the pattern of individuation for the whole Soviet population. The practice of revelation by deeds came to constitute the background against which the phenomena of everyday life of millions of Soviet people made sense, thus enabling these people to talk about their individual life experiences in a very particular way, intelligible to all of them, but hardly understandable to those Western observers who did not share in the same individualizing practice.

REVEAL ONESELF: THE OBJECTIVE OF INDIVIDUATION

We turn now from the very beginning of individualization—practices of individuation that single out an individual unit from the primary group —to describe the structure of these practices in greater detail. Expressions such as *proiavit' litso* and *proiavit' sebia,* which may be translated as "to reveal the [essential] features" or "to reveal oneself," capture the aim of Stalinist individuation, though *litso* holds specific difficulties for translation.[34]

Our analysis of these linguistic formulas begins with the verbs *proiavit'* and *vyiavit',* both of them very important to Soviet discourse on the purges. *Proiavit'* means "to show, to make manifest some of the inner qualities and feelings," says a modern Russian dictionary.[35] The examples given include "to demonstrate courage" or "reveal one's love in caresses."

33. Kotkin, *Magnetic Mountain,* 301.
34. The usual translation of *proiavit' litso,* "reveal the nature or essence" of somebody, misses the connotation of exterior features, which *litso* implies. On this difficulty, and translating *litso* as a "face" (to be unmasked in the purge process) see Sheila Fitzpatrick, "Two Faces of Anastasia," in *Everyday Subjects,* ed. Christina Kiaer and Eric Naiman (Ithaca: Cornell University Press, forthcoming).
35. Article on *proiavit',* in *Slovar';* the second—recent—meaning of *proiavit'* is "to develop a film."

This widespread mundane use seems, however, to be a recent development. Selishchev, in his classic study of the language of revolutionary Russia, registers the redefinition of the verb *vyiavliat'* (to make manifest), a synonym of *proiavliat'* in vernacular usage and derived from the same root.[36] According to Selishchev, this term of specialized philosophical language came into widespread popular use in the 1920s, adopting a new, mundane sense of "to make public," "to expose," "to reveal." From our standpoint, one of the examples of new usage that he supplies is particularly telling. Describing a screening of a student collective, a newspaper writes: "The students were revealed [*vyiavliali*] in their social aspect in order to discern what they would be like on entering [posteducation] life."[37]

Other examples of usage from the purges and screenings in the Party suggest a progressive internalization of the object to be revealed—from the openly visible "social aspect" or "class features" to a "self," and later to a "personality." In the early days, it would seem, testing the class nature of each Communist was a universal requirement while revealing the individual self (*proiavit' sebia*) was an imperative for specific Party members only. For example, in 1921, only Communists working in Party offices were supposed to supply the purge commission with three letters of recommendation that would describe "how they revealed themselves [*proiavili sebia*] in social and personal life."[38] Similarly, Communists were to be expelled in the 1924 screening of Soviet office cells if they *ne proiavili sebia,* that is, if they did not "reveal themselves" as active builders of communism.[39] However, even when this requirement to *proiavit' sebia* did not concern simple workers or the rank-and-file Party members in general—for these, a check on social origin would generally do—some Party idealists would insist that *proiavit' sebia* was the aim of life of each Communist nevertheless. When others were at most saying "might," Solts contended in 1924 that "a Communist *should* be active. . . . The joy of life consists in the full revelation of

---

36. The root word *iav'* means "reality," while adjective *iavnyi* means "manifest, obvious." *Proiavliat'* and *vyiavliat'* are imperfective forms of the verbs *vyiavit'* and *proiavit'* respectively; *ob'iavliat'* (to declare, to proclaim) comes from the same root, as does *iz'iavliat'* (to express). All these verbs connote putting something into the open, into plain visibility.

37. A. Selishchev, *Iazyk revoliutsionnoi epokhi: Iz nabliudenii nad russkim iazykom poslednikh let, 1917–1926* [Language of the revolutionary epoch: some observations on the Russian language of recent years, 1917–1926] (Moscow: Rabotnik prosveshcheniia, 1928), 49.

38. "Instruktsiia" (1921), 14.

39. Resolution on the screening adopted by the XIII Party Congress quoted in Iaroslavsky, ed., *Kak provodit' chistku partii,* 135.

one's self [*proiavlenie sebia*]. . . . This revelation of oneself in one's life, the assertion of one's will—that's when a man feels that he lives, and does not merely exist."[40] This choice of the spectacular few, who managed to reveal their selves to the public, became the compulsory fate of everybody only following the Stalinist intensification of individuation in the mid-1930s.

The 1929 purge still, however, aimed at only "revealing the class features" (*proiavit' klassovoe litso*) of each Communist, or at "revealing the class face" of each, as it could be translated also.[41] The difficulty in translation stems from the richness of meanings of the word *litso* in contemporary Russian. Its five registered meanings are: (1) "the face, the front part of the human head"; (2) metaphorically, "individuality, the distinctive features of something or someone" as in the expression *sokhranit' svoe litso v iskusstve*, "keep one's individuality in art"; (3) "the top, front, outward side of something" as in *litso dvortsa*—"the facade of the palace"; (4) "a human person as an individual," as in "juridical person" or "noble individual"; (5) a grammatical category, as for instance in "first person singular."[42]

Which of these senses governs the term *litso*, when it appears in the expression *klassovoe litso* in the purge literature? Let us juxtapose this usage to other similar usages from the 1920s and 1930s. First, both groups and individuals could have a *litso* in the 1920s and 1930s. Stalin, for example, implied that the opposition had a certain "face": *litso* in his usage was a feature of Trotskyites, who, in the beginning before they were persecuted by the Party, openly spoke about their programs and went to the working class "with a raised visor" as they "were not afraid to show their class face" to the working class.[43] Kuromiya cites a record of the speech of the Moscow Party secretary in 1929, who asserted that one-man management introduced in industry to replace the rule of the "triangle" (industrial manager, Party secretary, trade union organizer) would not render the Party cells "depersonalized," or better, "defaced" (*obezlicheny*). The audience cried out objections, apparently thinking that the cells would lose their "political face," that is, their manifest class role in supervising industrial development.[44] A 1928 book on the face of factory workers presents another ex-

40. Solts, "O partiinoi etike," 272.
41. Iaroslavsky, ed., *Kak provodit' chistku partii*, 8.
42. Article on *litso*, in *Slovar'*.
43. Stalin, "O nedostatkah partiinoi raboty,"1(XIV):198. The passage plays on the multiple meanings of *litso*, suggesting that since the Trotskyites have lowered the visor, only the gruesome helmet is visible, not their true face; it hints too at the oppositionists' bellicose aspirations.
44. Kuromiya, *Stalin's Industrial Revolution*, 178.

ample of *litso*. The text demonstrated how this collective face was to be studied. It described patterns of workers' lifestyles, calculated percentages of workers in different trades and skill grades, and analyzed trends in their typical occupational change and migration—these were supposed to reveal the profile of the workers in question as a group.[45]

Now, these instances of usage sound somewhat strange to a contemporary Russian speaker, but they are very revealing in terms of what the Bolsheviks were looking for when they sought to reveal each Communist's "class *litso*" during the purges. In all of these examples, one common meaning of *litso* stands out: individuality, a set of specific features that distinguishes a group or a person from others. The cell is afraid to lose its distinctive feature, its role in Communist production; Stalin chides the Trotskyites for hiding the features that distinguish them from the majority of the Party. The factory workers of peasant origin are distinguished from all other workers by their shared features revealed in the graphs and tables of the book. We may initially suppose that the procedure of revealing *klassovoe litso* of a Communist had the same meaning: establishing an image of individual features as a class fighter. This usage corresponds to the second meaning of the modern Russian word.

This second meaning is the result of a very recent development in the Russian language.[46] Except for this second meaning and the fifth one— "grammatical category," which is also the understandable latter-day addition—the term *litse* in the ancient Russian language contained three out of five contemporary meanings. These three remaining meanings of *litso* all relate in a certain extent to the original translations of the Greek word *prosopon,* or the Latin word *persona,* which does not apply to the second meaning at all.[47] Yet the recently added second meaning—as captured, for

---

45. N. Semenov, *Litso fabrichnykh rabochikh, prozhivaiushchikh v derevniakh, i politprosvetrabota sredi nikh* [Face of factory workers living in villages, and their political education] (Moscow, 1929).

46. "Up until the XIX century, *litso* did not have the meaning of 'individual character'[*oblik*] or distinct features" (V. V. Vinogradov, "Lichnost'," in his *Istoriia slov* [History of words] [Moscow: Tolk, 1994], 279). I use the 1994 ed., which has the best commentary on *litso* and *lichnost'* and includes its 1946 version in eleven numbered paragraphs (V. V. Vinogradov, "Iz istorii slova *lichnost'* v russkom iazyke do serediny XIX veka" [On the history of the word *Lichnost'* in Russian before the mid-19th century], *Doklady i soobshcheniia filologicheskogo fakulteta MGU* [Philological Department of Moscow University notes] 1 [1946]: 10–12) with the unpublished notes; I cite both works.

47. There are some curious features about the ancient term *litse,* whose now forgotten meanings include "a cheek," "a mask," "a color," "a drawing," "evidence," with the most interesting being an equivalent of the Greek term *eidos* in Biblical

instance, in the late Soviet era dictionary quotation from Lenin: "There are quite a lot of parties in Russia, and the [Bolshevik] Party has quite distinct political features [*politicheskoe litso*] in the eyes of the people"[48]—still carries by implication a major connotation of the other meanings of the term *litso*, that is, of outwardness, plain visibility, immediate givenness to sight.

Thus, the aim of the 1929 purge was "to reveal the class nature" or "essence" of each Communist. Inessential features were not to be taken into account, as Iaroslavsky stressed so often at that time: "revealing the class Party features" of an individual was opposed to "rummaging in his personal life."[49] He reproved the numerous instances of creating different ad

---

translations—"outward appearance, countenance" (see S. G. Barkhudarov, ed., *Slovar' russkogo iazyka XI–XVII vv.* [Dictionary of the Russian language, 11th–17th centuries] [Moscow: Nauka, 1975–92], article on *litse;* and Vinogradov, *Istoriia slov*, 279).

Among Russian words related to the root word *litso, oblichie,* its synonym in the meanings of "the front of the human being," or of "outward appearance," was the most ancient derivative from the same root *lich-*. It is registered in 11th-century sources, translating Greek *idea,* and was also used to translate *eidos* and *eikon* (Barkhudarov, ed., *Slovar' russkogo,* article on *oblichie*). *Lichina* was another medieval term (first registered in the 14th century) linked to *litse.* It designated the masks of the Russian popular minstrels [*skomorokhi*], who were denounced by the Church for their pagan rites and plays, hence the term's derogatory connotation. The word could also mean the image or depiction of a human. A seemingly simple word *lik,* in the sense of "depiction" and "image," is registered only in the 17th-century sources. A completely etymologically unrelated *lik* meaning "a choir"—compare with *likovat',* to sing, to rejoice"—existed since 11th century; *lik* in the meaning of "image" is an homonymic later creation (all data from respective articles in Barkhudarov, ed., *Slovar' russkogo*).

Of the later creations, very close to *litso* is *oblik* (in the sense of outward appearance), which was also a frequently used term for an entity revealed during the purges. Thus, an editorial in *Pravda* (February 27, 1937) wrote about *oblik* as an ideal image of a Communist: for the masses, it said, the *oblik* of the Communist is of "a man to whom the interests of the people are superior to any others." This word was most often used in Bolshevik discourse in the stable expression *moral'nyi oblik,* "moral character."

The interesting connections between the early Russian concept of the person and the original Greek one (also tied to the masks of Greek theater) include the fact that at least three meanings of ancient word *litso* come from the Greek word *prosopon,* and that among related terms the earliest ones, *lichina* and *oblichie,* could both designate the pagan mask. See Marcel Mauss's essay in Michael Carrithers, Steven Collins, and Steven Lukes, eds., *The Category of the Person* (Cambridge: Cambridge University Press, 1985).

48. Article on *litso,* in *Slovar'.*

49. See *Biulleten' TsKK* (August–September 1929): 4: "*vyiavit' klassovoe partiinoe litso, i menshe vsego kasalis' lichnoi zhizni*"; see also Iaroslavsky, *Rabota TsKK VKP(b)*, 122. The 1929 purge instructions insist on the same.

hoc commissions to inspect the everyday life of the rank-and-file Communists and insisted on having official purge commissions concentrate on serious biographical issues of work and social activism. Solts, also writing for
the 1929 purge, clarified that the central question of the purge was to decide whether a given Communist would remain in the Party, and this big
question did not merit concentration on particular insignificant misdeeds.[50]

This essence or nature was not deeply hidden; the connotations of the
term *litso* implied its availability to the public gaze. And thus a purge aimed
at "revealing essential class features," since this phrase can still carry the
relevant connotation of outwardness. By contrast, the 1933 purge had another objective: the "self" (*sebia*) rather than *litso* was to be revealed. Even
if the 1933 purge also strove to reveal the individuality of a given Communist—"how different Communists revealed themselves in action"—
its object of concern was already posited deeper: *sebia* (oneself, themselves)
does not have the connotation of outward appearance, which *litso* has. The
purge stopped concentrating on *litso* and now centered on the hidden self,
or even on Conscience, as some usage suggested. The Party brochure published during the height of individuation drives sought to teach what questions an individual Communist should try to figure out beforehand, what
the self-criticism meeting might be interested to know: "Do you support
the Party discipline by your Conscience, by your devotion to the revolution,
by your endurance, by your self-sacrifice and heroism? In what, where, and
when did you *reveal [proiavil] this Conscience*, this devotion to the Party
and the revolution, this endurance, this self-sacrifice, this heroism?"[51] This
quote captures some points in the transition to the internalization of the
object revealed by the purge or self-criticism meeting: among the features
discussed only Conscience may be taken as an inner one; others are still
manifest features of outward behavior.

It would be tempting to claim that the change in discourse reflected an
underlying shift in practices. Tempting, but rather misleading: we cannot
assert with full certainty that genealogy of social origin always displayed a
Communist's "class features" while revelation by deeds displayed the revolutionary self or Conscience. Of course, "essential class features" usually
involved obvious matters of political or work biography but could include
close scrutiny of the recently demonstrated deeds. The shift to concern
with the self may have elicited another pragmatic change, however: in order

50. Solts, "K chistke," 33.
51. Emelian Iaroslavsky, *Chego partiia trebuet ot kommunista* [What the Party
demands from a Communist] (Moscow, 1936), 52; emphasis added.

to arrive at the knowledge of the self, the whole totality of deeds—rather than the set of most important ones that revealed essential class features—was to be scrutinized. Thus, the scope of phenomena subject to examination expanded: "If we say that the Communists are the most avant-garde, the most conscientious, the most revolutionary part of the working class, then it should be proven in deed [*dokazat' na dele*], resolutely, in all the spheres of life. . . . From this follows the Party demand on the Communist in personal life: live in such a way that your life may serve as an example for neighboring non-Party members."[52]

This transition from analysis of "essential class features" to the analysis of the self, revealed in demonstrated deeds in all spheres of life, was perhaps facilitated by the discovery that establishing the class essence—or, better, "revealing the class face"—does not guarantee the loyalty of the Party member. Starting from the 1933 purge, one of the main subversions was seen as *dvulichie* and *dvurushnichestvo*, as "double-facedness" and "double-dealing."[53] In 1937 the need to discover double-dealers justified the emphasis on renewed self-criticism in Stalin's speech that called for heightened vigilance. Apparently a check of outward appearances did not reveal double-dealing enemies.[54] They had two faces; and the hidden one was to be unveiled by the analysis of actual deeds. Frequently, this was called "unmasking the true face."[55]

Therefore, a search for a true self hidden under the outward appearance of loyalty also contributed to an emphasis on the revelation of inner, invisible qualities. Analysis of demonstrated deeds sought to uncover something more profound than outward features: certain hidden psychological states were to be imputed as the source of observable behavior. These states came to be designated as evil or good motives. Curiously, as some would suggest, the appearance of these states as a feature of every individual's

52. Ibid., 78, 81.

53. 1933 purge instructions "Instruktsiia" (1933), sec. "The Objects of the Purge," pars. 2 and 4, 7, says about hidden enemies: "in reality (*na dele*, literally meaning 'in deed') they oppose the Party," hence the analysis of the deeds is needed. On the origins of the term *dvurushnichestvo*, literally—"double-handedness," see Vinogradov, *Istoriia slov.*

54. For Stalin's rhetoric, see his speech on "new type of wreckers" at the February–March 1937 plenum, "O nedostatkakh partiinoi raboty," 1(XIV):189–224. Zhdanov's speech in *XVIII Steno/39*, 519, similarly cites "double-dealing, the veiling of their subversive activity by outward agreement with the Party line, by outward readiness to fight for implementing Party decisions."

55. Fitzpatrick, "Two Faces of Anastasia." Perhaps "unmasking the persona" would sound more English, but "true face" is closer to the Russian original.

psyche marked the end of the Great Terror. The ruling of the Supreme Court of December 31, 1938 stated the need to prove the *intent* of antirevolutionary activities in order to condemn the accused.[56] Criminal prosecution was now supposed to concentrate on the study of criminal motives, and to deliberate to what extent these motives corresponded to the "personality" of the criminal. Now the guilty verdict could not be produced simply on the basis of one's acts or their "objective consequences." Rather, analysis of the objectively registered deeds was supplemented by analysis of the subjective motives revealed in these deeds. "Personality" was then understood as the internal general structure of this motivation.

As a result, Western commentaries noted, the Soviet legal system came to be distinguished from its Western counterparts by the extent to which "the whole personality of the criminal is to be taken into account." Individualization of the criminal was the result of the wish "to convict or acquit the accused solely on the basis of his personal qualities, (including his attitudes toward his community)."[57] The criminal's acts came to be considered as revealing the deeper structure of his motivation and personality, and it was this structure, not the acts as such, that was to be tried by the community. The term *lichnost'* came to designate this deep structure as the object to be revealed. This Russian word, which previously had mostly meant "an individual" or "a person" in ordinary usage, acquired a new, inner, subjective sense, when it emerged as part of the stable expression *lichnost' prestupnika*, "the personality of the criminal."

How was this objectification of a deep subjective self to be carried out? A typical discussion of the reasons that led to the formation of "a criminal personality" cited failures in the moral formation of the individual. These were ascribed to different *kollektivy*—a family, a high school, a worker's collective, and so on—which had failed to do their job of shaping the new individual properly. Psychological reasons for the formation of the "criminal personality" were to be discussed during the court proceedings. There it was necessary to examine "to what extent the antisocial deed corresponds

56. Harold Berman, *Justice in the USSR*, 2d ed. (Cambridge, Mass.: Harvard University Press, 1962), 253.

57. Ibid., 251, 258. The author notes the occasional sacrifice of the law's individualizing intent to the desire to integrate community through legal measures. But intense individualization is visible in many case. For example, negligence does not refer to an act with consequences that any reasonable individual should have foreseen (a standard for the Anglo-American legal system), but to an act with consequences that this particular individual in his specific life situation could have foreseen (254–256).

to or contradicts the whole pattern of a given personality [*lichnost'*], its views, tendencies, ideals, and inclinations."[58] To facilitate this deliberation, *kharakteristiki*, that is, formal references, authored by the *kollektivy* at the place of work and the place of lodging were to be solicited.

The study of hidden motives and the deep structure of personality called *lichnost'* became almost a popular pastime starting from the 1950s. Simultaneously, social sciences singled out moral motives and attitudes as central to personality. They were captured in a concept of "directedness" (*napravlennost'*), frequently defined as the intraindividual sum of motives, attitudes, and orientations.[59] Official philosophers took "directedness" as the most important component of personality, casting the "Socialist directedness" as the definitive feature of the Soviet type of the individual.[60] Some psychologists echoed these definitions, saying that "the structure of personality is defined by its directedness more than anything else."[61] Other psychologists, disgruntled by this denigration of biological factors in human personality, criticized them for "vulgar sociologism" but still had to integrate such physiological phenomena as temperament, capacities, and "character" with moral "directedness" in their own conceptions of personality.[62] Analysis of inner moral features became essential for the study of the individual.

By the 1970s, the transition from revealing a certain visible essence of the individual to an inner hidden self was already complete. This inner structure of the self was revealed by observable deeds and captured by the

58. A. B. Sakharov, *O lichnosti prestupnika i prichinakh prestupnosti v SSSR* [On the personality of the criminal and the causes of crime in the USSR] (Moscow, 1961), 141.

59. See I. S. Kon, *Sotsiologiia lichnosti* [Sociology of personality] (Moscow: Politizdat, 1967), 40; he does not use the term but speaks rather of the "inner structure of personality."

60. See G. L. Smirnov, *Sovetskii chelovek: formirovanie sotsialisticheskogo tipa lichnosti*, 3d enlarged ed. (Moscow: Politizdat, 1980), ch. 4; "socialist directedness," in the opinion of the author, consists of three main groups of features: rigorous Communist beliefs, labor for the common good as the highest aim in life, and collectivism (in English, see *Soviet Man: The Making of a Socialist Type of Personality*, trans. Robert Daglish [Moscow: Progress, 1973]).

61. L. I. Bozhovich, *Lichnost' i ee formirovanie v detskom vozraste* [Personality and its formation in childhood years] (Moscow, 1968), 422.

62. See K. K Platonov, *Struktura i razvitie lichnosti* [Structure and development of personality] (Moscow, 1986), 24. For yet another typical attempt of integrating moral motives with biological features in one single concept of "personality" see A. G. Kovalev, *Psikhologiia lichnosti* [Psychology of personality], 3d ed. (Moscow, 1970).

word *lichnost'*. As a typical truism of the late Soviet days put it, *Vo vsekh delakh i deistviiakh proiavliaetsia lichnost' cheloveka*—"In all acts and activities the personality of the individual is revealed."[63] The historical development of the term *proiavit' sebia*—an objective of the individuation—points in the same direction of increasing internalization. In the dictionaries, *proiavit' sebia* figures as a stable idiomatic expression, with interesting differences between respective interpretations of this demand to "reveal oneself" in the Stalinist and late Soviet editions. The 1960s dictionary provides the following: "to make manifest one's abilities, capacities." The 1935 dictionary supplies "to make manifest to others one's merits and deficiencies, to earn a reputation" (*zarekomendovat' sebia*).[64] Both definitions stress showing previously unrevealed features. But there is a different quality to the revelation in the two cases. Using the Latin categories of scholastics, we note in the early Stalinist definition that what is manifested is *esse*, the actually present qualities of action or phenomena that are manifestly apparent. Their hiddenness lies, perhaps, in the fact that the action or quality was not practiced before in the public gaze. In the late Soviet case it is *posse*, the potentialities, that lie hidden and dormant within a person's soul and become manifest by means of external action. *Proiavlenie sebia* has moved from the manifest, outer qualities of action to its hidden, inner, personal features, that never show up directly themselves but only through the mediation of visible acts.

But what precisely showed up when *lichnost'* was revealed? Was it the individual, the personality, the self? All of these simultaneously? Let us study this most central term of Russian culture, by concentrating on its linguistic—and "moral"?—history, that is, on its heroic and mundane dimensions.

LICHNOST'

Russian lexicologists agree that the term *lichnost'* appeared in the middle of the eighteenth century but acquired its modern meaning only in the middle of the nineteenth. The addition of the suffix *-ost'* to the adjective *lichnyi*, meaning "personal," or " pertaining to one's face," depending on what sense of *litso* one invokes, turned it into an abstract noun. The suffix

63. V. Momov and A. I. Kochetov, *Samovospitanie, samoutverzhdenie, samokontrol'* [Self-training, self-assertion, self-control] (Moscow, 1975), 31; it was part of the series *To the Young About Ethics*.

64. See articles on *proiavit' sebia* in *Slovar'*; and in Ushakov's *Tolkovyi slovar'*.

in question is one of the most popular (English language equivalents are *-ity* and *-ness*) for the creation of abstract nouns in the Russian language; large numbers of new words were created with its help in the eighteenth and nineteenth centuries. The English word "personal-ity" thus seems to be the literal equivalent of *lichn-ost'*.

However, Raymond Bauer noted in his classic study that the Russian concept of *lichnost'* was more concrete than its literal equivalent and thus was closer to the English concept of "person." *Lichnost'* signified a unique set of present features that made up this or that specific individual. Western psychologists understood "personality" in a more general sense, that is, as "all those traits which are essential to understanding a given individual." [65] Therefore, the Russian word *kharakter* seemed to translate the English word "personality" better, while *lichnost'*, designating that inimitable set of features that made a given person unique, was better translated as "an individual" or "a person." I mostly follow Bauer's proposed translation here, except for interpreting archaic Russian usages or those that clearly imply personality as the object of study for scientific psychology.

As a term, *lichnost'* was registered at the end of the eighteenth century in the *Dictionary of the Russian Academy:* it was defined there as "a relation in some respect to someone's own person [*litso*] proper," and the following use is given as an illustration: "Justice is alien to personality" (*pravosudiiu nesvoistvenna lichnost'*). [66] Some lexicological commentaries suggest that the compilers of the dictionary may simply have filled all the possible slots of the root family of related words, even though the word *lichnost'* was not yet used by the general public. In their opinion, creating a new word with the suffix *-ost'* was very easy, while making a proposed new usage widespread was a difficult enterprise. [67] Others suppose that the word *lichnost'* was already—if rarely—used in the middle of the eighteenth century, and that the academic definition captured one of the two original meanings, that which implied the opposite of impersonality in bureaucratic

65. Bauer, *New Man*, 164.

66. *Slovar' Akademii rossiiskoi, proizvodnym poriadkom raspolozhennyi* (St. Petersburg, 1789–94). So far, the earliest usage was registered in the letters of Antioch Kantemir in 1742. See a useful article found in Vinogradov's archives and published in his 1994 *Istoriia slov* (A. V. Kokorev, "Iz istorii russkogo literaturnogo iazyka pervykh desiatiletii XVIII veka" [From the history of the Russian literary language in the first decades of the 18th century], 309).

67. V. V. Veselitsky, *Otvlechennaia leksiksa v russkom literaturnom iazyke XVIII–XIX vekov* [Abstract lexicon of Russian literary language, 18th–19th centuries] (Moscow: Nauka, 1972), 81.

procedure.[68] This meaning—defined as "the relation of one person to another"—was still registered in the 1847 dictionary, though it disappeared later. The example of usage from 1847 now evokes a certain feeling of strangeness: "No personality [*lichnosti*] may be tolerated in [military or civil] service."[69] The second original meaning, still preserved in modern usage as part of a stable idiomatic expression, concerns personal offenses or barbs. This idiomatic usage—*pereiti na lichnosti*—means "to switch to producing personal insults" and is close to the English expression "to get personal." But in the late eighteenth–early nineteenth century, when *lichnost'* seems to have predominantly meant "critical remarks about some person," it was not yet part of stable idiom.

Translations of Rousseau and the writings of the Russian Enlightenment at the end of the eighteenth century influenced these two meanings of *lichnost'*. The first major literary text that uses the word is usually said to be Radishchev's treatise *On Man*, which included expressions like "Where is the old 'you,' where is your particularity [*osobennost'*], your person [*lichnost'*]?" and "such a manifest personality [*lichnost'*], such a singular I."[70]

---

68. Iu. S. Sorokin, *Razvitie slovarnogo sostava russkogo literaturnogo iazyka, 30e–90e goda XIX veka* [Development of the lexical content of Russian literary language, 1830s–1890s] (Moscow: Nauka, 1965), 201.

69. Budagov, *Istoriia slov*, 149. "Justice is no respecter of persons" is a comparable English maxim, misleading in its own way.

70. Alexander Radishchev, *Polnoe sobranie sochinenii* (Moscow, 1938–52), 2:47 and 190, quoted in Sorokin, *Razvitie slovarnogo sostava*, 201.

The Russian word *osobnost'* existed at least from the 15th century, in common with other Slavic languages (cf. *osobnost* and *osobistosc*, meaning "personality" in Czech and Polish respectively). It meant "separateness," "particularity," and connoted personhood; its root words are *osoba* (notable person, person with a high social status) or *osob'* (a species). Even if early usage from the late 18th century sometimes made *osobnost'* and *lichnost'* synonyms (e.g., as in Radishchev), *osobnost'* faded by the mid-19th century (Slavophiles tried unsuccessfully to use it rather than *lichnost'*, which for them seemed excessively pervaded by the Western influence). One of its last instances can be found in Herzen's writing in the 1850s: "Moscow has lost its particularity [*osobnost'*]" (Alexander Herzen, *Sobranie sochinenii* [Moscow, 1954–65], 2:187 in Sorokin, *Razvitie slovarnogo sostava*, 203). The modern Russian word *osobennost'* that designates particularity or specificity is devoid of all connotation of personhood.

Persona is another Russian word that declined in use with the rise of *lichnost'*. This term is registered already in the 14th century, widely used in the 16th, predominantly in Ukrainian and southwestern Russian sources, but scorned at the Muscovite court for that reason until Peter the Great made it fashionable, in the sense of "noble individual" or "individual of high social rank" (Kokorev, "Iz istorii," 307). A variation, frequently rendered as *persuna*, designated in the 16th and 17th centuries a painting with an image of the person. See a picturesque description in a 17th-century poem—*na persunu mila drugu nasmotriusia* (M. N. Speransky, "Iz

Here, it seems, the connotation of particularity and uniqueness is beginning to be stressed. The works of Karamzin, another central figure of the Russian Enlightenment, demonstrate similar usage.[71] Modern lexical analysis considers these expressions of Radishchev and Karamzin to be more dependent on the meaning of the root *lich-* (face, juridical person) than the modern understanding of a person as a unique individual, and thus distant from modern usage. In effect, the more radical contemporary commentaries claim that the term *lichnost'* in the texts of the Russian Enlightenment and the modern term should be considered homonyms. In this tradition, a transfer from the eighteenth-century notion of *lichnost'* to the modern concept of *lichnost'* meaning "person" becomes a linguistic revolution.[72]

The main extension of the word's meaning happened in the 1820s, when a notion of the unique individual superseded the notion of "everything relating to a person." The new notion drew on the writings of the Romantics and German idealist philosophers, who imagined the individual as radically opposed to society, "a monad perceiving the world in a way uniquely granted to it."[73] Translation of German philosophical terms posed a formidable problem for the Russian interpreters and seems to have forced a reconceptualization of *lichnost'*. Thus, the German term *Selbstheit* was rendered by such Russian terms as *lichnost'*, *sebialiubie* (self-love), and *samoliubie* (self-esteem).[74] Similarly, *Persönlichkeit*, a term from Kant and Fichte, was translated in a philosophical treatise published in 1819 as *lichnost'*, as part of a very interesting sentence: "The liberty of man is the personality [*lichnost'*], or unconditioned indivisibility."[75] Modern individualism was almost there: the notion of a single atom of action, a unit of society that cannot be further subdivided, and a subject of free action—all were inherent in this obscure formulation. In the end, a new meaning reflecting "the personal qualities of someone, personal dignity and self-

materialov dlia istorii ustnoi pesni" [From the sources for the history of oral song], *Izvestiia AN SSSR, seriia sotsialnykh nauk* [USSR Academy of Sciences, social science series notes] 10 [1932]: 922).

71. Vinogradov, *Istoriia slov*, 288.

72. Budagov, *Istoriia slov*, 149, on the thesis originally put in V. V. Veselitsky, *Razvitie otvlechennoi leksiki v russkom literaturnom iazyke pervoi treti XIX veka* [Development of the abstract lexicon of Russian literary language in the first third of the 19th century] (Moscow: Nauka, 1964).

73. Vinogradov, "Iz istorii slova *lichnost'*," par. 7, and expanded version, in his *Istoriia slov*, 273, 291–292.

74. Ibid., 285.

75. A I. Galich, *Istoriia filosofskikh sistem* [History of philosophical systems] (St. Petersburg, 1819), quoted in Veselitsky, *Razvitie otvlechennoi leksiki*, 118.

hood [*samobytnost'*], exposure of personal qualities and features, personal essence"[76] was developed in the 1820s and 1830s.

Lexicologists mention some curious points about this early modern usage. First, the term *lichnost'* was initially employed together with the designation of its possessor and was rarely used in the nominative, on its own, as, for example, in *lichnost' Shekspira* meaning "the person of Shakespeare."[77] Second, this usage also allowed for speaking about collective persons, as in the following expression: " the person of a people [*lichnost' naroda*] that subsumes single persons" (*lichnosti*).[78] Alexander Herzen also wrote about Russia as a "political person" (*politicheskaia lichnost'*).[79] Soon, however, the word *lichnost'* rid itself of any need to be accompanied by the name of its possessor, and Vissarion Belinsky, a founder of Russian literary criticism, could write: "before all else a man is a particularity [*osobnost'*], a person [*lichnost'*], an individual [*individual'nost'*]." *Lichnost'* thus became the term for a generic phenomenon, an ideal, a principle. Belinsky himself claimed that the sense in which he used the word was derived from the French term *personnalité*, with the further connotation of uniqueness, the specificity of each person.[80]

His contemporary, Shevyrev, described the notion of *lichnost'* as central to Russian belles lettres of the mid-nineteenth century. In the old days, summed up Shevyrev in 1848, *lichnost'* meant a personal barb, an offense; now the word came to designate the personal right to human dignity and respect.[81] Indeed, in the 1840s *lichnost'* was taken to be the central concept of a whole new worldview, on the basis of which scientific disciplines and humanities were rethought. For example, the history of Russia was reconceptualized in works of such authors as Kavelin and Aksakov on the basis

76. Ibid.
77. Sorokin, *Razvitie slovarnogo sostava*, 204.
78. Vissarion Belinsky, *Polnoe sobranie sochinenii* (Moscow, 1953–59), 3:348, quoted in Sorokin, *Razvitie slovarnogo sostava*, 204.
79. Herzen quoted in Budagov, *Istoriia slov*, 150. Perhaps the usage implying "collective personality" came from German translations also. Understanding of *Individualität* as "a richness in novel features" allowed Germans to refer to the "personality of the state" (Adam Müller in 1804) and then "individuality of the nation" that founded Pietisitic patriotism as "love to imagined ideal Fatherland" (see W. H. Bruford, *The German Tradition of Self-Cultivation* [Cambridge: Cambridge University Press, 1975], 84–86).
80. Belinsky, *Polnoe sobranie sochinenii*, 3:328 and 9:226–227, quoted in Sorokin, *Razvitie slovarnogo sostava*, 204.
81. Ibid., 202; and Vinogradov, *Istoriia slov*, 299.

of this notion.[82] This elaboration of the high ideal of *lichnost'* was continued in the tradition of the revolutionary radicals of the 1860s, who stressed
personal freedom and unique individual achievement. The radicals introduced the rhetoric of the "developed person," the "thinking person," the
"saintly person."[83] The Romantic claim for the higher meaning of the term
lichnost' had been reasserted once again, but on slightly different grounds:
only individuals who possessed well developed moral or intellectual qualities were worthy of the high title of *lichnost'*; the rest of the people were
consigned to wage the life of ordinary masses.

Yet, these masses had their revenge: they robbed the term *lichnost'* of its
uniquely heroic or saintly meaning and appropriated it for the most mundane discourse. Modern lexicologists are surprised by the unusual speed
with which this term of high literary discourse was adopted by popular usage in the two decades of the 1830s and 1840s.[84] Almost from the first appearance of its first modern meaning—the unique set of elevated individual
features essential to a particular person and characteristic of him or her—
lichnost' also came to mean the person as such, every single person on the
street, taken as an atom of society, an abstract subject of action and individual rights. Conservative literary figures like Bulgarin were the first to
lament this "lowering" of the meaning of the term. According to his angry
article of 1835, for example, "*lichnost'* became a synonym for 'somebody'
[*kogo-to*], for any person [*litso*], for a man as such [*chelovek voobsche*]."[85]
This second meaning of *lichnost'* in the sense of any particular citizen was
already captured in the Dal' dictionary in the mid-nineteenth century.
Dostoyevsky's texts offer particularly disheartening examples of *lichnost'*
used in this sense: "One, an unsightly individual [*lichnost'*] in a greasy suit,
fell from the chair as soon as he tried to seat himself at the table, and remained on the floor until the end of the supper."[86] By the end of the nineteenth century, the second meaning firmly prevailed in everyday popular
discourse, as demonstrated by Chekhov's sentence: "An individual [*lichnost'*] of grim countenance entered the train."[87]

These two senses of *lichnost'*—the expression of the unique set of qual-

82. Vinogradov, "Iz istorii slova *lichnost'*," par. 9, in his *Istoriia slov*, 273, and
296–298.
83. Ibid., par. 11, 273, and 300.
84. Sorokin, *Razvitie slovarnogo sostava*, 205.
85. Quoted in ibid., 204.
86. Quoted in Vinogradov, *Istoriia slov*, 303.
87. Quoted in Sorokin, *Razvitie slovarnogo sostava*, 204.

ities of a given individual (hereafter "the first meaning," roughly equivalent to the English word "person"), and of each human being as a subject of action in everyday life and as a carrier of individuality ("the second meaning," roughly equivalent to the English word "the individual")— have coexisted since then. They constitute the two predominant contemporary meanings out of the four given in the dictionary of modern Russian.[88] The twentieth century did not significantly alter these main meanings of the word *lichnost'*, but it has inserted them into a very specific discourse that had its doctrinal origin in Marxist writings. We will now trace the history of the term *lichnost'* in official Soviet discourse.

THE STALINIST INDIVIDUAL: FORMATION OF A HERO

Immediately after the 1917 Revolution, many Bolsheviks claimed that one of its fundamental aims was the development of *lichnost'*, understood mainly in the first, higher sense. "The Basic Principles of the United Labor School," written by Lunacharsky and adopted by the Commissariat of Education in 1918, stressed this objective. Of course, its immediate goal was to weed out bourgeois egoism by creating "tightly fused *kollektivy*" and to develop a capacity for collective sentiments. However, this struggle with egoism, claimed the school program further, "does not harness individualization. The individual [*lichnost'*] remains the highest value of socialist culture. But this individual can develop all its endowments only in a harmonic and solidary society of equals." Thus, the aim of Communist education was conceived as fostering a development of a specific collectivist individual: "Socialist education, by uniting the wish to construct psychological *kollektivy* with a subtle individualization [*tonkaia individualizatsiia*], engenders an individual who is proud of the development of all capacities in himself in order to serve society."[89]

The doctrinal objective of a "harmonious individual" was pretty clear:

88. The other two are "offensive remarks" (a meaning said to be archaic); and the rare one characteristic of peasant speech where *lichnost'* takes on the physical sense of the word *litso* and means "face" (a meaning noted to be "vulgar") (article on *lichnost'*, in *Slovar'*).

89. Anatolii Lunacharsky, "Osnovnye printsipy edinoi trudovoi shkoly" (October 1918), in *Direktivy VKP (b) i postanovleniia sovetskogo pravitel'stva o narodnom obrazovanii : sbornik dokumentov za 1917–1947 gg.* [Party and government decisions on education: a collection of documents for 1917–1947], ed. N. I. Bodyrev (Moscow: APN RSFSR, 1947), 2:268. See also Sheila Fitzpatrick's discussion of the context of its appearance in her *Commissariat of Enlightenment* (Cambridge: Cambridge University Press, 1970), 30–33.

to create a developed individuality, so that the new society would surpass all the previous ones in the radiance of talents it produced. This justification by creativity and self-development was part of the German Romantic heritage that the intelligentsia radicals of the nineteenth century bestowed on their Bolshevik successors.[90] Yet unlike its German Romantic counterpart, Soviet self-fashioning was supposed to be achieved in the collective, by eliminating all the obstacles to human development that were characteristic of capitalist society, where people are disunited because of private property. Socialism, it seemed, would foster all those sides of creative individuality that were suppressed by capitalist alienation and would stifle none of those positively creative features that had already been produced by human civilization. Lunacharsky's works are very representative in this respect: throughout his long career he posited the development of creative individuality as an essential feature of socialism. To give yet another example, in 1928 he argued against the then recently published book by Füllop-Miller on the suppression of the free individual in Soviet Russia.[91] On the contrary, Lunacharsky would claim, the Soviet Union creates a collectivist individual, a "granular" individual who is part of the bigger whole that helps develop individual uniqueness: "Here the most original individuals [*individualnosti*] develop, capable of contributing to a joint concerto, similar to the way in which everybody in the orchestra plays his own melodic line and all together produce a symphony."[92]

Maintaining the dialectical balance between the assertion of the individual and the development of the collective was a rather difficult enterprise, however. On the one hand, socialist society was supposed to eventually produce spectacular individuals. On the other, those stressing the role

90. Indeed, the works of Schiller and Goethe almost sound like Russian revolutionary manifestoes. Schiller's program for the "wholeness," the all-round development of personality, resulting in the creation of unique artistic individuality, was spelled out in his Sixth Letter on Aesthetic Education (1795). The same objective was captured in the words of Goethe's Wilhelm Meister: "At the back of my mind, it has been my wish and intention since my youth to develop to the full my own self, the powers that are in me. My ideas have not changed" (see Bruford, *German Tradition of Self-Cultivation*, 37, 56). The Bolsheviks simply wished to grant this opportunity of self-development to everybody.

91. Lunacharsky polemicizes against the now classic study of the early Soviet culture, René Füllop-Miller, *The Mind and Face of Bolshevism* (1928).

92. Anatolii Lunacharsky, *Vospitanie novogo cheloveka* [Raising a new man] (Leningrad, 1928), 47. Richard Stites describes the implementation of this metaphor into life in the 1920s: Persimfans, the First Symphonic Orchestra, really performed without a conductor, representing the model of the new civilization for listeners (see his *Revolutionary Dreams* [New York: Oxford University Press, 1989]).

of existing individuals too much were suspect of privileging them over the revolutionary collectivities. In 1920, for example, Party critics complained that Lunacharsky's play *Oliver Cromwell* presented history as an outcome of the acts of heroic individuals (*lichnosti*) instead of the "work of the collectives."[93] This criticism repeated the cliché from Party members' everyday usage, pervaded by the doctrinal opposition between the heroic individual and the masses. This opposition was clearly stated in the classic piece by Stalin, *Anarchism or Socialism?* (1907), and it came to be one of the tenets of popular Marxism.

As Robert Tucker suggests, it was the first major theoretical work of a religiously enlightened mind that had just been converted to secular doctrine and thus provided clear-cut oppositions for a rigid logical analysis of the world.[94] Stalin repeated for the Georgian-speaking audience a line of argumentation on "the role of the individual in history" that Plekhanov had made in the original pamphlet with the identical title, published abroad in 1894: not single individuals but masses make history. Plekhanov "dialectically" kept but overturned what many radicals believed to be the central opposition of the German Romantics, between a unique individual and a faceless mass: individuals, Plekhanov insisted, may make a historical contribution if they learn the aspirations of the masses and the laws of history and act according to them. Stalin also set this materialist position against the anarchist theory that a conspiratorial organization might instigate a successful rebellion in any country. He wrote:

> The cornerstone of anarchism is the *individual* [*lichnost'*], whose emancipation, according to its tenets, is the principal condition for the emancipation of the masses, the collective body [*kollektiv*]. According to the tenets of anarchism, the emancipation of the masses is impossible until the individual is emancipated. Accordingly its slogan is: "Everything for the individual." The cornerstone of Marxism, however, is the *masses*, whose emancipation, according to its tenets, is the principal condition for the emancipation of the individual. That is to say, according to the tenets of Marxism, the emancipation of the individual is impossible until the masses are emancipated. Accordingly, its slogan is: "Everything for the masses."[95]

93. *Vestnik teatra* [Theater herald] 38 (1920), quoted in Anatolii Lunacharsky, *P'esy* [Plays] (Moscow: Iskusstvo, 1963), 600. See more on the context of this exchange in Fitzpatrick, *Commissariat of Enlightenment*, 153–158.
94. Robert C. Tucker, *Stalin as Revolutionary, 1879–1929* (New York: Norton, 1973), 118.
95. J. V. Stalin, *Works* (Moscow: Foreign Languages Publishing House, 1952–55), 1:299.

Stalin was not the first or only one to pick up this line of argument, but his formulation became a part of the prized truth for the Bolsheviks after the revolution.[96] As a result, this post-Romantic opposition between the individual and the masses pervaded Bolshevik official discourse. Much as Stalin had denounced anarchism in 1907 and critics denounced Lunacharsky's play in 1920, the Party masses denounced "the cult of the individual" (*kul't lichnosti*) during the Fifteenth Party Congress, which triumphantly brought down the leftist opposition and dubbed its victory "the victory of *kollektivy* over the individuals."[97] One speaker articulated this thesis in a most stark manner in his speech at the congress:

> The discussion has dealt a stern blow to some residues of authoritarianism [*sic!*] in the Party. It has counterposed the work of *kollektivy* to the cult of the individual [*kul'tu lichnosti*] that some comrades (there were quite a lot of them in the opposition) developed and furthered, and on the basis of which they held on to their leaders' coattails."[98]

The message was clear to those sitting in the congress hall: Zinoviev and Trotsky were accused of cultivating an idea of their personal infallibility and creating small replicas of themselves in the local Party organizations,

96. Lenin did it in his 1901 theses (unpublished until 1936). Anarchists, in Lenin's opinion, valorized individual heroism too much, and were just "bourgeois individualists turned inside out" (Lenin, *Polnoe sobranie sochinenii*, 5:377–378, quoted in V. S. Kruzhkov, *O proizvedenii I. V. Stalina "Anarkhizm ili sotsializm?"* [On Stalin's work "Anarchism or Socialism?"] (Moscow: Znanie, 1952), 8.
97. The invention of the term "the cult of the individual" is generally ascribed to the German Romantics. Thus, Schlegel wrote: "It is just his individuality that is the primary and eternal element in man. To make a cult of the formation and the development of this individuality would be a kind of divine egotism." Lilian Furst gives Novalis as an example of the cult of unique artistic personality development: "The outer adventures only act as stimuli, opening the hitherto shut doors and windows of his soul so that Heinrich [von Offerdingen] gradually comes to take possession of his latent potentialities, to find his own individuality. This cult of the individual penetrated every aspect of German Romantic thought" (Schiller and Novalis quoted in Lilian R. Furst, *Romanticism in Perspective* [London: Macmillan, 1969], 65, 66, 321; note, however, that the English word "cult" translates the German originals' *Beruf*).
As suggested earlier, the Bolsheviks seem to have picked up this usage from the Romantics, who took it from the Stoic doctrine of the cultivation of the soul. Thus, Bruford writes on Humboldt: " 'Bildung' meant for him the weeding of his mental and emotional garden, the Ciceronian 'cultura animi' in its original sense, that of the Greek 'paideia' as it was understood in the Hellenistic age" (*German Tradition of Self-Cultivation*, 14).
98. Ianson's speech in *Piatnadtsatyi s"ezd VKP(b). dekabr' 1927g.: Stenograficheskii otchet* [15th Party Congress, December 1927: stenographic report] (Moscow: Politizdat, 1961), 1:530.

whom they firmly controlled. These smaller Trotskys and Zinovievs also pretended to be infallible and attempted to control the lower rank and file in their turn. Now this "Party aristocracy," consisting of the few well known professional—and, as some would say, heroic—revolutionaries, who had assumed that they could oppose the opinion of the Party masses, was discursively challenged by these masses. The Central Committee and the Central Control Commission, filled with new promotees who unanimously voted for the line that the majority allegedly espoused, expelled those spectacular individuals who seemed to allow themselves too much. The Party members understood by the "cult of the individual" a prioritization of the individual over the masses, a position hardly tenable for a Marxist-Leninist.

In line with this doctrinal vision, when Moscow was inciting the rank-and-file revolt against the authoritarian rule of the local leaders, it frequently did it under the slogan of rejecting "the cult of the individual." Thus, it is not surprising to find statements on fighting *kul't lichnosti* in 1937. *Pravda* in a series of editorials, covering the ongoing self-criticism campaign, mentioned frequent cases of the unacceptable "cult of the individual" of numerous local leaders, for example, in the Urals and in Chechnia. In fact, in the Nadterechnyi district of Chechnia some collective farms were even given the names of the first and second secretaries of the district Party committee, while one collective farm had been named after its Party organizer Issaev.[99] In another instance Musaev, the head of the Party organization in Ufa, the capital of the republic of Bashkiria, was criticized for fostering the cult of his person, when he allowed the publication of a book full of laudatory articles on himself. This smacked of serious crimes, hinted *Pravda*, since the Udmurtia Party chief, who encouraged similar brochures praising himself, had recently been exposed as the "enemy of the people."[100] As a result the masses were taught when to use the marker of the "cult of the individual": such talk was one of the battle cries available to the disgruntled rank and file in their possible assault on their authoritarian bosses.

By now it should be abundantly clear that Khrushchev, who used the same label, *kul't lichnosti*—conventionally translated as the "cult of personality"—and who is usually credited with inventing the term, simply followed the Stalinist canon. Khrushchev's minimal innovation consisted in extending the canon that he had previously learned from his semi-educated

99. *Pravda*, February 9, 1937.
100. *Pravda*, March 28, 1937.

seminarian teacher, to explain that teacher's own activity, and to ascribe the "cult of the individual" to Stalin himself. And yet it was not a true innovation, since Stalin himself suggested the possibility of such an extension, seemingly embarrassed by the cult of his own *lichnost'* when it concerned his physical rather than political body, to invoke the famous opposition from medieval political theology.[101] In his 1938 letter to the publishing house Detizdat (children's literature), which had proposed printing a set of didactic stories on Stalin in his childhood, similar to the already issued children's book of stories about Lenin, Stalin insisted that the project be discontinued lest it increase the harmful "cult of individuals" (*kul't lichnostei*, in the plural). The justification was doctrinally clear: "Heroes make the people, transform the crowd into the people, say the SRs [Socialist Revolutionaries]. The people makes heroes, the Bolsheviks answer the SRs." Thus, stories about an infallible individual called Stalin waging heroic struggles and effecting a revolution should not be published.[102] Even if the innumerable books about Stalin's self-aggrandizing psyche and his thirst for personal power were completely true, the doctrinal statements he made were in line with the dominant discourse. Stalin had helped to elaborate it initially, and he had to support it.

Nevertheless, if dialectical discourse insisted that adulation of exceptional and infallible self-fashioned individuals was unacceptable in the Marxist discourse, it simultaneously affirmed the point that the masses might and eventually would produce exceptional individuals from their own ranks. One of the first Soviet brochures on the problem of *lichnost'*, written in 1945 by the official philosopher Georgii Gak, is thoroughly representative in this respect. While the first part of the brochure studied the oppression of the individual under capitalism, citing examples from the novels of Alexander Cronin and Louis-Ferdinand Céline, the second was dedicated to the freedom of the individual in the USSR, which was understood as the development of the natural talents of the common people. The pamphlet gave the following justifications to support its claim that individual freedom flourished in the USSR to the fullest. First, there was the recent "mass promotion of talented people from the masses" into responsible positions. Soviet newspapers published biographies of these talented indi-

101. Kantorowicz, *King's Two Bodies.*
102. The letter itself remained unpublished from the 1930s until its release to the press in 1953 (I. V. Stalin, "Pis'mo v Detizdat," in *Sochineniia* 1(XIV):274). The Socialist Revolutionaries, a prominent socialist party, are here ascribed the "anarchist" position also.

viduals arising in the midst of the common people, a phenomenon that allegedly did not happen in the capitalist West. "Nowhere does the individual [*lichnost'*] have such acclaim as in the USSR," was the punch line. Second, the heroic Stakhanovite movement, demonstrating spectacular superhuman achievements in production, also meant above all "the development of the intellectual powers of the individual, his abilities, and his talents."[103]

Another early brochure specifically concerned with the problem of the individual, by a constitutional lawyer named Iakov Umansky, addressed individual rights to a certain extent. According to the author, these rights were guaranteed by the Soviet Constitution of 1936, and since "the position of the individual in the state gives us an opportunity to judge the level of democracy in a given country," the Soviet Union was a developed, albeit socialist, democracy. But the main point of attention was still the development of talents among the masses. Thus, Ivan Korobov and P. Kalinkina (with personal name not revealed, however) were cited as workers who had become famous for their shock work and thus had been elected to the Supreme Soviet. Tatiana Fedorova and T. Lysenko, although born peasants, had studied and become a renowned engineer and the most famous biologist, respectively, while the Soviet ace of air combat against the Germans, Pokryshkin, had been a modest fitter before the war. "They are the heroes of our time, the heroes of Stalin's epoch," stated the brochure.[104]

To support his point that Soviet society is capable of producing spectacular heroes, Umansky quoted Stalin, but in a very interesting manner. In an interview given to Roy Howard in 1936, to which Umansky referred, Stalin had provided the most thorough treatment of the topic of "personal freedom":

> Your question implies that socialist society denies personal freedom [*lichnaia svoboda*]. This is not true. . . . We have built this society not to curtail personal freedom, but to make the individual [*lichnost'*] feel really free. We have built it for real personal freedom, freedom without parentheses. I cannot imagine what personal freedom an unemployed person may have, when he walks around hungry and cannot find a way to apply his labor power. Real freedom exists only where exploitation is eliminated, where there is no oppression of some people by other people, where there is no unemployment and beggary, where a man is not afraid

103. G. M. Gak, *Sotsialisticheskoe obshchestvo i lichnost'* [Socialist society and the individual] (Moscow: Pravda, 1945), 16.
104. Ia. N. Umansky, *Lichnost' v sotsialisticheskom obshchestve* [The individual in socialist society] (Moscow, 1947), 16.

that tomorrow he might lose his job, his lodging, his bread. Only in such a society are real—rather than mere paper—personal freedom, and freedom of any other kind, possible.[105]

Now, we can easily interpret these assertions by Stalin as formulating the familiar doctrine of human rights so as to involve not only political rights but also and primarily social rights, which provide the ground for the exercise of political ones. Soviet propaganda of the Brezhnev years tediously repeated this point in its ideological war with the Western mass media. Umansky did not ignore these social rights altogether either. But while quoting Stalin, he omitted his last lines on social rights and concentrated on Stalin's notion of "real personal freedom," that he explained in the following way:

> Socialist society ensures the all-sided development of the abilities of its members, by bringing them up with a sense of human dignity, honor, courage, heroism, and acute socialist Conscience. . . . Freedom of the individual in the Soviet state consists in the real opportunity for each working man to reveal [*proiavit'*] all his physical and spiritual powers in order to achieve his own material or cultural well-being and in order to strengthen socialist society.[106]

Here the standard point about masses eventually giving birth to developed individuals cannot be made clearer. Consequently, the author interprets freedom of the individual as the real opportunity "to reveal all his physical and cultural powers," and thus to reveal oneself. This account is obviously still related to the Romantic ideal of self-perfection and the sought wholeness of individual development.[107] But opportunity is not the same as an achieved goal: the crucial point is that only a Soviet hero, rather than each person on the street, can be considered an individual. In the first Soviet brochures about *lichnost'*, everybody is capable of becoming a developed indi-

---

105. Stalin, "Beseda s g-nom Roy Govardom," in *Sochineniia* 1 (XIV): 127–128.
106. Umansky, *Lichnost' v sotsialisticheskom obshchestve*, 10–11.
107. It is also very close to the Soviet conception of personality in official psychology, which Bauer described in 1952, and which implied the following image of personal development. At the base of personality lies a certain physiological "temperament" (the same word in English and Russian), a set of basic dynamic psychosomatic qualities. These qualities develop differently in different individuals and thus create different personalities, the process of personality formation being dependent on the conditions of education and on innate capacities and abilities. Hence, the aim of the educator is to diagnose endowments hidden in a given individual and foster them, to help them develop to the fullest (Bauer, *New Man*, 164).

vidual in the Soviet Union, but so far only some of the common folk have managed to achieve this state, by becoming renowned heroes.

Speeches and writings of Mikhail Kalinin, a former peasant who became the chairman of the Presidium of the Supreme Soviet of the USSR, are indicative of the idea of heroic individual also. Mel'nikova's study of Kalinin's published sources suggests that he had started using the word *lichnost'* after the individual heroic feats of the Soviet people during the war called for that usage.[108] "The All-union elder," as he was frequently called in Soviet newspapers, did not use the word *lichnost'* at all until 1945! His statements, however, demonstrate a steadily increasing attention to matters of individual life, starting from an almost zero degree of concern for the individual. In 1924–30 the collective prevails over the individual: the linguistic constructions that Kalinin employs suggest that the individual is almost dissolved in the collective. At that time only groups function as actors in Kalinin's discourse: "masses," "strata," "people," "the teaching profession," "professors," and so on. In 1930–38 the first signs appear of an individualization of Kalinin's attention: these are stories about individuals, but still without mentioning their names. The short period of 1938–41 (before the war, but after the Great Terror) marks a sudden attention to describing differences between individuals, and even ascribing to them the right to make mistakes and have human weaknesses—a result of the individuation drive, we might say. The years of the war, 1941–45, bring numerous descriptions of the heroic feats of Soviet soldiers accompanied by accounts of the heroes' lives, giving particular names in each case. Finally, the word *lichnost'* appears in 1945 for the first time, though in a curious conjunction. It often attends class enemies or their activities, as in such expressions as "the person of a czar" (*lichnost' tsaria*) or "bourgeois intellectuals preached the natural egoism of the individual" (*lichnosti*). Nevertheless, Mel'nikova concluded that apparently by 1945 the social need to reflect in language the existence of bright singular individuals had materialized, and this need had led to the universal use of the term *lichnost'* in everyday Soviet discourse.[109]

Let us sum up this peculiar image of human development, suggested by

108. N. A. Mel'nikova, "K voprosu o stanovlenii i razvitii termina *lichnost'* v sovetskoi pedagogicheskoi publitsistike" [On the development of the term *lichnost'* in Soviet pedagogical literature], *Voprosy prikladnoi lingvistiki* [Problems of applied linguistics (Dnepropetrovsk University)] 2 (1970): 63–70.
109. Ibid., 67. The author also notes that Krupskaia also used the term *lichnost'* mainly to characterize the members of political groups, competing with the Bolsheviks, as "bright individuals" who, however, held erroneous views.

this study of Stalin's usage and high official discourse. Stalin and his ideologists most frequently used *lichnost'* to refer to spectacular heroic persons, rather than to a feature of each citizen of the USSR. On the one hand, these persons could oppose or try imposing their wills on the masses, and in this case they were subject to end up in the dustbin of history. On the other hand, among the winning masses, anybody could develop his or her innate talents to become a *lichnost'* understood as a spectacular individual; but in the meantime—until common people revealed their talents in spectacular deeds—they were not called *lichnosti*. Human freedom, then, was seen as the opportunity to develop innate capacities and become this illustrious developed individual.

And yet the second meaning of the word *lichnost'* in the sense of an individual as such was also inherent in Stalinist discourse. Indeed, becoming a spectacular individual, among many things, implies becoming an individual as such, one of the singularized atoms among the human mass. This opposition between two meanings appeared later as a clash between two sociological definitions of *lichnost'* in the 1960s. According to the first position, an individual must possess some "essential features [*svoe litso*]: an independence of thought, considered judgments and views, originality of feelings, willpower, internal self-control, and passion. A person [*lichnost'*] is an integration of socially relevant features, representing the essence of the given society in the individual; an individually unrepeatable and potentially infinite combination of active capacities of man."[110] The second position almost repeated this definition of *lichnost'* as an integrated set of relevant human qualities but rejected the notion of a compulsory need to be unique.[111]

Georgii Smirnov, an official philosopher who wrote the canonical text on the specificity of "the Soviet individual," adjudicated this clash in favor of the nonheroic and nonunique understanding of *lichnost'*. The first understanding, in his opinion, denied many Soviet people the right to be called *lichnost'*. On the contrary, argued Smirnov, "*lichnost'* is a social image

110. G. V. Osipov, ed., *Sotsiologiia v SSSR* [Sociology in the USSR] (Moscow: Mysl', 1965), 1:433–434. The introduction to pt. 4, where this definition appears, was apparently written by the editor.

111. "*Lichnost'* is a concrete expression of the essence of man, that is, an integration of socially relevant features, that are related to the essence of the given society, and that are realized in a given individual in a certain manner" (ibid., 2:492). Curiously enough, this definition appears in the glossary of sociological terms at the end of the two-vol. set; the absence of stated author and similarities of style suggest that Osipov was its author.

[*sotsialnyi oblik*] of each man, expressed in concrete individual characteristic. The features of *lichnost'* can be different—more or less bright, deep,
original, but their presence is inescapable and compulsory in every man because of his inclusion into the net of social relations."[112] Thus, latter-day
Soviet ideology downplayed the role of the unique and heroic individual
and defined individuality as a quality of each member of Soviet society.

The roots of this denigration of unique individuals lie in the demand for
mass individuation. The modest practitioner Makarenko, spared the great
tasks of producing heroes that concerned those at the apex of power in
Stalin's days, and wrestling with the wearying task of producing normal
Soviet citizens, is once again our best example.

MAKARENKO'S AVERAGE INDIVIDUAL

Makarenko's famous exposition of the meaning of the term *kollektiv* was
in fact part of a larger discussion of methods of bringing up a New Man that
he put into his 1932 unfinished book on the methods of education in the labor colony. The section that precedes the one discussing the *kollektiv* cen-
ters on the problems of *lichnost'* as the goal of education, and it is our focus here.

Makarenko insists that the work of a Soviet pedagogue should be driven
by the sole aim of creating a man that a socialist society needs, and perhaps
even a specific professional—a doctor, an engineer, a turret lathe operator
—if such would be the social order. "The design [*proektirovka*] of a person
as a product of education should be made according to the order of society,"
writes Makarenko.[113] Mass production of individuals with preset features
is his main objective, a view, which, as he understands, is not shared by the
majority of other educationalists in the USSR. Indeed, it met opposition
from such people as Lunacharsky, who ascribed standardization to the capitalist world, rather than to Soviet society, different from capitalism precisely in bringing up harmoniously developed and "subtly individualized"
persons.[114] Makarenko ridicules this majority of educators in his descrip-

112. Smirnov, *Sovetskii chelovek*, 58. The same authorship of the two opposing
quotes did not preclude Smirnov from casting these opposites as representative of
different groups of scholars; later authors simply repeated Smirnov's opinion.

113. In the mood typical of the day he aspires to find prepared drawings of personality types and then work according to them. They do not yet exist but, Makarenko hopes, Soviet social science will supply them soon (Makarenko 5:467).

114. See earlier discussion of Lunacharsky in this chapter, and the accompanying note 90.

tion of the history of their attempts to create a New Soviet Man: "Having gained speed on Western European pedagogical springboards, they jumped very high and easily took such ideal heights like 'harmonious individual.'"[115] Later they had to substitute a "man-Communist" for this ideal, and by the 1930s the goal was lowered to the modest one of "a fighter, full of initiative."

Still, even this aim is hardly achievable, given the prevalent methods of upbringing, copied from Rousseau and entailing a one-to-one interaction between child and pedagogue.[116] In Makarenko's opinion, the Soviet educational system did not have enough money to behave like the petit-bourgeois father of some Emile and assign each child an individual pedagogue, nor, perhaps, should it even strive to employ such methods, which smack of bourgeois liberalism. And, since the Soviet state cannot afford to spend much on everyone, it needs "a method that will be general and common but will also allow each individual [*lichnost'*] to develop his abilities, to move along the line of his propensities."[117]

The notion of "the production of individuals" may seem justifiably ominous to a modern reader, for whom anti-utopias like Huxley's *Brave New World* and Orwell's *1984* reflect the worst tendencies in modern civilization. While these tendencies are present in Makarenko, his main concern is not so much with fashioning each individual to fit the standard mass pattern, but with the need to make orderly individuals out of chaotic masses, with minimal expense and as quickly as possible. In other words, his concern is not with producing conformity among individuals, but with producing individuals at all (who may happen to conform to certain standards, but this outcome is one of the possible corollaries of the production process).

Of course, the individual that Makarenko is poised to produce is the Soviet individual, as the following quotation shows:

> They say to us: "Produce a healthy, literate—and if possible—educated man who is well developed and has initiative, who is orderly in hygiene and everyday life and, most important, who conscientiously takes part in the joint work of the *kollektiv* and of the class, an active agent of our construction who is ready to join the ranks of the military to defend our cause against the bourgeois armies."[118]

115. Makarenko 5:463.
116. Makarenko 5:480.
117. Makarenko 5:467.
118. Ibid.

But apart from the line on *kollektiv* and class, this description of the desired individual is very thin. Orderly, literate, hygienic, docile in labor, and ready to defend the nation—all these qualities do not exceed the basic requirements for the modern individual, understood as in the capitalist West, simply as a unit of action. We can scarcely even call it the New Soviet Man, save for the willingness to take part in socialist construction, and Makarenko envisions objections coming from the less pragmatic Communist educationalists.

> Many pedagogues would say—this is not enough! We need a harmonious individual! But I say: if we could ensure the mass manufacturing of such a product, this would be remarkable. . . . And the Party, and the army, and the business managers would be very grateful to us.[119]

The agencies that commission Makarenko's products are clearly named in the last sentence. Dealing with huge masses of uprooted peasants and recalcitrant workers, these agencies earnestly called for modern orderly agents of individual action. Makarenko wishes to satisfy their pragmatic demands and forget, for the time being, about the ideal of the higher individual that the Revolution dreamed of creating. In a sense, he wishes to produce *lichnost'* in the second, widespread sense of the term, as a unit for individual action, but not in the first sense, as a unique individuality that would distinguish itself from all others, satisfying high heroic and revolutionary aspirations. Of course, Makarenko says, this individual (in the second sense of the Russian word) whom he would like to create, this basic peg on which to hang social obligations and individual responsibility, may also develop his or her abilities and reveal endowments in a unique manner and to an unprecedented extent, and thus become *lichnost'* in the higher sense. This possibility is left to the future personal effort of each individual, originally produced en masse.

For the time being, the tasks of the day demand the formation of a simple docile individual, and the invention of a method for its mass production. As we already know, Makarenko invented this method: he was the Soviet Ford of the mass assemblage of *lichnost'*. The name of this method is the *kollektiv*. It was equivalent to Ford's conveyor belt in its revolutionary impact upon mass production: if a cheap model-T helped radically to alter human material life, an inexpensive mass-produced individual influenced spiritual life in a no less radical way.

119. Ibid.

The methods of producing *lichnost'* within a kollektiv are best described in one of the sections of Makarenko's 1938 *Problems of Soviet School Education* called "The Pedagogy of Individual Action."[120] This section is usually taken as a concise statement of Makarenko's method of "parallel action," proposed in opposition to the Rousseau-influenced method of "direct action" practiced by certain Soviet pedagogues who relied on direct communication between individual teacher and student for inculcating "conscious discipline." As we remember, Makarenko considered this direct appeal to individuals akin to pedological sermons and deemed them very ineffective, since the influence of the pedagogue swiftly evaporated in his or her absence.[121] Makarenko's method, by contrast, had staying power: the *kollektiv* that he had set up dutifully policed itself and thus supported the standards of "conscious discipline," even when left on its own.

"Parallel action" implies that pedagogical influence simultaneously affects both the individual and the collective. A pedagogue influences the collective but a second, unnoticed, influence on the individual also occurs, parallel to this primary influence. Makarenko stresses that his initial mistake consisted in thinking that one should first set up a *kollektiv* and only then start working on the *lichnost'* of individual members. Practice taught him, however, that setting up one part of the opposition "collective versus individual" without the other is simply impossible: by creating the *kollektiv*, one creates a corollary *lichnost'*. Once the *kollektiv* is formed—once people come to exist in "constant association of [shared] work, friendship, ideology, and everyday life"[122]—the pedagogy of forming a Soviet individual is already in place.

Thus a teacher, writes Makarenko, should not relate to individuals at all but should always address statements about individuals to the whole group of which they are members. His favorite statements are "Volkov of your detachment has stolen," or "Petrenko of your detachment is always late." Rewards and punishments apply to the group as a whole, as we remember, and the commander of a detachment frequently suffers arrest for the misdeeds of his or her detachment. Rewards, says Makarenko, work even better than punishments: when all members of a detachment that has distin-

120. Other sections are "Methods," "Discipline, regime, punishment, rewards" and "Labor education: Relations, style and tonality of the *kollektiv*." The section that we describe follows the disciplinary one and precedes the one on matters of style in group life.
121. Makarenko 5:134.
122. Makarenko 5:160.

guished itself receives theater tickets, comrades shame the bad members for not deserving the reward the group (nevertheless) has won. "In essence," writes Makarenko, this is a form of acting precisely on the individual [*vozdeistvie na lichnost'*], but the [discursive] formulation parallels this essence. In real terms we deal with the individual but claim that we do not have anything to do with it."[123]

Soviet pedagogy, following Makarenko, also dubbed this method of parallel development of the collective and the individual as a method of *avansirovanie lichnosti cherez kollektiv*, that is, "advancing the individual through the *kollektiv*," with the verb having the same meaning as in "advancing money." *Lichnost'* is advanced not in the sense that it is developed, but in the sense that it is allocated, and allocated to a single person in a very curious form—as an advance, a prepayment for work yet to be done. It is allocated to a single body that may now work in a disciplined manner to repay this initial advance. Makarenko also calls his method "cultivating a single individual" (*kul'tivirovat' otdel'nuiu lichnost'*), with the same sense as "cultivating plants," implying an agricultural metaphor related to Cicero's *cultura animi*.[124] Perhaps we should not mix metaphors, but if we do, a general picture of the following kind emerges: pedagogues allocate *lichnost'* first, investing or positioning it—sowing it—in the collective field and then help it grow and flourish there.

This very strange method of cultivation has two aspects. First, Makarenko lays bare the contradictory mechanism of cultivation: the discourse is overtly collectivist, while the underlying aim of the educational practice is the allocation and perfection of individuals. "Collectivist individuals" thus become possible: they espouse collectivist values and repeat the statements of collectivist discourse in which they had been socialized, while in practice they act individually in order to support this collectivism in discourse. And the method prepares individuals for the schizophrenic split, registered by students of Soviet society: in public one is overtly collectivist, but in the security of private life, where the public fails to interfere, one may become an unconstrained egoist.[125]

---

123. Makarenko 5:164. The original text in Russian is *na samom dele my imeem delo s lichnostiu, no utverzhdaem chto do lichnosti nam net nikakogo dela*.

124. Makarenko 5:170.

125. As Stephen White perceptively stated, the visible obedient participant in Communist rituals and the invisible truth-teller and gain-seeker share the same body, but it is not obvious what part of the double individual is more "real." A Soviet citizen keeps oscillating between the two, seemingly real in both incarnations (see his *Political Culture and Soviet Politics* [New York: St. Martin's Press, 1979], 111).

The second aspect is that the method hardly applies to individual plants: the pedagogical effort directed to a specific individual always goes through the mediation of the group; cultivating every single individual occurs by means of mass cultivation. Even in watering specific plants or uprooting specific weeds, the agent that will do it is the primary group: "We officially touched the individual [*individualnost'*] only through the primary *kollektiv*. Such was our *instrumentarium*, and in practice we always had a particular colonist in mind."[126]

In terms of practical advice, Makarenko suggests very few forms of cultivating the individual, which is surprising given the detailed description of methods of *kollektiv*-building. His examples of "individual work" include only analysis of the *kollektiv* by itself, and a small number of disciplinary narratives. None of these stories demonstrates anything close to the agricultural metaphor of the cultivation of personality, or even to the economic metaphor of its advance allocation; rather, these stories present instances of allocation to the collective of different degrees of the right to correct and punish the culpable individual. "Advancing the individual through the *kollektiv*" or its "cultivation" becomes a simple process of designating the atom to be straightened out by a group, plus the subsequent correction itself, and nothing else.

The process of group-enforced correction follows each round of the collective self-analysis of Makarenko's colony, a further perfection of self-criticism as performed by the Party cells. The council of commanders regularly meets and compiles lists of colonists according to four categories of demonstrated zeal: *aktiv*, "reserve," *passiv*, and "swamp."[127] After assigning them, the activists try to influence the "most backward," that is, members of the swamp, that is, to "activate" them by means of a veiled threat: "We say to Petrov, 'You are in the swamp,' and we try to activate him. Some time passes, and he distinguishes himself in something [*sebia proiavil*], gets interested, distinguishes himself again, and he transfers to the *passiv* or to the reserve."[128] The exact term, we notice, is *proiavit' sebia* once

---

This oscillation is also nicely captured in the concept of "modal schizophrenia" that Katerina Clark ascribes to the literature of Socialist Realism (*The Soviet Novel*, 37).

126. Makarenko 5:170.

127. Indeed, this is a more sophisticated version of the usual practice of choosing the names of the best members of the *kollektiv* to be included in the publicly displayed "red list of honor" (*doska pocheta*), or the worst into the "black list of dishonor." Makarenko's colony assigned a category to each colonist, hence the need for intermediary designations.

128. Makarenko 5:173.

again: under group pressure, Petrov has to reveal himself after the collective objectifies him as a slacker, or as a potential saboteur. He has to do something about this objectification, about this dangerous self that the collective ascribed to him; thus, he reveals another self to the public, by distinguishing himself through enthusiastic work effort. Thus, the advancement of *lichnost'* first allocates a personal definition to a member of a group who thus becomes singled out—or, better, individuated. After the member changes the manifest behavior, suggesting by this move a change of *lichnost'*, the group allocates a different definition.

Makarenko furnishes the following short narrative as an example of work on the individual (*individual'naia rabota*) proper.

> I learn that a boy has offended a girl, and I know that my reprimanding lectures are of no use. Thus I write a note to him—"to come to my office at 11 P.M."—and send it by a "communication technician," not saying anything except that he should deliver it to X. He will tell X everything anyway, after that the detachment will shame him [*razdelaet*]; he will come at 11 very upset; I will say to him: "Have you understood?—You may go." [129]

A less gentle method involved inviting the whole detachment to a tea party in Makarenko's office, and not mentioning the offense that led to this invitation: "during this conversation, while sipping cups of tea and joking, communards are thinking about who might be to blame." [130] After the party the communards return to the sleeping ward and say, "Everything turned out to be fine, X, but see how you let us down." After a while Makarenko would invite the detachment for a tea party once again. This time chats over tea would be really joyful, as the communards would proudly report that they had spotted the problem and had fixed it. In serious cases, open accusations of individuals were practiced: Makarenko would get the transgressor together with a group of activists and openly state the accusation, while the activists would finish the job of shaming: "He does not care about what I say, but . . . he listens to his comrades." [131]

The gradations of "advancing the individual through the collective"

---

129. Makarenko 5:182.

130. The basic mechanism of Russian culture is set up in operation here: first, the group asks the familiar question *Kto vinovat?* [Who is to blame? (the title of the famous novel by Herzen)]; then it deliberates on the question *Chto delat'?* [What is to be done? (the title of both Chernyshevsky's and Lenin's revolutionary classics)].

131. Makarenko 5:182–184.

reflect the simple logic of increasing pressure by degrees: a pedagogue may call an individual to come to his office without summoning the collective, and the collective will do its educative job on its own; a pedagogue summons all without telling the collective who is to blame (as a result of this, the group shaming of the transgressor is more intense, since members of the collective lose their personal time, while the misdeed also threatens the position of the group in competition with other collectives); a transgressor is clearly designated by the pedagogue in the presence of the shaming collective.

The culmination, an acute conflict between a resisting individual and a shaming group, is a situation that Makarenko called "the explosion" (*vzryv*). The pedagogue polarizes and strains relations between an individual and a collective to such an extent that a sudden "conversion" of individual to group-shared values occurs.[132] An excerpt describing "the explosion" appeared in the first edition of *The Pedagogic Poem* but was then withdrawn from later editions by Makarenko himself, perhaps because other outcomes to such conflict had proved possible. Bowen mentions one example that startled him as a commentator who was usually predisposed favorably to Makarenko. A communard named Chobot committed suicide after the colonists and then Makarenko had forbidden his marriage to Natasha, a fellow communard. The colonists did not resent this suicide at all. Chobot was an incorrigible individualist who often demonstrated his defiance of the *kollektiv*. "The colony," comments Bowen, "was relieved at getting rid of what was becoming an embarrassment to them."[133] However, this nonchalant incitement to suicide itself became an embarrassment for later generations of Soviet teachers. Those who evaluated the transferability of Makarenko's methods in the early 1980s clearly got rid of "the explosion," because, in their words, its successful execution required the "personal talents" of Makarenko.[134]

132. Makarenko 5:507, also 231 and 253.
133. Bowen, *Soviet Education*, 101.
134. Kurakin, Liimets, and Novikova, *Kollektiv i lichnost' shkol'nika*, 58. At the end of the section on work on the individual Makarenko describes a situation that required his "talents"; he could not recommend it to every follower but admitted that he had practiced it. Once a *kollektiv* was after the victim, and stopping it became essential, Makarenko would lie as the last resort in order to escape turning the lamb over to the wolves. He would say at the colonists' assembly: "She did not steal; I can see it in her eyes" and use his personal authority to save the potential victim. When the colonist came to thank him personally afterwards, he would say: "Why are you thanking me, when you are a thief?" This covert threat of repeating the awful group-shaming procedure, mentions Makarenko, worked wonders: "It gave her

Collective expulsion and sacrifice, thus, seem to function as the ultimate means of individuation in Makarenko's advancement of the person, as they functioned in the self-criticism sessions of 1937.[135] A milder version, a separation from the *kollektiv*, figures in his arrangement of other techniques of punishment. Individual communards who were full members of the commune could be punished only by "arrest," a measure that had no value beyond temporary separation from the *kollektiv*. "A man feels contrition for the fact that he was condemned by the *kollektiv*, knowing that he did wrong, that is, there is no dejection in punishment, but just a feeling of disengagement from the *kollektiv*." Arrested individuals had to spend up to ten hours in Makarenko's office. Makarenko went about his business, while the communards had to organize their own arrest themselves, that is, stay in the office for all the assigned time and police themselves. They could talk with Makarenko about the weather or production plans but never about the reason for their arrest. An arrest became "an honorable duty," since by performing a ritual of symbolic separation the member restored the *kollektiv*'s challenged unity through self-subjugation to the group ritual.

Of course, along with group pressure hierarchical surveillance plays an additional role in bringing up the colonists. In order to apportion the application of group pressure to a given individual correctly, Makarenko compiled personal files on each colonist. Makarenko burned old files accompanying the referred individuals that were sent to him by courts and other punitive bodies. He considered these to be of no use, because the strength of the transformative experience of life in the *kollektiv* did not depend on

---

over to me completely as the *pedagogical object*" (Makarenko 5:186). Perhaps here is the essence of his system: using the threat of group violence against a transgressor in order to make each single individual a docile object. People become *ob-jects* in the etymological sense of this word, thrown away and out in front of the group, which stands against them as a crowd of spectators. Such is the fate of the Soviet individual.

135. I found no satisfactory theory of sacrifice that would suit Soviet experience. Rene Girard, *Violence and the Sacred*, trans. Patrick Gregory (Baltimore: Johns Hopkins University Press, 1977) is very suggestive—that the essence of scapegoating lies in finding an acceptable victim who will not or cannot retaliate and that the act of sacrifice stops the bloody communal feud—but it falls short in the Soviet case. Rather, the Soviet group gives out its members for sacrifice in order to satisfy the bloodthirsty interests of the wider society and thus prevent the extermination of the group as a whole. In the collective correction episodes described above, the objects of this pent-up violence are individuals who dare to challenge the group's dearly earned place in that bloodthirsty society. Perhaps the same mechanisms operate in those empires based on brutal conquest and periodic collections of ransom.

the prehistory of the colonist.[136] Instead, he started a new file, one that contained nothing but information on the transgressions against law and order within the colony.[137] At the end of each day, an elder from each study class submitted a disciplinary report on the behavior of members of each detachment. A joint list of transgressors of that day was compiled by the pedagogue on duty and passed on to Makarenko. He distributed this information to the respective personal files and added his personal comments, if he had any. In this manner, *lichnosti*—as slots for the files in Makarenko's card catalogue—were constructed. In the words of one of the later commentators, Makarenko used to say: "How can one direct two hundred children without a card file? This is uncultured."[138] But he did not emphasize this personal card file and, in line with his doctrine of "parallel action," rarely mentioned it in his novels or pedagogical writings. The colonists may have not known about it at all. They came to know who they were through a different procedure, not by reading their files, but by asking the primary group to define them, for example, by looking at the blackboard where the results of the self-analysis of the *kollektiv* were presented every week.

Vinogradova has also described another "moving" way to figure out who one was: a specific ritual of admission into the *kollektiv* took place when new entrants appeared. During the ritual a commander introduced the novice to a detachment and then introduced each member to the novice, by giving a short description of each. "He should briefly state all the truth as to what he thinks about each one. To deceive and to withhold all truth is impossible for the commander." As a result of this truth-telling exercise, all are "very excited and attentive" and "await with impatience" the commander's description. The scope of this description followed what the commander had to observe in the novice's comportment in order to be able to describe her or him, should the next introductory round happen soon: the commander "should know what air a person breathes, whom he befriends, his habits, his level of [personality] development, his capacities, how he studies, what

136. No more "genealogy of social origin," we might say.
137. Entering new life was also marked by a specific rite of passage. The communards sent to recruit new entrants to the colony among numerous street waifs and railroad hoboes staged a ritual burning of the old clothes of the new recruits on arrival to the colony—to signify the start of a new life for the unsuspecting waifs who had hoped simply for a couple of days' food and lodging. The new entrants were then led through the shower and given new clean military-style clothes (which the tastes of the day judged beautiful).
138. Vinogradova, "Voprosy oranizatsii obshchego obrazovaniia," 254.

he reads, where and how he works, in what leisure circles he participates." The commander follows the novice everywhere: "in the cinema, in the bath, in the theater."[139] When this comprehensive understanding of the everyday comportment of each colonist thus emerges into the open during the admittance of the next novice into the detachment, everyone has a chance to check what has changed by listening to the commander's brief description of each individual.

On the basis of this information, a council of commanders constructs regular lists of the "analysis of the *kollektiv*." By listening to external judgment authorized by the *kollektiv*, individuals know who they are; and commanders who are not in sync with the detachment's opinion will not be elected or reelected. The group's opinion of each individual is objectified in the commander's description, which then becomes solid knowledge for future judgment and assessment. The description creates an individual as an object of public knowledge and offers the only knowledge of the self available to the person who has not learned the practices of solitary self-knowing, like introspection, or confession in diaries or private letters. The *lichnost'* that emerges depends wholly on the existence of the *kollektiv*. If the *kollektiv* that evaluates the given individual dissolves, she or he will never know this "true" self, since there will be nobody to pronounce the truth on it.

Thus the creation of *lichnost'* first of all requires the creation of the *kollektiv*. As Makarenko stressed, they are bound to emerge simultaneously; but the creation of the group deliberating on the personal features of the individuals comprising it is the founding move that sets this two-level machinery going. The critical importance of its two-level process emerged clearly in places that tried repeating Soviet successes or in marginal parts of the USSR itself, where the problem of individualization of the populace arose on the agenda rather late. In Vietnam, for example, socialist competition between workers' collectives was instrumental in bringing about the "socialist type of individual," boasted a Vietnamese dissertation on the importance of the Soviet model. Particularly, the worker collective's competition during the war, the role of the army collectives as subjects of education, and the postwar role of the collectives of the Union of Vietnamese Women (10 million members, created in the summer of 1976) turned out to be decisive in the formation of the new type of the individual.[140]

---

139. Ibid., 248.
140. Chan Van Chyong, "Ispol'zovanie istoricheskogo opyta KPSS po formirovaniiu lichnosti sotsialisticheskogo tipa v sovremennykh usloviiakh vo Vietname"

In order to form the socialist individual over the course of a single generation in the Soviet far north, certain "difficulties" had to be overcome. To set up "labor collectives" among the northern nomadic tribes, elements of kinship structures were regrouped to create Soviet institutions: "production cooperatives," "kinship Soviets," and Soviet courts based on customary law were created. They allowed "tying the existing traditions and habits to the formation of the socialist type of individual." Apparently, this transformation only entailed consolidating disparate kinship groups into bigger entities and instigating mechanisms of group discussions of single individuals, once the newly set Soviet production and government units had to gather for normal working routine, "normal" meaning these discussions.[141] A 1992 book dealing with standard Soviet solutions to the problems of "forming a *lichnost'* " describes the Party's efforts in the 1960s–80s to instigate better types of *kollektivy* and collective activities fostering more developed *lichnosti* and mentions the practices of individual self-perfection only in the case of "the individualization of leisure activities."[142]

Makarenko's techniques that aimed at objectifying an individual by means of group pressure corresponded to the general matrix of Soviet power. He stressed the crucial point: if one forms a *kollektiv*, one also forms a specific individual; engendering *kollektiv* and *lichnost'* are two sides of the same coin. And though some latter-day reformers took Makarenko's advice to heart and followed it closely, the broader Soviet society in his days moved along the lines of the formation of the Soviet individual, parallel to what Makarenko proposed but largely independent of his influence, by leaps and jumps, by trial and error, through the efforts of multiple agencies

---

[Use of the CPSU's historical experience in the formation of the socialist individual in contemporary Vietnam] (abstract, Candidate of Science diss., Plekhanov Institute of National Economy, Moscow, 1987).

141. V. S. Lukovtsev, "Formirovanie novogo tipa lichnosti v usloviiakh perekhoda narodnostei severa ot patriarkhal'no-rodovogo stroiia k sotsializmu" [Formation of the new type of individual during the northern people's transition from patriarchal-kinship mode to socialism] (abstract, diss., Moscow Higher Party School of the Central Committee, 1975). On the *kollektiv* among the peoples of the far north, see David Anderson, "Bringing Civil Society to an Uncivilized Place: Citizenship Regimes in Russia's Arctic Frontier," in *Civil Society*, ed. Chris Hann and Elizabeth Dunn (London: Routledge, 1996). For a general overview see Yuri Slezkine, *Arctic Mirrors* (Ithaca: Cornell University Press, 1994).

142. L. S. Iakovlev, *Stanovlenie lichnosti: opyt, problemy (60e–80e gody).* [Development of the person: experience, problems (1960s–80s)] (Saratov: Saratov University Press, 1992). The book seems to have been finished before August 1991, as the Party is sympathetically described as an actor that makes mistakes, its socialist course being basically correct.

and diverse activists. In the beginning of this chapter we described the most important process in this respect: individuation as it happened during the purges and self-criticism sessions of the 1930s. Makarenko provided a succinct formulation of this generic movement that happened not only in his colony but in the broader society as well.

THE MEANS OF INDIVIDUATION: *OBLICHENIE* AS A PRACTICE

As a basic mechanism of Soviet individuation, the *kollektiv's* deliberation about the deeds of its members in order to ascertain their individual inner qualities was, I contend, so obvious to many and so readily adopted because this self-revelation as proposed by the Bolsheviks was predicated on an age-old Russian practice. This was the practice of *oblichenie*, a practice of the Orthodox Christian Church for publicizing sins and accusing the sinners. Having been directed toward a new object called *lichnost'*, the recast practice was not simply replicated, but altered; yet the alterations involved no radical break with the past.

Oblichit' pervades the discourse of the purges together with *proiavit' sebia*, but if the latter constituted the intended result of the purge process, the former was the means. At that time, *oblichit'* had the dominant meaning "to accuse" or "to condemn." Strictly speaking, *oblichit'* was the central practice of Soviet self-criticism. When self-criticism merged with the practice of purging in the deadly configuration of 1937, *oblichenie* (a noun from the verb *oblichit'*) became the focal practice of this configuration. Before it came to be institutionalized in the purges, however, *oblichenie* had been most visibly represented among the insurrectionary practices inherited by the Bolsheviks from the Russian revolutionaries of the 1860s and 1870s who were their direct predecessors. Rather than stress doctrinal and biographical continuities, let us focus only on the practical continuity relevant to our study. With their attention to *oblichitel'naia proza*, a genre of critical secular literature that appeared after the Crimean War of 1853–56 and that sought to reveal the crimes of the government, the radicals supplied Lenin with an obvious means of revolutionary activity.[143] In 1902 Lenin picked up the practice of *oblichenie*, already in the stock of revolutionary techniques available at the time, and made it the central practice of Bolshevik tactics.

In his classic pamphlet *What Is To Be Done?*, echoing the title of Cherny-

---

143. See, Pisarev, "Realisty," 3:8. Next to this "denouncing prose" also existed "denouncing poetry."

shevsky's revolutionary novel, Lenin attempted to effect a certain transformation of the practice of *oblichenie* to suit Bolshevik aims. First, *oblichenie* was to stop being the elevated practice of a few revolutionary intellectuals and become a widespread activity of simple Russian folk, and of workers in particular. They, asserted Lenin, were already capable of revealing injustices in their local workers' newspapers. The task was only to endow these spontaneous revelations with a political quality, that is, to link revelations of injustices at a given factory or in a given governmental office to each other as parts of the general system of oppression and exploitation, by giving them a doctrinal Marxist interpretation. The most urgent task of the Bolshevik Party was to organize political revelations (*politicheskie oblicheniia*), wrote Lenin in the third chapter of his manifesto, comparing an old and new tactic in the workers' movement:

> Why do the Russian workers still manifest little revolutionary activity? . . . We must blame ourselves, our lagging behind the mass movement, for still being unable to organize sufficiently wide, striking, and rapid revelations [*oblicheniia*] of all the shameful outrages. When we do that (and we must and can do it), the most backward worker will understand or will feel, that the students and religious sects, the peasants and the authors are being abused and outraged by the same dark forces that are oppressing and crushing him at every step of his life. . . . As yet we have done very little, almost nothing to bring before the working masses prompt revelations [*oblicheniia*] on all possible issues.[144]

Before 1917 the Bolsheviks had difficulties in carrying out this plan, but by the end of the first tumultuous years of the Revolution and the Civil War *oblichenie* was already part of the repertoire of numerous revolutionary activists. Thus, Trotsky's usage suggested that the letters from the worker-correspondents to the press were instances of familiar prerevolutionary "public revelations" (*publichnye oblicheniia*), while the self-criticism campaign of 1928 was pervaded by this term.[145] One of the industrialists, speaking at the June 1928 Central Control Commission plenum that dealt with self-criticism, proposed publishing only those "accusatory materials" (*oblichitel'nye materialy*) that had been approved by the workers' meetings and thereby acquired the status of truth, as opposed to unfounded libel.[146] Other commentators from that period would allege that bosses had already

144. V. I. Lenin, "What Is to Be Done?" (1902), in his *Collected Works* (Moscow: Progress, 1964), 4:414, translation modified.
145. Trotsky, *Problems of Everyday Life*, 65.
146. *III Plenum/28*, 41.

worked out their own ways of escaping the consequences of the workers' revelations. For example, some of them, "accused of misdeeds" (*oblichennye v prostupkah*) would represent the revealed deficiencies as the fault of the whole enterprise rather than their personal fault.[147]

In the mid-1930s the practice of "self-criticism" was reinvigorated, as *oblichenie* was applied not only to management, but to anyone who could be taken for a potential wrecker or spy. As already mentioned, the *oblichenie* that figured so heavily in the self-criticism campaigns is obviously directly linked to the currently dominant meaning of the word: "to expose wrongs or misdeeds" or "to accuse of having sinful or incriminating qualities." Viewed from a different angle, however, the same practice reveals its other aspect that mattered so much in the Stalinist intensification of individuation. Indeed, *oblichit'* also has a different meaning, that is, "to expose, to reveal." Perhaps, nobody captured this meaning more felicitously than Vladimir Dal' in an example of nineteenth-century usage in his famous *Dictionary of the Living Russian Language:* "Deeds, and not words, reveal the man, indicate his real face and his real person."[148] This aspect of exposure, of publicizing the self is very close to the Stalinist insistence on revealing the real person by his or her deeds. In this sense, the word *oblichenie* may be said to almost literally mean "en-personation" (*ob-lichenie*), the endowment of someone with *litso* (face or juridical person) or *lichnost'* (personality).[149]

147. Ingulov, *Samokritika i praktika ee provedeniia*, 31.

148. In Russian, *Dela, a ne slova, oblichaiut cheloveka, pokazyvaiut podlinnoe litso i lichnost' ego* (Vladimir Dal', *Tolkovyi slovar' zhivago velikorusskago iazyka* [Dictionary of the living Russian language (1859)], 5th ed. [Moscow: Russkii Iazyk, 1980], 3:596).

149. Whereas the English prefix *re-* usually refers to action repeated or pointed back, the prefix *ob-* in Russian has a different meaning: it designates (1) transformation, process of becoming something; (2) action applied to entire surface of object or to series of objects; (3) indicating action or motion about an object (B. O. Unbegaun, ed., *Oxford Russian-English Dictionary* [Oxford: Clarendon, 1984])—none has a direct tie with action pointed back. Hence translating *ob-lichenie* as "de-masking," in a false analogy with *re-velare*, is unwarranted. *Slovar'* gives nine meanings of *ob-*, none of which directly mean retraction. Tseitlin, *Staroslavianskii slovar'*, in the commentary on the early Slavonic word *oblichie*, proposes to connect it with Russian or Czech *obraz* (image; in Greek *eikon, morphon*), which etymologically comes from *ob-rezati*, to "cut by sides," to "put into cut form." Also, a medieval Russian word, *oblichie*—both a pagan mask and a human face or external appearance—is about endowment with the mask, rather than about un- or demasking. Barkhudarov (ed., *Slovar' russkogo*, 79) gives a telling example from 12th-century usage: "It is not appropriate for men to dress up in women's clothes, nor to play in masks [*oblichiia* in Russian, *prosopeia* in Greek, *persona* in Latin].

Consider, for example, the following episode. An autobiography of the shock worker Nikita Izotov, *My Life—My Work*, published in 1934, and one of the first in its genre, merited a special supplement.[150] Pasted on the inside of the back cover of the book was an exact copy of the front page of the newspaper *Mechanized Mine* of April 4, 1933, entirely devoted to Izotov undergoing the purge. The narrative informs us that the hall was filled to the limit because everybody wanted to know the secrets of Izotov's heroism. After he recounted his biography, questions about his current activities were posed from the presidium and from the hall. Izotov answered them, giving details about the secrets of his mastery. Then his disciples spoke about their teacher. In the end the Party secretary spoke, summing up the meeting and characterizing Izotov as "a teacher and leader," and gave Izotov back his Party card to the sound of the audience's applause. Now, the constitutive element of this ritual, *oblichenie* as a publicizing of a heroic self, is easy to see. But the really curious detail is the fact that Izotov's autobiographical account had to be published together with this insert carrying a public seal of approval of Izotov's *lichnost'*; his individuality may have not emerged simply by means of his account, it had to be supported by the purge evidence.

Oblichenie as a publicizing of the self became so common in Soviet culture that its role as the shared background for actors is easy to overlook. For example, few authors, if any, notice the individualizing component in the atrocious purge rituals, as demonstrated by the insert of the Izotov book. If 17 percent of the Party members were expelled in the most extensive universal purge of 1933–34 and 6.6 percent were demoted to the lower status of "sympathizers," 76.4 percent or approximately 850,000 of them were affirmed (even if only temporarily) as possessing a revolutionary self.[151] Of even more significance is the fact that both the affirmed and the expelled—the elect and the reprobate, to use the language of a different epoch and a different culture—were subjected to the procedure for publicizing their selves.

THE STRUCTURE OF *OBLICHENIE*

Let us now retrace the history of the word *oblichenie*, which will allow us to see the relevant distinctions of Soviet life in a clearer light. This term has

---

Ob-lichenie is thus about putting the mask or image on, rather than about taking the mask off.

150. Nikita Izotov, *Moia zhizn'—moia rabota* [My life—my work] (Kharkov, 1934).

151. Figures from *XVII Steno/34*, 287.

an awesome conceptual history: it entered the Russian language very early with Biblical translations and church books, and the complicated pattern of its early meanings may be represented as follows.[152] Church Slavonic had two verbs, *oblichati* and *oblichiti* (in imperfective and perfective form), which in Russian translations of the Bible and of church texts were most frequently employed to translate three Greek terms: the verbs *paradeigmatidzo, demosieuo,* and *elendzo.*[153]

Paradeigmatidzo meant "to point out somebody as a bad, shameful example," or "to make somebody an object of public ridicule"; the latter usage being more characteristic of the New Testament. The obvious example of usage comes in the Russian translation of Matthew 1:19: "And her husband, Joseph, . . . unwilling to put her to shame, resolved to send her away quietly . . . ," where the Russian *oblichati* is used to translate the Greek *paradeigmatisai.* Another example, from the eleventh-century code of Prince Iaroslav, reads: "If he is afraid to reveal his sins, on the Last Day he will have to reveal himself not in front of one or two people, but in front of all the watching universe" (*oblichaet sebia* translating *paradeigmatidzetai*). *Demosieuo* was related to the word *demos* (people) and had a straightforward connotation of publicness. Its meanings include "to convert into public property," "to make accessible to everyone," "to popularize." The relevant examples of Russian translations include a quotation from the writings of Saint Gregory of Nazianzus: "revealing the spirit of this canon" (*oblichaia* translating *demosieuo*). Another example comes from *Kormchaia,* a Russian compilation of Byzantine canons and secular laws, where a paragraph in the canons adopted by the Council of Carthage mentions the characteristic usage "revealed to everybody" (*vsem chelovekom oblichivshiu* translating *demosieusavtos*). The Latin version, given by Sreznevsky, is *publicante.*

---

152. All the examples of usage in the following exposition in this section come from the articles on *oblichiti* and *oblichati* in I. I. Sreznevsky, *Materialy dlia slovaria drevne-russkago iazyka po pismennym pamiatnikam* [Materials for the dictionary of the ancient Russian language according to written sources] (St. Petersburg, 1893–1912); and Barkhudarov, ed., *Slovar' russkogo.* Some translations also mention corresponding Latin translations of the same terms, which are very useful for our study.

153. There is a complication with the first meaning of *oblichiti* usually given as "to shape into form," "to give an image," which at least in one example is a translation of the Greek *exeikonismenon,* coming from *eikon,* image (an interesting anomaly that requires further exploration). A noun *oblichie* translated Greek *eikon* in the sense of "similitude," "depiction," and *idea/eidos* in the sense of "image, " "appearance."

Elendzo did not necessarily connote publicness but simply meant "to accuse somebody," "to scold somebody," "to criticize." It directly implied a negative evaluation of the person, a criticism of sins and misdeeds. Examples of usage include the famous dictum from Matthew 18:15: "If your brother sins against you, go and tell him his fault, between you and him alone" (*oblichi—elendzon auton*). Among numerous others the most illuminating for an English reader would be those that have Latin versions given. A quotation from Patericon of Synai says "neither shame, nor accuse" (*ni sramiti, ni oblichati* in Russian, *ni pudefacere, ni arguere* in Latin; the relevant last verb is *auton elendzai* in Greek). The hagiography of Saint Alexander says: "Even a friend will not accuse him" (*oblichit* in Russian, *accusaretur* in Latin).

At first this maze of meanings looks unpromising. But there is some logic to it. *Paradeigmatidzo* comes closest to the Russian *oblichiti/oblichati*, insofar as it carries both a connotation of publicness (shared with *demosieuo*) and a connotation of making an accusation (shared with *elendzo*). The two remaining Greek verbs polarize these two connotations. Therefore, in order to accentuate the distinction we drop the most fruitful verb, *paradeigmatidzo*, and retain the other two to signify their respective opposed connotations. Referring to *oblichenie* in the sense of *demosieuo*, we stress its aspect of publicness, and in the sense of *elendzo* we stress the interchange between a critic and the object of criticism. This fine distinction—*oblichenie* as making public versus *oblichenie* as criticism—helps us analyze historical sources.

For example, let us take a look at relevant examples of usage from the late sixteenth and early seventeenth centuries, using Gruzberg's historical lexicon.[154] *Oblichenie* in the sense of the criticism of sins seems to predominate. Thus, Prince Andrei Kurbsky writes to Ivan the Terrible: "You . . .

154. See A. A. Gruzberg, *Chastotnyi slovar' russkogo iazyka vtoroi poloviny XVI—nachala XVII veka.* [Frequency dictionary of the Russian language, late 16th–early 17th centuries] (Perm, 1974). I am grateful to Claudio Ingerflomm for suggesting this lexicon to me and follow Gruzberg's cites of sources (interested readers may wish to check the latest editions of some works).
The lexicon also supplies data on frequency of recorded usage, drawing on 27 major written works from the period to provide examples of the standard meanings at that time. In these texts the words (noun-agent) *oblichitel'* or *oblichnik* appear 2 times each; (noun-process) *oblichenie* is used 24 times, (imperfective form of vb.) *oblichati* 37 times, and (perfective form) *oblichiti* 43 times. This is a rather frequent use given the highly doctrinal origin of the word; in comparison, *obvinit'* (to accuse) is mentioned only 6 times, *ukoriat'* (to reproach)—17, and such most widely used word as *pokazat'* (to show)—153 times.

were not ashamed of God's punishment and exposure of [your] wrongs" (*oblicheniia*) and a little later adds, "only your conscience cries out at you and convicts you [*oblichaiushcha*] for your sinful deeds and incalculable blood-letting." [155] Ivan responds in turn by invoking the normative biblical stance on revelations, saying that "prophets predicted God's words and revealed (*oblichaiushche*) the sins and the violations of canons." [156] Apparently, he sees himself doing the same when he writes about the alleged innocence of his executed enemies: "Is it that they may not be revealed (*ikh oblichit'*) in their wrongs, . . . whatever they have done?" [157] In *Stoglav*, a collection of regulations on ecclesiastical life adopted under Ivan, we also find a doctrinal statement on exposing heresies: "Those people who start teaching others [using heretical books] and are later revealed (*oblicheny*) in that activity, should be excommunicated by the bishops according to holy canons." [158]

Later sources repeat the stress on the divine function of revealing sins, as when "God had wished to convict [*oblichiti*] his [the usurper Boris Godunov's] insolence." [159] At certain moments, this function can be taken over by the metropolitans (false Dmitrii "chased the metropolitan Kirill out of Rostov, because he feared his exposures" [*oblicheniia*]) [160] or even by the lower clergy. Thus we learn about "traitors to God and brigands, who, having observed the sternness of monks," were unable "to withstand their exposures (*oblichenie*)." [161]

The second aspect of the practice of *oblichenie*—publicizing something, bringing it into the open—can also be illustrated by a number of examples. Usually these examples depict the revelation of some negative feature of a person or of a general condition of existence. Thus, Ivan writes that the "insatiable anger and unrelenting mind" of his enemies revealed itself

155. *Sochineniia kniazia Kurbskogo* [Works of Prince Kurbsky], Russkaia istoricheskaia biblioteka [Russian historical library] 1, no. 31 (St. Petersburg, 1914), 146, 152.

156. *Poslaniia Ivana Groznogo* [Epistles of Ivan the Terrible] (Moscow-Leningrad: Akademiia Nauk SSSR, 1951), 200.

157. Ibid., 31.

158. *Stoglav* (Kazan', 1862), 186.

159. *Vremennik Ivana Timofeeva* [A chronicle of Ivan Timofeev], Russkaia istoricheskaia biblioteka 13, no. 1 (Leningrad, 1925), 298.

160. "Piskarevsky letopisets'" [Piskarevsky chronicler], in *Materialy po istorii SSSR*, vol. 2, *Dokumenty po istorii XV–XVII vekov* [Materials on the history of the USSR, vol. 2, Documents of 15th–17th centuries] (Moscow, 1955), 117.

161. *Inoe skazanie* [The other chronicle], Russkaia istoricheskaia biblioteka 13, no. 1 (Leningrad, 1925), 100.

(*oblichisia*), and they were executed according to their guilt.[162] Addressing Kurbsky directly, he rejects the prince's argument that the czar himself had started a fire in the Kremlin, takes this argument as a sign of Kurbsky's sinister mind, and concludes: "In all this your treason is revealed (*oblichaetsia*)."[163] The process of publicizing is obvious, though what gets publicized is morally reprehensible. Here and in other examples cited in Gruzberg, revealed qualities include "untruth," "ugliness," "treason," "anger," "insolence," "scheming." Gruzberg offers no instances of usage where a positive quality would be revealed. We have to rely on Sreznevsky to claim that it was not absent altogether. For example, an indigenous Russian collection of texts from the fourteenth century mentions the following: "Revealing (*oblichaia*) the depths of the heart."[164]

Frequently, the rigid distinction between *oblichenie* as criticism and *oblichenie* as publicizing seems to be mostly a convenient analytical tool, since many examples combine instances of both, as in the following passage:

> He [false Dmitrii] ordered them to be executed by diverse tortures, but they, not afraid of tortures, exposed his wrongs (*oblichashe*) in front of all the people. And he ordered that their joints . . . be hacked with an ax, that others have their legs and hands cut off, and that some be put into boiling tar and expelled from the city. But they shouted and revealed (*oblichashe*) in front of all people that he was a true thief, a servant of the boyars' Elagin children, the son of a shoemaker. Aren't they martyrs, aren't they saints? And in older times the martyrs suffered under their torturers in the same way.[165]

This chronicle description of the heroic feat of *oblichenie* of the false czar depicts martyrs who accused the alleged czar of being an impostor (*oblichenie* as criticism); thus, they simultaneously publicly revealed his true essence (*oblichenie* as publicizing). Furthermore, in doing so they revealed themselves as heroes (*oblichenie* also, but of a different kind, it involves publicizing themselves). Yet the fact that we need to mention the self-publicizing aspects of the practice of *oblichenie* in this example points to a larger trend: in the course of Russian history the publicizing aspect of *oblichenie* was gradually becoming obscured by the prevalence of *oblichenie* conceived as criticism. Perhaps medieval and then modern Russia was more concerned with publicizing negative rather than positive features.

162. *Poslaniia Ivana Groznogo*, 42.
163. Ibid., 36.
164. Sreznevsky, *Materialy*, article on *oblichati*, col. 521.
165. "Piskarevsky letopisets'," 130.

THE HISTORY OF *OBLICHENIE*

The farther back into Russian history we go, the more stress on publicizing aspects of *oblichenie* we encounter. For example, *oblichiti* in the early Russian legal codes meant "to publicize a sin" and was often related to ecclesiastical authorities. Thus, an extensive version of the code of Prince Iaroslav says: "If a girl engages in sexual intercourse or becomes pregnant [while she still lives] with her father or mother, while she is a widow, after having found [her] out [*oblichivshe*], put her in a church house."[166] Now, this is a curious *oblichenie*. The standard modern commentary in the most recent academic edition of this code says that "in order to enforce the sanction, one needs *oblichenie*. This term usually designated not the court proceedings, but the public disclosure of a misdeed."[167] However, even if this disclosure was not related to secular courts, it may have been related to the proceedings of ecclesiastical courts, since the commentator supports his claim by citing the 34th canon rule of Saint Basil the Great: "Our fathers have ruled not to publicize [*oblichati*] adulterous wives."[168] It seems likely that *oblichenie*—as the first one in the triad reveal-admonish-excommunicate that lay at the foundation of canon law—was taken as a necessary ecclesiastical routine.

A little later (paragraph 36 in modern demarcation) the code of Iaroslav brings up *oblichenie* as a public rite once again: "If the wife steals from her husband, and she is exposed [*oblichiti*], then the metropolitan gets three *grivnas* [an ancient monetary unit] and the husband punishes her, but there is no divorce." The commentary tries to explain the puzzling payment to the metropolitan, since in marriage affairs the husband was the sole authority: "Apparently it was tied to the suggested exposure [*oblichenie*] of the wife, that is, to publicizing her misdeeds."[169] If indeed the metropolitan received payments for *oblichenie*, then, by implication, it becomes part of his church services and duties. Therefore, it seems that this paragraph simply deals with yet another instance of the application of church canons.

---

166. "Ustav kniazia Iaroslava" [Code of Prince Iaroslav], in *Rossiiskoe zakonodatel'stvo X–XX vekov*, vol. 1, *Zakonodatel'stvo drevnei Rusi* [Russian laws of 10th–20th centuries, vol. 1, Laws of ancient Russia] (Moscow, 1984); in English see "The Statute of Grand Prince Iaroslav," in *Reinterpreting Russian History*, ed. Daniel H. Kaiser and Gary Marker (New York: Oxford University Press, 1994), 51.

167. "Ustav kniazia Iaroslava," 195.

168. Neither the commentary nor the code of Iaroslav itself distinguishes between proceedings or sanctions of secular and church courts but lumps them together. Hence the confusion.

169. "Ustav kniazia Iaroslava," 191, 202.

Oblichenie in the sense of *demosieuo* pervades the code. Further in the document, five paragraphs that deal with the reasons for legal divorce employ two verbs—*oblichitisia* and *ob"iavitisia*—apparently as synonyms.[170] The particle *-sia* in the end of the word signifies the reflexive form of a verb, as in French *s'ouvrir* or in German *sich öffnen*. "If a wife hears from other people that they plot against the czar, or against the prince, but she does not tell her husband about this, and later is exposed [*oblichitsia*], divorce them," says the code. Exactly the same meaning is expressed by the verb *obiavitsia*, two clauses later: "If a woman plots against her own husband with poison or with other people, . . . and later this is exposed [*obiavitsia*], divorce [them]." This is a very interesting correspondence, since *ob"iaviti* and *oblichiti* go hand in hand in the Stalinist texts too.[171]

Apart from applying ecclesiastical canons, bishops also had a high duty to admonish and criticize the powerful, and here *oblichenie* in the sense of *elendzo* moves into the forefront. When Saint Theodosius of Pechera, the founder of Russian monasticism, said to princes of Kiev: "We must expose your wrongs (*oblichati*) and advise on the salvation of the soul, and it is appropriate for you to follow this advice,"[172] he was only repeating in Russian an apostolic statement on the relation between Church and state. Saint John Chrysostom, a martyr who had suffered at the hands of the unruly Byzantine emperor whose sins he had denounced, became the paradigmatic example for Russian church hierarchs up to the time of Ivan the Terrible. Church historians single out many bishop-exposers (*oblichiteli*) who followed in Chrysostom's footsteps on Russian soil in revealing the sins of the princes.[173]

Once the bishops also took on the ecclesiastical duty of revealing heresies, *oblichenie* became even more dependent on the sense of *elendzo*.

170. *Ob"iaviti* means "to declare," but also "to make manifest," as it comes from the same root as *vyiavit'* or *proiavit'*.

171. "Ustav kniazia Iaroslava," pars. 57 and 59, 192 (adapted from Kaiser's translation in *Reinterpreting Russian History*, 53). In Stalin's era *oblichenie* often had the final aim of "revealing a Communist self" or of *proiavit' sebia*. Making manifest is the action that unites the two verbs in the synonymical pair, by doing so they reflect the central quality of Soviet culture. Whereas early Russian practices of *oblichenie* aimed at making manifest sins or certain transgressions (apparently only by women who flouted household rules and church canons, which betrays a certain misogyny), the Soviet practices aimed at manifesting individuals rather than acts.

172. Georgii Fedotov, *Sviatye Drevnei Rusi* [Saints of ancient Russia] (Moscow: Moskovskii rabochii, 1990), 66.

173. Ibid., 113, 125.

Among many renowned clerics, the canonical position of a fighter for the orthodoxy of Russian faith belongs to Saint Joseph of Volokolamsk. Contemporary historiography conventionally presents him as the head of the "party of denouncers" (*partiia oblichitelei*) in late fifteenth- to early sixteenth-century Muscovy.[174] His fourteen letters against the so-called heresy of Judaizers were conveniently assembled in a single volume tellingly entitled *The Enlightener* (Prosvetitel'), and they served for centuries as the example of rhetoric for those aspiring to reveal some new brand of heretical schisms and deviations. Under Joseph's leadership the party of denouncers achieved illustrious results. In 1503 Joseph managed to persuade the grand prince of Moscow to burn the heretics condemned at the Church Council in Moscow, for the first time in Russian history.

For such successes of the denouncers of heretics, many liberal historians have concluded, Russia had to pay a high price.[175] In exchange for the agreement of the state to execute the heretics, the Church surrendered its right to oppose princely power. Though not officially proscribed, the right or duty of condemning the misdeeds of the powerful was thereafter rarely practiced. Daniel, a successor to Saint Joseph at the Volokolamsk monastery, and later a powerful metropolitan of Muscovy, became the head of the party of "evil Josephites" who concentrated solely on fighting the diverse heresies they found around them. He was also the first to start revealing the sins even of the lowest laity, as contemporary commentaries point out, but his prolific writings do not contain a single criticism of the grand prince.[176]

174. Lur'e, "Iosif Volotsky kak publitsist."

175. George P. [Georgii] Fedotov, *The Russian Religious Mind*, vol. 2, *The Middle Ages* (Belmont, Mass.: Nordland, 1975), ch. 12.

176. See Ia. S. Lur'e, *Ideologicheskaia bor'ba v russkoi publitsistike kontsa XV–nachala XVI veka* [Ideological struggle in Russian literature, 15th–16th centuries] (Leningrad: Akademiia Nauk SSSR, 1960), 503; and V. I. Zhmakin, *Sochineniia mitropolita Daniila* [Works of the metropolitan Daniel] (Moscow, 1881). Researchers note a certain "vulgarization" of the rhetorical style in his writings. Among the church hierarchs, the metropolitan Daniel was the first to extensively use debasing epithets ("swine," etc.) to characterize the alleged heretics (and the habit apparently became addictive). Curiously, Ivan the Terrible picked up his literary style from the writings of *oblichiteli*, i.e., St. Joseph and the metropolitan Daniel, as Lur'e claims (ibid., 509). Likhachev implies that this was a lucky development since Ivan IV, in his opinion, had enriched the nascent secular Russian literature by mixing into it both elements of the elevated Church Slavonic discourse and elements of lowly speech, which, if taken together, provide a humorous effect. Thus, Ivan labels his opponent Prince Kurbsky an "Ethiopian face" in a well-known excerpt (Dmitrii Likhachev, "Stil' proizvedenii Groznogo i stil' proizvedenii Kurbskogo" [Styles of Ivan the Terrible and Kurbsky], in *Perepiska Ivana Groznogo s*

Altogether, the rule of Ivan the Terrible had undercut the tradition of *oblichenie* in the sense of bishops revealing the sins of princes but institutionalized *oblichenie* in the sense of revealing the sins of heretics. After he was crowned as czar, Russia witnessed a series of final clashes between the Church and state power. The death of the metropolitan Philip (Kolychev), who was canonized later for his heroic attempts to denounce the czar's terror, marked a final watershed: after that, church hierarchs did not dare to utter an *oblichenie* of the czar's wrongs in public. The exposure and punishment of heresies, however, became the joint activity of Church and state. Later battles included those waged against the Old Believers after the Great Schism of 1667, and against numerous rationalist and mystical sectarians of the eighteenth and nineteenth centuries. These battles, together with an increasing number of encounters with Roman Catholic and Protestant churches, led to the establishment of polemical theology (*oblichitel'noe bogoslovie*—literally, "accusatory theology") as a compulsory part of church education in the first half of the nineteenth century.[177] A typical practical guide on *oblichenie* of the schismatics and sectarians would outline their creeds, cite their central arguments, and propose the lines of counterargumentation.[178] Quite a few future revolutionary radicals may have picked up the style and manner of dogmatic argumentation from this "critical" discipline.[179] This was not the only source of critical *oblichenie*, however: millions of peasant schismatics and sectarians of different

---

Andreem Kurbskim [Correspondence between Ivan the Terrible and Andrei Kurbsky] [Moscow: Nauka, 1979], 192, 201). Perhaps. Four centuries later the ruthlessness of Bolshevik discourse lashing out against enemies in the 1920s startled lexicographers who charted their use of particularly low epithets for members of other working-class parties or members of the opposition within the Party (Selishchev, *Iazyk revoliutsionnoi epokhi*, 68–69). The 1930s brought the flourishing of this "enriched Russian language" (if we follow Likhachev's argument to the end). Innumerable resolutions to "kill the Trotskist vermin" filled newspapers in 1937, as if applying the skill of murderous rhetoric learned from 16th-century *oblichiteli*.

177. Freeze, *Parish Clergy*, 122. However, this theological discipline was primarily taught in the Spiritual Academies, the highest educational institutions of the Church. Seminaries, being schools of lower level, did not offer special classes of "accusatory theology."

178. See N. Ivanovsky, *Rukovodstvo po istorii i oblicheniiu raskola: S prisovokupleniem svedenii o sektakh ratsionalnykh i misticheskikh* [Handbook of history and exposure of the schism: accompanied by information on rationalistic and mystical sects] (Kazan, 1892).

179. Laurie Manchester argues in her forthcoming book *Secular Ascetics: Clerical Mentalities in the Russian Intelligentsia* that even if the number of Bolsheviks of direct seminarian background was not substantial, the seminarian approach to life decisively shaped the general worldview of the intelligentsia in the end of the

breeds waged the retaliatory war of denunciation against the enthroned Antichrist.[180]

After Ivan the Terrible, *oblichenie* in the sense of revealing the sins of the powerful did not disappear altogether. In fact, it passed to the laity. Aristocratic dissidents appeared first, with Prince Kurbsky perhaps epitomizing this kind of *oblichenie* of czars.[181] And the secular practice of *oblichenie* of the sins of the powerful also became the province of fools for Christ, also known as "the holy fools." The religious phenomenon of fools for Christ is usually considered predominantly Russian, with some antecedents in Byzantium and back to the lines of Saint Paul claiming that in this world being true to God resembles madness (1 Corinthians 3:18). Mortifying their flesh, and living on the streets even in deadly cold, these fools were habitually regarded in Russia as having the gift of prophecy and the right to reveal ultimate truths hidden by appearances. The high point of their popularity coincides with the rule of Ivan the Terrible. Fletcher, an English diplomat describing his visit to Moscow in 1588, noted their sheer number and the "rude libertie" of denouncing the czar in public that they enjoyed.[182] The hagiography of the famous fool for Christ, Basil the Blessed (who lent his name to the central cathedral on Red Square in Moscow), even pictures him feeding Ivan the Terrible with raw meat during Lent, accusing the czar by this act of bloodthirsty terror.

19th century. For a partial exposition of the argument see her "Secularization of the Search for Salvation."

180. There are even curious direct connections between sectarians and Bolsheviks (though their significance to the transposition of practices is at best ambiguous): the founding II Congress of the Russian Social Democratic Party (1903) adopted a special resolution on cooperation with the sectarians, authored by Bonch-Bruevich, a future secretary of Lenin. The sectarians delivered prohibited revolutionary Bolshevik newspapers across the Russian borders through their established conspiratorial channels (see A. I. Klibanov, *History of Religious Sectarianism in Russia [1860s–1917]* [Oxford: Pergamon Press, 1982], 5).

181. If Ivan the Terrible learned his literary style from the writings of Joseph Volotsky, then Kurbsky is said to have been under the influence of the worst enemy of the Josephites, Maxim the Greek (Lur'e, *Ideologicheskaia bor'ba*, 509).The latter, having been released in 1551 from internment in the Volokolamsk monastery, where he had to undergo strict penance after his first trial in 1526, immediately produced a series of "revealing discourses" [*oblichitelnye slovesa*] including the famous "Discourse Diffusely Expounding with Pity on the Disorder and Excess of Tsars and Rulers of Recent Times" and "Instructive Chapters to Those Ruling Properly." I borrow this translation of the titles from Jack V. Haney, *From Italy to Muscovy* (Munich: W. Fink, 1973).

182. Quoted in A. S. Ivanov, *Vizantiiskoe iurodstvo* [Fools for Christ in Byzantium] (Moscow: Mezhdunarodnye otnosheniia, 1994), 148.

Fools for Christ not only exposed the sins of the czar and of the powerful; evidence suggests that they directed their zeal primarily against the laity of lower status.[183] Fletcher writes that they approached people on the streets and pointed out their misdeeds; the accused would habitually accept the revelation and admit: "This is according to my sins." Through fools for Christ, the practice of secular *oblichenie* was becoming firmly rooted among ordinary people. Even after these holy madmen were banned by the Church and persecuted in the seventeenth and eighteenth century, many fools for Christ still led an underground existence and were extremely popular. Stories of religious feats in the nineteenth century include accounts of many officially unrecognized but locally praised fools for Christ.[184]

All these last examples of bishops' activities or of secular *oblichenie* seem to suggest the prolonged historical predominance of *oblichenie* as criticism over *oblichenie* in the sense of making public. And yet the publicizing of the self was frequently involved in what seemed to be standard accusatory practices. To give a relevant example, I point out the element of *oblichenie* as *demosieuo* in the activity of the famous "elders." These monks, preaching to and revealing the sins of the simplest people, drew the attention of many a writer. *Oblichenie* was part and parcel of their everyday activity. Leonid, the first elder of Optyna Pustyn', a center of this new type of spirituality attracting massive pilgrimage, justified his acts to an inquiring local bishop who suspected something "Jesuitical" in the elder's habit of daily accepting confessions from pilgrims, in the following manner: "God has brought him to me for sincere penance, for me to expose his wrongs [*obli-*

183. See this argument developed in ibid., 150.

184. See Efim Poselianin, *Podvizhniki v russkoi tserkvi v deviatnadtsatom veke* [Popular heroes of the Russian Church in the 19th century] (Moscow, 1901). In another notable example, Chernyshevsky spends at least a dozen pages in his autobiography describing the local fool for Christ, Antonushka, as one of the few people who "had decisively influenced" his childhood. Apparently, the young son of a priest was startled by *oblichenie*, coming from a person who was an example of honest, if coarse and ignorant, devotion to Christ. In his own words: "Why did I dedicate so many pages to him? Because I would like to deduce the great philosophical truths from the role he played in the city of Saratov, I would like to elevate him to a type of world-historical significance. . . . [In Antonushka] I sought convictions, more satisfactory than the mixture of Golubinsky and Feofan Prokopovich with Rollaine [French historian of Rome] in Trediakovsky's translation, and books of all tendencies, from St. Dimitrii Rostovsky to Dickens and Belinsky" (Nikolai Chernyshevsky, "Avtobiografiia," in *Polnoe sobranie sochinenii* [Complete works] [Moscow, 1939], 1:596–597). Note how in Chernyshevsky's education coarse religious zeal and seminary literature intertwine with secular enlightenment and criticism of powers that be.

chit'] and admonish; how can I not admit him?"[185] This example seems to present us with a clear-cut *oblichenie* in the sense of *elendzo*.

However, consider a similar, but more detailed, account that Dostoyevsky provides in *The Brothers Karamazov*. A certain lady with "feeble faith" comes to the elder Zossima to seek advice after her confession. The elder, however, exposes the lady's hidden motive to solicit praise for her goodness. He admonishes her to engage herself in the deeds of "active love" instead of just making a sincere confession. These deeds will demonstrate her real Christian virtue, while the deed of just a confession reveals her hypocrisy. In the end the lady accepts that the elder had revealed her true self: "You have pointed out myself to me, you have perceived me, and explained myself to me."[186] Thus, Zossima's *oblichenie* has both aspects simultaneously: he has accused the lady of hypocrisy and in doing so, he has made public her (unworthy) self. Furthermore, Zossima's exhortation to prove faith by many real deeds, rather than by simple personal observance of piety, is very close to the Stalinist canon of revealing the self in the totality of deeds.

The publicizing aspects of *oblichenie* were there but not emphasized. The long preoccupation of pointing out misdeeds, or with the publication of sins, made it hard to notice. Only the Soviet regime challenged this predominance of accusation over the publication. When the Russian Revolution intensified the practice of *oblichenie*, it also refocused it: the publicizing component of *oblichenie* gained, if not the upper hand then, at least, equal status with the accusing aspect of the practice. Perhaps, this happened because the practice was employed by some practitioners to reveal a new object. Instead of the sins of the powerful, or the untruths of the heretics, it now revealed the individual, a new notion that developed in the nineteenth century.

OBLICHENIE AND PUBLIC PENANCE

Two further points suggest a connection between the practice of revelation by deeds and Tertullian's doctrine of *publicatio sui*. First, the early Chris-

---

185. D. D. Sokolov, *Optinskoe starchestvo i ego vliianie na monashestvuiushchikh i mirian* [Elders of Optina Pustyn' and their influence on monasticism and laity] (Kaluga, 1898), 23.

186. Fyodor Dostoyevsky, *Sobranie sochinenii* [Collected works], ed. G. M. Fridlender and M. B. Khrapchenko (Moscow: Pravda, 1984), 11:67.

tian practices of public penance that were used to achieve the *publicatio sui* effect had declined in the West but survived as the doctrinally central church practice for erasing sins in Orthodox Russia. Second, Latin versions of expressions containing the word *oblichenie* in the sense of *demosieuo* relentlessly use terms related to the word "public." Furthermore, the relevant examples are usually accompanying official judgments on sins, that is, they involve ecclesiastical courts allocating penance. Apart from the example already presented above (*publicante*), Sreznevsky also gives the following examples from the church canons: "to reveal the falsely written words" (*oblichati—demosieuesthai—publicari*) and "Our fathers have ruled not to publicize adulterous wives" (*oblichati—demosieuein—publicari*).[187]

Tertullian used the Latin phrase *publicatio sui* in *De Poenitentia*—one of the first Christian treatises on the doctrine and practice of penance—to designate a penitent's self-knowledge in the community of early Christians during the rite of *exomologesis,* a precursor of penance allocated by church courts. Only by going public, by publicizing one's self in public penance, can one come to know it: the self is constituted by this special kind of deed. Foucault says in his commentary on Tertullian:

> Publish oneself, that means that he has two things to do. One has to show oneself as a sinner. . . . But this *exomologesis* was also a way for the sinner to express his will to get free from this world, to get rid of his own body, . . . and get access to a new spiritual life. . . . The punishment of oneself and the voluntary expression of oneself are bound together. . . . In a few words, penance in the first Christian centuries is a way of life acted out at all times out of an obligation to show oneself.[188]

Penitents in a public ritual revealed their sinful self to the community and in so doing took an essential step toward liberating the self from the sins and, in a sense, acquired a new, true self imbued with Christian conscience.

The structural congruence among Tertullian's *publicatio sui* and the revelation by deeds practiced by the Bolsheviks is striking. What both cases reveal is the saintly self, which emerges by rejection of sinful behavior, and the possession of which is now tested through the analysis of special deeds. The arena where revelation happens is also similar: in *publicatio sui* it is the community of early Christians, a group with exclusive membership that

187. Sreznevsky, *Materialy,* col. 521. The first phrase is from the 63d canon of the Council in Trullo; the last, already cited, is part of the 34th canon of Basil the Great. See note 168.
188. Foucault, "About the Beginning," 214.

deems all other memberships worthless; in *oblichenie* it is the *kollektiv*. The how of the practice involves undergoing a certain highly demanding ritual. Tertullian's description of exomologesis stresses its rigor,[189] and in Stalinist purges, the ritual is even more exacting. The deeds discussed during purges are not those of the specific penitential kind, but those performed in the totality of a given Communist's life. The end result of both practices may be captured by either Russian *proiavit' sebia* or Latin *publicatio sui:* the true self is publicized, revealed by deeds.

Despite the decline of public penance as an actual church practice in Russia following the establishment of the Holy Synod in the eighteenth century (described in chapter 2), the spread of *oblichenie* may well have preserved the publicizing aspects of the ritual of public penance, either as part of popular religiosity or in its secular versions. These aspects of public penance were later actualized and intensified, when the practice of *oblichenie* was picked up by the revolutionaries, while the final institutionalization of this practice after 1917 had far-reaching consequences. Might it not be the case that after a period of corruption and laxity, the demanding early Christian practice was restored in its full rigor after the Bolshevik revolution?

The Russian Revolution may have effected a change similar to the Protestant Reformation, which also intensified an early Christian practice to reinvigorate the ailing religiosity. Luther made Augustine's solitary confession into the central practice of what became Protestant culture, paving the way for a mystical communion with God for any believer who dared to reject the Catholic priests' claim to mediate. In so doing, he received credit for helping develop the individualism of Western culture. The Bolsheviks similarly radicalized those ecclesiastical practices that were available to them in their culture, based on Eastern Christianity and the centrality of public penance. Instead of using the aristocratic models of individualization copied from Western models of confessional practices and solitary self-reflection, they turned the Orthodox practice of *oblichenie,* nearly defunct in the official Russian Church, into the predominant Soviet mechanism of bearing witness to one's achievement of lay sainthood and "assurance of grace." The radical reformation of ecclesiastical practices in this case also yielded an individual, but of a specific kind. If the Western individual was born as a confessing animal, its Soviet counterpart came to be a penitent beast.

---

189. See this description in chapter 2 text and its accompanying note 90.

CODA

Let us recapitulate the main steps of the argument. The Stalinist dictum was that freedom of the individual in the Soviet state lay in the real opportunity to reveal the individual self. The Stalinist epoch in Soviet life witnessed an individuation drive as an attempt to bring this individual self into existence. And it succeeded. Before, *lichnost'* hardly existed for the vast masses of the population, neither as a discursive term nor as a phenomenon in the everyday life. Demanding that every Party member and then every citizen reveal the self, the Stalinist regime made this revelation obligatory and enforced this revelation. Thus, it made the mass use of the word *lichnost'* possible and taught the populace how to recognize *lichnost'* in oneself. In this sense, the regime granted *lichnost'* to the masses, it gave each Soviet citizen the possibility to become an individual self. In the sense in which Heidegger would speak of freedom, the regime freed *lichnost'* for existence.

"Freedom is the essence of truth itself," wrote Heidegger in one of his enigmatic essays where he mulled over the relationship between the fundamental practices of showing and revealing, on the one hand, and objects showing up as a result of these practices, on the other. The freedom in question was not a freedom of the human being; rather, it was the freeing quality of the disclosive space where phenomena appear, the freeing quality that allows things to be, lets them be. "Freedom reveals itself as the 'letting-be' of what is."[190] Heidegger is speaking of the move that brings certain background practices into place, the move that thus enables objects of a certain culture, or any other sphere of shared intelligibility, to appear against this background. This move sets up the human world of intelligible objects and perspectives for action that make sense, the world in which free human action will take place.

This initial move offers the possibility for the negative and positive freedom of a human being, as it creates the world in which an individual may freely act. But the freedom to set up this world does not belong to any single human being:

> Freedom is not what common sense is content to let pass under that name: the random ability to do as we please, to go this way or that in our choice. Freedom is not license in what we do or do not do. Nor, on

190. Martin Heidegger, "On the Essence of Truth," in *Existence and Being*, trans. R. F. C. Hull and Alan Crick (London: Vision, 1959), 330, 333.

the other hand, is freedom a mere readiness to do something requi-
site and necessary. . . . Over and above all this ("negative" and "positive" freedom) freedom is a participation in the revealment of what-
is-as-such.[191]

Heidegger's insight illuminates Stalinist discourse from an unexpected
angle. The pronouncements of Stalin's ideologists on "the freedom of the
individual" in the USSR as an opportunity to reveal the self may be reinterpreted as pointing to this initial freeing of the "individual" into existence, to engendering of individuality as a phenomenon of everyday life.
Soviet individuals had to be created first, had to be freed from nonexis-
tence, and then could start caring about the negative or positive freedom of
their acts, and about providing the standard set of human rights and liber-
ties for each individual in the country. Stalinist formulations then could be
related to this freedom to exist at all, rather then to freedom as conceived
in liberalism.

But if, following Heidegger, we may say that the freedom of *lichnost'* of
which Stalinist discourse spoke was the freeing of *lichnost'* into the open—
the initial freedom of the move that set up the culture where *lichnost'* appeared as a mass phenomenon of everyday life and as a subsequent subject of rights and obligations—why wouldn't this epoch of *kul't lichnosti*,
which is now habitually understood as "the cult of personality" (that is, of
Stalin's persona), be better understood as the time of the cultivation of each
single individual, in Makarenko's phrase?

191. Ibid.

FIGURE 1.   Maxim Gorky on a visit to Makarenko's labor colony, named after
him, in 1928. Makarenko is second from the left. (Courtesy Anton Makarenko,
Sochineniia [Moscow: Academy of Pedagogical Sciences of RSFSR, 1950–52])

FIGURE 2.   The first band of colonist-musicians assembles against the background of the former monastery building where Makarenko's colony was stationed in the late 1920s. (Courtesy Anton Makarenko, *Sochineniia* [Moscow: Academy of Pedagogical Sciences of RSFSR, 1950–52])

FIGURE 3.   An assembly of the colony's council of commanders. Makarenko is fifth from the left. (Courtesy Anton Makarenko, *Sochineniia* [Moscow: Academy of Pedagogical Sciences of RSFSR, 1950–52])

FIGURE 4.   Comradely admonition: children with slogans shame those who "refuse to liquidate their illiteracy." The central slogan has names of those shamed. (Courtesy National Library of Russia; photo from the album *Svetom oktiabria* [In the light of October] [Moscow, 1967])

FIGURE 5.   A group of workers joins the Party collectively in the wake of Lenin's death, Leningrad Mint, 1924. (Courtesy St. Petersburg Archive of Cinema, Photo, and Audio Documents)

FIGURE 6.   Another comradely admonition: a comrades' court in a collective farm, early 1930s. Its targets are truants and job shirkers (seated in the center). (Courtesy National Library of Russia; photo from the journal *Za tempy, kachestvo, proverku* [Tempos, quality, control] 9–10 [1933]: 35)

FIGURE 7. An assembly of the leaders of class collectives in a standard girls' school, 1952. (Courtesy National Library of Russia; propaganda materials on Young Pioneers, inventory no. EI-12142)

FIGURE 8. Mutual surveillance in action: sanitary patrols check the hygienic condition of their classmates, 1952. (Courtesy National Library of Russia; propaganda materials on Young Pioneers, inventory no. EI-12142)

FIGURE 9. Individualization: S. A. Grigoriev's "Discussion of an F grade," late 1940s. (Courtesy NLR collection of reprints)

FIGURE 10. Another instance of individualization: S. A. Grigoriev's "Joining the Komsomol," late 1940s. (Courtesy NLR collection of reprints)

FIGURE 11.   Changing emphasis in Party purges (front page of a satirical journal, January 1933):

WIFE: "Why are you worried? So it's yet another purge, and once again they'll ask you what you were doing before 1917 . . ."

HUSBAND: "That'd be nothing indeed. If only they'd never ask what I am doing *now*." (Courtesy *Krokodil* 1 [1933]: 1)

FIGURE 12.   Graphic representation of the purge: L. Alekhin's "Screened!,"
late 1930s. In a positive affirmation of the self, a Party secretary hands back a
comrade's Party card. (Courtesy NLR collection of reprints)

FIGURE 13.   A model purge: a secretary of the Oktiabr'sky district Party committee, Andreasian (standing), undergoes a purge in the presence of Aaron Solts
(seated in the center, gray-haired), Moscow, 1933. (Courtesy *Ogonek* 15 [1933]: 15)

FIGURE 14.   A standard purge: a Party member undergoes a purge at the Volo-
darsky Textile Factory, Leningrad, July 1933. The audience listens and asks questions. (Courtesy St. Petersburg Archive of Cinema, Photo, and Audio Documents)

FIGURE 15. An assembly of the turbine workshop of the Kirov Tractor Plant during the Party purge, 1933. Note a curious orchestra in the right corner. (Courtesy St. Petersburg Archive of Cinema, Photo, and Audio Documents)

FIGURE 16. The Party court embodied: the presidium of the Vasileostrovsky district control commission, Leningrad, 1934. (Courtesy St. Petersburg Archive of Cinema, Photo, and Audio Documents)

FIGURE 17.   Verification of Party documents, the Central district committee,
Leningrad, 1936. The subject sits with her back to the camera. (Courtesy
St. Petersburg Archive of Cinema, Photo, and Audio Documents)

FIGURE 18.   The height of the individualization drive: a public reading of Stalin's March 1937 speech announcing the appearance of a new type of wrecker and a secret ballot multicandidate Party reelection campaign. (Courtesy private collection of Natalia Lebina)

FIGURE 19.   Self-immolation of the Party: a Party reelection conference of the
Krasnogvardeisky district committee, Leningrad, May 1937. Note the onlookers'
unusually close attention. Among the leaders, who will withstand revelation by
deeds? How many will survive? (Courtesy St. Petersburg Archive of Cinema,
Photo, and Audio Documents)

FIGURE 20.   A group of delegates to the Leningrad Party reelection conference,
May 1937. Seated next to Zhdanov (with mustache, center front) is the Leningrad
Party secretary, Ugarov (to Zhdanov's right), who was promoted to Moscow, then
shot in 1939 on counterrevolutionary charges. How many others in this picture
did not survive the terror? (Courtesy St. Petersburg Archive of Cinema, Photo,
and Audio Documents)

FIGURE 21.   Results of the reelection campaign. The first plenum of the newly
elected Moskovsky district Party committee, Leningrad, May 1937. (Courtesy
St. Petersburg Archive of Cinema, Photo, and Audio Documents)

FIGURE 22.   A benign face of power. The Lenin Pass undertaken by a Komsomol
member at the Elektrosila Factory, 1972. (Courtesy St. Petersburg Archive of
Cinema, Photo, and Audio Documents)

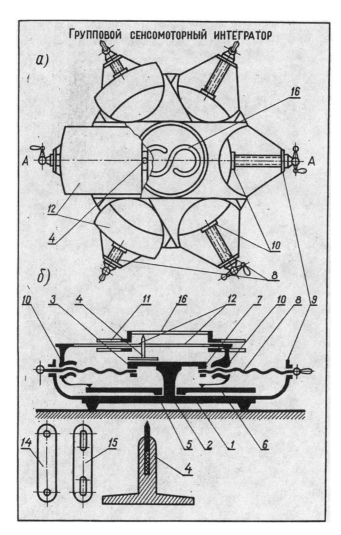

ГРУППОВОЙ СЕНСОМОТОРНЫЙ ИНТЕГРАТОР

FIGURE 23. A diagram of Soviet power. Drawing of a Sensory-Motor Integrator. (Courtesy Leonid Umansky, "Senso-motornyi integrator," *Voprosy psikhologii* 1 [1969]: 128–130)

6 Working on Oneself
The Individual as a Subject of Knowledge and Action

HISTORY OF WORKING ON ONESELF

In the late Soviet era "working on oneself" (*rabota nad soboi*) came to refer to techniques of individual self-training. This was not so before. For example, Lenin's writings demonstrate this usage, as well as the earlier usage for practices of transforming the collective as a body. On the one hand, in *What Is To Be Done?* Lenin spoke of the "need for a long methodical manufacturing of a professional revolutionary out of oneself."[1] On the other hand, in his speech at the Eleventh Party Congress (1922) he said: "the crux of the matter is that the avant-garde should not be afraid of working on itself, of remaking itself,"[2] which left unclear whether he meant individuals or the collectivity. In a more clearly collectivist vein, Iaroslavsky, writing on the objective of the 1929 general purge, noted:

> To a certain extent we are all people of the past with all the drawbacks from the past, and a great deal of work should be done on all of us. We should ourselves work on ourselves and on those who come to us [i.e., non-Communists] . . . We should accept people as they are, and see whether they are suitable for the struggle for socialism, . . . [whether they are ready] to sacrifice themselves if the Cause requires it.[3]

Subjecting oneself to a higher cause, with an ultimate willingness to die for that cause if the need arises, is the doctrinal aim, stated here clearly, as in many other similar writings on the moral obligation of a Communist, but the practices underlying this claim can be still more or less collectivist.

1. Lenin, *Polnoe sobranie sochinenii*, 6:125–127.
2. Ibid., 45:137.
3. Iaroslavsky, ed., *Kak provodit' chistku partii*, 10.

Individual practices of self-transformation and self-perfection were not at the forefront of the Bolsheviks' discussions in the 1920s and 1930s; rather, collectivist discourse encouraged paying more attention to collective self-perfection of the group.[4] During these early days, the closest thing to an idea of individual self-perfection was probably found in discourse on individual self-education, the minimal form of self-fashioning allocated to Party members by the dominant discourse.[5]

Thus, Nadezhda Krupskaia's *Organization of Self-Education* (1922) gave central significance to the practices of individual reading.[6] She jokingly compared the method of studying *Das Kapital*, predominant then among Party members, to trying to kill bears with one's bare hands, and proposed the following four stages of learning before setting off on the hunt. First, one should understand every word in the text; that is, use a dictionary to look up unknown words and remember them in the stable expressions in which they recur in the text. Second, one should take copious notes from the text; the Russian word for these notes, *konspekt*, then became the symbol of Soviet scholastic procedure, designating an auxiliary means that facilitates seeing the truth, almost in direct correspondence with the Latin origin of this term (*con-spect*).[7] Third, one should "represent for oneself the whole line of thinking of the author," reading the book as a single logical narrative. Fourth, upon finishing the book, one should give oneself an account (*otdat' sebe otchet*) of the text read.

A section on these four phases was reprinted in a slightly changed version in Krupskaia's "How to Work Independently with a Book" (1939), a brochure that appeared following the November 1938 resolution of the Central Committee on the introduction of compulsory individual reading of the just published *Short Course of the History of the Communist Party*. This section on the basic techniques of reading was inserted in a broader context, which advertised "systematic reading" as a kind of a rigorous self-

4. See chapter 4 on discourse of self-criticism and purges.
5. Krupskaia, who published two brochures on learning reading skills in 1919 and 1922, stressed in their later versions (e.g., 1935) that earlier conditions and scanty resources had forced Communists to call for "mutual help" in self-education, since not everyone had an individual book (Nadezhda Krupskaia, "O samoobrazovanii" (1935) [On self-education], in *Pedagogicheskie sochineniia* [Pedagogical works] [Moscow, 1960], 9:559–566).
6. Krupskaia, "Organizatsiia samoobrazovaniia" (1922), in ibid., 59–86.
7. This practice persisted well into the 1980s: higher education students, taking compulsory classes on Marxism, had to submit their *konspekty* of the classics for inspection by a teacher.

discipline, reminiscent of Norbert Elias's recent argument on modernization as the advent of the possibility of prolonged, consistent, and methodical action.[8] Along with the consistent reading of a single text, the brochure recommended consecutive reading of a series of texts. Not only should one avoid skipping pages or moving back and forth in chaotic fashion; one should also design a plan of reading, comprising several texts, and follow it methodically.

Another detail stressed by the brochure was the linking of knowledge collected from the text to everyday life, in a systematic manner.[9] This injunction is highly reminiscent of historical instances of dogmatic religious education. In the English case, Thomas Hobbes held the preaching of "seditious ministers" to be among the causes of the Civil War. William Perkins, the father of Calvinist "covenant theology" in England, wrote in the 1580s, in his book *The Whole Treatise of the Cases of Conscience* that the duty of the preacher was "to apply . . . the doctrines rightly collected [out of the Bible] to the life and manners of men in simple and plain speech."[10] According to Robert C. Tucker, Stalin was drawn to Lenin precisely by this project of linking the everyday experiences of workers to the Marxist word. The chief stock-in-trade of Stalin as revolutionary were his impressive knowledge of the fundamentals of Marxism and an ability to explain them very simply to ordinary workers, writes Tucker. "[T]he seminary experience gave him a cathechistic approach to teaching and a facility for finding homely examples which must have been effective in his worker classes."[11] This "cathechistic" style characterized Stalin's later writings too, which often consisted of short lists of concise dogmatic answers to explicitly posed basic questions. The interesting point for us here is that the campaign that followed the November 1938 Central Committee resolution on individual reading, which used brochures of the "how to read properly" type, may also have aimed at the individualization of faith, as seditious ministers had done in revolutionary England.

Krupskaia also seems to have been the first to furnish a special treatise on the individual self-training of a Leninist. Her exhortations to the young

8. See Helmut Kuzmics, "The Civilizing Process"; and Norbert Elias, "Violence and Civilization," in *Civil Society and the State*, ed. John Keane (London: Verso, 1988).

9. This is emphasized also in the earlier 1935 brochure of Krupskaia, 565.

10. Quoted in Walzer, *Revolution of the Saints*, 145.

11. See Robert C. Tucker, *Stalin as Revolutionary, 1879–1929* (New York: Norton, 1973), 116.

Communists who aspired to become real Leninists did not call for much more than knowledge of revolutionary theory and its application in everyday life, both private and public; reading was to supply the needed theoretical knowledge. She wrote: "One must tie one's life to working for the cause of communism, direct oneself by revolutionary theory, be sober in one's way of life and not afraid to persevere. [Do those things, and] then you'll become a Leninist."[12] Three main features are obvious here: learning doctrinal theory, subjecting one's life to doctrinal requirements, and steadfastly carrying them out. Not much of a difference from the English Puritan individual, we might say. Another zealous Communist, M. N. Liadov, suggested what the Bolshevik self-perfection implied in 1925. "One should stage the October [Revolution] within oneself,"[13] he wrote during the Party ethics campaign, because inside each Bolshevik a petit-bourgeois with anti-collectivist intentions was hiding. Liadov suggested: "We should each look into ourselves and sweep out [this] petit-bourgeois with the Bolshevik broom. To learn to understand the will, the interests of the *kollektiv*, to define one's own will and interests by them—this is a first approach to creating a new life."[14]

Liadov and Krupskaia, of course, belonged to a select group of top Party functionaries who specifically concerned themselves with self-training and self-perfection in the 1920s and 1930s. Others at the top could simply ignore it, concentrating on the pressing needs of the day. On the mass level, self-fashioning was ascribed to singular and illustrious individuals, who represented the radiant future. For example, published descriptions of model lives of Stakhanovites, who had allegedly fashioned themselves to become almost superhuman, contain indications of other practices of working on oneself. These descriptions highlight the element of will, mentioned in Liadov, to the utmost degree. Thus, Izotov stresses subjecting oneself to collective aims; we know, he writes "that everything [in the building of socialism] depends on our will."[15] A. K. Busygin similarly accords the effort of will a special place in his account of "learning to study." A former peasant who had arrived at the Donbass coal mines only in the late 1920s, he

---

12. Nadezhda Krupskaia, "Podgotovka lenintsa" [Preparation of a Leninist (speech at the 6th Komsomol Congress, 1924)], in *Izbrannye proizvedeniia* (Moscow, 1988), 26.

13. M. N. Liadov, "Voprosy byta" (1925) [Problems of everyday life], in *Partiinaia etika*, ed. A. A. Guseinov et al. (Moscow: Politizdat, 1989), 310.

14. Ibid., 326.

15. Izotov, *Moia zhizn'*, last ch.

describes his own difficulties in concentrating his attention during studies, in sitting in the same place with a book in his hands for hours, and in memorizing. Having encountered these difficulties, he asked himself, "Do they come from a lack of willpower?" By straining his will, he concentrated on studies and achieved spectacular successes: he entered the Industrial Academy, got elected to the USSR Supreme Soviet, and—last but not least—wrote the very book that the reader was now holding in his hands.[16]

All these examples are, however, far from demonstrating the general condition of self-fashioning and self-perfection in the USSR before the Second World War. The Stakhanovites and zealous Bolsheviks represent those who may be called "the spectacular few" among the indifferent many. Those many were mostly unconcerned with working on oneself to reach the spectacular heights of Bolshevik self-sacrifice—until the demanding standard of revealing oneself in one's deeds was imposed upon them during the purges. Iaroslavsky's series of brochures, *What the Party Demands from a Communist*, distributed during that period, offers us a first glimpse into the mass practice of self-fashioning.[17] A question is directed to the reader; "You, the Communist, ask yourself:. Do you match these demands? Do you underpin Party discipline with your Conscience, your dedication to the revolution, your self-control [*vyderzhka*], your self-sacrifice and heroism?"[18] Familiar allusions to self-sacrifice and strengthening of the will, which a reader might ignore as yet another instance of high rhetoric, are less important than the concrete mundane practice of questioning oneself, imposed on every reader. The questions asked foreshadow those that may be posed at the coming purge meetings: the purge procedure is rehearsed within one's soul. In 1945 the imposed practice changes a little bit: instead

16. A. K. Busygin, *Zhizn' moia i moikh druzei* [My life and the life of my friends] (Moscow: Profizdat, 1939), 68. Writing during the campaign to strengthen individual reading practices, Busygin also explains how he reads *The Short Course:* as if following Krupskaia's recommendations, he takes copious notes and writes down questions and thoughts that occur to him.

17. *Chego partiia trebuet ot kommunista;* first published in Ukraine in 1934, then generally in 1935 and 1936. In 1945 a similar brochure, but adjusted to the needs of the day, appeared (*Chego partiia trebuet ot kommunistov v dni otechestvennoi voiny* [What the Party demands from Communists in the days of the patriotic war] [Moscow, 1945]). In 1925 and 1926, Iaroslavsky edited essays in 3 distinct editions with a similar intention, *Kakim dolzhen byt' kommunist* [What the Communist ought to be]. The 1920s brochures often have discussion articles; the 1930s works are part catechism on Party rules, part confessional: description of the program and the statute, and a Communist's main obligations.

18. Iaroslavsky, *Chego partiia trebuet ot kommunista*, 1936 ed., 51.

of putting questions to oneself, the brochure demands that "each Communist is obliged to keep his eye on himself, screen himself" (*sledit' za soboi, proveriat' sebia*) as to whether one is working in the way required by the Party.[19] The first mass-imposed practices of individual self-care seem to be internalized practices of collective self-analysis and collective self-criticism during the purges. This is the minimum, demanded of every Communist, while the heights of self-perfection and self-sacrifice are left to zealots, who wish to pursue them.

Later Soviet sources describing the history of self-training would claim that individual "working on oneself" had been practiced in the 1920s and 1930s, but without much fuss: spectacular individuals had silently achieved self-renunciation and subjection of the self to the collective will. "The active relation to oneself was typical of the spiritual character of a new man," wrote one of the commentators in the 1980s, but "those who, having perceived its value, engaged in self-training, were less than anything else inclined to write or talk about it."[20] Their reticence, asserted the commentaries, reflected their suspicion of its value, since heretofore self-training had turned out bourgeois individualists and religious fanatics. Instead of talking about self-training, which was so dangerously connected to the dark past of humankind, an early Soviet zealot quietly applied these techniques of self-training to himself in order to transform himself into a collectivist individual, always disposed to submit himself to the collective will: "To merge with the common, to partake in the people-wide cause—such was a leitmotif that pervaded the new relation of man to the world and to himself, that stimulated and directed self-training."[21]

The convoluted and half-hearted literature on self-training of the 1930s gave way to straightforward and explicit recommendations on self-training after the Second World War, in the wake of the 1948 speech by Zhdanov on the problems of cultural development. They perfunctorily repeated one paragraph from this speech, which mentioned "working on oneself." In his attack on the editorial boards of the journals *Zvezda* and *Leningrad*—which had lost the sense of Bolshevist self-criticism and become false *kollektivy*, Zhdanov said—and apart from the usual official incantations about

19. Iaroslavsky, *Chego partiia trebuet ot kommunistov v dni otechestvennoi voiny*, 1945 ed., 27.

20. I. A. Dontsov, *Samovospitanie lichnosti: Filosofsko-eticheskie problemy* [Self-training of the individual: philosophical and ethical problems] (Moscow: Politizdat,1984), 207.

21. Ibid., 212.

the need for collective self-criticism, Zhdanov also added a few surprising new lines on the need for individual self-analysis:

> Comrade Stalin repeatedly pointed out that the most important factor in our development is the necessity for every Soviet citizen to assess the sum total of his work every day, and fearlessly examine himself; to analyze his work, manfully criticize his failings and mistakes, ponder on how to achieve better results of his own work, and to work cease-lessly at improving oneself.[22]

Zhdanov's paragraph was surprising in that Stalin hardly ever men-tioned "working on oneself" in his speeches, and he never dealt with the mundane issue of assigning the task of everyday self-review to an individual. Perhaps Zhdanov simply ascribed it to Stalin, as everything coming from the top had to be connected with the Leader.[23] In any case, this single passage seems to have opened up a flood of literature on working on one-self, which faithfully quoted the originating word of the leader. Popular brochures on the training of the will, a main component of the process of working on oneself, appeared in the late 1940s—early 1950s, followed by first scholarly monographs on self-training of the late 1950s—early 1960s.[24] These paved the way for a truly voluminous literature on self-training published during the 1960s and 1970s.

Perhaps, the real initial impetus to the literature on individual self-development came from the widespread publicity given to instances of in-dividual heroism during the Second World War, and the subsequent post-war interest in training heroes with strong willpower.[25] "Training of the

22. Zhdanov, *Doklad o zhurnalakh* Zvezda *i* Leningrad; translated in *The Central Committee Resolution*, 66.

23. I was unable to find Stalin's original injunction. Numerous Soviet com-mentators on Zhdanov's speech curiously omit Stalin's original statement (if it ever existed); if Stalin's published writings held anything resembling a statement on "working on oneself," the code of writing at the time demanded its compulsory citation.

24. E.g., A. T. Kovalev, *Volia i ee vospitanie (v pomoshch' uchiteliu)* [The will and its training (guidance for the teacher)] (Simferopol: Krymizdat, 1949); and Iu. A. Samarin, *Vospitanie voli i kharaktera* [Training of the will and character] (Leningrad: Znanie, 1952); these simpler early recommendations suggest that if one decides to work on oneself, one should construct a plan of self-perfection, and start fulfilling it without further procrastination (*Vospitanie voli*, 34).

25. The mass usage of *lichnost'* coincided with heightened attention to heroes and willed behavior. As noted in chapter 5, Kalinin also started giving detailed bio-graphical descriptions of individuals only during the war, recounting heroic deeds, and first used the word *lichnost'* in 1945.

will" literature seems to have responded to this interest and satisfied it. According to one calculation, about fifty dissertations were defended on this
topic in the 1940s and 1950s.[26] Of course, the Stalinist regime glorified the
concept of the will, and we have quoted above excerpts from Stakhanovites
Izotov and Busygin who achieved spectacular feats "by sheer will."[27] Later
Soviet commentators disapproved of this "nonscientific" amorphous concept that included many elements not pertaining to will power strictly defined, as a "conscious goal-oriented efforts, that facilitate subjecting the life
activity of man to his will, [that facilitate] overcoming of difficulties."[28]
Later Soviet theorists stressed the aspect of overcoming an obstacle, while
earlier sources called any protracted effort carried out in accordance with
higher Conscience "willed." For example, the following instances of the absence of will were cited in the 1949 pamphlet: easy receptivity to external
influences, apathy, indecision, lack of perseverance and endurance, surrender to sudden impulses, and "negativism," that is, a consistent rejection of
orders coming from the outside.[29]

One important example of the mass propaganda of practices of individual self-training in order to transform oneself into a hero was the hugely
popular journal *Iunost'* (Youth) in 1955; its title clearly indicated its intended readers. The first issue of *Youth* did not have an editorial but opened
with an article by Ivan Kozhedub, a Soviet ace air fighter, who pondered the
right means for the moral education of a Communist, for training one's will
and becoming a hero. Kozhedub started his article with the question that
haunted the postwar generations of Soviet youth, "Who should one be?"
(*Kem byt'?*). And he ended it with the motto that was familiar—I am not
exaggerating—to every Soviet citizen born after the war: "One should live
one's life in such a way that one does not end in the excruciating pain of
having lived one's years aimlessly." This statement was attributed to Pavel
Korchagin, Kozhedub's personal hero and a central character from Nikolai
Ostrovsky's model novel of socialist realism, *How Steel Was Tempered.*

In the middle of the first issue, letters of another famous Komsomol
writer from the 1930s, Boris Gorbatov, appeared. Gorbatov had earned lit-

26. L. I. Ruvinsky, *Samovospitanie lichnosti* [Self-training of the individual]
(Moscow: Mysl', 1984), 89.
27. On the notion of the Stakhanovites breaking the laws of nature by sheer
will, see Katerina Clark, *The Soviet Novel* (Chicago: University of Chicago Press,
1981); and Siegelbaum, *Stakhanovism.*
28. Ruvinsky, *Samovospitanie lichnosti*, 93.
29. Kovalev, *Volia i ee vospitanie*, 24.

erary acclaim at a very young age for his novel *The Cell* (1930), describing the life of a Komsomol group in high school. His following career as a Komsomol zealot writer and a heroic wartime correspondent also made him particularly suitable for deification. In effect, the comments that the *Youth* editor, Valentin Kataev (himself an author of the renowned 1930s classic *Time, Forward!*), attached to these letters formed an editorial manifesto. Kataev offered the letters to the reader as an opportunity for thinking about oneself, by comparing oneself to how "your peer thought and felt" in "the heroic 1930s." The letters, written by Gorbatov to his beloved, were filled with philosophical ramblings, dealing with such topics as self-training and the formation of a new man. If readers, following Kataev's advice, compared their own thoughts with the letters cleverly selected by the editors— containing only very intelligent comments by Gorbatov, burning with the earnest desire to perfect humankind—they were bound to end up with feelings of self-deficiency and the realization that they needed to perfect themselves. The first picture insert in the journal reproduced the popular paintings of young Lenin passing his graduation exam at St. Petersburg University, and of Zoia Kosmodemianskaia, a heroic woman partisan of the Great Patriotic War.

The third issue of *Youth* carried another landmark in popularizing techniques of individual self-training. "Thoughts on Self-Training" by Nikolai Ostrovsky were compiled posthumously from scattered notes in his archives. "Some strange people think that it is possible to be a Bolshevik without working every day, every hour on training one's will, one's character. One must constantly tend to this matter in order not to slide into the swamp of petit-bourgeoisification [*meshchanstvo*]. The true Bolshevik constantly forges and polishes himself."[30] Ostrovsky's notes were intended to popularize the techniques of working on oneself, to make them accessible to everybody. Individual self-criticism, hero-identification, and working out a program of personal development were among the techniques suggested in this dense, one-page article. Before discussing these techniques in detail in the next section, I should mention that all of them were employed to effect a transformation of the self that would make self-sacrifice possible. This was the end result of Communist individual self-training.

And yet, with the advent of the thorough ritualization of life in the late Soviet regime, two difficulties with spreading individual self-training tech-

30. Nikolai Ostrovsky, "Mysli o samovospitanii" [Thoughts on self-training], *Iunost'* 3 (1955): 71.

niques among the Soviet population arose. First, the number of genuinely charismatic situations for the practice of Communist heroism diminished when the Second World War ended. Thus, zealotry within the Soviet Union was now supposed to be practiced in mundane situations, which undercut its appeal.[31] Soviet didactic literature endlessly ruminated on the problem of heroism in everyday life. Second, an inherent danger was always present in individual self-training: though it was supposed to result in subjection to collectivist values, it might also stop short of accepting these values and, on the contrary, revert to blatant unconstrained egoism.

Thus, the Party became ambiguous on matters of unconstrained popularization of methods of self-development and, as we shall see, tried to link the techniques of self-training to the ritualized occasions of public evaluation of the individual. This linkage effectively meant the death knell for official propaganda on self-training: in the routinized Brezhnevite political system, anything linked to official rituals smacked of morbidity and staleness. A poll conducted in 1976–78 found that among the official means of training, literature on self-training least influenced the population; *kollektivy*, mass media and didactic novels were rather more effective in molding the New Soviet Man.[32] Still, the last wave of Soviet books on self-fashioning appeared after the 1983 plenum of the Party's Central Committee which once again dealt with the need to instill the practices of Communist self-training among the recalcitrant populace. These books carried the following introductions typical of the genre: "Merely wishing to work on oneself is not enough to make this work effective; one must know how to do it. . . . This book is addressed to a most broad circle of readers, because everybody should practice self-training."[33]

It seems that in practice the spread of techniques of self-training progressed, albeit not as fast as the educationalists wanted. Self-training and self-fashioning had already taken root after years of propaganda and zealots' experimentation. Volkogonov, who had interviewed young workers on the methods of self-training they actually employed, wrote in 1985 that these included two main techniques: first, self-planning for a day, or a year, with an accounting of the results achieved at the end of the time

31. One of the last upsurges of popular aspirations was linked to Cuba in 1962, where the early Soviet revolutionary experience seemed to live again; combat in Che Guevara brigades fed the imagination of later Communist zealots.
32. Dontsov, *Samovospitanie lichnosti*, 212.
33. A. T. Kovalev, *Lichnost' vospityvaet sebia* [The individual trains himself] (Moscow: Politizdat, 1983), 7.

period; second, hero-identification. When young workers faced a difficult situation, they asked themselves what their favorite model hero would do in such a case and acted upon the answer. These were the main popular recipes for "self-training of courage," though as Volkogonov noted, the detailed techniques for carrying it out were hard to elaborate.[34]

Volkogonov also restated for didactic purposes what "the standard of heroic behavior" meant in Soviet discourse, in words that resembled the earlier words of Krupskaia, Iaroslavsky, or Ostrovsky. According to him, "the phenomenon of heroism" included three components: first, life for the sake of society, with sacrifice as an ultimate goal; second, self-discipline as "an expression of the ethical freedom of man, his mastery over himself"; third, constant struggle with one's own base motives and intentions, which resulted in acts of "building oneself."[35] Let us turn to these elements in detail as they were reflected in manuals on self-training and scholarly works on the topic.

THE STRUCTURE OF PRACTICES OF WORKING ON ONESELF

The literature on self-training, although less efficient in its transformation of the popular life than the work of *kollektivy* or didactic novels, nevertheless laid bare the practices of self-training, common to them all, to the fullest degree. The first recognized scholarly monograph on the subject of individual self-training appeared in 1958.[36] As with any major work founding a field, it set the terms of discourse and delimited the field of described phenomena but was unable to give a detailed analysis of practices. The works that followed began to fill this gap. A. I. Aret's 1961 book is usually considered the most exhaustive enumeration of possible practices of working on oneself, and the best exposition of the elements involved in individual self-analysis.[37] L. I. Ruvinsky reworked this list of practices on the basis of the "activity approach," predominant in Soviet psychology, and thus provided the strictly "scientific" basis for thinking on this topic. Though I use two highly systematic Ruvinsky works, one from 1982 (an introduc-

34. Dmitrii Volkogonov, *Fenomen geroizma* [Phenomenon of heroism] (Moscow, 1985), 256–258.

35. Ibid., 250–251.

36. A. T. Kovalev and A. A. Bodalev, *Psikhologiia i pedagogika samovospitaniia* [Psychology and pedagogy of self-training] (Leningrad: Leningrad University, 1958).

37. A. Ia. Aret, *Ocherki po teorii samovospitaniia* [Essays on the theory of self-training] (Frunze: Kirghiz State University, 1961).

tion to the psychology of individual self-training for the students at pedagogical institutes) and one from 1984 (a most up-to-date account of the
state of the Soviet social science of methods of individual self-training) as
the two primary sources,[38] I also rely on some other works of minor figures
in the field, who proposed interesting methodological variations and twists
of argument within the general paradigm.

Different authors set up varying typologies of phases in individual self-
training, but they fell into three stages: first, the stages of self-cognition and
self-evaluation; second, the stage of self-compulsion or self-stimulation,
leading to self-training of the will proper; and finally, the stage of self-
control or self-command.[39] The process of working on oneself starts with
the realization of certain personal deficiencies, revealed in the process of
self-evaluation; then, during the second stage, the means of effecting the
personal transformation are applied; the third stage designates the telos of
individual self-development, the condition of self-control. This condition,
however, is not static but rather is a dynamic state of constant balancing
and counteracting certain tendencies to deviation from the desired standard. In each case, it is surprising to find to what extent all methods of
individual self-fashioning are embedded in or subjugated to the communal practices of self-revelation, ultimately stemming from the practices of
oblichenie.

The first stage of working on oneself—self-cognition resulting in self-
evaluation—is directly concerned with the communal review of the individual. Among six methods of self-cognition, most meticulously described
by Aret, the first one bears the rather long name of "recognizing oneself by
means of others." This meant comparing oneself to relevant others (a most
widespread method of self-knowing: in Aret's sample, which comprised
students of two high school classes, 82.5 percent practiced such comparison) but also listening to what others may say about you.[40] Many people
also, in Aret's opinion, first come to know about their personal qualities
through the judgments of outside observers. Thus, 40 percent of the interviewed students stated that their information about themselves came from

---

38. L. I. Ruvinsky and A. E. Solov'eva, *Psikhologiia samovospitaniia* [Psychol-
ogy of self-training] (Moscow: Prosveshchenie, 1982). L. I. Ruvinskii, *Samovospitanie lichnosti.*

39. In Russian, the first stage involves *samopoznanie* or *samoootsenka;* the second *samo-prinuzhdenie* or *samo-stimulirovanie,* the third and final *samoooblada-
nie,* literally "self-possession."

40. Aret, *Ocherki,* 70. Given the survey's primitive character and small sample,
I quote the percentages only to illustrate Aret's opinions.

their fellow students, 22 percent cited parents, and 13 percent named teachers, as sources.[41] Aret lists a number of standard school-life situations when this augmentation of knowledge of oneself may occur: school grading; comment during labor training classes; distribution of awards and punishments; socialist competition and discussion of its results; discussion of candidates for the school's elected bodies; occasions of discussing those joining the Young Pioneers and Komsomol; routine class discussions of study successes, of failures in discipline and other misdeeds; criticism of individuals during public assemblies.

A modern reader may be completely surprised by this thorough installation of the surveillance mechanism into everyday life: all of these occasions remind us of the attenuated purge sessions, when the *kollektiv* discussed a given individual. Routine Soviet school life simply employs them in a milder form. But this is not enough. Aret describes with enthusiasm a recent pedagogical invention, "hours for the mutual discussion of an individual," which was implemented in high school no. 12 in the city of Frunze, where he conducted his research. During these hours, comrades discuss the positive or negative features of each individual in a given class. Peers speak out and give the individual under discussion valuable advice about working on him- or herself. These discussions elicit great interest, says Aret.[42] It is hard not to notice how this "enlightening" procedure most obviously restages 1937 in a minuscule version, revealing the secret of other cited instances of "recognizing oneself by means of others." The same familiar practice of *oblichenie* becomes routinized and institutionalized in dozens of ritualized settings.[43]

Other methods (and simultaneously substages in the process) of self-cognition less directly depend on communal review. Thus, the second

41. Ibid., 70–71. In the capitalist countries, says Aret, opinions about others are not freely shared, and research data on individuals are covered up; as a result, people go to phrenologists and chiromants in order to know themselves. In our socialist country, people bravely tell each other what they think about each other, so self-cognition is not a problem.

42. Ibid., 72. Another novel version of "recognizing oneself through others" is discussing one's moral evaluation (*kharakteristika*), issued on graduation, with the teacher who wrote it.

43. Of course, sociology long ago theorized this acquisition of the self through others: for example, George Herbert Mead's concept of the development of an individual self included recognizing oneself through interaction with another, learning to interact with many others, and adopting the position of the generalized other. Yet it did not envisage permanent successive monitorings of each self by others in an institutionalized setting.

244 / *Working on Oneself*

method of self-cognition is solitary self-reflection and self-observation. Individuals react to the public statements and direct their gaze on their features and their own past deeds, as well as the feelings and motives that accompanied them. The third method is self-analysis proper, when they break down observed deeds into elements that may be taken as indicative of those personal features. The revelation by deeds mechanism is in full swing. The object of self-analysis, Aret emphasizes, should be concrete expressions of personality in observed acts, rather than emotional experience or sentiments.[44] Legitimate objects of self-analysis may include the outward appearance of students' material possessions and study materials, checked for their cleanliness or tidiness; manner of speech and handwriting; the history of getting a particular grade or of some good or bad deed, and so on. According to Aret, 74 percent of his respondents engage in this type of self-analysis, and "this happens particularly after committing a bad deed."[45]

The fourth method, self-accounting, or self-report, involves transforming self-analysis into a routine procedure, staged at the end of the day, year, or some other time period.[46] Individuals recount acts within this period that demonstrate the features of their personality and record which features they corrected or perfected. Final self-reports occur rarely, usually at some transformative moment in individuals' lives, while current self-accounting is more frequent. According to Aret, 70 percent of his pupils practiced it at the end of each day.[47]

The fifth method of self-cognition is "criticism and self-criticism." Aret, however, is not concerned with confusion arising from the application of this term from Party discourse to individual self-training, nor does he clarify whether this method involves individuals criticizing themselves or peers criticizing each other. Therefore a quote from Ostrovsky may illustrate this

44. This point is stressed by others also. For example, Ruvinsky writes that self-analysis should concern facts, rather than "lived experience." Analysis of sentiments and sensations is useless, because "one can judge himself objectively only according to his real deeds," rather than according to self-delusions (Ruvinsky and Solov'eva, *Psikhologiia samovospitaniia*, 68). To the best of my knowledge, most authors of Soviet books on self-training ignore the analysis of desires, which Foucault thought to be the predominant mechanism of self-cognition in the West.

45. Ibid., 76.

46. Ruvinsky later distinguishes between current and final self-accounting [*samo-otchet*]. See *Psikhologiia samovospitaniia*, 69.

47. Aret, *Ocherki*, 76. Practices of self-training seem to have changed very little between Stalin's time and the thaw of the 1960s: Zhdanov's speech in 1948 pointed out individual self-accounting in the end of the day as desirable; 13 years later Aret finds a majority of the young Soviet citizens already practicing it.

method of self-cognition: "It seems to me that for self-training one should first summon oneself to one's own harsh and impartial trial. One should clearly . . . discover one's own deficiencies and vices. . . . Self-criticism is a very effective means, given to us by the Party, for retraining the people."[48] Once again, we recognize internalization of communal mechanisms as the means for individual self-fashioning.

The sixth method of self-cognition is the final construction of self-evaluation. Individuals once again compare the intermittent results of self-analysis with the collective evaluation and establish an "objective" self-evaluation. To sum up the logic of individual self-cognition: the referential group tells individuals of deficiencies in the self; self-examination allows them to analyze their conduct as separate acts they consider revelatory of character traits that were criticized by the group; then a comparison of the resulting self-judgment with the group judgment once again gives them self-knowledge and the basis for formulating a judgment on the objectives of further personal self-perfection. With some variations, later Soviet sources in general recommended this six-step procedure as a way to achieve self-knowledge.[49]

With the aims of the stage of self-cognition achieved, the second stage of working on oneself—the stage of self-transformation or self-perfection—begins. Self-injunction, or self-stimulation, are the first steps to take. The goal is to bring oneself to start acting. One of Ruvinsky's student respondents described it as follows:

> A traitorous voice whispers: why work? Do what is more interesting, joyful, and so on. I start to persuade myself. I recollect all the reasons for the serious systematic work on oneself, I find more reasons, and it feels as if I am gaining strength. I push the hesitations aside. I fulfill my tasks.[50]

48. Ostrovsky, "Mysli o samovospitanii," 71. Aret's main concern is at what age to start this self-criticism. Unlike his colleague Sambros, who advocates its introduction among 2d- and 3d-yr. pupils (8–9 year-olds), Aret recommends starting the practice among preschoolers.

49. The literature that followed Aret's study differed somewhat from his model. Many works shorten its six proposed methods of self-study in their schemes of self-cognition. For example, a book of the youth guidance genre proposed the following four stages of self-knowing: self-observation, self-comparison with others to check self-observation, self-analysis, and self-criticism. Next came a test of self-evaluation against the group opinion on the individual, revealing whether the individual self-evaluation was set too high or too low (Momov and Kochetov, *Samovospitanie, samoutverzhdenie,* 24–25).

50. Ruvinsky, *Samovospitanie lichnosti,* 73.

Issuing a command to oneself clearly represents an internalization of the predominant situation of external injunction in Soviet society and was, therefore, of the first to have been thoroughly conceptualized by Soviet science.[51] Apart from self-commanding, other means of self-injunction include such techniques as self-reminder, self-encouragement, self-suggestion, and so on.

After self-injunction comes the stage of working on oneself narrowly defined, of transforming oneself by special techniques. Here the typical two primary techniques are "personal planning" and of "hero-identification."[52] Adopting obligations, or self-promises, in the form of internal personal pledges, and adopting a list of personal rules of conduct needed to meet these obligations, are among the most widespread means of working on oneself.[53] Aret wrote that 81 percent of tenth-graders and 64 percent of sixth-graders in his sample adopted these personal programs of development. However, he also found the scope of these programs wanting: junior pupils chose programs that centered on physical training and sports, while senior pupils dropped these to focus on perfecting personal relations within a *kollektiv*; that is, they tried to correct their moral character.[54] To replace such spontaneous one-sided planning, Aret recommended a multifaceted approach that combined moral with physical development. He referred to a recent decision of the October 1959 plenum of the Komsomol, recommending the adoption of "a unified program of personal development" by each member. A bit later, in 1969, the Central Committee of the Komsomol institutionalized the system of the "Lenin Pass" (*Leninskii zachet*) in every one of its primary organizations; thus, it applied to every high school class. The public ritual of the Lenin Pass included institutionalized adoption of annual obligations for self-improvement. These obligations were to be written down

51. Works on giving commands to oneself appeared earlier than those dealing with other aspects of working on oneself (see T. I. Agafonov, "K voprosu o psikhologii samoprikaza" [On the problem of the psychology of giving a command to oneself], *Uchenye zapiski Krasnodarskogo Pedagogicheskogo Instituta* [Learned notes of the Krasnodar Pedagogical Institute] 2 [1957]).

52. In fact, Soviet educationalists did not use exactly these terms; they preferred to speak about "working out personal rules of conduct" and "adopting personal programs of action" in the first case, and of "imitation of the ideal" in the second case.

53. Personal rules, in contrast to personal programs, were sets of personal mottoes—Never Give Up, Finish Whatever You Started, and the like. Kovalev offers 16 model rules, concocted out of the personal rules of Tolstoy and Ushinsky, found in their diaries (Kovalev, *Lichnost' vospityvaet sebia*, 132)

54. Aret, *Ocherki*, 105.

on a standard printed form, called "the composite personal plan" (*lichnyi kompleksnyi plan*),[55] according to the three main dimensions of personal development: moral, labor, and intellectual. Some versions of these plans included "military-patriotic" and "aesthetic" dimensions as well.

Of course, adoption of personal programs by the Komsomol members was neither novel nor surprising as a method of self-training. Planning was a central feature of Soviet life; personal planning was recommended even by the earliest sources on working on oneself—witness Krupskaia's recommendations on systematic reading plans. Ostrovsky also insisted on personal planning: after harsh self-criticism, the next step in self-development was programming: "one needs to establish for oneself a life goal, perhaps breaking it down into separate sequential steps," so that achieving these subgoals becomes feasible.[56] The novelty of the 1970s lay in the authorities' order: the obligatory adoption of self-programming by all Komsomol members took in virtually all young Soviet citizens.

Along with self-planning, hero-identification was another major technique of self-transformation.[57] Hardly ever institutionalized, it was nevertheless recommended by almost every source on self-training.[58] Earlier sources were not very specific: the original 1958 monograph recommended

55. Every Soviet schoolchild had state-printed diaries and schedules to regulate life at school: on entering the first grade, a pupil bought a standard printed diary with empty graphs for the six study days and filled in the classes, setting up a mechanical routine each week; there were appropriate slots for grades given for written and oral presentations, and disciplinary comments by teachers. Each two-page spread that covered a week was supposed to be signed by a parent at the end of this week, and then by a teacher, who checked the parent's signature.

56. Ostrovsky, "Mysli o samovospitanii."

57. Christel Lane described the phenomenon of ritualized heroism in the later Soviet society. Using Sherry Ortner's definition of heroes (who supply a given culture's strategies for successful living), she focused on such phenomena as the existence of officially certified living Heroes of Socialist Labor, an award title established in 1938. See Christel Lane, *The Rites of the Rulers* (Cambridge: Cambridge University Press, 1981). We deal here with a different aspect: a personal technique of identifying with a hero.

58. The only exception to this universal rule was Aret, who keeps silent on these matters. Perhaps his Lutheran background—which may explain his unparalleled preoccupation with internal techniques of self-analysis—also stops him from recommending hero-identification, a ritualistic Russian technique of imitating Christ in outward behavior. (Aulis Iakubovich Aret, apparently an Estonian by birth and prewar citizenship, was widely published in Estonian pedagogical journals until the late 1930s. His writings reappear only in the late 1950s, in the publications of the Kirghiz Republican University in the city of Frunze, where Aret headed the laboratory on self-training until his death. Did the move to Frunze result from evacuation or exile?)

hanging a picture of Korchagin on the wall above one's study table and adopting a personal motto from one of the heroic novels of socialist realism.[59] However, this was already deeply ingrained in Soviet culture and, thus perhaps did not require special attention and institutionalization. In the poem of Vladimir Mayakovsky that constituted part of the compulsory school program in literature, one learned the way to identify: "To a youth, who is thinking about his future life, about who to copy in one's life, / I say: Model it on Comrade Dzerzhinsky!"[60] Ostrovsky similarly advised following "high models of spiritual and moral grandeur": ancient Greeks, explorers, and revolutionaries like Marx, Engels, Lenin, and Stalin. For Ostrovsky himself, the model was a generalized figure of the Old Bolshevik, "an individual, who is morally highly organized, with a willed attitude."[61]

Ruvinsky supplied a most systematic description of the technique of hero-identification in his primer for pedagogical institutes of higher education. There are three stages of transforming a "pedagogical image" into a "personal ideal." First, the pedagogical image exists as an orienting pattern: we know it, but do not necessarily follow it. Then it becomes procedural reality: we copy it but do not accept it as a moral value. The third stage arrives when—passing through comparison and mimesis, we arrive at full identification—we accept the image as a personal value, willingly imitating it in everyday conduct.[62] Ruvinsky gives an example of an image that allegedly elicited hero-identification at this time: Rakhmetov, a literary creation of Chernyshevsky, who was a personal hero for Lenin, is said to be followed by many modern Soviet youths as well. However, laments Ruvinsky, kids usually choose to follow the external aspects of Rakhmetov's self-training—they fast or sleep on nails. The main aim of the technique of hero-identification should be different: rather than thoughtlessly repeating Rakhmetov's feats, one should use such exercises to form an internal world similar to Rakhmetov's. The 1988 brochure for schoolchildren also called for transforming the personally chosen hero (Arctic travelers and pilots were advised) into a "dear and intimate" companion. However, one need not copy this hero in inventing special exercises, as some children did—pinching their fingers in the door in imitation of Aleksei Maresiev's

59. Kovalev and Bodalev, *Psikhologiia i pedagogika samovospitaniia*, 68.
60. In Russian, *Iuntsu, obdumyvaiushchemu zhitie, sdelat' by zhizn's kogo, / skazhu: delai ee s tovarishcha Dzerzhinskogo!*
61. In Russian, *s volevoi ustanovkoi* (Ostrovsky, "Mysli o samovospitanii").
62. Ruvinsky and Solov'eva, *Psikhologiia samovospitaniia*, 80.

feats, for example[63]—one should simply be persevering in fulfilling whatever goals one set oneself in everyday life.

Altogether, techniques of both personal planning and hero identification serve as the central components in the second stage of working on oneself, which was also often called "the training of the will." Programs are props for the training of will, while heroic mimesis is a practical means to help overcome difficulties. Nevertheless, the telos of the process of working on oneself—self-control—was considered to have been attained during the third and final stage of self-training, when self-restraint and self-renunciation were already practiced with ease.[64] Though this condition of self-control was generally supposed to be the final aim of individual development, a further degree of perfection was also recommended by some authors within this stage. Certain special exercises were suggested, highly reminiscent of religious exercises to fight passions and ward off temptations.

Earlier sources even used religious language. In 1955 N. S. Lukin advised "fleeing from temptations" as a means of self-training for self-control in teenagers, while Aret recommended switching one's attention to better, higher matters if a mean thought appeared.[65] Some curious later sources secularized Orthodox self-training techniques to a certain extent, while avoiding religious terms. Thus, a Bulgarian author writing for the Soviet audience added to the usually recommended control of acts another injunction: "a man should always control his thoughts, moods, emotions." He proposed two means: first, ordering the external world and family life and adopting a strict personal "regime of the day" one could order one's thoughts and feelings; second, if still bothered by the disorderly thoughts

63. A hero of Boris Polevoi's novel *A Story of a Real Man* (1947), the pilot Maresiev parachuted when the Germans shot down his plane and landed with both legs broken, but crawled in the snowy forest back to Soviet positions. After the amputation of both legs, he returned to the ranks of air fighters, wearing artificial limbs.

64. As may now be obvious from my terminology, I adapt four coordinates that Foucault used to analyze ethical practices in the *History of Sexuality*, vols. 2–3: (1) "ethical substance"—those elements of human life that become objects of ethical concern; (2) "a mode of subjection"—the approach that brings the ethical substance into conformity with a certain ethical rule; (3) *travail ethique*—the practical efforts that transform the ethical substance; (4) "telos"—a certain standard, an aim of ethical transformation. I interpret the fourfold Soviet schema as follows: (1) deeds; (2) *oblichenie*, or revelation in accordance with Marxist teaching; (3) self-planning and hero-identification; (4) self-renunciation, or self-control.

65. N. S. Lukin, *Vospitanie vyderzhki u podrostkov* [Training of self-control in teenagers] (Moscow, 1955), 73; quoted in Aret, *Ocherki*, 116–119.

and passions, one could employ special exercises of controlled physical motion and of emotional suppression in order to ward them off.[66] Rather than offer such extravagant quasi-monastic recipes, the majority of advocates of self-control recommended consistent and methodical fulfillment of planned personal objectives, by means of mimesis of an adopted heroic model.

Let us now survey the overall picture of recommended practices of self-fashioning. Even if in reality only a few willing Soviet individuals carried out the full set of techniques of self-training as the indifferent majority accepted it in part and some recalcitrant individuals rejected it, the logic behind the imposition of these techniques of "working on oneself" reveals a lot about a shared background for individual self-development in Soviet society. Three particular aspects of this logic deserve stress: the initial collective sanction as an impetus for individual self-reflection; the subsequent progressive internalization of the communal mechanisms as a personal means of self-perfection; and, finally, subordination of resulting inner self-analysis to the control of actions.

The first aspect—the collective sanction, or public statement of an individual's deficiencies—elicits a yearning for self-training. Many authors write about the dependence of successful self-training on the development of the *kollektiv*. Referring to Makarenko's four stages of *kollektiv*-building, they clearly posit self-training in the fourth stage of this development: when members of the *kollektiv* zealously police one another and also start to police themselves more successfully.[67] To escape a collective and untimely *oblichenie*, it is better to train yourself to control your own behavior. In the early Soviet days many people were for the first time forced to attend to themselves, or to reflect on their personal features, as a result of the intervention of the reference group; in later Soviet society, this intervention ushered in practices of self-care and self-transformation among children.

Ruvinsky distinguishes among age groups, or chronological stages of personal development of the capacity to analyze oneself. The initial willingness to perfect oneself appears already in a young child, who, upon being criticized for misdeeds, corrects his or her behavior accordingly. However, children do not establish ties between their external behavior and internal features of their personality. Teenagers who are twelve to fifteen years old may already establish the relationship between their deeds and features of their characters, but only in the next stage do youngsters start measuring

---

66. Momov and Kochetov, *Samovospitanie, samoutverzhdenie,* 27–29.
67. See Kovalev and Bodalev, *Psikhologiia i pedagogika samovospitaniia,* 11–12; Ruvinsky and Solov'eva, *Psikhologiia samovospitaniia,* 84–86.

their internal features as revealed in their deeds, against the highest standards set by the "Moral Code of the Builder of Communism."[68]

Another typology of the development of revelation by deeds similarly captures different types of reactions to external prodding by the *kollektiv*. Some people have only a "procedural-situational" capacity for self-analysis; they correct their acts upon criticism, but their self-concept is not affected. Others are capable of a "feature-situational" analysis: they see the relation between deeds and self but use certain deeds as rigid indicators of certain personal qualities and usually possess inadequate self-evaluation, since one deed, or even a specific series of deeds, rarely represent an objective expression of the complicated personality. The most widespread type of self-analysis is "feature-conservative": individuals have a stable self-concept after analyzing the expression of self in multiple and various deeds but do not change it to reflect new information that may conflict with it. The desirable fourth type of self-analysis, "feature-dynamic," belongs to individuals who have a constant dynamic relationship between the self and deeds: they constantly adjust the self-concept after thorough analysis of recently performed deeds.[69]

These types outline the historical stages of individualization in Soviet history. Type one is characteristic of peasants who become workers who become Communists, and are surprised to find out that they have some personal features that do not satisfy the local Control Commission; as a result they simply stop performing this suspect behavior in public.[70] Type two is characteristic of an early Bolshevik for whom specific zealous or heroic deeds speak of a unique *lichnost'*. Type three is a feature of those who had passed the purge, or its milder equivalents in mundane Soviet life: once one's self is assured, one does not worry until the next purging. Type four is the ultimate achievement of Soviet individualization: a modern subject who constantly readjusts his or her self-concept by staging internal mini-trials over his or her demonstrated deeds.

The second aspect—the internalization of the *kollektiv*'s influence and mechanisms to achieve self-order—replicates processes in the broader society. In fact, Aret explicitly claims that "any means of training becomes a means of self-training, if a man applies it to himself."[71] Ruvinsky also

68. Ruvinsky, *Samovospitanie lichnosti*, 27.
69. Ruvinsky and Solov'eva, *Psikhologiia samovospitaniia*, 65–66.
70. On dissimulation, see note 119 below.
71. Aret, *Ocherki*, 26. Another point that should not be overlooked: Aret repeats a number of times that self-transformation techniques in his compendium may be practiced by both the individual and the *kollektiv*.

supports the thesis that techniques of working on oneself are "in essence, means of training, translated into the language of the theory of self-training"[72]—save for such techniques of self-influence that lead to negative results, since these are not means of self-building, but rather means of self-destruction (say, paranoid self-delusion). Earlier sources on working on oneself advocated more group-based and group-supported techniques of self-care than later ones. For example, I. A. Samarin recommends practicing self-accounting not only alone, but in front of a friend, or of a Komsomol cell.[73] Perhaps, greater efficiency of self-training is the reason for hooking it up with collective surveillance. In order to achieve effective self-transformation, advises the first scholarly treatise on the topic,

> a creation of successful conditions for everyday practice of working on oneself in the *kollektiv* . . . is of decisive importance. Our experience tells us that these conditions are: a staging of self-accounts and adopting of obligations in front of the authoritative *kollektiv*, staging a review of the concrete aspects of the student's activity that is delayed in time and of which he is warned beforehand.[74]

Aret's typology of the six methods of knowing oneself breaks down the universal ritual of *oblichenie* and reifies its constituent elements. Later Soviet sources take for granted that separate elements of these community-based training—and shaming—techniques have been internalized, and thus have become means of self-training. Perhaps there is no better example for this progressive internalization than the representation of internal self-criticism in Ostrovsky, to which I have already alluded: an external purge is restaged within one's soul.

The third important generic aspect of Bolshevik practices of working on oneself—its subordination of self-cognition techniques to action—left inner self-analysis with a curious status. It was to be practiced, but with a certain restraint and suspicion. As a result, many Soviet people seemed not to even know what self-knowing was exactly. In one of the high school classes for which Aret gives data, only 20 percent of the interviewed students could correctly define the term "self-cognition" (*samopoznanie*). Others proposed the following explanations: "cognition of everything by oneself," "studies outside school," and so on. Only a few of those interviewed (13 out

---

72. Ruvinsky, *Samovospitanie lichnosti*, 50; apparently this "translation" involves only adding the word "self-" in the beginning of the word that describes a given means of training.

73. Samarin, *Vospitanie voli*, 36.

74. Kovalev and Bodalev, *Psikhologiia i pedagogika samovospitaniia*, 87.

of 39) practiced some of the specifically internal techniques of self-cognition
—individual self-reflection, say, or self-analysis—while the 82 percent
practiced a simple comparison of oneself with others. But the result of the
application of this uncomplicated technique of "recognizing oneself through
others" was startling: 64.5 percent of the interviewed believed that they
knew themselves well![75] Apparently, individuals gained self-knowledge
primarily through self-comparison with others and direct judgments others made about them.

This finding mirrors one in Western Sovietology. Alex Inkeles, writing
after a series of standard psychological tests comparing modal personality features of the general American public with those of Russian émigrés
concluded in 1958: "Russians displayed rather low and unintense self-
awareness and little painful self-consciousness. They showed rather high
and secure self-esteem, and were little given to self-examination and doubt
of their inner selves. . . . The organization of their personality depended for
its coherence much more heavily on their intimate relatedness to those
around them."[76] Americans, according to Inkeles, on the contrary, were
prone to acute self-awareness and, since they were constantly doubting
their inner qualities, resorted to substantial self-examination in order to
resolve these issues.

Soviet educationalists gave some reasons for this curtailment of internal
self-examination. Aret wrote that "because self-analysis was at the service
of reactionary-idealist psychology," Soviet pedagogical thought had a lot of
reservations about it. Practiced without these reservations, self-analysis
could easily evolve into *samokopanie*, the "fruitless self-rummaging," so
typical of Russian intellectuals and aristocrats and a favorite object of Bolshevik attacks. For the Bolsheviks, self-analysis that was practiced for the
sake of self-analysis, and that never resulted in practical action, was a feature of the capitalist education of a bourgeois individual. For example, Lunacharsky wrote: "Eternal self-rummaging, expressed in lengthy confessions to a priest, in which people analyzed their soul, was a process of
capitalist self-discipline."[77] By contrast, the Bolsheviks espoused the ideal
of the man of productive action, rather than of fruitless endless confes-

75. Aret, *Ocherki*, 69–70.
76. Alex Inkeles, "Modal Personality and Adjustment to the Soviet Sociopolitical System" (1958), in *Social Change in Soviet Russia* (Cambridge, Mass.: Harvard University Press, 1968), 116, 120–121.
77. Anatolii Lunacharsky, *Istoriia zapadno-evropeiskoi literatury v ee vazhneishikh momentakh* [History of Western European literature in its most important moments] (Moscow, n.d.), 1:7.

sions. A dictionary article on *samokopanie* gives an example of usage from the novel of Boris Gorbatov: "Aleksei hates sissies and their intellectualist self-rummaging."[78] Ostrovsky expressed a similar preference for deeds over words: "It is difficult to imagine a more disgusting character than a honey-exuding sentimentalist who all of his life . . . indulges in sentimental outpourings of words, and at the same time is not capable of a single courageous deed."[79]

For the same reason, the use of diaries presented a problem. Aret held diaries useful, but with important reservations. Diaries, of course, were supposed to record events that were revealing about one's personality, including both one's deeds and the sentiments accompanying these deeds. But in this respect, only Herzen's and Feliks Dzerzhinsky's diaries could serve as models. Diaries of individuals that recorded a complicated stream of consciousness, such as those of Tolstoy and Dobroliubov, were useful to read only in adapted versions with additional commentaries on Communist self-training; otherwise they could be ineffectual or even harmful.[80] Later Soviet sources were also ambiguous on the issue of diaries, and Ruvinsky even cited Diesterweg's radical claim that diaries were completely useless.[81]

To make a Soviet reader in the 1980s understand why unrestrained self-analysis was suspect, one of the books on self-training quoted the following excerpt from a letter, written by a Komsomol zealot to his brother in the 1930s:

> Where did you get the idea that a man works out the way of his own development by means of a diary, by means of organizing and studying his own self? . . . No, my dear, what is most valuable in man's life is his work and not his diary. . . . Because knowing and loving one's work, . . . keeping in step with the multimillion member collective, is the main thing in contemporary training and self-training. And the diary is not a method of self-training, but a method of self-rummaging. It is suitable for the 'intellectuals' (in the derogatory sense of the word), who 'study' themselves and dig in the depths of their own psychology,—here am I, a mean and weak-willed man; here is the misdeed I committed.[82]

78. Article on *samokopanie*, in *Slovar'*. Gorbatov is a very suitable source for quotes on "self-digging"; as we noted before, he was one of the best examples of the Komsomol zealot.

79. Ostrovsky, "Mysli o samovospitanii."

80. Aret, *Ocherki*, 85.

81. Ruvinsky, *Samovospitanie lichnosti*, 55.

82. S. Chekmarev, *Stikhi, pis'ma, dnevnik* [Poems, letters, diary] (Moscow, 1959), 141–142; quoted in Dontsov, *Samovospitanie lichnosti*, 201.

The Soviet author who cited this passage himself found the practice of keeping a diary useful (Stakhanov, had one, after all!), but useful only to the extent that the diary was at the service of practical revolutionary activity, subordinating self-analysis to the needs of practical action.

Thus, ambiguity resulted from an obvious contradiction: internal self-analysis was a legitimate part of the process of self-cognition, on the one hand; but, on the other, protracted self-analysis smacked of possessing a nonactive, nonrevolutionary self. Therefore, Aret provided the following precautions for those who practiced self-analysis: one should "not allow an excessively deep self-analysis, particularly one that concerns trifles and inessential sides of the personality; one should not allow one-sided self-analysis, when it is directed toward a few features of personality, neglecting others; one should not get excited by the analysis of the negative features of one's own behavior and personality; one's analysis should come to practical conclusions: [set] tasks and implement them energetically."[83] The recommendations of the 1970s and 1980s echoed Aret: self-analysis should accompany practical action to transform the self, rather than being an end in itself. The danger in self-analysis was clearly captured by a suggestive metaphor of later days: one should engage in self-analysis like a doctor, define what is wrong and go right to work on it.[84] As the metaphor implies, the fear is that drawing out and refining the diagnosis might cause the patient—the soul to be cured—to die.

CHRISTIAN ANTECEDENTS OF WORKING ON ONESELF

At this point in the examination of a curious object that constantly preoccupied the Soviet regime, while remaining largely unnoticed in the West, we come on two obvious questions. First, how does this working on oneself, with which the Soviet pedagogues bothered themselves so much, relate to the previous Orthodox Christian practices of self-perfection and self-transformation?—was Soviet Russia different from the Orthodox Russia, or will we find on a pragmatic level some type of a continuum between the two? Second, and more interestingly, how does Bolshevik working on oneself relate to all the intense self-examination techniques of the aristocracy and the intelligentsia, expressed, for example, in the novels of Tolstoy and Dostoyevsky that brought Russian culture its initial world acclaim?—

83. Aret, *Ocherki*, 76.
84. Momov and Kochetov, *Samovospitanie, samoutverzhdenie*, 24–25.

isn't it strange that confessional practices that first made Russia famous play such a subservient and negligible role in the Bolshevik set of practices of self-perfection? Exploring the antecedents will help us better understand the change that the Russian Revolution ushered in.

Let's first take a closer look at Orthodox Christian techniques of self-perfection. Comparing them to the Bolshevik set, we see neither an easy continuum nor a radical break. Indeed, some features of Communist self-training find striking parallels in an earlier Orthodox Christian literature on self-perfection. Communal prodding toward self-reflection, internalizing *oblichenie*, and subordinating inner self-analysis to the correction of deeds exist there also. But some features of self-training seem of a generic — rather than of specifically Orthodox — Christian origin. Furthermore, important differences in self-fashioning practices hint at the changes that the Revolution effected in the preexisting Orthodox Christian background.

First, the similarities. As in the Communist program, the initial move to a Christian concern with oneself frequently comes as a result of an external initiative. In idiomatic language, *oblichenie* should make people "attend to themselves." For example, a father advises a son in the most popular medieval book of household governance: "If someone accused [*oblichit*] me of a sin or impiety or gave me spiritual advice, or if somebody ridiculed or reproached me, all these I lovingly accepted and attended to myself" (*sebe vnimakh*).[85] If this heightening of attention to oneself and the correction of misdeeds does not happen, further admonition follows; if several admonitions prove also to be in vain, expulsion of the sinner is the last resort. The triad reveal-admonish-excommunicate offers an opportunity to attend to oneself after each move of its machinery.

In similar terms, Joseph Volotsky described the process of an individual attending to himself following an accusation from the brethren in his monastery. Elder brothers were supposed to practice *oblichenie;* while the novices had to listen to revelations concerning them that came from others, and to inspect themselves closely. "The entering juniors do not expose, nor prohibit, but only attend to themselves [*sebe vnimaiut*] and accept advice from all parties," [86] wrote Joseph in his statute. Sources from the fourteenth and fifteenth centuries translate *vnimat' sebe* as "to go deep into

85. A. Orlov, ed., *Domostroi — po konshinskomu spisku* (Moscow, 1908), 65.
86. "Dukhovnaia Gramota prepodobnogo Iosifa," col. 578. An expression *otov-siudu sebe zazirati* in the end of this phrase is very revealing: literally, "they look at themselves from all sides."

oneself," "to immerse oneself into oneself," as represented in the following examples: "People do not attend to themselves [*vnimaiut sebe*], and
they slumber as if they were immortals"; "Divine ways are unknown: because of that we should immerse ourselves in ourselves [*sebe vnimat'*] and
lament our misdeeds."[87]

Tikhon Zadonsky highlighted and popularized the practice of attending
to oneself perhaps more than any other writer. This interesting eighteenth-
century monk, one of only four saints canonized by the Russian Church
between the seventeenth and twentieth centuries, was famous for his
preaching to the common people, and may have been instrumental in the
spread of self-awareness techniques. Billington, in one of the surprisingly
few Western commentaries on Tikhon, mentions that his aim was to bring
monastic life out to the people; he centered on "inward renewal and reded-
ication," concerns that Billington ascribes to German pietistic influence on
Tikhon.[88] Orthodox theological commentaries on Tikhon also stress his
pastoral zeal, his utterly emotional style ("from the overflow of heart his
lips talk," says one of the commentaries), and the specific discursive strategies he employed to be understood by simple folk.[89] In explaining the Bible
he used many analogies, and instead of providing peasants with a string of
theological syllogisms that were hardly digestible, Tikhon rhetorically
poured out all the divine truths at once, juxtaposing them in their shining
beauty, so that peasants might "enter the . . . room, where one sees all the
[divine] beauties simultaneously and enjoys them."[90]

Tikhon left a sixteen-volume oeuvre, but bits and pieces of it were reprinted in the nineteenth century in small booklets of ten to fifteen pages
that were intended for the lower classes' consumption. The booklet that is
of particular interest to us, *Attend to Oneself*, has a very strange form.[91] It
opens with the assertion: "You ask: what does this expression [the one
in the title of the booklet] mean?" The answer, however, does not follow.

87. Examples from Barkhudarov, ed., *Slovar' russkogo*.
88. J. H. Billington, *The Icon and the Axe* (New York: Vintage, 1966), 202. His
thesis on Pietistic influence is challenged in Nadejda Gorodetzky, *Saint Tikhon
Zadonsky* (London: SPCK, 1951), 98.
89. Archimandrit Evlogii, *O sviatitele Tikhone Zadonskom i ego tvoreniiakh*
[On St. Tikhon Zadonsky and his works] (Moscow, 1898), 11. Also see Georges
Florovsky, *Puti russkago bogoslovia* [Ways of Russian theology] (Paris: YMCA-
Press, 1937), 123–125.
90. Evlogii, *O sviatitele*, 11.
91. Tikhon Zadonsky, *Vnimai sebe* [Attend to yourself] (St. Petersburg, 1894).

Instead, the reader gets a series of further questions on matters of piety, each followed by the same exhortation: "Attend to yourself!" For example:

> You call yourself a Christian; but do you perform deeds appropriate to a Christian? Attend to yourself. You believe in God. But do you pay homage to Him with a clear conscience? Attend to yourself. . . . You promised in baptism to serve Christ faithfully and truthfully, but do you remember and keep your promises? Attend to yourself.[92]

This discursive strategy is ingenious: instead of telling an interested reader what attending to oneself means, Tikhon makes him or her live it out in the actual experience of reading the booklet. In response to Tikhon's questions, the reader effectively attends to him- or herself, and thus, by responding, performs the answer to the question posed in the first line of the booklet. Furthermore, this potentially novel experience (of attending to oneself) is immediately named by the exhortation following each question. It is indeed hard to imagine a speech act that could have more performative force. After reading the booklet, the person not only knows what attending to oneself means but has also already practiced it.

Perhaps the booklet simply reifies the process of *oblichenie,* directed from a priest to a Christian.[93] As the text progresses, the questions become more and more inquisitive, expressing suspicion that the interlocutor is not being honest with himself or herself:

> You raise your hands to God? . . . But don't you desecrate them by robbery, thievery, and other injustice? Attend to yourself. . . . Do you call with your mouth the holy and dreadful name of God? But don't you disgrace it by mean speech, libel, censure, flattery, lies, and other vices? Attend to yourself. Do you position your body in God's prayer? But do you position your spirit there? Isn't it the case that your tongue says

---

92. Ibid., 3.

93. Interpreting Foucault, Dreyfus and Rabinow suggest that confessional practices lie at the heart of the contemporary "interpretive turn" in the social sciences: when the scientific community uses the wider society's practices to gain social knowledge, they acquire the familiar guise of "hermeneutics." The practice of revelation by deeds may engender a corresponding method of knowing in the human sciences. Endowing the reader with an immediate, directly experienced knowledge of the phenomenon in question, without ever explicitly defining what this phenomenon is, Tikhon follows the methodology of homiletics—the art of preaching, yet another discipline taught at the seminaries together with hermeneutics, exegesis of the meaning of sacred texts. Perhaps Tikhon's homiletics may now be secularized to form the basis of a very specific kind of interpretive inquiry, distinct from hermeneutics.

one thing in the prayer, while your mind thinks of another? Attend to yourself.[94]

The booklet objectifies *oblichenie* and basically entrusts the act of final condemnation to its readers themselves, following the act of attending to oneself. Self-condemnation thus becomes a first step on the way to self-perfection. To put it slightly differently, external *oblichenie* that engendered internal attention to oneself, as represented in the example from the medieval household manual, is now internalized as a result of the reading of the book. One attends to oneself, having positioned an imaginary accuser within oneself.

It is interesting to juxtapose Tikhon's fiery rhetoric to the themes of self-training in the 1936 pamphlet by Iaroslavsky that we have already quoted:

> You, the Communist, ask yourself: do you understand Party discipline in the same way [as described above in the pamphlet]? Do you live up to these demands? Do you underpin Party discipline with your Conscience, your dedication to the revolution, your self-control, your self-sacrifice, and heroism?[95]

The affinities are striking. The only difference is that Iaroslavsky exhorts the reader to "ask yourself," rather than "attend to yourself." But there is no functional difference here: the common aim is concern with the self.

Yet Iaroslavsky's brochure was more effective than Tikhon's simply because the same performative effects happened in a different general context; his questions were posed in the tense atmosphere of the purges, when each Party *kollektiv* demanded saintly behavior from its members. In Makarenko's terms, its context was the fourth phase of *kollektiv*-building that demanded attending to oneself from everybody: therefore, it was no longer entrusted to the vicissitudes of the dissemination of a printed text. Rather it was carried out as a result of the interaction of every *kollektiv*. Makarenko's method of the "advancing of individual" started with Tikhon's and Iaroslavsky's *oblichenie* techniques, and it was inescapably effective: "We say to Petrov: 'You are in the swamp,' and we try to activate him. Some time passes, and he distinguishes himself in something [*sebia proiavil*], gets interested, distinguishes himself again, and he transfers to the *passiv* or to the reserve."[96] Poor Petrov; in earlier days attending to oneself had not involved such a frightening force.

94. Tikhon Zadonsky, *Vnimai sebe*, 5.
95. Iaroslavsky, *Chego partiia trebuet ot kommunista,*1936 ed., 51.
96. Makarenko 5:173.

260 / Working on Oneself

In contrast to these obvious similarities in communal prodding toward self-fashioning and in attempts to make the recalcitrant populace internalize *oblichenie* techniques, there is a more complicated relation between Orthodox Christian and Bolshevik core practices of self-transformation. Not all the Bolshevik practices have clear analogues in the Orthodox set. Let us examine the two important works of Orthodox moral theology of the nineteenth century—a textbook by Ioann Ianyshev, chair of moral theology in the St. Petersburg Spiritual Academy, and a treatise on Christian moral living by Bishop Theophanus (Govorov)—to outline this complex relationship. Ianyshev's work is more systematic and logical, being the product of a scholarly mind; Theophanus's is more emotional.

At least one of the two main Bolshevik techniques of working on oneself—hero-identification—finds an obvious antecedent in Orthodox moral theology and its injunction to imitate Christ if one wishes to attain the heights of Christian living. Theophanus writes: "One should seek the highest degree of perfection in Jesus Christ, one should posit this [search] as an aim for oneself. . . . An obligation to strive for perfection is the same as the obligation to imitate the Lord Jesus Christ, imagine Him in oneself, imprint his perfection in oneself."[97] Furthermore, the telos of this self-perfection—self-sacrifice or, in a milder version, self-control in order to subjugate oneself to a higher cause—is also identical in Bolshevik and Orthodox sources. Thus, in the words of Theophanus, the main law of life of the Christian individual is "czardom over oneself with self-sacrifice to God." This self-control—he uses the very word *samoobladanie* that also figures heavily in the Communist literature as the term to designate the telos of working on oneself—is expressed in the way in which a true Christian sacrifices everything to God: his spirit, his body, his material possessions and status. First, a Christian sacrifices his spirit: his mind, in that he thinks what God says; his will, in that he wishes what God orders; his heart, in that he loves what God wills him to love. The sacrifice of the body involves ascetic exercises and chastity, and subjection of lower bodily motions to the command of higher faculties of the spirit.[98] In the less emotional language of Ianyshev, *samo-sobrannost'* ("self-gatheredness" or "self-control") is "a constant effort of the self . . . to submit to itself and consequently to its own moral sentiment the movements of instrumental forces of a Christian, both spiritual and corporeal, which are accustomed to vile

97. Theophanus (Govorov), *Nachertanie khristianskogo nravoucheniia* [Outlines of Christian moral teaching], (Moscow, 1891), 456.
98. Ibid., 459.

activity, are subject to external impressions and tend to dissipate on external objects."[99]

These injunctions are almost as demanding in force and scope as the brochures of such Communist zealots as Krupskaia, Liadov, and Iaroslavsky. They, as we remember, wished the Communist to sacrifice everything to the Party cause, and live conscientiously in both public and private lives. The Party takes the place of God, but self-renunciation in favor of the higher cause remains. We should note, however, that this self-renunciation that the Russian nineteenth-century moral theology advocated, and that the zealous Bolsheviks also accepted as a most worthy aim, does not have necessarily Orthodox roots. Indeed, the telos of self-renunciation seem to be common to all brands of Christianity; it is a phenomenon of generic quality stemming from the practice of imitating Christ.

Of course, types and styles of self-renunciation could differ, and there were predominantly Russian types of *imitatio Christi*. The first two canonized Russian saints, Boris and Gleb, had established a typically Russian type of sainthood—voluntary martyrdom, captured in the Greek term *kenosis*—when they meekly submitted themselves to the knives of their slaughterers in imitation of Jesus Christ.[100] Another type of specifically Russian sainthood, fools for Christ—discussed in the previous chapter—imitated Christ's access to otherworldly truth through mortification of flesh and intentional neglect of common sense. However, these exceptional types of sainthood are rather far away from the Bolshevik resolute and stern self-renunciation in methodic action required to change the world. Thus, the Bolsheviks were closer to a generic self-renunciation required of any Christian. Apparently, this imitation of Christ could rather easily blend with an imitation of spectacular Party heroes, who had already achieved self-renunciation, and, in the later Soviet years, with a technique of identification with a self-chosen hero.

In contrast to hero identification, the second central technique of Bolshevik self-fashioning—self-planning—is largely absent from Orthodox writings on moral theology. Of course, there is some marginal mention of

99. I. L. Ianyshev, *Pravoslavno-khristianskoe uchenie o nravstvennosti* [Orthodox Christian teaching on morals], 2d ed. (St. Petersburg, 1906), 435.

100. Sergei Averintsev, "Vizantiia i Rus': dva tipa dukhovnosti" [Byzantium and Russia: two types of spirituality], *Novyi Mir*, September 1988, 231. For a recent fundamental exposition on *kenosis* see Vladimir Toporov, *Sviatost' i sviatye v russkoi dukhovnoi kul'ture*. Vol. 1, *Pervyi vek khristianstva na Rusi* [Sainthood and saints in Russian spiritual culture, vol. 1, First century of Christianity in Russia] (Moscow: Gnosis, 1995), esp. 413–507.

planning in rationalist Ianyshev. He states: "Every day, having gathered oneself together in internal deeds—having gathered the spirit, as they say —having appraised beforehand the task of the day, one should set about his business." In later stages of self-perfection, says Ianyshev, this "plan" will be unnecessary, since God will point a Christian in the required direction in every mundane situation.[101] Still, even this quote can be hardly taken as a definitive demand for planning oneself, rather than for simply planning daily activities. Furthermore, we find nothing like self-planning in Theophanus, save modest references to the need for order in mundane affairs.[102]

The absence of self-programming in Orthodox writings should not overshadow yet another, and a more profound, difference between them and the Communist treatises on working on oneself. Nineteenth-century theologians were primarily concerned with the control of passions and thoughts, rather than with control of actions. Both Theophanus and Ianyshev spend far more time discussing techniques of spiritual combat with passions than techniques of subjecting observable deeds to a certain standard. And Ianyshev's treatise describes attention to oneself as a means of controlling passions and sentiments, with specific techniques recommended in this incessant struggle. Most sections concern guidance in introspective exercises. In Theophanus, the section on individual self-care is contained in the last chapter dealing with the rules of Christian living. Previous chapters concern "attaining [pious] sentiments and dispositions" in those who prepare for baptism, and maintaining these pious sentiments in those who already dwell in God. These sentiments include adoring God and its creations, the feeling of awe at the sight of the immensity of His power, and so on. The last chapter, from which we quoted extensively, discusses how to evoke proper feelings and dispositions in those dwelling in God by means of partaking in the visible Church. Though it mentions the visible Church practices, it sets out the exposition's aim in the titles of sections: "to evoke sentiments and dispositions," that is, to control thoughts and passions rather than acts.

This aim stands in stark contrast to the Bolsheviks who concentrated on controlling acts in directing internal feelings rather than in controlling feelings as such. Were the Bolsheviks more realistic, when they imposed on the Russian populace their demand of controlling external actions, than the theologians who requested intense spiritual combat? It would seem so. High theology seemed to stand in contrast even to beliefs of those Ortho-

---

101. Ianyshev, *Pravoslavno-khristianskoe uchenie o nravstvennosti,* 449.
102. Theophanus, *Nachertanie,* 471.

dox clergy who preached to the simple folk and thus knew the popular demand better. Tikhon Zadonsky, for example, did not give much attention
to the passions either; his questions in the booklet I cite are more concerned
with external acts that contradict the stated fundamentals of the faith. In
another booklet, entitled *On the Goal of Good Deeds*, he wrote:

> Our faith requires from us the demonstration of this faith in our deeds.
> . . . And even if the faith in Christ alone will save us without regard to
> our deeds (Jacob 2:18) . . . , this faith cannot be idle. There is no saving
> faith in the person who does not perform good deeds, but only some
> oral, hypocritical, or—as the apostle teaches—dead faith.[103]

Summing up, one can say that the Bolshevik set of self-fashioning
practices retains the Christian telos of individual self-perfection—self-
renunciation and self-sacrifice. It also incorporates the main practical means
of attaining this telos in Christian sainthood—that is, imitation of Christ
—though in a transformed guise of the technique of hero identification.
However, personal planning seems to be an utterly modern phenomenon that the Bolshevik set adds to the age-old monastic practices. Thus,
the novelty of the Bolshevik recasting of the Orthodox practices of self-
perfection consists in the joining of hero-identification with modern planning, which results in the Bolshevik insistence on the methodical character
of everyday conduct as a means to restructure and train oneself.[104] Another
novelty is the immense intensification of the popular religious preoccupation with controlling deeds by following Christ, and a corresponding
diminution of concern for disciplining the passions.

Of course, temptations and evil passions were also found in the soul of
the Bolshevik, as Makarenko wrote:

> The residues of capitalism are still numerous and often spread in the
> society in a treacherously unnoticeable way. Imperceptible to the eye,

---

103. Tikhon Zadonsky, *O kontse dobrykh del* (St. Petersburg, 1875), 11. Pastoral literature stresses good works as most helpful in keeping faith alive. Joseph
Volotsky defended his strict monastic discipline against critics who cited the biblical statement that man will be saved by simply willing (*proizvolenie*) to live like a
Christian—by faith alone. Temptations in the monastery, Joseph said, required a
special discipline of deeds: if you simply stand near the ditch, the devil will push
you in ("Dukhovnaia Gramota prepodobnogo Iosifa," col. 560).
104. Whether the Bolsheviks' love for the nice Methodist touch of self-planning
comes from their doctrinaire Marxist roots and thus from secular planning techniques, or whether some sectarian influence of reform in the Orthodox Christian
background brought in Methodist-like overtones, is beyond the scope of this book.
Further research is undoubtedly needed.

they reside in the deeply hidden motives of deeds, intentions, desires.
. . . Sometimes they reveal themselves in open behavior that is clearly
out of harmony with the general style of our life. . . . The bacilli-carriers
are ordinary people, sincerely Soviet, who do not even know what enemy they carry within.[105]

But these passions and motives were not to be cured by spiritual combat.
They were to be eliminated by the communal control of deeds, by the *kollektiv.* Cheap and economic means of fighting residual capitalist motives
within an individual soul included such communal measures as "drastic
suppression, protest, delicate persuasion, or silent shunning in the hope of
[their] natural decay."[106]

Inkeles was very insightful in this respect once again. He wrote that
Russians were highly aware of their impulses, such as sex, oral gratifica-
tion, aggression, dependence. They freely accepted them as natural, gave in
and lived them out, with external control being more important than self-
control.[107] Individual motives and impulses were to be controlled by communal surveillance, rather than internal self-control. Of course, diligent
educationalists strove to promote individual self-control by each Soviet
citizen and displace the conditions of the 1940s and 1950s that Inkeles
described. If vile passions were not to be dealt with as such, their consequences were to be surely eliminated by the internalized techniques of
communal control, when an individual consciously and persistently policed
his or her acts in public.

EFFACEMENT OF THE CONFESSIONAL CULTURE

But what of the true introspection and deep inner confession? Did not they
exist alongside the means of internalized communal fashioning of the self?
For example, the Russian propertied classes espoused Western confessional
modes of self-knowledge at least from the eighteenth century on. Educated
Russian clergy used confession also. It would be hard to imagine that these
aristocratic or clerical confessional techniques were effaced in a day. And
yet they were eventually marginalized, given the prevalence of revelation
by deeds in Soviet life.

In what follows I concentrate on aristocracy and trace the relationship

---

105. Anton Makarenko, "O kommunisticheskoi etike" [On Communist ethics],
in Makarenko 5:429.
106. Ibid.
107. Inkeles, *Social Change in Soviet Russia,* 115.

between the Communist and the prerevolutionary aristocratic techniques of self-fashioning. In outlining this hypothetical connection, I rely on two brilliant studies usually classified as literary analysis: Lidia Ginzburg's magisterial work on the origins of psychological prose and Irina Paperno's study of Chernyshevsky. Consistent with the main tenets of the Tartu school of semiotic analysis of behavior, they tell us a lot about the features of Russian culture, particularly self-fashioning techniques. Rarely examined by social and political analysis, these techniques have long interested literary scholars.[108]

Following Ginzburg, we may point to the massive introduction of confessional methods of self-cognition and self-analysis to Russia through the translation of the enormously influential work of John the Mason.[109] His manual on confession and self-analysis of emotions and desires effectively became the main guide for many actors of the burgeoning Russian enlightenment. Aristocratic origins, membership in Masonic lodges, and enlightened activism or patronage of the arts and science frequently combined in many prominent figures of Russian high society in the late eighteenth-early nineteenth century. Diaries of the poet Vasily Zhukovsky, a close friend of Pushkin, are the epitome of the influence of John the Mason, according to Ginzburg. The question "Who am I?" (*Kakov ia?*) is a continuous subject of Zhukovsky's notes. He concludes each day by writing down his thoughts and describing emotions he felt, in order to answer this question. Introspection with accompanying minute analysis of inner feelings is his main method of self-knowledge.

The popularity of German Romanticism and idealist philosophy in early nineteenth-century Russia added a further twist to this practice. The circle of the young aristocrat Mikhail Bakunin practiced introspection but attached high metaphysical significance to even the most infinitesimal movements of the soul. Members of the circle cultivated sentimentality within themselves; a strongly felt emotion was a sign of the presence of the metaphysical quality, a medium through which some category of the Hegelian

108. For a comparable classic study in this respect, though not in the field of Slavic literatures, see Greenblatt's *Renaissance Self-Fashioning*.
109. Lidia Ginzburg, *O psikhologicheskoi proze* (Leningrad, 1977), 39. An English version exists (*On Psychological Prose*; trans. and ed. Judson Rosengrant [Princeton: Princeton University Press, 1991]), but I cite the original Russian ed.
Aret claims that John the Mason's work was the first widespread manual on the analysis of emotions but points out that Novikov, a central actor in the Russian Enlightenment and also a Mason, advised writing down not thoughts but good deeds at the end of the day (Aret, *Ocherki*, 41).

absolute spirit expressed itself in this-worldly fashion. Belinsky, a founder of modern literary criticism in Russia and a member of the circle in his younger years, describes the tears and blushes that people cultivated, when they met. Lengthy confessions to each other, accompanied by tears of passion, were the rule of the day. This stressed sensitivity was taken to be a clear sign of the beautiful soul and its elevated life, in line with the highest aspirations of humankind, which itself was only one moment in the self-development of the absolute spirit. "Life in the absolute, where my personal self found more than it lost," in Bakunin's own words, was the transformative experience for the future anarchist.[110]

This emphasis on the analysis and cultivation of emotions, their careful exposition in confessions to friends or to one's diary, reached its apogee in the narrative methods of Tolstoy and Dostoyevsky, writes Ginzburg. Their technique of the "stream of consciousness," that registered every single thought or movement of soul of a literary character, representing them as long sequences of bright, distinct elements of lived experience, was the culmination of the confessional tradition and thus found immediate and enthusiastic reception in Western Europe. However, within Russia, this tradition was powerfully challenged by the anti-introspective style of the new revolutionary radicals.

Belinsky and Chernyshevsky, the two central figures in the formation of Russian radicalism, serve as the best examples of this new style. Having frequented Bakunin's circle, Belinsky was appalled by his own inability to cultivate high emotions within his soul, which earnestly yearned for them. Since Belinsky was poorer than Bakunin or other aristocrats in this circle, his introspective search for grand emotions was constantly interrupted by the mundane things of life such as creditors, brawls with laundresses, fights against dirt or laziness. The sudden understanding that petty emotions consumed most of his life and kept him from achieving spiritual grandeur was even worse. Belinsky concluded that his life was doomed to be filled by these petty emotions on base topics.[111]

His salvation came in the doctrine of *Tat*, a German word for "deed" and a category of Hegel's conception of practice. Unlike mere words, this act or deed held a means to change the world, either within or outside oneself. Belinsky found the practices in which he had engaged in Bakunin's circle heretofore—those of "getting deep into oneself" (*samo-vnikanie*)

110. Ginzburg, *O psikhologicheskoi proze*, 53.
111. Ibid., 97.

and "speaking oneself out" (*samo-vygovarivanie*)—abhorrent: engaging in these futile exercises, people failed to change the world and to save from petty and trivial endeavors those, who—like Belinsky—could not cultivate great Romantic passions because of the time they spent in petty troubles. Thus, reasoned Belinsky, external action could free them from conditions that produced internal disharmony (such a project twenty years later was called emancipation from alienated existence). Confessions to friends, as a consequence of this reconceptualization, abate in Belinsky's letters and completely disappear after his marriage, a deed of very specific significance, as we shall see in the following discussion. What is most important, however, is Belinsky's rejection of the fruitless practices of confession and adoption of a pragmatic stance of changing the world in order to attain spiritual harmony—at the least, changing one's most proximate environment.

Chernyshevsky takes Belinsky one step further: he starts analyzing the self according to demonstrated deeds. The early diaries of Chernyshevsky preserve for us his psychological ramblings. They are driven by an emotion similar to Zhukovsky's ("who am I?"); they are concerned with self-definition and self-improvement. Coming from the family of a provincial priest, Chernyshevsky experienced many problems similar to those of Belinsky. His diaries are very sparse in descriptions of his feelings, since Chernyshevsky was bothered by a "disease," which he thought was his personal deficiency. He calls it "insensitivity to the world." Walking the streets of St. Petersburg in the 1840s, the student Chernyshevsky encounters what he knows to be objects of sublime beauty, but nothing moves in his soul in reaction to them. He searches the depths of his soul for the signs of any stirrings of elevated feelings but cannot find anything.

This quest for sentiments is all the more important because young Chernyshevsky wholeheartedly supports the Schillerian standard of "aesthetic intuition," shared by Russian high society at the time. "Cultivation of ideal love for sublime beauty" was taken to be the aim of self-development; failure to achieve it was the failure of self-fulfillment.[112] Chernyshevsky is looking for this ideal love, but the absence of feelings in his soul bothers him greatly. Therefore, having failed to detect great feelings by introspection, he develops an alternative approach to assure himself that he is in love. The case of falling in love with Natalia Lobodovskaia is very telling in this respect. The initial impression that this woman, his friend's wife, produces on him, makes Chernyshevsky suspect that he might be in love. Fur-

112. Paperno, *Chernyshevsky*, 60.

ther introspection, however, yields nothing. In view of the initial impression fading rather fast, Chernyshevsky sets out upon the streets of the city to prove that he *is* in love, after all.

He wishes to compare her with the ideal beauty as portrayed in the pictures of gorgeous women exhibited in the windows of art galleries. He will attain assurance in feelings by inverse reasoning: if she turns out to be the ideal beauty, then Chernyshevsky is in love. Chernyshevsky meticulously compares the details of the portraits with his mental image of Natalia; the form of her nose particularly gives him a lot of trouble, since it does not correspond to publicly approved standard of beauty.[113] Not particularly satisfied by the results of his search, he decides to register his emotions in her presence. Introspection is of no help, as always, so he relies on a different technique. Chernyshevsky demetaphorizes the expression "the heart throb" and secretly measures his pulse, while looking at Lobodovskaia!

All of these strange grapplings with the reality of internal emotions, all of these attempts somehow to assess them, lead him to begin evaluating his elusive internal feelings through external media. From then on, Chernyshevsky analyzes external criteria of bodily comportment to arrive at judgments on the availability of internal sentiments. Outward appearances become the sole way to arrive at knowledge of the internal self. His later diaries are filled with detailed descriptions of physical settings where certain emotions allegedly occurred. Sometimes, Chernyshevsky even draws meticulous spatial schemes of the respective positions of those present at a meeting or a tea party. "Insensitivity to the world" within Chernyshevsky's soul is overcome by the painstaking description of its external characteristics.

Physical comportment and acts start to matter more in his accounts of feelings than anything else. An act of marriage, for example, defines his feelings toward his wife, no matter what happens to Chernyshevsky afterwards. In line with the teaching of the French socialists, which he espoused by the time of his marriage, he recasts marriage as a means of liberating a woman, of emancipating her from familial bondage that had oppressed her heretofore, and making her equal and happy. Thus, love resulting in marriage becomes not only the primary act of Romantic self-fulfillment for the mid-nineteenth-century Russian radicals, but also a civic duty. Chernyshevsky's marriage had liberated his wife from the house of her father and saved her from the destiny of staying there forever, since she had slim

---

113. Ibid., 72.

chances of marriage, because of her reputation as a frivolous woman[114]—
what could be more revealing than this act in showing that he was truly in
love? Hardly any further action, and certainly no idle introspective inquiry,
could challenge Chernyshevsky's assurance in his feelings toward his wife.

The standard of evaluating one's feelings through one's deeds and the
standard of attaining internal harmony through outward action merged in
the figure of Rakhmetov, one of the central characters of Chernyshevsky's
What Is To Be Done? The reader does not know anything about the internal life of Rakhmetov and observes only his external deeds. But they are
enough: Rakhmetov's deeds reveal his heroic self. Lenin later confessed, in
a famous phrase, that Rakhmetov "had ploughed him up anew," because
his image of a revolutionary individual offered a model to follow in life.
Lenin was not alone; Paperno says that Lenin's predecessors, the radicals of
the 1860s, also took Rakhmetov as a singular model hero, as a model of
conduct to copy and imitate, with *What Is To Be Done?* as their Bible.[115]
Apparently, one hardly needed introspection to become a revolutionary.

The imperative behind the image of Rakhmetov was clear: subject personal life to the demands of the higher cause. Pisarev, another prominent
radical of the 1860s, highlighted this aspect in his famous essay, "The Realists." If Chernyshevsky supplied the model of revolutionary ascetic behavior in the figure of Rakhmetov, Pisarev explained what was central to
Rakhmetov's internal world. According to Pisarev, "people of the last generation," in which the reader could easily recognize the young Bakunin or
Herzen, were interested in their feelings, which they immediately transformed into outward behavior without any mediating control. Their outpourings of uninhibited emotion contrasted with the psychic structure of
the New Man, the Realist, who controls his intended actions by seeing
whether they correspond to his stated principles.[116] Announcing control of
actions by doctrinal insight, radical discourse supplemented Chernyshevsky's insistence on the analysis of the self through demonstrated deeds with
stress on self-control as the telos of self-transformation. Anticipating the
Bolshevik future, and in part resembling the Christian past, the discourse
proposed a novel combination of practices of working on oneself.

The reinvigorated standard of Christian piety demonstrated in deeds,

114. Russian radicals shared with French socialists the mythology of marrying
a prostitute and thus saving her; see ibid., 100.
115. Ibid., 28.
116. Pisarev, "Realisty," 3:8.

270 / Working on Oneself

asserted by revolutionary radicals, may have been closer to the masses than the strange confessional practices of the aristocracy or of educated clerics. A control of acts through which faith was allegedly expressed became the way to assure the possession of a higher Conscience, and analyzing these acts became the way to know oneself. Among revolutionary radicals, and later, among the Bolsheviks, one hardly any longer needed confession or introspection to know oneself. Once the Russian Revolution swept away or marginalized the strata that practiced these confessional techniques, it paved the way to an almost unchallenged hegemony of the practice of revelation by deeds.

DISSIMULATION

The compulsory introduction of practices of revelation by deeds had an unintended practical consequence. Independent of all the theorizing on working on oneself, and almost contrary to the recipes of Communist self-perfection, another popular practice—that of dissimulation and deception—grew to become the central unofficial means of individual self-fashioning and self-manipulation.[117]

Ken Jowitt has grasped this peculiarity of what he calls Leninist regimes, in which, he says, dissimulation ties public and private together.[118] Jowitt appears to assume that dissimulation is used to shield a pregiven "private" life from official surveillance and interference. My contrasting contention is that this "private" sphere itself came into being under Stalin: dissimulation was the practice that established it. Dissimulation, therefore, would appear not as a derivative of a split between public and private in Soviet Russia, but as a central practice constitutive of this split.

Workers and peasants moving into Party and Soviet offices, now filled with comradely vigilance, immediately learned the dubiousness of certain modes of conduct, which they had to conceal both at work and at home.[119]

117. Although, we might suspect, the general expansion of individual dissimulation happened in the 1920s and 1930s, discussion of this most widespread of Soviet practices logically follows that of the intensification of mutual surveillance.

118. Kenneth Jowitt, *New World Disorder* (Berkeley: University of California Press, 1992), 72.

119. The CCC continuously registered instances of workers astonished at a summons for Party prosecution of age-old activities that had suddenly become criminalized; many of the workers had been recently promoted. Smidovich's mention of Morgunov in chapter 4 is one example. See another typical case in *Biulleten' TsKK* 6–7 (1927): 13: a Communist with two wives was startled by the CCC interference into his personal life (*v nedoumenii sprashival, kakoe otnoshenie k partii . . . imeiut momenty iz lichnoi zhizni*). Detailed statistics on the stratification of Party crimes

The form of their dissimulation was new, but the practice itself was not. As many studies have shown, Russian peasants had practiced collective dissimulation against their feudal masters and the czar's officials for ages.[120] This dissimulation did not substantially differ from similar "weapons of the weak" as found, for example, in a contemporary Malaysian village: the weak of the peasant world collectively practice dissimulation against the strong.[121] The novel aspect of Bolshevik dissimulation was that it was primarily practiced individually against the members of the peer group, not collectively against superiors. This dissimulation was also different from the aristocratic one, so well practiced in courtly intrigue, in that it was not secondary to the already existing individual self; on the contrary, in many cases Soviet dissimulation was instrumental in constructing the Soviet individual. That is, many Bolsheviks who joined the Party ranks after the Revolution individualized themselves primarily by dissimulation. Let me clarify this paradoxical point.

This individualizing aspect of dissimulation draws on *pritvorstvo* rather than *litsemerie*. Both mean "dissimulation" but have different connotations. *Litsemerie* is linked to English word "hypocrisy" (from the same underlying Greek term), and it conveys the connotation of playacting or, literally, "changing faces"—a later stage in the genealogy of a dissimulating individual. *Pritvorstvo* comes from the Church-Slavonic verb *pritvoriati*, which in modern times came to mean "to dissimulate" with connotations of "to close the door" or "to close oneself off."[122] Peasants who became workers who became Bolshevik officials found it easier to close themselves

---

in the CCC report to the XV Party Congress show the CCC's particular interest in workers promoted to managerial and bureaucratic posts: 11.5 percent of recent worker promotees were tried by the Party collegiums in 1926–27 (the average for Party members working in Soviet offices was 10.2); of Party members working on the factory shopfloor, only 5.1 percent were tried. The move from shopfloor into a Soviet or Party office increased a worker's chances of being put on Party trial by a factor of 2.25 (see figures in Guseinov et al., eds., *Partiinaia etika*, 450–451).

120. See Michael Confino, *Société et mentalités collectives en Russie sous l'ancien régime* (Paris: Institut d'Etudes slaves, 1991), 99–133, particularly 132 on "cette confrontation latente et dissimulée." Also see a brilliant analysis of a complicated dissimulation game between peasants and czarist authorities in Daniel Field, *Rebels in the Name of Tsar* (Boston: Unwin Hyman, 1989).

121. James C. Scott, *Weapons of the Weak* (New Haven: Yale University Press, 1985).

122. Sreznevsky, *Materialy*, does not register the meaning of dissimulation for *pritvoriati*; originally, it related to the entrance of the church (*pritvor*), later also "door" and "cover." *Slovar'* first registers *pritvoritsia* in the sense of dissimulation in the 17th century.

272 / Working on Oneself

off from mutual surveillance than to transform their inner qualities or change their behavior completely. In some cases, of course, where surveillance was all-pervasive, there was no choice short of a restructure. But the majority simply stopped practicing suspect behavior in public; that is, they retracted certain parts of their conduct from the public gaze, and these parts constituted the almost completely invisible, most private spheres of their lives.[123] Once many Bolsheviks suddenly found themselves in this situation of life broken down into two parts—the hidden private, and the visible official—they started to individualize themselves by this practice of closure: retracting or hiding suspect behavior became the only practice that they practiced on their own, individually, without any recourse to collectively approved skills and with little, if any, guidance from dominant ideology.[124] Later, they also came to invest these hidden areas of their life with specific meaning; a further study is needed to examine the question of whether it was done by means of confessional practices or by replicating the practices of revelation by deeds in these unofficial spheres. This section simply examines the origins of this dissimulative split.

The initial stage of the retraction of behavior and constitution of hidden areas is still collective, in full accordance with peasant skills. The Central Control Commission officials who supervised the anti-alcoholism campaign in 1924–25 noted that "persecuted by repression, open drinking [pianka] becomes a hidden vice—'having just a drop' [vypivka], with all the precautions taken."[125] Though the next example may seem unrelated, Stalin also suspected the oppositionists of the same relocation of denounced activities into the secrecy of their houses and hangouts. Openly repenting after the Fourteenth Party Congress that rebuked attempts to form a unified left opposition within the Party, the followers of Zinoviev and Kamenev started to build "a party within the Party." The two most widely known charges against them were staging alternative meetings in 1926 dedicated to the October Revolution, and attempting to unite into a strong oppositional block by the time of the next Party congress. Although the extent of

---

123. That is, a Soviet dissimulator fell under the first type of "from deeds to self" analysis, in Ruvinsky's classification: a change in acts did not affect self-concept. But since we cannot assume that many peasants even in the 1930s had a self-concept, it is better to apply another of Ruvinsky's categories: self-training among children starts with the desire to correct those acts that are frowned on, before there is any knowledge of the self.

124. Of course, this ideology designated modes of conduct that were suspect, but it did not and could not give any advice on how to hide them.

125. Iaroslavsky et al., eds., O bor'be s naslediem proshlogo, 25.

these factional activities that led to the leftists' denunciation and expulsion at the Fifteenth Congress may be debatable, one thing is obvious. After agreeing to obey Party discipline, Zinoviev and Kamenev had continued to engage in activities that were clearly "factional" in the opinion of the majority of the Party, even if these activities were simply meeting behind closed doors. That is, they had dissimulated submission to Party will.

Group dissimulation was easy to break down. Since it had been practiced by peasants for ages and then picked up by professional revolutionaries, the methods for its uncovering had also been tried before. One only needed strong will and resources to challenge these group lies by planting informers, subjecting weaker suspects to methods of "harsh interrogation," and so on. An individual dissimulator was rather more difficult to catch; this dissimulator in turn became the primary concern of the saintly regime.

For example, Makarenko found the problem of individual dissimulation to be the central one plaguing his colony. His main concern as a chief pedagogue, he writes, was not to look after those who openly challenged the colony rules (the *kollektiv* would take care of these), but those who were hardly noticeable in everyday life. The open transgressors, undergoing the correctional influence of the *kollektiv*, entered life as normal Soviet citizens; those who hid themselves in the "mimicry of Soviet behavior and even Marxist phraseology," [126] were highly likely to turn petit bourgeois. They "start a petty family, find a warm place of work by some contriving, abandon the ranks of the Komsomol, and lose all ties with society." In the worst case, upon graduating from the colony, these dissimulators immediately revealed the "slow deep rotting" developing within their individual psyches: they started building their own houses, breeding swine, speculating on the black market—all atrocious instances of anti-collectivist behavior.[127] These inconspicuous people were usually categorized in Makarenko's colony as a "swamp" and thus merited special attention from the rest of the *kollektiv*. Surveillance in their regard was more intensive and, we may well suspect, probably made them better at dissimulation.

Now we can add another interesting fact: the first widely publicized Soviet use of the expression "working on oneself" came as part of the title of Konstantin Stanislavsky's book on playacting.[128] The system of Stanislav-

126. Makarenko 5:429.
127. Makarenko 5:171.
128. K. S. Stanislavsky, *Rabota aktera nad soboi* [An actor working on himself] (Moscow: Khudozhestvennaia literatura, 1938), translated as *An Actor Prepares* by Elizabeth Reynolds Hapgood (London : Eyre Methuen, 1946). Her translations of

sky, the cornerstone of Soviet realist theater, was one of the orthodoxies in Soviet cultural life and was propagated with utmost force in the 1930s and 1940s. An explanation for this phenomenon follows the usual line of argument on the Great Retreat: Stalinist culture gave merit to traditional values that restored order, that had been challenged in the first years of revolutionary experimentation; verisimilitude in theater was one of these values.[129] And yet another interpretation is equally plausible. Actors in Stanislavsky's theater were supposed to inhabit a different person, in the feat of total identification with an imaginary character. They effected the total merger by the introduction of an "as if" clause: the point was not to believe in the reality of an assigned role, but simply to act out all the consequences as if this role were their natural persona.[130] In part, they were to recall and relive their feelings in incidents of their own lives analogous to the situation of the imaginary character. Whether average Soviet citizens appropriated Stanislavsky's *instrumentarium* of "working on oneself" or whether Stanislavsky's system just nicely fitted the practices of the wider society, is hard to decide, but the affinity between the two is startling: always on stage, always in the limelight, Soviet citizens tended to irreproachably perform the public role ascribed by the general plot, with some adopting it as a real identity and living it out as truthfully as they could.[131]

It is hard to estimate to what extent individual dissimulation was widespread, for obvious methodological reasons. But the heightening of Party discourse against individual dissimulators may serve as one useful indicator of the seriousness of this problem. In fact, it seems hardly coincidental that the February 1937 speech of Stalin ushering in the height of Party

---

later parts of this work also have suggestive titles: *Building a Character* (1949) and *Creating a Role* (1961).

129. See Nicholas Timasheff, *The Great Retreat* (New York: Dutton, 1946).

130. A third section of *Rabota aktera nad soboi* (on acting as such) is specifically concerned with "as if" clause, which works wonders, according to Stanislavsky.

131. Another favorite Stanislavsky technique of "staying alone in public" was to block an actor's view of the pit by a projectile, making the public easier to ignore (*Rabota aktera nad soboi*, 172). Though reminiscent of Makarenko's method of putting the transgressor "under the chandelier," the technique offers a way out to Makarenko's victims: to reduce the pressure of the collective gaze, concentrate on the small lighted space around yourself. And Makarenko unwittingly validates it. A young commander particularly fearful of accounting for her misdeeds "under the chandelier" spent two hours in his office crying: "How could she appear in front of the general assembly?" But all went well. Now, he says, she is an actress in Kharkov drama theater (Makarenko 5 : 157), not noticing that this dissimulator's skills, produced in the colony, found easy professional application afterwards.

self-criticism was overwhelmingly concerned with the problem of dissimulation. Khrushchev, making a speech on the changes in the Party statute
at the Nineteenth Party Congress in 1952, also dubbed "deception of the
Party" the most serious of crimes.[132] His own behavior, however, shows
that almost any Communist at the time could have been dissimulating to a
certain extent: when four years later Khrushchev denounced Stalin, he only
proved that he had been keeping some thoughts and doubts strictly to himself during all the preceding years. In the early 1950s official discourse (and
Khrushchev in person) indicated the worst-kept secret: dissimulation was
most widely practiced. As one newspaper article put it, repeating the standard Stalinist truth, dissimulators had "two faces" (*dva litsa*), one for society and one for themselves.[133]

Another indirect sign of universal spread of individual dissimulation was
the appearance of the literary figure of successful careerist dissimulator in
what Vera Dunham called the "middlebrow fiction" of socialist realism.[134]
Novels seem to distinguish two different types of dissimulators: the intellectual from old days, who is bound to lose, and the newly upwardly mo-
bile careerist. The former, for example, appears in Ilya Ehrenburg's novel
Out Of Chaos (1933), which depicts the construction of the famous Kuz-
netsk foundries.[135] The main character, the manager Safonov, is an individualist who strongly detests the human anthill he has to supervise during this construction. But he confines his criticisms only to his private diary
and delivers loyal speeches in public. Ehrenburg's verdict on such a split
character is obvious: Safonov commits suicide. Intellectuals cannot survive
the dissimulatory posture imposed on them by the new circumstances.

Latter-day dissimulators are radically different from Safonov. They are
formed as individuals by the practice of dissimulation. Their double-faced
life is not a painful split forced upon their heretofore unitary self; on the
contrary, this split is normal for them because they originate as individuals by means of this split. These dissimulators can only be spotted when
they suddenly let their strict self-control go and break their utmost secrecy.

132. Nikita Khrushchev, *Doklad XIX s"ezdu partii ob izmeneniiakh v ustave KPSS* [Report to the 19th Party Congress on changes in the CPSU statute] (Moscow: Gospolitizdat, 1952), 24.

133. Iu. Filonovich, "Eto ne chastnoe delo" [This is not a private affair], *Komsomolskaia Pravda*, September 20, 1950.

134. See Vera Dunham, *In Stalin's Time* (Cambridge: Cambridge University
Press, 1976).

135. This novel is analyzed in Edward Brown, *Russian Literature Since the
Revolution* (Cambridge, Mass.: Harvard University Press, 1982), 198.

They may, for instance, confide to their lovers their "innermost secrets," at least, in those novels that tried to encourage people to vigilant denunciations of such "double-facers." Thus, in one of the narratives Dunham finds a careerist who reveals his true intimate heart to a mistress:

> Soon we will finish our work here. . . . I shall receive a sizable bonus. And on to Moscow. . . . You and I, we will have a Bluthner piano, a Telefunken set, and crystal, real French crystal. . . . So that all these things should come alive, we need the poetry of an electric push-button behind which stands the charm of the French word *comfort* and the convenience of the American word *service.*
>
> Oddly enough, the spoiled and idle belle cuts him down to size . . . :
> "May I ask you one more intimate question? . . . Why are you in the party? A petite bourgeois (*meshchanka*) is asking you that! . . . You are even worse than I am. . . . You are a slave of possessions, you are a shell, which does not contain any pearl but dirt."[136]

The poor dissimulator, having revealed some of his most intimate dreams, elicits nothing but an adequate image of the structure of his self: he is a shell, which hides only dirt under the surface appearance. The shells are routinely denounced.

Another postwar novel hints at a newer reality: if you are not a shell, you cannot survive. Not only because of terror that eliminates unskillful dissimulators or nondissimulators but also because a new dynamic is now at work: dissimulators, having become the dominant type of Soviet individual, force everyone to become one. Those who did not learn to dissimulate "naturally" will be made to learn dissimulation by force. Even the residual Bolshevik saints are forced to adopt a dissimulative posture. A novel called *First and Last,* implying the first in knowledge and the last in citizenship, tells the story of a young ensign of the naval academy. He is a diesel engine addict, spends all his time working on the engine, and forgets about serving the community. When forced by his superiors and peers to care about something other than technical tasks, the ensign defends his right to serve the Socialist Motherland the way he sees fit. This does not work very well. A sly villain, the insidious friend of the ensign, who occupies a powerful position at the top,

> proffers advice, the kind that oils the wheels of any deal. He leans confidently over and whispers: "You know what? Don't argue against these truths. They say all these things. Well, let them. You should agree with

136. Dunham, *In Stalin's Time,* 50.

them. It isn't difficult, is it? That way it will be much more peaceful. It's only a conditional agreement. It does not bind you to anything serious."[137]

How perfectly he lays out the secrets of the trade of dissimulation. But the ensign rejects them. The result is quick to follow: the ensign is the only one to graduate as merely a lieutenant junior grade; his peers turn away from him and the head of the academy refuses to shake hands with him. The story ends with public punishment of the deviant. And now, this is a strange deviance! In the late Stalinist society the refusal to play by the unwritten rules of dissimulation is abnormality to be punished. The ultimate judge of what is normal is no longer some doctrinal ideal, but the community that imposes standard norms of behavior, the saintly congregation that covertly admonishes its members to dissimulate in order to fit into these norms.

This may well be one the first novels that foretell the future of Soviet society: the collective of saints turns out to be the collective of accomplices, who merely produce a saintly image of themselves but consistently demand the display of loyalty to these images both at work and at home. Later, in the 1960s and 1970s, these demands will somehow shift to reflect realistic assumptions of what can be expected from the members of the congregation. Minor subversions of saintly ideals will not matter so long as the primary loyalty holds, and this is the loyalty to the mechanism of mutual surveillance that ensures the preponderance of the *kollektiv* in establishing the standards: what should be obeyed and how it should be obeyed. With the aging of the Soviet regime the acuteness of substantive demands will subside; finally the *kollektiv* will not demand much more than loyalty to the procedure of display of loyalty itself—an ultimate ritualization of life.[138]

According to Inkeles and Bauer's description of the "Stalinist formula of social control," the Soviet regime did not attempt to reduce discontent but rather strove to "isolate and suppress open disloyalty."[139] That is, the system concerned itself not with feelings, but with acts, said the authors. A Soviet citizen controlled his comportment and communication, but "his doubts, fears and compromises may continue to work corrosively on his inner, deeper self," resulting in a "split state of mind . . . characteristic of the

---

137. Ibid., 203.
138. Aleksei Yurchak theorizes the same phenomenon as "pretense misrecognition" in "The Cynical Reason of Late Socialism: Power, Pretense, and the *Anekdot*," *Public Culture* 9 (1997).
139. Alex Inkeles and Raymond A. Bauer, *The Soviet Citizen* (Cambridge, Mass.: Harvard University Press, 1959), 282.

majority."[140] One of the psychological devices that mended this split, according to Inkeles and Bauer, was self-indoctrination. Through reinforcing images of a monolithic society a typical Soviet citizen persuaded himself that an individual deviant had no chances of survival.[141] And yet, contrary to their expectations, the authors found this self-indoctrination obvious to many: "since most such processes are largely unconscious [in the West], it is somewhat surprising that a considerable number of respondents described them so accurately."[142]

Given the fundamental quality of the structure of the dissimulative split in the behavior of typical Soviet citizens, such surprise may be unfounded. If citizens perceived the split in conscious self-reflection, then the next step would be to consciously mend it by offering some rationalization why certain behavior had to be hidden. In this respect, self-analysis and self-accounting were techniques, taught in official life, but independently applied to mend the split between official and hidden intimate spheres. What Western authors called "self-indoctrination" was a first conscious attempt to deal individually with one's split self, to do something about it, to transform it, if not to perfect it. Here the long genealogy of independent and hidden self-building begins. One of the steps in this long development was individual perfection of the mechanism for constant switching between the intimate and the official, a curious kind of unofficial self-training, a process that comes later than the initial stage of dissimulation conceived as "closing off" (*pritvorstvo*), and one that we may more aptly call dissimulation as "changing faces" (*litsemerie*). In the end, this latter-day dissimulation came to be practiced almost automatically: sitting at a Komsomol meeting, one raises one's arm in a ritualized vote without reflection, while being immersed in reading Aleksandr Solzhenitsyn; switching of faces becomes an embodied skill.[143]

140. Ibid., 286.
141. Among the interviewees of the Harvard study of former Soviet citizens, none had ever stated open disloyalty to the regime while living in the Soviet Union.
142. Ibid., 288.
143. A description of this typical situation is borrowed from Yurchak, "The Cynical Reason of Late Socialism," 171.

7 The Collective in Mature Soviet Society

The remaining two chapters examine the constellation of background practices that underlay the formation of mature Soviet society—the intertwining of the practices of the *kollektiv*'s formation and collective self-examination, and of the individuals' practices of self-recognition and of working on oneself. How did these practices come to found the widely shared perception of the Soviet system's monolithic unity and at the same time engender alternative and more or less independent spheres of life beyond this facade of unity? It was not that cracks appeared in this monolith, according to the popular metaphor. Rather, the facade of monolithic unity formed above and contained disunity and disarray at deeper levels. In the grand mass called the Soviet Union, a rigid surface covered—as with the planet itself—a fluid core. Within the deeper levels, practices that created unity at the surface advanced aims different from the official ones. They allowed for spaces of discourse that would be intolerable at the surface. These practices interconnected in new and strange ways, which finally led to the reabsorption and implosion of the surface into an all-melting core.

THE COLLECTIVIZATION-OF-LIFE DRIVE REVISITED

During the 1950s the all-out collectivization-of-life drive of the 1930s took off with new vigor in official life. Indeed, the reforms associated with Khrushchev's name aimed at heightening the collectivization of life to the utmost. The post-1953 liberalization—usually represented as the curtailment of the power of the secret police, and the elimination of centralized terror—was accompanied by the profound consolidation of the practices of what many Western commentators called "social control" or "social pressure":

279

the practices of mutual surveillance profoundly intensified and admonition came to rule the day.

Four grand strategies evolved. First, intensify collectivist mechanisms in existing *kollektivy*. Second, tie them together by means of inter-*kollektiv* surveillance into a mega-*kollektiv*. Third, create *kollektivy* out of those human groups that still managed to escape collectivization. Fourth, spot and force into a *kollektiv* those rare individuals who still somehow existed on their own in the interstices of the system. If they resist joining any officially registered *kollektiv*, flush them out to the penal system, which strategy number three will collectivize.

Let us discuss them one by one. Examples of the first strategy—that of the intensification of collectivist mechanisms in the already existing *kollektivy*—are numerous, with changes in industry and agriculture being the most telling ones. The collective responsibility of labor *kollektivy* in industry was heightened by a wage reform in the early 1960s, in which collective bonuses became a sizable part of wages, while the system of individual norms and wages, so characteristic of the Stalin industrialization, was largely dismantled. This collective bonus was to be allocated among individual laborers by a decision of the *kollektiv*. In practice, this most often meant that the size of individual bonuses was decided by the management, but the discursive justification for the wage reform came from the idea of sharing collectively earned income. As a corollary, where little or no bonus was earned, additional measures were introduced to produce communal pressure on those who were allegedly at fault. In addition to the usual barrage of appeals to create a public opinion around job-shirkers so that they become ashamed to come late to work or do their jobs unconscientiously, note the Khrushchev-era invention of "public personnel departments."

These personnel departments, composed of older workers who had worked at a given enterprise for a number of years, fought the high turnover of the labor force by "talking" to those who wanted to abandon this enterprise for better working conditions at another. Some departments were tellingly called "councils of workers' honor," revealing their primary means of activity—collective shaming.[1] As is well known, the problem of labor turnover became serious in the late 1950s. Filtzer notes that even if turnover in 1956 was 25 percent lower than the record figure of 1932, it was still very high: one in three factory workers changed jobs in 1956, up from

1. Yu. E. Volkov, *Tak rozhdaetsia kommunisticheskoe samoupravlenie: Opyt konkretno-sotsiologicheskogo issledovaniia* [Birth of Communist self-government: an essay in empirical sociology] (Moscow, 1965), 182.

one in eight in 1953.[2] Speeches of personnel department members recast job-changing as an example of "profit-seeking individualism," and they started monitoring "the job flitters." Faced with the problem of fortifying their admonitions to make them more effective, workers' collectives pressed for organizational innovations, so that a job-flitter who escaped one *kollektiv* would be punished by another or would have no place to which to move.

The Soviet press was filled with such grassroots proposals as recording job changes against the wish of the *kollektiv* as "violations of labor discipline" in labor cards, the compulsory work permit that each Soviet citizen had to submit to obtain a job. Some workers demanded that the "flitters" who wanted to leave a given enterprise file for permission not with management but with the workers' collective; others insisted that the *kollektiv* be granted the right to punish the flitters, since the management frequently failed to do so. If admonition was ineffective, the workers were ready to use force themselves.[3] The most radical proposal demanded the introduction of a specific "labor passport" in addition to the usual internal citizen's passport and the labor card already in existence. Entries in this new document were to be made by the decision of the worker's collective and would comment on the disciplinary qualities of the worker. Even later Soviet sources looked at these proposals as constricting freedom and lauded the Brezhnev era, which, though it brought some centralization of control and a restoration of hierarchy, repealed these fearsome policies.[4]

In agriculture, the intensification of collectivization was carried out in two policies—the abrupt curtailment of private plots and ownership of cattle in 1958–59, and the creation of the "link" as the main unit of collective work effort.[5] If the attack on private property rested on doctrinal grounds and did not really intensify horizontal surveillance, the link was a direct attempt to create a supra-*kollektiv*. As the name suggests, "the link" was a group of agricultural brigades that united existing primary labor collectives in Soviet agriculture. The link coordinated all stages of the production process and thus undertook to deliver the final product in cooperation. Paid by the sales of the final product on the market rather than by the completion of intermediate tasks according to contracts, as the brigade would be, the link was envisaged as the panacea for Soviet agriculture.

2. Filtzer, *Soviet Workers and De-Stalinization,* 47.
3. Ibid., 55.
4. Iakovlev, *Stanovlenie lichnosti,* 62.
5. Karl Eugen Wadekin, *The Private Sector in Soviet Agriculture,* 2d ed. (Berkeley: University of California Press, 1973), esp. ch. 9.

282 / *The Collective in Mature Soviet Society*

First, interbrigade pressure would eliminate the need for external discipline, since the link's income would depend on the joint work effort of many brigades; second, given the fact that the link was paid on final sales, the widespread practice of false accounting and forged target data would stop.[6]

The second strategy of the 1950s' collectivization-of-life drive was intensification of means of inter-*kollektiv* surveillance, tying the whole Soviet people into a single mega-*kollektiv*. Signs of times of the 1950s and 1960s were the "people's patrols" and the "comrades' courts." Although in existence since the early days of Soviet rule, these forms of surveillance, admonition, and control came into full bloom during the 1950s. The ideology underlying the formation of both bodies was very close to that of the Central Control Commission discussed in chapter two. Neither people's patrols nor comrades' courts were envisaged as punitive bodies; they could refer the violator to authorities for criminal prosecution, but only after other means of influence had failed. Their aim was to correct behavior and admonish people to live righteously. For example, one of the many local Soviet propagandists, describing the comrades' courts' activity, wrote:

> No court is more demanding than a court of one's comrades, with whom one labors in the same workplace, shares joys and sorrows, and to whom one is suddenly revealed as not exactly the same person they trusted and thought they knew. No punishment is more effective than that imposed by a friendly hand, because it is imposed not in order to punish, but in order to help those who have made a misstep to return to the right path.[7]

According to the 1961 handbook for the judges of comrades' courts, they were supposed to establish the guilt of the defendant for themselves and be persuaded of his or her guilt before holding a session of the comrades' court. The primary aim of the proceedings was subjecting the guilty to the influence of the community attending the trial, with a concomitant aim of making a defendant "confess his misdeeds publicly at the trial and ask for forgiveness," if possible.[8] Both colleagues and neighbors of the defendant

6. On Khrushchev's infatuation with "links" and further literature on them, see George Breslauer, *Khrushchev and Brezhnev as Leaders* (London: Allen and Unwin, 1982), 94.

7. D. Shchepakin, *Obshchestvennyi poriadok v rukakh naroda* [Public order in the hands of the people] (Tula, 1965), 35. The alleged continuity between early revolutionary ideas of correction and the contemporary 1950s drive was achieved by citing Feliks Dzerzhinsky, who pronounced almost the same in the early 1920s.

8. Berman, *Justice in the USSR*, 290.

were supposed to be present at and participate in this shaming procedure. According to the 1961 statute, the courts could not detain or convict an individual, since their aim was training the new citizen. However, they could extract a public apology from offenders; warn them in a comradely way or subject them to "social censure"; impose reprimands (possibly published in a local newspaper) and fines of up to fifty rubles, more than half an average monthly salary at the time; recommend to management their transfer to a lower-paid job (and request their dismissal if they worked with money or children); recommend expelling troublemakers from their state apartments upon request of their neighbors; and request offenders to restore a victim's losses if these were under fifty rubles.[9]

Harold Berman wrote on the rationale for these disciplinary developments:

> It is an effort to effectuate an internalization of official values in the minds and hearts of the people, by enlisting their direct intervention in proceedings of a legal nature. The use of procedures derived from the official law is thought to be an effective means of reintegrating the offender into the collective, and the use of the collective itself to administer those proceedings is thought to have educational value for all who participate.[10]

Of course, this statement also applies to activities of the Control Commissions of the 1920s. In the long durée of Soviet history, attempts to give the collective the power to correct the individual and employ mutual surveillance and admonition recur with tedious constancy. Describing these attempts, I used the case of the CCC, since parallels between its precepts and the principles of the church courts are especially suggestive but—as is now clear—Soviet history holds any number of similar examples. Furthermore, as the example of the comrades' courts demonstrates, the origin of the spread of collective surveillance and admonition techniques through the body social was not confined to a single definitive locality: the comrades' courts coexisted with and even outlived the CCC. Nor were these two bodies the only two exceptional springs of burgeoning surveillance. Rather, both—as well as many others—represented nascent streams of mutual

9. Peter H. Juviler, *Revolutionary Law and Order* (New York: Free Press, 1976), 81. The penultimate paragraph was by far the most threatening, used in communal wars over scarce lodging. Swamped by complaints on the abuses, local Soviets had to create special bodies, "social councils dealing with comrades' courts" that effectively became appeals courts overviewing the comrades' courts' decisions.

10. Berman, *Justice in the USSR*, 297.

surveillance in the most diverse areas of its application, which later combined into one great disciplinary flow.

The exact historical origin of the comrades' court is of less interest (some claim that Trotsky was first to authorize the creation of comrades' courts in the Red Army in 1918 in order to enforce discipline) than the fact that through them—already in 1919—officials tried to install the system of comradely admonition in industry.[11] The Trade Union Statute of 1919, which relied on comrades' courts in order to enforce discipline in the enterprise, was repealed only in 1922 with the advent of NEP.[12] Revived in 1928 to assist the renewed collectivization drive in industry, comrades' courts took over some cases in civil law (45,000 existed in 1938).[13] Courts created in rural areas at the same time spread like wildfire and in 1931 approximately 30,000 of them functioned, imposing sanctions for violations of labor discipline in the newly formed collective and state farms.[14] The end of the Great Terror largely eliminated these bodies, but they were once again revived under Stalin in 1951, when small infractions of labor discipline became subject to their enforcement. Khrushchev therefore was merely continuing the general Party strategy over these years, which aimed to stimulate mass participation in corrective efforts (unless, of course, this participation threatened the very cohesion of the body social, as it did in 1935–38). After Khrushchev's campaign to bring comrades' courts into full force at the end of the 1950s, they were supposed to be created in every labor collective with 50 or more members, and in every ZhEK (a Soviet hous-

11. On the origins of comrades' courts see ibid., 288.

12. See V. A. Aksenov, "K voprosu o kharaktere vliianiia tovarishcheskikh distsiplinarnykh sudov na rabochie kollektivy promyshlennykh predpriiatii v nachale 2oh godov" [On the influence of comrades' disciplinary courts on the workers' collectives in industrial enterprises in the early 1920s] (Institute of Scientific Information on Social Sciences [INION] of the Russian Academy of Sciences ms 26673, Gorky University, 1986).

13. Berman, *Justice in the USSR*, 288.

14. See V. M. Savitsky and N. M. Keiserov, "Razvitie pravovykh form organizatsii i deiatel'nosti tovarishcheskikh sudov" [Development of the legal forms of organization and proceedings of the comrades' courts], *Sovetskoe gosudarstvo i pravo* [Soviet state and right] 4 (1961): 37. "The Statute of the Comrades' Court in the Collective Farm," adopted in Saratov district, cited only three disciplinary penalties—"warning," "public shaming," and "putting the name of a violator on a black [shaming] board" (vs. "red" [laudatory] board). In fact, disciplinary measures often led to beatings, detainment, exiles, and expropriations, perfunctorily condemned by the brochure as excesses (V. Pomerantsev, *Tovarishcheskie sudy v kolkhozakh* [Comrades' courts in the collective farms], 2d ed. [Saratov, 1931], 6 and 93).

ing unit). In 1965, at the height of comrades' courts activity, 52,000 people staffed 5,580 courts in Moscow alone.[15] Of course, many of these existed only on paper, but the effort to tangle all citizens in a net of paralegal comradely admonition is evident.

The story of the "people's patrols" (also known under the acronym DND, which stood for Voluntary People's Regiments in Russian) is similar. The 1959 Central Committee resolution "On Laborers' Participation in the Enforcement of Public Order in the Country" officially authorized the creation of people's patrols on the basis of "existing local initiatives" and "revolutionary traditions." These initiatives were really an extension of earlier practice: since 1954 special new regiments of Komsomol and Party activists walked the streets of some Soviet cities, helping the police enforce law and order and fighting street "hooliganism." Once again, in the long durée of Soviet history they were hardly novel. For example, an eager historian, who wished to cast the appearance of people's patrols as an end result of the long development of a specific form of Communist self-government had little trouble in doing so. The first revolutionary detachments enforcing law and order were said to have appeared as early as 1905, during the first Russian revolution and then easily reestablished themselves in 1917. These brigades existed until 1922 but were on the wane in the years of NEP. In 1928 they came back to vigorous life under the name of Osodmil (society for assisting the militia); they were renamed Brigadmil (brigades of assistance to militia) in 1932. During the Second World War "groups of public order" were formed to search for spies and paratroopers as well as deserters from the Soviet army. In 1946 these groups merged with Brigadmil but were largely inactive until the 1954 Komsomol initiative for patrolling the streets. Leningrad, Rostov-on-Don, Gorlovka (Donetsk Basin), and Penza were the first cities to experiment with regular people's patrols.[16]

In a familiar vein, official discourse stressed that people's patrols did not exist to punish; they were to correct and to fight capitalist residues in people's lives. As an imaginary worker said in a propagandist brochure, the Soviet people were still defending the gains of the Revolution. "Only our aims are somehow different: we do not walk with gun in hand. Our aim is to fight the vestiges of capitalism, an enemy of a very dangerous kind. Our

---

15. Theodore H. Friedgut, *Political Participation in the USSR* (Princeton: Princeton University Press, 1979), 252.
16. Data from N. V. Dement'ev, *Trudiashchiesia na strazhe obshchestvennogo poriadka* [Laborers on guard for public order] (Moscow: Profizdat, 1959), 10–16.

main weapon is persuasion and training."[17] Indeed, the statute of people's patrols adopted in March 1960 stated that persuasion and warning are the first two methods of its work. However, the statute also authorized members of the patrol to warn and then demand "the discontinuation of the violation of the public order," to check documents if necessary, to detain people for short periods of time and send notices of their violations to their places of work or habitation, and to turn violators over to regular police if necessary. Its members could also enter any establishment (with management's permission) in pursuing patrol objectives, and could stop and commandeer private cars for the patrol's purposes.[18] By July 1960, 80,000 people's patrols numbering 2.5 million members were reported. By 1965 this official number grew to 130,000 patrols with 4.5 million members.[19] Once again, the figures are doubtless grossly exaggerated since in actual terms only a tiny fraction of this mass was active in patrolling, but the spread of the intention to make people take part in social control is notable. The table of regional differences in the Russian republic in 1963 stated that from 1.83 to 3.12 percent of the total population formally enlisted in people's patrols and thus could be called to fulfill a citizen's duty at any time.[20]

A strange isomorphism, one might say. People's patrols played the same role in the monolithic body of the multimillion collective called the Soviet Union as the *aktiv* did in any small *kollektiv:* they constituted a fearful core of mutual surveillance, which one joined from time to time in order to enforce the standards that one otherwise reluctantly suffered when they were imposed by others. The people's patrols were more meticulous and closer to the people: they were the people policing itself, and thus escape was hardly possible from their omniscient gaze and omnipresent power. The first activists of the people's patrols acutely felt the exhilaration of this omnipotence and poeticized it.

For example, the narrative of the first Komsomol patrol that appeared in Leningrad in 1954 is starkly frank on these matters. The city assembly of the Party *aktiv* noted that individual members of Komsomol were reluctant to approach and correct the violators of socialist law and order. Following this "insightful guidance," in three days one of the district Komsomol committees organized a Komsomol patrol detachment one hundred

---

17. Ibid., 30.
18. M. M. Levina, ed., *Druzhinniku: Sbornik zakonodatelnykh i inykh materialov* [To a patrolman: a collection of legal and other documents] (Moscow, 1963), 30.
19. Shchepakin, *Obshchestvennyi poriadok,* 7.
20. Ibid., 11.

members strong and sent them to patrol Nevsky Prospekt and the central recreational parks of the northern capital. Having initially been "soft" and "irresolute" toward the violators, and only later coming to appreciate the taste of power, the patrol declared war on hooligans and delinquents.

In the words of one of the first patrol's members, "the violators, detained by the Komsomol members, understood that besides the militia, a new, more severe and ruthless force had appeared in the streets."[21] This force was more ruthless indeed, for two reasons. First, the scope of censured behavior extended well beyond codified legal or administrative delicts. The patrols could reprimand or detain people "for dressing in a slovenly matter or wearing loud clothes"; "for buying photo cards from private speculators"; for dancing in a "stylish" way with the "unnatural jerky movements" that fashion-conscious youth then favored;[22] for gathering in a crowd of fans outside an actor's residence; for littering city streets; for offering a cigarette to a minor; for riding public transport without a ticket or violating the prescribed order of entering through the front door and exiting through the rear door; for playing cards in the "dark alleys" of the city parks, and so on.[23]

Second, the patrols were more ruthless than the police because they were invisible; members often wore civilian clothes and struck when the offender least expected it. The aim, however, was not so much to hide the members among the general public; this made little sense since they were recruited from the general public anyway. The aim was to transform the general public into a hidden regiment of the people's patrol. Every citizen—with or without papers as a member of the people's patrol—could now strike an offender if she or he thought it right. In the words of the poem about the Leningrad patrols, "Not only patrols should detain hooligans; let every passer-by become a patrolman!"[24]

The first accounts of the Komsomol patrols are of course stylized narratives, produced to elicit imitation—models for the same activities in other Soviet cities. It is interesting to compare the initial accounts with the nitty-

21. Yu. Osipov and F. Pristavakin, *Komsomol'skii patrul'* [Komsomol patrol], 2d ed. (Leningrad: Znanie, 1959), 7.

22. "Tastes are to be discussed since they could be implanted," was the rationale (ibid., 11). On the conflict between "socialist good taste" and *styliagi* see the exposition below.

23. Ibid., 26–29.

24. The original in Russian of the poem by I. Chistov, quoted in ibid., 40: *ikh* [i.e., hooligans] *brat' dolzhny ne tol'ko patruli, / pust' patrulem liuboi prokhozhii stanet!*

gritty of the usual work of the people's patrol brigade of the Moscow Mytishchi Machine Plant in 1960, registered in their journal of daily activity. The scope of censured activities is very wide; the level of penetration is deep: surveillance and censure run wild. Members of the patrol

> interfered with and stopped the quarrel of the residents of 41 Rumiantsevskaia Street. . . . Established strict following of queuing order in the taxi line and warned the cabbies about the inadmissibility of picking out favored passengers. . . . Established order in the ticket office of the railway club, then reprimanded the orchestra musicians for playing music of base quality. . . . Picked up and delivered a drunkard to the drunk tank. . . . In the buffet of Mytishchi railroad station issued a strict warning to a bartender for distributing spare glasses to those who brought their own alcohol to the premises. . . . Noted that the driver of an automobile, license plate UN 00–32, was illegally transporting people and so informed the police.[25]

These activities, so wide-ranging in their penetration of so many spheres of everyday life, so meticulous in their wish to root out each vestige of capitalism demonstrated in non-Communist behavior, still seem rather innocent. Obviously, petty repressive power given over to the people looks more benign than the mad terror of Stalinist days. The people proscribed but they did not kill. They might censure a thousand a day, but that is not equivalent to killing even one, common sense tells us. However, the next example will demonstrate how dangerously close the former came to the latter.

In the famous case of the city of Nikolaev, two leaders of the local people's patrol brigade, Mednik and Shaposhnikov, were accused of sadism and convicted on charges of exceeding their legal jurisdiction. According to press reports of the court proceedings, they terrorized the city by detaining people at their whim. They frequently beat the detained. They installed controls at the entrances of local restaurants and compiled a photo album of "women of easy virtue," that is, of those young women who entered restaurants without prior authorization from the patrol leadership. Their power seemed

---

25. Understandably, taxi drivers preferred customers who wanted to go a long distance or looked likely to tip well; workers in buffets made money from selling food to go with drinks, as well as from redeeming the deposit on empty alcohol bottles; and the unfortunate driver was charging a fee to transport people. The statements come from V. Surov, *Svoei respubliki storozha: Budni dobrovol'nykh narodnykh druzhin po okhrane obshchestvennogo poriadka* [Watchmen of their own republic: everyday work of the people's patrols] (Moscow: Sovetskaia Rossiia, 1960), 21.

invulnerable and total. After they clashed with TV journalists during a soccer match, breaking their cameras, the local Party leaders defended the patrolmen, saying that, understandably, people's patrols could not "pussy-foot around the violators of public order."[26] But Mednik's days were numbered once one of his beaten victims died from the inflicted wounds, after having been detained on the grounds of "violating the order of a taxi queue." Although Mednik burned the victim's passport and erased the records of his detention, journalists eager for revenge after their recent fight did all they could to report the story in the central newspapers and bring him to trial.[27] Since the mass media workers had a personal stake in revelations, and since the conflict between journalists and local Party leadership had already gotten out of control and splashed onto the pages of the Moscow press, they finally succeeded. How many similar stories went unreported or were suppressed?

An activity that may at first seem ridiculously down-to-earth and inconsequential, like enforcing order in a taxi queue or detaining an individual for the strange fashion of his jacket, contained an intense threat: the famous "steel battalions of the proletariat" of Lenin's *State and Revolution* —enforcing social order without scruples—could easily subject millions of people to their own petty but profound terror. And even if the official reports of the people's patrols recounted "peaceful discussions" and "debates" with recalcitrant young style-seekers over matters of taste, perhaps the reality was closer to quick and simple action: on encountering a "stylishly" dressed fellow, a *styliaga* according to the parlance of the day, the patrol's members would detain him, cut his longish hair and cut his tight fashionable trousers into strips. "No joke!" adds the journalist Artemy Troitsky, who first recounted to Western audiences this typical experience, suffered by thousands.[28] Chaotic and sporadic fierce terror against some was replaced by milder but more extensive everyday bullying of all, which always threatened to become terror again when its perpetrators felt immune from justice.

In fact, we can take the episode of the *styliagi* scare as the first test of mutual surveillance and admonition on the scale of the whole country, which demonstrated their formidable power. A *styliaga*, according to news-

26. "Pod maskoi druzhinnika" [Under the mask of a patrolman], *Komsomolskaia Pravda*, October 6, 1960.

27. "Pokroviteli prestupnikov" [Protectors of criminals], *Izvestiia*, June 23, 1961.

28. Artemy Troitsky, *Back in the USSR* (Boston: Faber and Faber, 1988), 13.

paper descriptions, and according to interviews with a few surviving genuine *styliagi*, wore "outrageous clothes": thick-soled shoes, tight trousers, a striped shirt with a bright tie and a stylish jacket. The unlikely model was Johnny Weissmüller from the film *Tarzan in New York*, which somehow managed to pass Soviet censorship in 1951.[29] Little groups of *styliagi* would walk down what they called "Broadway," that is, the right side of Gorky Street between Red and Pushkin Squares in Moscow, displaying themselves in full gear, and end up in some restaurant where they would pass the time till three or four in the morning.

One surprising thing about the *styliagi* is that they were better off before Stalin's death in 1953 than after. They were under solid protection, because many of them were sons and daughters of the few families of the top Soviet elite. Fred Starr, who documented the merger of *styliagi* with jazz culture in the 1950s, notes,

> [M]any elite children adopted the upbeat new mode of behavior and dress to flaunt their privileges. Nikita Khrushchev's children were arguably the founders of "style hunting" in 1940, but soon after the war the new cult of youthful assertiveness spread to the Gromykos and other prominent families. . . . What had begun as a fad among children of the elite before the death of Stalin had burgeoned into a full-scale revolt by alienated Soviet youths.[30]

Now, the revolt in question may be slightly exaggerated, since the genuine *styliagi* were very few. Aleksei Kozlov, a future leader of the Soviet jazz-rock group *Arsenal*, and at the time a devoted *styliaga* (which meant that he was one of the few who wore their stylish outfits seven days a week) recalled that in public transportation on his way to "Broadway" people would call him a parakeet or a monkey and shame him. For that reason, said Kozlov, there were few women among *styliagi*; it was unbelievably more difficult for a woman to withstand the popular pressure.[31] This pressure grew by the end of the 1950s. The baggy-trousered crowds would now not only shame a *styliaga* on the street but approach him to "discuss" tastes, and fairly often the exchanges erupted into violence. People's patrols only institutionalized this practice.

More a product of Soviet moral panic than a real movement, the phe-

---

29. The film passed precisely because no official censor found anything scandalous in it, one might suggest.

30. Frederick S. Starr, *Red and Hot* (Oxford: Oxford University Press, 1983), 238–239.

31. Troitsky, *Back in the USSR*, 10.

nomenon of *styliagi* served as a referent for a huge public campaign that raged all over the Soviet Union in the late 1950s and looked for *styliagi* everywhere. Kozlov says that he knew no more than fifty people who were as devoted as he was. Others put on their flashy clothes only once a week to show up on Gorky Street in Moscow. But with the new emphasis on egalitarianism and the downgrading of leaders officially approved, the masses threw themselves into regulating the "scum," as *styliagi* were popularly called. A campaign against *styliagi* started up in the pages of the Soviet press and on the streets of Soviet cities.

The mechanism of this campaign is described in an article, "Who of Them Is a *Styliaga?*," which appeared in *Komsomolskaia Pravda* in 1956, at the height of moral panic. A Komsomol activist named Antonov was designated as a *styliaga* by his comrades in the provincial town of Batyrevo. He demonstrated a "somehow abnormal behavior among the club youth. He differed from the rest in everything: in haircut, in his suit and in his raised collar." The dispute between Antonov and the local satirical journal, which ridiculed his appearance, could not be resolved at the local level. The district Komsomol committee sent a photo of Antonov to *Komsomolskaia Pravda* to figure out whether he was a *styliaga*. The newspaper ruled that he was not and lamented the avalanche of letters that described the excessive collective zeal demonstrated during this campaign. For example, in Odessa some members were expelled from Komsomol for having mustaches. The head of the Odessa Komsomol city committee gave the following rationale for the expulsions: first a mustache, then a bright tie, and you get a *styliaga!*[32]

After the whole commonwealth started to wage war on *styliagi*, the latter went into hiding. From time to time they would reappear in public spaces for a moment, as guerrilla fighters against uniformity, only to retreat immediately afterwards into safe privacy. By the early 1960s the campaign against *styliagi* subsided; apparently, because they were all reformed, at least in public. *Styliagi* became the first victims of conformism as enforced by the masses, and they were not nonconformists by any means. When they appeared, the mechanism of enforced conformity was not yet fully in motion; there were still spaces in the grid of mutual surveillance. Under Khrushchev's policies of expanding socialist self-government these spaces were successfully eliminated. The dinosaurs of Stalin's epoch, *styliagi* simply had to learn to dissimulate to survive, and many did.

32. E. Rusakova, "Kto iz nikh styliaga?" [Who of them is a *styliaga?*], *Komsomolskaia Pravda*, August 11, 1956.

Apparently, employing mutual surveillance to control the behavior of the people on the streets and in their apartments was not enough. The horizontal control fever achieved its height in the KPGK, the committee of Party-state control. Khrushchev, introducing the new body at the November 1962 Central Committee plenum, stated that unification of the bodies of state and Party control, which had existed separately since 1934, into this single overarching agency was necessary for fighting the frequent collusion between Party and state officials to deceive the central authorities and mistreat the common people. Khrushchev stressed that the new body was in fact a reborn CCC-WPI (central control commission and worker-peasants' inspectorate), which Stalin allegedly destroyed in order to take over and control the people's power.[33] Now the people were to get it back. In 1963–64, 3,280 local commissions of KPGK started up and in turn directed about 700,000 "groups of support" in factories and offices. Those groups formally enlisted the services of 4 million activists.[34] Activists on the shop floor were supervised by a local Control Commission, which then reported directly to Moscow.

Jan Adams described the system of penalties imposed by commissions of the KPGK. Once again, as in the other cases of comradely admonition reviewed so far, the main aim was seen as prophylactic rather than retributive, prevention rather than punishment. Penalties, however, became harsher and included public reports of offending officials and suspension of their administrative orders; hailing offenders before a comrades' court; withholding an official's pay for damages; issuing reprimands; imposing fines, and requesting suspension from work, or, in serious cases, requesting dismissal.[35] When admonition failed, the KPGK was to be linked to coercion in a way closer than any other body of mutual surveillance. If the controllers suspected some grave offense, they were supposed to turn their investigation materials over to criminal prosecutors. As the statute of the KPGK proclaimed, "the KPGK, the whole immense army of its activists, must build its work in such a manner that bureaucrats and work-stallers,

33. For changes to the committees of Party and state control between 1934 and 1962, see Grey Hodnett, "Khrushchev and Party-State Control," in *Politics in the Soviet Union*, ed. Alexander Dallin and Alan F. Westin (New York: Harcourt, Brace and World, 1966).

34. Data from *Kommunist* 6 (1964): 68. These figures were cited by almost every Western observer writing on the KPGK. See, e.g., Jan S. Adams, *Citizen Inspectors in the Soviet Union* (New York: Praeger, 1977), 185; and William J. Conyngham, *Industrial Management in the Soviet Union* (Stanford: Hoover Institute, 1973), 181.

35. Adams, *Citizen Inspectors*, 180.

idlers, bribers, thieves, speculators, and dissimulators become aware of their inescapable punishment and tremble [*trepetali*] before the great power of the Soviet public."[36]

The extent of public participation in the work of the KPGK was reflected in the ratio of paid staff to activists, which was 1:34. An average regional commission would have 10–15 paid staff members and 350–500 activists participating in its everyday activities, not counting those formally listed as members of "support groups" in the enterprises and bureaucracies. The net of potential control was cast very wide, even though "advantages of social participation were offset by an extremely loose overall structure and serious difficulties in communication."[37] Once the KPGK started waging actual campaigns, it attempted to subject other governmental bodies to its requirements and orders. The "intensification of the use of chemistry in agriculture" campaign of 1963 was exclusively conducted by the KPGK, as were the purges of the Party apparatus in Georgia and Armenia in 1964. The courts, local soviets, and bodies of standard administrative control were required to follow the orders of the KPGK commissions in these cases.[38] Of course, the KPGK commissions were ineffective, since they were overwhelmed by "signals" demanding a raid in a given enterprise (about 500,000 denunciations flooded in, of which only 140,000 were actually investigated); and of course, many of the 1 million raids proudly boasted for 1964 were conducted *pro forma*, but one thing was becoming increasingly clear. Headed by the former KGB chief, the KPGK was encroaching on more and more prerogatives of the Party and state bodies, often carrying out raids to boost its own status; its license to popular activism led to an easy transformation of the "vigilant activist" into "an unrestrained vigilante."[39] It is hard to decide whether KPGK could have initiated a new all-out purge on the model of 1937, but the potential—clear enough to frighten contemporaries who recalled the earlier events—was definitely present.[40] One of the

36. "Polozhenie o KPGK" [KPGK statute], in *Polozhenie ob organakh part-goskontrolia: gruppakh i postakh sodeistviia, Komsomol'skom prozhektore* [Statutes of the bodies of Party-state control: "groups of support," and "the Komsomol searchlight"] (Moscow: Politizdat, 1964), 6.

37. Adams, *Citizen Inspectors*, 186.

38. Ibid., 199. The figure of Shelepin, the former KGB chief who headed the newly organized KPGK, made these purges even more fearful. Shevardnadze's rise to power in Georgia was connected with these purges also.

39. Paul M. Cocks, "The Rationalization of Party Control," in *Change in Communist Systems*, ed. Chalmers Johnson (Stanford: Stanford University Press), 176.

40. Grey Hodnett in a famous article discussed the pros and contras of this argument (see Hodnett, "Khrushchev and Party-State Control"). Squeezing middle

first things accomplished by the new leadership of Brezhnev and Aleksei Kosygin in 1965 was the dismantling of the KPGK and the creation of a new body called the Committee of People's Control, safely subordinated to the Council of Ministers, and with clearly delineated functions confined to economic supervision.

The comrades' courts, the people's patrols, the KPGK: perhaps by now the thrust of the second strategy of the 1950s' collectivization of life— spreading horizontal control throughout the whole body social—has become clear. Khrushchev's reforms used mutual surveillance as a decisive means to tie together the primary *kollektivy* into a mega-*kollektiv* called the Soviet people. The third grand strategy of filling the gaps in surveillance was the creation of *kollektivy* out of all remaining groups that did not yet practice mutual surveillance to support saintly ideals. The army, the prison, the vocational school, the sports team—indeed, every site where people regularly met for a substantial period of time was to recast itself as a *kollektiv*. Like the postwar transformation of high schools (described in chapter 3), the reform of the penitentiaries is illuminating, not only because of the changes that the authorities sought to effect (they should come as no surprise after the previous exposition) but also because of the reactions that these changes induced in recalcitrant groups.

Until the 1950s the main unit of the corrective labor system was the *lagpunkt*, the camp. The camp usually consisted of a number of "labor battalions" (*roty*), each numbering three hundred to four hundred people, headed by three appointed supervisors, who were not prisoners. In the late 1950s this system was transformed and differentiated. First, four types of "corrective labor colonies" with regimes differing in severity were created for mature inmates. Second, "training labor colonies" were established for delinquents fourteen to seventeen years old. Third, the "prisons," strictly called, incarcerated only the minority of the convict population.[41] A system of "detachments" (*otriady*) also replaced the heretofore existing "battalions." In the early 1950s Kitoy, Idel, and Moscow regional camps had experimented with the new detachment system, and an order of the USSR

<hr>

managers in between attacks coming from the top and from the bottom: is this not an essentially Stalinist strategy?

41. Convicts were held in prisons only on their way to the colonies, or as punishment for violating the colonies' disciplinary regime (Juviler, *Revolutionary Law and Order*, 106). Prisons had only two regimes, strict and special; corrective labor colonies were divided into those with common, intensified, strict and special regimes.

Ministry of Internal Affairs made it compulsory in June 1957. As a brochure for law students explained retrospectively in 1962, under the previous penal system "the mass of inmates was depersonalized. Particular features of specific individuals or groups of inmates were not taken into account."[42] Although assigned the tasks of "correction and training" of the inmates, the camp administration was mostly unable to perform them, since only two people, the director of the camp and his political deputy, supervised this activity, which therefore mainly took the form of random mass lectures on the ideals of the new life. The administration's attention was inevitably drawn only to individual violators of the established regime in the camp, with the mass of the convicts being left unattended.

The creation of the system of detachments was supposed to change this perilous condition and introduce "individual treatment" of the inmates. A detachment of 50–110 inmates was headed by a detachment leader and was then broken into smaller subunits called brigades. Everything was done in full accordance with Makarenko: the detachment became "a primary *kollektiv* of inmates" that had a single production objective and became collectively responsible for its achievement. Penal reformers faithfully quoted Makarenko—"A [collective] bedroom should be an additional form of labor, production, and political training"[43]—and ruled that each brigade was to be allocated a separate bedroom, for the orderliness and cleanliness of which the brigade was also collectively responsible. This rearrangement of working and living environment and of human groups was supposed to heighten discipline, decrease the number of violations, eliminate shirking of work, and promote the meeting of production norms.[44] The results of

42. Yu. M. Tkachevsky, *Otriadnaia sistema v ispravitel'no-trudovykh koloniiakh* [Detachment system in corrective labor colonies] (Moscow: Moscow State University, 1962), 4.

43. Makarenko 5:12, cited in ibid., 8.

44. Nothing is entirely novel: among the first signs of experiments with the detachment system, researchers found "detachments" of 300–600 people in Dmitrovlag in 1934. A detachment's members lived, worked, and underwent "political and cultural education" together, were collectively responsible for internal discipline and for meeting production targets. See M. G. Detkov, *Soderzhanie karatel'noi politiki sovetskogo gosudarstva i ee realizatsiia pri ispolnenii ugolovnogo nakazaniia v vide lisheniia svobody v tridtsatye—piatidesiatye gody* [Punitive policy of the Soviet state and its realization in penitentiary detention in the 1930s–50s] (Domodedovo: Academy of the Russian Ministry of Internal Affairs, 1992), 57.

Apparently, the influx of terror victims and the press's loss of interest in reeducation in labor camps after the mid-1930s combined to limit the experiments. For an official representation of camp reeducation, see the model book *The Stalin Chan-*

this transformation, boasted the reformers, were immediate: "If earlier, before the introduction of detachments, many violators of the regime . . . remained unknown to the administration . . . , nowadays this is impossible."[45] The *kollektiv,* whether of the brigade or of the whole detachment, was expected to identify and influence the open violators of the regime and thus improve the "individual treatment" of each inmate.

The *aktiv* was also in the process of being formed. Camps were ordered to create "councils of the *aktiv*" in September 1954; the members of these councils were to be people "who had firmly committed themselves to the road of correction" and were to be elected by the inmates at open assemblies.[46] But after two *aktiv* leaders of one of the Khabarovsk camps were killed by criminals in 1955 in a widely publicized case, the system was called into question. The solution adopted was to segregate inmates according to type, with corresponding assignment to a colony with the appropriate regime. The killers were defined as "recidivist" criminals, who were to be locked up in the colonies with the harshest regime.[47] Thus, differentiation of the system of penal colonies and the intensification of their collectivization went hand in hand.

Comrades' courts were introduced in the colonies of the "common," that is, less harsh, regime only, with seven to nine activists shaming a violator and deciding on the penalty. The court's members were supposed to be elected only by open vote, which apparently was intended to give the prison administration the possibility of influencing the decision of who would become members of the court.[48] In 1955 some other "advanced" forms of training of the socialist individual were applied to penitentiaries: socialist competition between prisoners' brigades was to be introduced; the appointment of special observers from the Soviet public to the prison administration was to ensure progress in the living and working conditions in the colonies, and the like.[49]

Finally, the fourth grand strategy of the collectivization of life drew in

nel, produced by a surprising staff of writers including even Mikhail Zoshchenko (Maxim Gorky, ed., *Kanal imeni Stalina* [Moscow, 1934]).

45. Tkachevsky, *Otriadnaia sistema,* 16.
46. Detkov, *Soderzhanie karatel'noi politiki,* 138.
47. Ibid., 91.
48. Since the administration drew up the list of candidates, open election (with mutual surveillance) became the means of rigging direct democracy. Yet, as we see later, such maneuvers alienated the rest of the inmates and helped form the prison's customary law system.
49. Detkov, *Soderzhanie karatel'noi politiki,* 140–145.

any remaining recalcitrant individuals who were still not part of any registered *kollektiv*. Homogenization of the body social and the elimination of those gaps in it that still escaped social control became the task of the "antiparasite" campaign. "The law against idlers" adopted in 1961 allowed administrative bodies to sentence an individual not legally registered at any job to forced labor. This law not only helped supply new sites of socialist construction in Siberia and the far north with cheap labor but also made it possible to flush out "persons hard to convict of specific crimes but still living in a shadow economy of private speculation, prostitution, handouts from rich parents, vagrancy, and begging." [50] Though largely waged in the central cities by police bodies, eager to send all troublemakers out of their region, the campaign fostered the role of the *kollektiv* in the homogenization of the body social more generally. "Neighbors' assemblies" could exile an undesirable neighbor for two to five years of forced labor following the decision of the comrades' court.[51] The same campaign also provided a legal pretext for ridding the central areas of all religious and political dissenters, along with generally undesirable people.[52] The next "homogenization purge" that occurred in 1966–67 under Brezhnev, in the guise of a struggle against "hooliganism," flushed out the remaining undesirables and settled them beyond a radius of a hundred kilometers from the central cities. Brezhnev was only finishing what his rowdy predecessor had left unaccomplished.[53]

KHRUSHCHEV'S NORMALIZATION

Khrushchev's name usually connotes a period of liberalization, relaxation, and the elimination of the most atrocious elements of the Stalinist repressive apparatus, and it is an apt label for the era. However, as we have seen, the name also applies to the profound extension of a system of communal

50. Juviler, *Revolutionary Law and Order*, 78.

51. After 1961 administrative bodies claimed this right because of widespread abuses and could act only if an idler did not find a job after a warning. After 1965 only criminal courts could send individuals to forced labor (Juviler, *Revolutionary Law and Order*, 76–77).

52. Ibid. The poet Joseph Brodsky was among this campaign's victims.

53. Ibid., 87. Observers who tracked changes in practices rather than Party speeches about a break from Khrushchev's era noted the continuity. According to Paul Cocks, Brezhnev dropped the excessive zeal and enthusiasm of mutual control but "retained and even augmented the vast army of public checkers" (Cocks, "Rationalization of Party Control," 188).

enslavement, a system more meticulous and thorough in its attention to each individual than the more openly repressive Stalinist one it replaced.

Let us listen to Khrushchev himself. From his speeches it is clear that he sought to install the system of comradely admonition everywhere, a system that would correct erring citizens and prevent crimes rather than punish those that have already occurred. His insistence on mutual control was constant, notwithstanding the twists and turns of government policies in the 1950s and 1960s. Speaking at the Twenty-first Party Congress in 1959, Khrushchev advocated "a new period of Communist construction" marked by the withering away of the state and the gradual growth of the elements of Communist self-government. "Social discipline" and "attitudinal homogeneity" were taken as prerequisites for this self-regulating society, according to the most meticulous study of Khrushchev's speeches in this period.[54] But how were these prerequisites to be achieved?

Khrushchev's description of the work of the people's patrols and comrades' courts is particularly telling:

> When comrades' courts work actively and the public itself nominates people to defend public order, it will be easier to fight the violators. One can discern such a violator not only when he has committed a misdeed or a crime, but when he merely deviates from norms of public behavior in a way that may [eventually] lead to antisocial acts. People [then] can influence him in time so that his vicious disposition is cut short. . . . The main thing is the prophylaxis, the work of training.[55]

In his speech at the Twenty-second Party Congress (1961), Khrushchev made the same point in a slightly different way: "It is necessary to heighten public attention and requirements to people's behavior. Because evil deeds are committed by people most of whom are members of one or another *kollektiv*. . . . We should more actively use the moral weight and authority of the public to fight violators of the norms and rules of common socialist life."[56] Khrushchev did not prescribe any new means for fulfilling this task; evidently he thought that surveillance within *kollektivy* and communal pressure in the interstices of social life between *kollektivy* could solve all the problems.

His speech at the November 1962 Central Committee plenum that authorized the creation of the KPGK was even more straightforward:

54. Breslauer, *Khrushchev and Brezhnev as Leaders*, 69.
55. Nikita Khrushchev, *Stroitel'stvo kommunizma* [Building communism] (Moscow, 1964), 7:103.
56. Ibid., 220.

We have 10 million Party members, 20 million Komsomol members, 66 million members of trade unions. If we could put all these forces into action, if we could use them in the interests of control, then not even a mosquito could pass unnoticed.[57]

A system of 96 million controllers watching each other so that not even a mosquito could escape notice—this is the disciplinary dream of Khrushchev. Instead of the chaotic and punitive terror of the Stalinist years, he wanted to see a relentless and rational system of preventive surveillance. We might add that he largely made this dream come true.

"The point of Soviet community effort—and this holds both for place of residence and place of work"—summed up one of the Western commentaries, "is to make the regime your neighbor by having your neighbor represent the regime."[58] Other Western observers described the activism of the Khrushchev years in similar terms. Breslauer noted: "'All the people' would be drawn into the process of monitoring the behavior of their immediate hierarchical superiors; however, they would also be mobilized *en masse* to monitor each other."[59] Conyngham: "The mass participation movement was so pervasive that it constituted in essence a silent social explosion affecting all public organizations in the Soviet Union and many areas of social life."[60] Juviler: "Stalin's grassroots social controls were flaccid and listless despite his totalitarianism. There was no community, even a pushed-together, mobilized one. . . . It was Khrushchev and Brezhnev who reintroduced a pervasive structure for social control with the popularization of justice and the push for grass roots influence of deviants."[61] Finally, according to Berman's synthetic formulation, the Stalinist dualism of law and terror was replaced by Khrushchev's dualism of law and social pressure. Under Stalin, one could trust that consideration of his or her case would be relatively fair, *if* the case ever made it to the People's Court. Under Khrushchev "one is free from arbitrary assault by the secret police but one is not free from the social pressure of the 'collective'. . . . The new dualism still stands in the shadow of the old."[62]

Khrushchev's liberalization was a corollary to other changes, the liberating potential of which is dubious at best. Viewed from the perspective of

57. Ibid., 401.
58. Friedgut, *Political Participation*, 239.
59. Breslauer, *Khrushchev and Brezhnev as Leaders*, 129.
60. Conyngham, *Industrial Management*, 68.
61. Juviler, *Revolutionary Law and Order*, 121.
62. Berman, *Justice in the USSR*, 88.

the trend toward increasing pervasive mutual surveillance in everyday life, 1957 was a direct outgrowth and continuation of 1937. If 1937 can be viewed as a first decisive attempt to install the overarching system of total mutual surveillance, with excessive zeal of comradely control turning to homicide and contributing to the chaotic terror, then 1957 marked the final achievement of the Stalinist goal: a fine-tuned and balanced system of total surveillance, firmly rooted in people's policing each other in an orderly and relatively peaceful manner.

Simultaneously, the list of the objects of legal concern was to be firmly established. This codification drive was one of the main puzzling features of Khrushchev's liberalization. For example, Juviler gives a laundry list of changes in the judiciary and penal systems under Khrushchev, documenting what he thought were obvious paradoxes. Khrushchev, "a Communist liberal" and a theoretician of self-government, introduced "harsher penalties including an unprecedented legal extension of the death penalty for nonpolitical crimes, far outdoing Stalin on that."[63] It was under Khrushchev that *not* informing authorities of an impending crime of which one knew (in cases of state treason or banditry) became itself a crime. Six new crimes were codified in 1961–62; these included falsifying plan figures, wrecking agricultural machinery, repeated theft, rebellion and terror in places of detention, attempts on a police officer's life, and—finally, after all the years since the Chubarov affair!—group rape with serious consequences. As a result, the end of Khrushchev "liberal" era witnessed an unprecedented growth in the number of criminal sentences: 2.8 million were convicted in 1961–63, almost as many as during the 1966–68 Brezhnev campaign against "hooliganism," generally considered to be a "very repressive" period.[64]

Of course, this extended codification of criminal behavior and the resulting sudden growth of criminals corresponded to the need to punish the violators according to the law, rather than the whim of the special courts or an individual's feeling of revolutionary justice. But filling the gaps in legislation, extending the death penalty for old crimes, and codifying new crimes, Khrushchev's regime moved swiftly to complete the total net of

63. Juviler, *Revolutionary Law and Order*, 82. Khrushchev introduced capital punishment for 16 crimes, including illegal operations with hard currency, printing counterfeit money, repeated bribery, and theft of public property in very large amounts. A famous 1960 case drew a retroactive death penalty for hard-currency operations; this 1960 law's specific target was recent scandalous deeds.

64. Ibid.

registration and suppression of misdeeds. This net was to be cast by both the punitive police bodies and the watchful Soviet people so that no misdeed escaped it, and no wish to commit a misdeed remained unanticipated, should this wish be ever registered by the Soviet public. The rationalized and extended system of Soviet legality came to rely on the network of mutual surveillance, which both reported those many deeds established as crimes and also spotted those deeds—even more numerous and not yet codified—that were dangerously close and thus could lead to crimes.

By 1985, of course, this system of "popular pressure" was thoroughly routinized. The people's patrols, subordinated now to the local soviets, became groups of obedient citizens strolling brightly lit alleys in demonstration of their loyalty to the absurd demands of the aging saintly regime, rather than expressing any real zeal for fighting petty hooliganism and crime. The 1977 statute of the comrades' courts firmly tied these bodies to the "public commissions on the comrades' courts" sections of the local soviets, which oversaw and guided their work. In many cases, instead of punishing transgressors, the comrades' courts became the means of their collective defense: by undergoing the undemanding public rite of confessing a crime and pleading for forgiveness and with the help of consenting members of the primary *kollektiv* to which the transgressor belonged, they could escape criminal prosecution. Express loyalty to the form now mattered more than substantive loyalty to the content of the doctrine, a state of affairs that sly citizens immediately turned to their advantage.[65]

But, as the Levada report noted in the late 1980s, a fundamental "transparency" had already been installed by previous zealous drives to heighten mutual control and admonition: Soviet individuals were "simple" by definition. They were open to the gaze of a neighbor and expressly possessed the same simple needs and interests as the neighbor did. This fundamental transparency meant "openness to understanding by those who were like oneself, and, in particular, to control from above."[66] Since mutual control was in operation everywhere, in the Brezhnev years it was only excessive surveillance and admonition that were safely stored in such special rou-

65. See documents on the comrades' courts and other public bodies of Khrushchev's era, suggesting their ritualized stagnation in the Brezhnev years, in I. I. Veremeenko and V. F. Vorob'ev, eds. *V pomoshch DND: Sbornik normativnykh aktov* [Handbook of the People's patrols: a collection of normative documents] (Moscow: Iuridicheskaia literatura, 1985).
66. Iurii Levada, ed., *Prostoi sovetskii chelovek* [A common Soviet individual] (Moscow, 1993), 26.

tinized bodies as the comrades' courts. They dealt only with cases of open defiance of surveillance and listened to the individual's ritualized public confession of a misdeed that restored the status quo. Furthermore, the secret police came to strike only in those rarest of cases when even these bodies of routinized admonition failed to bring public confession of loyalty to the regime.

Let us sharpen the argument presented so far. Stalin's regime still allowed for the existence of random patches of individual human freedom. Chaos and inefficiency frequently characterized the management of the "quicksand society" of Stalin's days: people could sometimes escape the imminent threat of terror by simply moving to another city,[67] by making a brilliant rhetorical counterblow during the purge assembly meeting,[68] by turning the tables on their persecutors through enlisting the help of some higher body on their behalf, and so on. After all, some people were never noticed or touched by the machinery of terror. Of course, a horrifyingly large number of people perished in the whirlpool of terror, but the survival of exiled Mikhail Bakhtin in the calm waters of provincial Saransk testified that even an extraordinary individual could still escape death, the application of which was rather uneven. Surveillance and repression were neither omniscient nor omnipresent. The painter Pavel Filonov, whom some would consider the Soviet equivalent of Pablo Picasso, starving in the late 1930s after the loss of his job because of his flirtation with the formalist school long before, was not summoned to the police or exiled to the far north as an "idler," as was the poet Joseph Brodsky some twenty years later.[69] Daniil Kharms, the epitome of Soviet absurdist prose and incessant experimentation with lifestyle, could walk the streets of Leningrad during the 1930s in the most extravagant attire unharrassed. There was no people's patrol to regulate his clothes.[70] Lest anyone misunderstand me, I do not argue that dying from hunger in your own room is better than life on a guaranteed food ration in a corrective labor colony. Nor do I claim that life under Stalin

67. See Kotkin, *Magnetic Mountain*, 334.

68. Fitzpatrick, "Two Faces of Anastasia."

69. A general introduction is Nicoletta Misler and John E. Bowlt, eds., *Pavel Filonov* (Austin, Tex.: Silvergirl, 1983).

70. He was interned shortly after the German invasion, possibly because of his German-sounding pseudonym, and died in the NKVD prison in February 1942. On his lifestyle see Svetozar Shishman, *Neskol'ko veselykh i grustnykh istorii o Daniile Kharmse i ego druziiakh* [Several funny and sad stories about Kharms and his friends] (Leningrad, 1991), 118, 157. The standard introduction is George Gibian, ed., *Russia's Lost Literature of the Absurd* (New York: Norton, 1971).

was better than life under Khrushchev. But what the earlier uneven and frequently chaotic terror still allowed for was a space of uncompromised human freedom and dignity that the later orderly mutual surveillance erased. The disciplinary grid became faultless and ubiquitous: any degree of freedom in private was to be paid for by an inescapable participation in the mutual enforcement of unfreedom and humiliation in public.

INFORMAL COLLECTIVES WITHIN OFFICIAL *KOLLEKTIVY*

The total collectivization of life had two corollaries: the creation of informal collectives within formal *kollektivy* and the creation of informal collectives outside the official terrain altogether, as if on the obverse side of social life. Let us first concentrate on the informal collectives that appeared within the borders of established *kollektivy*.

One of the most interesting reactions to the introduction of official *kollektivy* happened in the prison world. The installation of the Khrushchev's machinery of "socialist self-government" in the penitentiary seemed to proceed rather smoothly until 1960–61. At the time, "the idea of self-government was pivotal in the doctrine of recasting criminals. A system of administrative positions that inmates could hold (brigade leaders, norm assignors, enforcers of internal discipline, etc.) was put into effect, and thus the personnel of the camp system delegated some of their functions to the inmates themselves."[71] But after 1960, as many reports noticed, the regime in Soviet labor colonies suddenly worsened: new strict penalties for the violation of internal rules appeared, additional sentences for prison rebellions harshened, and prisoners received less food and fewer letters from the outside.[72] Whatever the cause, the harshening of the policies of the penal system in the early 1960s set up a resistant community within the colony, an informal *kollektiv* bound together by the war against the penal authority. Recent interviews with political prisoners who served their terms in the 1960s and 1970s revealed a startling fact about the prison reform of the late 1950s and early 1960s: instead of creating a "system of collective self-government," it formed a rigid underground caste society, which charac-

71. V. F. Abramkin and V. Chesnokova, "Tiuremnyi zakon" [Prison law], in *Tiuremnyi mir glazami politzakliuchennykh* [The prison world in the eyes of political prisoners], ed. V. F. Abramkin (Moscow: Sodeistvie, 1993), 14.

72. E.g., multiple references to the famous dissident Anatolii Marchenko's opinion on that, cited in Juviler, *Revolutionary Law and Order*, 106. See also Abramkin and Chesnokova, "Tiuremnyi zakon," 13.

terized the Soviet prison until its last days and apparently persists in the Russian penitentiary.

In their pioneering study based on these interviews, Abramkin and Chesnokova have proposed that descriptions of the camp system, so familiar to us now through the works of the victims of Stalinism of the Solzhenitsyn generation, were not true of the Soviet penal system of the 1960s. In the 1920s–40s, the camp system did not know the homogenous body of inmates as it existed in the 1960s; rather, the most familiar feature before the 1950s was the division of prisoners into "the politicals" and "ordinary criminals." The latter brutally oppressed the former. The criminals had their own communal organization guided by rigid "thieves' laws" that helped them survive in prison; in fact, life there was part of the normal life of the professional criminal. By contrast, "the politicals" had to defend themselves individually, thrown by the machinery of terror into a milieu totally novel for them. Also, the criminals were officially considered to be "socially close" while the political prisoners were, of course, "socially alien." Therefore, the camp administration relied on criminals to suppress the politicals and enforce discipline in the camps, which led to the worst possible terror waged by the criminals against the rest of the camp population. Solzhenitsyn's and Shalamov's stories capture the politicals' hatred of the criminals and sense of powerlessness in the face of the others' in-camp preponderance.

This imbalance of power in the prison world did not outlast the 1950s. According to Abramkin and Chesnokova, the first shift occurred in 1947 when Stalin proclaimed an offensive against the blossoming criminal community. Prison officials relied on former soldiers, imprisoned during or after the Second World War, and on renegade criminals who did not recognize the unwritten common law of the criminal community, to fight the primary upholders of this law, professional criminals who were called *avtoritety* (authorities).[73] The late 1940s witnessed a bloody war between the traditional criminal "authorities" and the challengers, supported by the prison administration. After 1953 with the prospect of mass release of the politicals and the amelioration of their treatment by the penal system, the politicals also joined the war on the domination of the criminals, and by the mid-1950s, according to interviews with the politicals of that time, it

73. A vote of existing "authorities" gave a criminal the title of *avtoritet*. Even under pressure in the camp, *avtoritety* never worked and became primary enforcers and adjudicators of thieves' law (against informing and cooperating with state authorities, and on setting rules of customary behavior and speech).

seemed that this domination was broken down completely. Official sources support this view. The 1958 classified brochure for penitentiary employees on the handling of the criminal elite stated that a penal officer should give an *avtoritet* two alternatives: either betray the thieves' law or spend the rest of life in prison. By the authors' estimates, by the late 1950s no more than 20 percent of the criminal *avtoritety* remained "clean," still refusing to work in production or cooperate with the prison administration in any matter.[74]

The late 1950s and early 1960s brought a surprising change: the power of the criminals within the penitentiary, which had been almost crushed, developed once again. By the mid-1960s the professional criminals' common law served as a model for the unwritten "prison law" that now bound the entire population of the Soviet corrective labor colonies, not just criminals alone. Abramkin and Chesnokova propose the following explanation. For some reason Khrushchev decided to reintroduce the system of slave labor in the Soviet penitentiary. (Many would argue that he was facing stark economic difficulties in 1960–61 after the extremely good results of the extensive growth of 1958–59.)[75] Therefore the liberalized penal system of post-Stalinist camps of the mid-fifties, which to a large extent relied on market elements—with its wage payment, abundance of goods in camp shops, and possibility of earning a reduction in sentence through hard work—was no longer suitable. The administrators of the Soviet penitentiary, ordered to squeeze more surplus value out of the inmates, were by and large the same people who ran the camps under Stalin. And they had to achieve the same economic results without violating the new professed doctrine of "socialist legality." The Abramkin and Chesnokova volume explains the rigidification and harshening of conditions of life in the colonies in the early 1960s as the means for securing more legal grounds for transforming a wage-earning inmate into a slave.

The collectivization of colony life and experiments with socialist self-government after 1961 seem to have followed the same objective. Instead of allowing inmates to arrange their life themselves within this framework, the penal administration used it as a cover for a more hierarchical discipline by effectively transforming the *aktiv* into a network of constant informers. This network, comprising all "voluntary prisoners' organizations" in the bureaucratic parlance of the day, was greatly expanded. "The idea of self-government acquired a totally novel quality" after that, write Abramkin

74. Abramkin and Chesnokova, "Tiuremnyi zakon," 12.
75. Breslauer, *Khrushchev and Brezhnev as Leaders*, 83–88.

and Chesnokova.[76] The authors are not clear when these multiple organi-zations of inmates originated, but they are sure that filling the numerous positions in the inmates' associations changed prison life. Inmates had to enroll in such organizations as the "section for the prophylaxis of law violations" (effectively the main spying squad), the "sanitary section," the "production section" (charged with increasing the productivity of labor), the "section for cultural and educational training" (repeating ideological dogmas), and diverse inmates' councils, ranging from the council of the colony to the council of the detachment. Enrolling in a section defined one as the individual who "had firmly stepped onto the road of correction." This enrollment became the only means for reducing one's sentence. In short, the novel demand imposed on members of the prison *aktiv* from the early 1960s was total collaboration with the penal administration. If before that becoming an activist meant certain administrative work for a period of one or two years, now it meant becoming a sentence-long associate of the camp administration.

The absence of the huge number of activists needed to fill the numerous positions in the "voluntary organizations" made the penal authorities re-sort to old methods. Often under the auspices of a complicit administra-tion, the "unprincipled thieves" (those who were themselves crushed by the bloody anti-*avtoritety* war of 1947–53) tortured and raped those in-mates who refused to fill the positions in a given corrective institution's "bodies of Communist self-government." Therefore, becoming part of the "voluntary organizations" of the colony frequently meant the abandon-ment of everything human in oneself: "The most startling phenomenon consists in the fact of a refusal of a man to adopt the way of correction offered by the administration, precisely because he wishes to remain a man."[77] Also, note the authors, joining the ranks of the prison activists in the 1960s meant betrayal of others and siding with the brutal and cunning official authorities, which contradicted the obvious precept that one can-not educate by pressuring to betray. The tiny layer of those who agreed to take these positions—and became the visible referent for the "successes of the socialist collective training" as practiced in the penal system—found themselves ostracized by the rest of the inmates.

As a result, a rigidly structured community of all inmates developed, guided by spontaneously produced customary laws based on joint resis-

76. Abramkin and Chesnokova, "Tiuremnyi zakon," 14.
77. Ibid., 17.

tance to the penitentiary pressure. "People immersed in this [penal] system started independently and at their own risk to build a new system, parallel to the administrative one. And they have built it. Now we have, on the one hand, moral authority and 'law,' honor and ritual; on the other— power based on sheer violence."[78] According to a hypothesis of Abramkin and Chesnokova, the closed communities of inmates who mostly were not professional criminals—following the model of thieves' law with its unconditional prohibition of betrayal and containment of arbitrary violence through communal institutions—tacitly worked out a body of rules, now known as "prison law" (*tiuremnyi zakon*), which applied to every inmate. One major innovation was introduced, however. If in thieves' law violation of customary norms was punished by death, in prison law a milder equivalent was adopted: collective homosexual rape to punish and stigmatize the violator.[79]

In the 1960s the Soviet prison society became divided into four main informal caste-like categories. First, the category of "thieves," professional criminals who guided themselves by thieves' law but established and enforced both it and prison law. For difficult questions of prison law, a professional criminal—an *avtoritet* recognized for a given corrective institution—would provide a verdict; in novel cases not covered by customary law, "thieves" would deliberate together. The second category, "men," to which the majority of the inmates belonged, was bound by prison law; in contradistinction to the caste of professional criminals, who were prohibited by thieves' law from working in prison, the men would work in socialist production. Third, the category of the "goats," those who collaborated with the administration, filling the positions of "voluntary inmates' organizations." They were despised but were rarely assaulted, since they were defended by the administration. Fourth, "the roosters," the downtrodden category of passive homosexuals stigmatized by collective rape. These were untouchable, in the most physical sense of the word,

78. Ibid., 18.
79. The authors consider stigmatization through homosexual rape part of a certain "humanization"—a curious comment, given the fact that the majority of people suddenly subjected to this humiliating ritual were ordinary inmates who never practiced murder. Neither criminals nor politicals practiced rape as means of stigmatization in Stalin's camps, nor in those of 1955–59. In fact, prisoners' interviews stress the availablity of a relatively decent and humane life (on conditions of relative freedom in the inner colony life in the mid 1950s see Abramkin, ed., *Tiuremnyi mir*, 11).

since touching them was considered contaminating and immediately transformed an inmate into a "rooster."[80] Roosters did the dirtiest jobs in the
cell or in the colony; constantly mistreated and harassed, they ate and slept
in specially designated areas. One could become a rooster through a violation of customary law (e.g., stealing from an inmate, nonpayment of card
debts, insulting another inmate by word or act) or by the violation of some
symbolic ritual that supported this law (e.g., touching roosters or doing
their work, such as sweeping floors or cleaning toilet bowls, not retaliating
with immediate violence on being called "a rooster" in public, and so on).
Whatever the origins of stigmatization by homosexual rape, one thing is
clear: the self-governing community in a cell or a prison used it as the ultimate threat and penalty.[81] The *kollektiv*, forming itself spontaneously
rather than under pressure from the administration, still took the ways of
group life advocated at the top with full seriousness but had different aims.

Of course, my conjecture that group life among inmates imitated official
models is necessarily of a purely chronological order. Given the compulsory introduction of the detachment system in corrective labor colonies in
1957, the fight with the criminals' prison influence largely completed by
1958, and the relative freedom that inmates enjoyed in 1955–59, it seems
highly likely that some embryos of real *kollektivy* may have been formed
in the penitentiary system during this period. When these *kollektivy* of inmates were put under intense pressure after 1960 to become adjuncts of
administrative surveillance, they solidified and resisted this pressure by
developing a system of collective defense. Hence the appearance of prison
law in the mid-1960s. The fact that this common body of informal norms
tying all the inmates together in a countercommunity did not exist up until the 1960s, even in the face of similar centralized pressure and brutal humiliation and torture of the 1930s and 1940s, suggests that the inmates had
no means of collective resistance before the late 1950s. That's why it seems

80. Those taking the active homosexual role or beating a rooster were exempt
from this rule.
81. To isolate a closed community's transgressors of customary law, some kind
of stigmatization ritual was bound to emerge. Abramkin offers two hypotheses on
how homosexual stigmatization began. The first takes criminal *avtoritety's* opinion
that "unprincipled thieves" (on a hint from prison administrators) used rape to in-
timidate inmates who refused to join the "voluntary associations." The other more
plausibly refers to the fact that in the 1930s–50s the label "goats" never applied to
members of the prison *aktiv* but only to passive homosexuals, suggesting that indignant cell communities used rape to retaliate against the first collaborators with
the administration (Abramkin, ed., *Tiuremnyi mir*, 272).

plausible that the prison reform designed to introduce elements of Communist self-government supplied those resources of collective resistance to the inmates.

We should not forget, however, that the informal *kollektivy* of inmates still functioned within the official framework, simultaneously supporting and challenging it. The inmates' detachment as a whole had to meet production tasks and cleanliness requirements, using internal pressure to punish individual inmates who subverted success in meeting these criteria, with stigmatization being the ultimate means. The authors are not entirely clear on this matter of an informal *kollektiv*'s cooperation with administration. For example, in their description of penal colonies for teenagers—where, in accordance with the previous exposition, we might expect development of an administration-defying community also—we find instead that the category of goats, collaborating with administration, is not so different from those who wage violence to uphold prison law in the cell. Perhaps in those corrective institutions that dealt with secondary socialization the informal *kollektivy*'s cooperation with official structures—or some sort of intraorganizational division of labor—was more open than in the penal colonies for adults. Consider the following description of the young delinquents' corrective institution in the 1970s: "Humiliation, torment, torture, rape— this is the Training Labor Colony's everyday reality. All of these happen with the consent and even with the support of an official 'educator' who uses this 'collective pedagogy' to support order, ensure the meeting of necessary criteria and the fulfillment of the production plan. The Training Labor Colonies have the largest percentage of 'roosters.'" According to Abramkin and Chesnokova, this number reached up to 30 percent of the inmates.[82]

Now compare this horrifying picture with the official description of the condition of Training Labor Colonies. The 1991 police handbook on the creation of the *kollektiv* in these juvenile corrective institutions admitted that though 60 percent of them had a *kollektiv*'s structure (councils of commanders, detachments, and so on), 79 percent of the polled officials of these colonies thought that a "real" *kollektiv* was lacking and needed to be cre-

82. Ibid., 261. A possible reason for the high percentage of stigmatization in teenage colonies and in common-regime corrective labor institutions, which held many first-time offenders, is that inmates did not bother to explain prison law to newcomers and minors. The majority of those raped and stigmatized had unwittingly made ritual transgressions—using the wrong word, touching the wrong place—of some of the numerous symbolic borders that supported customary law.

ated.[83] In the euphemistic language of the Makarenko pedagogy, most officials considered that the actually existing *kollektivy* in their colonies were positioned between the first and second stages of their development: the *aktiv* (and the reserve) were applying disciplinary demands to the rest, without observing them themselves.[84] However, the reliance of the administration on an informal *aktiv*, that is, people who use violence to make the rest conform to the prescribed regime and fulfill planned objectives, was not unique to the teenage corrective colonies.

In fact, it was also the feature of another major resocialization agency. The whole system of *dedovshchina*, or "eldership"—the hazing informally practiced in the Soviet army—relied on the existence of the informal *aktiv* who would teach and coerce new recruits into helping fulfill the planned targets of the regiments. In contradistinction to the teenage penal colonies' *kollektivy*, there was steady rotation into and out of the informal *aktiv* of a military regiment: after a year of service soldiers themselves became part of the *aktiv* and started oppressing the new arrivals. This informal hazing system, evidently also installed in the 1950s, came to be the main feature of army training. If only 40 percent of the recruits knew about it before joining the army in the 1970s, by 1991 all of them, and 90 percent of their parents, were aware of what awaits new recruits.[85] Both the teenage colony and the army served as primary means of resocialization, a kind of a terrifying school of Soviet citizenship, almost in accord with the widespread proverb: "There are only two schools of life, the army and the prison."

Once again, since the subject was not discussed in the Soviet days, we rely on the pioneering study of Belanovsky and Marzeeva, who interviewed Moscow University students who had served in the armed forces.[86]

83. E. M. Danilin, *Ispol'zovanie sistemy A. S. Makarenko v deiatel'nosti VTK* [Using Makarenko's system in the work of Training Labor Colonies] (Moscow: VNII MVD, 1991), 34.

84. Ibid., 35.

85. Yu. I. Deriugin, "Dedovshchina: sotsial'no-psikhologicheskii analiz iavleniia" [The eldership: a socio-psychological analysis of the phenomenon], *Psikhologicheskii zhurnal* [Journal of psychology (Moscow)] 11, no. 1 (January–February 1990): 112.

86. S. A. Belanovsky and S. N. Marzeeva, "Armiia kak ona est'" [The army as it is], in *Dedovshchina v armii: Sbornik sotsiologicheskikh dokumentov* [The eldership in the army: a collection of sociological documents], ed. S. A. Belanovsky (Moscow: Institute of Economic Prognostication, 1991). Apparently only one essay broke the silence in 1977, by the dissident journalist Kirill Podrabinek (now reprinted in Belanovsky, ed., *Dedovshchina*, 195–212). Official Soviet sources on military psychology or soldiers' *kollektivy* mentioned "informal relations" within the army but usually simply commented on the need to fight them (see V. V. Sheliag

According to the authors, the Soviet army had three codes of behavior, one based on the written Disciplinary Statute, another based on the informal system of eldership, and the third based on national or territorial identities (*zemliachestva*). The Disciplinary Statute, which had a number of disciplinary penalties for not obeying the orders of a superior (reprimand, disciplinary work, guardhouse, and military prison), was in effect only in the sergeants' and professional schools, and to a lesser extent in the elite regiments and among the border guards. The eldership system developed as a means to enforce disciplinary compliance in those regiments where hierarchical status was not or could not be enforced. In essence, it was a system of exploitation of new recruits by second-year soldiers, "the elders," who forced the younger ones to carry out all the disciplinary assignments and keep barracks and military equipment at the required levels of cleanliness and operation. The elders did none of this "lowly" work themselves and punished those of the younger recruits who volunteered to tell the officers about this system of exploitation. In the majority of regiments the Disciplinary Statute functioned only during combat, and on guard duty, but not in everyday barracks life. The third system of mores, based on ethnic subgroups, could challenge the general dominance of eldership by defending fellow Georgians or fellow Chechens against its encroachments but did not substantially subvert the eldership system among the Slavic recruits.[87]

Researchers have singled out six caste-like categories of recruits in the eldership system.[88] As in an informal *kollektiv*, new entrants did all the everyday work, were deprived of food and sleep, and were continuously harassed and mistreated by "the elders," who thus produced docile soldiers eager to fulfill any, even the most absurd, order supported by communal terror.[89] Those who refused to obey these rules were ruthlessly beaten. Those who obeyed but then informed the officers were immediately cast out

---

et al., eds., *Military Psychology: A Soviet View,* translated under the auspices of the U.S. Air Force [Washington, D.C.: U.S. Government Printing Office, 1976]).

87. According to the authors, as the USSR was falling apart and ethnic conflicts broke out on its periphery, ethnic ties replaced eldership ties in many regiments (ibid.). Since 1991 the Russian army has drawn conscripts only from the Russian Federation; without many ethnic subgroups from the Caucuses who challenged the eldership system, it may now be as powerful as before.

88. An interested reader should study Belanovsky and Marzeeva, "Armiia kak ona est'," 10−18.

89. Frequently reported "disciplinary" exercises involved humiliation for the sake of instilling unquestioned obedience: awakened in the middle of the night, new recruits were required to crawl and bark under the barrack bunk beds at the elders' command or act as "cars," with elders sitting on their backs, and so on.

and, according to some accounts, were stigmatized by homosexual rape.[90] These outcasts lived the existence of new recruits throughout their two years of service and could never become "elders." The most disturbing side of this system was that after being victims for six to twelve months, recruits themselves became perpetrators of brutal violence (those who refused to beat were themselves beaten by still elder soldiers) and perhaps even came to accept it by the end of their service as a natural order of things.[91] The army thus functioned as the largest Soviet resocialization agency, which instilled unquestioned obedience through communal terror.[92] Using the same means of mutual surveillance and pressure as in prison law, insiders presented barracks mores as the will of the genuine community of soldiers.

There are strong reasons to think that this system of the barracks mores also developed in conjunction with Khrushchev's drive to instill "socialist self-government" in an army regiment. The documentation of its historical origins is scarce, but both Deriugin and Belanovsky date it from the mid-1950s at the earliest. Commentaries have suggested that the decisive shift occurred when the moral authority of the officers deteriorated within the army as a result of Khrushchev's reduction of the officer corps and their social status; thus they could not enforce the formal discipline required by the statute. Simultaneously, from the mid-1950s the army could not rely on docile uneducated recruits predominantly of a peasant origin as it had previously, since the technical requirements of modern warfare made the

90. See the 1989 public appeal to Yazov, the USSR Minister of Defense (Belanovsky, ed., *Dedovshchina*, 187), claiming that homosexual rape affected *all* army regiments. To explain the transfer of Soviet prison mores into the army, Deriugin suggests that they came with the many recently amnestied young criminals recruited in the late 1950s drafts (Deriugin, "Dedovshchina," 109); Belanovsky suggests that they came from "construction battalions," which included a "junk labor force" of weak and unfit recruits who found themselves between hammer and anvil, with pressure from ethnic subgroups and recruits from young delinquents' colonies (Belanovsky and Marzeeva, "Armiia kak ona est'," 17). It also seems plausible that the army, like the prison, could invent homosexual rape as a means of stigmatization in a parallel and unrelated manner.

91. In VTsIOM's sample in the all-union surveys of the late 1980s, 28 percent of males agreed that eldership was useful and brought up "real males" and that "the army is the model for the construction of society" (Levada, *Prostoi sovetskii chelovek*, 117).

92. According to the estimates of Belanovsky and Marzeeva, half the army regiments were not combat units but reserves of "a human contingent that was gathered under compulsion, now unmanageable and not engaged in any useful activity" ("Armiia kak ona est'," 4).

education of soldiers essential to its success. Education also contributed to a leveling of status between officers and soldiers; urban recruits frequently challenged the officers' and sergeants' authority, while these had to rely on the informal mechanisms of the soldiers' milieu, making compliance effective through oppression.[93] However, both explanations proposed above fail to explain why the soldiers themselves organized barracks life or why army units introduced collective responsibility for violations committed by a single member.[94] It seems that the development of the informal soldiers' *kollektiv* occurred simultaneously with other developments in the general collectivization-of-life drive of the 1950s.

COLLECTIVES ON THE OBVERSE SIDE

The second type of informal *kollektivy* existed not within the formal ones, but as if on the obverse side of the social life. Each of their members was also a member of some formal *kollektiv*, but the intermember ties in the informal networks cut across these formal borders. According to many accounts, the post-1953 thaw brought back the enjoyment of conversation. With the fear of denunciation to the secret police substantially reduced, people gathered just "to chew the fat" (*trepatsia*): parties of thirty to forty people would get together for no other reason than the pleasure of unrestrained communication.[95] Their communication often took the form of a loyal critique of the regime's disfunctions. And from these gatherings, in full accord with Habermas's schema, a public sphere of belles lettres emerged from interfamily communication and in its turn later became politicized.[96]

Stadiums filled with people eager to listen to poets like Yevtushenko, Rozhdestvensky, or Voznesensky. People hand-copied popular poems and circulated the manuscripts by the thousands. They sent millions of let-

93. Chesnokova proposed this hypothesis, mentioned in a note in Belanovsky, ed., *Dedovshchina*, 7.
94. Though officers do not live in the barracks and leave self-policing to the regiments and sergeants, young sergeants cannot challenge the power of their elders. Thus the system still guides the regiments at night.
95. See Liudmila Alekseeva, *Istoriia inakomysliia v SSSR: Noveishii period* (Moscow: Vest', 1992), 200. Its English version (not entirely congruent to the Russian one) is in [Ludmila Alexeeva,] *Soviet Dissent: Contemporary Movements for National, Religious, and Human Rights*, trans. Carol Pearce and John Glad (Middletown, CT.: Wesleyan University Press, 1985), 270.
96. Habermas, *Structural Transformation*.
97. See the very beginning of Felix Kuznetsov, *Kakim byt'?: literatura i nravstvennoe vospitanie lichnosti* [Whom to be?: literature and moral education of the

ters to the authors of popular novels, published in "thick" journals.[97] And they held an equal number of private discussions of those novels. In fact, the first *samizdat* journals were just an extension of the practice of hand-copying poems and short stories.[98] Eventually, when literary discussions in the informal sphere of belles lettres suddenly faced the problem of the political trial of two authors, Andrei Siniavsky and Yuri Daniel, they turned political: the same practices and channels of circulation now carried information about politics and opposition to the regime. The public sphere of letters became the political public sphere. *The Chronicle of Current Events*, compiled illegally and circulated through the underground network, became its primary medium.

The political dissent movement that took off shortly after the trial of Siniavsky and Daniel was more like a secret society than a network. It was a congregation of equals united in the fight against the unjust regime and, like many dissenters throughout Russian history, these postwar political dissidents of different brands seemed to have one common feature—a quasi-Protestant intense inner belief, which caused them to act according to the professed ideals. Hence the intense moral tonality of the movement, though beliefs varied.

The majority of the dissidents of the first wave of the 1960s were "children of the thaw," that is, they espoused ideals close to the Communist ones.[99] Their profile resembles that of the Huguenots in sixteenth-century France. Both groups were dissatisfied with ritualized reality and strove to live according to the Cause, as gathered from an individual reading of the Word: the Bible in the Huguenot case and the texts of Marx and Lenin in the Soviet case. Both attempted to use their positions as citizens and magistrates to reform the ritualized system from within: people like Roy Medvedev were the de Mornays of the USSR. Both were repressed; but if the Catholics' attempt to rid themselves of the troublesome Huguenots took up one night (of St. Bartholomew), the work to straighten out Communist dissidents in postwar Russia demanded a series of demonstration trials. In the face of mounting repression many dissenters publicly repented and

---

individual] (Moscow: Sovetskii pisatel', 1962), which cites three "typical" letters out of a zillion written to Anatolii Kuznetsov, a popular author of "young prose."

98. Alekseeva, *Istoriia inakomysliia v SSSR*, 196. I could not find a parallel description in its English-language ed.

99. K. Zhitnikov, "The Decline of the Democratic Movement," in *The Political, Social, and Religious Thought of Russian Samizdat*, ed. Michael Meerson-Aksenov and Boris Shragin (Belmont, Mass.: Nordland, 1977).

turned to full-blown dissimulation. Others converted to liberalism, which revealed for them the "true" character of the Soviet regime as violating essential human rights. Some lapsed into religious mysticism. Eventually two crippling blows by the KGB (1973–74 and 1980–81) swept most members of this community either into prisons or out of the country. But while it existed on the outskirts of official society, the dissidents' milieu apparently shared the mechanisms of broader Soviet society. Mutual admonition supported ideals alternative to the official ones but still dogmatic; the dissidents seemed to play the same game but with ideals of a directly opposite kind. In short, here too we find the *kollektiv*, albeit a secret one. As Zhitnikov noted on the mores of the early opposition, "A body of judgments is being formed which has a powerful emotional agitation at its base and which allows neither discussion nor factual comparison."[100]

Observers usually invoke the high moral tone of the early dissent movement of the late 1960s to explain the failure of the KGB to plant informers among the dissidents.[101] However, once one of them repented and thus initiated the wave of arrests among the secret society of dissenters in 1973, the strategy of their communication changed. Later dissidents, facing the constant threat of secret police repression, cohered as a network rather than as a secret society. In this network each individual knew an adjacent friend but rarely knew a friend of a friend. No one knew all the members of the network. Asking the names of a friend's friends was highly improper. Seemingly decapitated by each blow from the KGB, the network was reborn each time. It united dissimulating individuals, and each new wave of repression brought more members who helped regenerate it.

Soviet nonpolitical subcultures, however, evolved as networks from the very start. Even though early subcultures were very similar to the early dissent movement in their quasi-religious zeal—for example, Frederick Starr noticed that "engagement with jazz had the intensity of the religious belief within the underground church"[102]—this engagement never led to a formation of special societies with circumscribed membership and rigid surveillance of the observed mores. Rather, the "drive for jazz was engendered by youth's craving for an authentic language of their own. . . . The

100. Ibid., 250. Inverting officially recommended practice in their self-fashioning as well, dissidents based their quest for justice on hero-identification and self-programming for heroic service and possibly for sacrifice.
101. Alekseeva, *Istoriia inakomysliia v SSSR*, 259.
102. Starr, *Red and Hot*, 260.

concept of 'hip,' of knowing the score without wanting to talk about it, united members of the young vanguard among the elders."[103] A similar force was at work in other widespread subcultures of the 1960s, distinct from the official charisma of the Leninist state: the mountain climbers, the bard singers, the hikers (in the professional version—the geologists), and so on.[104] These thrived on the authenticity of rough experience, ideals of "true friendship" and the sense of a true adventure.

Of course, these subcultures were very close to Dick Hebdige's conception of subculture as a loose community that reappropriates an alien and imposed language for aims of resistance through ritual and style.[105] The difference from the English experience lies in the fact that many Soviet subcultures had to become institutionalized with time in order to continue meeting without the KGB arresting their members incessantly. They often became "clubs." Thus, an amorphous "youth club of interests" of the Gorky Automobile Factory split in 1962 into registered separate units: "discussion club," "jazz club," "Russian language study club," "patriotic club," "performance arts club" and so on.[106] Each brought together people with different interests. Once institutionalized, however, the clubs were forced to become formalized *kollektivy* with all the required attributes, in order to win the uneasy tolerance of the KGB. They created an *aktiv*, drew up an annual plan of officially accepted activities, and put representatives of the local authorities in their governing bodies. As a result of this formalization, a countercore of club members, different from the officially registered *aktiv*, developed within the official structures of the clubs, defying state intervention and informally advocating a code of behavior for the rest of subculture. This code was close to the one of the informal *kollektiv* of prisoners: we fulfill your requirements and demonstrate loyalty, and you do not interfere in our internal affairs.

In the face of the state repression of the Brezhnev years, it was almost impossible for subcultures to escape state penetration. Even rock culture could not escape it: the first rock club was registered in Leningrad and officially convened the first rock festival in 1983.[107] Under the slogan of fight-

103. Ibid., 242.
104. See Richard Stites, *Russian Popular Culture* (Cambridge: Cambridge University Press, 1992), ch. 5, for a more detailed description of some of them.
105. Dick Hebdige, *Subculture* (London: Methuen, 1979).
106. Iakovlev, *Stanovlenie lichnosti*, 112.
107. Strictly speaking, there was an earlier rock festival in Tbilisi in 1980, not advertised as such. Troitsky describes both in *Back in the USSR*.

ing for peace, each participating rock group presented in its program one song dealing directly with peace, while a jury meted out awards for the best contribution of "young talents" to this eternal struggle. Nevertheless, subcultures—even after being squeezed into the official format of "clubs"—never evolved into true underground *kollektivy*. Some degree of collective responsibility for the acts of individual club members existed, of course. But because club members did not have planned production targets to meet, and because all of them belonged to primary work *kollektivy* somewhere else, the clubs did not follow the example of the prison or the army and did not produce their own internal humiliating means of discipline. The underground *kollektiv* enforcement did not take root. The underground *aktiv* existed, but it had neither the means nor really any need to enforce compliance with mores alternative to the Soviet system.

Therefore, subcultures survived by means of dissimulation. For example, almost every member of the rock culture had an official job and was attached to some business *kollektiv*, which could straighten him or her out if necessary. In the time off from work an individual could hang out with friends and espouse alternative values, if they were not politically offensive. A minimal demonstration of loyalty at work, in the guise of an obedient member of the *kollektiv*, satisfied both the regime and the individual.[108] Subcultures became informal communities that united individuals who dissimulated loyalty in their official *kollektivy*, while being united in their free time into loose networks devoted to alternative values. They were less of a *kollektiv* than any other group discussed in this section.

The tight *kollektiv* spontaneously emerged in one other and very important cultural form, that of a friendship network. Given its ubiquity and salience, remarkably little sociological analysis has been published on issues of friendship in the Soviet Union. Vladimir Shlapentokh remarked that friendship was never an official Soviet value;[109] its absence from official discourse may explain the obvious gap in scholarship. There were no *Pravda* editorials on friendship; it was exalted only in functional terms, as a means of fulfilling the plan or meeting planned objectives. Shlapentokh cited data from Kogan's 1981 empirical study on friendship to compare the difference between Soviet and American perceptions of friendship and the great

108. Rock musicians tried to minimize the interference of their job *kollektivy* by choosing only certain jobs. They were becoming "a generation of street cleaners and night watchmen," sang Boris Grebenshchikov, who led the most popular rock group, *Aquarium*.
109. Shlapentokh, *Public and Private Life*, 171.

importance of friendship ties for Soviet society. According to this study, 16 percent of respondents met friends every day, 32 percent—once or several times a week, 31 percent—several times a month. For the United States of the same times, the median was substantially lower: bachelors met four times a month.[110] Shlapentokh also noted that friendship played an important role in "beating the system," that is, in finding access to scarce resources and escaping state punishment, and therefore—among the young in particular—became a specific value.

Our previous exposition indicated that close interpersonal friendship may have always been suspect in the eyes of the powers that be because of its potential contribution to creating "false *kollektivy*" that challenged the official ones. Of course, cases of "sacred friendship" were sometimes lauded in the official sources, but praise of relationships between several individuals was to be of secondary importance and subordinate to the praise of friendship as the phenomenon of the *kollektiv*, be it friendship between different *kollektivy*—of the USSR republics, or among countries of the Soviet bloc—or within certain *kollektivy*, where friendship, however, was conceived very abstractly, in almost Christian terms, as the love individual member of the *kollektiv* felt for all the rest.

Perhaps because of this official unease with matters of friendship, the only scholarly Soviet study that directly addressed the subject, written by the sociologist Igor Kon, was more concerned with expounding historical views and philosophical doctrines on friendship from Cicero to Hegel than with actually examining the peculiarities of Soviet friendship.[111] By the end of the book, nevertheless, Kon offered a classification of generational differences in attitudes to friendship in the Soviet Union, summing up the research data available in disparate studies. Children befriended each other on a situational basis, being brought together in the *kollektivy* of the kindergartens, or in play-groups in the same yard; their friendship was "a contact cooperation." Teenagers developed a novel yearning for understanding and sought approval in friendship (in general, they expected to be valued more by their friends than they valued themselves). Adults, whose families usually monopolized intimate life, divided their allegiance between friendships surviving from early days and new, mostly intellectual, bonds. As a result, mature friendships were not as demanding as the intimate friendships of the young; but they still satisfied two basic needs of an indi-

110. Ibid.
111. I. S. Kon, *Druzhba: etiko-psikhologicheskii ocherk* [Friendship: an essay in ethics and psychology], 2d ed. (Moscow: Politizdat, 1987).

vidual: to trust another person unconditionally and to talk about one's problems.[112] Unconditional trust and a chance to confide and discuss personal problems at any time—these two features made mature Soviet friendship an unofficial moral value, different from the value of friendship in the West.[113] "As a moral relationship friendship emerges only after the interpersonal tie stops being considered as a pure expression of emotional attraction, social duty, or the result of a rational calculation," concluded Kon.[114]

Bringing Shlapentokh's and Kon's accounts together, we may consider the following hypothesis: trust in a friend and the possibility of discussing one's problems became suspect values, because friends did not abandon each other even when the *kollektiv* attacked one of them. "Beating the system" together included beating the collective pressure. No other description of friendship was more widespread in the Soviet Union than the proverbial "a friend in need is a friend indeed." In late Soviet society, communal pressure played the role of the secret police of earlier days in testing the solidity of friendships.[115] A friend, by definition, then, was an individual who would not let you down even under direct menace to him- or herself; a person to whom you could securely entrust your controversial thoughts since she or he would never betray them, even under pressure. Friendship thus in a sense became an ultimate value, produced in resistance struggles in the Soviet Union: any ascribed category of human relationship could crumble under the threat of terror—children denounced parents, wives betrayed husbands or vice versa. By contrast, a "friend" was not an ascription but an achievement; it was a definition forged by terror and thus represented a dearly earned status. It characterized a person who withstood terror and did not betray. Milder but more widespread struggles in later Soviet society tested its worth as a moral value, but the obligation to with-

112. Ibid., 187, 210, 251.
113. On views of Adam Smith and Adam Ferguson that helped form the Anglo-American perception of friendship, see Allan Silver, "'Two Different Sorts of Commerce'—Friendship and Strangership in Civil Society," in *Public and Private in Thought and Practice*, ed. Jeff Weintraub and Krishnan Kumar (Chicago: University of Chicago Press, 1997).
114. Kon, *Druzhba*, 324.
115. Another test of friendship, which of course fused friends for life, was common experience of trench warfare in the Second World War. Anecdotal data suggest that threats of state violence hardly affected wartime friendships, but a historical study would be useful. On ideological laxity that allowed the themes of authentic feelings to be expressed in public in 1943–45 see Dunham, *In Stalin's Time*, 7; and Stites, *Russian Popular Culture*, 101.

stand pressure in order to be called a true friend persisted.

Networks of friends pervaded official *kollektivy* and transcended their established borders. There were dyadic and triadic relationships forged in joint resistance to the pressure of the same *kollektiv*. Furthermore, bigger groupings of friends united these dyads and triads into larger, stable, tight, and semi-closed interpersonal networks, transcending the borders of *kollektivy*. In a recently published study, Kasianova proposes the phrase "a group of diffuse interaction" to designate this widespread phenomenon.[116] She borrows the term from Talcott Parsons's dichotomy of diffuse and concrete interaction. In concrete interaction individuals choose an environment of people that will somehow contribute to the realization of their own specific aims; this interaction is instrumental and goal-oriented. In diffuse interaction, individuals choose friends based on criteria that summarily characterize them as individuals; to a certain extent Parsons's typology repeats the Kantian distinction between treating another individual as a means to an end or an end in him- or herself. In diffuse interaction people choose their contacts on the basis not of fleeting role or status features, but of personality features.[117]

Russians do not like concrete interaction, writes Kasianova. "And on the contrary, we feel OK in a group that interferes in our personal life, rummages in our views and motives, and attempts to form our persona. We allow it to this group, we give this right to it."[118] The reasons for this admission of a diffuse group into the most personal matters of an individual's life are twofold. First, a diffuse group of friends will always unconditionally defend another friend against the threats or calumnies. "What are you telling us? We know this man. He couldn't have done it. This is a misunderstanding," would be the typical response of a diffuse group, according to Kasianova. "And they would be completely right, because they really know

116. Kseniia Kasianova, *O russkom natsional'nom kharaktere* [On Russian national character] (Moscow, 1993). Kasianova applied the Minnesota Multiphasic Personality Inventory test to her Soviet sample and used her personal anecdotal knowledge and randomly assembled texts of philosophers of the Russian Idea and Orthodox religious writings to interpret its results, in order to outline broad continuities. Though at times the book's method verges on mystical exegesis that is hard to defend in a scholarly community—it turns up such fictional essences as "Russian epileptoid personality"—Kasianova's study is an invaluable informed insider's description of late Soviet society. And very few among the 1970s writers can compete with Kasianova in the knowledge of classical sociology.

117. Ibid., 249–250.

118. Ibid., 254.

[the individual in question]. They will not let him down, they cannot do it, they simply *have no right* to do it. No social welfare system ever or anywhere could guarantee a man such confidence and freedom as that given by the support of a group of a diffuse type."[119] Second, the diffuse group is tolerant toward individuals who belong to it and ensures authentic communication without any need to dissimulate: "In this group a man can be himself: playing a role or impersonating some intended other is simply impossible. Consequently, only one variant of behavior is possible—they should accept you as you are, such as you have become to this very moment, with your drawbacks, sins, and weaknesses."[120] Leniency toward one another and unconditional support among members make diffuse groups an extraordinarily important phenomenon in a society founded on communal pressure that enforces official saintly standards.

In our terminology, the diffuse groups that Kasianova describes function as informal authentic *kollektivy.* They cohere as stable networks of free individuals drawn together by mutual interest and respect, who therefore cherish one another's opinions. Defending the constituent members is their first obvious feature; but the second feature is even more important. Diffuse groups have such freedom to penetrate their constituent individuals' lives because they allow all to be who they are—but not the right to be anyone. Diffuse groups allow members to be who they are in the sense that they reveal to each of them who they are; they endow each individual with a person. As will become clear later, they function as the primary arenas of informal *oblichenie*, revealing the person of all members of a diffuse group with all their particular "weaknesses" and "drawbacks."

The next chapter takes up this function of authentic *oblichenie*, which supplied people in the late Soviet society with the sense of who they were; now let us point to the interconnections among these stable semi-closed diffuse groups. According to Kasianova, at the base of each group lies a certain consensus on values.[121] Separate diffuse groups, however, may be linked by people of high moral authority who start a debate on these values, an "exchange of the elements of consensi" that lie at the foundation of

119. Ibid. Interestingly, Kasianova does not discuss the situation when the individual in question really commits a crime, treating an outsider's accusation as necessarily unfounded and unjust.

120. Ibid.

121. At one point, Kasianova, in an instance of usage reminiscent of Orthodox theology, calls diffuse groups "catholic [i.e., gathered] individuals," *sobornye lichnosti* (ibid., 320).

each diffuse group. She cites examples of such high moral authority, or *avtoritet* in Russian: Aleksandr Solzhenitsyn and Andrei Sakharov.[122] Because *avtoritet* "arises more and more exclusively in the sphere of informal relations . . . (since the informal sphere has monopolized the function of moral evaluation now), this status is perceived by the state and its defenders as dangerous."[123] Hence, while the state tolerated informal *kollektivy* called diffuse groups or friendship networks even though they subverted the official system—rarely doing so openly, and thus to an extent supporting the system—it brutally suppressed attempts at the interlinking and unification of diffuse groups and at the establishment of a whole quasi-public sphere of informal exchanges on values that smacked of organized opposition.

ZINOVIEV'S SYNTHESIS:
THE INFORMAL LIFE OF THE FORMAL *KOLLEKTIV*

Alexander Zinoviev's conceptualization of informal activity within the formal business *kollektiv* is exceptional in how it brings the background practices of mutual surveillance and admonition into the foreground, which no other author has done with such clarity and force.[124] His account, though not directly applicable to the functioning of such informal *kollektivy* as the prison cell and the army unit, the secret society and the diffuse group, is still very illuminating and disturbing. Not specifying an abstract feature common to them all, it points rather to the sets of family resemblances common to some of these diverse reincarnations of the *kollektiv*. In the para-

122. Kasianova contrasts "authority" in English, "power of a legitimate type," with *avtoritet*, "a phenomenon of a purely informal order. In its pure form it is based exclusively on the respect a concrete individual pays to another concrete individual" (ibid., 264). She seems to overvalue one meaning of "authority" stressed in Weberian sociology, denigrating its meaning of "moral influence" similar to the Russian term. Note also the similarity between Kasianova's definition and prison community usage.
123. Ibid., 327.
124. Western scholars hold Alexander Zinoviev in disrepute for two basic reasons. First, the early works in his favorite genre of "literary-sociological sketch" were not scientific, as he embarrassingly insisted, but far removed from the standards of positivist research. Second, after the Soviet Union collapsed he made radical charges about the Western conspiracy to ruin Russia, a move that many took for a political blunder. I disregard works of his later, "nationalist" period and largely ignore the intricate texture of his early novels but argue that *Kommunizm kak real'nost'*—a 1980 book where Zinoviev became as systematic as he possibly could—is the best introduction to Soviet life available.

doxical presentation of Zinoviev, the best phenomena are suspected to contain the worst, while the basest phenomena are suddenly revealed to harbor most elevated elements.

Unlike the Soviet sources that had to represent *kollektivy* in accordance with the ritualized canon, Zinoviev realistically describes the actual workings of the mechanism that Makarenko's thought helped set into motion after the 1920s and 1930s. Zinoviev starts with a definition of the *kollektiv* that is very reminiscent of Makarenko's, stressing the systemic features of functionally differentiated units that have ruling bodies.[125] "Two or more people form an integral communal individual if, and only if, the following conditions are fulfilled: (1) this group of people relates to the environment as a unit; (2) there takes place within it the same distribution of 'body' and 'brain' functions as observed in the case of the individual person, the former being governed by the latter; (3) there is a division of functions among the individuals who are governed."[126] At this point the expositions of Makarenko and Zinoviev part ways, however.

Zinoviev addresses the group that lives as a formal *kollektiv*, corresponding to Makarenko's theory to the letter in its outward appearance as a group striving for collective good. Its informal life, however, is pervaded by cynical strife for individual recognition and increasing each member's own material wealth. Because resources and wages are allocated to the *kollektiv* as a whole, Soviet individuals must constantly sharpen their talents at what Zinoviev calls "prevention": rather than compete for distinction in a given activity, the point is to ensure that no neighbor gets more than they themselves do. The life of the *kollektiv* is an eternal battle for recognition where each tries to stop others from distinguishing themselves. "We would obtain a graphic example of this kind of struggle if we could somehow attach competing runners to each other and give them the means of stopping each other from running."[127]

This struggle consumes all the energy of the *kollektiv*'s members:

> At the level of the primary collective people not only work, they spend time in the company of people they know well. They swap news, amuse

125. On Makarenko's definition—"a goal-oriented complex of persons that possesses the organs of the *kollektiv*"—see chapter 3. Also compare Zinoviev's to the Soviet social psychologists'definitions that follow Makarenko's (also cited in chapter 3).

126. Alexander Zinoviev, *The Reality of Communism*, trans. Charles Janson (London: Gollancz, 1984), 64.

127. Ibid., 120.

themselves, do all kinds of things to preserve and improve their position, have contacts with other people on whom their well-being depends, go to innumerable meetings, get their vacation vouchers, living space and supplementary food-stuffs. . . . The commune takes people in their entirety, squeezes all spiritual juice out of them and spits them out afterwards onto the street and into private life as exhausted, drained, bad-tempered, bored and empty husks.[128]

The responsibility of the *kollektiv* for its members reminds Zinoviev of the army. Hence the system of mutual surveillance and collective correction of members' behavior is in place; and hence the internal structure of the *kollektiv*. Surveillance and correction are primarily carried out by the *aktiv:* "They form a particular mafia of their own, bound together by collective guarantee and mutual support. They are the carriers, the mouthpieces, and the creators of public opinion within the collective. They are elected to the local trade union committee, to the housing committee, to the management of the mutual aid fund. They control the distribution of trips and loans and prizes. They spread rumors and gossip. They compile secret dossiers on every member of the collective."[129] The *passiv*, the category to which the majority of the members belong, partake in the consumption of the goods allocated to the *kollektiv* but do not engage in social activism.

The following mechanism inevitably produces the *kollektiv*'s outcasts.[130] An individual's misdeed marks him or her off from the *kollektiv*. Then follows an admonishment to become normal ("become as we all are and then we will forgive you"), using threats and cajolery. Simultaneously, ridicule and slander stigmatize the potential outcast. For many—cherishing the opportunity that the *kollektiv* gives them to exculpate themselves—reintegration into the *kollektiv* is next. For others, expulsion: "Enemies of society are not born. They are made. And they are made by the will and wish of society itself. The collective singles out a certain type of individual for future sacrifice, and involves him in its life in such a way that his projection into the role of the enemy is an inevitable consequence."[131] The reasons for these ritual expulsions escape the members of the *kollektiv*, ac-

---

128. Ibid., 114; translation changed. Zinoviev calls the primary *kollektiv* a "commune."

129. Ibid., 133.

130. Zinoviev's original term *otshchepentsy*, literally, "the split-offs," appears in the English version as "renegades" (ibid., 133). I choose "outcasts" since it better expresses the action of splitting them off and away from the collective body.

131. Ibid., 135–136.

cording to Zinoviev. They are three. First, the *kollektiv* needs to demonstrate monolithic unity to itself and to the outside from time to time. Second, it needs to train itself periodically to express this unity. Third, it teaches the majority of its members unquestioned obedience by means of these rituals.

Zinoviev describes in fine detail the elements of the actual ritual of communal expulsion and punishment. First comes an acceptable interpretation of the "guilt" of the outcast. No matter how absurd, all accept it because it is convenient for them. "It affords them psychological justification, . . . and gives them arguments for the punishment of the victim. They themselves are both judges and executioners." [132] Also, notes Zinoviev, by participating in the collectively waged shaming on the basis of absurd charges, individuals escape the individual guilt that they otherwise would feel after punishing an innocent person; nobody feels individually responsible for collective action. Then comes the ritual punishment:

> (1) denigrate the victim in every possible way; (2) express one's astonishment at his behavior; (3) confess one's own fault in the sense that one has 'overlooked things,' and 'displayed a liberal attitude' without 'paying due attention to certain things and signals'; (4) punish those who are deemed guilty of having 'overlooked things'; (5) take prophylactic measures.[133]

Zinoviev's dense summary seems unparalleled in that it sums up the points about the informal laws of functioning of the formal *kollektiv* in the workplace, similar in the power of its insights to Abramkin's or Belanovsky's analyses of the informal *kollektivy* in the prison and in the army. However, Zinoviev also highlights two features of the formal *kollektiv* that other analyses did not make central to their exposition. These are the description of the *kollektiv*'s "intimate life" and the hypothesis on the role of hierarchical organizations supervising *kollektivy:* both, to an extent, serve as checks against the ever present threat: a possible devolution of the *kollektiv* into what Zinoviev calls "a mafia-type group."

First, the intimate life of the *kollektiv* brings together the manager and the subordinates and gives subordinates the force of an effective shaming community, informed of the most minute and intimate details of the lives of its members, a community capable of incriminating everybody, including the manager. "The intimate life does not embrace only productive or

132. Ibid., 136–137.
133. Ibid., 137.

official activity. It includes social activity as well (meetings, evenings, journeys), and also personal relations and activities emerging from these: gossip, visiting, love affairs, drinking orgies, local groups and mafias, collective guarantees, mutual services." People eat, drink, and make love in the *kollektiv:* "because of this there is nothing left in the intimate life of the man which is unknown to the collective, from the condition of his bowels to his love affairs."[134] Through this total transparency of life, individuals move intimately close to the *kollektiv,* becoming "one's own," possessing a set of known vices that are tolerated but potentially brought up for shaming if the need arises. An intimacy of group life develops, which in effect is "mutual coercion, mutual humiliation and mutual surveillance. . . . In actual fact, the principle of these 'warm' and 'friendly' relations is this: 'We are all nonentities'. . . . I know of no more loathsome phenomenon in human relationships than the intimate nearness of Soviet people."[135]

Thus, the hierarchical surveillance carried out by the superior *kollektivy* that guide the lower *kollektivy* is, paradoxically, not wholly vicious. Even though it makes the *kollektiv* what it is, a body united by collective responsibility and a joint plan—since periodic checks from above ensure that the manager maintains the necessary outward image of the cell and the meeting of the planned objectives—it also prevents the dissolution of the *kollektiv* into a group where the strong would blatantly dominate the weak. Zinoviev proposes an empirically testable hypothesis: if a *kollektiv* achieves real self-rule, without any hierarchical body overseeing its exercise, then the *kollektiv* will immediately devolve into "a closed shop" (*chastnaia lavochka*), into a "mafia," and the former *kollektiv* now runs as "a gang." The *aktiv* becomes the "strong" and, together with the manager, starts to brutalize and terrorize the weak. "The mafia becomes the sover-

134. Ibid., 123. A typical network in the late 1950s that later evolved into a dissenters' community of the 1960s looked disturbingly similar to Zinoviev's description: "A normal Moscow circle numbered forty to fifty 'close friends.' Although divided into smaller subgroups, the entire group regularly gathered for parties that were held at the slightest excuse and everyone knew everything about everybody else. All these circles were connected with similar circles and the links led to Leningrad, Novosibirsk and other cities. Everyone gathered around the table and imbibed tea and more than tea. Affairs were begun; families were formed and broken up" (Alexeeva, *Soviet Dissent,* 269). For one of the most depressing depictions of sexual promiscuity that tied informal *kollektivy* together, see Liudmila Petrushevskaia, "Svoi krug" [Our circle], in her *Bal poslednego cheloveka* [The last man's ball] (Moscow: Lokid, 1996).

135. Zinoviev, *Reality of Communism,* 124.

eign ruler and rules according to its own communal laws, virtually ignoring the limitations imposed by formal laws."[136] The upper echelons of power keep the primary *kollektivy* from devolving into these gang-modeled communities. The majority of the *kollektiv* may appeal to the higher echelons, produce their shaming evidence of the managers' license and transgressions, and thus depose the managers if they monopolize too much power.[137]

Zinoviev's model allows us to make some additions to Pierre Bourdieu's view on the mechanisms of cohesion in communities bound by mutual surveillance. Bourdieu has described the mechanism of "collective misrecognition" with the help of which Kabyle communities in Algiers maintain themselves. This mechanism is strikingly reminiscent of the Soviet society of the 1960s, as represented in Zinoviev's theorization. Bourdieu argues that a group united by shared mores, or a certain "code of honor," necessarily misrecognizes the objective conditions of its own existence, and practices of what he calls "serial constraint" or "cross censorship" enforce and support this misrecognition. In other words, everybody watches everybody else, immediately inflicting punishment for even a minimal violation in public of the professed beliefs of the group.[138]

As we already noted, the unanimity of the 1960s–1980s was achieved in the USSR through the imposition of exactly this kind of serial constraint. "There is nothing that groups demand more insistently and reward more generously than this reverence of what they claim to revere."[139] Even if many did not believe in Communist ideals in their hearts by the late 1960s,

136. Ibid., 200.

137. And, once hierarchical supervision disappears, a *kollektiv* turns into a gang, according to Zinoviev's hypothesis. Among Soviet social psychologists, Leonid Umansky talked about the *anti-kollektiv* characterized by internal infighting and developing out of the *kollektiv* under certain conditions (see his "Poetapnoe razvitie gruppy," 83). In Makarenko's definition a gang would be a false *kollektiv*. More research is needed on this topic, of course.

138. As Bourdieu noticed, earlier studies of gift-giving practices by Mauss and Levi-Strauss had uncovered an equivalent exchange within every act of voluntary gift-giving but missed the fact that "gift exchange is one of the social games that cannot be played unless the players refuse to acknowledge the objective truth of the game . . . and unless they are predisposed to contribute, with their efforts, their marks of care and attention, and their time, to the production of collective misrecognition" (Bourdieu, *Logic of Practice*, 105–106). In other words, acknowledgment of the fact of equivalent exchange collapses the act of gift-giving. Therefore, communal suppression of this fact is essential.

139. Bourdieu, *Logic of Practice*, 109.

they continued to engage in cross-censorship that each suffered reluctantly but without failing to impose on others. Virtually all helped to impose on others the constraints they themselves experienced from others, and breaking off was unimaginable. Bourdieu does not explain why and how this mechanism of serial constraint may collapse but he suggests the necessary avalanche-like pace of its collapse, in a sentence strikingly applicable to the disintegration of Soviet officialdom during the perestroika years, 1987–91:

> The fact that the primary belief of the strongly integrated communities is the product of serial constraint that the group applies to itself, which may be suffered with great impatience . . . but without ever being able to spark off a revolt that could call them into question, explains why breaks . . . happen in a sudden, collective form, with circular control losing its efficacy as soon as there is a glimpse of the real possibility of breaking it.[140]

Following Zinoviev, we may suggest that this collapse also has another quality. It happens when the threat of punishment for disobedience to hierarchical supervision fades, and when the *aktiv* of a given group finds direct suppression of the oppressed group's discontent cheaper and more effective than upkeep on the system of universal collective surveillance. By gaining the obvious power positions, the *aktiv* stands apart from the network of surveillance and thus its members liberate themselves, while simultaneously resorting to manipulation and sometimes open brutal suppression of discontent among the group's weak members. In other words, radical social change happens when the *aktiv* finds it easier and more profitable to turn the entrusted factory or office into "a closed shop" rather than run it as a fictive collective of equals. In general terms, groups run as gangs eclipse groups run as *kollektivy*.

140. Ibid., 111.

8 The Individual in Mature Soviet Society

The *oblichenie* practices that constitute the background for transforming an individual into an object of action and knowledge underwent two parallel developments in the 1960s. First, *oblichenie* gradually became routinized and ritualized in the official sphere. Among these routinized forms were periodic Party and workplace *kollektivy* meetings to assess individual Communists during the ritual of "individual report" (*individual'nyi otchet*), on the one hand, and school meetings that evaluated each high school student, on the other. The latter, because they dealt with the very important sphere of youth socialization, were institutionalized in 1969 in the annual rite of the Lenin Pass. Second, simultaneously with this ritualization, *oblichenie* was displaced into the unofficial sphere, where it was also practiced intensely. In all these case, however, self-revelation in the eyes of the relevant community was now inseparably linked together with self-fashioning techniques, and the end result of the joint influence of this ensemble of practices constituted what we may strictly call Soviet individualization.

The standard Party procedure of routinized *oblichenie* is visible in a typical brochure from that time.[1] On a number of standard occasions the deliberations of some relevant Party assembly gave individual Communists the chance to come to know themselves. First, a Communist encountered

---

1. Here is one of many similar provincial publications, notable only for the mediocrity of its style and banality of its problems: R. V. Gataulin and G. Z. Safin, *Za vysokoe zvanie kommunista: Iz opyta raboty partiinykh komissii Tatarskoi ASSR* [For the high title of Communist: the work of Party Commissions of the Tatar Autonomous Republic] (Kazan', 1980).

the ritual of collective deliberation about him- or herself while joining the Party. From January 1962 on, special "Party commissions," attached to a district Party committee, were established as voluntary social bodies that routinely screened all potential candidates. A Party commission consisted of retired Party activists who would examine the candidates' motives for joining and their knowledge of the Party Statute, program, and history.

These Party commissions eventually started reviewing Party members as well, as a means of "training young Communists." For example, in one of the district committees of Tatarstan, the local Party commission solicited and reviewed "individual self-reports" of 1,864 Party members (or 42 percent of local membership) in 1977 alone. At meetings of primary Party organizations, the commissions staged discussions of 1,281 Communists and, at meetings of the Party bureaus, of 583 more.[2] Both forms—prerecruitment screening and collective discussion of individual Communists during the individual report sessions—were highly routinized and conducted without any zeal. Serious consideration of the individual was exceptional. Rather, we may suspect, the ritual involved scarcely anything more than a perfunctory five-minute presentation of self in front of the commission (or Party assembly), followed by an array of customary questions to the individual, with a subsequent unanimous vote to let him or her pass the rite. However, the routinized form unobtrusively reinforced the "normal," that is, habitualized, way of how one would and should know oneself.

In contrast to the boring proceedings on the individual reports, a consideration of the "personal case" (*personal'noe delo*) was frequently more agitated and less routine. This euphemistic phrase designated an active consideration of a specific misdeed of a Communist in a Party court and, beginning in the 1960s, it involved the following procedure. A Party committee received a denunciation and forwarded it to the district Party commission, which conducted a preliminary investigation and discussed the denunciation with its target and its author. Then members of the Party commission convened a meeting of the primary Party organization, where they presented the case and asked the cell's approval of the proposed penalty. "Taking into consideration" the character of the misdeed, its established motives, and the degree of sincere contrition, the cell ruled on the penalty. It then forwarded the "personal case" to the district Party committee, which either ratified the cell's decision or returned the case to the Party commission for additional consideration.[3] Examples of "personal cases" offered in-

2. Ibid., 62.
3. Ibid., 73.

clude the proverbial Party crimes of the 1970s, that is, those few that merited Party attention when all other requirements of loyal behavior were fulfilled: alcoholism, loss or mutilation of the Party card, use of state resources for private gain, and "loss of connection with the Party organization." The last pretext regularly allowed cells to expel those retired Communists who did not show up at Party meetings at all.

After the imposition of the penalty, the Party commission was supposed to ensure that the guilty comrade "underwent correction in practical deeds, under the watchful control of the *kollektiv*."[4] Of course, it had imposed no special deeds of penance; the Communist was expected to express his or her earnest desire for self-correction by every deed of his or her normal life. Nevertheless, this was clearly still the familiar requirement of performing penitential deeds before the eyes of the community, and not necessarily in a merely ritualized form as we might expect. For example, in 1972 the Party commission of the city of Naberezhnye Chelny decided to review the 3,740 Communists who had reprimands registered in their Party cards and were undergoing penalty. By September 1974, only 1,503 remained on the rolls as undergoing penalty; others, having been screened, were ruled "corrected" and their penalty records eliminated from their Party cards. The truly "recalcitrant"—those whose reprimand records had not been lifted even five years after the penalty was imposed—numbered only 25, down from 485 in 1972, to the commission's joy.[5] Of course, this was part of bureaucratic politics; imposing and relieving reprimands frequently meant no change in the real life of, say, a worker of the Kamaz automobile plant in Naberezhnye Chelny. What is surprising, however, is the longevity of the penitential forms that existed throughout all the turmoil of the purges and the Great Terror, of the war years and of the collectivization-of-life drive of Khrushchev's time. The logic of the ecclesiastical court remained in the Party's life up until its very last days. The ritualized triad reveal-admonish-excommunicate indelibly inscribed the routinized means of individualization.

The same mechanism of collective deliberation on the individual structured another, non-Party, ritual of the 1970s: that of the Lenin Pass, nominally staged by every Komsomol primary organization. It is hard to assess the extent of this ritual's spread in such relatively recalcitrant settings as industrial or agricultural enterprises, but we can be sure that this complicated procedure took place in at least one milieu, which was under special

4. Ibid., 84.
5. Ibid., 34.

control of the powers that be: every student in every high school had to pass through it once a year.[6]

The Lenin Pass first occurred in 1969, to mark the preparation for the centennial of Lenin's birth, and to strengthen the faltering zeal of the Komsomol, whose membership now included almost all young people aged fourteen to twenty-eight in the Soviet Union. A brochure of the Komsomol Central Committee gave a prehistory for the pass. In 1933, it stated, a Komsomol cell in a Moscow automobile plant invented this procedure when its activists started to discuss how the members of the cell were following Lenin's commandments in real life. And, it added, Krupskaia noticed this initiative in a special article that stressed its outstanding quality: members of the cell gave individual accounts at the general assembly of the cell of how each implemented Lenin's guidelines in concrete acts. This practice began again in 1964 within the Komsomol committees of the Leningrad Metal Works and the Moscow Stankolinia Factory in the form of individual self-reports in public on the topic of "How Do We Study Communism?" A special resolution in 1969 supported and institutionalized the initiatives of some regional organizations of the Komsomol in the late 1960s, which had also taken up this type of individual self-examination in public.[7]

The Lenin Pass comprised four components: the adoption of an "individual composite plan" by each Komsomol member at the beginning of the year; its implementation during the year; special Lenin's Classes at which veterans of the Party or of the Second World War were present, and where certain works of Lenin were discussed; and, finally, the "social-political attestation" of each member at the end of the year. We have already dealt with the individual composite plan, said to be "the basic form of forecasting the social development of an individual" (*lichnosti*).[8] Many city committees of the Komsomol printed standard versions of these plans of personal self-development, with subsections headed "study plans," "ideological work,"

6. The next section draws on four brochures on the Lenin Pass: *Leninskii zachet "Resheniia XXVI s"ezda v zhizn'"* (Voroshilovgrad, 1976); *Leninskii zachet v komsomol'skoi organizatsii srednikh shkol* (Leningrad, 1978); *Leninskii zachet v sisteme kommunisticheskogo vospitaniia molodezhi* (Leningrad, 1980); *Leninskii zachet v shkole* (Piatigorsk, 1985). Many, many more exist.

7. *Leninskii zachet* [The Lenin Pass] (Moscow: Molodaia Gvardiia, 1977), 26–30. This collection of essays was published by the Central Committee of Komsomol; the bibliography at the end of the book has 220 sources on the Lenin Pass, after only eight years of its existence.

8. Ibid., 34. For discussion of individual composite plans see an excerpt on Aret and Ruvinsky in chapter 6.

"labor training," and so on. After students compiled the plans at a special class meeting and submitted them to the teacher (some schools practiced reading self-obligations aloud in public), individuals allegedly went out to fulfill them. Given the high level of dumb ritualization of life at that time, it is hard to believe that many actually did so; perhaps the only reminders of the Lenin Pass during the year were quarterly Lenin's Classes, where students were supposed to listen to narratives of heroic deeds related by visiting veterans and thus practice hero-identification.[9]

The decisive stage of the Lenin Pass arrived with discussion of each classmate's fulfillment of the individual composite plan at the end of the year. This discussion took place at a Komsomol meeting, but under various forms: with or without "sponsors" present, with or without preliminary discussion of each individual by a specially appointed attestation commission, consisting of five or six members of the school *aktiv*, which then offered its opinion to the meeting. Teachers, attending the proceedings of this Komsomol attestation of each member, were to interfere only if they encountered "youthful maximalism," which was the latter-day Soviet euphemism for a group's desire to sacrifice one of its members.

Structurally, the Lenin Pass—in preparation for which all students had to perfect themselves—echoed the 1930s purge literature. Even the criticism of its deficiencies followed the canons of the purge instructions. The didactic literature on the Lenin Pass lamented that attestation committees did not exist as permanent bodies; that they were hastily assembled a week before the pass rite; that the final evaluations were written not by the assemblies, but by the fatigued teachers; and that often attestation meetings left off comparing a given individual's plans with demonstrated deeds or discussing individual development, to look into irrelevant issues and obscure knowledge.[10]

"Youthful maximalism" remained under strict control, however, which saved these meetings from becoming the meat grinder that self-criticism

---

9. To establish "Soviet traditions" and shore up intergenerational authority, in the late 1960s Brezhnev's leadership authorized the creation of high school museums of military regiments and industrial enterprises in the schools named after them, attaching groups of military or labor veterans (or current worker activists in the same enterprise) as *shefy* (sponsors) and often calling these groups to the schools to participate in all kinds of events, including Lenin's Classes (see Iakovlev, *Stanovlenie lichnosti*, 77).

10. Party literature during the 1920s–30s purges similarly criticized mistakes such as the devolution of a purge meeting into an examination of irrelevant or quizzical knowledge (see *Otchet TsKK RKP(b) XIV s"ezdu partii*, 57).

sessions had been in 1937. The difference between the routinized Lenin Pass and the frenzied collective self-examination sessions of 1937 lies in the absence of an intent to spot enemies. More than anything else, the Lenin Pass presented an annual review of each individual. It did not emphasize searching for enemies within the *kollektiv* but stressed the evaluation of each individual member. In relevant Greek terms for collective self-criticism and purging that we used in chapter five to analyze the practice of *oblichenie*, it now peacefully stressed the aspect of *demosieuo*, with the aspect of *elendzo* almost defunct. Still, staging of the Lenin Pass was extremely attractive for the regime, because it combined the central elements in the process of training and self-training, discussed in the previous chapter: group shaming and victimization on the one hand, and self-planning, self-accounting, and hero-identification, on the other. In one neat and compact ritual, it offered the growing generations all the elements of the Soviet civilizing experience.

Notwithstanding the obvious truths that the Lenin Pass usually meant boring routine and, as a consequence, was highly inefficient in inculcating Communist values into the everyday life of the Soviet citizens, its radical novelty consisted in the fact of institutionalization itself. Even if young people did not subscribe to values offered to them in such a stale form, they did learn the background practices of Soviet life—and observe them to the extent of performing them obediently in public every year. For a civilization based on Eastern Christian penitential rites, a very important event occurred in 1969. If the 1933 purge made revelation by deeds the compulsory matrix of individuation, which eventually made its way into different official Soviet procedures, 1969 quietly finished this job of pragmatic dissemination: the annual review of the individual's deeds and collective deliberation on the individual self finally imposed a routinized socialization rite on every student. But few citizens perceived the novelty of the final solidification of the institutional matrix of the annual review of deeds of Conscience in 1969: this solidification happened so easily and was almost unnoticed because it only expressed in an annual compulsory rite what was already practiced in many other milieus on a regular basis anyway.[11]

Having described the habitualization of *oblichenie* in the official rites of late Soviet society, we now notice its curious displacement and diffusion. People followed the officially authorized practices with the sole aim of

11. And, I suggest, having rejected Communist values in 1991, many Russian citizens did not, could not, or (in some cases) would not as easily reject the habitual practices that had always served as background for these values.

demonstrating loyalty outwardly, and the constant underlying thought of retreating into the unofficial sphere as soon as possible. The irony of the situation lay in the fact that there, in the unofficial milieu, they took over and implemented these practices to the fullest degree to attain aims different from the official ones. Thus ritualized in the official sphere, *oblichenie* found a place in diffuse groups and informal communities.

Oblichenie penetrated secret societies, subcultures, informal groups, and networks of friends. Its presence in the diffuse groups discussed above was the most important phenomenon, and we will use their example to illustrate the point. Diffuse groups came to be indispensable once they had become the primary arenas where the individual's sense of self was revealed and perfected. To paraphrase Kasianova, these groups allowed people to be who they were, since—as we suggested—it was primarily through the medium of these groups that people came to know who they were. Thanks to the existence of these diffuse groups, deliberation on the individual self in the official *kollektivy* hardly mattered anymore; the diffuse group's evaluation, by contrast, had become essential. Friends allowed their stable and semi-closed diffuse group to rummage in their private lives, because exposure was a precondition for the emergence of their sense of themselves.

We can even point to a curious informal annual ritual in the life of a diffuse group: the birthday celebration. As Levada's research demonstrated, members of younger generations considered their individual birthday the central holiday of a calendar year, while older generations ascribed such value to some community or family holiday: Victory day, New Year's Day, and the like.[12] Indeed, the birthday party plays a very central role in Soviet and post-Soviet culture. First of all, birthdays involve considerable expenditure on the part of the celebrant, who has to prepare sumptuous meals and a liberal quantity of libations for the invited guests, and they in return must bring sizable presents. Second, community rearrangement techniques are in full gear: intrigue flourishes in the choice of guests. Invitations for some and not for others: exclusion of the nondesirables is one of the rules of the successful birthday party. Third, birthdays structure the flow of time. The importance of birthdays is so high that a high school student's

12. Levada, *Prostoi sovetskii chelovek*, 36–37: among the youngest, 73 percent picked birthdays, and among those 65 or older, 40 percent picked May 9 (Soviet holiday commemorating the victory in the Second World War). The imbalance may also reflect teenagers' greater need to assess and assert themselves; see Kon, *Druzhba* on the emotional functions of friendship for teenagers.

calendar often consists in a series of friends' birthday celebrations, rather than any other events. Personal planning carefully marks and memorializes these birthday dates.

All this frantic activity of preparation and celebration surrounds the central informal rite of the event—the revelation of the celebrant's self. It recasts the habitual toasting routine of Russian celebrations to include a sequence of obligatory toasts by participating guests, who in their speeches will evaluate and laud the achievements of the celebrant. Of course, some toasts may go astray and produce merely a brief well-wishing remark; some guests may violate the canon of positive evaluation and produce the dangerous "X is great, but" speech. Both the deviations and their normal suppression by those present, however, only confirm the rule: the most important is the community's judgment, revealed in their toasts. The inherent license to insult the celebrant during the toast, or to mention some one or two particular faults, only makes the expressed evaluations seem more real.

It is striking that all the elements of the *oblichenie* practice are in operation here. An annual peer review of deeds happens, and an individual listens to the community judgment not so much with fear and trembling (since prebirthday community rearrangement and normal suppression of deviations from the routine assure mostly positive evaluations) as with intense attention: it endows the celebrant with a new self. In other words, it is a scene of annual rebirth. This is very close to Mircea Eliade's account of the reenactment of the myth of the birth of the world in sacred holidays in religious civilizations.[13] During the birthday party, a celebrant lives in "a sacred time," with ordinary temporality suspended. That's why a Russian wakes up on the birthday morning with a feeling that today birds should be singing and the sun should shine differently: it is the day of the ritual after which the world will not quite be the same.

Kasianova's book may once again offer us some insight on what exactly the birthday celebration evaluates. In her discussion of the functioning of a diffuse group, she describes how what she calls "personality-based status" —*lichnostnyi status* in Russian, and a synonym for *avtoritet*, as it turns out later—emerges in such a group.[14] Relying on conceptual distinctions taken

---

13. See Mircea Eliade, *The Sacred and the Profane* (New York: Viking, 1958).

14. Kasianova, *O russkom natsional'nom kharaktere*, 264–265. Kasianova's focus is the emergence of individual moral authority rather than general mechanisms of a group's evaluation of its members. But she describes both, since the group's evaluation is a precondition for high moral authority. As we noted, Kasianova holds that those who have moral authority within their groups often transfer it in the informal sphere of ties between diffuse groups.

from Kingsley Davis's analysis of stratification, Kasianova defines "prestige" as the moral approval attached to someone's social status and "role" as the way in which one meets the requirements of his or her status. Kasianova proposes the third term, "reputation" (*reputatsiia*) or "personality-based status," which combines prestige, roles, *and* "an evaluation . . . of still unrealized possibilities and capacities of an individual, his deeds of a purely moral character, not tied to statuses or roles."[15] Her example of a "purely moral" deed is help offered to a total stranger.

She is not clear, however, on the general interrelationship among prestige, role-playing, and moral evaluation in creating a composite reputation, but it seems that in her description of Russian culture the moral component definitely predominates: "What matters in the reputation is not the results achieved by an individual at a given time, but what he strives for, that is, which *values* he accepts and implements."[16] Reputation, then, emerges from a "diffuse group" deliberating on the predominantly moral character of the individual revealed in his or her deeds. Evaluation in Russian diffuse groups focuses primarily on moral matters and replicates the matrix of evaluation during the purge or any other instance of official *oblichenie*, shifting it into an informal *kollektiv*, where it is practiced more meaningfully than in the stale official sphere.

A PERSON AND AN INDIVIDUALITY

After discussing the fate of *oblichenie*, its ritualization in the official sphere and its expansion into unofficial life, particularly into the life of diffuse groups, we turn now to another very important phenomenon that became widespread from the 1950s on. Individualization by distinction followed individuation by revelation of the self. *Otlichie* joined *oblichenie*, to reveal distinctive features of this individual self in a group of similar persons.[17] In other words, after becoming an individual as a result of *oblichenie*, one could become a unique individual, by means of *otlichie*. The mass-produced individual emerging from Makarenko's factory, needed a finish-

---

15. Ibid. The original text is Kingsley Davis, "A Conceptual Analysis of Stratification," *American Sociological Review* 7, no. 3 (1942): 312–321.

16. Ibid.

17. *Otlichie* captures both primary meanings of "distinction": to be distinct from others and to be the best. And it is yet another offspring of that extremely rich family of the root *lich-* (face, persona): by getting a distinction, a Russian gets a different face and an individuality distinct from that of anyone else.

ing touch, the individual gloss to mark him or her as different from the other products on the conveyor belt.[18]

This achievement of a distinct individuality proceeds in stages. First, one distinguishes oneself from society at large by joining an informal group that defines itself against and in opposition to this broader society. Second, as a member of the group one attempts to excel within it, distinguishing oneself there by unique achievements or by a unique style of action. In the language of Pierre Bourdieu, the initial differentiation of social subgroups marks the boundaries of the diverse "fields" of action, and then individual distinction—distinguishing oneself from other players in the same field—becomes the primary stake in the game in each of these emerging fields.[19]

The new possibility for distinguishing oneself and acquiring a distinct individuality also marked the appearance of scientific discourse on the term *individualnost'*. This term had been in use in colloquial Russian for quite a long time. *Individualnost'*, as defined in the 1956 edition of the most authoritative dictionary, meant "particularity, distinctive features [*otlichitel'nye cherty*], inherent in a give individual," first, and served, second, as a synonym of the term "the individual." It is curious that in mid twentieth-century standard usage, one gains "individuality" by *otlichie*, not by *oblichenie*.[20] And yet the first philosophical monographs and sociological works on the problem of individuality appeared only after Khrushchev. For example, Georgii Gak, one of the authors of early Stalinist brochures on the problem of *lichnost'* discussed above, published a whole dialectical materialist treatise on the problem of *individualnost'* in 1967. Of course, he reminded the reader that *lichnost'* is "the whole ensemble of human relations," according to the canonical definition from Marx. One ensemble

18. Of course, *otlichie* and *otlichnik* are old Russian words that quickly fit into Soviet usage. For example, by the end of a 1933–35 campaign of *otlichnichestvo*, a competition for individual distinction among industrial workers, 2.8 percent of them managed to earn the title of *otlichnik*, based on the demonstrated results of their work (Siegelbaum, *Stakhanovism*, 52). The spread of *otlichie* may parallel that of *oblichenie* throughout the Soviet era, but for analytical reasons I cast *oblichenie* in a founding role, setting the stage for the later *otlichie*. Lexicographic evidence suggests the same: words related to *otlichie* began to appear after the 15th century (and the verb *otlichiti* itself is registered only in the end of the 17th), while *oblichenie* was part of the original Church Slavonic, dating back to the earliest available sources (see Barkhudarov, ed. *Slovar' russkogo*).

19. Pierre Bourdieu, *Distinction*, trans. Richard Nice (Cambridge, Mass.: Harvard University Press, 1984).

20. Even this 1956 dictionary does not ascribe "individuality" to the ordinary self; its first six examples of usage dealt with particularities of artistic genius and the seventh, scientific work (article on *individualnost'*, in *Slovar'*).

may differ from others, however, because of varying degrees of development of universal human capacities in particular human beings; Gak captures vast differences in what he calls "types of personality" (*tipy lichnosti*). But there are "degrees of individuality" even within the same "type of personality." "Individuality" itself is a metaphysical category that applies to human individuals and to any individual phenomenon that has "unrepeatable expressions of the common," features that make it unique.[21]

In application to the human being specifically, according to Gak, a citizen's individuality rests in four sets of relations: in unique features of the set of human capacities, in his or her unique character traits and features of temperament, in individual opinion [*sic*], and in individual tastes revealed in patterns of consumption. Among these four, the Soviet state should take account of the first set of features only, since the suggested pragmatic aim of Gak's philosophical treatise is to establish the precise "individual treatment" of each Soviet citizen, in order "to position people in production in accord with their individual endowments."[22] The "individual approach" that figured so heavily in the Party resolutions at the time of the Great Purges reaches out now to include the most unique features of the human individual; people should have vocations and positions precisely in accord with their individuality.

The first main type of self-revelation through distinction is informal individualization through professional distinction. Professional self-expression through one's personal achievement and style of work turned up in Leopold Haimson's analysis of the Soviet novels concerned with science during the Khrushchev era: "While continuing to feel loyal to the foundations of their social order—to socialism and its values as they variously choose to define them—many of the members of this new generation appear driven by the compelling urge to discover and defend an area of personal autonomy, to find a channel, however narrow, for uncontrolled, unmanipulated individual expression."[23] However, this Soviet image of scientific self-expression is by no means like Cavendish's solitary aristocratic exercises in chemistry at his isolated estate, closed to the outside world. Moshe Lewin suggested the preconditions for this flourishing of professional self-definition—namely, the formation of "invisible colleges"

21. G. M. Gak, *Dialektika kollektivnosti i individual'nosti* [A dialectics of collectivity and individuality] (Moscow, 1967), 12. In chapter 5 I discuss Gak's 1945 brochure.

22. Ibid., 3.

23. Leopold Haimson, "The Solitary Hero and the Philistines," in *The Russian Intelligentsia*, ed. Richard Pipes (New York: Columbia University Press, 1962), 109.

of scientists in the 1960s and 1970s.[24] Though Lewin borrowed the term from the work of Derek de Solla Price, which dealt with Western scientists, in the Russian context it applied to the formation of informal arenas of professional *otlichie*. This professional acclaim was hard to earn, since it lay in recognition from an "invisible college" of a given scientist's individual style and originality in solving scientific problems. The community that effectively deliberated and granted this informal status never convened at the meetings of the USSR Academy of Sciences but existed in the interstices of the system, in the letters and exchanges of those who already possessed this professional recognition themselves.

The same individualization through creative style would seem to apply to diverse artistic communities and subcultures. For example, Frederick Starr holds that improvisation in jazz, highly individual in nature, accentuated the drive for personal expression and individuality, and that in the Soviet jazz community individualization occurred through "inner-directedness" and escape into privacy from "the lonely crowd."[25] Yet, as his own analysis of the *styliagi* subculture tightly linked with the jazz milieu in the late 1950s suggests, these subcultures were more concerned with outward appearances than with internal self-development. Therefore, while Starr's thesis is perhaps true in relation to culture producers, "the development of inner-directedness" was hardly characteristic of culture consumers. Among consumers, distinction by style of consumption goods, or possessions, mattered more than distinction by qualities of creative action. Hence, the second main type of individualization by distinction—individualization through distinction in the style of possessions—evolved and was practiced by broader audiences than individualization by professional distinction.

Style-conscious youths displayed their clothes and thereby their "individuality." Being authentic here meant not individually designing oneself in an ek-static project (Starr uses existentialist vocabulary—though not precisely these terms—to characterize the subcultures of the 1950s and 1960s),[26] but joining the right subculture, distinct from the rest of the world, and then earning individual distinction within this subculture. Far from the individual self-projection of the existentialist, this individualiza-

24. Moshe Lewin, *The Gorbachev Phenomenon* (Berkeley: University of California Press, 1990), 66, 73.
25. Starr, *Red and Hot*, 239.
26. In effect, he seems to read the values of the American beat generation into the contemporaneous generation of Russian youth.

tion through consumption style was closer to what historian Caroline Bynum found in twelfth-century Western Europe: it was individualization through choosing a group ideal to follow, a religious order to join.[27] Of course, once a part of this community (of jazz musicians, mountain climbers, scuba divers, and so on), one could excel within this order and distinguish oneself from the rest of this community.

In the initial stages of the Soviet subcultural *otlichie* through style, there were few affirmations of the individual at the expense of the group. The individual did not cast off inhibiting patterns of the greater society but rather accepted new patterns in the time free from officially required activities and tried to excel in a way authorized by the relevant underground community. Furthermore, the evaluation of the success of individualization here totally depended on the community: to be "most hip" or "most cool," one needed the judgment of those who could understand the standards of hipness or coolness. Though types of charismatic appeal that underlay the formation of various underground communities differed, the arenas of distinction through style that they created functioned very similarly. However, these different underground milieus soon gave way to a broader community of style appreciation.

For instance, the simplest way to excel in the *styliagi* subculture, of course, was to get the "hippest" clothes. But once the *styliagi* were nearly wiped off the streets in the campaign of the late 1950s, the press registered the appearance of a different class of style-seekers. The "crown princes," as the press called them then, were working-class youths who behaved like good socialist citizens at their job sites but in their spare time searched for stylish clothes by trading for them with foreigners in black market deals. This spread of style-seeking heralded the new era: *otlichie* through clothes became available to every Soviet citizen. Vasilii Aksenov, who later became a renowned émigré writer, wrote a piece in 1960 dealing with the puzzle of why among many young workers "becoming a real man" amounted to getting stylish clothes. If a *styliaga* lurked within every working-class youth, the problem was not suppressing the impulse, as among wealthy youths, but understanding it, and then correcting it:

> How did . . . the sons of ordinary working families come to lead such a life? . . . [The struggle against them] cannot be reduced to what used to be done several years ago when every young fellow with welted pockets and every girl with dyed hair was hauled off to a patrol post.

27. See Bynum, *Jesus as Mother*, 83.

We must proceed differently, and we must first of all understand why moths flying toward the dangerous flame of an attractive life appear among our serious, intelligent young people.[28]

Of course, simple economic capacity may have contributed to the desire to acquire and hoard material possessions, since Soviet society was becoming increasingly affluent. And yet use of consumer items as a means of self-definition was relatively novel, and the adoption of this strategy by the majority of the Soviet urban youth was a formidable development. Good Western clothes, stylish dance, and a stylish strolling gait challenged the monotonous conformity of the general Soviet public but revealed a stylish self to the underground community as well. Distinction through style was transformed into distinction through possessions, since the latter provided a relatively easy means of self-definition. Rather than excelling in feats of unique creativity, one could simply buy distinctive clothes. Instead of sweating over writing a unique book, one could simply demonstrate to awe-struck guests one's unique collected library, whether the books were ever opened or not.[29]

A corollary development to the strengthening of informal individualization through consumption was the slackening of attention to the practices of *oblichenie*. In a consumer-based culture, becoming an "individuality" was easier than anything else: instead of undergoing demanding sacrifices for the Motherland—to be revealed as a highly moral self—one could leave these sacrifices to others and scrimp a bit to buy or barter for yet another consumer article. Given that the revelation of self was assured by participation in the routinized rites of official *oblichenie*, in which each had to take part to a certain extent, one could safely consider one's own sense of self constructed and progress to embellish the revealed self with distinctions in consumption. Distinction achieved in the unofficial sphere was superimposed on the sense of the moral self routinely granted in the official sphere. "X is just a normal student, who has a great collection of rock music," would be the relevant community's frequent remark about some down-to earth Soviet youth.

Relieved of the need to test the moral basis of their self-evaluation,

28. Vasilii Aksenov, "Printsy, nishchie dukhom" [Princes, who are spiritual beggars] *Literaturnaia gazeta* [Literary gazette (Moscow)], September 7, 1960, as cited in Allen Kassof, *The Soviet Youth Program* (Cambridge, Mass.: Harvard University Press, 1965), 158–159.

29. On individualization through personal collections, see Svetlana Boym, *Common Places* (Cambridge, Mass.: Harvard University Press, 1994), 159.

many individuals in late Soviet society seemed to have lost any interest in the basic mechanisms of *oblichenie* (practiced meaningfully only in small diffuse groups), and turned instead to a full-fledged struggle for consumer distinction, so well described in Zinoviev. Ritualized support of the system allowed more and more freedom in private, including freedom from Conscience. Not surprisingly, this development elicited the disgust of official authors and critics of the regime alike, as both groups grew more and more concerned about the disintegration of the moral foundation of the person. Self-revelation through distinction, easily obtained in a flourish of possessions and stylish behavior—and a neat finesse past substantial *oblichenie*—drew universal scorn. Borrowing a metaphor from the nineteenth-century radical Dmitrii Pisarev, the language of the 1960s described this behavior as a problem of the empty nutshell: the pursuit of external distinction hid the void within.

CONFESSIONAL PROSE AND SELF-FASHIONING

Official ideologists sensed this absence of moral criteria, so central for *oblichenie*, from the sphere of *otlichie* and sounded the alarm: these style-seekers lacked inner spirituality and higher moral values.[30] Among the members of literary officialdom, the critic Felix Kuznetsov took up the campaign against the "surrogate emancipation of the self."[31] According to Kuznetsov, the search for oneself through the display of jeans, jargon, and motorbikes, poeticized in the novels of Vasilii Aksenov, was the best example of this surrogate individualization. Aksenov was part of the group of young authors who started publishing after 1956 and were usually subsumed under the label of "new" or "confessional prose" (*ispovedal'naia proza*). Kuznetsov's overview of confessional prose written in 1967, when this movement seemed already a thing of the past—and when many of its primary proponents, under fire from Soviet authorities, had recanted in public for creating "unrealistic heroes" and "superficial plots"[32]—was an

30. On style-seekers' lack of *dukhovnost'* (inner spirituality) see Rusakova, "Kto iz nikh stiliaga?" and on *dukhovnost'* in traditional everyday mythology as against Enlightenment rationalism and the cultivation of the body see Boym, *Common Places*, 84.

31. The term occurs in Felix Kuznetsov, "K zrelosti: Konets chetvertogo pokoleniia" [Toward maturity: the end of the fourth generation], *Iunost'* [Youth] 11 (November 1967): 85.

32. Khrushchev directly attacked Aksenov, who was among those authors invited to attend Khrushchev's famous March 1963 meeting with members of "creative intelligentsia," where avant-garde trends in art were denounced. Aksenov

attempt at public repentance for his own infatuation with this prose in the early 1960s.

To keep himself on the safe side, Kuznetsov appealed to the unquestionable authority of Pisarev—who demanded that literary movements should be interpreted as reflecting the social needs of an epoch—and reasoned that confessional prose was a necessary initial stage in the development of post-Stalin literature. According to Kuznetsov, confessional prose was the reaction of the young writers to the prevalence of the unthinking "functional man" that pervaded the novels of Stalinist socialist realism. The confessionalists, on the contrary, brought back the questioning individual, to reflect on themselves and their own value as human beings.[33] In Kuznetsov's opinion, the revelations of the Twentieth Party Congress made blind faith in Communist ideals impossible and subjected high rhetoric and ritual beliefs to scrutiny from the point of view of real life. Heightened interest in the simple things in life such as clothes, bikes, and music was a corollary of this denigration of lofty ideals.

Indeed, the schism between words and deeds, revealed in 1956, somehow engendered the eruption of "confessional prose." As the name of the movement implies, authors of this current—Anatolii Kuznetsov, Vasilii Aksenov, Anatolii Gladilin, and Chinghiz Aitmatov, to name but a few—brought back into Soviet literature confessional techniques largely obliterated during the Stalinist years. But this confession was of rather strange quality, as a Western critic remarked, comparing Aksenov's writings to beat prose in the United States: "One of the important characteristics of . . . Kerouac's prose is that it is highly autobiographical. . . . This is true of Aksenov; although he to some extent tries to hide it . . . ; but his prose cannot be labeled 'confessional' as can Kerouac's. In this respect Kerouac follows Henry Miller and Anaïs Nin, constantly analyzing himself, always occupied with his inner thoughts and desires."[34] This commentary did not expound on how Aksenov himself wrote, but by implication it was clear that he did not

---

publicly recanted in the *Pravda* issue of April 3, 1963, and promised to create more acceptable characters. See J. J. Johnson, Jr., "V. P. Aksenov: A Literary Biography," in *Vasiliy Pavlovich Aksenov*, ed. Edward Mozejko (Columbus, Ohio: Slavica, 1986), 36.

33. This process is rather confusingly called "a self-recognition of the self" (*samoosoznanie sebia*) but, in the usage of the 1950s, "self-recognition of the *kollektiv*" was possible also; hence Kuznetsov's need to stress that the individual is both agent and object of analysis.

34. Per Dalgard, "Some Literary Roots of Aksenov's Writings," in *Vasiliy Pavlovich Aksenov*, ed. Edward Mozejko (Columbus, Ohio: Slavica, 19186), 82.

analyze his own thoughts and desires. Then what was confessional about confessional prose?

As Felix Kuznetsov wrote: "A hypertrophied attention to the individual [*lichnosti*], first of all to one's own personality [*lichnosti*], more precisely to the personality of a peer, a wish to understand and assert it—this is the idée fixe of confessional prose."[35] An exegesis may help interpret this rather confusing passage. Authors of confessional prose did not write about themselves but they supplied lengthy narratives of the inner reflections of their main characters. Many wrote in the first person singular. Confessional prose consistently pictured hesitant young men, who continuously reflected on their lives and realized that they did not know what they wanted. Having spent hours deliberating over their goals in life, they ended up confessing that they had none.

From our perspective, a very interesting feature of this confessional style is that intense self-questioning usually stays within the confines of the individual soul. For example, when pressed to comment on the same matters in speech, Aksenov's characters adopt an ironic stance. They do not restate their private thoughts; rather they repeat clichéd versions of acceptable public values in an obviously ridiculing way. The inner monologue of a character—disclosed to the reader—frequently remains a mystery to other characters in these novels. If one character in the novel fathoms another's thoughts, often the second character's deeds give them away. The aversion to explicit confession of internal states in public speech comes from a specific feature of confessional prose: confession is the means of inner reflection on deeds, not on intentions and desires. Furthermore, confession is not an end in itself, rather, it is subordinate to action and almost seems to follow the official Soviet guides' recommendations for working on oneself. Thus, we conclude, confessional prose was "confessional" only because little of this internal reflection had figured in Soviet novels previously but would hardly qualify as "confessional" in the sense of the works of Augustine, Montaigne, or Rousseau.

Indeed, confessional prose devoted a huge number of pages to characters who talk, but their talk centered on the main issue of the epoch: comparing words and deeds. The words were secondary and subservient to the deeds: they represented the deeds, clashed with the deeds, analyzed the deeds and their relation to other words that preceded these deeds. Confession was not an aim in itself, it was rather the means for revealing doubt that deeds then

---

35. Kuznetsov, "K zrelosti," 85.

would test. "In the stream of arguments, aphorisms, puns and outpourings, in the continuous disputation that constituted the essence of the confessional novels, the same wish was reflected: to test words in their solidity, to segregate the real from the unreal, life from mist, core from surface," wrote the critic Lev Anninsky. "The word contrasted with the deed. The deed was superior to everything. And the deed done was somehow simple, tangible, authentic in a tactile way."[36] To demonstrate that this split between words and deeds was the common denominator for all types of "young prose" at the time, Anninsky balances Aksenov's confessional prose against the "silent" prose of Iulian Semenov. In Aksenov's stories protagonists constantly spoke, while in Semenov they were silent most of the time. And yet both writers shared the same objective, in Anninsky's opinion: their heroes tested words in action. When Semenov's heroes finally opened their mouths, they exploded in tirades reminiscent of the "talkers"; when the "talkers" went to work, they did their jobs "in ferocious silence."[37] Words weren't to be trusted after 1956; hence verbalization was more suspect than ever. Yet deep internal reflection on the grand schism between words and deeds in confessional novels gave the name to confessional prose.

The reflection contained in confessional prose, according to Kuznetsov, represented only the first step in the "spiritual emancipation of the individual," which—as became clear by 1967, the date of Kuznetsov's repenting article—should culminate in the individual adoption of those revolutionary ideals that had survived the test of real life and could thus become the core values of the new type of person. The confessionalists only doubted everything, they had yet to take the second step and work out a firm individual faith in Communist ideas, based on true, unspoiled Leninism. In Kuznetsov's opinion, the mid-1960s heralded the maturation of confessional prose writers, who started depicting the second stage of personality development: in many novels characters imbued with "revolutionary spirit" reappeared. These new heirs of the Russian Revolution differed from the heroes of the Stalin era in that they "read Lenin but not according to a school program" and passed "from convictions based on [blind] faith to convictions based on knowledge and individual thought."[38]

It is rather interesting to juxtapose to this voice of officialdom the writings of Lev Anninsky, who had fame as a critic of liberal leanings. Surpris-

36. Lev Anninsky, *Iadro orekha: Kriticheskie ocherki* [The nut's kernel: critical essays] (Moscow: Sovetskii pisatel', 1965), 89.

37. Ibid.

38. Kuznetsov, "K zrelosti," 86.

ingly, Anninsky also questioned Aksenov's rejection of hortatory rhetoric about values in favor of individualization through such mundane aspects of life as jeans, jazz, and jargon. Indeed, the establishment and the democratic opposition joined ranks in the common fight against "surrogate individualization." According to Anninsky, many young writers after 1956 started to concern themselves with matters of individuality, searching for its core.[39] Yet, by 1965, the search—already in full swing for almost a decade—had hardly produced any definitive findings. Novels by Vasilii Aksenov and his friends in the confessional prose movement were hallmarks of this search but also demonstrated its lack of results. According to Pisarev's metaphor— which appeared in the title of Anninsky's 1965 book—the young writers dealt with the nutshell but not with its inside. Whether people listen to Tchaikovsky or jazz, Anninsky reasoned, speak in "ode-like rhetoric or intimate lyrics," wear wide trousers or tight jeans didn't matter. "External forms" are unimportant compared to "the process of inner and spiritual straightening up of oneself," inducing "the capacity of the individual to take responsibility for himself, to be himself."[40]

Anninsky reproached Aksenov for stopping at nutshells because, when it came to final conclusions, it turned out that Aksenov's heroes had no aim in life. They were unable to define the core of their personhood. Anninsky saw this core as a substantive goal individuals should strive to achieve, some service to the common good. In a false etymology of the Latin term *individuum*, Anninsky proposed that this term implied the indivisibility of the human individual from the common cause. He concluded: "An individual [*lichnost'*] emerges at the intersection of social ties. . . . Using the old term of Planck, one may call the individual a quantum of the historical stream: a quantum is indivisible, but it exists only in a stream; a stream of light consists only of quanta." Anninsky's verdict on Aksenov's characters is final: since they have no connection to any socially useful goal, they are not "individuals" in the full sense of the word; they "only imitate life."[41]

Anninsky did not quite advocate Kuznetsov's solution—to accept the values of the Bolshevik revolution after personally testing them for soundness—but he came close to it. A human being, in Anninsky's version, becomes an individual in choosing to serve some external value, as opposed to accepting values automatically supplied by the official ideology. Beneath

---

39. See Anninsky, *Iadro orekha*, 8: "the history of the individual [*lichnosti*]— that's what is hiding in each poet. In the origin [of poetry] lies the individual."
40. Ibid., 97.
41. Ibid., 99, 98.

both writers' views on individualization is the conscious choice to serve some external value cherished by a larger community. The difference lies only in the source of the values, whether official Marxist or—in the case of Anninsky—covertly liberal ideology.

In their war against the "surrogate emancipation" of the individual, both Kuznetsov and Anninsky missed what was essential to the plot of Akse-nov's novels: attention to consumer objects gave him, gave his characters a context in the search for moral value. But, I argue, their objective was elusive, hidden in the folds of text poeticizing these outward signs of individualization through distinction. On the one hand, the novel's heroes immerse themselves in jeans, jazz, and bikes, all of them consumer goods previously unimaginable in Soviet prose. On the other, outward distinction is not their primary aim in life. Critics eager to pick a novelist who would serve as an obvious referent for the moral panic of the time tended to overlook these complexities in order to combat individualization through consumerism. A closer look at Aksenov's novel *A Ticket to the Stars* (1961), which made him the leader of "confessional prose," will help reveal the link between consumerism and higher values.[42]

Between the two novels that brought Aksenov fame, *The Colleagues* (1960), which largely conformed to the canons of socialist realism, and *A Ticket to the Stars*, which nearly all critics took to be primarily concerned with clothes, restaurants, and other outward signs of distinction in the youth subculture, Aksenov wrote his essay on "crown princes" that dealt with similar issues.[43] Working-class kids looked for restaurants and smart clothes to prove themselves "real men." Now, it is clear that in this article published in September 1960 Aksenov did not take this quest as a wholly worthwhile endeavor; he might almost have called it "surrogate individualization," as other critics did, and not only for ideological reasons.

Aksenov could not stand mindless aping of fashion in the place of active self-fashioning, and that's what seemed to worry him in the youth culture. Rejecting fashion in clothes as the only and cheapest means of self-fashioning, he wrote lines almost reminiscent of Pavel Korchagin: "In the course of one's life, one should struggle with oneself and learn to make sacrifices, to work, to love, to fight the dark past, and all this to the fullest

42. Analysis of the novel's background of shared practices is particularly useful, since many contemporaries took it as the first adequate example of the language and issues concerning the younger generations. On its reception as a realist novel, see V. P. Skobelev and L. A. Fink, eds., *Vasilii Aksenov: Literaturnaia sud'ba* [Vasilii Aksenov: literary fate] (Samara: Samara University, 1994).

43. See Aksenov, "Printsy, nishchie dukhom."

degree."[44] "The dark past" of course here meant the vestiges of capitalism and was possibly just the usual incantation, required for the public press, rather then an assault on the style-seekers' blind consumerism. And yet there is a genuine affinity between this essay, which denounced style-seeking, and *A Ticket to the Stars*, which seemingly affirmed it. The essay on "crown princes" ended with an appeal to working-class youths: "You are wrong, kids! Can't you see anything in the sky but a restaurant signboard?" The novel, which appeared nine months later in the journal *Youth*, in fact contained the different ideal in its very title: looking at the sky, you ignore restaurant signboards and see the stars. Instead of mindlessly hopping from one café to another, you follow a star in the sky.[45]

But, leaping ahead, I should say that these stars do not symbolize some substantive socially useful goals for Aksenov. "Struggling with oneself," in Aksenov's version of reform, is not supposed to lead individuals to bury themselves in service to some externally set social values. Dmitrii Denisov, the chief protagonist of *A Ticket to the Stars*, has no socially useful goal in life, no matter how hard he tries to find one in his unending self-questioning. However, this constant search for an elusive goal suggests a rather simple solution for Dmitrii's problem. The means itself becomes the end; the process becomes the goal. Self-fashioning itself can be said to have become the chief value of Aksenov's hero, and therefore the name of the star to which he aspires is autonomous self-definition.

Autonomy, of course, figures heavily in the novel. Many debates between the two brothers Denisov in *Ticket to the Stars* revolve around this elusive concept.[46] The elder brother, Victor, hesitates whether to undertake an unauthorized experiment that might undermine the results of his own work of the last three years, which is about to be published in a dissertation. Furthermore, it might call into question the achievements of some very powerful colleagues:

> And what can be more beautiful, more exhilarating to a man than independence [*samostoiatelnost'*]? A man who once gets that feeling of independence (to me it's a combination of arrogance, determination and a

44. Ibid.
45. Many commentaries noticed the stars' central symbolism as the novel's protagonist stopped liking fake decorative stars on the ceiling of the Tallinn café where he spent much of his time and chose real ones.
46. When Aksenov chose the names, did he have in mind the Denisov brothers who had led one of the most famous dissident communes of the Old Believers in Russia's far north? See Robert O. Crummey, *The Old Believers and the World of Antichrist* (Madison: University of Wisconsin Press, 1970).

special sort of heart tremor) will tremble over it, as he would tremble over a delicate, fragile vase. . . . But once he drops it, he might as well say, It's a sign of good luck and so much for the better, after all, for I could not relax for one minute worrying all the time that the damned thing might get cracked, and so to hell with it![47]

After a lengthy struggle with himself, Victor makes a decision to conduct this experiment, which is also Victor's first experience of autonomy; the novel is explicit about it through a play of words, since *opyt* means both "experience" and "experiment" in Russian. As he would later admit, "in my case I have to fight against myself without mercy for my hide."[48]

Here a generally unnoticed reconceptualization of the struggle with oneself occurs. The struggle with vestiges of the past—with "the past" defined as capitalism, of course—which the Communist Aksenov recommended nine months earlier in the *Literary Gazette* article, now becomes a struggle with "the past" defined as the Stalinist heritage, the inability to make an independent decision. Indeed, 1956 is a very important date, directly referred to in text. The director of Victor's lab, who finally congratulates him on the successful completion of the risky experiment, says: "For four years, I've watched you and your like with mixed feelings, I could not understand you too well. What are they after, I wondered? Is it just to take everything to pieces, to reject everything? But now I believe I can see what you are after and I believe it is the same thing that I am after myself."[49] Given the year of the publication of the novel, 1961, calling everything into question "four years ago" implies the aftermath of the Twentieth Party Congress. And 1956 is very significant for another reason. Victor's younger brother, Dmitrii, grew up after Stalin's death; part of his secondary schooling occurred after 1956 when all established ideals were called into question. As a result, he takes autonomy as a natural condition, in Victor's words. Dmitrii does not have to fight himself to acquire it; he simply cannot imagine life without it.

His first debate with his older brother starts by rejecting the automatic, robotlike progression through life in a vocation that his brother had accepted at the suggestion of their parents, the fate that their parents had intended for them both: "Why, in your whole life, you've never even once taken an important decision, never accepted a serious risk. To hell with

47. Vasili [Vasilii] Aksenov, *A Ticket to the Stars*, trans. Andrew R. MacAndrew (New York: Signet, 1963), 29.

48. Ibid., 150.

49. Ibid., 124.

that! Before we are even born, everything is worked out for us, our whole future is all mapped out. Ah, no, that just ain't for me! I'd rather be a tramp and suffer all sorts of setbacks than go through my whole life being a nice little boy doing what others tell me."[50]

The problem is that Dmitrii does not know what he wants. The arbitrary nature of his decisions shows up in the title of the first part of the novel, "Heads or Tails." Teenagers constantly toss coins to figure out what to do. Aksenov almost stresses that what matters for Dmitrii and his friends is not the substance of activity but their own autonomy, their own decision to undertake it. Victor also invokes the metaphor of tossing the coin. On the verge of the decision to undertake the experiment, Victor says to himself: "It is my labor, all my own, the product of my own thinking. It is also, if you wish, the toss of a coin—heads or tails."[51] Here tossing signifies the risk of failing, but it also connotes an attribute of independent decision-making.

When the capacity to make decisions independently solidifies, and one knows what one wants, one no longer needs to toss a coin. This happens when Dmitrii juggles a coin while tossing it before setting on a trip to Tallinn: he is sure he should go there. In another episode at the end of the novel, when two Dmitrii's friends resolutely—and of course, independently—decide to take on decent careers, he thinks: "Well, so Yurka and Alik have decided what they were going to do next. They haven't even had to toss a coin either."[52] And, as the later exposition shows, Dmitrii himself will no longer need to toss coins either. This claim may be puzzling, since he still does not know what to do: "But what about me? Well, I have to sadly admit that thus far I have no program for my further life. It must be a case of arrested development."[53] Nor will a life program in the form of a choice of professional vocation appear by the end of the novel. This absence of a life goal allowed Anninsky to call Dmitrii an empty shell. But this absence of a life program, this rejection of the choice of a vocation is the very choice that Aksenov ascribes to his main protagonist. It *is* his life program.

Reflecting on his current goals and his temporary job as a seasonal fisherman in an Estonian village, Dmitrii thinks:

> Ah, if I only knew myself what I wanted. Well, I guess, I'll find out some day. Now I want to go catching fish without being bothered. I want to feel that I am strong and tough. I want to stand in the wheel-

50. Ibid., 25.   51. Ibid., 109.   52. Ibid., 171.
53. Ibid., 171–172.

house in the middle of the black sea and listen to a symphony. Let the spray fly in my face. Give me a chance to digest it all. I want to have arguments with the skipper and roar with laughter with my pals. Don't ask me such questions. I want the palms of my hands to become as rough as the soles of my boots from handling the lines. And when I fall asleep, all I want to see is pilchards, pilchards, and pilchards. I want— I want to leave 1793 [another fishing boat, which Dmitrii's boat is trying to beat in the socialist competition] far behind in every respect. I want to go out into the Atlantic next year."[54]

Here all the main tenets of confessional prose appear with utmost clarity: no lying words and high rhetoric, just sound, simple deeds. A hero looks for authentic experience that cannot be subverted by any changes in official doctrine. He rejects any demands that he account in words for what he wants ("Don't ask me such questions"). Confessional prose does not trust confessions. It trusts deeds.

Curiously enough, these last two passages also demonstrate the interrelationship of officially prescribed techniques of self-revelation and self-fashioning with the most essential definition of Dmitrii's independent self. In fact, Soviet techniques of self-fashioning suffer the same fate as the practices of *oblichenie:* ritualized in the official sphere, they are taken over and remolded for private purposes. Dmitrii knows that winning in socialist competition is yet another officially approved way to acquire the approved public self, endowed by the community. But he participates in the competition for private purposes. He just needs it for himself, to be himself for himself. He also knows that Soviet people are expected to engage in self-programming. And by the end of the novel his friends do have life programs, informally adopted. But rather than submit their individual plans for later official public review, Dmitrii and his friends engage in self-programming to know and form themselves in a diffuse group.

The end of the novel suddenly reappropriates another Soviet self-fashioning technique, hero identification, for the private aims of Dmitrii. After Victor's death during his experiments with space flight, Dmitrii goes back to Moscow for his brother's funeral and cannot find any rest for two days, incessantly circling the streets of the city. Suddenly, an obvious thought dawns on him: he should visit the apartment where his family lived before he left for Tallinn and Victor left for his space experiments. The building is under repair but Dmitrii finds a way to enter it and ends up

54. Ibid., 151.

on the windowsill where his elder brother used to lie for hours watching the stars. He takes his brother's posture, lies down on the sill, and sees a narrow strip of sky shaped like a railway ticket punched through with stars:

> "Wonder whether Vic ever thought of that?"
>
> I looked and looked up there and my head began to spin and everything that had happened to me in my life and that is still going to happen started to spin too and I no longer knew whether it was me stretched on my back with my head on the windowsill or whether it was someone else. And the real, real stars, so full of great meaning, are turning above me. Whatever happens, this is now my ticket to the stars. Whether he knew it or not, Victor has left this ticket to me.[55]

This concluding scene is indeed filled with "loftiest meaning," as the British translator interpreted Aksenov's words *vysochaishii smysl* in the same episode.[56] A scene of quasi-religious exhilaration occurs. Dmitrii identifies with his brother and, through him, with something bigger, with the stars and the universe. He finally finds the "loftiest meaning" that Aksenov's interpreters generally failed to recognize in his characters. But what is it?

A series of considerations can help us answer this question. First, looking at the stars, Dmitrii does not see "a restaurant signboard" either, though as we know he likes restaurants a lot. Everything is rotating, and he is only able to notice that what is rotating with the stars is his life: whatever has happened to him and whatever is going to happen. In looking at the stars, he sees himself. By choosing to adopt his brother's posture, he chooses the stars and thus chooses himself. By watching the stars, Dmitrii finally chooses his life program.

Second, if his brother lying on the windowsill saw the object of his professional endeavors, to a certain extent (stars as the goal of space flight), Dmitrii encounters simply a charismatic opening, with no relation to the mundane world whatsoever. Getting a ticket to the stars through hero-identification, he still has not gotten a vocation, a fate he has avoided throughout the novel. He does not see the cosmos with its romantic patina of travel and conquest, dear to so many Soviet youths at that time, either. But his vocation is there nevertheless; he has received it, in the form of the ticket to the stars, from his brother.

Third, Dmitrii so far has always refused to imitate his brother (Victor

---

55. Ibid., 175–176.
56. Here I find the English version more accurate (Vasili [Vasilii] Aksenov, *A Starry Ticket*, trans. Alec Brown [London: Putnam, 1962], 224).

even laments this failing at one point);[57] hero-identification was never his choice. Now this means of official self-fashioning suddenly occurs to the rebellious Dmitrii after two days of intensive unrest, as an obvious relieving solution. It is a result of an independent and natural—should we say, authentic?—decision that does not involve even a thought about tossing a coin. It's a must. Rejected until the last page of the novel, the technique of hero-identification becomes the essential choice for Dmitrii, his life program. The subtle point here, however, is that Dmitrii chooses a specific technique of Soviet self-fashioning, hero-identification, not as a means to some external goal; rather Dmitrii's choice implies that self-fashioning is a goal in itself. Among many types of activity that could become his life goal, he chooses—since the novel ends at this episode, after trying every substantive definition of a goal and rejecting them all—self-fashioning itself as the goal of activity.

57. "They exhorted me to follow certain worthy examples and later pointed to me as a model for my young brother Dimka to emulate. . . . But Dimka just sneezed at the model offered him" (Aksenov, *A Ticket to the Stars*, 109).

9 Conclusion

Our Foucaultian study of the origins of individualism in the Russian setting yields interesting comparisons between the Russian and what may be termed Western European, or—more broadly—Western cases. Adopting Dreyfus and Rabinow's distinction between objectifying practices (to make individuals the objects of knowledge and action) and subjectifying practices (to make them the subjects who act and know), and drawing out the distinction—as Foucault does to a certain extent—we may formulate two broad comparative hypotheses.

The first hypothesis states that objectification of the individual in Russia relied on practices of mutual horizontal surveillance among peers, rather than on the hierarchical surveillance of subordinates by superiors that characterized the West. More precisely, this surveillance operated through three practices: revelation of sins, admonition to right behavior, and excommunication. Before 1917 only bodies on the margins of society joined these three practices, for example, in the operation of the ecclesiastical courts and in some monasteries arranged according to the statute of Saint Joseph of Volokolamsk. After the Revolution these practices pervaded almost every social body. As they spread far and wide, to be sure, these practices adapted to new aims or diverse interpretations.

Heightened admonition in mature Soviet society enforced discipline, whereas the atrocities of the Great Terror in the 1930s happened against the background of a direct merger of practices of revelation and excommunication, unmediated by admonition, that is, contrary to what the New Testament would require. The irony of history, however, consists in the fact that this profound terror was linked to an attempt to install mutual surveillance to the fullest, that is, to use admonition to unify each Party cell or workers' collective. The universal introduction of gentle disciplinary means happened by means of the wildest bloodshed. Khrushchev merely completed the job started under Stalin when he ultimately helped spread admonition throughout the whole body social in the 1950s and 1960s and let it mediate the murderous coupling of revelation and excommunication.[1]

In a parallel development, the background practice of revelation of sins (*oblichenie*) was intensified and recast to reveal new objects: first, the revolutionary self of a Bolshevik and later the person of each Soviet individual. Its publicizing aspect achieved equal prominence with the heretofore prevalent accusatory aspect, whereas in the late Soviet days the accusatory element even took second place. *Oblichenie* brought about a specific Soviet kind of individual, formed in the public gaze of his or her peers. They evaluated this individual in the specific setting of the purge or, in some of its later, routinized versions such as the Party member's individual report or the high school student's Lenin Pass.

The second hypothesis holds that Russian subjectifying practices formed from practices of self-knowledge characteristic of Eastern Christianity— from penitential practices rather than the confessional practices that constitute the background for self-knowledge in Western Christianity. To state this second comparison slightly differently, the Western individual was produced by confessing matters of sex, or by some parallel hermeneutic analysis of desire: by confessing to a priest, to a psychoanalyst, to a diary. By contrast, the Russian individual was produced by submitting to consideration by the relevant group that reviewed his or her morality, a procedure rooted in the practices of penance in the public gaze.

In our analysis of the Soviet techniques of self-fashioning we rely on Foucault's discussion of the two potential technologies of the self inherent in early Christianity. The first one is "the truth technology of the self oriented toward the manifestation of the sinner," expressed in the early Christian rite of *exomologesis:* the truth about the sinner manifested itself in visible deeds.[2] In Foucault's suggestive phrase, this penitential technology

1. It seems that Russians would do better if they got rid of the age-old preoccupation with the famous questions "What is to be done?" and "Who is to blame?," especially when they are combined in the question "What is to be done concerning those who are to blame?" made possible by the murderous merging of revelation and excommunication practices. Perhaps, dissociating the practices that constitute the paradigmatic triad "reveal-admonish-excommunicate" and remolding each separate element of this triad to suit new, different aims, might form other groupings of practices that could preclude the possibility of the reemergence of the deadly constellation of 1937.

2. Foucault, "About the Beginning," 222.

of self-knowledge expresses "the ontological temptation of Christianity," since being manifests itself directly without the mediation of words. The second technology of the self—an expression of "the epistemological temptation of Christianity"—was a different truth technology, which involved "discursive and permanent analysis of thought." This confessional technology was an aspect of the early Christian practice of *exaugoresis*, which concerned itself with knowledge stated in words rather than with visible being. According to Foucault, the second technology eclipsed the first in Western Europe after some "conflicts and fluctuation."[3] A contrary development occurred in Russia: there the first, penitential technology survived and predominated in the Christian East.

Soviet subjectifying practices—like the Soviet objectifying practices based on mutual surveillance—also included a series of components that were recast to suit new aims and were merged together in novel configurations. Before submitting oneself to the judgment of peers on the success of one's self-fashioning demonstrated in deeds, an individual could work on him- or herself primarily through the secular equivalent of Christian *imitatio Dei*, by choosing a personal hero and imitating this hero in everyday life. This Christian means of self-fashioning was amended, however, by its coupling with a secular technique of self-planning or self-programming, which was superimposed on hero identification following the doctrinal requirements of the Bolshevik discourse. Coupled together, self-programming and hero-identification, eventually judged by the relevant community, became the primary means of self-fashioning.

With the ritualization of life in Soviet official sphere, I argue, the practices of hero identification and submitting individual morality to the judgment of the relevant community moved into the informal sphere of networks, subcultures, and friendship. However, new means of self-fashioning also developed, characteristic only of this informal sphere. The first development was the spread of individual dissimulation, the practice protecting the individual from any interference, which resulted in the creation of a secret sphere of intimate life, available to the gaze of the closest friends or family members but sometimes kept secret even from them. This proliferation of secret, intimate spheres, created and controlled only by the individual, prepared the way to the easy public assertion of the value of privacy after 1991. We must not forget, however, that the sphere of Soviet privacy originated in dissimulation, unlike its counterpart in the West.

3. Ibid.

Therefore, the meaning of statements that use the phrase *chastnaia zhizn'* (a rough equivalent of "private life" in English) in Russian may be radically different from those in English or French.[4]

The second means of informal self-fashioning was individualization through distinction in style or possessions. This individualization revealed the presence of a nonmoral self and thus drew the censure of official ideologists and critical intelligentsia alike, who labeled it a "surrogate individualization." Even so, in debates over distinction through style a reconceptualization of self-fashioning occurred: instead of serving as the means to obtain a higher moral self, self-fashioning became an end in itself, a value cherished on its own. And the concomitant spread of the practices of autonomous self-fashioning contributed to a preparation of the grounds for an easy and almost natural assertion of autonomy as one of the ultimate values of human existence in the post-1991 discourse.

A summary overview of these Soviet practices reveals a picture of bustling activity, unintentionally preparing the post-Soviet adoption in discourse of all "core ideas" of Western individualism, as Lukes conceptualizes it. Small pragmatic changes made possible the whole-hearted support of such novel values as privacy and autonomy, while self-development was a value in the Soviet discourse since its inception. Furthermore, the Soviet attention to the individual within the collective examined in chapter 5 was one step away from the assertion of the unconditional self-worth or dignity of the individual as such. This final assertion of this first item on Lukes's list came about in a bare reversal of the ideology of official collectivism after 1991.

Having summed up the argument, I should now stress some important methodological aspects of this study of background practices in the Soviet Union. The continuity of practices between the Soviet Union and Russia seems tremendous, yet this continuity was far from being a matter of simple constancy. Even age-old practices—like the penitential revelation of self in the public gaze—were recast when they became the background for Soviet culture. One might better speak about reformation than about continuity in this case.

Two types of such reformation of background practices were indicated by our study. First, the existing practices were recast to achieve novel tar-

4. See the more detailed exposition on private life in Oleg Kharkhordin, "Reveal and Dissimulate: A Genealogy of Private Life in Soviet Russia," in *Public and Private in Thought and Practice*, ed. Jeff Weintraub and Krishan Kumar (Chicago: University of Chicago Press, 1997).

gets. For example, as I tried to show, the Bolshevik purge commission was not the simple reincarnation of the ecclesiastical court of the early Christians. Rather, the publicizing aspect of the practice of *exomologesis* was emphasized to such an unprecedented degree, while the practice itself was brought to reveal a new object called a Higher Conscience, that this double transformation yielded a novel institutional form, a regular review of the sainthood of each individual. This form in its turn was displaced to new locales, such as the review of the individual in a friends' network, or produced multiple reactions, such as individual dissimulation. If all these developments speak of a continuity, this is a continuity in a very Nietzschean sense. As he wrote in *The Genealogy of Morals:*

> whatever exists, having somehow come into being, is again and again reinterpreted to new ends, taken over, transformed and redirected by some power superior to it. . . . The evolution of a "thing," a custom, an organ, is thus by no means its progressus towards a goal, even less a logical progressus by the shortest route and with the smallest expenditure of force—but a succession of more or less profound, more or less mutually independent processes of subduing, plus the resistances they encounter, the attempts at transformation for the purpose of defense and reaction, and the results of successful counteractions. The form is fluid, but the "meaning" is even more so.[5]

Second, archaic practices were not only remolded to suit new aims and displaced into new milieus, they were regrouped with other practices in new configurations. For example, *imitatio Dei* was not simply copied in the Bolshevik self-fashioning; rather it was joined with methodical self-planning and was thus radicalized and recast to yield a new practice of Soviet individual self-development. Practices merged in the novel way, and this built a novel way of life, which, however deep its roots in the resources from the past, was radically different in its reformation of these resources. So the continuities are there, but the breaks engendered by the reformations of the first and the second type are also very important. The change in background practices escapes the simplistic conceptualization in dichotomous terms of either a "total continuity" or a "radical break."

Radical breaks occurred, of course, but usually at the level of revolutionary discourse, keen on stressing the revolutionary difference of the new society from the old one. Pragmatic changes were rather slow to follow and often took shapes other than those prescribed for them by the

5. Friedrich Nietzsche, "On the Genealogy of Morals," second essay, sec. 12, in *On the Genealogy of Morals,* ed. W. Kaufmann (New York: Vintage, 1967), 77.

grand official discourse. As we discovered, pragmatic changes that underlay the construction of the new Soviet culture stemmed more from the transformation of the perennial practices of Eastern Christianity than from the vision contained in the grand Marxist discourse. However, not all Soviet discourses were so radically off the mark. Soviet discourses that dealt specifically with the change in practices—like Makarenko's novels and pedagogical advice—and therefore had lower status than official Marxism were more intimately tied with this pragmatic change. Some willing experimenters intentionally implemented Makarenko's advice in practice. And many more of those who "followed" Makarenko adopted his discourse because it reflected what was already underway in their milieu.

Still, even such small discourses on pragmatic reshuffling of the collective and the corollary remaking of the individual in the Soviet Union could not fully account for or elicit the changes in background practices. These changes rarely went exactly according to Makarenko's or similar prescriptions and often even defied these small discourses at the conscious rearrangement of practices. First, nonauthorized practices, like individual dissimulation and self-fashioning through distinction in style, emerged in reaction to or concomitantly with pragmatic changes that the authorities in different fields tried to elicit. Second, though ritualized and thus frequently ineffective in the official sphere, authorized practices were reappropriated and successfully restaged in the unofficial sphere to achieve aims different from—and sometimes even contrary to—the official aims. For example, mutual surveillance was practiced in the dissident movement to create a secret society espousing values opposite to the official ones. Similarly, self-recognition through judgment of the relevant community—utterly ritualized and thus a sham in the official Soviet life of the 1970s and 1980s— was transposed to be meaningfully practiced within friends' networks.

To sum up, this proliferation and intertwining of authorized, nonauthorized, and displaced authorized practices together constituted the slowly changing background for the political and social actors in the Soviet society. This background existed almost unnoticed and unaccounted for by both Soviet social sciences and by the Western studies of Soviet life. On the one hand, Soviet scholars followed the grand official Marxist discourse, perfunctorily disregarding small discourses on pragmatic changes in constructing the new Soviet culture—that supplied at least glimpses of the current constellation of background practices— as documents of secondary importance. Who would think that a standard 1960s instruction on the disciplinary regime in an industrial enterprise is more important than *State and Revolution?* On the other hand, Western scholars, with a few exceptions, were busily translating Soviet documents, enumerating Soviet institutions and policies, and describing the behavior of Soviet leaders, which they then analyzed in terms of organizational efficiency or of ideological acceptability (from the standpoint of either Western democratic theory or Marxism's originating grand discourse). In this respect, too, everyday practices that constituted the background for a correct understanding of these documents or these institutions were ignored.

The failure of official Soviet discourse to account for Soviet life is not surprising, given that it focused on the dogmatic exegesis of a few sacred Marxist texts, rather than on the study of what people were actually doing. The failure of Western scholarly discourse in the same respect is more puzzling, given the honest commitment to scientific analysis and the amount of time and resources spent on this activity. However, this failure suggests that reflections on the background practices of a culture or, more precisely, on the differences in background practices between the culture studied and that to which a researcher belongs, should perhaps precede comparisons of foreground phenomena like the content of discourse or the official form of institutions. In other words, examining differences in backgrounds may be a necessary prerequisite to examining differences in foreground phenomena.

Cross-cultural comparisons of background practices need not be as crude as the two hypotheses stated in the beginning of this conclusion, of course. First, two formal axes of "horizontal versus hierarchical surveillance" and "confessional versus penitential practices" do not exhaust all relevant background comparisons even within cultures related to Christianity, let alone comparisons between them and, say, cultures connected to Buddhism or Islam.[6] Other axes may present themselves. Second, these comparisons of cultural backgrounds may perhaps reveal differences of degree, rather than differences of kind. The two hypotheses outlined above are rather crude because they overlook the obvious fact that Russian culture still allows a certain use of confessional modes of self-knowledge and undoubtedly employs hierarchical surveillance. For example, few readers will be unaware that I pass over the residues of prerevolutionary confession among the Soviet population and the phenomenal import of confessional techniques coming through Western films, novels, and music in the post-Stalin era. Furthermore, hierarchical surveillance—even if subordinate in its significance to

6. See Christian Jambet's very interesting study of technologies of the self in Christianity and Islam, "The Constitution of the Subject and Spiritual Practice" in *Michel Foucault Philosopher*, trans. Timothy J. Armstrong (New York: Routledge, 1992).

the horizontal one—also operated with unusual ferocity in Soviet Russia, and such familiar elements of the Soviet regime as piece rates, internal passports, and secret police files are elements of it. Similarly, Western culture is not a uniform universal, and it relies to a certain extent on horizontal surveillance and on penitential analysis of visible deeds. Comparisons—if they are to be drawn as meticulous comparisons, rather than as initial crude generalizations—should perhaps account for this difference of degree and note, say, that subjects in Russian culture rely on penitential modes of self-knowledge in 70 percent of their life situations, while in the balance they use confessional techniques. By contrast, Anglo-Americans may turn out to rely on confessional techniques in 70 percent of life situations, and on penitential techniques in 30 percent. This comparison is still not refined enough, and problems of operationalization abound, but I hope that the general thrust of the argument is obvious.

This book describes a difference between cultural backgrounds as a stark difference in quality in order to alert the reader to this difference and thus, perhaps, open space for further research. In so doing I pursue a rather well established investigative procedure. John Austin, in his theory of "doing things with words," first radically contrasts the performative and constative utterances but ends his famous article on performatives by saying that each utterance has performative and constative aspects, and that further research will perhaps reveal the degrees and modes of differences in these qualities of each utterance.[7] Later Austin's theory, as well as John Searle's theory of speech acts, which meticulously accounted precisely for these differences, developed in the space opened up by this initial formulation.

The present book too sets out its distinctions, in the hope of moving the debate on differences between respective cultures beyond overused and tired comparisons of collectivist Russia vis-à-vis the individualist West. More generally, this book tries to add to an ongoing discussion of the study of practices and will fulfill its aim if it recedes into its background.

7. J. L. Austin, "Performative Utterances," in *Philosophical Papers* (Oxford: Clarendon Press, 1961).

Bibliography

STENOGRAPHIC RECORDS OF PARTY PLENUMS
AND CONGRESSES (IN CHRONOLOGICAL ORDER)

Otchet TsKK RKP(b) XIV s"ezdu partii [Central Control Commission report to the 14th Party Congress]. Moscow, 1925.

VI Plenum TsKK sozyva XIII s"ezda, 11–13 dekabria 1925 [6th Central Control Commission plenum, December 11–13, 1925]. Moscow, 1926.

XIV s"ezd VKP(b): Stenograficheskii otchet [14th Party Congress (December 1925): stenographic report]. 3d ed. Moscow: Gosizdat, 1926.

XV s"ezd VKP(b): Stenograficheskii otchet [15th Party Congress (December 1927): stenographic report]. 2 vols. Moscow: Politizdat, 1961.

III Plenum TsKK sozyva XV s"ezda 25–29 avg. 1928 [3d Central Control Commission plenum, August 25–29, 1928]. Moscow: Izdatel'stvo TsKK-NK RKI, 1928.

XVII s"ezd VKP(b): Stenograficheskii otchet [17th Party Congress: stenographic report]. Moscow, 1934.

III Plenum KPK pri TsK VKP(b) [3d Committee of Party Control plenum]. Rostov-on-Don, 1936.

XVIII s"ezd VKP(b): Stenograficheskii otchet [18th Party Congress (March 1939): stenographic report]. Moscow: Politizdat, 1939.

KPSS v rezolutsiiakh i resheniiakh s"ezdov, konferentsii i plenumov TsK [Resolutions and decisions of CPSU's congresses, conferences, and central committee plenums]. 9th ed. Moscow: Politizdat, 1983–85.

REFERENCE BOOKS FOR PARTY WORKERS
(IN CHRONOLOGICAL ORDER)

Spravochnik partiinogo rabotnika [Reference book of Party officials]. 1st and 2d eds. Moscow: Gosudarstvennoe izdatel'stvo, 1921–22.

Spravochnik dlia KK RKP(b) i organov RKI [Reference book for the Control

Commissions and bodies of the Worker-Peasants' Inspectorate]. 1st ed. Moscow: Izdatel'stvo NK RKI, 1924.

Spravochnik dlia KK VKP(b) i organov RKI, [Reference book for the Control Commissions and bodies of the Worker-Peasants' Inspectorate]. 2d ed. Moscow: Izdatel'stvo TsKK-NK RKI, 1927.

Spravochnik rabotnika KK-RKI: Rukovodiashchie materialy i direktivy o rabote organov KK-RKI [Reference book for officials of the Control Commissions and Worker-Peasants' Inspectorate: guiding materials and directives on the work of bodies of the CC-WPI]. Moscow-Leningrad: Tekhnika upravleniia, 1931.

Spravochnik rabotnika KK-RKI [Reference book for officials of the Control Commissions and Worker-Peasants' Inspectorate]. 3d expanded ed. Moscow-Leningrad: Tekhnika upravleniia, 1932.

Spravochnik rabotnika KK-RKI [Reference book for officials of the Control Commissions and Worker-Peasants' Inspectorate]. 4th ed. Moscow: Vlast' Sovetov, 1933.

GENERAL LITERATURE

Abramkin, V. F., and V. Chesnokova. "Tiuremnyi zakon" [Prison law]. In *Tiuremnyi mir glazami politzakliuchennykh* [The prison world in the eyes of political prisoners], ed. V. F. Abramkin. Moscow: Sodeistvie, 1993.

Adams, Jan S. *Citizen Inspectors in the Soviet Union: The People's Control Committee.* New York: Praeger, 1977.

Aksenov, V. A. "K voprosu o kharaktere vliianiia tovarishcheskikh distsiplinarnykh sudov na rabochie kollektivy promyshlennykh predpriiatii v nachale 2oh godov" [On the influence of comrades' disciplinary courts on the workers' collectives in industrial enterprises in the early 1920s]. Institute of Scientific Information on Social Sciences (INION) of the Russian Academy of Sciences ms 26673. Gorky University, 1986.

Aksenov, Vasilii. "Printsy, nishchie dukhom" [Princes, who are spiritual beggars]. *Literaturnaia gazeta* [Literary gazette], September 7, 1960.

———. *A Ticket to the Stars,* trans. Andrew R. MacAndrew. New York: Signet, 1963. Also published as *A Starry Ticket,* trans. Alec Brown (London: Putnam, 1962).

Akulenko, V. V. "Iz istorii russkoi obshchestvenno-politicheskoi terminologii nachala XX veka" [Notes on the history of Russian social and political terms of the beginning of the 20th century]. *Uchenye Zapiski Khar'kovskogo Gosudarstvennogo Universiteta* [Learned works of Kharkov University] 109 (1960).

Akvilonov, Evgenii. *Tserkov': Nauchnyia opredeleniia tserkvi i apostolskoe uchenie o nei kak o tele khristovom* [The church: its scientific definitions and apostolic teaching on the body of Christ]. St. Petersburg, 1894.

Aleksandrov, V. I., A. P. Bodrilin, and E. I. Dumasheva. "K voprosu o poniatii

kollektiv" [On the concept of the collective]. In *Uchenye zapiski MOPI* [Learned notes of Moscow Regional Pedagogical Institute] 302 (1971).
Alekseeva, Liudmila. *Istoriia inakomysliia v SSSR: Noveishii period.* Moscow: Vest', 1992. Originally published as *Soviet Dissent: Contemporary Movements for National, Religious, and Human Rights*, trans. Carol Pearce and John Glad (Middletown, Conn.: Wesleyan University Press, 1985).
Alikhanov, G. *Samokritika i vnutripartiinaia demokratiia* [Self-criticism and intraparty democracy]. Leningrad, 1928.
Allison, David B., ed. *The New Nietzsche: Contemporary Styles of Interpretation.* Cambridge, Mass.: MIT Press, 1985.
Almazov, A. I. *Tainaia ispoved' v pravoslavnoi vostochnoi tserkvi: Opyt vneshnei istorii* [Private confession in the Eastern Orthodox Church: an essay of external history]. 3 vols. Odessa, 1894.
Anderson, David. "Bringing Civil Society to an Uncivilized Place: Citizenship Regimes in Russia's Arctic Frontier." In *Civil Society: Challenging Western Models*, ed. Chris Hann and Elizabeth Dunn. London: Routledge, 1996.
Andreeva, G. M. *Sotsial'naia psikhologiia* [Social psychology]. Moscow: Moscow University, 1980.
Anninsky, Lev. *Iadro orekha: Kriticheskie ocherki* [The nut's kernel: critical essays]. Moscow: Sovetskii pisatel', 1965.
Aret, A. Ia. *Ocherki po teorii samovospitaniia* [Essays on the theory of self-training]. Frunze: Kirghiz State University, 1961.
Armstrong, Timothy J., trans. *Michel Foucault Philosopher: Essays from French and German.* New York: Routledge, 1992.
Asmolov, A. G. *Psikhologiia individual'nosti* [Psychology of individuality]. Moscow, 1986.
———. *Psikhologiia lichnosti* [Psychology of the personality]. Moscow: Moscow University, 1990.
Averintsev, Sergei. "Vizantiia i Rus': dva tipa dukhovnosti" [Byzantium and Russia: two types of spirituality]. *Novyi Mir*, September 1988.
Barkhudarov, S. G., ed. *Slovar' russkogo iazyka XI–XVII vv.* [Dictionary of the Russian language, 11th–17th centuries]. Moscow: Nauka, 1975–92.
Barsov, N. I. *Sushchestvovala li v Rossii inkvizitsiia?* [Did the Inquisition exist in Russia?]. St. Petersburg, 1892.
Bauer, Raymond A. *The New Man in Soviet Psychology.* Cambridge, Mass.: Harvard University Press, 1952.
Beck, W., and F. Godin. *Russian Purge and the Extraction of Confession.* London, 1951.
Bekhterev, V. M. *Kollektivnaia refleksologiia* [Collective reflexology]. Moscow: Kolos, 1921.
Belanovsky, S. A., and S. N. Marzeeva. "Armiia kak ona est'" [The army as it is]. In *Dedovshchina v armii: Sbornik sotsiologicheskikh dokumentov*, ed.

S. A. Belanovsky [The eldership in the army: a collection of sociological documents]. Moscow: Institute of Economic Prognostication, 1991.

Bellah, Robert N. *Beyond Belief: Essays on Religion in a Post-Traditionalist World.* Berkeley: University of California Press, 1970.

Benjamin, Walter. "On Language as Such and on the Language of Man." In *Reflections: Essays, Aphorisms, Autobiographical Writings,* trans. Edmund Jephcott. New York: Harcourt Brace Jovanovich, 1978.

Berdiaev, Nikolai. *Istoki i smysl russkogo kommunizma* [Origins and meaning of Russian communism]. Paris: YMCA-Press, 1955.

Berman, Harold. *Justice in the USSR.* 2d ed. Cambridge, Mass.: Harvard University Press, 1962.

Billington, J. H. *The Icon and the Axe: An Interpretive History of Russian Culture.* New York: Vintage, 1966.

Bourdieu, Pierre. *Distinction: A Social Critique of the Judgment of Taste.* Trans. Richard Nice. Cambridge, Mass.: Harvard University Press, 1984.

———. "From Rules to Strategies." In *In Other Words.* Stanford: Stanford University Press, 1990.

———. *The Logic of Practice.* Stanford: Stanford University Press, 1990.

Bowen, James. *Soviet Education: Anton Makarenko and the Years of Experiment.* Madison: University of Wisconsin Press, 1962.

Boym, Svetlana. *Common Places: Mythologies of Everyday Life in Russia.* Cambridge, Mass.: Harvard University Press, 1994.

Bozhovich, L. I. *Lichnost' i ee formirovanie v detskom vozraste* [Personality and its formation in childhood years]. Moscow, 1968.

Breslauer, George. *Khrushchev and Brezhnev as Leaders: Building Authority in Soviet Politics.* London: Allen and Unwin, 1982.

Brooks, Jeffrey. "Revolutionary Lives: Public Identities in *Pravda* During the 1920s." In *New Directions in Soviet History,* ed. Stephen White. Cambridge: Cambridge University Press, 1992.

Brower, R. A. *On Translation.* Cambridge, Mass.: Harvard University Press, 1959.

Brown, Edward. *Russian Literature Since the Revolution.* Cambridge, Mass.: Harvard University Press, 1982.

Bruford, W. H. *The German Tradition of Self-Cultivation: Bildung from Humboldt to Thomas Mann.* Cambridge: Cambridge University Press, 1975.

Brzezinski, Zbigniew. *The Permanent Purge: Politics in Soviet Totalitarianism.* Cambridge, Mass.: Harvard University Press, 1956.

Buck-Morss, Susan. *The Origins of Negative Dialectics: Theodor W. Adorno, Walter Benjamin, and the Frankfurt Institute.* New York: Free Press, 1977.

Budagov, R. A. *Istoriia slov v istorii obshchestva* [History of words in the history of society]. Moscow, 1971.

Budassi, S. A. "Modelirovanie lichnosti v gruppe (na veroiatnostnykh strukturakh)" [Modeling an individual within a group (in probability structures)]. Abstract, Candidate of Science dissertation, Moscow State Pedagogical Institute, 1972.

Busygin, A. K. *Zhizn' moia i moikh druzei* [My life and the life of my friends]. Moscow: Profizdat, 1939.

Bynum, Caroline Walker. *Jesus as Mother: Studies in the Spirituality of the High Middle Ages.* Berkeley: University of California Press, 1982.

Cartwright, Dorwin, and Alvin Zander, eds. *Group Dynamics: Research and Theory.* 3d ed. New York: Harper and Row, 1968.

Chan Van Chyong. "Ispol'zovanie istoricheskogo opyta KPSS po formirovaniiu lichnosti sotsialisticheskogo tipa v sovremennykh usloviiakh vo Vietname" [Use of the CPSU's historical experience in the formation of the socialist individual in contemporary Vietnam]. Abstract, Candidate of Science dissertation, Plekhanov Institute of National Economy, Moscow, 1987.

Chernyshevsky, Nikolai. "Avtobiografiia." In *Polnoe sobranie sochinenii* [Complete works]. Vol. 1. Moscow, 1939.

Clark, Katerina. *The Soviet Novel: History as Ritual.* Chicago: University of Chicago Press, 1981.

Cocks, Paul M. "Politics of Party Control: The Historical and Institutional Role of Party Control Organs in the CPSU." Ph.D. dissertation, Harvard University, 1969.

———. "The Rationalization of Party Control." In *Change in Communist Systems,* ed. Chalmers Johnson. Stanford: Stanford University Press, 1970.

Confino, Michael. *Société et mentalités collectives en Russie sous l'ancien régime.* Paris: Institut d'Etudes slaves, 1991.

Conquest, Robert. *The Great Terror.* Cambridge, Mass.: Harvard University Press, 1969.

Conyngham, William J. *Industrial Management in the Soviet Union: The Role of the CPSU in Industrial Decision-Making, 1917–1970.* Stanford: Hoover Institute, 1973.

Crummey, Robert O. *The Old Believers and the World of Antichrist: The Vyg Community and the Russian State, 1694–1855.* Madison: University of Wisconsin Press, 1970.

Dalgard, Per. "Some Literary Roots of Aksenov's Writings: Affinities and Parallels." In *Vasiliy Pavlovich Aksenov: A Writer in Quest of Himself,* ed. Edward Mozejko. Columbus, Ohio: Slavica, 1986.

Danilin, E. M. *Ispol'zovanie sistemy A. S. Makarenko v deiatel'nosti VTK* [Using Makarenko's system in the work of Training Labor Colonies]. Moscow: VNII MVD, 1991.

Davidson, Arnold I. "Archaeology, Genealogy, Ethics." In *Foucault: A Critical Reader,* ed. David Couzens Hoy. Oxford: Blackwell, 1986.

Davies, R. W. *The Industrialization of Soviet Russia.* Vol. 2: *The Soviet Collective Farm, 1929–30.* London: Macmillan, 1980.

Davis, Natalie Zemon. "Boundaries and the Sense of Self in Sixteenth-Century France." In *Reconstructing Individualism: Autonomy, Individuality and the Self in Western Thought*, ed. Thomas C. Heller, Morton Sosna, and David E. Wellbery. Stanford: Stanford University Press, 1986.

Deleuze, Gilles. "Active and Reactive." In *The New Nietzsche: Contemporary Styles of Interpretation*, ed. David B. Allison. Cambridge, Mass.: MIT Press, 1985.

———. *Foucault*. Trans. Sean Hand. Minneapolis: University of Minnesota Press, 1988.

———. "What is a *dispositif?*" In *Michel Foucault Philosopher*, trans. Timothy J. Armstrong. New York: Routledge, 1992.

Dement'ev, N. V. *Trudiashchiesia na strazhe obshchestvennogo poriadka* [Laborers on guard for public order]. Moscow: Profizdat, 1959.

Deriugin, Yu. I. "Dedovshchina: sotsial'no-psikhologicheskii analiz iavleniia" [The eldership: a socio-psychological analysis of the phenomenon]. *Psikhologicheskii zhurnal* [Journal of psychology (Moscow)] 11, no. 1 (January–February 1990).

Detkov, M. G. *Soderzhanie karatel'noi politiki sovetskogo gosudarstva i ee realizatsiia pri ispolnenii ugolovnogo nakazaniia v vide lisheniia svobody v tridtsatye–piatidesiatye gody* [Punitive policy of the Soviet state and its realization in penitentiary detention in the 1930s–50s]. Domodedovo: Academy of the Russian Ministry of Internal Affairs, 1992.

DiFranceisco, William, and Zvi Gitelman. "Soviet Political Culture and 'Covert Participation' in Policy Implementation." *American Political Science Review* (September 1984).

Dontsov, A. I. *Psikhologiia kollektiva: Metodologicheskie problemy issledovaniia* [Psychology of the collective: methodological problems of research]. Moscow: Moscow University, 1984.

Dontsov, I. A. *Samovospitanie lichnosti: Filosofsko-eticheskie problemy* [Self-training of the individual: philosophical and ethical problems]. Moscow: Politizdat, 1984.

Dostoyevsky, Fyodor. *The Brothers Karamazov*. Trans. Constance Garnett. New York: Modern Library, 1960.

———. *Sobranie sochinenii* [Collected works]. Ed. G. M. Fridlender, M. B. Khrapchenko. Moscow: Pravda, 1984.

Dreyfus, Hubert L. *Being-in-the-World: A Commentary on Heidegger's Being and Time*. Cambridge, Mass.: MIT Press, 1991.

———. "Foucault and Heidegger on the Ordering of Things." In *Michel Foucault Philosopher*, trans. Timothy J. Armstrong. New York: Routledge, 1992.

Dreyfus, Hubert L., and Paul Rabinow. *Michel Foucault: Beyond Structuralism and Hermeneutics*. 2d ed. Chicago: University of Chicago Press, 1983.

———. "What is Maturity? Habermas and Foucault on 'What is Enlightenment?'" In *Foucault: A Critical Reader*, ed. David Couzens Hoy. Oxford: Blackwell, 1986.

Dubner P., and M. Kozyrev. *Kollektivy i kommuny v bor'be za kommunisti-cheskie formy truda* [*Kollektivy* and communes in the struggle for Communist forms of labor]. Moscow-Leningrad, 1930.

Dunham, Vera. *In Stalin's Time: Middleclass Values in Soviet Fiction.* Cambridge: Cambridge University Press, 1976.

Elagin, N. *Predpolagaemaia reforma tserkovnogo suda* [Proposed reform of the church court]. 2 vols. St. Petersburg, 1873.

Eliade, Mircea. *The Sacred and the Profane.* New York: Viking, 1958.

———, ed. *The Encyclopedia of Religion.* New York: Macmillan, 1987.

Elkonin, D. B. "Detskie kollektivy" [Children's collectives]. In *Uchebnik pedologii dlia pedologicheskikh tekhnikumov,* chast 2: *Pedologiia shkolnogo vozrasta* [Handbook of pedology for the students of pedological schools, part 2: pedology of the school age], ed. M. N. Shardakov. Leningrad, 1931.

Engelstein, Laura. "Combined Underdevelopment: Discipline and the Law in Imperial and Soviet Russia." *American Historical Review* 98 (April 1993).

Erickson, John H. "Penitential Discipline in the Orthodox Canonical Tradition." In *The Challenge of Our Past: Studies in Orthodox Canon Law and Church History.* Crestwood, N.Y.: St. Vladimir's Seminary Press, 1991.

Evlogii, Archimandrit. *O sviatitele Tikhone Zadonskom i ego tvoreniiakh* [On St. Tikhon Zadonsky and his works]. Moscow, 1898.

Fainsod, Merle. *Smolensk Under Soviet Rule.* Cambridge, Mass.: Harvard University Press, 1958.

Fateev, P. S. *E. M. Iaroslavsky.* Moscow, 1980.

Fedotov, Georgii. *Sviatye Drevnei Rusi* [Saints of ancient Russia]. Moscow: Moskovskii rabochii, 1990. Also published in an authorized amended version as *The Russian Religious Mind,* 2 vols. (Belmont, Mass.: Nordland, 1975).

Festinger, Leon, Stanley Schachter, and Kurt Back. *Social Pressures in Informal Groups: A Study of Human Factors in Housing.* New York: Harper and Brothers, 1950.

Field, Daniel. *Rebels in the Name of Tsar.* Boston: Unwin Hyman, 1989.

Filonovich, Iu. "Eto ne chastnoe delo" [This is not a private affair]. *Komsomolskaia Pravda,* September 20, 1950.

Filtzer, Donald. *Soviet Workers and De-Stalinization: The Consolidation of the Modern System of Soviet Production Relations, 1953–64.* Cambridge: Cambridge University Press, 1992.

Fitzpatrick, Sheila. "Ascribing Class: The Construction of Social Identity in Soviet Russia." *Journal of Modern History* 65, no. 4 (1993).

———. "The Civil War as a Formative Experience." In *Bolshevik Culture: Experiment and Order in the Russian Revolution,* ed. Abbott Gleason, Peter Kenez, and Richard Stites. Bloomington: Indiana University Press, 1985.

———. *The Commissariat of Enlightenment: Soviet Organization of Education and the Arts Under Lunacharsky, October 1917–1921.* Cambridge: Cambridge University Press, 1970.

————. *The Cultural Front.* Ithaca: Cornell University Press, 1992.

————. "The Problems of Class Identity in NEP Society." In *Russia in the Era of NEP,* ed. Sheila Fitzpatrick et al. Bloomington: Indiana University Press, 1991.

————. *Stalin's Peasants: Resistance and Survival in the Russian Village After Collectivization.* New York: Oxford University Press, 1994.

————. "Two Faces of Anastasia: Narratives and Counter-Narratives of Identity in Stalinist Everyday Life." In *Everyday Subjects,* ed. Christina Kiaer and Eric Naiman. Cornell University Press, forthcoming.

Fitzpatrick, Sheila, and Robert Gellately, eds. *Accusatory Practices: Denunciation in Modern European History, 1789–1989.* Chicago: University of Chicago Press, 1997.

Florence, Maurice. "Foucault, Michel, 1926 –." In *The Cambridge Companion to Foucault,* ed. Gary Gutting. Cambridge: Cambridge University Press, 1994.

Floria, B. N. "Ispovednye formuly o vzaimootnosheniiakh tserkvi i gosudarstva v Rossii XVI–XVII vv." [Relations between church and state through confessional formulae: Russia, the XVI–XVII centuries]. In *Odysseus: Man in History, 1992.* Moscow, 1994.

Florovsky, Georges. *Puti russkago bogoslovia* [Ways of Russian theology]. Paris: YMCA-Press, 1937.

Flynn, Thomas. "Foucault's Mapping of History." In *The Cambridge Companion to Foucault,* ed. Gary Gutting. Cambridge: Cambridge University Press, 1994.

Foucault, Michel. "About the Beginning of the Hermeneutic of the Self." *Political Theory* 21, no. 2 (May 1993).

————. *The Archaeology of Knowledge,* trans. A. M. Sheridan Smith. New York: Pantheon, 1972.

————. "The Concern for Truth." In *Michel Foucault: Politics, Philosophy, Culture. Interviews and Other Writings, 1977–1984,* ed. Lawrence D. Kritzman. New York: Routledge, 1988.

————. "The Confession of the Flesh." In *Power/Knowledge: Selected Interviews and Other Writings 1972–77,* ed. Colin Gordon. New York: Pantheon, 1980.

————. *Discipline and Punish: The Birth of the Prison,* trans. Alan Sheridan. New York: Pantheon, 1978.

————. The History of Sexuality. Vol. 1, *An Introduction.* Trans. Robert Hurley. New York: Pantheon, 1978.

————. Vol. 2, *The Use of Pleasure.* Trans. Robert Hurley. New York: Pantheon, 1985.

————. Vol. 3, *The Care of the Self.* Trans. Robert Hurley. New York: Pantheon, 1986.

————. "Nietzsche, Genealogy, History." In *Language, Counter-Memory, Practice,* ed. Daniel Bouchard. Ithaca: Cornell University Press, 1977.

————. *The Order of Things: An Archaeology of the Human Sciences.* New York: Pantheon, 1971.

————. "Polemics, Politics, and Problemizations." In *The Foucault Reader,* ed. Paul Rabinow. New York: Pantheon, 1984.

————. "The Politics of Crime." *Partisan Review* 3 (1976).

————. "Questions of Method." In *The Foucault Effect: Studies in Governmentality,* ed. Graham Burchell et al. Chicago: University of Chicago Press, 1991.

————. "Why Study Power: The Question of the Subject." Afterword to *Michel Foucault: Beyond Structuralism and Hermeneutics,* by Hubert L. Dreyfus and Paul Rabinow. 2d ed. Chicago: University of Chicago Press, 1983.

Frank, S. L. *Dukhovnye osnovy obshchestva: Vvedenie v sotsial'nuiu filosofiiu* [Spiritual foundations of society: introduction to social philosophy]. Moscow: Respublika,1992.

Freeze, Gregory L. *The Parish Clergy in Nineteenth-Century Russia: Crisis, Reform, Counter-reform.* Princeton: Princeton University Press, 1983.

————. *The Russian Levites: Parish Clergy in the Eighteenth Century.* Cambridge, Mass.: Harvard University Press, 1979.

Friedgut, Theodore H. *Political Participation in the USSR.* Princeton: Princeton University Press, 1979.

Gak, G. M. *Dialektika kollektivnosti i individual'nosti* [A dialectics of collectivity and individuality]. Moscow, 1967.

————. *Sotsialisticheskoe obshchestvo i lichnost'* [Socialist society and the individual]. Moscow: Pravda, 1945.

Gataulin, R. V., and G. Z. Safin. *Za vysokoe zvanie kommunista: Iz opyta raboty partiinykh komissii Tatarskoi ASSR* [For the high title of Communist: the work of Party Commissions of the Tartar Autonomous Republic]. Kazan', 1980.

Gerasimova, Katerina. "Zhil'e kak sotsial'nyi institut: Leningrad, 1918–1941" [Habitat as a social institute: Leningrad, 1918–1941]. Master's thesis, Faculty of Political Sciences and Sociology, European University at St. Petersburg, 1997.

Geroi Oktiabria [Heroes of the October Revolution]. Moscow, 1967.

Getty, J. Arch. *Origins of the Great Purges: The Soviet Communist Party Reconsidered, 1933–1938.* Cambridge: Cambridge University Press, 1985.

Getty, J. Arch, and Roberta T. Manning, eds. *Stalinist Terror: New Perspectives.* Cambridge: Cambridge University Press, 1993.

Gibian, George, ed. *Russia's Lost Literature of the Absurd: A Literary Discovery.* New York: Norton, 1971.

Gier, Nicholas F. *Wittgenstein and Phenomenology: A Comparative Study of the Later Wittgenstein, Husserl, Heidegger, and Merleau-Ponty.* Albany, N.Y.: State University of New York Press, 1981.

Ginzburg, Lidia. *O psikhologicheskoi proze.* Leningrad, 1977. Also published as *On Psychological Prose*, trans. and ed. Judson Rosengrant (Princeton: Princeton University Press, 1991).

Goffman, Erving. *Frame Analysis: An Essay on the Organization of Experience*. New York: Harper and Row, 1974.

———. *The Presentation of Self in Everyday Life*. Garden City, N.Y.: Doubleday, 1959.

Golikova, N. B. *Politicheskie protsessy pri Petre I* [Political trials during the reign of Peter the Great]. Moscow, 1957.

Golubinsky, E. E. *Istoriia russkoi tserkvi* [History of the Russian church]. 2 vols. Moscow, 1900–1912.

Gorodetzky, Nadejda. *Saint Tikhon Zadonsky: Inspirer of Dostoevsky*. London: SPCK, 1951.

Gralia, Ieronim. *Ivan Mikhailovich Viskovaty: kar'era gosudarstvennogo deiatelia v Rossii XVI v.* [Viskovaty: career of a state official in 16th-century Russia]. Moscow, 1994.

Greenblatt, Stephen. *Renaissance Self-Fashioning: From More to Shakespeare*. Chicago: University of Chicago Press, 1980.

Grigoriev, B. G. *Boets i letopisets revolutsii* [The warrior and chronicler of the revolution]. Moscow, 1960.

Gross, Jan T. "Social Control Under Totalitarianism." In *Toward a General Theory of Social Control*, ed. D. Black. Vol. 2. New York: Academic Press, 1984.

Gruzberg, A. A. *Chastotnyi slovar' russkogo iazyka vtoroi poloviny XVI— nachala XVII veka* [Frequency dictionary of the Russian language, late 16th–early 17th centuries]. Perm, 1974.

Guseinov, A. A., M. V. Iskrov, and R. V. Petropavlovsky, eds. *Partiinaia etika: Dokumenty i materialy diskussii dvadtsatykh godov* [Party ethics: documents and materials of Party discussions of the 1920s]. Moscow: Politizdat, 1989.

Gutting, Gary. "Michel Foucault: A User's Manual." Introduction to *The Cambridge Companion to Foucault*, ed. Gary Gutting. Cambridge: Cambridge University Press, 1994.

———, ed. *The Cambridge Companion to Foucault*. Cambridge: Cambridge University Press, 1994.

Habermas, Jürgen. *The Structural Transformation of the Public Sphere*. Cambridge, Mass.: MIT Press, 1989.

Haimson, Leopold. *The Russian Marxists and the Origins of Bolshevism*. Cambridge, Mass.: Harvard University Press, 1955.

———. "The Solitary Hero and the Philistines: A Note on the Heritage of the Stalin Era." In *The Russian Intelligentsia*, ed. Richard Pipes. New York: Columbia University Press, 1962.

Hall, Edward T. *The Silent Language*. Garden City, N.Y.: Doubleday, 1959.

Halliburton, John. "'A Godly Discipline': Penance in Early Church." In *Confession and Absolution*, ed. Martin Dudley and Geoffrey Rowell. London: SPCK, 1990.

Haney, Jack V. *From Italy to Muscovy: The Life and Works of Maxim the Greek*. Munich: W. Fink, 1973.

Havelock, Eric. *Preface to Plato*. Cambridge, Mass.: Harvard University Press, 1962.

Hebdige, Dick. *Subculture: The Meaning of Style*. London: Methuen, 1979.

Heidegger, Martin. "On the Essence of Truth." In *Existence and Being*, trans. R. F. C. Hull and Alan Crick. London: Vision, 1959.

Hodnett, Grey. "Khrushchev and Party-State Control." In *Politics in the Soviet Union: 7 Cases*, ed. Alexander Dallin and Alan F. Westin. New York: Harcourt, Brace and World, 1966.

Hoy, David Couzens. "Power, Repression, Progress: Foucault, Lukes, and the Frankfurt School." In *Foucault: A Critical Reader*, ed. David Couzens Hoy. Oxford: Blackwell, 1986.

Iakovlev, L. S. *Stanovlenie lichnosti: opyt, problemy (60e–80e gody)* [Development of the person: experience, problems (1960s–80s)]. Saratov: Saratov University Press, 1992.

Ianyshev, I. L. *Pravoslavno-khristianskoe uchenie o nravstvennosti* [Orthodox Christian teaching on morals]. 2d ed. St. Petersburg, 1906.

Iaroslavsky, Emelian. *Chego partiia trebuet ot kommunista* [What the Party demands from a Communist]. 3d ed. Moscow, 1936.

———. *Chego partiia trebuet ot kommunistov v dni otechestvennoi voiny* [What the Party demands from Communists in the days of the patriotic war]. Moscow, 1945.

———. *Kakim dolzhen byt' kommunist* [What the Communist ought to be]. 3d ed. Moscow, 1926.

———. "O partetike: Doklad na II Plenume TsKK RKP(b)" [On Party ethics: report to the 2d CCC plenum (October 5, 1924)]. In *Partiinaia etika: Dokumenty i materialy diskussii dvadtsatykh godov*, ed. A. A. Guseinov et al. Moscow: Politizdat, 1989.

———. "O partetike: Predlozheniia prezidiuma TsKK II Plenumu TsKK 3 oktiabria 1924 g." [On Party ethics: proposals of the CCC presidium to the 2d CCC plenum, October 3, 1924]. In *Partiinaia etika: Dokumenty i materialy diskussii dvadtsatykh godov*, ed. A. A. Guseinov et al. Moscow: Politizdat, 1989.

———. *Rabota TsKK VKP(b): Doklad, zakliuchitelnoe slovo i rezoliutsii po dokladu XVII Moskovskoi gubpartkonferentsii* [Work of the CCC: report, concluding remarks, and resolutions on the 17th Moscow regional Party conference report]. Moscow-Leningrad, 1929.

———. *Za bolshevistskuiu proverku i chistku partii* [Bolshevik verification and purging of Party ranks]. Moscow, 1933.

———, ed. *Kak provodit' chistku partii* [How to conduct the Party purge]. Moscow, 1929.

Iaroslavsky, Emelian et al., eds. *O bor'be s naslediem proshlogo (p'anstvo i religioznye predrassudki sredi chlenov partii)* [Fighting the residues of the past (alcoholism and religious prejudices among Party members)]. Moscow: TsKK, 1925.

Ikonnikov, S. N. *Sozdanie i deiatel'nost' ob"edinennykh organov TsKK-RKI v 1923–1934 gg.* [Creation and activities of the CCC-WPI in 1923–34]. Moscow: Nauka, 1971.

Il'enko, S. G., and M. K. Maksimova. "K istorii obschestvenno-politicheskoi leksiki Sovetskogo perioda" [Toward the history of the social and political lexicon of the Soviet period]. *Uchenye Zapiski LGPI* [Learned works of the Leningrad Pedagogical Institute] 165 (1958).

Ingulov, S. *Samokritika i praktika ee provedeniia* [Self-criticism and the practice of its implementation]. Moscow: Gosizdat, 1928.

———. *Samokritika v deistvii* [Self-criticism in action]. Moscow-Leningrad: Gosizdat, 1930.

Inkeles, Alex. "Modal Personality and Adjustment to the Soviet Sociopolitical System (1958)." In *Social Change in Soviet Russia*. Cambridge, Mass.: Harvard University Press, 1968.

Inkeles, Alex, and Raymond A. Bauer. *The Soviet Citizen: Daily Life in a Totalitarian Society*. Cambridge, Mass.: Harvard University Press, 1959.

Inoe skazanie [The other chronicle]. Russkaia istoricheskaia biblioteka [Russian historical library] 13, no. 1. Leningrad, 1925.

Iovchuk, M. T., ed. *Sotsialisticheskoe promyshlennoe predpriiatie-shkola vospitaniia kommunisticheskoi soznatel'nosti* [Socialist industrial enterprise as the training school for the Communist conscience]. Sverdlovsk, 1953.

Ivanov, A. S. *Vizantiiskoe iurodstvo* [Fools for Christ in Byzantium]. Moscow: Mezhdunarodnye otnosheniia, 1994.

Ivanovsky, N. *Rukovodstvo po istorii i oblicheniiu raskola: S prisovokupleniem svedenii o sektakh ratsionalnykh i misticheskikh* [Handbook of history and exposure of the schism: accompanied by information on rationalistic and mystical sects]. Kazan, 1892.

Izotov, Nikita. *Moia zhizn'—moia rabota* [My life—my work]. Kharkov, 1934.

Jambet, Christian. "The Constitution of the Subject and Spiritual Practice." In *Michel Foucault Philosopher*, trans. Timothy J. Armstrong. New York: Routledge, 1992.

Janik, Allan, and Stephen Toulmin. *Wittgenstein's Vienna*. New York: Simon and Schuster, 1973.

Jay, Martin. *Adorno*. Cambridge, Mass.: Harvard University Press, 1984.

Jeremiah. "Otvet liuteranam sv. Ieremii" [St. Jeremiah's response to the Lutherans]. *Khristianskoe chtenie* [Christian reading (St. Petersburg)] 2 (1842).

Johnson, J. J., Jr. "V. P. Aksenov: A Literary Biography." In *Vasiliy Pavlovich Aksenov: A Writer in Quest of Himself*, ed. Edward Mozejko. Columbus, Ohio: Slavica, 1986.

Joseph (Volotsky). "Dukhovnaia Gramota prepodobnogo Iosifa" [Spiritual

Statute of St. Joseph]. *Velikie Chetii Minei,* September 1–13,. St. Petersburg, 1868.

Jowitt, Kenneth. *New World Disorder: The Leninist Extinction.* Berkeley: University of California Press, 1992.

Juviler, Peter H. *Revolutionary Law and Order: Politics and Social Change in the USSR.* New York: Free Press, 1976.

K proverke, peresmotru i ochistke partii [Toward the checking, screening, and purging of the Party]. Irbit, 1921.

Kalistratov, Iu. *Za udarnyi proizvodstvennyi kollektiv* [For the shock production collective]. Moscow, 1930.

Kasatkin, A. A. "Novye slova ruskogo proiskhozhdeniia v italianskom iazyke" [New words of Russian origin in the Italian language]. *Uchenye zapiski LGU* [Learned works of Leningrad University] 161 (1952).

Kasianova, Lidia. *O russkom natsional'nom kharaktere* [On Russian national character]. Moscow, 1993.

Kassof, Allen. *The Soviet Youth Program: Regimentation and Rebellion.* Cambridge, Mass.: Harvard University Press, 1965.

Kharkhordin, Oleg. "The Corporate Ethic, the Ethic of *Samostoiatelnost'*, and the Spirit of Capitalism: Reflections on Market-Building in Post-Soviet Russia." *International Sociology* 9, no. 4 (December 1994).

———. "Reveal and Dissimulate: A Genealogy of Private Life in Soviet Russia." In *Public and Private in Thought and Practice,* ed. Jeff Weintraub and Krishan Kumar. Chicago: University of Chicago Press, 1996.

Khomiakov, A. A. *Kritika i samokritika v deiatel'nosti partiinykh organizatsii* [Criticism and self-criticism in the activity of party organizations]. Moscow, 1984.

Khrushchev, Nikita. *Doklad XIX s"ezdu partii ob izmeneniiakh v ustave KPSS* [Report to the 19th Party Congress on changes in the CPSU statute]. Moscow: Gospolitizdat, 1952.

———. *Stroitel'stvo kommunizma* [Building communism]. Vol. 7. Moscow, 1964.

Klibanov, A. I. *History of Religious Sectarianism in Russia (1860s–1917).* Oxford: Pergamon Press, 1982.

Kollektiv Severo-Donetskoi v borbe s zimnei stikhiei [North Donetsk Railroad collective in the struggle with winter]. Moscow, 1940.

Kolomiets, V. P. *Stanovlenie individual'nosti: sotsiologicheskii aspekt* [Development of individuality: sociological aspects]. Moscow: Moscow University, 1993.

Kon, I. S. *Druzhba: etiko-psikhologicheskii ocherk* [Friendship: an essay in ethics and psychology]. 2d ed. Moscow: Politizdat, 1987.

———. *Sotsiologiia lichnosti* [Sociology of personality]. Moscow: Politizdat, 1967.

———, ed. *Slovar' po etike* [Dictionary of ethics]. 3d ed. Moscow: Politizdat, 1975.

Konnikova, T. E. *Organizatsiia kollektiva uchashchikhsia v shkole* [Organizing the collective of pupils in school]. Moscow: Russian Academy of Pedagogical Sciences, 1957.

Kosher, Rudy. "Foucault and Social History." *American Historical Review* 98 (April 1993).

Kostina, M. D. "Organizatsiia i vospitanie uchashchikhsia pervykh i vtorykh klassov" [Organizing and training of 1st- and 2d-year pupils]. *Izvestiia Akademii Pedagogicheskikh Nauk* [Academy of Pedagogical Sciences reports] 94 (1957).

Kotkin, Stephen. *Magnetic Mountain: Stalinism as Civilization*. Berkeley: University of California Press, 1995.

Kovalev, A. G. *Psikhologiia lichnosti* [Psychology of personality]. 3d ed. Moscow, 1970.

Kovalev, A. T. *Lichnost' vospityvaet sebia* [The individual trains himself]. Moscow: Politizdat, 1983.

———. *Volia i ee vospitanie (v pomoshch' uchiteliu)* [The will and its training (guidance for the teacher)]. Simferopol: Krymizdat, 1949.

Kovalev, A. T., and A. A. Bodalev. *Psikhologiia i pedagogika samovospitaniia* [Psychology and pedagogy of self-training]. Leningrad: Leningrad University, 1958.

Kravchenko, Viktor. *I Chose Freedom*. New York: Scribner's, 1946.

Krupskaia, Nadezhda. *Izbrannye proizvedeniia* [Selected works]. Moscow: Politizdat, 1988.

———. *Pedagogicheskie sochineniia* [Pedagogical works]. 10 vols. Moscow, 1960.

Kruzhkov, V. S. *O proizvedenii I. V. Stalina "Anarkhizm ili sotsializm?"* [On Stalin's work "Anarchism or Socialism?"]. Moscow: Znanie, 1952.

Kurakin, A. T., H. J. Liimets, and L. I. Novikova. *Kollektiv i lichnost' shkol'nika* [The collective and the personality of the pupil]. Tallin, 1981. 2 issues.

Kuromiya, Hiroaki. *Stalin's Industrial Revolution: Politics and Workers, 1928–1932*. Cambridge: Cambridge University Press, 1988.

———. "Worker's Artels." In *Russia in the Era of NEP*, ed. Sheila Fitzpatrick et al. Bloomington: Indiana University Press, 1991.

Kuznetsov, Felix. "K zrelosti: Konets chetvertogo pokoleniia" [Toward maturity: the end of the fourth generation]. *Iunost'* [Youth] 11 (November 1967).

———. *Kakim byt'?: literatura i nravstvennoe vospitanie lichnosti* [Whom to be?: literature and moral education of the individual]. Moscow: Sovetskii pisatel', 1962.

Laitin, David D. *Politics, Language, and Thought: The Somali Experience*. Chicago: University of Chicago Press, 1977.

Lane, Christel. *The Rites of the Rulers: Ritual in Industrial Society—The Soviet Case*. Cambridge: Cambridge University Press, 1981.

Larin, Iurii. *Stroitel'stvo sotsializma i kollektivizatsiia byta* [Socialist construction and the collectivization of everyday life]. Leningrad, 1930.

Lenin, V. I. *Polnoe sobranie sochinenii* [Complete works]. 55 vols. 5th ed. Moscow: Gospolitizdat, 1967–70.
———. "What Is to Be Done?" (1902). In *Collected Works.* Vol. 4. Moscow: Progress, 1964.
Leninskii zachet [The Lenin Pass]. Moscow: Molodaia Gvardiia, 1977.
Leninskii zachet v sisteme kommunisticheskogo vospitaniia molodezhi [The Lenin Pass in the system of the Communist training of youth]. Leningrad, 1980.
Leonov, M. A. *Kritika i samokritika—dialekticheskaia zakonomernost' razvitiia sovetskogo obshchestva* [Criticism and self-criticism—the dialectical law of the development of Soviet society]. Moscow: Pravda, 1948.
Levada, Iurii, ed. *Prostoi sovetskii chelovek* [A common Soviet individual]. Moscow, 1993.
Levin, Eve. *Sex and Society in the World of Orthodox Slavs, 900–1700.* Ithaca: Cornell University Press, 1989.
Levina, M. M., ed. *Druzhinniku: Sbornik zakonodatelnykh i inykh materialov* [To a patrolman. a collection of legal and other documents]. Moscow, 1963.
Lewin, Moshe. *The Gorbachev Phenomenon.* Berkeley: University of California Press, 1990.
———. *Russian Peasants and Soviet Power.* London: Allen and Unwin, 1968.
Liadov, M. N. "Voprosy byta" (1925) [Problems of everyday life]. In *Partiiniaia etika: Dokumenty i materialy diskussii dvadtsatykh godov,* ed. A. A. Guseinov et al. Moscow: Politizdat, 1989.
Likhachev, Dmitrii. "Stil' proizvedenii Groznogo i stil' proizvedenii Kurbskogo" [Styles of Ivan the Terrible and Kurbsky]. In *Perepiska Ivana Groznogo s Andreem Kurbskim* [Correspondence between Ivan the Terrible and Andrei Kurbsky]. Moscow-Leningrad: Akademiia Nauk SSSR, 1979.
Lukes, Steven. *Individualism.* London: Blackwell, 1973.
Lukovtsev, V. S. "Formirovanie novogo tipa lichnosti v usloviiakh perekhoda narodnostei severa ot patriarkhal'no-rodovogo stroiia k sotsializmu" [Formation of the new type of individual during the northern people's transition from patriarchal-kinship mode to socialism]. Abstract, dissertation, Higher Party School of the Central Committee, Moscow, 1975.
Lunacharsky, Anatolii. *Istoriia zapadno-evropeiskoi literatury v ee vazhneishikh momentakh* [History of Western European literature in its most important moments]. Vol. 1. Moscow, n.d.
———. "Osnovnye printsipy edinoi trudovoi shkoly" [Basic principles of united labor school]. In *Direktivy VKP (b) i postanovleniia sovetskogo pravitel'stva o narodnom obrazovanii: sbornik dokumentov za 1917–1947 gg.* [Party and government decisions on education: a collection of documents for 1917–1947], ed. N. I. Bodyrev. Vol. 2. Moscow: APN RSFSR, 1947.
———. *P'esy* [Plays]. Moscow: Iskusstvo, 1963.

———. *Religiia i sotsialism*. 2 vols. St. Petersburg: Shipovnik, 1908–10.

———. *Vospitanie novogo cheloveka* [Raising a new man]. Leningrad, 1928.

Lur'e, Ia. S. *Ideologicheskaia bor'ba v russkoi publitsistike kontsa XV–nachala XVI veka* [Ideological struggle in Russian literature, 15th–16th centuries]. Leningrad: Akademiia Nauk SSSR, 1960.

———. "Iosif Volotsky kak publitsist i obshchestvennyi deiatel'" [St. Joseph Volotsky as a moralist and public figure]. In *Poslaniia Iosifa Volotzkogo* [Epistles of St. Joseph Volotsky]. Moscow-Leningrad: Akademiia Nauk SSSR, 1959.

———. "Kratkaia redaktsiia Ustava Iosifa Volotskogo—pamiatnik ideologii rannego iosiflianstva" [Short version of Joseph Volotsky's statute—a monument of the ideology of early Josephites]. *Trudy otdeleniia drevne-russkoi literatury* [Works of the section on ancient Russian literature (Leningrad)] 12 (1956).

Machado, Roberto. "Archaeology and Epistemology." In *Michel Foucault Philosopher*, trans. Timothy J. Armstrong. New York: Routledge, 1992.

Makarenko, Anton. *Sochineniia* [Works]. 7 vols. Moscow: Academy of Pedagogical Sciences of RSFSR, 1950–52.

Manchester, Laurie. "The Secularization of the Search for Salvation: The Self-Fashioning of Orthodox Clergymen's Sons in Late Imperial Russia." *Slavic Review* 57, no. 1 (spring 1998).

Mastrantonis, George. *Augsburg and Constantinople*. Brookline, Mass.: Holy Cross Orthodox Press, 1982.

Mauss, Marcel. "The Category of the Person." In *The Category of the Person*, ed. M. Carrithers et al. Cambridge: Cambridge University Press, 1985.

Meerson-Aksenov, Michael, and Boris Shragin, eds. *The Political, Social, and Religious Thought of Russian Samizdat*. Belmont, Mass.: Nordland, 1977.

Mel'kumov, A., ed. *Voprosy partiinogo stroitel'stva: Materialy i dokumenty* [Problems of party building: materials and documents]. Moscow: Gosizdat, 1927.

Mel'nikova, N. A. "K voprosu o stanovlenii i razvitii termina *lichnost'* v sovetskoi pedagogicheskoi publitsistike" [On the development of the term *Lichnost'* in Soviet pedagogical literature]. *Voprosy prikladnoi lingvistiki* [Problems of applied linguistics (Dnepropetrovsk University)] 2 (1970).

Mezentsev, S. P. *Kritika uchit, pomogaet, vospityvaet* [Criticism teaches, helps, trains]. Moscow, 1976.

Miliukov, Pavel. *Ocherki po istorii russkoi kul'tury*. Vol. 2: *Tserkov' i shkola* [Sketches on the history of Russian culture. Vol. 2, Church and school]. Moscow, 1897. Translated as *Outlines of Russian Culture* (Philadelphia: University of Pennsylvania Press, 1942).

Misler, Nicoletta, and John E. Bowlt, eds. *Pavel Filonov: A Hero and His Fate, Collected Writings on Art and Revolution, 1914–1940*. Austin, Tex.: Silvergirl, 1983.

Momov, V., and A. I. Kochetov. *Samovospitanie, samoutverzhdenie, samo-*

kontrol' [Self-training, self-assertion, self-control]. Part of the series entitled *To the Young About Ethics.* Moscow, 1975.

Morris, Colin. *The Discovery of the Individual, 1050–1200.* New York: Harper and Row, 1973.

Moskalenko, I. M. *TsKK v bor'be za edinstvo i chistotu partiinykh riadov* [CCC in the struggle for the unity and purity of Party ranks]. Moscow: Politizdat, 1973.

Naiman, Eric. *Sex in Public: The Incarnation of Early Soviet Ideology.* Princeton: Princeton University Press, 1997.

Nietzsche, Friedrich. "On the Genealogy of Morals." In *On the Genealogy of Morals* and *Ecce Homo*, ed. W. Kaufmann. New York: Vintage, 1967.

O chistke partii [On the Party purge]. Moscow: Partizdat, 1933.

O chistke partii. Saratov, 1935.

"O publichnom pokaianii" [On public penance]. *Pravoslavnyi Sobesednik* [Orthodox conversant] 5, no. 1 (January–April 1868).

Orlov, A., ed. *Domostroi — po konshinskomu spisku* [A book of household governance]. Moscow, 1908.

Osipov, Yu., and F. Pristavakin. *Komsomol'skii patrul'* [Komsomol patrol]. 2d ed. Leningrad: Znanie, 1959.

Ostrovsky, Nikolai. "Mysli o samovospitanii" [Thoughts on self-training]. *Iunost'* 3 (1955).

Paden, William E. "Theaters of Humility and Suspicion: Desert Saints and New England Puritans." In *Technologies of the Self: A Seminar with Michel Foucault*, ed. Luther H. Martin, Huck Gutman, Patrick H. Hutton. Amherst: University of Massachusetts Press, 1988.

Panasenko, G. V., and Iu. N. Belokopytov. "Formirovanie poniatiia kollektiva v filosofii i drugikh obshchestvennykh naukakh" [Formation of the concept of the collective in philosophy and other social sciences]. Moscow University, 1985. Institute of Scientific information on Social Sciences ms 20323, Russian Academy of Sciences.

Paperno, Irina. *Chernyshevsky and the Age of Realism: A Study in the Semiotics of Behavior.* Stanford: Stanford University Press, 1988.

Pelikan, Jaroslav. *The Spirit of Eastern Christendom (600–1700).* Chicago: University of Chicago Press, 1974.

Petrovsky, A. V. *Lichnost', deiatel'nost', kollektiv* [The individual, the act, the collective]. Moscow: Politizdat, 1982.

———, ed. *K voprosu o diagnostike lichnosti v gruppe* [On diagnosing an individual within a group]. Moscow, 1973.

———. *Psikhologicheskaia teoriia kollektiva* [Psychological theory of the collective]. Moscow: Pedagogika,1979.

Petrovsky, V. A. "Emotsinal'naia identifikatsiia v gruppe i sposob ee vyiavleniia" [Emotional identification in a group and methods of its registration]. In *K voprosu o diagnostike lichnosti v gruppe*, ed. A. V. Petrovsky. Moscow, 1973.

Petrushevskaia, Liudmila. "Svoi krug" [Our circle]. In *Bal poslednego che-loveka* [The last man's ball]. Moscow: Lokid, 1996.

Pisarev, Dmitrii. "Realisty." In *Sobranie sochinenii* [Collected works]. Vol. 3. Moscow, 1956.

"Piskarevsky letopisets'" [Piskarevsky chronicler]. In *Materialy po istorii SSSR*. Vol. 2, *Dokumenty po istorii XV–XVII vekov* [Materials on the history of the USSR, vol. 2, Documents of 15th–17th centuries]. Moscow, 1955.

Pitkin, Hanna. *Wittgenstein and Justice: On the Significance of Ludwig Wittgenstein for Social and Political Thought.* Berkeley: University of California Press, 1972.

Pizzorno, Alessandro. "Foucault and the Liberal View of the Individual." In *Michel Foucault Philosopher*, trans. Timothy J. Armstrong. New York: Routledge, 1992.

Platonov, K. K. "Obshchie problemy teorii grupp i kollektivov" [General problems of the theory of groups and *kollektivy*]. In *Kollektiv i lichnost'*, ed. K. K. Platonov. Moscow: Nauka, 1975.

——— *Struktura i razvitie lichnosti* [Structure and development of personality]. Moscow, 1986.

———, ed. *Kollektiv i lichnost'* [The collective and the individual]. Moscow: Nauka, 1975.

Pol'tov, M. "Partiinyi sud" [Party court]. *Sbornik materialov Peterburgskogo komiteta RKP, vypusk 1: ianvar'–iiul'* [A collection of the documents of the Petersburg Party committee] 1 (January–July 1920).

Polanyi, Michael. *Personal Knowledge.* Chicago: University of Chicago Press, 1958.

"Polozhenie o KPGK" [KPGK statute]. In *Polozhenie ob organakh partgoskontrolia: gruppakh i postakh sodeistviia, "Komsomol'skom prozhektore* [Statutes of the bodies of Party-state control: "groups of support" and "the Komsomol searchlight"]. Moscow: Politizdat, 1964.

Pomerantsev, V. *Tovarishcheskie sudy v kolkhozakh* [Comrades' courts in the collective farms]. 2d ed. Saratov, 1931.

Ponomarev, V. *Nas vyrastil Stalin* [We were brought up by Stalin]. Sverdlovsk, 1951.

Popov, Ardalion. *Sud i nakazaniia za prestupleniia protiv very i nravstvennosti po russkomu pravu* [Court procedure and punishment for crimes against faith and morals in Russian law]. Kazan, 1904.

Poselianin, Efim. *Podvizhniki v russkoi tserkvi v deviatnadtsatom veke* [Popular heroes of the Russian church in the 19th century]. Moscow, 1901.

Poslaniia Ivana Groznogo [Epistles of Ivan the Terrible]. Moscow-Leningrad: Akademiia Nauk SSSR, 1951.

Pospelov, P. N. *Bol'shevistskaia samokritika—osnova partiinogo deistviia* [Bolshevist self-criticism—the foundation of party action]. Moscow: Partizdat, 1937.

Rajchman, John. "Foucault: the Ethic and the Work." In *Michel Foucault Philosopher*, trans. Timothy J. Armstrong. New York: Routledge, 1992.

Ramazanov, V. M. *Vnoshu predlozhenie: O kritike i samokritike v rabote partiinykh organizatsii* [Making a motion: on criticism and self-criticism in the work of Party organizations]. Rostov-on-Don, 1989.

Ratner, V. I. *Pervichnye organizatsii partii* [Primary Party organizations]. Moscow, 1953.

Ratnikov, V. P. *Kollektiv kak sotsial'naia obshchnost'* [The collective as a social unity]. Moscow, 1978.

Reese, Roger. "The Red Army and the Great Purges." In *Stalinist Terror: New Perspectives,* ed. J. Arch Getty and Roberta T. Manning. Cambridge: Cambridge University Press, 1993.

Rezvitsky, L. I. *Lichnost', individualnost', obshchestvo: Problema individuali-zatsii i ee sotsial'no-filosofskii smysl* [The individual, individuality, society: the problem of individualization and its meaning in social philosophy.]. Moscow, 1984.

Rittersporn, Gabor. *Stalinist Simplifications and Soviet Complications: Social Tensions and Political Conflicts in the USSR, 1933–53.* Philadelphia: Harwood, 1991.

Roberts, Alexander, and James Donaldson, eds. *The Ante-Nicene Fathers: Translations of the Writings of the Fathers Down to A.D. 325.* Grand Rapids, Mich.: Eerdmans, 1951.

Rochlitz, Rainer. "The Aesthetics of Existence: Post-Conventional Morality and the Theory of Power in Michel Foucault." In *Michel Foucault Philosopher,* trans. Timothy J. Armstrong. New York: Routledge, 1992.

Rol' kollektiva RKP pri novoi ekonomicheskoi politike [The role of the collective of the Russian Communist Party during the New Economic Policy]. Petrograd, 1922.

Rosenberg, William G. *Bolshevik Visions: First Phase of the Cultural Revolution in Soviet Russia.* Ann Arbor, Mich.: Ardis, 1984.

Roshchevsky, P. I. *Skvoz' Grozy* [Through the storms]. Sverdlovsk, 1967.

Rowell, Geoffrey. "The Anglican Tradition: From the Reformation to the Oxford Movement." In *Confession and Absolution,* ed. Martin Dudley and Geoffrey Rowell. London: SPCK, 1990.

Ruvinsky, L. I. *Samovospitanie lichnosti* [Self-training of the individual]. Moscow: Mysl', 1984.

Ruvinsky, L. I., and A. E. Solov'eva. *Psikhologiia samovospitaniia* [Psychology of self-training]. Moscow: Prosveshchenie, 1982.

Rybakov, B. A. "Vointstvuiushchie tserkovniki XVI veka" [Militant clerics of the 16th century]. *Antireligioznik* [The anti-religious] 3 (1934).

Ryle, Gilbert. "Knowing How and Knowing That." *Proceedings of the Aristotelian Society* 46 (1945–46).

Sakharov, A. B. *O lichnosti prestupnika i prichinakh prestupnosti v SSSR* [On the personality of the criminal and the causes of crime in the USSR]. Moscow, 1961.

Salisbury, Harrison. *The 900 Days: The Siege of Leningrad.* New York: Harper and Row, 1969.

Samarin, Iu. A. *Vospitanie voli i kharaktera* [Training of the will and character]. Leningrad: Znanie, 1952.

Savitsky, V. M., and N. M. Keiserov. "Razvitie pravovykh form organizatsii i deiatel'nosti tovarishcheskikh sudov" [Development of the legal forms of organization and proceedings of the comrades' courts]. *Sovetskoe gosudarstvo i pravo* [Soviet state and right] 4 (1961).

Sbornik materialov Peterburgskogo komiteta RKP [A collection of the documents of the Petersburg Party committee]. St. Petersburg, 1920.

Schaff, Philip, and Henry Wace, eds. *A Select Library of Nicene and Post-Nicene Fathers*. Grand Rapids, Mich.: Eerdmans, 1954.

Scott, James C. *Weapons of the Weak: Everyday Forms of Peasant Resistance*. New Haven: Yale University Press, 1985.

Searle, John. "The Background." In *Intentionality: An Essay in the Philosophy of Mind*. Cambridge: Cambridge University Press, 1983.

———. "Collective Intentions and Action." In *Intentions in Communication*, ed. Philip R. Cohen, Jerry Morgan, and Martha E. Pollack. Cambridge, Mass.: MIT Press, 1990.

———. *The Construction of Social Reality*. New York: Free Press, 1995.

———. "Literal Meaning." In *Expression and Meaning*. Cambridge: Cambridge University Press, 1979.

Seligman, Adam. *Innerworldly Individualism: Charismatic Community and Its Institutionalization*. New Brunswick, N.J.: Transaction, 1994.

Selishchev, A. *Iazyk revoliutsionnoi epokhi: Iz nabliudenii nad russkim iazykom poslednikh let, 1917–1926* [Language of the revolutionary epoch: some observations on the Russian language of recent years, 1917–1926]. Moscow: Rabotnik prosveshcheniia, 1928.

Semenov, N. *Litso fabrichnykh rabochikh, prozhivaiushchikh v derevniakh, i politprosvetrabota sredi nikh* [Face of factory workers living in villages, and their political education]. Moscow, 1929.

Shchepakin, D. *Obshchestvennyi poriadok v rukakh naroda* [Public order in the hands of the people]. Tula, 1965.

Shishman, Svetozar. *Neskol'ko veselykh i grustnykh istorii o Daniile Kharmse i ego druziiakh* [Several funny and sad stories about Kharms and his friends]. Leningrad, 1991.

Shlapentokh, Vladimir. *Public and Private Life of the Soviet People: Changing Values in Post-Stalin Russia*. Oxford: Oxford University Press, 1989.

Siegelbaum, Lewis H. "Production Collectives and Communes." *Slavic Review* 45, no. 1 (1986).

———. *Stakhanovism an the Politics of Productivity of Productivity in the USSR, 1935–1941*. Cambridge: Cambridge University Press, 1988.

Silver, Allan. "'Two Different Sorts of Commerce'—Friendship and Strangership in Civil Society." In *Public and Private in Thought and Practice: Perspectives on the Grand Dichotomy*, ed. Jeff Weintraub and Krishnan Kumar. Chicago: University of Chicago Press, 1997.

Skobelev, V. P., and L. A. Fink, eds. *Vasilii Aksenov: Literaturnaia sud'ba* [Vasilii Aksenov: literary fate]. Samara: Samara University, 1994.

Slepov, L. *Kritika i samokritika v rabote partiinykh organizatsii* [Criticism and self-criticism in the work of party organizations]. Moscow, 1956.

Slezkine, Yuri. *Arctic Mirrors: Russia and the Small Peoples of the North.* Ithaca: Cornell University Press, 1994.

Slovar' sovremennogo russkogo literaturnogo iazyka [Dictionary of contemporary Russian literary language]. 17 vols. Moscow: Institut russkogo iazyka, 1955–68.

Smidovich, Sofia. "O Korenkovshchine" (1926) [On Korenkovism]. In *Partiinaia etika: Dokumenty i materialy diskussii dvadtsatykh godov,* ed. A. A. Guseinov et al. Moscow: Politizdat, 1989.

Smirnov, G. L. *Sovetskii chelovek: formirovanie sotsialisticheskogo tipa lichnosti.* 3d enlarged ed. Moscow: Politizdat, 1980. Also published as *Soviet Man: The Making of a Socialist Type of Personality,* trans. Robert Daglish (Moscow: Progress, 1973).

Sochineniia kniazia Kurbskogo [Works of Prince Kurbsky]. Russkaia istoricheskaia biblioteka 1, no. 31. St. Petersburg, 1914.

Sokolov, D. D. *Optinskoe starchestvo i ego vliianie na monashestvuiushchikh i mirian* [Elders of Optina Pustyn' and their influence on monasticism and laity]. Kaluga, 1898.

Solts, Aaron. *Dlia chego partii nuzhna samokritika?* [Why does the Party need self-criticism?]. Moscow: Partizdat, 1933.

———. "Doklad Kontrol'noi Komissii na X s"ezde RKP (b)" [CCC report to the 10th Party Congress]. In *Partiiniaia etika: Dokumenty i materialy diskussii dvadtsatykh godov,* ed. A. A. Guseinov et al. Moscow: Politizdat, 1989.

———. "Iz otcheta Tsentral'noi Kontrol'noi Komissii na XI s"ezde RKP(b)" [CCC report to the 11th Party Congress]. In *Partiiniaia etika: Dokumenty i materialy diskussii dvadtsatykh godov,* ed. A. A. Guseinov et al. Moscow: Politizdat, 1989.

———. "K chistke" (1929) [Toward the purge]. In *Kak provodit' chistku partii,* ed. Emelian Iaroslavsky. Moscow, 1929.

———. "O partinoi etike" (1924) [On Party ethics]. In *Partiiniaia etika: Dokumenty i materialy diskussii dvadtsatykh godov,* ed. A. A. Guseinov et al. Moscow: Politizdat, 1989.

———. "Otchet TsKK na X s"ezde RKP(b)" [CCC report to the 10th Party Congress]. In *Partiiniaia etika: Dokumenty i materialy diskussii dvadtsatykh godov,* ed. A. A. Guseinov et al. Moscow: Politizdat, 1989.

Sorokin, Iu. S. *Razvitie slovarnogo sostava russkogo literaturnogo iazyka, 30e–90e goda XIX veka* [Development of the lexical content of Russian literary language, 1830s–90s]. Moscow: Nauka, 1965.

Sreznevsky, I. I. *Materialy dlia slovaria drevne-russkago iazyka po pismennym pamiatnikam* [Materials for the dictionary of the ancient Russian language according to written sources]. St. Petersburg, 1893–1912.

Stalin, I. V. "Doklad na aktive MO o rabote aprel'skogo ob"edinennogo plenuma TsK i TsKK 13 aprelia 1928 g." [Report on the April unified plenum
of the CC and CCC at the meeting of Moscow Party organization's *aktiv*].
In *Lenin i Stalin o partstroitel'stve* [Lenin and Stalin on party building].
Vol. 2. Moscow, 1941.

———. *I. V. Stalin, Sochineniia* [Works]. Ed. Robert H. McNeal. Vols. 1–3
(XIV–XVI). Stanford: Hoover Institute, 1967.

———. "O nedostatkakh partiinoi raboty i merakh likvidatsii trotzkistskikh i
inykh dvurushnikov" [On weaknesses in Party work and measures for the
liquidation of Trotskyites and other double-dealers]. In *I. V. Stalin, Sochineniia*, ed. Robert H. McNeal. Vol. 1 (XIV). Stanford: Hoover Institute,
1967.

———. "Protiv oposhleniia lozunga samokritiki" [Against perverting the
slogan of self-criticism]. In *Lenin i Stalin o partstroitel'stve*. Vol. 2. Moscow, 1941.

———. "Zakliuchitel'noe slovo na Plenume TsK VKP(b) 5 marta 1937 g."
[Concluding remarks at the Central Committee plenum, March 5, 1937].
In *I. V. Stalin, Sochineniia*, ed. Robert H. McNeal. Vol. 1 (XIV). Stanford:
Hoover Institute, 1967.

Stanislavsky, K. S. *Rabota aktera nad soboi* [An actor working on himself].
Moscow: Khudozhestvennaia literatura, 1938. Also published as *An Actor
Prepares*, trans. Elizabeth Reynolds Hapgood (London: Eyre Methuen,
1946).

Starr, Frederick S. *Red and Hot: The Fate of Jazz in the Soviet Union, 1917–
1980*. Oxford: Oxford University Press, 1983.

"The Statute of Grand Prince Iaroslav." In *Reinterpreting Russian History:
Readings 860 – 1860s*, ed. Daniel H. Kaiser and Gary Marker. New York:
Oxford University Press, 1994.

Stites, Richard. *Revolutionary Dreams: Utopian Vision and Experimental Life in the Russian Revolution*. New York: Oxford University Press,
1989.

———. *Russian Popular Culture: Entertainment and Society Since 1900*.
Cambridge: Cambridge University Press, 1992.

Stoglav. Kazan', 1862.

Surov, V. *Svoei respubliki storozha: Budni dobrovol'nykh narodnykh druzhin po okhrane obshchestvennogo poriadka* [Watchmen of their own
republic: everyday work of the people's patrols]. Moscow: Sovetskaia
Rossiia, 1960.

Suvorov, N. S. *K voprosu o tainoi ispovedi i dukhovnikakh v vostochnoi
tserkvi* [On private confession and confessors in the Eastern Church].
Iaroslavl', 1886.

———. *O tserkovnykh nakazaniiakh: Opyt issledovaniia po tserkovnomu
pravu* [On church penalties: an investigative essay on ecclesiastical law].
St. Petersburg, 1876.

————. *Ob"em distsiplinarnogo suda i iurisdiktsii tserkvi v period vselen-skikh soborov* [Scope of disciplinary court and church jurisdiction in the time of the ecumenical councils]. Iaroslavl', 1884.

————. *Uchebnik tserkovnogo prava* [Introduction to ecclesiastical law]. 5th ed. Moscow, 1913.

Taylor, Charles. "Foucault on Freedom and Truth." In *Foucault: A Critical Reader,* ed. David Couzens Hoy. Oxford: Blackwell, 1986.

Tentler, Thomas N. *Sin and Confession on the Eve of the Reformation.* Princeton: Princeton University Press, 1977.

Tertullian. "On Repentance." In *Tvoreniia Tertulliana* [Works of Tertullian]. St. Petersburg, 1847.

Theophanus (Govorov). *Nachertanie khristianskogo nravouchenia* [Outlines of Christian moral teaching]. Moscow, 1891.

Thorniley, Daniel. *The Rise and Fall of the Soviet Rural Communist Party, 1927–39.* London: Macmillan, 1988.

Thurston, Robert. "Reassessing the History of Soviet Workers: Opportunities to Criticize and Participate in Decision-Making." In *New Directions in Soviet History,* ed. Stephen White. Cambridge: Cambridge University Press, 1992.

Tikhon (Zadonsky). *O kontse dobrykh del* [On the goal of good deeds]. St. Petersburg, 1875.

————. *Vnimai sebe* [Attend to yourself]. St. Petersburg, 1894.

Timasheff, Nicholas. *The Great Retreat.* New York: Dutton, 1946.

Tkachevsky, Yu. M. *Otriadnaia sistema v ispravitel'no-trudovykh koloni-iakh* [Detachment system in corrective labor colonies]. Moscow: Moscow State University, 1962.

Toporov, Vladimir. *Sviatost' i sviatye v russkoi dukhovnoi kul'ture.* Vol. 1, *Pervyi vek khristianstva na Rusi* [Sainthood and saints in Russian spiritual culture. Vol. 1, First century of Christianity in Russia]. Moscow: Gnosis, 1995.

Troeltsch, Ernst. *Making of the Soviet System: Essays in the Social History of Interwar Russia.* New York : Pantheon, 1985.

Troitsky, Artemy. *Back in the USSR: The True Story of Rock in Russia.* Boston: Faber and Faber, 1988.

Trotsky, Leon. "Voprosy byta." *Pravda,* August 17, 1923. Translated in *The Problems of Everyday Life* (New York: Monad Press, 1973).

Tucker, Robert C. *Stalin as Revolutionary, 1879–1929: A Study in History and Personality.* New York: Norton, 1973.

Umansky, Ia. N. *Lichnost' v sotsialisticheskom obshchestve* [The individual in socialist society]. Moscow, 1947.

Umansky, Leonid. "Poetapnoe razvitie gruppy kak kollektiva" [Stages of development of a group as the collective]. In *Kollektiv i lichnost',* ed. K. K. Platonov. Moscow: Nauka, 1975.

Umansky, Leonid, A. S. Chernyshev, and B. V. Tarasov. "Senso-motornyi integrator" [Sensory-motor integrator]. *Voprosy psikhologii* [Problems of psychology (Moscow)] 1 (1969).

Unfried, Berthold. "Die Konstituierung des stalinistischen Kaders in *Kritik und Selbst-Kritik.*" *Traverse* 3 (1995).

"Ustav kniazia Iaroslava" [Code of Prince Iaroslav]. In *Rossiskoe zakonodatel'stvo X–XX vekov.* Vol. 1, *Zakonodatel'stvo drevnei Rusi* [Russian laws of the 10th–20 centuries, vol.1, Laws of ancient Russia]. Moscow, 1984.

Vasmer, Max. *Etimologicheskii slovar' russkogo iazyka.* 4 vols. Moscow: Progress, 1986. Originally published as *Russisches etymologisches Worterbuch* (Heidelberg, 1950–58).

Veremeenko, I. I., and V. F. Vorob'ev, eds. *V pomoshch DND: Sbornik normativnykh aktov* [Handbook of the People's patrols. a collection of normative documents]. Moscow: Iuridicheskaia literatura, 1985.

Verkhovskoi, P. V. *Uchrezhdenie dukhovnoi kollegii i dukhovnyi reglament; k voprosu ob otnoshenii tserkvi i gosudarstva v Rossii* [Establishment of the spiritual college and the Spiritual Reglament: on church-state relations in Russia]. 1916. Reprint, Farnborough: Gregg, 1972.

Veselitsky, V. V. *Otvlechennaia leksiksa v russkom literaturnom iazyke XVIII–XIX veka* [Abstract lexicon of Russian literary language, 18th–19th centuries]. Moscow: Nauka, 1972.

———. *Razvitie otvlechennoi leksiki v russkom literaturnom iazyke pervoi treti XIX veka* [Development of the abstract lexicon of Russian literary language in the first third of the 19th century]. Moscow: Nauka, 1964.

Veyne, Paul. "Foucault and the Going Beyond (or the Fulfillment) of Nihilism." In *Michel Foucault Philospher,* trans. Timothy J. Armstrong. New York: Routledge, 1992.

Viktorsky, G. "Samokritika v sisteme sovetskoi demokratii" [Self-criticism in the system of Soviet democracy]. In *Sovetskaia demokratiia,* ed. I. M. Steklov. Moscow: Sovetskoe Stroitel'stvo, 1929.

Vinogradov, V. V. *Istoriia slov* [History of words]. Moscow: Tolk, 1994.

———. "Iz istorii slova *lichnost'* v russkom iazyke do serediny XIX veka" [On the history of the word *Lichnost'* in Russian before the mid-19th century]. *Doklady i soobshcheniia filologicheskogo fakulteta MGU* [Philological Department of Moscow University notes] 1 (1946).

Vinogradova, M. D. "Voprosy oranizatsii obshchego obrazovaniia v shkole kommuny im. FED" [Problems of educational organization in the Dzerzhinsky commune school]. *Izvestiia Akademii Pedagogicheskikh Nauk RSFRSR* [Reports of the Academy of Pedagogical Sciences of the RSFSR] 102 (1959).

Viola, Lynn. "The Second Coming: Class Enemies in the Soviet Countryside, 1927–35." In *Stalinist Terror: New Perspectives,* ed. J. Arch Getty and Roberta T. Manning. Cambridge: Cambridge University Press, 1993.

Vogel, Ezra. *Canton Under the Communist Rule.* Cambridge, Mass.: Harvard University Press, 1969.

Volkogonov, Dmitrii. *Fenomen geroizma* [Phenomenon of heroism]. Moscow, 1985.

———. *Lenin.* 2 vols. Moscow, 1995.

Volkov, Yu. E. *Tak rozhdaetsia kommunisticheskoe samoupravlenie: Opyt konkretno-sotsiologicheskogo issledovaniia* [Birth of Communist self-government: an essay in empirical sociology]. Moscow, 1965.

Vremennik Ivana Timofeeva [A chronicle of Ivan Timofeev]. Russkaia istoricheskaia biblioteka 13, no. 1. Leningrad, 1925.

Wadekin, Karl Eugen. *The Private Sector in Soviet Agriculture.* 2d ed. Berkeley: University of California Press, 1973.

Wahl, François. "Inside or Outside Philosophy?" In *Michel Foucault Philosopher,* trans. Timothy J. Armstrong. New York: Routledge, 1992.

Walzer, Michael. "The Politics of Michel Foucault." In *Foucault: A Critical Reader,* ed. David Couzens Hoy. Oxford: Blackwell, 1986.

———. *The Revolution of the Saints: A Study in the Origins of Radical Politics.* New York: Atheneum, 1968.

Ware, Timothy. *The Orthodox Church.* Harmondsworth: Penguin, 1980.

Watkins, Oscar D. *A History of Penance, Being the Study of the Authorities.* London: Longmans, Green, 1920.

———. "Penance, Anglican." In *Encyclopaedia of Religion and Ethics,* ed. James Hastings. New York: Scribner's Sons, 1908–26.

Wesson, Robert G. *Soviet Communes.* New Brunswick, N.J.: Rutgers University Press, 1963.

White, Stephen. *Political Culture and Soviet Politics.* New York: St. Martin's Press, 1979.

———, ed. *New Directions in Soviet History.* Cambridge: Cambridge University Press, 1992.

Williams, Robert C. "Collective Immortality: The Syndicalist Origins of Proletarian Culture, 1905–1910." *Slavic Review* 39, no. 3 (September 1980).

Wittgenstein, Ludwig. *Philosophical Investigations,* trans. G. E. M. Anscombe. Oxford: Blackwell, 1953.

Wolin, Richard. *Walter Benjamin, an Aesthetic of Redemption.* New York: Columbia University Press, 1982.

Wolin, Sheldon S. "On the Theory and Practice of Power." In *After Foucault: Humanist Knowledge, Postmodern Challenges,* ed. Jonathan Arac. New Brunswick, N.J.: Rutgers University Press, 1988.

Yurchak, Aleksei. "The Cynical Reason of Late Socialism: Power, Pretense, and the *Anekdot.*" *Public Culture* 9 (1997).

Zhdanov, A. A. *Doklad o zhurnalakh* Zvezda *i* Leningrad. Moscow: Ogiz, 1946. A bilingual edition of the second speech is published in *The Central Committee Resolution and Zhdanov's Speech on the Journals* Zvezda *and* Leningrad, trans. F. Ashbee and I. Tidmarsh (Royal Oak: Strathcona, 1978).

———. "Podgotovka k vyboram v verkhovnyi sovet SSSR po novoi izbiratel'noi sisteme i sootvetstvuiushchaia perestroika partiino-politicheskoi raboty" [Preparations for the elections of the USSR Supreme Soviet according to the new electoral system and the corresponding restructuring of the Party's political work]. In *O perestroike partiino-politicheskoi raboty: K itogam Plenuma TsK VKP(b) 26 fevralia 1937 g.* [On restructuring the Party's political work: results of the CC plenum, February 26, 1937]. Moscow: Partizdat, 1937.

———. "Rech' na Iubileinom Plenume TsK VLKSM" [Speech at the jubilee plenum of the Komsomol CC]. *Komsomolskaia Pravda*, November 4, 1938.

Zhitnikov, K. "The Decline of the Democratic Movement." In *The Political, Social, and Religious Thought of Russian Samizdat*, ed. Michael Meerson-Aksenov and Boris Shragin. Belmont, Mass.: Nordland, 1977.

Zhmakin, V. I. *Sochineniia mitropolita Daniila* [Works of the metropolitan Daniel]. Moscow, 1881.

Zinoviev, Alexander. *The Reality of Communism*. Trans. Charles Janson. London: Gollancz, 1984.

Znamensky, I. *Prikhodskoe dukhovenstvo v Rossii so vremeni reformy Petra* [Parish clergy in Russia since Peter's reforms]. Kazan, 1873.

Zotova, O. I. "Razvitie teorii kollektiva v sovetskoi nauke" [Development of the theory of the collective in Soviet science]. In *Kollektiv i lichnost'*, ed. K. K. Platonov. Moscow: Nauka, 1975.

Index

Abelard, Pierre, 6, 8
Abramkin, V. F., 304–7, 308n, 309, 325
Adams, Jan, 292
Admonition: and Central Control
Commission, 43, 44, 45, 46, 48, 49,
52, 54, 55; and collectivization, 280,
282; and comrades' courts, 282, 283,
284; and ecclesiastical courts, 52,
53, 54; and Great Terror, 47; and
Khrushchev's reforms, 298; and the
kollektiv, 281, 282, 322, 324; and
KPGK, 292; and merger of self-
criticism and purging, 155, 163;
and mutual surveillance, 355; and
oblichenie, 256; and political dissent,
315
Adorno, Theodor, 30, 31
Aitmatov, Chinghiz, 344
Aksakov, S. T., 188
Aksenov, Vasilii, 341, 343–54
Alienation, 80, 191, 267
Almazov, A. I., 68
Anarchism, 192, 193, 266
Andreeva, Galina, 97, 99
Anninsky, Lev, 346–48
Archaeology, and Foucault's method-
ology, 13–20, 22–23, 25–26, 28
Aret, A. I., 241–44, 245n, 246, 247n,
249, 251n, 252, 255, 265n
Aristocracy, 253, 255, 264–65, 266,
270, 271

Artel's, 78, 93, 96, 107–8
Atheism, 44n, 55
Augustine, Saint, 6, 228, 345
Austin, John, 362
Authorship, 21, 25

Background practices, 9–13, 15, 16,
20, 24, 33, 34, 162, 174, 175, 279,
358, 359, 360, 361
Bakhtin, Mikhail, 302
Bakunin, Mikhail, 265, 266, 269
Balsamon, Theodore, 69
Basil the Great, Saint, 51n, 121, 220
Bauer, Raymond A., 2, 167, 185, 197n,
277–78
Bekhterev, V. M., 77, 91
Belanovsky, S. A., 310, 312, 325
Belinsky, V., 188, 266–67
Benjamin, Walter, 30–32
Bentham, Jeremy, 114, 118
Berdiaev, Nikolai, 55–56
Berger, Peter L., 45n, 106
Berman, Harold, 283, 299
Bible, 49, 53, 62, 118, 178n, 216, 217,
257, 314
Billington, J. H., 257
Birthdays, 335–36
Black market, 39n, 273
Body: and Foucault's methodology, 18,
20; and the *kollektiv*, 79, 85, 91; and
monastic practices, 117; and Party

Conflict Commissions, 46–47; and conscience, 59; and corruption, 36, 40, 139; as court, 37–40, 42, 48, 54, 55; and cult of the individual, 194; and definition of social position, 169; and democracy, 37, 42n; and disciplinary practices, 36–49; dissolution of, 42, 292; and education, 43, 46; and emphasis on curing rather than punishment, 36–37, 42–43, 48, 51; and expulsion, 42n, 43, 44, 45, 47–48, 52; and factionalism, 40, 41, 45, 46; founding of, 37, 59; and industrialization, 41; and Komsomol (Young Communist League), 46–47, 151; and KPGK, 292; and lack of staunchness, 45; and misuse of funds, 41n, 139; and mutual surveillance, 131–32, 283; and New Economic Policy (NEP), 40, 44; and Party ethics, 40, 41, 43, 44; and Party illnesses, 36, 38, 40, 41n, 42–43, 138–39, 153n; and Party unity, 136–37, 139; and people's patrols, 285; and petty-bourgeois elements, 36, 40, 139; and prohibition of religious practices, 36, 41n, 140; and property relations, 36, 139; and purges, 42, 46, 48, 60, 136–37, 140n, 142; and self-criticism, 147, 151–53, 213; and sexual misconduct, 35, 36, 41n, 140; and Worker-Peasants' Inspectorate, 38n, 42n, 292

Chekhov, Anton, 189

Cheliabinsk, 159–60

Chernyshevsky, Nikolai, 58–59, 206n, 212–13, 225n, 248, 265, 266–69

Chesnokova, V., 304–7, 309, 313n

China, Cultural Revolution in, 145

Christianity: and confession, 5–7, 56, 61–69, 71–72, 228, 356, 357, 361; and Council of Trent, 6, 61; and cultural difference, 361; Eastern, 6, 50, 53, 61, 67, 68, 74, 228, 356, 357, 360; and ethics, 56; and imitation of Christ, 261, 263, 357, 359; and indulgences, 68, 69; and Lateran

Council, 6, 56, 61, 68, 74; and monasticism, 61, 67, 263; and *oblichenie*, 216–28; and penitential practices, 61, 63–73, 226–28, 356–57, 361; and relations with state, 49–50, 53; and self-analysis, 6; and self-knowledge, 61, 63; and self-renunciation, 261, 263; and sexuality, 23–24, 61, 69, 356; Western, 6, 50, 61, 67–68, 74, 356. *See also* Catholicism; Protestantism; Russian Orthodox Church

Chrysostom, John, Saint, 221

Cicero, 204

Cinema, 115n, 290

Civil law, 53, 284

Civil rights, 53

Civil War, 36, 39n, 112, 133, 134, 147, 213

Clark, Katerina, 59, 205n

Class features, 176, 177, 178–81

Class relations, 129–30, 168–69, 178, 312

Clubs, as sites for subcultures, 316–17

Cocks, Paul, 297n

Collectives: definition of, 76–78, 92, 93; and social psychology, 76–77. *See also Kollektivy*

Collectivism, 78–80, 94, 96, 98, 132; and individualism, 1, 2, 362; and individuality, 8, 190–93, 198, 203–4, 206–7, 210–11, 236, 240, 358, 360; and self-training, 240; and self-transformation, 231–32, 236

Collectivization, 41, 83, 84, 133, 167, 169, 279–82, 294, 296, 303, 305, 313, 331; agricultural collectivization, 83, 281

Comintern, 82, 145

Commissariat of Education, 190

Commissariat of Internal Affairs, 145

Committee of Party Control, 134

Committee of People's Control, 294

Committee of Soviet Control, 134

Communal evaluation, of individuals, 243, 245, 250, 264

Communes, 84, 110

Compositor:	G&S Typesetters
Text:	10/13 Aldus
Display:	Aldus
Printer and binder:	Thomson-Shore, Inc